Koren Talmud Bavli

THE NOÉ EDITION

BERAKHOT
DAF 17B THROUGH DAF 34B

Steinsaltz Center

KOREN

תלמוד בבלי

KOREN TALMUD BAVLI

THE NOÉ EDITION

ברכות

BERAKHOT

Daf 17b through Daf 34b

COMMENTARY BY

Rabbi Adin Even-Israel
Steinsaltz

EDITOR-IN-CHIEF

Rabbi Dr Tzvi Hersh Weinreb

SENIOR CONTENT EDITOR

Rabbi Dr Shalom Z Berger

EXECUTIVE EDITOR

Rabbi Joshua Schreier

STEINSALTZ CENTER
KOREN PUBLISHERS JERUSALEM

Supported by the Matanel Foundation

Koren Talmud Bavli, The Noe Edition
Vol. 1.2: Tractate Berakhot, Daf 17b through Daf 34b
Paperback, ISBN, 978-965-7765-23-4

First Hebrew/English paperback edition, 2019

Koren Publishers Jerusalem Ltd.
PO Box 4044, Jerusalem 91040, ISRAEL
PO Box 8531, New Milford, CT 06776, USA
www.korenpub.com

Steinsaltz Center

Steinsaltz Center is the parent organization of institutions established by Rabbi Adin Even-Israel Steinsaltz

PO Box 45187, Jerusalem 91450 ISRAEL
Telephone: +972 2 646 0900, Fax +972 2 624 9454
www.steinsaltz-center.org

Hardcover design by Ben Gasner

This book was published in cooperation with the Israel Institute for Talmudic Publications.

הִנֵּה יָמִים בָּאִים, נְאֻם אֲדֹנָי יֱהוִה, וְהִשְׁלַחְתִּי רָעָב בָּאָרֶץ,
לֹא־רָעָב לַלֶּחֶם וְלֹא־צָמָא לַמַּיִם, כִּי אִם־לִשְׁמֹעַ אֵת דִּבְרֵי יהוה.

Behold, days are coming – says the Lord God – I will send a hunger to the land, not a hunger for bread nor a thirst for water, but to hear the words of the Lord. (AMOS 8:11)

The Noé edition of the Koren Talmud Bavli
with the commentary of Rabbi Adin Steinsaltz (Even-Israel)
is dedicated to all those who open its covers
to quench their thirst for Jewish Knowledge,
in our generation of Torah renaissance.

This beautiful edition is for the young, the aged,
the novice and the savant alike,
as it unites the depth of Torah knowledge
with the best of academic scholarship.

Within its exquisite and vibrant pages,
words become worlds.

It will claim its place in the library of classics,
in the bookcases of the Beit Midrash,
the classrooms of our schools,
and in the offices of professionals and business people
who carve out precious time to grapple with its timeless wisdom.

For the Student and the Scholar

DEDICATED BY LEO AND SUE NOÉ

Steinsaltz Center

Executive Director, Steinsaltz Center
Rabbi Meni Even-Israel

Managing Editor
Rabbi Jason Rappoport

Senior Content Editor
Rabbi Dr. Shalom Z. Berger

Translators
Amy Fay Kaplan Benoff
Betzalel Philip Edwards
Rabbi Elli Fischer
Gila Hoch
Stephen Lauber
Elie Leshem
Rabbi Eli Ozarowski
Gavriel Reiss
Yosef Rosen
Jay Shapiro
Rabbi Ami Silver
Eliana Kinderlehrer Silver
Avi Steinhart
Amiel Vick
Rabbi Abe Y. Weschler
Rabbi Yaakov Komisar
Rabbi Adin Krohn
Rabbi Jason Leib
Sally Mayer
Rabbi Jonathan Mishkin
Rabbi Noam Shapiro
Rabbi Michael Siev
Rabbi David Strauss

Editors
Mali Brofsky
Rabbi David Jay Derovan
Rabbi Dov Karoll

Copy Editors
Aliza Israel, *Coordinator*
Bracha Hermon
Shira Finson
Ita Olesker
Nechama Unterman

Language Consultants
Dr. Stephanie E. Binder, *Greek & Latin*
Rabbi Yaakov Hoffman, *Arabic*
Dr. Shai Secunda, *Persian*

KOREN

Design & Typesetting
Raphaël Freeman, *Design & Typesetting*
Dena Landowne Bailey, *Typesetting*
Tani Bayer, *Jacket Design*

Images
Eliahu Misgav, *Illustration*
Yehudit Cohen, *Image Acquisition*

Digital Edition
Raphaël Freeman, *Team Leader*
Eliyahu Skoczylas, *Senior Architect*
Tani Bayer, *User Interface Design*
Dena Landowne Bailey, *Concept*
Rabbi Hanan Benayahu, *Concept*
Laura Messinger, *Commercial Liaison*

Introduction by the Publisher

The Talmud has sustained and inspired Jews for thousands of years. Throughout Jewish history, an elite cadre of scholars has absorbed its learning and passed it on to succeeding generations. The Talmud has been the fundamental text of our people.

It is thus a privilege to present the *Noé Edition Koren Talmud Bavli*, an English translation of the talmudic text with the brilliant elucidation of Rabbi Adin Even-Israel Steinsaltz. The depth and breadth of his knowledge are unique in our time. His rootedness in the tradition and his reach into the world beyond are inspirational.

Our intentions in publishing this new edition of the Talmud are threefold: First, we seek to fully clarify the Talmud page to the reader – textually, intellectually, and graphically. Second, we seek to utilize today's most sophisticated technologies, both in print and electronic formats, to provide the reader with a comprehensive set of study tools. And third, we seek to help readers improve their process of Talmud study.

To achieve these goals, the *Noé Edition Koren Talmud Bavli* is unique in a number of ways:

- The classic *tzurat hadaf* of Vilna, used by scholars since the 1800s, has been reset for greater clarity, and opens from the Hebrew "front" of the book.
- Full *nikkud* has been added to both the Talmud text and Rashi's commentary, allowing for a more fluent reading with the correct pronunciation; the commentaries of *Tosafot* have been punctuated.
- Upon the advice of many English-speaking teachers of Talmud, we have separated these core pages from the translation, thereby enabling the advanced student to approach the text without the distraction of the translation.
- The Vilna pages were read against other manuscripts and older print editions, so that texts which had been removed by non-Jewish censors have been restored to their rightful place.
- The English translation, which starts on the English "front" of the book, reproduces the *menukad* Talmud text alongside the English translation (in bold) and commentary and explanation (in a lighter font).
- The Hebrew and Aramaic text is presented in logical paragraphs. This allows for the Hebrew reader to refer easily to the text alongside and where the original text features dialogue or poetry, the English text is laid out in a manner appropriate for the genre.
- Critical contextual tools surround the text and translation: personality notes, providing short biographies of the Sages; language notes, explaining foreign terms borrowed from Greek, Latin, Persian, or Arabic; and background notes, giving information essential to the understanding of the text, including history, geography, botany, archeology, zoology, astronomy, and aspects of daily life in the talmudic era.

- Halakhic summaries provide references to the authoritative legal decisions made over the centuries by the rabbis. They explain the reasons behind each halakhic decision as well as the ruling's close connection to the Talmud and its various interpreters.
- Photographs, drawings, and other illustrations have been added throughout the text – in full color in the Standard and Electronic editions, and in black and white in the Daf Yomi edition – to visually elucidate the text.

This new, travel-sized edition, allows the learner to fulfil the precept we recite twice daily, "speak of them when you sit at home and when you travel on the way." Using these volumes, we hope to open the world of Talmud to people all over the world, wherever they may be, and to share in their successes as they master page after page, volume after volume, and tractate after tractate. We pray that this edition will be a great source of learning and, ultimately, greater *avodat Hashem* for all Jews.

Matthew Miller, Publisher
Koren Publishers Jerusalem
Jerusalem 5779

Contents

Berakhot Part Two **119**

Image Credits **234**

For the vocalized Vilna Shas layout, please open as a Hebrew book.

Introduction to **Perek III**

When you go forth in camp against your enemies, then you shall keep yourself from every evil thing. If there be among you any man, that is not clean by reason of that which chance him by night, then shall he go abroad out of the camp, he shall not come within the camp. But it shall be, when evening comes on, he shall bathe himself in water; and when the sun is down, he may come within the camp. You shall have a place also without the camp, where you shall go forth abroad. And you shall have a paddle among thy weapons; and it shall be, when you sit down abroad, you shall dig with it, and shall turn back and cover that which comes from you. For the Lord your God walks in the midst of your camp, to deliver you, and to give up your enemies before you; therefore your camp shall be holy; that He see no unseemly thing in you, and turn away from you.

(Deuteronomy 23:10–15)

This chapter is, in a sense, a continuation of the previous chapter. The previous chapter also dealt with problems that arise as a result of circumstances that hinder the recitation of *Shema*. However, those hindrances were primarily generated by external factors that prevent one from reciting *Shema* properly. In this chapter, hindrances of a different sort will be discussed; i.e., cases where one is in a place or a situation where it is inappropriate to engage in sacred activities.

One problem discussed in this chapter is how one should act as far as *Shema* and prayer are concerned in various conditions of mourning, both in terms of the mourner himself and in terms of those engaged in burial of the deceased.

Another problem related to the mitzvot of *Shema* and prayer is a by-product of their very essence; when a person accepts the fundamental tenets of his faith and stands before his Creator, he should do so while clean and ritually pure. However, there are circumstances which render a person ritually impure or constitute an unclean environment. Precise determinations are necessary to establish when those circumstances completely exempt one from the obligation to recite *Shema* and pray and when the obligation is merely postponed.

The verses in Deuteronomy, which warn a person to avoid ritual impurity and filth in an army camp, apply everywhere, at all times. A Jew is always obligated to acknowledge: "For the Lord your God walks in the midst of your camp," especially when engaged in sacred activities.

In *halakha*, this was consolidated into three categories: Ritual impurity, unseemly matters, and filth. Ritual impurity is not, in essence, tied to a concrete flaw; nevertheless, it is a spiritual flaw from which it is incumbent upon the person to purify himself before entering the camp. The Torah directive with regard to ritual impurity resulting from a seminal emission leads directly to the discussion of the ordinance instituted by Ezra. This ordinance established that one who is ritually impure due to a seminal emission, including a husband who engaged in conjugal relations with his wife, is forbidden to recite *Shema*, pray, or study Torah until he immerses himself and becomes ritually pure. Even though it never gained widespread acceptance, in many senses several appropriate modes of conduct with regard to caution and ritual purity while studying Torah and praying were established by virtue of that ordinance.

The concept of unseemly matters also has far-reaching applications. It includes any exposed limb in the human body that is usually covered. On the one hand, this was instituted to prevent arousing sexual desire while engaged in sacred activity. However, there is another aspect, as it says in the Torah: All nakedness involves contempt for God, and consequently, covering that nakedness is an acknowledgement of the sanctity of the matters in which one is involved.

What is true with regard to spiritual flaws also applies to actual filth. The Torah commandment to be vigilant about cleanliness within the camp was formulated as a general directive to avoid every evil thing. That includes avoiding all sights or smells that provoke disgust or unpleasantness, which should be avoided at all times, especially when reciting *Shema* and praying.

Defining and illuminating these elements, and determining their precise parameters, are the primary focus of this chapter.

מתני׳ מִי שֶׁמֵּתוֹ מוּטָּל לְפָנָיו – פָּטוּר מִקְּרִיאַת שְׁמַע, וּמִן הַתְּפִלָּה וּמִן הַתְּפִילִּין, וּמִכׇּל מִצְוֹת הָאֲמוּרוֹת בַּתּוֹרָה.

MISHNA **One whose deceased** relative **is laid out** unburied **before him is exempt from the recitation of** ***Shema*****,**[NH] **from** the ***Amida*** **prayer, and from** the mitzva to don **phylacteries, as well as all** positive **mitzvot mentioned in the Torah,** until the deceased has been buried.

נוֹשְׂאֵי הַמִּטָּה וְחִלּוּפֵיהֶן וְחִלּוּפֵי חִלּוּפֵיהֶן, אֶת שֶׁלִּפְנֵי הַמִּטָּה וְאֶת שֶׁלְּאַחַר הַמִּטָּה; אֶת שֶׁלִּפְנֵי הַמִּטָּה צוֹרֶךְ בָּהֶם – פְּטוּרִין, וְאֶת שֶׁלְּאַחַר הַמִּטָּה צוֹרֶךְ בָּהֶם – חַיָּיבִין, וְאֵלּוּ וָאֵלּוּ פְּטוּרִים מִן הַתְּפִלָּה.

With regard to **the pallbearers**[H] **and their replacements and the replacements of their replacements, those** located **before the bier** who have not yet carried the deceased **and those** located **after the bier. Those before the bier who are needed** to carry the bier **are exempt** from reciting *Shema*; **while those after the bier,** even if **they are** still **needed** to carry it, since they have already carried the deceased, they are **obligated** to recite *Shema*. However, both **these and those are exempt from** reciting the ***Amida*** **prayer,**[N] since they are preoccupied and are unable to focus and pray with the appropriate intent.

קָבְרוּ אֶת הַמֵּת וְחָזְרוּ, אִם יְכוֹלִין לְהַתְחִיל וְלִגְמוֹר עַד שֶׁלֹּא יַגִּיעוּ לַשּׁוּרָה – יַתְחִילוּ, וְאִם לָאו – לֹא יַתְחִילוּ.

After **they buried the deceased and returned, if they** have sufficient time to **begin** to recite *Shema* **and conclude before they arrive at the row,** formed by those who attended the burial, through which the bereaved family will pass in order to receive consolation, **they should begin. If** they do **not** have sufficient time to conclude reciting the entire *Shema*, then **they should not begin.**

הָעוֹמְדִים בַּשּׁוּרָה, הַפְּנִימִיִּים – פְּטוּרִים, וְהַחִיצוֹנִים – חַיָּיבִים. (נָשִׁים וַעֲבָדִים וּקְטַנִּים פְּטוּרִים מִקְּרִיאַת שְׁמַע וּמִן הַתְּפִילִּין וְחַיָּיבִין בִּתְפִלָּה וּבִמְזוּזָה וּבְבִרְכַּת הַמָּזוֹן.)

And **those standing in the row, those** in the **interior** row, directly before whom the mourners will pass and who will console them, **are exempt** from reciting *Shema*, while **those** in the **exterior** row, who stand there only to show their respect, **are obligated** to recite *Shema*. **Women, slaves and minors are exempt from the recitation of** ***Shema*** **and from phylacteries, but are obligated in prayer,** ***mezuza*** **and Grace after Meals.**

גמ׳ מוּטָּל לְפָנָיו – אִין, וְשֶׁאֵינוֹ מוּטָּל לְפָנָיו – לָא;

GEMARA We learned in the mishna that one whose deceased relative is laid out before him is exempt from the recitation of *Shema* and other positive mitzvot. The Gemara deduces: When the corpse is **laid out before him, yes,** he is exempt, but when the corpse is **not** physically **laid out before him, no,** he is not exempt from these mitzvot.

וּרְמִינְהִי: מִי שֶׁמֵּתוֹ מוּטָּל לְפָנָיו – אוֹכֵל בְּבַיִת אַחֵר, וְאִם אֵין לוֹ בַּיִת אַחֵר – אוֹכֵל בְּבֵית חֲבֵירוֹ, וְאִם אֵין לוֹ בֵּית חֲבֵירוֹ – עוֹשֶׂה מְחִיצָה וְאוֹכֵל, וְאִם אֵין לוֹ דָּבָר לַעֲשׂוֹת מְחִיצָה – מַחֲזִיר פָּנָיו וְאוֹכֵל, וְאֵינוֹ מֵיסֵב וְאוֹכֵל, וְאֵינוֹ אוֹכֵל בָּשָׂר וְאֵינוֹ שׁוֹתֶה יַיִן, וְאֵינוֹ מְבָרֵךְ וְאֵינוֹ מְזַמֵּן,

The Gemara **raises a contradiction** from a *baraita*: **One whose deceased** relative **is laid out before him eats in another room.**[H] **If he does not have another room, he eats in the house of a friend. If he does not have a friend's house** available, **he makes a partition** between him and the deceased **and eats. If he does not have material** with which **to make a partition, he averts his face** from the dead and **eats. And** in any case, **he does not recline while he eats,** as reclining is characteristic of a festive meal. **Furthermore, he neither eats meat nor drinks wine, and does not recite** a **blessing** before eating, **and does not** recite the formula to **invite** the participants in the meal to join together in the Grace after Meals [*zimmun*], i.e., he is exempt from the obligation of Grace after Meals.

וְאֵין מְבָרְכִין עָלָיו וְאֵין מְזַמְּנִין עָלָיו, וּפָטוּר מִקְּרִיאַת שְׁמַע וּמִן הַתְּפִלָּה וּמִן הַתְּפִילִּין וּמִכׇּל מִצְוֹת הָאֲמוּרוֹת בַּתּוֹרָה; וּבְשַׁבָּת – מֵיסֵב וְאוֹכֵל בָּשָׂר וְשׁוֹתֶה יַיִן, וּמְבָרֵךְ וּמְזַמֵּן, וּמְבָרְכִין עָלָיו וּמְזַמְּנִין עָלָיו, וְחַיָּיב בְּכׇל הַמִּצְוֹת הָאֲמוּרוֹת בַּתּוֹרָה; רַבָּן שִׁמְעוֹן בֶּן גַּמְלִיאֵל אוֹמֵר: מִתּוֹךְ שֶׁנִּתְחַיֵּיב בְּאֵלּוּ נִתְחַיֵּיב בְּכוּלָּן.

And there is no need for others **to recite a blessing** beforehand **on his behalf, nor do others invite him** to join in Grace after Meals, as he cannot be a member of the quorum of three required to recite the formula. **He is exempt from the recitation of** ***Shema*****,** from the ***Amida*** **prayer and from phylacteries, and from all mitzvot mentioned in the Torah. On Shabbat,** however, **he reclines** at the meal as per his custom, **and eats meat and drinks wine, and recites blessings and** recites the formula to **invite** the participants in the meal to join together in the Grace after Meals, **and others may recite blessings on his behalf and invite him** to join in Grace after Meals, **and he is obligated in all mitzvot mentioned in the Torah. Rabban Shimon ben Gamliel says: Just as he is obligated** on Shabbat **to** fulfill **these** mitzvot associated with Shabbat meals, **he is obligated to** fulfill **all** mitzvot.

NOTES

One whose deceased relative is laid out unburied before him is exempt from the recitation of *Shema* – מִי שֶׁמֵּתוֹ מוּטָּל לְפָנָיו פָּטוּר מִקְּרִיאַת שְׁמַע: In the Jerusalem Talmud, the verse: "That you may remember the day when you came forth out of the land of Egypt all the days of your life" (Deuteronomy 16:3) was cited in support of this *halakha*. Remember the Exodus on days that you are involved with the living and not on days when you are involved with the dead (Jerusalem Talmud, *Berakhot* 3:1).

Both these and those are exempt from reciting the *Amida* prayer – אֵלּוּ וָאֵלּוּ פְּטוּרִים מִן הַתְּפִלָּה: Although the bier no longer requires their services, nevertheless they are exempt from the obligation to pray because they are engaged in performance of a mitzva and the principle is: One who is engaged in a mitzva is exempt from a mitzva (*Magen Avraham*).

HALAKHA

One whose deceased relative is laid out unburied before him is exempt from the recitation of *Shema* – מִי שֶׁמֵּתוֹ מוּטָּל לְפָנָיו פָּטוּר מִקְּרִיאַת שְׁמַע וכו׳: A mourner is exempt from reciting *Shema* and prayer, and performing all other positive mitzvot, until the deceased he is mourning is buried (Rambam *Sefer Ahava*, *Hilkhot Keriat Shema* 4:3, *Sefer Shofetim*, *Hilkhot Evel* 4:6; *Shulḥan Arukh*, *Oraḥ Ḥayyim* 71:1).

The pallbearers – נוֹשְׂאֵי הַמִּטָּה: The pallbearers and their replacements, all of whom are needed to carry the bier, are exempt from reciting *Shema* and performing other positive mitzvot. If the replacements are not needed to carry the bier, they are obligated (Rambam *Sefer Ahava*, *Hilkhot Keriat Shema* 4:4; *Shulḥan Arukh*, *Oraḥ Ḥayyim* 72:1, *Yoreh De'a* 358:1). However, all of the pallbearers are exempt from prayer. (*Shulḥan Arukh*, *Oraḥ Ḥayyim* 106:1).

One whose deceased relative is laid out before him eats in another room – מִי שֶׁמֵּתוֹ מוּטָּל לְפָנָיו אוֹכֵל בְּבַיִת אַחֵר וכו׳: One whose deceased relative has not yet been buried, may not eat in the same house in which the body is located. In exigent circumstances, when there is no alternative, one may avert his face from the deceased and eat (Rambam *Sefer Shofetim*, *Hilkhot Evel* 4:6; *Shulḥan Arukh*, *Yoreh De'a* 341:1). On weekdays he is exempt from reciting blessings and does not join others in a *zimmun* (*Shulḥan Arukh*, *Oraḥ Ḥayyim* 199:5).

HALAKHA

One who watches over the deceased – הַמְשַׁמֵּר אֶת הַמֵּת: One who is watching over the deceased, even if he is not a relative, is exempt from reciting it and exempt from all mitzvot in the Torah. However, if there were two people watching over the deceased in shifts, while one watches, the other recites *Shema* and vice-versa (Rambam *Sefer Ahava, Hilkhot Keriat Shema* 4:3; *Shulḥan Arukh, Oraḥ Ḥayyim* 71:3).

One may not walk in a cemetery with phylacteries on his head – לֹא יְהַלֵּךְ אָדָם בְּבֵית הַקְּבָרוֹת וּתְפִילִּין בְּרֹאשׁוֹ: It is prohibited to enter a cemetery or to come within four cubits of the deceased with exposed phylacteries, but if they are covered, it is permissible (Rambam *Sefer Ahava, Hilkhot Tefillin UMezuza VeSefer Torah* 4:23; *Shulḥan Arukh, Oraḥ Ḥayyim* 45:1, and see 71:7).

One may not walk in a cemetery with…a Torah scroll in his arm and read from it – לֹא יְהַלֵּךְ...וְסֵפֶר תּוֹרָה בִּזְרוֹעוֹ וְקוֹרֵא: It is prohibited to enter a cemetery with a Torah scroll, or to read the Torah in a cemetery, or to read it within four cubits of the deceased (Rambam *Sefer Shofetim, Hilkhot Evel* 14:13; *Shulḥan Arukh, Yoreh De'a* 282:4).

Prayer before the deceased – תְּפִלָּה בִּפְנֵי הַמֵּת: It is prohibited to recite *Shema* in a cemetery or within four cubits of the deceased. The same is true with regard to reciting all other sacred matters (*Mishna Berura*). One who recited *Shema* in the presence of the deceased is penalized by the Sages and they decreed that he did not fulfill his obligation (*Magen Avraham*). The *Ra'avad* ruled that he fulfilled his obligation. Since the Rambam ruled that he must repeat *Shema*, the ruling is that he repeats *Shema* but does not repeat its blessings (*Be'er Heitev*).

וַאֲמַר רַבִּי יוֹחָנָן: מַאי בֵּינַיְיהוּ – תַּשְׁמִישׁ הַמִּטָּה אִיכָּא בֵּינַיְיהוּ,

Rabbi Yoḥanan said: What is the practical difference **between** the apparently identical statements of Rabban Shimon ben Gamliel and the first *tanna*? **The** practical difference **between them is** with regard to **conjugal relations.** The first *tanna* holds that although there is no mourning on Shabbat, since refraining from addressing his wife's conjugal rights would not be a public display of mourning, conjugal relations are prohibited. Rabban Shimon ben Gamliel holds that since there is no mourning on Shabbat, he must fulfill the mitzva of addressing his wife's conjugal rights.

קָתָנֵי מִיהַת ״פָּטוּר מִקְּרִיאַת שְׁמַע וּמִן הַתְּפִלָּה וּמִן הַתְּפִילִּין וּמִכָּל מִצְוֹת הָאֲמוּרוֹת בַּתּוֹרָה״! אֲמַר רַב פַּפָּא: תַּרְגְּמָא אַמַּחֲזִיר פָּנָיו וְאוֹכֵל. רַב אַשִׁי אָמַר: כֵּיוָן שֶׁמּוּטָּל עָלָיו לְקוֹבְרוֹ – כְּמוּטָּל לְפָנָיו דָּמֵי, שֶׁנֶּאֱמַר: ״וַיָּקָם אַבְרָהָם מֵעַל פְּנֵי מֵתוֹ״, וְנֶאֱמַר: ״וְאֶקְבְּרָה מֵתִי מִלְּפָנָי״ – כָּל זְמַן שֶׁמּוּטָּל עָלָיו לְקוֹבְרוֹ כְּמוּטָּל לְפָנָיו דָּמֵי.

In any event, the *baraita* **teaches** that **one is exempt from the recitation of *Shema*, from** the *Amida* **prayer and from phylacteries, and from all mitzvot mentioned in the Torah.** This is an apparent contradiction of our mishna which states that one is exempt only when the deceased is laid before him. To resolve this contradiction, **Rav Pappa said: Explain** the *baraita* as applicable only to the particular case when **one turns his face** away **and eats,** with the deceased laid out before him. In the other cases, when he is in a different room, he is obligated in all mitzvot. **Rav Ashi says:** The phrase: The deceased is laid out before him, is not to be taken literally, but rather, **since it is incumbent upon him to bury the deceased,** and he is not yet buried, it is **as if he is laid out before him, as it is stated: "And Abraham rose up from before his dead"** (Genesis 23:3), **and** when Abraham speaks with the Hittites, **it is stated: "So that I may bury my dead from before me"** (Genesis 23:4). **As long as it is incumbent upon him to bury him,** it is **like he is laid out before him.**

מֵתוֹ – אִין, אֲבָל מְשַׁמְּרוֹ – לָא,

From the mishna one can infer that when **his deceased** relative is laid out before him, **yes,** he is exempt from mitzvot. **But,** if it is not his relative and he is only **watching over** the deceased, **no,** he is not exempt.

וְהָתַנְיָא: הַמְשַׁמֵּר אֶת הַמֵּת אַף עַל פִּי שֶׁאֵינוֹ מֵתוֹ – פָּטוּר מִקְּרִיאַת שְׁמַע וּמִן הַתְּפִלָּה וּמִן הַתְּפִילִּין וּמִכָּל מִצְוֹת הָאֲמוּרוֹת בַּתּוֹרָה. מְשַׁמְּרוֹ – אַף עַל פִּי שֶׁאֵינוֹ מֵתוֹ, מֵתוֹ – אַף עַל פִּי שֶׁאֵינוֹ מְשַׁמְּרוֹ.

The Gemara challenges: **Wasn't it taught** in a *baraita*: **One who watches over the deceased,**[H] **even if it is not his deceased** relative, **is exempt from the recitation of *Shema*, from prayer and from phylacteries, and from all mitzvot mentioned in the Torah?** The Gemara responds that these two sources should not be understood as contradictory, but as complementary. In both the cases, he is exempt; where **one watches over** the deceased, **but it is not his deceased** relative, as well as the case where **it is his deceased** relative, **but he is not watching over** the deceased.

מֵתוֹ וּמְשַׁמְּרוֹ אִין, אֲבָל מְהַלֵּךְ בְּבֵית הַקְּבָרוֹת – לָא, וְהָתַנְיָא: לֹא יְהַלֵּךְ אָדָם בְּבֵית הַקְּבָרוֹת וּתְפִילִּין בְּרֹאשׁוֹ וְסֵפֶר תּוֹרָה בִּזְרוֹעוֹ וְקוֹרֵא, וְאִם עוֹשֶׂה כֵּן עוֹבֵר מִשּׁוּם ״לוֹעֵג לָרָשׁ חֵרֵף עוֹשֵׂהוּ״!

The Gemara further challenges: We concluded that, in both cases, if it is **his deceased** relative or if he was **watching over** the unrelated deceased, **he is** exempt from mitzvot. **However, one walking in a cemetery is not** exempt. **Wasn't it taught** explicitly in a *baraita*: **One may not walk in a cemetery with phylacteries on his head**[H] **and a Torah scroll in his arm and read** from it?[H] **If one does so he commits** a transgression **due to** the verse: **"He who mocks the poor blasphemes his Creator"** (Proverbs 17:5). As the deceased is incapable of fulfilling mitzvot, fulfilling a mitzva in his presence is seen as mocking him.

הָתָם תּוֹךְ אַרְבַּע [אַמּוֹת] הוּא דְּאָסוּר, חוּץ לְאַרְבַּע אַמּוֹת חַיָּיב, דְּאָמַר מָר: מֵת תּוֹפֵס אַרְבַּע אַמּוֹת לִקְרִיאַת שְׁמַע, הָכָא – חוּץ לְאַרְבַּע אַמּוֹת נַמִי פָּטוּר.

The Gemara answers: **There,** when one walks in a cemetery, **within four cubits** of a grave, **that is prohibited.** However, **beyond four cubits** from a grave, **one is obligated** in prayer and phylacteries. **As the Master said: The deceased occupies four cubits** with regard to the exemption from the **recitation of *Shema*.** One who walks within four cubits of the deceased is exempt. **Here,** however, in the case where it is either his deceased relative or he is watching over an unrelated deceased, **beyond four cubits he is also exempt.**

גּוּפָא: הַמְשַׁמֵּר אֶת הַמֵּת אַף עַל פִּי שֶׁאֵינוֹ מֵתוֹ – פָּטוּר מִקְּרִיאַת שְׁמַע וּמִן הַתְּפִלָּה וּמִן הַתְּפִילִּין וּמִכָּל מִצְוֹת הָאֲמוּרוֹת בַּתּוֹרָה. הָיוּ שְׁנַיִם – זֶה מְשַׁמֵּר וְזֶה קוֹרֵא, וְזֶה מְשַׁמֵּר וְזֶה קוֹרֵא. בֶּן עַזַּאי אוֹמֵר: הָיוּ בָּאִים בִּסְפִינָה – מַנִּיחוֹ בְּזָוִית זוֹ וּמִתְפַּלְּלִין שְׁנֵיהֶם בְּזָוִית אַחֶרֶת.

The Gemara discusses the **matter** of the *baraita* **itself.** It was taught in the *baraita*: **One who watches over the deceased, even though it is not his dead** relative, **is exempt from the recitation of *Shema*, from** the *Amida* **prayer**[H] **and from phylacteries, and from all mitzvot mentioned in the Torah.** The *baraita* continues: If **two** individuals **were** watching over the deceased, **this one watches and that** one **recites** *Shema*, and then **that** one **watches and this** one **recites** *Shema*. **Ben Azzai says:** If **they were traveling** with the deceased **on a boat, they** are permitted **to set** the deceased **down in this corner** of the boat **and both pray in another corner** of the boat.

מַאי בֵּינַיְיהוּ? אָמַר רָבִינָא: ״חוֹשְׁשִׁין לַעֲכְבָּרִים״ אִיכָּא בֵּינַיְיהוּ. מָר סָבַר: חָיְישִׁינַן, וּמָר סָבַר: לָא חָיְישִׁינַן.

The Gemara asks: **What is** the practical difference **between these** two opinions? **Ravina said:** The practical difference **between them is** whether or not one need be **concerned about mice** even inside the boat. The first **Sage holds that we are concerned** about mice everywhere, and it is therefore inappropriate to leave the deceased unguarded, even on a boat, lest he be eaten by mice. **The other Sage,** ben Azzai, **maintains that we are not concerned about mice** on a boat.

תָּנוּ רַבָּנַן: הַמּוֹלִיךְ עֲצָמוֹת מִמָּקוֹם לְמָקוֹם – הֲרֵי זֶה לֹא יִתְּנֵם בְּדִסַּקַּיָא וְיִתְּנֵם עַל גַּבֵּי חֲמוֹר וְיִרְכַּב עֲלֵיהֶם, מִפְּנֵי שֶׁנּוֹהֵג בָּהֶם מִנְהַג בִּזָּיוֹן. וְאִם הָיָה מִתְיָרֵא מִפְּנֵי גּוֹיִם וּמִפְּנֵי לִסְטִים – מוּתָּר, וּכְדֶרֶךְ שֶׁאָמְרוּ בַּעֲצָמוֹת כָּךְ אָמְרוּ בְּסֵפֶר תּוֹרָה.

The Gemara discusses other issues concerning the dignity of the deceased. **The Sages taught: One who transports bones from place to place**[HN] **may not place them in a saddlebag** [*disakaya*][L] **and place them on the donkey's back and ride on them,** as in doing so **he treats** the remains **disgracefully. However, if he is afraid of gentiles** or **highwaymen** and therefore must move quickly, **he is permitted** to do so. **And just as they said with regard to bones, so they said with regard to a Torah scroll.**[H]

אַהַיָּיא? אִילֵימָא אַרֵישָׁא – פְּשִׁיטָא, מִי גָּרַע סֵפֶר תּוֹרָה מֵעֲצָמוֹת! אֶלָּא אַסֵּיפָא.

With regard to this last statement, the Gemara asks: **To what** section of the *baraita* does the parallel to a Torah scroll refer? **If you say** that this refers to **the first clause** of the *baraita*, this is **obvious. Is a Torah scroll less** important **than bones** of the dead? Certainly one may not treat a Torah disgracefully. Rather, this statement must refer **to the latter clause** of the *baraita*, that in a dangerous situation, one is permitted to ride on a Torah scroll as well.

אָמַר רַחֲבָה אָמַר רַב יְהוּדָה: כָּל הָרוֹאֶה הַמֵּת וְאֵינוֹ מְלַוֵּהוּ – עוֹבֵר מִשּׁוּם ״לֹעֵג לָרָשׁ חֵרֵף עֹשֵׂהוּ״. וְאִם הִלְוָהוּ מַה שְּׂכָרוֹ? אָמַר רַב אַסִי, עָלָיו הַכָּתוּב אוֹמֵר: ״מַלְוֵה ה׳ חוֹנֵן דָּל״, ״וּמְכַבְּדוֹ חֹנֵן אֶבְיוֹן״.

Raḥava said that **Rav Yehuda said: One who sees the deceased** taken to burial **and does not escort him**[H] **has committed a transgression due to** the verse: **"He who mocks the poor blasphemes his Creator." And if he does escort him, what is his reward? Rav Asi said: The verse says about him: "He who gives to the poor gives a loan to the Lord,** and the Lord will repay him" (Proverbs 19:17), and: "He who oppresses the poor blasphemes his Creator, **but he who is gracious to the poor honors Him"** (Proverbs 14:31).

רַבִּי חִיָּיא וְרַבִּי יוֹנָתָן הֲווּ שָׁקְלִי וְאָזְלִי בְּבֵית הַקְּבָרוֹת, הֲוָה קָשַׁדְיָא תְּכֶלְתָּא דְּרַבִּי יוֹנָתָן. אֲמַר לֵיהּ רַבִּי חִיָּיא: דַּלְיֵיהּ, כְּדֵי שֶׁלֹּא יֹאמְרוּ ״לְמָחָר בָּאִין אֶצְלֵנוּ וְעַכְשָׁיו מְחָרְפִין אוֹתָנוּ״.

The Gemara relates that **Rabbi Ḥiyya and Rabbi Yonatan were walking in a cemetery and the sky-blue string of Rabbi Yonatan's** ritual fringes **was cast** to the ground and dragging across the graves. **Rabbi Ḥiyya said** to him: **Lift it,** so the dead **will not say: Tomorrow,** when their day comes, they will **come to** be buried with **us, and now** they are **insulting us.**[H]

אֲמַר לֵיהּ: וּמִי יָדְעִי כּוּלֵּי הַאי? וְהָא כְּתִיב: ״וְהַמֵּתִים אֵינָם יוֹדְעִים מְאוּמָה״! אָמַר לֵיהּ: אִם קָרִיתָ – לֹא שָׁנִיתָ, אִם שָׁנִיתָ – לֹא שִׁלַּשְׁתָּ, אִם שִׁלַּשְׁתָּ – לֹא פֵּירְשׁוּ לְךָ: ״כִּי הַחַיִּים יוֹדְעִים שֶׁיָּמוּתוּ״ – אֵלּוּ צַדִּיקִים שֶׁבְּמִיתָתָן נִקְרְאוּ חַיִּים, שֶׁנֶּאֱמַר: ״וּבְנָיָהוּ בֶן יְהוֹיָדָע בֶּן אִישׁ חַי רַב פְּעָלִים מִקַּבְצְאֵל הוּא הִכָּה אֵת שְׁנֵי אֲרִאֵל מוֹאָב וְהוּא יָרַד וְהִכָּה אֶת הָאֲרִי בְּתוֹךְ הַבּוֹר בְּיוֹם הַשָּׁלֶג״;

Rabbi Yonatan **said to him: Do the dead know so much? Isn't it stated: "And the dead know nothing"** (Ecclesiastes 9:5)? Rabbi Ḥiyya **said to him: If you read** the verse, **you did not** read it **a second time, and if you** read it **a second time, you did not** read it **a third time, and if you** read it **a third time, they did not explain it to you** properly. The meaning of the verse: "For the living know that they will die, and the dead know nothing and have no more reward, for their memory has been forgotten" (Ecclesiastes 9:5): **For the living know that they will die, these are the righteous, who even in their death are called living.** An allusion to this is **as it is stated: "And Benayahu, son of Yehoyada, son of a valiant man of Kabze'el, who had done mighty deeds, he smote the two altar-hearths of Moab; he went down also and slew a lion in the midst of a pit in time of snow"** (II Samuel 23:20).

A donkey carrying a saddlebag

HALAKHA

One who transports bones from place to place – הַמּוֹלִיךְ עֲצָמוֹת מִמָּקוֹם לְמָקוֹם: One who transports the bones of the deceased should not ride upon them. However, as long as he does not sit on them, he is permitted to place them on the animal that he is riding (*Tosafot*). And if he was transporting them through a dangerous area, he may ride directly on them (Rambam *Sefer Shofetim, Hilkhot Evel* 14:14; *Shulḥan Arukh, Yoreh De'a* 403:10).

One who transports a Torah scroll – הַמּוֹלִיךְ סֵפֶר תּוֹרָה: One who travels from one place to another with a Torah scroll must not place it in a sack on the donkey's back and ride on it. Rather, he should hold it on his lap, opposite his heart. If he fears bandits, he may ride on it. Even in that case, halakhic authorities disagree whether or not it is permissible to sit directly on top of the Torah scroll. Some hold that it is preferable that the Torah scroll be stolen rather than have it treated with disrespect (*Bah*), while others disagree (*Shakh*). In dangerous circumstances, all necessary steps are permitted (*Shulḥan Arukh, Oraḥ Ḥayyim* 282:3).

One who sees the deceased and does not escort him – כָּל הָרוֹאֶה הַמֵּת וְאֵינוֹ מְלַוֵּהוּ: One who sees a funeral procession is obligated to escort the deceased for a distance of at least four cubits, as less than that, it is not considered that he moved at all. If one fails to escort him, he violates the prohibition derived in the Gemara from the verse: "He who mocks the poor" (*Shulḥan Arukh, Yoreh De'a* 361:3).

Ritual fringes in a cemetery – צִיצִית בְּבֵית הַקְּבָרוֹת: In places where the custom is to attach ritual fringes to one's regular clothing, one may enter a cemetery with that garment, but he must make certain that the ritual fringes do not drag over the graves, in accordance with the opinion of Rabbi Ḥiyya. Nowadays, when the garment with the ritual fringes is designated exclusively for prayer, one is prohibited from wearing it in a cemetery even if the ritual fringes do not drag across the graves. If one wears the garment beneath his clothing, it is permitted to enter the cemetery (*Shulḥan Arukh, Yoreh De'a* 23:1).

NOTES

One who transports bones from place to place – הַמּוֹלִיךְ עֲצָמוֹת מִמָּקוֹם לְמָקוֹם: During the mishnaic era, burial consisted of two stages. First, the body was buried in the ground. After the flesh decomposed, the bones were removed and placed in stone sarcophagi. That is why it was common for bones to be transported from one place to another.

LANGUAGE

Saddlebag [*disakaya*] – דִּסַּקַּיָא: The root of the word disakaya is the Greek **δισάκκιον**, *disakion*, which means a double bag, i.e., two bags tied together.

"בן איש חי", אטו כולי עלמא בני מתי נינהו? אלא, "בן איש חי" – שאפילו במיתתו קרוי חי; "רב פעלים מקבצאל" – שריבה וקבץ פועלים לתורה; "והוא הכה את שני אראל מואב" – שלא הניח כמותו לא במקדש ראשון ולא במקדש שני;

He was referred to in the verse as **son of a living man.** The Gemara wonders: **Is that to say,** the fact that the Bible referred to him with that appellation, **that all others are children of the dead? Rather,** the verse should be explained as follows: **The son of a living man** who lives forever, **who even in death is referred to as living. Man of Kabze'el who had done mighty deeds, as he accumulated and gathered many workers for** the sake of the **Torah. Who killed the two lion-hearted men** [*Ariel*] **of Moab,** as after his death **he left no one his equal, in either the First Temple or the Second Temple** periods, as the Temple is called *Ariel* (see Isaiah 29:1), and the two *Ariel* refers to the two Temples.

"והוא ירד והכה את הארי בתוך הבור ביום השלג" – איכא דאמרי: דתבר גזיזי דברדא ונחת וטבל, איכא דאמרי דתנא סיפרא דבי רב ביומא דסיתוא.

The Sages disagreed over the interpretation of the rest of the verse: **"And who descended and slew the lion in the pit on the snowy day." Some say** that this means **that he broke blocks of hail and descended and immersed himself** in the water to purify himself. **Others say that he learned** all of **the *Sifra*,** the halakhic midrash on the book of Leviticus **of the school of Rav,** on **a winter's day.**

"והמתים אינם יודעים מאומה" – אלו רשעים שבחייהן קרויין מתים, שנאמר: "ואתה חלל רשע נשיא ישראל". ואי בעית אימא, מהכא: "על פי שנים עדים או (על פי) שלשה עדים יומת המת". חי הוא! אלא: המת מעיקרא.

In contrast to the righteous, who are referred to as living even after their death, the verse states explicitly: **"The dead know nothing." These are the wicked,** who even **during their lives are called dead,** as the prophet Ezekiel **said** in reference to a king of Israel who was alive: **"And you are a slain, wicked prince of Israel"** (Ezekiel 21:30). **And if you wish, say** instead that the proof is **from here: "At the mouth of two witnesses or three witnesses the dead shall be put to death"** (Deuteronomy 17:6). This is puzzling. As long as the accused has not been sentenced to death, he **is alive. Rather,** this person who is wicked is considered **dead from the outset.**

בני רבי חייא נפוק לקרייתא איעקר להו תלמודייהו, הוו קא מצערי לאדכוריה. אמר ליה חד לחבריה: ידע אבון בהאי צערא? אמר ליה אידך: מנא ידע? והא כתיב: "יכבדו בניו ולא ידע"!

The Gemara relates a story on this topic: **The sons of Rabbi Ḥiyya went out to the villages** to oversee the laborers. **They forgot what they had learned and were struggling to recall it. One** of them **said to the other:** Does **our** deceased **father know of our anguish? The other said to him: From where would he know? Isn't it written: "His sons are honored yet he shall not know it,** they come to sorrow and he shall not understand them" (Job 14:21)? The dead do not know.

אמר ליה אידך: ולא ידע? והא כתיב: "אך בשרו עליו יכאב ונפשו עליו תאבל", ואמר רבי יצחק: קשה רמה למת כמחט בבשר החי.

The other said back **to him:** And do the dead truly **not know? Isn't it written: "Only in his flesh does he feel pain, in his soul does he mourn"** (Job 14:22)? Based on this verse **Rabbi Yitzḥak said:** Gnawing **maggots are as excruciating to the dead**[N] as the stab of **a needle to the flesh of the living.** The dead must have the capacity to feel and know.

אמרי: בצערא דידהו – ידעי, בצערא דאחרינא – לא ידעי.

In order to reconcile this contradiction **they said:** They **know of their own pain but do not know of the pain of others.**

ולא? והתניא: מעשה בחסיד אחד שנתן דינר לעני בערב ראש השנה בשני בצורת והקניטתו אשתו והלך ולן בבית הקברות. ושמע שתי רוחות שמספרות זו לזו, אמרה חדא לחברתה: חברתי, בואי ונשוט בעולם ונשמע מאחורי הפרגוד מה פורענות בא לעולם. אמרה לה חברתה: איני יכולה שאני קבורה במחצלת של קנים, אלא לכי את ומה שאת שומעת אמרי לי. הלכה היא ושטה ובאה. ואמרה לה חברתה: חברתי, מה שמעת מאחורי הפרגוד? אמרה לה: שמעתי, שכל הזורע ברביעה ראשונה ברד מלקה אותו. הלך הוא וזרע ברביעה שניה. של כל העולם כולו – לקה, שלו – לא לקה.

The Gemara challenges this: **And** is it so that the dead do **not** know of the pain of others? **Wasn't it taught** in a *baraita*: There was **an incident involving a pious man who gave a poor man a dinar on the eve of Rosh HaShana during drought years, and his wife mocked him** for giving so large a sum at so difficult a time? **And** in order to escape her incessant mockery, **he went and slept in the cemetery.**[N] That night in his dream (Ritva, *HaKotev*, Maharsha), **he heard two spirits conversing with each other. One said to the other: My friend, let us roam the world and hear from behind the heavenly curtain** [*pargod*],[L] which separates the Divine Presence from the world, **what calamity will befall the world. The other spirit said to her:** I **cannot** go with you, **as I am buried in a mat of reeds,**[NB] **but you go, and tell me what you hear. She went, and roamed, and came back. The other spirit said: My friend, what did you hear from behind the heavenly curtain? She replied: I heard that anyone who sows during the first rainy season** of this year, **hail will fall and strike his** crops. Hearing this, the pious man **went and sowed** his seeds **during the second rainy season.** Ultimately, the crops of **the entire world were stricken** by hail **and his** crops **were not stricken.**

NOTES

Gnawing maggots are excruciating to the dead – קשה רמה למת: It is not that the body of the deceased feels the pain. Rather, his soul regrets the decomposition of his body, which served as its sanctuary (*Sefer Ḥasidim*, Rashba in his Responsa).

There was an incident involving a pious man… and he went and slept in the cemetery – מעשה בחסיד אחד...והלך ולן בבית הקברות: Nearly all of the commentaries interpret this incident and those that follow, as dream-like visions of unique individuals. Some even explained that his sleeping in the cemetery itself was symbolic. In the wake of the quarrel with his wife, he was forced to descend from his lofty spiritual level to occupy himself with worldly matters and concerns for his livelihood (*HaKotev*).

In a mat of reeds – במחצלת של קנים: Since the soul of the deceased maintains a connection with the body for as long as the body is intact (*Shabbat* 152b), and since the body of the girl buried in a mat of reeds was protected from decomposition for an extended period, her soul remained connected to her body (*Tziyyun LeNefesh Ḥayya*).

LANGUAGE

Curtain [*pargod*] – פרגוד: The *pargod*, in one sense, refers to a type of screen. The word most likely comes from the Greek **παραγαύδιον** or the Latin *paragauda*, a garment with a purple border, which is derived from the Persian *parigund*.

BACKGROUND

A mat of reeds – מחצלת של קנים: Mats are made from a variety of materials, the choicest being manufactured from the soft, inner portion of the reed, and the coarser, cheaper mats being manufactured from entire reeds tied together. Such mats were generally used as partitions or to cover roofs. There were also several different types of shrouds, and earlier generations were quite strict about burying the deceased in expensive fabrics, at times even beyond the means of the bereaved. Later, at the behest of Rabban Shimon ben Gamliel, they would also bury them in less expensive fabrics. Only the poorest of families, however, would be reduced to burying their deceased in cheap mats made from reeds, which is why the girl's mother was ashamed when this information was made public.

לַשָּׁנָה הָאַחֶרֶת הָלַךְ וְלָן בְּבֵית הַקְּבָרוֹת, וְשָׁמַע אוֹתָן שְׁתֵּי רוּחוֹת שֶׁמְּסַפְּרוֹת זוֹ עִם זוֹ. אָמְרָה חֲדָא לַחֲבֶרְתָּהּ: בּוֹאִי וְנָשׁוּט בָּעוֹלָם וְנִשְׁמַע מֵאֲחוֹרֵי הַפַּרְגּוֹד מַה פּוּרְעָנוּת בָּא לָעוֹלָם. אָמְרָה לָהּ: חֲבֶרְתִּי, לֹא כָּךְ אָמַרְתִּי לָךְ: אֵינִי יְכוֹלָה שֶׁאֲנִי קְבוּרָה בְּמַחֲצֶלֶת שֶׁל קָנִים? אֶלָּא לְכִי אַתְּ וּמַה שֶּׁאַתְּ שׁוֹמַעַת בּוֹאִי וְאִמְרִי לִי. הָלְכָה וְשָׁטָה וּבָאָה. וְאָמְרָה לָהּ חֲבֶרְתָּהּ: חֲבֶרְתִּי, מַה שָּׁמַעַתְּ מֵאֲחוֹרֵי הַפַּרְגּוֹד? אָמְרָה לָהּ: שָׁמַעְתִּי, שֶׁכָּל הַזּוֹרֵעַ בִּרְבִיעָה שְׁנִיָּה שִׁדָּפוֹן מַלְקֶה אוֹתוֹ. הָלַךְ וְזָרַע בִּרְבִיעָה רִאשׁוֹנָה. שֶׁל כָּל הָעוֹלָם כּוּלּוֹ – נִשְׁדַּף, וְשֶׁלּוֹ לֹא נִשְׁדַּף.

The following year, on the eve of Rosh HaShana, the same pious man **went and slept in the cemetery** at his own initiative, and again **he heard the two spirits conversing with each other. One said to the other: Let us roam the world and hear from behind the heavenly curtain what calamity will befall the world. She said to her: My friend, have I not** already **told you** that **I cannot, as I am buried in a mat of reeds? Rather, you go, and tell me what you hear. She went, and roamed, and returned. The other** spirit **said to her: My friend, what did you hear from behind the curtain? She said to her: I heard that those who sow during the second rainy season blight will strike his** crops. That pious man **went and sowed during the first rainy season.** Since everyone else sowed during the second rainy season, ultimately, the crops **of the entire world were blighted and his** crops **were not blighted.**

אָמְרָה לוֹ אִשְׁתּוֹ: מִפְּנֵי מָה אֶשְׁתָּקַד שֶׁל כָּל הָעוֹלָם כּוּלּוֹ לָקָה וְשֶׁלְּךָ לֹא לָקָה, וְעַכְשָׁיו שֶׁל כָּל הָעוֹלָם כּוּלּוֹ נִשְׁדַּף וְשֶׁלְּךָ לֹא נִשְׁדַּף? סָח לָהּ כָּל הַדְּבָרִים הַלָּלוּ. אָמְרוּ: לֹא הָיוּ יָמִים מוּעָטִים עַד שֶׁנָּפְלָה קְטָטָה בֵּין אִשְׁתּוֹ שֶׁל אוֹתוֹ חָסִיד וּבֵין אִמָּהּ שֶׁל אוֹתָהּ רִיבָה. אָמְרָה לָהּ: לְכִי וְאַרְאֵךְ בִּתֵּךְ שֶׁהִיא קְבוּרָה בְּמַחֲצֶלֶת שֶׁל קָנִים.

The pious man's **wife said to him: Why is it that last year,** the crops **of the entire world were stricken and yours were not stricken, and now** this year, the crops **of the entire world were blighted and yours were not blighted? He related to her the entire story. They said: It was not** even **a few days** later **that a quarrel fell between the pious man's wife and the mother of the young woman** who was buried there. The pious man's wife **said to her** scornfully: **Go and I will show you your daughter,** and you will see that **she is buried in a mat of reeds.**

לַשָּׁנָה הָאַחֶרֶת הָלַךְ וְלָן בְּבֵית הַקְּבָרוֹת וְשָׁמַע אוֹתָן רוּחוֹת שֶׁמְּסַפְּרוֹת זוֹ עִם זוֹ. אָמְרָה לָהּ: חֲבֶרְתִּי, בּוֹאִי וְנָשׁוּט בָּעוֹלָם וְנִשְׁמַע מֵאֲחוֹרֵי הַפַּרְגּוֹד מַה פּוּרְעָנוּת בָּא לָעוֹלָם. אָמְרָה לָהּ: חֲבֶרְתִּי, הַנִּיחִינִי, דְּבָרִים שֶׁבֵּינִי לְבֵינֵךְ כְּבָר נִשְׁמְעוּ בֵּין הַחַיִּים. אַלְמָא יָדְעִי!

The following year, he again **went and slept in the cemetery, and heard the same spirits conversing with each other. One said** to the other: **My friend, let us roam the world and hear from behind the heavenly curtain what calamity will befall the world. She said to her: My friend, leave me** alone, as **words that** we have privately exchanged **between us have already been heard among the living. Apparently,** the dead **know** what transpires in this world.

דִּילְמָא אִינִישׁ אַחֲרִינָא שָׁכֵיב וְאָזֵיל וַאֲמַר לְהוּ.

The Gemara responds: This is no proof; **perhaps another person,** who heard about the conversation of the spirits secondhand, **died** and he **went and told them** that they had been overheard.

תָּא שְׁמַע: דִּזְעֵירִי הֲוָה מַפְקִיד זוּזֵי גַּבֵּי אוּשְׁפִּיזְכְתֵּיהּ, עַד דְּאָתֵי וְאָזֵיל לְבֵי רַב, שְׁכִיבָה. אֲזַל בַּתְרָהּ לַחֲצַר מָוֶת. אֲמַר לָהּ: זוּזֵי הֵיכָא? – אֲמַרָה לֵיהּ: זִיל שְׁקָלִינְהוּ מִתּוּתֵי בְּצִנּוֹרָא דְּדַשָּׁא בְּדוּךְ פְּלָן, וְאֵימָא לָהּ לְאִימָּא תְּשַׁדַּר לִי מַסְרְקַאי וְגוּבְתַאי דְּכוּחְלָא בַּהֲדֵי פְּלָנִיתָא דְּאָתְיָא לִמְחָר. אַלְמָא יָדְעִי! –

With regard to the deceased's knowledge of what transpires, **come** and **hear** a proof, as it is told: **Ze'iri would deposit** his **dinars with his innkeeper. While he was going and coming to** and from **the school of Rav, she died,** and he did not know where she had put the money. **So he went after her to** her grave in **the cemetery**[N] **and said to her: Where are the dinars? She replied: Go and get them from beneath the hinge of the door in such and such a place, and tell my mother** that **she should send me my comb**[B] **and a tube of eyeshadow**[B] **with such and such a woman who will die and come here tomorrow. Apparently,** the dead **know** what transpires in this world.

דִּלְמָא דּוּמָה קָדֵים וּמַכְרִיז לְהוּ.

The Gemara rejects this proof: **Perhaps** the angel **Duma,** who oversees the dead, **comes beforehand and announces to them** that a particular individual will arrive the next day, but they themselves do not know.

תָּא שְׁמַע: דַּאֲבוּהּ דִּשְׁמוּאֵל הָווּ קָא מַפְקְדִי גַּבֵּיהּ זוּזֵי דְּיַתְמֵי, כִּי נַח נַפְשֵׁיהּ לָא הֲוָה שְׁמוּאֵל גַּבֵּיהּ. הָווּ קָא קָרוּ לֵיהּ בַּר אָכֵיל זוּזֵי דְּיַתְמֵי. אֲזַל אַבַּתְרֵיהּ לַחֲצַר מָוֶת. אֲמַר לְהוּ: בָּעֵינָא אַבָּא. אֲמַרוּ לֵיהּ: אַבָּא טוּבָא אִיכָּא הָכָא. אֲמַר לְהוּ: בָּעֵינָא אַבָּא בַּר אַבָּא. אֲמַרוּ לֵיהּ: אַבָּא בַּר אַבָּא נַמִי טוּבָא אִיכָּא הָכָא. אֲמַר לְהוּ: בָּעֵינָא אַבָּא בַּר אַבָּא אֲבוּהּ דִּשְׁמוּאֵל, הֵיכָא? – אֲמַרוּ לֵיהּ: סְלֵיק לִמְתִיבְתָּא דִּרְקִיעָא. אַדְּהָכִי חַזְיֵיהּ לְלֵוִי דְּיָתֵיב אַבָּרַאי. אֲמַר לֵיהּ: אַמַּאי יָתְבַתְּ אַבָּרַאי, מַאי טַעְמָא לָא סָלְקַתְּ? אֲמַר לֵיהּ, דְּאָמְרִי לִי: כָּל כִּי הֲנָךְ שְׁנֵי דְּלָא סְלִיקַתְּ לִמְתִיבְתָּא דְּרַבִּי אָפֵס וְאַחֲלִישְׁתֵּיהּ לְדַעְתֵּיהּ – לָא מְעַיְּילִינַן לָךְ לִמְתִיבְתָּא דִּרְקִיעָא.

The Gemara cites another proof: **Come** and **hear,** as it is told: **They would deposit the money of orphans with Shmuel's father** for safekeeping. **When Shmuel's father died, Shmuel was not with him,** and did not learn from him the location of the money. Since he did not return it, Shmuel **was called: Son of** him who **consumes the money of orphans.** Shmuel **went after** his father **to the cemetery and said to** the dead: **I want Abba.** The dead **said to him: There are many Abbas here. He told them: I want Abba bar Abba. They said** to him: **There are also many** people named **Abba bar Abba here. He told them: I want Abba bar Abba, the father of Shmuel. Where** is he? **They replied: Ascend to the yeshiva on high. Meanwhile, he saw** his friend **Levi**[P] **sitting outside** the yeshiva, away from the rest of the deceased. **He asked him: Why do you sit outside? Why did you not ascend** to the yeshiva? **He replied: Because they tell me** that for **all those years** that **you didn't enter the yeshiva of Rabbi Afes,**[P] **and** thereby **upset him, we will not grant you entry to the yeshiva on high.**

NOTES

To the cemetery [*ḥatzar mavet*] – לַחֲצַר מָוֶת: Some interpreted *ḥatzar mavet* as referring to a cemetery (Rashi). Others explained this passage as a vision, as Shmuel was a priest and certainly did not go to a cemetery (*Ahavat Eitan*). Rather, *ḥatzar mavet* is a place where the dead who have yet to find rest in a more sublime world are in abeyance.

BACKGROUND

Comb – מַסְרֵק:

Comb from Eretz Yisrael in the mishnaic period

Tube of eyeshadow – גּוּבְתָא דְּכוּחְלָא:

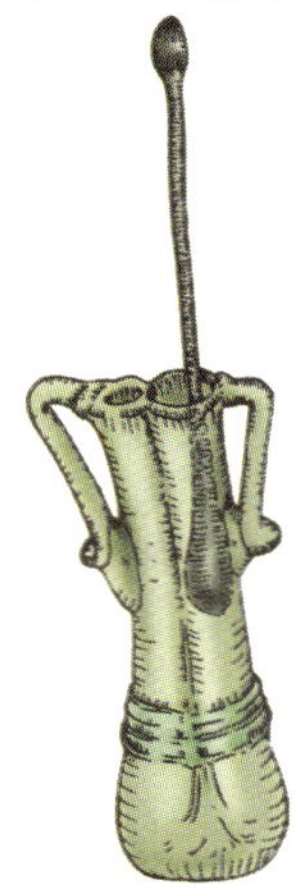

Tube of eyeshadow from the talmudic era

PERSONALITIES

Levi and Rabbi Afes – לֵוִי וְרַבִּי אָפֵס: The complicated chain of events that culminated in Levi not attending Rabbi Afes' yeshiva was set into motion by the will of Rabbi Yehuda HaNasi, in which he appointed Rabbi Ḥanina to succeed him at the helm of the yeshiva. Rabbi Ḥanina, however, foreswore the appointment in order to honor Rabbi Afes, who was Rabbi Ḥanina's senior in age, if not in wisdom. When Rabbi Afes was appointed to head the yeshiva, Rabbi Ḥanina could not attend as a student, so he sat outside the yeshiva. Rabbi Afes' friend Levi, who was his junior and who was not averse, in principle, to learning from him, joined Rabbi Ḥanina to keep him company. Rabbi Afes, however, was unaware of the reason for Levi's absence and was insulted. Shmuel and his father, who were close friends of Levi, likely knew that he had done so out of respect for Rabbi Ḥanina.

אַדְּהָכִי וְהָכִי אֲתָא אֲבוּהּ, חַזְיֵיהּ דַּהֲוָה קָא בָּכֵי וְאַחֵיךְ. אֲמַר לֵיהּ: מַאי טַעְמָא קָא בָּכֵית? אֲמַר לֵיהּ: דִּלְעַגַל קָא אָתֵית. מַאי טַעְמָא אַחֵיכַתְּ? – דַּחֲשִׁיבַתְּ בְּהַאי עָלְמָא טוּבָא, אֲמַר לֵיהּ: אִי חֲשִׁיבְנָא – נְעַיְּילוּהּ לְלֵוִי, וְעַיְּילוּהוּ לְלֵוִי.

Meanwhile, Shmuel's **father came** and Shmuel **saw that he was crying and laughing.** Shmuel **said to** his father: **Why are you crying?** His father **replied:** Because **you will come here soon.** Shmuel continued and asked: **Why are you laughing?** His father replied: Because **you are extremely important in this world.** Shmuel **said to him: If I am important, then let them grant Levi entry** to the yeshiva. **And** so it was **that they granted Levi entry** to the yeshiva.

אֲמַר לֵיהּ: זוּזֵי דְּיַתְמֵי הֵיכָא? אֲמַר לֵיהּ: זִיל שָׁקְלִינְהוּ בְּאַמְתָא דְּרֵחַיָּא, עִילָּאֵי וְתַתָּאֵי – דִּידַן, וּמִיצְעֵי – דְּיַתְמֵי. אֲמַר לֵיהּ: מַאי טַעְמָא עֲבַדְתְּ הָכִי? – אֲמַר לֵיהּ: אִי גַּנּוּבֵי גַּנָּבֵי – מִגַּנְבוּ מִדִּידַן, אִי אָכְלָה אַרְעָא – אָכְלָה מִדִּידַן. אַלְמָא דְּיָדְעִי! – דִּילְמָא שָׁאנֵי שְׁמוּאֵל, כֵּיוָן דַּחֲשִׁיב – קָדְמִי וּמַכְרְזִי "פַּנּוּ מָקוֹם".

Shmuel **said to** his father: **Where is the orphans' money? He said to him: Go** and **retrieve it from the millhouse,** where you will find **the uppermost and the lowermost** money **is ours, and** the money **in the middle** belongs to **the orphans.** Shmuel **said to him: Why did you do that? He replied: If thieves stole, they would steal from our** money on top, which the thief would see first. **If the earth swallowed up** any of it, it would swallow **from our** money, on the bottom. **Apparently,** the dead, in this case Shmuel's father, **know** when others will die. Since Shmuel did not die the next day, clearly the angel Duma could not have informed them (*Tosafot*). The Gemara responds: **Perhaps Shmuel is different,** and **because he is so important they announce beforehand: Clear place** for his arrival.

וְאַף רַבִּי יוֹנָתָן הֲדַר בֵּיהּ, דְּאָמַר רַבִּי שְׁמוּאֵל בַּר נַחְמָנִי אָמַר רַבִּי יוֹנָתָן: מִנַּיִן לַמֵּתִים שֶׁמְּסַפְּרִים זֶה עִם זֶה? שֶׁנֶּאֱמַר: "וַיֹּאמֶר ה׳ אֵלָיו זֹאת הָאָרֶץ אֲשֶׁר נִשְׁבַּעְתִּי לְאַבְרָהָם לְיִצְחָק וּלְיַעֲקֹב לֵאמֹר", מַאי 'לֵאמֹר' – אָמַר הַקָּדוֹשׁ בָּרוּךְ הוּא לְמֹשֶׁה: לֵךְ אֱמוֹר לָהֶם לְאַבְרָהָם לְיִצְחָק וּלְיַעֲקֹב שְׁבוּעָה שֶׁנִּשְׁבַּעְתִּי לָכֶם כְּבָר קִיַּימְתִּיהָ לִבְנֵיכֶם.

In any case, with regard to the crux of the issue, **Rabbi Yonatan also reconsidered** his opinion, **as Rabbi Shmuel bar Naḥmani said** that **Rabbi Yonatan said: From where** is it derived **that the dead converse with each other? As it is stated: "And the Lord said to him, this is the land that I swore to Abraham, Isaac and Jacob, saying:** I will give it to your offspring" (Deuteronomy 34:4). **What is the** meaning of **"saying"?** It means that **God told Moses: Go and tell Abraham, Isaac, and Jacob,** that **the oath that I swore to you I have already fulfilled for your descendants.**

Perek **III**
Daf **19** Amud **a**

LANGUAGE

His skull [*arneka demoḥei*] – אַרְנְקָא דְמוֹחֵיהּ: *Arneka* is from the Greek ἀρνακίς meaning sheepskin. Ultimately, it included other items as well, especially, purses made from sheepskin.

NOTES

After the biers of Torah scholars – אַחַר מִטָּתָן: The standard explanation of this phrase is as a euphemism for "after their death," as the Sages said: The righteous, even after their death, are called alive (Maharsha). Variant readings have this explicitly as "after their death." Others explain: After the Torah scholars have strayed, which has an etymological similarity in Hebrew, from the path of righteousness evoking the verse: "Those who turn aside unto their crooked ways" (Psalms 125:5; see Rabbeinu Ḥananel).

וְאִי סָלְקָא דַּעְתָּךְ דְּלָא יָדְעִי – כִּי אֲמַר לְהוּ מַאי הָוֵי? – אֶלָּא מַאי, דְּיָדְעִי? – לָמָּה לֵיהּ לְמֵימַר לְהוּ? – לְאַחֲזוּקֵי לֵיהּ טִיבוּתָא לְמֹשֶׁה.

And if it should enter your mind that the dead **do not know, then what of it if he tells them?** The Gemara rejects this: **Rather what** will you say, **that they know?** Then **why does he need to tell them?** The Gemara replies: This is not difficult, as he is telling them so that **they will give credit to Moses.**

אָמַר רַבִּי יִצְחָק: כָּל הַמְסַפֵּר אַחֲרֵי הַמֵּת כְּאִלּוּ מְסַפֵּר אַחֲרֵי הָאֶבֶן. אִיכָּא דְּאָמְרִי: דְּלָא יָדְעִי; וְאִיכָּא דְּאָמְרִי: דְּיָדְעִי וְלָא אִיכְפַּת לְהוּ.

On this subject, **Rabbi Yitzḥak said: Anyone who speaks** negatively **after the deceased it is as if** he **speaks after the stone.** The Gemara offers two interpretations of this: **Some say** this is because the dead **do not know, and some say** that **they know,** but **they do not care** that they are spoken of in such a manner.

אִינִי? וְהָא אֲמַר רַב פַּפָּא: חַד אִישְׁתָּעֵי מִילְּתָא בַּתְרֵיהּ דְּמָר שְׁמוּאֵל וּנְפַל קַנְיָא מִטִּלְלָא וּבְזַעָא לְאַרְנְקָא דְמוֹחֵיהּ!

The Gemara asks: **Is that so? Didn't Rav Pappa say:** There was once **someone who spoke** disparagingly **after** the death of **Mar Shmuel and a reed fell from the ceiling, fracturing his skull?**[L] Obviously, the dead care when people speak ill of them.

שָׁאנֵי צוּרְבָא מֵרַבָּנַן, דְּקוּדְשָׁא בְּרִיךְ הוּא תָּבַע בִּיקָרֵיהּ.

The Gemara rejects this: This is no proof that the dead care. Rather, a **Torah scholar is different, as God** Himself **demands** that **his honor** be upheld.

אָמַר רַבִּי יְהוֹשֻׁעַ בֶּן לֵוִי: כָּל הַמְסַפֵּר אַחַר מִטָּתָן שֶׁל תַּלְמִידֵי חֲכָמִים נוֹפֵל בְּגֵיהִנָּם, שֶׁנֶּאֱמַר: "וְהַמַּטִּים עֲקַלְקַלּוֹתָם יוֹלִיכֵם ה׳ אֶת פּוֹעֲלֵי הָאָוֶן שָׁלוֹם עַל יִשְׂרָאֵל", אֲפִילּוּ בְּשָׁעָה שֶׁשָּׁלוֹם עַל יִשְׂרָאֵל "יוֹלִיכֵם ה׳ אֶת פּוֹעֲלֵי הָאָוֶן".

Rabbi Yehoshua **ben Levi said** similarly: **One who speaks** disparagingly **after the biers of Torah scholars**[N] and maligns them after their death will **fall in Gehenna, as it is stated: "But those who turn aside unto their crooked ways, the Lord will lead them away with the workers of iniquity; peace be upon Israel"** (Psalms 125:5). **Even** if he speaks ill of them **when there is peace upon Israel,** after death, when they are no longer able to fight those denouncing them (*Tosafot*); nevertheless **the Lord will lead them away with the workers of iniquity,** to Gehenna.

תנא דבי רבי ישמעאל: אם ראית תלמיד חכם שעבר עבירה בלילה – אל תהרהר אחריו ביום, שמא עשה תשובה. ׳שמא׳ סלקא דעתך? אלא: ודאי עשה תשובה. והני מילי – בדברים שבגופו, אבל בממונא – עד דמהדר למריה.

On a similar note, **it was taught in the school of Rabbi Yishmael: If you saw a** Torah **scholar transgress a prohibition at night, do not think** badly **of him during the day; perhaps he has repented**[N] in the meantime. The Gemara challenges this: **Does it enter your mind** that only **perhaps** he has repented? Shouldn't he be given the benefit of the doubt? **Rather, he has certainly repented.** The Gemara notes: **The idea** that one must always give a Torah scholar the benefit of the doubt and assume that he has repented refers specifically to **matters** affecting **himself, but,** if one witnesses a Torah scholar committing a transgression **involving the property** of another, one is not required to give him the benefit of the doubt. Rather, he should not assume that he has repented **until** he sees him **return** the money to **its owner.**

ואמר רבי יהושע בן לוי: בעשרים וארבעה מקומות בית דין מנדין על כבוד הרב, וכולן שנינו במשנתנו. אמר ליה רבי אלעזר: היכא? אמר ליה: לכי תשכח.

Since matters relating to the respect due Torah scholars were raised, the Gemara continues, citing **Rabbi Yehoshua ben Levi,** who **said: There are twenty-four places in which the court ostracizes**[N] **over** matters of **respect** due **the rabbi, and we learned them all in our Mishna. Rabbi Elazar said to him: Where** are those cases to be found? Rabbi Yehoshua ben Levi **said to him: When** you look, **you** will **find** them.

נפק דק ואשכח תלת: המזלזל בנטילת ידים, והמספר אחר מטתן של תלמידי חכמים, והמגיס דעתו כלפי מעלה.

He went out, analyzed, and found three examples: **One who demeans** the ritual of **washing of the hands, one who speaks** disparagingly **after the bier**[H] **of Torah scholars, and one who is arrogant vis-à-vis Heaven.** The Gemara cites sources for each of these cases.

המספר אחר מטתן של תלמידי חכמים מאי היא? דתנן, הוא היה אומר: אין משקין לא את הגיורת ולא את המשוחררת; וחכמים אומרים: משקין. ואמרו לו: מעשה בכרכמית, שפחה משוחררת בירושלים והשקוה שמעיה ואבטליון! – ואמר להם: דוגמא השקוה; ונדוהו, ומת בנדויו, וסקלו בית דין את ארונו.

What is the source for **one who speaks** disparagingly **after the biers of Torah scholars? As we learned** in the mishna: Akavya ben Mahalalel[P] **would say:** In the case of a woman whose husband suspects her of adultery, who was warned by her husband not to seclude herself with another man and she did not listen (see Numbers 5), the court **does not administer** the bitter water potion of a *sota* to **a convert or an emancipated** maidservant.[H] **And the Rabbis say:** The court **administers** the bitter water potion to them. **And** the Rabbis **said to him** as proof: **There is the story of Kharkemit, an emancipated maidservant in Jerusalem, and Shemaya and Avtalyon administered her** the bitter waters. Akavya ben Mahalalel **said to** the Sages: That is no proof. Shemaya and Avtalyon, who were also from families of converts, required the maidservant **to drink** the potion because she was **like them** [*dugma*].[NL] **And** since Akavya ben Mahalalel cast aspersion on the deceased Torah scholars, **he was ostracized and died** while **he** was still under the ban of **ostracism. And** in accordance with the *halakha* with regard to one who dies while under a ban of ostracism, the court **stoned his coffin.** Apparently, one who deprecates a deceased Torah scholar is sentenced to ostracism.

NOTES

Perhaps he has repented – שמא עשה תשובה: It is to be understood as follows: One who sees a Torah scholar sin should not think badly of him. One must assume that the scholar certainly, and not just might have, repented (Rav Yoshiya Pinto).

Ostracism – נדוי: Ostracism is a lesser degree of excommunication. The primary *halakhot* that apply at this level of excommunication are that the individual must conduct himself as if he is in mourning and he is not included in a prayer quorum. This does not preclude the individual, however, from hiring laborers or hiring himself out as a laborer; in that sense, it is business as usual. The same is true in terms of studying and teaching Torah. On the other hand, one who does not take the necessary steps to have his ostracism lifted is then excommunicated. At that stage, all contacts with him are severed. The courts resorted to ostracism primarily in two cases: when an individual failed to pay his debts and there were no other measures at their disposal to compel him to pay, or as punishment for disparaging the Torah or Torah scholars.

They required her to drink the potion because she was like them – דוגמא השקוה: Some explain the phrase to mean that instead of the actual bitter waters, they had her drink colored water in order to scare her into confessing (Rabbeinu Ḥananel). According to Akavya they did so because, as descendants of converts themselves, they did not want it publicized that a convert does not drink the bitter waters. He was ostracized either for casting aspersion upon them (Rambam), or for suspecting that they acted improperly as substitution of colored water for the bitter waters was liable lead people to treat the actual bitter waters with disdain (Ra'avad).

PERSONALITIES

Akavya ben Mahalalel – עקביא בן מהללאל: One of the first *tanna'im* and a contemporary of Hillel the Elder (some 100 years before the destruction of the Temple), Akavya ben Mahalalel maintained stringent opinions that were at odds with most of the Sages of his generation. His eminence in Torah is evidenced by the fact that his fellow Sages told him that if he reneged upon three laws that they found unacceptable, he would be appointed head of the *beit din* of Israel. He famously replied: I would rather be called a fool for my entire life than be wicked for a single hour.

This firmness was based upon his piety and a profound fear of Heaven, as well as the conviction that he must pass on the *halakha* as he received it from his teachers. However, he told his son (who was also a Sage) to accept the opinion of the majority. Few of his halakhic and aggadic statements are recorded in the Mishna.

LANGUAGE

Like them [*dugma*] – דוגמא: From the Greek δεῖγμα, *deigma*, meaning form or sample. Some, based on parallel sources, have a variant reading, *dukhma* or *dukma* from the Greek δοκιμή, *dokimè*, meaning test.

HALAKHA

Twenty-four places in which the court ostracizes over matters of respect due the rabbi…One who speaks disparagingly after the bier, etc. – בעשרים וארבעה מקומות בית דין מנדין על כבוד הרב, והמספר אחר מטתן וכו׳: It is incumbent upon the court to ostracize one against whom there is testimony that he maligned a Torah scholar, even if he only did so verbally or not in his presence (Rema). His ostracism is not lifted until he appeases the scholar on whose account he was excommunicated. If he maligned a Torah scholar after his death, the court ostracizes him until he repents (Rambam *Sefer HaMadda, Hilkhot Talmud Torah* 6:14; *Shulḥan Arukh, Yoreh De'a* 243:7; 334:43).

Administering the bitter waters to a convert or an emancipated maidservant – השקיית הגיורת והשפחה המשוחררת במי סוטה: A convert and an emancipated maidservant are administered the bitter water potion just like any other Jewish woman, in accordance with the opinion of the Rabbis, who constitute the majority in the dispute with the lone dissenting opinion (Rambam *Sefer Nashim, Hilkhot Sota* 2:6).

והמזלזל בנטילת ידים מאי היא? דתנן, אמר רבי יהודה: חס ושלום שעקביא בן מהללאל נתנדה, שאין עזרה ננעלת על כל אדם בישראל בחכמה ובטהרה וביראת חטא כעקביא בן מהללאל, אלא את מי נדו – את אלעזר בן חנוך שפקפק בנטילת ידים; וכשמת – שלחו בית דין והניחו אבן גדולה על ארונו, ללמדך: שכל המתנדה ומת בנדויו – בית דין סוקלין את ארונו.

And **what is** the source for **one who demeans** the ritual of **washing of the hands?**[H] **We learned** later in the same mishna: **Rabbi Yehuda said:** That story related with regard to the ostracism of Akavya ben Mahalalel is completely untrue; **God forbid that Akavya ben Mahalalel was ostracized, as the Temple courtyard is not closed on any Jew,** meaning that even when all of Israel made the pilgrimage to Jerusalem, when each of the three groups that gathered to offer the Paschal lamb filled the courtyard, leading the Temple administration to close the courtyard, there was no one there as perfect **in wisdom, purity and fear of sin as Akavya ben Mahalalel. Rather, whom did they excommunicate? Elazar ben Ḥanokh,** because he **doubted** and demeaned the rabbinic ordinance of **washing of the hands. And when he died, the court sent** instructions **and they placed a large rock upon his coffin** in order **to teach you that one who is ostracized and dies in** a state of **ostracism, the court stones his coffin,**[H] as if symbolically stoning him. Apparently, one who makes light of the ritual of washing of the hands is sentenced to ostracism.

המגיס דעתו כלפי מעלה מאי היא? דתנן, שלח לו שמעון בן שטח לחוני המעגל: צריך אתה להתנדות, ואלמלא חוני אתה גוזרני עליך נדוי, אבל מה אעשה שאתה מתחטא לפני המקום ועושה לך רצונך כבן שמתחטא לפני אביו ועושה לו רצונו, ועליך הכתוב אומר "ישמח אביך ואמך ותגל יולדתך".

What is the source for the third case, **one who is arrogant vis-à-vis Heaven?** The mishna relates that Ḥoni HaMe'aggel, the circle-drawer, drew a circle and stood inside it, and said that he would not leave the circle until it rained, and he went so far as to make demands in terms of the manner in which he wanted the rain to fall. After it rained, **Shimon ben Shataḥ,** the *Nasi* of the Sanhedrin, relayed to **Ḥoni HaMe'aggel:** Actually, **you should be ostracized** for what you said, **and if you were not Ḥoni, I would have decreed ostracism upon you, but what can I do? You nag God and He does your bidding, like a son who nags his father and** his father **does his bidding** without reprimand. After all, the rain fell as you requested. **About you, the verse states: "Your father and mother will be glad and she who bore you will rejoice"** (Proverbs 23:25). Apparently, one who is arrogant vis-à-vis Heaven would ordinarily merit excommunication.

ותו ליכא? והא איכא דתני רב יוסף: תודוס איש רומי הנהיג את בני רומי להאכילן גדיים מקולסין בלילי פסחים; שלח ליה שמעון בן שטח: אלמלא תודוס אתה גוזרני עליך נדוי, שאתה מאכיל את ישראל קדשים בחוץ!

The Gemara challenges this: **And are there no more** cases of excommunication or threats of excommunication? **Surely there are** additional cases like the one in the *baraita* **taught by Rav Yosef:** It is told that **Theodosius of Rome,**[P] leader of the Jewish community there, **instituted the custom for the Roman** Jews **to eat whole kids,** young goats roasted with their entrails over their heads, as was the custom when roasting the Paschal lamb, **on the eve of Passover,**[H] as they did in the Temple. **Shimon ben Shataḥ sent** a message **to him: If you were not Theodosius,** an important person, **I would have decreed ostracism upon you,** as it appears as if **you are feeding Israel consecrated food,** which may only be eaten in and around the Temple itself, **outside** the Temple.

במשנתנו קאמרינן, והא ברייתא היא.

The Gemara responds: This case should not be included, as Rabbi Yehoshua ben Levi said that there were twenty-four cases **in our Mishna,** and **this is** merely **a** ***baraita.***

ובמתניתין ליכא? והא איכא הא דתנן: חתכו חוליות ונתן חול בין חוליא לחוליא, רבי אליעזר מטהר, וחכמים מטמאים, וזהו תנורו של עכנאי;

The Gemara asks: **And are there none in the Mishna? Isn't there that which we learned** in the mishna: **One who cut** an earthenware oven horizontally **into** ring-shaped **pieces and put sand between the pieces, Rabbi Eliezer deems** the oven **ritually pure,** i.e., it is no longer susceptible to ritual impurity. He holds that, although the fragments of the oven were pieced together, it is not considered an intact vessel but, rather, as a collection of fragments, and a broken earthenware vessel cannot become ritually impure. **And the Rabbis deem it ritually impure.** Since the oven continues to serve its original function, it is still considered a single entity and a whole vessel despite the sand put between the pieces. **And this is** called **the oven of *akhnai*, snake.**[HB]

מאי עכנאי? אמר רב יהודה אמר שמואל: מלמד, שהקיפוהו הלכות כעכנאי זה וטמאוהו;

The Gemara asks: **What is** the meaning of oven of the **snake? Rav Yehuda said** that **Shmuel said:** It is called snake **to teach that** the Rabbis **surrounded** Rabbi Eliezer **with** *halakhot* and proofs **like a snake** surrounds its prey, **and declared** the oven and its contents **ritually impure.**

HALAKHA

One who demeans the ritual washing of the hands – והמזלזל בנטילת ידים: One must be vigilant with regard to the ritual washing of the hands, as the court is required to ostracize anyone who demeans that ritual, i.e., one who never in his life did so; Rashi, *Tosafot*. He will become impoverished and be uprooted from the world, in accordance with the mishna cited here (Rambam *Sefer Ahava, Hilkhot Berakhot* 6:19; *Shulḥan Arukh, Oraḥ Ḥayyim* 158:9).

One who is ostracized and dies in a state of ostracism, the court stones his coffin – שכל המתנדה ומת בנדויו בית דין סוקלין את ארונו: One who was ostracized due to contempt for Torah and mitzvot and died in that status, the court places a stone on his coffin, his relatives do not rend their clothing, he is not eulogized, and none of the rites instituted to honor the deceased are practiced. On the other hand, consoling the mourners, which is to honor the living, is permitted (*Shakh* based on the Ramban; Rambam *Sefer HaMadda, Hilkhot Talmud Torah* 7:4; *Shulḥan Arukh, Yoreh De'a* 334:3).

Eating whole kids on the eve of Passover – גדיים מקולסין בלילי פסחים: It is prohibited on Passover eve to eat a goat that was roasted whole, as it appears as if one is eating consecrated food outside of the Temple. Whether or not one is permitted to eat the meat if it was sliced and then roasted depends upon the local custom (Rambam *Sefer Zemanim, Hilkhot Ḥametz UMatza* 8:11; *Shulḥan Arukh, Oraḥ Ḥayyim* 476:1).

The oven of *akhnai* – תנורו של עכנאי: An oven that was cut into segments and sand was placed between the segments; if he subsequently plastered the surface of the oven, it has the legal status of a vessel and is susceptible to ritual impurity, as per the opinion of the Rabbis (Rambam *Sefer Tahara, Hilkhot Kelim* 16:3).

PERSONALITIES

Theodosius – תודוס: Theodosius of Rome, who lived in the time of Shimon ben Shataḥ and King Alexander Yannai, was, apparently, the leader of the Jewish community in Rome. He was also charged with overseeing the transport of Jewish contributions to the Temple and the Sages. Theodosius was also a Sage, as evidenced by the inclusion in the Gemara of one of his aggadic statements with regard to the sanctification of God's name. Due to his renown and status as a leader, Shimon ben Shataḥ adopted a tone of respect when addressing him and did not excommunicate him.

BACKGROUND

The oven of *akhnai* – תנורו של עכנאי: According to Rabbi Eliezer, if an oven was cut, according to the parallel lines in the illustration, it is considered a broken vessel incapable of contracting ritual impurity, even if it was later reassembled.

Likeness of the stove of *akhnai*

וְתַנְיָא: אוֹתוֹ הַיּוֹם הֵבִיאוּ כׇּל טְהָרוֹת שֶׁטִּיהֵר רַבִּי אֱלִיעֶזֶר וּשְׂרָפוּם לְפָנָיו, וּלְבַסּוֹף בֵּרְכוּהוּ!

And it was taught in a *baraita*: **On that day, they gathered all of the ritually pure** food items that had come into contact with the oven **that Rabbi Eliezer had declared ritually pure, and burned them before him,** and because he did not accept the decision of the majority, **in the end they "blessed,"** a euphemism for ostracized, **him.** This is another case that ended in ostracism.

אֲפִילּוּ הָכִי, נִדּוּי בְּמַתְנִיתִין לָא תְּנַן. אֶלָּא בְּעֶשְׂרִים וְאַרְבָּעָה מְקוֹמוֹת הֵיכָא מַשְׁכַּחַתְּ לַהּ? – רַבִּי יְהוֹשֻׁעַ בֶּן לֵוִי מְדַמֵּה מִילְּתָא לְמִילְּתָא, וְרַבִּי אֶלְעָזָר לָא מְדַמֵּה מִילְּתָא לְמִילְּתָא.

The Gemara answers: **Even so, we did not learn** the ruling with regard to his **ostracism in the mishna.** The Gemara asks: Then **where do you find** the **twenty-four places** mentioned in Rabbi Yehoshua ben Levi's statement? The Gemara responds: **Rabbi Yehoshua ben Levi likens one matter to another** similar **matter.** Whenever he would encounter a case in a mishna where one of the Sages expressed himself inappropriately in reference to other Sages, he concluded that they should have been excommunicated. **Rabbi Elazar does not liken one matter to another** similar **matter,** and therefore located only three explicit cases of ostracism.

״נוֹשְׂאֵי הַמִּטָּה וְחִלּוּפֵיהֶן״. תָּנוּ רַבָּנַן: אֵין מוֹצִיאִין אֶת הַמֵּת סָמוּךְ לִקְרִיאַת שְׁמַע, וְאִם הִתְחִילוּ אֵין מַפְסִיקִין. אִינִי? וְהָא רַב יוֹסֵף אַפְּקוּהוּ סָמוּךְ לִקְרִיאַת שְׁמַע! – אָדָם חָשׁוּב שָׁאנֵי.

We learned in the mishna that **the pallbearers and their replacements** are exempt from the recitation of *Shema*. On this subject, the Gemara cites that which the **Sages taught** in a *baraita*: **The deceased may not be taken out** to be buried **adjacent to** the time for **the recitation of *Shema*,**[H] but should be buried later. **And if they** already **started** to take him out, **they need not stop** in order to recite *Shema*. The Gemara challenges: **Is that so? Didn't they take Rav Yosef out** to be buried **adjacent to** the time for **the recitation of *Shema*?** The Gemara resolves this contradiction: The case of **an important person is different,** and they are more lenient in order to honor him at his burial.

״שֶׁלִּפְנֵי הַמִּטָּה וְשֶׁלְּאַחַר הַמִּטָּה״. תָּנוּ רַבָּנַן: הָעוֹסְקִים בְּהֶסְפֵּד, בִּזְמַן שֶׁהַמֵּת מוּטָל לִפְנֵיהֶם – נִשְׁמָטִין אֶחָד אֶחָד וְקוֹרִין, אֵין הַמֵּת מוּטָל לִפְנֵיהֶם – הֵן יוֹשְׁבִין וְקוֹרִין וְהוּא יוֹשֵׁב וְדוֹמֵם, הֵם עוֹמְדִים וּמִתְפַּלְּלִין וְהוּא עוֹמֵד וּמַצְדִּיק עָלָיו אֶת הַדִּין, וְאוֹמֵר: רִבּוֹן הָעוֹלָמִים, הַרְבֵּה חָטָאתִי לְפָנֶיךָ וְלֹא נִפְרַעְתָּ מִמֶּנִּי אֶחָד מִנִּי אֶלֶף, יְהִי רָצוֹן מִלְּפָנֶיךָ ה׳ אֱלֹהֵינוּ שֶׁתִּגְדּוֹר פִּרְצוֹתֵינוּ וּפִרְצוֹת כׇּל עַמְּךָ בֵּית יִשְׂרָאֵל בְּרַחֲמִים.

In the mishna, we learned the *halakha* with regard to the pallbearers and their obligation to recite *Shema*, and a distinction was made between those **who are before the bier and** those **after the bier. Our Rabbis taught** in a *baraita*: **Those involved in eulogy**[H] **must slip away** from the eulogy **one by one while the deceased is laid out before them and recite** *Shema* elsewhere. And **if the deceased is not laid out before them,** the eulogizers must **sit and recite** *Shema* **while** the bereaved **sits silently. They stand and pray and he stands and justifies God's judgment, saying: Master of the Universe, I have sinned greatly against You, and You have not collected even one one-thousandth** of my debt. **May it be Your will, Lord our God, to mercifully repair the breaches in our** fence **and the breaches of Your nation, the House of Israel.**

אָמַר אַבַּיֵי לָא מִבְּעֵי לֵיהּ לְאִינִישׁ לְמֵימַר הָכִי דְּאָמַר רַבִּי שִׁמְעוֹן בֶּן לָקִישׁ וְכֵן תָּנָא מִשְּׁמֵיהּ דְּרַבִּי יוֹסֵי לְעוֹלָם אַל יִפְתַּח אָדָם פִּיו לַשָּׂטָן

Abaye said: A person should not say that, as Rabbi Shimon ben Lakish said, and it was also taught in the name of Rabbi Yosei: One must never open his mouth to the Satan,[HN] i.e., one must not leave room for or raise the possibility of disaster or evil. This formula, which states that the entire debt owed due to his transgressions has not been collected, raises the possibility that further payment will be exacted from him.

וְאָמַר רַב יוֹסֵף: מַאי קְרָאָה – שֶׁנֶּאֱמַר: ״כִּמְעַט כִּסְדוֹם הָיִינוּ״, מַאי אַהְדַּר לְהוּ נָבִיא – ״שִׁמְעוּ דְבַר ה׳ קְצִינֵי סְדוֹם״.

And Rav Yosef said: What is the verse from which **it** is derived? **As it is stated: "We should have almost been as Sodom,** we should have been like unto Gomorrah" (Isaiah 1:9), after which **what did** the prophet **reply to them? "Hear the word of the Lord, rulers of Sodom;** give ear unto the law of our God, people of Gomorrah" (Isaiah 1:10).

״קָבְרוּ אֶת הַמֵּת וְחָזְרוּ וְכוּ׳״. אִם יְכוֹלִים לְהַתְחִיל וְלִגְמוֹר אֶת כּוּלָּהּ – אִין, אֲבָל פֶּרֶק אֶחָד אוֹ פָּסוּק אֶחָד – לָא. וּרְמִינְהוּ: קָבְרוּ אֶת הַמֵּת וְחָזְרוּ, אִם יְכוֹלִין לְהַתְחִיל וְלִגְמוֹר אֲפִילּוּ פֶּרֶק אֶחָד אוֹ פָּסוּק אֶחָד!

We learned in the mishna that, in a case when **they buried the deceased and returned,**[H] if they have sufficient time to begin to recite *Shema* and conclude before they arrive at the row formed by those who came to console the bereaved, they should begin. Here, the Gemara clarifies: This is the case only **if they can begin and complete** recitation of *Shema* **in its entirety. However,** if they can only complete **one chapter or one verse,** they should **not** stop to do so. The Gemara **raises a contradiction** from that which we learned in the *baraita*: After **they buried the deceased and returned, if they can begin** the recitation of *Shema* **and finish even a single chapter or verse,** they should begin.

הָכִי נַמִי קָאָמַר: אִם יְכוֹלִין לְהַתְחִיל וְלִגְמוֹר אֲפִילּוּ פֶּרֶק אֶחָד אוֹ אֲפִילּוּ פָּסוּק אֶחָד עַד שֶׁלֹּא יַגִּיעוּ לַשּׁוּרָה – יַתְחִילוּ, וְאִם לָאו – לֹא יַתְחִילוּ.

The Gemara responds: **That is also what** the *tanna* of the mishna **said** and this is the conclusion drawn from his statement: **If one can begin and conclude even one chapter or one verse before they arrive at the row** of consolers, **they should begin. And if not, they should not begin.**

HALAKHA

The deceased may not be taken out to be buried adjacent to the time for the recitation of *Shema* – אֵין מוֹצִיאִין אֶת הַמֵּת סָמוּךְ לִקְרִיאַת שְׁמַע: The deceased may not be taken out for burial adjacent to the time when *Shema* must be recited, so that its recitation will not be abrogated. If the funeral procession already began, it is not interrupted to recite *Shema*. Nowadays, the custom is that even an important person is not taken out for burial adjacent to the time when *Shema* must be recited (*Taz*). There are those who are lenient with regard to the nighttime *Shema*. They begin the funeral procession adjacent to the time of its recital because one has the whole night to recite the *Shema* and in order to avoid delaying the burial until the next day. This opinion was cited by the Rema and adopted by the *Magen Avraham* (Rambam *Sefer Ahava, Hilkhot Keriat Shema* 4:4; *Shulḥan Arukh, Oraḥ Ḥayyim* 72:2 and *Yoreh De'a* 358:2).

Those involved in eulogy with regard to reciting *Shema* – הָעוֹסְקִים בְּהֶסְפֵּד לְעִנְיַן קְרִיאַת שְׁמַע: If the deceased was laid out before those engaged in eulogizing him, they slip out one at a time and recite *Shema* and pray. If the deceased is not before them, they recite *Shema* and pray where they are assembled, with the exception of the mourner who sits in silence (Rambam *Sefer Ahava, Hilkhot Keriat Shema* 4:5; *Shulḥan Arukh, Oraḥ Ḥayyim* 72:3).

One must never open his mouth to the Satan – לְעוֹלָם אַל יִפְתַּח אָדָם פִּיו לַשָּׂטָן: It is inappropriate for one to say that God has not punished him enough for his sins, as he thereby opens his mouth to Satan, as per the statements of Abaye and Reish Lakish (*Shulḥan Arukh, Yoreh De'a* 376:2, Rema).

They buried the deceased and returned – קָבְרוּ אֶת הַמֵּת וְחָזְרוּ וכו׳: If those who returned from the burial and are proceeding to form a row to console the mourners have enough time to recite even the first verse of *Shema*, they should begin and recite as much of *Shema* as they can (*Baḥ*). Some say that once they begin they should recite *Shema* in its entirety (*Beit Yosef*). If there is concern that the time for reciting *Shema* will pass, they should recite it (*Rema*) as per the *baraita* and the Gemara's conclusion (Rambam *Sefer Ahava, Hilkhot Keriat Shema* 4:6; *Shulḥan Arukh, Oraḥ Ḥayyim* 72:4).

NOTES

One must never open his mouth to the Satan – לְעוֹלָם אַל יִפְתַּח אָדָם פִּיו לַשָּׂטָן: The reason is that once a person justifies God's judgment, there is no more room for the attribute of mercy to be applied in his case. However, this restriction applies only to the future, but with regard to the past, it is an act of righteousness to declare that God punished him for his sins (*HaKotev*).

״הָעוֹמְדִים בַּשּׁוּרָה וכו׳״. תָּנוּ רַבָּנַן: שׁוּרָה הָרוֹאָה פְּנִימָה – פְּטוּרָה, וְשֶׁאֵינָהּ רוֹאָה פְּנִימָה – חַיֶּיבֶת, רַבִּי יְהוּדָה אוֹמֵר: הַבָּאִים מֵחֲמַת הָאָבֵל – פְּטוּרִין, מֵחֲמַת עַצְמָן – חַיָּיבִין.

We learned in the mishna that **those standing in the row,**[H] those in the interior row, are exempt from reciting *Shema* and the others are obligated. **The Sages taught** this more expansively in the *Tosefta*: The consolers standing in **a row** from **which** one **sees inside** the area where the mourners are passing **are exempt, and** those standing in a row from which **one does not see inside are obligated. And Rabbi Yehuda** elaborates and **says:** The consolers standing in the row **who come on account of the bereaved**[N] **are exempt,** while those who come **on account of their own** curiosity **are obligated** to recite *Shema.*

אָמַר רַב יְהוּדָה אָמַר רַב: הַמּוֹצֵא כִּלְאַיִם בְּבִגְדוֹ פּוֹשְׁטָן אֲפִילּוּ בַּשּׁוּק, מַאי טַעְמָא – ״אֵין חָכְמָה וְאֵין תְּבוּנָה וְאֵין עֵצָה לְנֶגֶד ה׳״ – כָּל מָקוֹם שֶׁיֵּשׁ חִילּוּל הַשֵּׁם אֵין חוֹלְקִין כָּבוֹד לָרַב.

We learned that some who come to console the bereaved are exempt from *Shema* as a means of honoring the deceased. The Gemara expands the discussion to raise the general question: To what degree does preserving human dignity takes precedence over mitzvot enumerated in the Torah? **Rav Yehuda said** that **Rav said: One who discovers diverse kinds** [*kilayim*], i.e., a prohibited mixture of wool and linen, **in his garment,**[H] **must remove them even in the** public **marketplace.** He may not wait until he reaches home. **What is the reason** for this? As it is stated: **"There is neither wisdom, nor understanding, nor counsel against the Lord"** (Proverbs 21:30). From here, the general principle: **Anywhere that there is desecration of the Lord's name, one does not show respect to the teacher,** is derived.

מֵתִיבִי: קָבְרוּ אֶת הַמֵּת וְחָזְרוּ, וְלִפְנֵיהֶם שְׁתֵּי דְרָכִים, אַחַת טְהוֹרָה וְאַחַת טְמֵאָה, בָּא בַּטְּהוֹרָה – בָּאִין עִמּוֹ בַּטְּהוֹרָה, בָּא בַּטְּמֵאָה – בָּאִין עִמּוֹ בַּטְּמֵאָה, מִשּׁוּם כְּבוֹדוֹ. אַמַּאי? לֵימָא: ״אֵין חָכְמָה וְאֵין תְּבוּנָה לְנֶגֶד ה׳״.

The Gemara cites several sources to challenge this principle. The Gemara **raised an objection** from a *baraita*: After **they buried the deceased and returned, and** on their way **there are two paths before them, one ritually pure and one ritually impure,** e.g., it passes through a cemetery, if the mourner **comes on the pure** path,[N] **they come with him on the pure** path; if **he comes on the impure** path, all of the funeral participants **accompany** him **on the impure** path in order to show **him respect. Why** would they do this? **Let us say** here too that, **"There is neither wisdom, nor understanding… against the Lord!"**

תַּרְגְּמַהּ רַבִּי אַבָּא בְּבֵית הַפְּרָס דְּרַבָּנַן.

Rabbi Abba explained that the *baraita* is referring to a path that passes **through an area where there is uncertainty with regard to the location of a grave or a corpse** [*beit haperas*].[BLH] For example, with regard to a field in which there is a grave that was plowed and no longer intact, the entire field is deemed impure due to concern that the plow scattered bones throughout the field. The field is impure only **by rabbinic law** but not according to Torah law. Since it is only prohibited by rabbinic law, one is permitted to walk through the field to show the mourner respect.

דְּאָמַר רַב יְהוּדָה אָמַר שְׁמוּאֵל: מְנַפֵּחַ אָדָם בֵּית הַפְּרָס וְהוֹלֵךְ; וְאָמַר רַב יְהוּדָה בַּר אַשִׁי מִשְּׁמֵיהּ דְּרַב: בֵּית הַפְּרָס שֶׁנִּדַּשׁ טָהוֹר.

The Gemara cites proof that the legal status of a *beit haperas* is unlike the legal status of impurity by Torah law: **Rav Yehuda said** that **Shmuel said: One** who passes through **a *beit haperas* may blow** on the dust before taking each step, so that if there is a bone beneath the dust, he will expose it, avoid it, **and walk.** One may not rely on that method of examination with regard to impurity by Torah law. **And Rav Yehuda bar Ashi said in the name of Rav: A *beit haperas* that has been trodden** underfoot,[H] creating a path, **is pure,** and one no longer need be concerned about bones. Clearly, the entire prohibition is a stringency decreed by the Sages.

NOTES

Those who come on account of the bereaved – הַבָּאִים מֵחֲמַת הָאָבֵל: Rabbi Yehuda's statement can be interpreted in two ways. One possibility is that Rabbi Yehuda is more stringent with regard to those standing in the first row. If they did not come on account of the bereaved, they are obligated to recite *Shema*. Alternatively, it is possible that Rabbi Yehuda is more lenient with regard to those in the second row if they came on account of the bereaved (*Talmidei Rabbeinu Yona*). Some say that Rabbi Yehuda is merely explaining the statement of the previous *tanna*. He distinguishes between those in the first row who are there in deference to the bereaved and those standing in the other rows (*Alfasi Zuta*).

He comes on the pure path – בָּא בַּטְּהוֹרָה: The Ra'avad's version reads: If the community comes on the pure path, the priest comes with them on the pure path, etc. He prefers that version because it explains why the priest does not simply go off on his own, as the mourner would not notice the absence of one individual and, therefore, would not perceive it as an affront. Rather, it is in deference to the community, as it is inappropriate for one individual to separate himself from the community (*Shitta Mekubbetzet*).

BACKGROUND

***Beit haperas* – בֵּית הַפְּרָס:** This term is a general term referring to a place in which, by rabbinic law, ritual impurity imparted by a corpse is dispersed. Typically, it refers to a field in which a grave was plowed, causing the bones to be scattered throughout the field. A second field that falls into this category is one where it is known that there is a grave, but its exact location is unknown. The third field in this category is one where it was customary to place the bier while the deceased was eulogized. The concern is that limbs might have fallen in the field and remained there.

LANGUAGE

***Beit haperas* – בֵּית הַפְּרָס:** There are several interpretations of this term. Some hold that it stems from the Hebrew *perisa*, meaning spreading or expansion, i.e., a field in which the ritual impurity is spread throughout the entire field (Rambam's Commentary on the Mishna). Others suggest that it stems from the fact that a broken or sliced [*parus*] source of ritual impurity was found in the field (Rashi). Yet others maintain that the field is given that name because people's feet [*parsot*] do not tread there (*Tosafot*). Another school of thought holds that the name is foreign in origin. Some say that it is from the Latin forum or from the Greek *πάρος*, *paros*, meaning in front of (*Mosaf HaArukh*).

HALAKHA

Those standing in the row – הָעוֹמְדִים בַּשּׁוּרָה: Those standing in the row of consolers; those in the interior row who are face-to-face with the mourners are exempt from reciting *Shema,* and those in the exterior rows who are not face-to-face with the mourners are obligated to recite it, in accordance with our mishna and the *Tosefta* here (Rambam *Sefer Ahava, Hilkhot Keriat Shema* 4:6; *Shulḥan Arukh, Oraḥ Ḥayyim* 72:5).

One who discovers diverse kinds [*kilayim*] in his garment – הַמּוֹצֵא כִּלְאַיִם בְּבִגְדוֹ: One who discovers a mixture of wool and linen, prohibited by Torah law, in the garment of another person, must remove the garment from him. He must do so even if they are in the marketplace, with no concern for the affront to his dignity, even if the individual in question was his teacher, as the dignity of a rabbi does not override the dignity of Heaven. If the mixture was only prohibited by rabbinic law, he may wait until the person wearing the garment returns home before removing it from him, as per the Gemara's conclusion that rabbinic decrees do not override human dignity. Furthermore, if the individual had worn the garment unwittingly, even if the mixture was prohibited by Torah law, human dignity takes precedence, and he should not remove the garment from him (*Tur* in the name of the Rosh; Rambam *Sefer Zera'im, Hilkhot Kilayim* 10:29; *Shulḥan Arukh, Yoreh De'a* 303:1).

Consoling the mourners in a *beit haperas* – נִיחוּם אֲבֵלִים בְּבֵית הַפְּרָס: A priest may enter a field in which a grave was plowed in order to console a mourner who is there (Rambam *Sefer Shofetim, Hilkhot Evel* 3:14; *Shulḥan Arukh, Yoreh De'a* 372:1).

A *beit haperas* that has been trodden underfoot – בֵּית הַפְּרָס שֶׁנִּדַּשׁ: One who passed through a field in which a grave was plowed, and a path had already been trodden, is ritually pure and eligible to offer the Paschal lamb. Similarly, if as he was passing through, he blew the dirt before him and did not encounter a bone capable of rendering him ritually impure, he is ritually pure and eligible to offer the Paschal lamb. The Sages did not apply their decree in a case involving *karet* (Rambam *Sefer Korbanot, Hilkhot Korban Pesaḥ* 6:8).

תָּא שְׁמַע, דְּאָמַר רַבִּי אֶלְעָזָר בַּר צָדוֹק: מְדַלְּגִין הָיִינוּ עַל גַּבֵּי אֲרוֹנוֹת שֶׁל מֵתִים לִקְרַאת מַלְכֵי יִשְׂרָאֵל, וְלֹא לִקְרַאת מַלְכֵי יִשְׂרָאֵל בִּלְבַד אָמְרוּ אֶלָּא אֲפִילּוּ לִקְרַאת מַלְכֵי אוּמּוֹת הָעוֹלָם, שֶׁאִם יִזְכֶּה – יַבְחִין בֵּין מַלְכֵי יִשְׂרָאֵל לְמַלְכֵי אוּמּוֹת הָעוֹלָם. אַמַּאי? לֵימָא: ״אֵין חָכְמָה וְאֵין תְּבוּנָה וְאֵין עֵצָה לְנֶגֶד ה׳״!

The Gemara cites additional proof with regard to the extent to which human dignity overrides mitzvot in the Torah. **Come and hear, as Rabbi Elazar bar Tzadok** the priest **said:** I and my fellow priests **would jump over coffins**[B] **of the deceased**[H] in order to hurry **towards kings of Israel** to greet them. **And they did not say** this **only towards kings of Israel, but** they said this **even towards kings of the nations of the world, so that if one will be privileged** to witness the redemption of Israel, **he will distinguish between kings of Israel and kings of the nations of the world.** The priest violated the Torah prohibition to become ritually impure through contact with the dead, in order to show respect for a king. And **why** is this? **Let us say** here too: **"There is neither wisdom, nor understanding, nor counsel against the Lord."**

כִּדְרָבָא, דְּאָמַר רָבָא: דְּבַר תּוֹרָה, אֹהֶל, כָּל שֶׁיֵּשׁ בּוֹ חֲלַל טֶפַח – חוֹצֵץ בִּפְנֵי הַטּוּמְאָה, וְשֶׁאֵין בּוֹ חֲלַל טֶפַח – אֵינוֹ חוֹצֵץ בִּפְנֵי הַטּוּמְאָה,

The Gemara responds to this challenge by saying that it must be understood **in accordance with** the opinion **of Rava, as Rava said: By Torah law, a tent** over a corpse, **as long as there is a handbreadth of space** between the corpse and the tent over it, **constitutes a barrier before** the spread of **impurity** and nothing above the tent can become ritually impure due to impurity imparted by the corpse. **And when there is not a handbreadth of space** between the corpse and the tent over it, the tent **does not constitute a barrier before** the spread of **impurity** and the "pressed" ritual impurity, can reach the heavens.

וְרוֹב אֲרוֹנוֹת יֵשׁ בָּהֶן חֲלַל טֶפַח, וְגָזְרוּ עַל שֶׁיֵּשׁ בָּהֶן מִשּׁוּם שֶׁאֵין בָּהֶן, וּמִשּׁוּם כְּבוֹד מְלָכִים לֹא גָּזְרוּ בְּהוּ רַבָּנַן.

Most coffins have a handbreadth of space. Consequently, their impurity does not spread above the coffin. However, the Sages **issued a decree regarding** coffins **in which there is** a handbreadth of space **because of** those coffins **in which there is not.** Nevertheless, **due to respect for kings,** the Sages **did not issue a decree** in a case involving **them** and the priests were permitted to jump over the coffins, as it is permitted by Torah law. Therefore, there is no proof from here regarding the question of whether or not human dignity overrides Torah law.

תָּא שְׁמַע: גָּדוֹל כְּבוֹד הַבְּרִיּוֹת שֶׁדּוֹחֶה [אֶת] לֹא תַעֲשֶׂה שֶׁבַּתּוֹרָה.

The Gemara cites an additional proof from a *baraita*: **Come and hear: Great is human dignity, as it overrides a prohibition in the Torah.**

וְאַמַּאי? לֵימָא: ״אֵין חָכְמָה וְאֵין תְּבוּנָה וְאֵין עֵצָה לְנֶגֶד ה׳״! – תַּרְגְּמָהּ רַב בַּר שַׁבָּא קַמֵּיהּ דְּרַב כָּהֲנָא בְּלָאו דְּ״לֹא תָסוּר״. אַחִיכוּ עֲלֵיהּ: לָאו דְּ״לֹא תָסוּר״ דְּאוֹרָיְיתָא הִיא!

The Gemara asks: **Why? Let us** also **say** here: **"There is neither wisdom, nor understanding, nor counsel against the Lord." Rav bar Shaba interpreted this** prohibition, which is overridden by human dignity, **before Rav Kahana** as referring **to the prohibition of:** "According to the Torah taught to you and the ruling handed down to you, you shall do, **you shall not deviate** to the left or the right from that which they tell you" (Deuteronomy 17:11). The Yeshiva students **laughed at him,** as the **prohibition of "you shall not deviate" is by Torah law,** like all other Torah prohibitions. Why should human dignity override it any more than any other Torah prohibition?

אֲמַר רַב כָּהֲנָא: גַּבְרָא רַבָּה אֲמַר מִילְּתָא לָא תָּחִיכוּ עֲלֵיהּ, כָּל מִילֵּי דְּרַבָּנַן אַסְמְכִינְהוּ עַל לָאו דְּ״לֹא תָסוּר״, וּמִשּׁוּם כְּבוֹדוֹ שָׁרוּ רַבָּנַן.

Rav Kahana replied to them: **A great man has spoken, do not laugh at him.** The Sages **based all rabbinic law on the prohibition of "you shall not deviate";**[N] **however, due to** concern for human **dignity, the Sages permitted** suspension of rabbinic law in cases where the two collide. All rabbinic decrees are predicated on the mitzva in the Torah to heed the judges in each generation and to never stray from their words. Therefore, when the Sages suspend a decree in the interest of preserving human dignity, human dignity is overriding a Torah prohibition. In any case, it only overrides rabbinic decrees.

תָּא שְׁמַע: ״וְהִתְעַלַּמְתָּ מֵהֶם״ – פְּעָמִים שֶׁאַתָּה מִתְעַלֵּם מֵהֶם וּפְעָמִים שֶׁאֵין אַתָּה מִתְעַלֵּם מֵהֶם;

The Gemara cites an additional proof from a *baraita*: **Come and hear:** With regard to the laws of returning a lost object, it is stated: "You shall not see the ox of your brother or his sheep go astray and ignore them; return them to your brother" (Deuteronomy 22:1). The *baraita* explains that the seemingly extraneous expression **and disregard them**[N] must be understood to give license that **at times you disregard** lost objects **and at times you do not disregard them.**

BACKGROUND

Coffins – אֲרוֹנוֹת: The ossuary is made of stone, as is its cover.

Stone ossuary from the end of the Second Temple era

HALAKHA

We would jump over the coffins of the deceased – מְדַלְּגִין הָיִינוּ עַל אֲרוֹנוֹת: A priest is permitted to run to greet the kings of Israel and disregard rabbinic decrees of impurity. Whether or not this allowance applies to gentile kings as well, see the Rambam and the *Magen Avraham* (Rambam *Sefer Shofetim, Hilkhot Evel* 3:14; *Shulḥan Arukh, Oraḥ Ḥayyim* 224:9, and see also the *Magen Avraham*).

NOTES

The prohibition of: You shall not deviate – לָאו דְּלֹא תָסוּר: Some explain that rabbinic decrees are overridden by concern for human dignity, despite the fact that the authority of rabbinic decrees and ordinances is itself based on a mitzva in the Torah. That mitzva only requires individuals to obey rulings of the Sanhedrin when there is a dispute between the Sages. However, the authority of rabbinic ordinances and decrees is alluded to by this prohibition and not based on it (*Alfei Menashe*).

And disregard them – וְהִתְעַלַּמְתָּ מֵהֶם: In the context in which it appears in the Torah, this phrase does not mean that one has license to ignore a lost object in certain circumstances. However, since the possibility of disregarding a lost object is mentioned, the inference is that this option exists in *halakha*, even though it is not the standard practice. The Sages interpreted it as an allusion to the established *halakha* that returning of a lost object is not incumbent upon every individual in every case.

HALAKHA

If he was a priest and the lost object was in the cemetery, or if he was an elder and it is beneath his dignity – אִם הָיָה כֹּהֵן וְהִיא בְּבֵית הַקְּבָרוֹת, אוֹ הָיָה זָקֵן וְאֵינָהּ לְפִי כְבוֹדוֹ: A priest who sees a lost object in a cemetery is not obligated to tend to its return. An elder for whom it is undignified to handle an object of that kind even if it belonged to him, is similarly exempt. This *halakha* also applies to the mitzva to assist its owner to unload an animal that collapsed under its burden (Rambam *Sefer Nezikin, Hilkhot Gezela VeAveda* 11:18. See also *Shulḥan Arukh, Ḥoshen Mishpat* 272:2–3).

Or if he had more work to do – אוֹ שֶׁהָיְתָה מְלַאכְתּוֹ מְרוּבָּה: One who earns a high salary and is concerned that he will lose it if he interrupts his work to tend to a lost object, if he stipulated before the court that he will be reimbursed for any lost wages, he is obligated to return the lost object. If, however, there is no court before which he could make that stipulation, his wages take precedence, as per the Gemara here and in *Bava Metzia* 30a (*Shulḥan Arukh, Ḥoshen Mishpat* 265:1).

הָא כֵּיצַד? אִם הָיָה כֹּהֵן וְהִיא בְּבֵית הַקְּבָרוֹת, אוֹ הָיָה זָקֵן וְאֵינָהּ לְפִי כְּבוֹדוֹ, אוֹ שֶׁהָיְתָה מְלַאכְתּוֹ מְרוּבָּה מִשֶּׁל חֲבֵרוֹ, לְכָךְ נֶאֱמַר: ״וְהִתְעַלַּמְתָּ״. אַמַּאי? לֵימָא: ״אֵין חָכְמָה וְאֵין תְּבוּנָה וְאֵין עֵצָה לְנֶגֶד ה׳״!

How so? If he was a priest and the lost object **was in the cemetery, or if he was an elder and it is beneath his dignity**[H] to tend to a lost object of that kind, **or if he had more work to do**[H] **than another person** and he does not want to set it all aside when another person is available to tend to the lost object. **Therefore,** with regard to those cases **it is stated: And disregard them** to permit one to refrain from returning the object. **Why? Let us say** here, too: Although handling the lost object would be beneath his dignity, **"there is neither wisdom, nor understanding, nor counsel against the Lord."**

שָׁאנֵי הָתָם, דִּכְתִיב: ״וְהִתְעַלַּמְתָּ מֵהֶם״. וְלִיגְמַר מִינַּהּ! – אִיסּוּרָא מִמָּמוֹנָא לָא יָלְפִינַן.

The Gemara answers: **There it is different, as it is written: "And disregard them,"** indicating that under certain circumstances one is permitted to disregard a lost object. In that case, there is a biblical directive that creates an exception to the prohibition: "You may not disregard" (Deuteronomy 22:3). We found a case in which human dignity overrides a Torah prohibition. The Gemara suggests: **Let us derive** a general principle that human dignity takes precedence over all mitzvot in the Torah **from this** case. This possibility is rejected: **We do not derive** *halakhot* pertaining to **prohibitions** from **monetary** laws, and the case of the lost object merely entails a monetary loss, unlike other prohibitions.

תָּא שְׁמַע:

The Gemara cites an additional proof from a *baraita*. **Come** and **hear** what was said in the Torah with regard to the Nazirite: "He shall not become impure for his father or his mother or his brother or his sister in their death, for the crown of his God is on his head" (Numbers 6:7). Since it was already written with regard to the Nazirite: "He shall not come upon a dead body" (Numbers 6:6), why is it necessary to elaborate and specify his parents and siblings?

״וּלְאַחוֹתוֹ״ מָה תַּלְמוּד לוֹמַר? הֲרֵי שֶׁהָיָה הוֹלֵךְ לִשְׁחוֹט אֶת פִּסְחוֹ וְלָמוּל אֶת בְּנוֹ וְשָׁמַע שֶׁמֵּת לוֹ מֵת, יָכוֹל יַחֲזוֹר וְיִטַּמֵּא – אָמַרְתָּ לֹא יִטַּמָּא.

The Sages derived through halakhic midrash that each of these relationships come to teach a specific nuance of the law. They learned: To **what** purpose **did the verse state: And his sister?** To teach that one **who was going to slaughter his Paschal** lamb **and to circumcise his son,** both of which are positive mitzvot that if he fails to fulfill them, he is punished with *karet*, **and he heard that** a relative **of his died, I might have thought** that **he** should **return and become ritually impure** with the impurity imparted by a corpse. **You said: "He shall not become impure"**; the death of his relative will not override so significant a mitzva from the Torah.

יָכוֹל כְּשֵׁם שֶׁאֵינוֹ מִטַּמֵּא לָהֶם כָּךְ אֵינוֹ מִטַּמֵּא לְמֵת מִצְוָה, תַּלְמוּד לוֹמַר: ״וּלְאַחוֹתוֹ״ – לַאֲחוֹתוֹ הוּא דְּאֵינוֹ מִטַּמֵּא,

I **might** have thought: **Just as he does not become impure for** his relatives, **so he does not become impure for a corpse with no one to bury it** [*met mitzva*]. **The verse states: "And his sister"; he may not become impure for his sister,** as someone else can attend to her burial,

Perek **III**
Daf **20** Amud **a**

HALAKHA

But he does become impure for a *met mitzva* – אֲבָל מִטַּמֵּא הוּא לְמֵת מִצְוָה: One is required attend to the burial of a corpse with no one to bury it and become impure through contact with that corpse. This is true even for a High Priest, a Nazirite and one en route to offer the Paschal lamb or circumcise one's son, in accordance with the conclusion of the *baraita* cited in the Gemara (Rambam *Sefer Shofetim, Hilkhot Evel* 3:8; *Shulḥan Arukh, Yoreh De'a* 374:1).

אֲבָל מִטַּמֵּא הוּא לְמֵת מִצְוָה, אַמַּאי? לֵימָא: ״אֵין חָכְמָה וְאֵין תְּבוּנָה וְאֵין עֵצָה לְנֶגֶד ה׳״.

but he does become impure for a *met mitzva*.[H] Here too, the question is asked: **Let us say** that the obligation to bury a *met mitzva*, which is predicated on the preservation of human dignity, should not override mitzvot explicitly written in the Torah, as it is stated: **"There is neither wisdom, nor understanding, nor counsel against the Lord."**

שָׁאנֵי הָתָם, דִּכְתִיב ׳וּלְאַחוֹתוֹ׳.

The Gemara answers: **There it is different, as it is explicitly written: "And his sister,"** from which we derive that although he may not become ritually impure to bury his sister, he must do so for a *met mitzva*.

וְלִיגְמַר מִינָּהּ! – שֵׁב וְאַל תַּעֲשֶׂה שָׁאנֵי.

The Gemara suggests: **Let us derive** a general principle that human dignity takes precedence over all mitzvot in the Torah **from this** case.[N] This possibility is rejected: This is a special case, because a case of **"sit and refrain from action"** [*shev ve'al ta'aseh*] **is different.**[N] Engaging in the burial of a *met mitzva* is not actually in contravention of a mitzva. Rather, by doing so he becomes ritually impure and is then rendered incapable of fulfilling that mitzva. We cannot derive a general principle from here that human dignity would also override a Torah prohibition in a case where that prohibition is directly contravened.

אֲמַר לֵיהּ רַב פַּפָּא לְאַבַּיֵי: מַאי שְׁנָא רִאשׁוֹנִים דְּאִתְרְחִישׁ לְהוּ נִיסָּא, וּמַאי שְׁנָא אֲנַן דְּלָא מִתְרְחִישׁ לָן נִיסָּא? אִי מִשּׁוּם תְּנוּיֵי – בִּשְׁנֵי דְּרַב יְהוּדָה כּוּלֵּי תְּנוּיֵי בִּנְזִיקִין הֲוָה, וַאֲנַן קָא מַתְנִינַן שִׁיתָּא סִדְרֵי! וְכִי הֲוָה מָטֵי רַב יְהוּדָה בְּעוּקָצִין ״הָאִשָּׁה שֶׁכּוֹבֶשֶׁת יָרָק בַּקְּדֵרָה״ וְאָמְרִי לָהּ ״זֵיתִים שֶׁכְּבָשָׁן בְּטַרְפֵיהֶן טְהוֹרִים״ אֲמַר: ״הֲוָיוֹת דְּרַב וּשְׁמוּאֵל קָא חָזֵינָא הָכָא״, וַאֲנַן קָא מַתְנִינַן בְּעוּקָצִין תְּלֵיסַר מְתִיבָתָא! וְאִילּוּ רַב יְהוּדָה, כִּי הֲוָה שָׁלֵיף חַד מְסָאנֵיהּ – אָתֵי מִטְרָא, וַאֲנַן קָא מְצַעֲרִינַן נַפְשִׁין וּמִצְוַח קָא צָוְחִינַן – וְלֵית דְּמַשְׁגַּח בָּן! –

The Gemara responds: In the context of the discussion whether or not human dignity overrides honoring God in the sense of fulfilling his mitzvot, **Rav Pappa said to Abaye: What is different about the earlier** generations, **for whom miracles occurred and what is different about us, for whom miracles do not occur? If it is because of** Torah **study; in the years of Rav Yehuda all of their learning was** confined to **the** order of ***Nezikin*****, while we learn** all **six orders!** Moreover, **when Rav Yehuda would reach in** tractate ***Okatzin***,[N] which discusses the extent to which the stems of various fruits and vegetables are considered an integral part of the produce in terms of becoming ritually impure, the *halakha* that **a woman who pickles a vegetable in a pot, and some say** when he would reach the *halakha* that **olives pickled with their leaves are pure,** because after pickling, it is no longer possible to lift the fruit by its leaves, they are no longer considered part of the fruit; he would find it difficult to understand. He **would say:** Those are **the disputes between Rav and Shmuel that we see here. And we,** in contrast, **learn thirteen versions of *Okatzin*. While,** with regard to miracles, after declaring a fast to pray for a drought to end, **when Rav Yehuda would remove one of his shoes**[N] **the rain would** immediately **fall, whereas we torment ourselves and cry out and no one notices us.**

אֲמַר לֵיהּ: קַמָּאֵי הָווּ קָא מָסְרִי נַפְשַׁיְיהוּ אַקְּדוּשַּׁת הַשֵּׁם, אֲנַן לָא מָסְרִינַן נַפְשִׁין אַקְּדוּשַּׁת הַשֵּׁם. כִּי הָא דְּרַב אַדָּא בַּר אַהֲבָה חַזְיֵיהּ לְהַהִיא כּוּתִית דַּהֲוַת לְבִישָׁא כַּרְבַּלְתָּא בְּשׁוּקָא, סְבַר דְּבַת יִשְׂרָאֵל הִיא, קָם קַרְעֵיהּ מִינָּהּ; אִגַּלַּאי מִילְּתָא דְּכוּתִית הִיא, שַׁיְימוּהָ בְּאַרְבַּע מְאָה זוּזֵי. אֲמַר לָהּ: מַה שְּׁמֵךְ? אֲמַרָה לֵיהּ: מָתוּן. אֲמַר לָהּ: מָתוּן מָתוּן אַרְבַּע מְאָה זוּזֵי שָׁוְיָא.

Abaye **said to** Rav Pappa: **The previous** generations were wholly **dedicated to the sanctification of God's name,** while **we are not** as **dedicated to the sanctification of God's name.** Typical of the earlier generations' commitment, the Gemara relates: **Like this** incident involving **Rav Adda bar Ahava** who **saw a non-Jewish woman who was wearing a garment made of a forbidden mixture of wool and linen** [*karbalta*][N] **in the marketplace.** Since he **thought** that **she was Jewish, he stood and ripped it from her. It was** then **divulged that she was a non-Jew** and he was taken to court due to the shame that he caused her, and **they assessed** the payment for the shame that he caused **her** at **four hundred *zuz*.** Ultimately, Rav Adda **said to her: What is your name? She replied: Matun.** In a play on words, **he said to her: Matun,** her name, plus ***matun*****,** the Aramaic word for two hundred, **is worth four hundred *zuz*.**

רַב גִּידֵּל הֲוָה רָגִיל דַּהֲוָה קָא אָזֵיל וְיָתֵיב אַשַּׁעֲרֵי דִּטְבִילָה, אֲמַר לְהוּ: הָכִי טְבִילוּ וְהָכִי טְבִילוּ. אָמְרִי לֵיהּ רַבָּנַן: לָא קָא מִסְתְּפֵי מָר מִיֵּצֶר הָרָע? אֲמַר לְהוּ: דַּמְיָין בְּאַפַּאי כִּי קָאקֵי חִיוָּרֵי.

It was also related about the earlier generations, that they would degrade themselves in the desire to glorify God. **Rav Giddel was accustomed to go and sit at the gates of the** women's **immersion** sites. **He said to them: Immerse yourselves in this way, and immerse yourselves in that way. The Sages said to him: Master,** do you **not fear the evil inclination? He said to them: In my eyes,** they **are comparable to white geese.**

רַבִּי יוֹחָנָן הֲוָה רָגִיל דַּהֲוָה קָא אָזֵיל וְיָתֵיב אַשַּׁעֲרֵי דִּטְבִילָה, אֲמַר: כִּי סָלְקָן בְּנוֹת יִשְׂרָאֵל וְאָתְיָין מִטְּבִילָה מִסְתַּכְּלָן בִּי, וְנֶהֱוֵי לְהוּ זַרְעָא דְּשַׁפִּירֵי כְּוָותִי. אָמְרִי לֵיהּ רַבָּנַן: לָא קָא מִסְתְּפֵי מָר מֵעֵינָא בִּישָׁא? אֲמַר לְהוּ: אֲנָא מִזַּרְעָא דְּיוֹסֵף קָא אָתֵינָא, דְּלָא שָׁלְטָא בֵּיהּ עֵינָא בִּישָׁא, דִּכְתִיב: ״בֵּן פּוֹרָת יוֹסֵף בֵּן פּוֹרָת עֲלֵי עָיִן״, וְאָמַר רַבִּי אַבָּהוּ: אַל תִּקְרֵי ״עֲלֵי עָיִן״ אֶלָּא ״עוֹלֵי עַיִן״.

Similarly, the Gemara relates that **Rabbi Yoḥanan was accustomed to go and sit at the gates of the** women's **immersion** sites. Rabbi Yoḥanan, who was known for his extraordinary good looks, explained this and **said: When the daughters of Israel emerge from their immersion, they will look at me, and will have children as beautiful as I. The Sages asked him: Master,** do you **not fear the evil eye? He said to them: I descend from the seed of Joseph over whom the evil eye has no dominion, as it is written: "Joseph is a bountiful vine, a bountiful vine on a spring** [*alei ayin*]**"** (Genesis 49:22). "*Ayin*" can mean both "spring" and "eye." **And Rabbi Abbahu said** a homiletic interpretation: **Do not read** it ***alei ayin*****, rather *olei ayin*****,** above the eye; they transcend the influence of the evil eye.

NOTES

Let us derive from this case – **וְלִיגְמַר מִינָּהּ:** The logical flow of the discussion is as follows: The *halakha* concerning lost objects constitutes a challenge to the principle that preventing desecration of God's name overrides concerns of human dignity. This challenge is in two stages. First, the Gemara cites the *baraita* as an example that contradicts the principle. The Gemara rejects the challenge by pointing out unique circumstances extant in the case in the *baraita*. The second stage is more general: Since there is one clear case, whatever the reason, where human dignity overrides a mitzva in the Torah, it can serve as a paradigm from which a general principle can be extrapolated. Employing the hermeneutic principle of analogy, even though the paradigm was derived from a proof unique to that case, once established, it can serve as the basis for a general principle. Therefore the rejection of the second stage is not based on emphasizing the unique aspect of the specific case but rather in proving that this case falls into a special category and, consequently, general conclusions may not be drawn.

"Sit and refrain from action" [*shev ve'al ta'aseh*] is different – **שֵׁב וְאַל תַּעֲשֶׂה שָׁאנֵי:** *Tosafot* pointed out the difficulty with this explanation. It explains the situation where one is en route to bring his Paschal lamb and becomes ritually impure due to contact with a corpse, i.e., where the mitzva is not uprooted directly by his action, but rather as a consequence of his status. However, that is not the case in a situation where a priest, and certainly the High Priest or a nazirite, becomes ritually impure as a result of tending to the burial of a *met mitzva*. There he directly violates the prohibition with his action. *Tosafot* (in *Bava Metzia* and *Shevuot*) explain that demeaning the dead is far more severe than the standard concern for human dignity. Alternatively, one could distinguish and assert that the cases of a priest and a Nazirite are not paradigmatic, as the prohibition in each of those cases is less severe than a standard prohibition. Since a nazirite can approach a Sage for dissolution of his nazirite vow, it is a conditional, non-absolute and, therefore, less severe prohibition. The prohibition in the case of the priest is, by definition, limited to the priest and, therefore, relative to universal prohibitions, is less severe.

In tractate *Okatzin* – **בְּעוּקָצִין:** The *halakhot* of ritual purity and impurity include numerous definitions with regard to what is considered part of the fruit or vegetable and what is considered ancillary to and not actually part of the fruit, e.g., the leaves, stem, peel, etc. In the *mishnayot* in tractates *Okatzin* and *Teharot* that deal with this issue, much attention is paid to the distinctions between the various parts and why one is considered part of the fruit while the other is not. This constitutes one of the most intricate areas of halakhic discourse.

Remove one of his shoes – **שָׁלֵיף חַד מְסָאנֵיהּ:** It is prohibited to wear shoes on a public fast proclaimed due to drought. As soon as Rav Yehuda began his preparations for the fast, removing one of his shoes, the rain immediately began to fall.

A garment made of a forbidden mixture of wool and linen [*karbalta*] – **כַּרְבַּלְתָּא:** Some say that this is a red garment, which is considered immodest and that is why Rav Adda ripped it off her (*Arukh*). According to Rashi, who explained that it is an expensive garment, it is inappropriate to walk in public dressed in such finery without wearing an outer layer to cover it (Maharshal).

רַבִּי יוֹסֵי בְּרַבִּי חֲנִינָא אָמַר מֵהָכָא: ״וְיִדְגּוּ לָרֹב בְּקֶרֶב הָאָרֶץ״ מַה דָּגִים שֶׁבַּיָּם מַיִם מְכַסִּין עֲלֵיהֶם וְאֵין עַיִן הָרָע שׁוֹלֶטֶת בָּהֶם – אַף זַרְעוֹ שֶׁל יוֹסֵף אֵין עַיִן הָרָע שׁוֹלֶטֶת בָּהֶם.

Rabbi Yosei, son of Rabbi Ḥanina, cited a different proof, from Jacob's blessing of Joseph's sons, Ephraim and Menashe: "The angel who redeems me from all evil shall bless the young and in them may my name be recalled, and the name of my fathers, Abraham and Isaac, **and may they multiply** [*veyidgu*] **in the midst of the earth"** (Genesis 48:16). *Veyidgu* is related etymologically to the word fish [*dag*]. **Just as the fish in the sea, water covers them and the evil eye has no dominion over them,** so **too the seed of Joseph, the evil eye has no dominion over them.**

וְאִי בָּעֵית אֵימָא: עַיִן שֶׁלֹּא רָצְתָה לִזּוֹן מִמַּה שֶּׁאֵינוֹ שֶׁלּוֹ – אֵין עַיִן הָרָע שׁוֹלֶטֶת בּוֹ.

And if you wish, say instead: Joseph's **eye, which did not seek to feast on that which was not his,** Potiphar's wife, **the evil eye has no dominion over him.**

מתני׳ נָשִׁים וַעֲבָדִים וּקְטַנִּים פְּטוּרִין מִקְּרִיאַת שְׁמַע

MISHNA **Women,**[H] **slaves, and minors,**[H] who have parallel obligations in various mitzvot, **are exempt from the recitation of *Shema***

HALAKHA

The obligation of women to recite *Shema* – נָשִׁים בְּחוֹבַת קְרִיאַת שְׁמַע: Women are exempt from reciting *Shema* and the accompanying blessings (*Mishna Berura*). They are not even obligated to do so by rabbinic law (*Mishna Berura*). There are those who ruled that women are obligated to recite the first verse of *Shema*, because it includes acceptance of the yoke of Heaven (*Beit Yosef* and *Baḥ; Shulḥan Arukh, Oraḥ Ḥayyim* 70:1).

The obligation of minors to recite the Shema – קְטַנִּים בִּקְרִיאַת שְׁמַע: The commentaries disagree whether the minors mentioned in the mishna as exempt from reciting *Shema* are only those who have not yet reached the age of training to fulfill mitzvot (Rabbeinu Tam) or whether even those who reached that age are exempt (Rashi). One should adopt the custom that a child who reached the age of training to fulfill mitzvot recites *Shema*, in accordance with the opinion of Rabbeinu Tam (*Shulḥan Arukh, Oraḥ Ḥayyim* 70:2).

Perek **III**
Daf **20** Amud **b**

וּמִן הַתְּפִילִּין, וְחַיָּיבִין בִּתְפִלָּה וּבִמְזוּזָה וּבְבִרְכַּת הַמָּזוֹן.

and from phylacteries,[H] but they **are obligated in** the mitzvot of **prayer,**[HN] ***mezuza,***[H] **and Grace after Meals.**[H] The Gemara explains the rationale for these exemptions and obligations.

גמ׳ ״קְרִיאַת שְׁמַע״, פְּשִׁיטָא! מִצְוַת עֲשֵׂה שֶׁהַזְּמַן גְּרָמָא הוּא, וְכׇל מִצְוַת עֲשֵׂה שֶׁהַזְּמַן גְּרָמָא נָשִׁים פְּטוּרוֹת!

GEMARA With regard to the mishna's statement that women are exempt from **the recitation of *Shema*,** the Gemara asks: That is **obvious,** as *Shema* is a **time-bound, positive mitzva, and** the halakhic principle is: **Women are exempt from any time-bound, positive mitzva,** i.e., any mitzva whose performance is only in effect at a particular time. *Shema* falls into that category as its recitation is restricted to the morning and the evening. Why then did the mishna need to mention it specifically?

מַהוּ דְּתֵימָא: הוֹאִיל וְאִית בָּהּ מַלְכוּת שָׁמַיִם – קָמַשְׁמַע לַן.

The Gemara replies: **Lest you say: Since** *Shema* **includes** the acceptance of the yoke of **the kingdom of Heaven,** perhaps women are obligated in its recitation despite the fact that it is a time-bound, positive mitzva. Therefore, the mishna **teaches us** that, nevertheless, women are exempt.

״וּמִן הַתְּפִלִּין״ פְּשִׁיטָא! – מַהוּ דְּתֵימָא: הוֹאִיל וְאִתְקַשׁ לִמְזוּזָה – קָמַשְׁמַע לַן.

We also learned in the mishna that women are exempt **from phylacteries.** The Gemara asks: That is **obvious** as well. The donning of phylacteries is only in effect at particular times; during the day but not at night, on weekdays but not on Shabbat or Festivals. The Gemara replies: **Lest you say: Since** the mitzva of phylacteries **is juxtaposed** in the Torah **to** the mitzva of ***mezuza,*** as it is written: "And you shall bind them as a sign upon your hands and they shall be frontlets between your eyes" (Deuteronomy 6:8), followed by: "And you shall write them upon the door posts of your house and on your gates" (Deuteronomy 6:9), just as women are obligated in the mitzva of *mezuza,* so too they are obligated in the mitzva of phylacteries. Therefore, the mishna **teaches us** that nevertheless, women are exempt.

HALAKHA

Those exempt from the mitzva of phylacteries – הַפְּטוּרִים מִתְּפִלִּין: Women and slaves are exempt from phylacteries. If women want to assume a stringency and don phylacteries they should be rebuked (Rambam *Sefer Ahava, Hilkhot Tefillin UMezuza VeSefer Torah* 4:13; *Shulḥan Arukh, Oraḥ Ḥayyim* 38:3).

Those obligated in prayer – הַחַיָּיבִים בִּתְפִלָּה: Everyone is obligated to pray, even women and slaves, in accordance with the *mishna*, and it is a mitzva to train minors to pray. Some rule that women fulfill their obligation by means of reciting an entreaty once daily. In the opinion of the Rambam, that is their obligation to pray by Torah law (*Magen Avraham*; Rambam *Sefer Ahava, Hilkhot Tefilla* 1:2; *Shulḥan Arukh, Oraḥ Ḥayyim* 106:1).

Those obligated in the mitzva of *mezuza* – הַחַיָּיבִים בִּמְזוּזָה: Everyone, including women and slaves, is obligated to affix a *mezuza* to his doorways. Even minors are trained to affix a *mezuza* to their doorways (Rambam *Sefer Ahava, Hilkhot Tefillin Mezuza VeSefer Torah* 5:10; *Shulḥan Arukh, Yoreh De'a* 291:3).

Those obligated in the mitzva of Grace after Meals – הַחַיָּיבִים בְּבִרְכַּת הַמָּזוֹן: Women are obligated to recite Grace after Meals in accordance with the *mishna*, and it is a mitzva to instruct minors to do so as well (Rambam *Sefer Ahava, Hilkhot Berakhot* 5:1; *Shulḥan Arukh, Oraḥ Ḥayyim* 186:1–2).

NOTES

Women's obligation in prayer – נָשִׁים בְּחוֹבַת תְּפִלָּה: This question is based on a more fundamental dilemma: Is prayer a mitzva by Torah or by rabbinic law? According to the opinion that it is rabbinic, the language of the Gemara: Like a time-bound positive mitzva is problematic. On the other hand, even those who hold that the basic mitzva of prayer is by Torah law, assert that the mitzva of turning to God is by Torah law, while the formula and the times for prayer are by rabbinic law. Therefore, it is possible for women to fulfill the mitzva of prayer by means of any request addressed to God.

״וְחַיָּיבִין בִּתְפִלָּה״ דְּרַחֲמֵי נִינְהוּ. – מַהוּ דְּתֵימָא: הוֹאִיל וּכְתִיב בָּהּ ״עֶרֶב וָבֹקֶר וְצָהֳרַיִם״, כְּמִצְוַת עֲשֵׂה שֶׁהַזְּמַן גְּרָמָא דָּמֵי – קָמַשְׁמַע לָן.

We also learned in the mishna that women, slaves, and children are **obligated in prayer.** The Gemara explains that, although the mitzva of prayer is only in effect at particular times, which would lead to the conclusion that women are exempt, nevertheless, since prayer **is** supplication for **mercy** and women also require divine mercy, they are obligated. However, **lest you say: Since** regarding prayer it is **written: "Evening and morning and afternoon** I pray and cry aloud and He hears my voice" (Psalms 55:18), perhaps prayer should be **considered a time-bound, positive mitzva** and women would be exempt, the mishna **teaches us** that, fundamentally, the mitzva of prayer is not time-bound and, therefore, everyone is obligated.

״וּבִמְזוּזָה״ פְּשִׁיטָא! – מַהוּ דְּתֵימָא: הוֹאִיל וְאִתְקַשׁ לְתַלְמוּד תּוֹרָה – קָמַשְׁמַע לָן.

We also learned in the mishna that women are obligated in the mitzva of *mezuza*. The Gemara asks: That too is **obvious.** Why would they be exempt from fulfilling this obligation, it is a positive mitzva that is not time-bound? The Gemara replies: **Lest you say: Since** the mitzva of *mezuza* **is juxtaposed** in the Torah to the mitzva of **Torah study** (Deuteronomy 11:19–20), just as women are exempt from Torah study, so too they are exempt from the mitzva of *mezuza*. Therefore, the mishna explicitly **teaches us** that they are obligated.

״וּבְבִרְכַּת הַמָּזוֹן״ פְּשִׁיטָא! – מַהוּ דְּתֵימָא: הוֹאִיל וּכְתִיב ״בְּתֵת ה׳ לָכֶם בָּעֶרֶב בָּשָׂר לֶאֱכֹל וְלֶחֶם בַּבֹּקֶר לִשְׂבֹּעַ״, כְּמִצְוַת עֲשֵׂה שֶׁהַזְּמַן גְּרָמָא דָּמֵי – קָמַשְׁמַע לָן.

We also learned in the mishna that women are obligated to recite the **Grace after Meals.** The Gemara asks: That too is **obvious.** The Gemara replies: **Lest you say: Since it is written: "When the Lord shall give you meat to eat in the evening and bread in the morning to the full"** (Exodus 16:8), one might conclude that the Torah established fixed times for the meals and, consequently, for the mitzva of Grace after Meals and, therefore, it **is considered a time-bound, positive mitzva,** exempting women from its recitation. Therefore, the mishna **teaches us** that women are obligated.

אָמַר רַב אַדָּא בַּר אַהֲבָה: נָשִׁים חַיָּיבוֹת בְּקִדּוּשׁ הַיּוֹם דְּבַר תּוֹרָה. – אַמַּאי? מִצְוַת עֲשֵׂה שֶׁהַזְּמַן גְּרָמָא הוּא, וְכׇל מִצְוַת עֲשֵׂה שֶׁהַזְּמַן גְּרָמָא נָשִׁים פְּטוּרוֹת! – אָמַר אַבַּיֵי: מִדְּרַבָּנַן.

Rav Adda bar Ahava[P] **said: Women are obligated to** recite **the sanctification of the** Shabbat **day** [***kiddush***][H] **by Torah law.** The Gemara asks: **Why?** *Kiddush* is **a time-bound, positive mitzva, and women are exempt** from **all time-bound, positive mitzvot. Abaye said:** Indeed, women are obligated to recite *kiddush* **by rabbinic,** but not by Torah **law.**

אָמַר לֵיהּ רָבָא: וְהָא ״דְּבַר תּוֹרָה״ קָאָמַר! וְעוֹד, כׇּל מִצְוֹת עֲשֵׂה נְחַיְּיבִינְהוּ מִדְּרַבָּנַן!

Rava said to Abaye: There are two refutations to your explanation. First, Rav Adda bar Ahava said that women are obligated to recite *kiddush* **by Torah law, and, furthermore,** the very explanation is difficult to understand. If the Sages do indeed institute ordinances in these circumstances, **let us obligate them** to fulfill **all** time-bound, **positive mitzvot by rabbinic law,** even though they are exempt by Torah law.

אֶלָּא אָמַר רָבָא: אָמַר קְרָא ״זָכוֹר״ ״וְשָׁמוֹר״ – כׇּל שֶׁיֶּשְׁנוֹ בִּשְׁמִירָה יֶשְׁנוֹ בִּזְכִירָה, וְהָנֵי נָשֵׁי, הוֹאִיל וְאִיתְנְהוּ בִּשְׁמִירָה – אִיתְנְהוּ בִּזְכִירָה.

Rather, Rava said: This has a unique explanation. In the Ten Commandments in the book of Exodus, **the verse said: "Remember** Shabbat and sanctify it" (Exodus 20:8), while in the book of Deuteronomy it is said: **"Observe** Shabbat and sanctify it" (Deuteronomy 5:12). From these two variants we can deduce that **anyone included in** the obligation to **observe** Shabbat by avoiding its desecration, **is** also **included in** the mitzva to **remember** Shabbat by reciting *kiddush*. **Since these women are included in** the mitzva **to observe** Shabbat, as there is no distinction between men and women in the obligation to observe prohibitions in general and to refrain from the desecration of Shabbat in particular, so too **are they included in** the mitzva of **remembering** Shabbat.

אֲמַר לֵיהּ רָבִינָא לְרָבָא: נָשִׁים בְּבִרְכַּת הַמָּזוֹן, דְּאוֹרַיְיתָא אוֹ דְּרַבָּנַן? לְמַאי נָפְקָא מִינָּהּ – לְאַפּוֹקֵי רַבִּים יְדֵי חוֹבָתָן. אִי אָמְרַתְּ (בִּשְׁלָמָא) דְּאוֹרַיְיתָא – אָתֵי דְּאוֹרַיְיתָא וּמַפֵּיק דְּאוֹרַיְיתָא, אֶלָּא אִי אָמְרַתְּ דְּרַבָּנַן – הָוֵי ״שֶׁאֵינוֹ מְחוּיָּיב בַּדָּבָר״, וְכׇל שֶׁאֵינוֹ מְחוּיָּיב בַּדָּבָר – אֵינוֹ מוֹצִיא אֶת הָרַבִּים יְדֵי חוֹבָתָן. מַאי?

Ravina said to Rava: We learned in the mishna that **women** are obligated in the mitzva of **Grace after Meals.** However, are they obligated **by Torah law** or merely **by rabbinic law? What difference does it make** whether it is by Torah or rabbinic law? The difference is regarding her ability **to fulfill the obligation of others** when reciting the blessing on their behalf. **Granted, if you say that** their obligation **is by Torah law,** one whose obligation **is by Torah law can come and fulfill the obligation** of others who are obligated **by Torah law. However, if you say** that their obligation is **by rabbinic law,** then from the perspective of Torah law, women **are** considered to be **one who is not obligated, and** the general principle is that **one who is not obligated** to fulfill a particular mitzva[H] **cannot fulfill the obligations of the many** in that mitzva. Therefore, it is important to know **what** is the resolution of this dilemma.[H]

PERSONALITIES

Rav Adda bar Ahava – רַב אַדָּא בַּר אַהֲבָה: A Babylonian *amora*, Rav Adda bar Ahava was among those who spanned the first and second generations of *amora'im*.

Looking at the various talmudic sources related to Rav Adda bar Ahava, it becomes clear that there were at least two, perhaps three, Sages referred to by that name. It appears that the reference in our Gemara is to the first and greatest Sage to go by that name. Rav Adda bar Ahava was one of Rav's greatest students; however, both Rav and Shmuel appreciated the extent of his righteousness and piety, and would rely on his merit in their belief that they would come to no harm. Future generations came to cite him as exemplifying behavior reflecting awe of Heaven. The Talmud tells of his modesty and the painstaking care he took with regard to the honor of Heaven, of his teachers, and of his fellows man.

It appears the calculation of the Hebrew calendar, referred to as *tekufat* Rav Adda, is named for this first Rav Adda, and, although Shmuel established his own calculation, Rav Adda's was far more accurate and now serves as the foundation for calculating the Jewish calendar.

HALAKHA

Women are obligated in the sanctification of the Shabbat day [*kiddush*] – נָשִׁים חַיָּיבוֹת בְּקִדּוּשׁ: Women are obligated to recite *kiddush* on Shabbat (*Rambam Sefer HaMadda, Hilkhot Avodat Kokhavim* 12:3; *Shulḥan Arukh, Oraḥ Ḥayyim* 271:2).

One who is not obligated to fulfill a particular mitzva – שֶׁאֵינוֹ מְחוּיָּיב בַּדָּבָר: One who is not obligated by Torah law to fulfill a specific mitzva cannot fulfill the obligation for someone obligated to fulfill that mitzva by Torah law with his blessing (Rambam *Sefer Ahava, Hilkhot Tefillin UMezuza VeSefer Torah* 1:11).

The essence of women's obligation to recite Grace after Meals – מַהוּת חִיּוּב נָשִׁים בְּבִרְכַּת הַמָּזוֹן: There is uncertainty as to whether the obligation of women to recite Grace after Meals is by Torah or rabbinic law. The dilemma raised in the Gemara remains unresolved and the ruling reached is consistent with the ruling in all cases of unresolved dilemmas. Therefore, women cannot fulfill the obligation for others obligated by Torah law in the mitzva of Grace after Meals (*Magen Avraham*; *Rambam Sefer Ahava, Hilkhot Berakhot* 5:15–16; *Shulḥan Arukh, Oraḥ Ḥayyim* 186:1).

תָּא שְׁמַע, בֶּאֱמֶת אָמְרוּ: בֵּן מְבָרֵךְ לְאָבִיו, וְעֶבֶד מְבָרֵךְ לְרַבּוֹ, וְאִשָּׁה מְבָרֶכֶת לְבַעְלָהּ; אֲבָל אָמְרוּ חֲכָמִים: תָּבֹא מְאֵרָה לְאָדָם שֶׁאִשְׁתּוֹ וּבָנָיו מְבָרְכִין לוֹ.

Come and hear from what was taught in a *baraita*: **Actually they said** that **a son may recite a blessing** on behalf **of his father,**[H] **and a slave may recite a blessing** on behalf **of his master, and a woman may recite a blessing** on behalf of **her husband, but the Sages said: May a curse come to a man** who, due to his ignorance, requires **his wife and children to recite a blessing on his behalf.**

אִי אָמְרַתְּ בִּשְׁלָמָא דְּאוֹרָיְיתָא – אָתֵי דְּאוֹרָיְיתָא וּמַפֵּיק דְּאוֹרָיְיתָא, אֶלָּא אִי אָמְרַתְּ דְּרַבָּנַן – אָתֵי דְּרַבָּנַן וּמַפֵּיק דְּאוֹרָיְיתָא?

From here we may infer: **Granted, if you say that** their obligation **is by Torah law,** one whose obligation **is by Torah law can come and fulfill the obligation** of others who are obligated **by Torah law. However, if you say** that their obligation is **by rabbinic law,** can one who is obligated **by rabbinic law, come and fulfill the obligation** of one whose obligation is **by Torah law?**

וּלְטַעֲמִיךְ, קָטָן בַּר חִיּוּבָא הוּא? – אֶלָּא, הָכָא בְּמַאי עָסְקִינַן – כְּגוֹן שֶׁאָכַל שִׁיעוּרָא דְּרַבָּנַן, דְּאָתֵי דְּרַבָּנַן וּמַפֵּיק דְּרַבָּנַן.

The Gemara challenges this proof: **And according to your reasoning,** is **a minor obligated** by Torah law to perform mitzvot? Everyone agrees that a minor is exempt by Torah law, yet here the *baraita* said that he may recite a blessing on behalf of his father. There must be another way to explain the *baraita*. **With what are we dealing here? With a case where** his father **ate** a quantity of food that did not satisfy his hunger, a **measure** for which one is only obligated **by rabbinic law** to recite Grace after Meals. In that case, one whose obligation **is by rabbinic law can come and fulfill the obligation** of another whose obligation **is by rabbinic law.**[N]

דָּרַשׁ רַב עֲוִירָא, זִמְנִין אֲמַר לָהּ מִשְּׁמֵיהּ דְּרַבִּי אַמִי וְזִמְנִין אֲמַר לָהּ מִשְּׁמֵיהּ דְּרַבִּי אַסִי: אָמְרוּ מַלְאֲכֵי הַשָּׁרֵת לִפְנֵי הַקָּדוֹשׁ בָּרוּךְ הוּא: רִבּוֹנוֹ שֶׁל עוֹלָם, כָּתוּב בְּתוֹרָתְךָ ״אֲשֶׁר לֹא יִשָּׂא פָנִים וְלֹא יִקַּח שֹׁחַד״, וַהֲלֹא אַתָּה נוֹשֵׂא פָנִים לְיִשְׂרָאֵל, דִּכְתִיב: ״יִשָּׂא ה׳ פָּנָיו אֵלֶיךָ״. אָמַר לָהֶם: וְכִי לֹא אֶשָּׂא פָנִים לְיִשְׂרָאֵל? שֶׁכָּתַבְתִּי לָהֶם בַּתּוֹרָה: ״וְאָכַלְתָּ וְשָׂבָעְתָּ וּבֵרַכְתָּ אֶת ה׳ אֱלֹהֶיךָ״, וְהֵם מְדַקְדְּקִים [עַל] עַצְמָם עַד כַּזַּיִת וְעַד כַּבֵּיצָה.

After citing the *halakha* that one who eats a quantity of food that does not satisfy his hunger is obligated by rabbinic law to recite Grace after Meals, the Gemara cites a related homiletic interpretation. **Rav Avira taught, sometimes he said it in the name of** Rabbi Ami, **and sometimes he said it in the name of** Rabbi Asi: **The ministering angels said before the Holy One, Blessed be He: Master of the Universe, in Your Torah it is written:** "The great, mighty and awesome God **who favors no one and takes no bribe**" (Deuteronomy 10:17), **yet You,** nevertheless, **show favor to Israel,**[N] **as it is written: "The Lord shall show favor to you** and give you peace" (Numbers 6:26). **He replied to them: And how can I not show favor to Israel, as I wrote for them in the Torah: "And you shall eat and be satisfied, and bless the Lord your God"** (Deuteronomy 8:10), meaning that there is no obligation to bless the Lord until one is satiated; **yet they are exacting with themselves** to recite Grace after Meals even if they have eaten **as much as an olive-bulk or an egg-bulk.** Since they go beyond the requirements of the law, they are worthy of favor.

מתני׳ בַּעַל קֶרִי מְהַרְהֵר בְּלִבּוֹ וְאֵינוֹ מְבָרֵךְ לֹא לְפָנֶיהָ וְלֹא לְאַחֲרֶיהָ; וְעַל הַמָּזוֹן מְבָרֵךְ לְאַחֲרָיו וְאֵינוֹ מְבָרֵךְ לְפָנָיו. רַבִּי יְהוּדָה אוֹמֵר: מְבָרֵךְ לִפְנֵיהֶם וּלְאַחֲרֵיהֶם.

MISHNA Ezra the Scribe decreed that one who is ritually impure because of a seminal emission may not engage in matters of Torah until he has immersed in a ritual bath and purified himself. This *halakha* was accepted over the course of many generations; however, many disputes arose with regard to the Torah matters to which it applies.[N] Regarding this, the mishna says: If the time for the recitation of *Shema* arrived and **one** is impure due to a **seminal emission,**[H] he may **contemplate** *Shema* **in his heart, but neither recites the blessings preceding** *Shema*, **nor the blessings following it. Over food** which, after partaking, one is obligated by Torah law to recite a blessing, **one recites a blessing afterward, but one does not recite a blessing beforehand,** because the blessing recited prior to eating is a requirement by rabbinic law. **And** in all of these instances **Rabbi Yehuda says: He recites a blessing beforehand and thereafter** in both the case of *Shema* and in the case of food.

גמ׳ אָמַר רָבִינָא, זֹאת אוֹמֶרֶת: הִרְהוּר כְּדִבּוּר דָּמֵי. דְּאִי סָלְקָא דַּעְתָּךְ לָאו כְּדִבּוּר דָּמֵי, לָמָּה מְהַרְהֵר?

GEMARA Ravina said: **That is to say,** from the mishna that **contemplation is tantamount to speech.**[H] **As if it would enter your mind** that **it is not tantamount to speech,** then **why** does one who is impure because of a seminal emission **contemplate?** It must be that it is tantamount to speech.

אֶלָּא מַאי הִרְהוּר כְּדִבּוּר דָּמֵי, יוֹצִיא בִּשְׂפָתָיו!

The Gemara rejects this: **But what** are you saying, that **contemplation is tantamount to speech?** Then, if one who is impure because of a seminal emission is permitted to contemplate, why does he not **utter** the words **with his lips?**

HALAKHA

A son may recite a blessing on behalf of his father – בֵּן מְבָרֵךְ לְאָבִיו: A minor can fulfill the obligation of an adult to recite Grace after Meals if the adult did not eat enough to leave him satisfied (Rambam *Sefer Ahava, Hilkhot Berakhot* 5:15–16; *Shulḥan Arukh, Oraḥ Ḥayyim* 186:2).

One who experienced a seminal emission with regard to the blessing of the Torah – בַּעַל קֶרִי בְּבִרְכוֹת הַתּוֹרָה: Based on the ordinance instituted by Ezra, one who experienced a seminal emission is prohibited from engaging in Torah study, praying, and reciting *Shema* until he immerses himself. However, in subsequent generations that ordinance was repealed and one who experienced a seminal emission was permitted to engage in all those activities without immersion or bathing in nine *kav* of water. That remains the prevalent custom. Nevertheless, one who chooses to immerse himself is praiseworthy. He must, however, make certain that, by doing so, he does not let the time for *Shema* or prayer pass or miss the opportunity to participate in communal prayer (Rambam *Sefer Ahava, Hilkhot Keriat Shema* 4:8; *Shulḥan Arukh, Oraḥ Ḥayyim* 88:1).

Contemplation is tantamount to speech – הִרְהוּר כְּדִבּוּר דָּמֵי: The halakhic authorities disagreed whether or not contemplation is tantamount to speech, and, if it is, in what instances. The *ge'onim* ruled in accordance with the opinion of Rav Ḥisda that contemplation is not tantamount to speech as that seems to be the opinion upon which the discourse in the Gemara was predicated. Others ruled that contemplation is tantamount to speech only after the fact, particularly if one mouths the words, even if he does so inaudibly, according to the ruling of the Rambam. Similarly, in exigent circumstances, one fulfills his obligation with contemplation (*Shulḥan Arukh, Oraḥ Ḥayyim* 62:3–4).

NOTES

One whose obligation is by rabbinic law can come and fulfill the obligation of another whose obligation is by rabbinic law – אָתֵי דְּרַבָּנַן וּמַפֵּיק דְּרַבָּנַן: In this *halakha* and in the homiletic interpretation of Rav Avira, a certain insight into rabbinic measures is provided. For all intents and purposes, there are two categories of mitzvot: mitzvot by Torah law and mitzvot by rabbinic law. However, here, it is clear that mitzvot by rabbinic law are an independent system in which there are specific obligations, i.e., mitzvot, as well as people obligated to fulfill them, who do not enter into the framework of mitzvot by Torah law.

Yet You show favor to Israel – וַהֲלֹא אַתָּה נוֹשֵׂא פָּנִים לְיִשְׂרָאֵל: The Rashbam notes that according to the literal meaning there is a distinction between *nesiat panim leYisrael* in the sense of showing favor to Israel, and *nesiat penei Yisrael*, in the sense of God rendering judgment in their favor (*Tosefot Rabbeinu Yehuda HaḤasid*).

Ezra's ordinances – תַּקָּנַת עֶזְרָא: The Gemara (*Bava Kama* 82a) cites a tradition with regard to the ten ordinances instituted by Ezra in order to enhance fulfillment of both mitzvot by Torah law and ancient customs. The emphasis in all the ordinances was enhancing the sanctity in the daily existence of the people. By Torah law, one who experienced a seminal emission is ritually impure and prohibited from eating *teruma* and consecrated foods. In his ordinance, Ezra instituted that the individual must purify himself before praying or engaging in Torah study. Although the ordinance was repealed several generations later, it remained the custom in many communities as well as a custom of the pious throughout the generations.

כִּדְאַשְׁכַּחַן בְּסִינַי.

The Gemara answers: **As we found at Mount Sinai.** There one who had sexual relations with a woman was required to immerse himself before receiving the Torah, which was spoken and not merely contemplated. Here, too, it was decreed that one who was impure due to a seminal emission may not recite matters of Torah out loud until he immerses himself.

וְרַב חִסְדָּא אֲמַר: הִרְהוּר לָאו כְּדִבּוּר דָּמֵי. דְּאִי סָלְקָא דַּעְתָּךְ הִרְהוּר כְּדִבּוּר דָּמֵי – יוֹצִיא בִּשְׂפָתָיו!

And Rav Ḥisda said that the opposite conclusion should be drawn from the mishna: **Contemplation is not tantamount to speech, as if it would enter your mind that contemplation is tantamount to speech,** then one who is impure because of a seminal emission should *ab initio*, **utter** *Shema* **with his lips.**

אֶלָּא מַאי – הִרְהוּר לָאו כְּדִבּוּר דָּמֵי, לָמָּה מְהַרְהֵר? – אָמַר רַבִּי אֶלְעָזָר: כְּדֵי שֶׁלֹּא יְהוּ כָּל הָעוֹלָם עוֹסְקִין בּוֹ וְהוּא יוֹשֵׁב וּבָטֵל.

The Gemara challenges this argument: **But what** are you saying, that **contemplation is not tantamount to speech? If so, why does he contemplate? Rabbi Elazar said: So that** a situation **will not** arise where **everyone is engaged in** reciting *Shema* **and he sits idly** by.

וְנִגְרוֹס בְּפִרְקָא אַחֲרִינָא! – אָמַר רַב אַדָּא בַּר אַהֲבָה: בְּדָבָר שֶׁהַצִּבּוּר עוֹסְקִין בּוֹ.

The Gemara asks: If that is the only purpose, **let him study another chapter** and not specifically *Shema* or one of the blessings. **Rav Adda bar Ahava said:** It is fitting that one engage **in a matter in which the community is engaged.**

Perek **III**
Daf **21** Amud **a**

וַהֲרֵי תְּפִלָּה דְּדָבָר שֶׁהַצִּבּוּר עֲסוּקִין בּוֹ, וּתְנַן: הָיָה עוֹמֵד בִּתְפִלָּה וְנִזְכַּר שֶׁהוּא בַּעַל קֶרִי – לֹא יַפְסִיק אֶלָּא יְקַצֵּר, טַעְמָא דְּאַתְחֵיל, הָא לָא אַתְחֵיל – לֹא יַתְחִיל!

The Gemara challenges: **And prayer,** which is also **a matter in which the community is engaged, and we learned** in the mishna: **One who was standing in prayer and remembered that he is one** who experienced a **seminal emission** and did not yet immerse himself **should not interrupt** his prayer, **rather he should abridge it.** The Gemara infers: **The reason is because he** already **began** to pray; **however,** if **he did not** yet **begin,** then **he should not begin,** even by means of contemplation.

שָׁאנֵי תְּפִלָּה, דְּלֵית בָּהּ מַלְכוּת שָׁמַיִם. וַהֲרֵי בִּרְכַּת הַמָּזוֹן לְאַחֲרָיו, דְּלֵית בָּהּ מַלְכוּת שָׁמַיִם, וּתְנַן: עַל הַמָּזוֹן מְבָרֵךְ לְאַחֲרָיו וְאֵינוֹ מְבָרֵךְ לְפָנָיו! אֶלָּא: קְרִיאַת שְׁמַע וּבִרְכַּת הַמָּזוֹן – דְּאוֹרַיְיתָא, וּתְפִלָּה – דְּרַבָּנַן.

The Gemara responds: **Prayer is different in that it does not contain** the acceptance of the yoke of **the kingdom of Heaven.** The Gemara rejects this: **And Grace after Meals does not contain** the acceptance of the yoke of **the kingdom of Heaven, and** yet **we learned** in the mishna: **Over food, one recites a blessing afterward, but does not recite a blessing beforehand. Rather,** the differences must be explained otherwise: **The recitation of** ***Shema*** **and Grace after Meals** are both mitzvot **by Torah law, while prayer** is only **by rabbinic law.** Therefore, one who is impure need not pray.

אָמַר רַב יְהוּדָה: מִנַּיִן לְבִרְכַּת הַמָּזוֹן לְאַחֲרֶיהָ מִן הַתּוֹרָה – שֶׁנֶּאֱמַר: "וְאָכַלְתָּ וְשָׂבָעְתָּ וּבֵרַכְתָּ".

Rav Yehuda said: From where is the mitzva **by Torah law** to recite **Grace after Meals,** derived? **As it is stated: "And you shall eat and be satisfied and bless the Lord your God"** (Deuteronomy 8:10).

מִנַּיִן לְבִרְכַּת הַתּוֹרָה לְפָנֶיהָ מִן הַתּוֹרָה – שֶׁנֶּאֱמַר: "כִּי שֵׁם ה׳ אֶקְרָא הָבוּ גֹדֶל לֵאלֹהֵינוּ".

And **from where is** the mitzva **by Torah law** to recite **the blessing over the Torah before it** is read, derived? **As it is stated: "When I proclaim the Lord's name, give glory to our God"** (Deuteronomy 32:3), meaning that before one proclaims the Lord's name by reading the Torah, he must give glory to God.

אָמַר רַבִּי יוֹחָנָן: לָמַדְנוּ בִּרְכַּת הַתּוֹרָה לְאַחֲרֶיהָ מִן בִּרְכַּת הַמָּזוֹן מִקַּל וָחוֹמֶר, וּבִרְכַּת הַמָּזוֹן לְפָנֶיהָ מִן בִּרְכַּת הַתּוֹרָה מִקַּל וָחוֹמֶר; בִּרְכַּת הַתּוֹרָה לְאַחֲרֶיהָ מִן בִּרְכַּת הַמָּזוֹן מִקַּל וָחוֹמֶר: וּמָה מָזוֹן שֶׁאֵין טָעוּן לְפָנָיו – טָעוּן לְאַחֲרָיו, תּוֹרָה שֶׁטְּעוּנָה לְפָנֶיהָ – אֵינוֹ דִּין שֶׁטְּעוּנָה לְאַחֲרֶיהָ; וּבִרְכַּת הַמָּזוֹן לְפָנֶיהָ מִן בִּרְכַּת הַתּוֹרָה מִקַּל וָחוֹמֶר: וּמַה תּוֹרָה שֶׁאֵין טְעוּנָה לְאַחֲרֶיהָ – טְעוּנָה לְפָנֶיהָ, מָזוֹן שֶׁהוּא טָעוּן לְאַחֲרָיו – אֵינוֹ דִּין שֶׁיְּהֵא טָעוּן לְפָנָיו.

Rabbi Yoḥanan said: We derived that one must recite **the blessing over the Torah after** it is read **from Grace after Meals** by means of an ***a fortiori*** **inference.**[N] **And** we derive the obligation to recite **a blessing before** partaking of **food** from **the blessing over the Torah** by means of an ***a fortiori*** **inference. The blessing over the Torah after** it is read **from Grace after Meals** by means of an ***a fortiori*** **inference: Food, which does not require a blessing beforehand** by Torah law, **requires a blessing afterward; Torah, which requires** a blessing **beforehand, is it not right that it requires** a blessing **afterward? And** similarly: **The blessing before** partaking of **food** from **the blessing over the Torah** by means of an ***a fortiori*** **inference: Torah, which requires no** blessing **afterward** by Torah law, **requires** a blessing **beforehand; food, which requires** a blessing **afterward, is it not right that it requires** a blessing **beforehand?**

NOTES

Deriving the blessing over the Torah after it is read from Grace after Meals by means of an *a fortiori* inference – לִימּוּד בִּרְכַּת הַתּוֹרָה וּבִרְכַּת הַמָּזוֹן מִקַּל וָחוֹמֶר: The *a fortiori* inference is a form of logical proof. In this example, there are two *halakhot* with regard to which there is incomplete information. The attempt is to prove that each can help fill in the missing details of the other. However, this comparative proof is based on the tacit presumption that one *halakha* is consistently more stringent than the other and consequently an *a fortiori* inference can be drawn between them. Refutation of that inference is accomplished by demonstrating that the two *halakhot* are not actually comparable and that there are inconsistencies in terms of their relative stringency and leniency. Although the refutation does not prove that the conclusions reached are incorrect, it does invalidate the means used to arrive at those conclusions.

אִיכָּא לְמִפְרַךְ: מַה לְּמָזוֹן – שֶׁכֵּן נֶהֱנֶה, וּמַה לַּתּוֹרָה – שֶׁכֵּן חַיֵּי עוֹלָם! וְעוֹד, תְּנַן: עַל הַמָּזוֹן מְבָרֵךְ לְאַחֲרָיו וְאֵינוֹ מְבָרֵךְ לְפָנָיו! תְּיוּבְתָּא.

The Gemara notes: The logic of this *a fortiori* inference **can be refuted: What** is true with regard **to food, where one derives pleasure** from eating,[N] is not true with regard to matters which offer no bodily pleasure. Therefore, the blessing over the Torah cannot be derived from the blessing over food. **And** similarly: **What** is true with regard to **Torah, that** provides **eternal life** to those who engage in its study, is not true with regard to matters that do not provide eternal life. Therefore, the blessing before partaking of food cannot be derived from the blessing over the Torah. **Furthermore, we learned** in the mishna: **Over food,** one who is impure due to a seminal emission **recites a blessing afterward, but does not recite a blessing beforehand.** The mishna does not derive the blessing recited before a meal from the blessing recited over Torah. Consequently, this is a **conclusive refutation** of Rabbi Yoḥanan's statement.

אָמַר רַב יְהוּדָה סָפֵק קָרָא קְרִיאַת שְׁמַע סָפֵק לֹא קָרָא – אֵינוֹ חוֹזֵר וְקוֹרֵא, סָפֵק אָמַר ״אֱמֶת וְיַצִּיב״, סָפֵק לֹא אָמַר – חוֹזֵר וְאוֹמֵר ״אֱמֶת וְיַצִּיב״. מַאי טַעְמָא – קְרִיאַת שְׁמַע דְּרַבָּנַן, ״אֱמֶת וְיַצִּיב״ דְּאוֹרָיְיתָא. –

Rav Yehuda said: One who is **uncertain whether he recited *Shema* or whether he did not recite it does not recite it again.** However, one who is **uncertain whether he recited: True and Firm** [***emet veyatziv***], the blessing that follows *Shema* in the morning, **must recite *emet veyatziv* again. What is the reason** for this? In his opinion, the obligation to recite ***Shema*** is only **by rabbinic law.** His ruling follows the principle that in cases of uncertainty involving rabbinic law, the ruling is lenient and he need not repeat it. However, since ***emet veyatziv*** is primarily a commemoration of the exodus from Egypt, it is a mitzva **by Torah law,**[N] and, in cases of uncertainty involving Torah law, the ruling is stringent and he must repeat it.

מְתִיב רַב יוֹסֵף: ״וּבְשָׁכְבְּךָ וּבְקוּמֶךָ״! – אֲמַר לֵיהּ אַבַּיֵי: הַהוּא בְּדִבְרֵי תוֹרָה כְּתִיב.

Rav Yosef raises an objection: How can you say that the obligation to recite *Shema* is only by rabbinic law when it is explicitly written: "And you shall recite them to your children and speak of them when you sit in your home and when you walk by the way, **when you lie down and when you rise**" (Deuteronomy 6:7)? **Abaye said to him: That** verse **was written with regard to matters of Torah.** One need not interpret the verse in the conventional manner, as obligating the recitation of *Shema*, but rather as referring to the general obligation to study Torah.

תְּנַן: בַּעַל קֶרִי מְהַרְהֵר בְּלִבּוֹ וְאֵינוֹ מְבָרֵךְ לֹא לְפָנֶיהָ וְלֹא לְאַחֲרֶיהָ, וְעַל הַמָּזוֹן – מְבָרֵךְ לְאַחֲרָיו וְאֵינוֹ מְבָרֵךְ לְפָנָיו.

From here, the Gemara attempts to resolve this issue by citing proof from the mishna. **We learned** in the mishna: **One who experienced a seminal emission** may **contemplate** *Shema* **in his heart, but neither recites the blessings preceding** *Shema,* **nor the blessings thereafter. Over food** which, after partaking, one is obligated by Torah law to recite a blessing, **one recites a blessing thereafter, but not beforehand.**

וְאִי סָלְקָא דַּעְתָּךְ ״אֱמֶת וְיַצִּיב״ דְּאוֹרָיְיתָא – לְבָרוֹךְ לְאַחֲרֶיהָ!

And if it would enter your mind that the obligation to recite ***emet veyatziv* is by Torah law, let him recite the blessing after** ***Shema.*** Since he does not recite the blessing, apparently, he is exempt.

מַאי טַעְמָא מְבָרֵךְ – אִי מִשּׁוּם יְצִיאַת מִצְרַיִם – הָא אַדְכַּר לֵיהּ בִּקְרִיאַת שְׁמַע.

The Gemara refutes this: **What is the reason that he recites** ***emet veyatziv*?** **If it is because** it deals primarily with **the exodus from Egypt, wasn't it** already **mentioned in the recitation of** ***Shema*,** in the portion of the ritual fringes?

וְנֵימָא הָא וְלָא לִבְעֵי הָא! – קְרִיאַת שְׁמַע עֲדִיפָא, דְּאִית בָּהּ תַּרְתֵּי.

The Gemara challenges: **And let him say this,** ***emet veyatziv,*** **and he will not need** to recite **that,** ***Shema.*** The Gemara responds: While one may commemorate the exodus from Egypt in either *Shema* or *emet veyatziv*, ***Shema*** **is preferable as it contains two** elements, both a commemoration of the exodus and an acceptance of the yoke of the kingdom of Heaven.

וְרַבִּי אֶלְעָזָר אָמַר: סָפֵק קָרָא קְרִיאַת שְׁמַע סָפֵק לֹא קָרָא – חוֹזֵר וְקוֹרֵא קְרִיאַת שְׁמַע, סָפֵק הִתְפַּלֵּל סָפֵק לֹא הִתְפַּלֵּל – אֵינוֹ חוֹזֵר וּמִתְפַּלֵּל. וְרַבִּי יוֹחָנָן אָמַר: וּלְוַאי שֶׁיִּתְפַּלֵּל אָדָם כָּל הַיּוֹם כּוּלּוֹ.

And Rabbi Elazar said a different opinion: One who is **uncertain whether he recited *Shema***[H] **or whether he did not recite** ***Shema,*** **must recite *Shema* again.**[N] According to his opinion, there is a mitzva by Torah law to recite *Shema.* However, if one is **uncertain whether he prayed**[H] **or whether he did not pray, he does not pray again,** as the obligation to pray is by rabbinic law. **And Rabbi Yoḥanan said:** He must pray again; **if only a person would pray throughout the entire day.**[NH]

NOTES

What is true with regard to food, where one derives pleasure from eating – מַה לְמָזוֹן שֶׁכֵּן נֶהֱנֶה: The distinction between food and Torah is not an arbitrary one and can be understood on a more profound level. The Gemara stated: What is true with regard to food, where one derives pleasure from eating, etc. Because that pleasure remains with him after the meal, it is reasonable that one would be required to recite a blessing after eating. And, the Gemara stated: What is true with regard to Torah that provides eternal life, etc. Therefore, one would be required to prepare himself beforehand, by reciting a blessing (*Shitta Mekubbetzet*).

***Emet veyatziv* is a mitzva by Torah law** – ״אֱמֶת וְיַצִּיב״ דְּאוֹרָיְיתָא: This does not mean that the formula of *emet veyatziv* is by Torah law; rather it means that commemorating the exodus from Egypt, which is a central theme in *emet veyatziv*, is a mitzva by Torah law (*Talmidei Rabbeinu Yona*). One does not fulfill any mitzva of commemoration by reciting *Shema,* other than the commemoration of the exodus from Egypt in the third paragraph. Consequently, one who recited the third paragraph of *Shema* is no longer obligated by Torah law to recite *emet veyatziv.*

One who is uncertain whether or not he recited *Shema* recites it again – סָפֵק קָרָא קְרִיאַת שְׁמַע חוֹזֵר: Some hold that Rabbi Elazar's opinion need not rely on the opinion that the reciting *Shema* is an obligation by Torah law. Even if the obligation is only by rabbinic law, it warrants repetition because it includes the acceptance of the yoke of the Kingdom of Heaven (*Tosefot HaRosh*).

If only a person would pray throughout the entire day – וּלְוַאי שֶׁיִּתְפַּלֵּל אָדָם כָּל הַיּוֹם כּוּלּוֹ: This statement is based on a specific understanding of the essence of prayer, and the *halakha* combines the statements of Rabbi Yoḥanan and Shmuel. If prayers are really based on the sacrifices then there is clearly no room for an added prayer, as that would be tantamount to adding a sacrifice that is not required (Rif, *Tosefot Rabbi Yitzḥak*). That is, indeed, why there can be no voluntary communal prayer. However, introducing a novel element to the prayer transforms the prayer into a type of free-will offering, which can be offered at any time in addition to the required daily sacrifices. Therefore, the *halakha*, based on the opinion of Rav Hai Gaon, is that one may only add prayers through introduction of a new element.

HALAKHA

One who is uncertain whether or not he recited *Shema* – סָפֵק קָרָא קְרִיאַת שְׁמַע: If one is uncertain whether or not he recited *Shema,* he must recite it again along with its accompanying blessings, because reciting *Shema* is an obligation by Torah law. The *halakha* is in accordance with the opinion of Rabbi Elazar, as the bulk of the *mishnayot, baraitot,* and statements in the Gemara are in accordance with his opinion (Rambam *Sefer Ahava, Hilkhot Keriat Shema* 2:13; *Shulḥan Arukh, Oraḥ Ḥayyim,* 67).

One who is uncertain whether or not he prayed – סָפֵק הִתְפַּלֵּל: One who is uncertain whether or not he prayed must pray again and is not required to introduce a new element to his prayer. When doing so, he stipulates: If I did not pray then, this prayer will fulfill my obligation; however, if I already prayed, this will be an added prayer (*Magen Avraham*). The *halakha* is in accordance with the opinion of Rabbi Yoḥanan who said: If only a person would pray throughout the entire day. Although prayer is not a Torah obligation, one who is uncertain whether or not he prayed may introduce a new element to his prayer and pray, as Rav Yehuda does not really disagree with Rabbi Yoḥanan (Rambam *Sefer Ahava, Hilkhot Tefilla* 10:6; *Shulḥan Arukh, Oraḥ Ḥayyim* 107:1).

If only a person would pray throughout the entire day – וּלְוַאי שֶׁיִּתְפַּלֵּל אָדָם כָּל הַיּוֹם כּוּלּוֹ: One is always permitted to recite a voluntary prayer, as long as he introduces a new element to that prayer, as per the opinion of Rabbi Yoḥanan (Rambam *Sefer Ahava, Hilkhot Tefilla* 10:6, *Shulḥan Arukh, Oraḥ Ḥayyim* 107:1).

ואמר רב יהודה אמר שמואל: היה עומד בתפלה ונזכר שהתפלל – פוסק, ואפילו באמצע ברכה. – איני? והאמר רב נחמן: כי הוינן בי רבה בר אבוה, בען מיניה, הני בני בי רב דטעו ומדכרי דחול בשבת, מהו שיגמרו? ואמר לן: גומרין כל אותה ברכה!

And Rav Yehuda said that **Shmuel said:** One **who was standing in prayer and remembered that he** already **prayed**[H] **must interrupt** his prayer, **even in the middle of a blessing.** The Gemara challenges this: **Is that so? Didn't Rav Naḥman say: When we were in the school of Rabba bar Avuh we raised a dilemma before him: Those students in the school of Rav** who **mistakenly recited a** blessing from the **weekday** *Amida* **on Shabbat,**[H] **what is** the ruling with regards to **completing** the weekday prayer? **And** Rabba bar Avuh **said to us:** The ruling is that **one must complete that entire blessing.** How then did Rav Yehuda say that one must interrupt his prayer even in the middle of a blessing?

הכי השתא! התם – גברא בר חיובא הוא, ורבנן הוא דלא אטרחוהו משום כבוד שבת, אבל הכא – הא צלי ליה.

The Gemara rejects this: **How can you compare** the two cases? **There,** on Shabbat, **the individual is one who is obligated** and should actually recite all eighteen blessings, **and it is the Sages who did not impose upon him**[N] **in deference to Shabbat** and instituted an abridged formula. **But here, didn't he** already **pray?** Therefore he can stop, even in the middle of a blessing.

ואמר רב יהודה אמר שמואל: התפלל ונכנס לבית הכנסת ומצא צבור שמתפללין, אם יכול לחדש בה דבר – יחזור ויתפלל, ואם לאו – אל יחזור ויתפלל.

And Rav Yehuda said that **Shmuel said:** One who already **prayed, and** then **enters a synagogue to find a congregation** standing and **praying,**[H] **if he is able to introduce a new element,** an expression or request, into his prayer, **he may pray again, and if not, he may not pray again.**

וצריכא: דאי אשמעינן קמייתא, הני מילי – יחיד ויחיד,

The Gemara notes: This concept is identical to Shmuel's previous statement regarding one who already prayed that he need not pray again. Nevertheless, both statements are **necessary. If he had taught us the first** *halakha*, we would have said that **applies only** to a case involving **an individual** who prayed **and an individual** who began to repeat the prayer,

Perek **III**
Daf **21** Amud **b**

או צבור וצבור, אבל יחיד לגבי צבור כמאן דלא צלי דמי – קמשמע לן; ואי אשמעינן הכא – משום דלא אתחיל בה, אבל התם דאתחיל בה, אימא לא – צריכא.

or a case where he prayed as part of **a congregation** and began to repeat it as part of **a congregation; however,** in a case where he initially prayed by himself and subsequently joined the congregation at the venue where it was praying, we might have said that **an individual vis-à-vis the congregation is** considered **as one who has not prayed.** Therefore, **he taught us** that in this case, too, one may not repeat the prayer. **And,** on the other hand, **if he had taught us here** only with regard to one who entered a synagogue, we would have thought that the reason he may not pray again is **because he did not** yet **begin** to recite the prayer, **but there, in the case where he** already **began** to recite the prayer, **say** that this is **not** the case and he may continue to repeat the prayer. Therefore, both statements are **necessary.**

אמר רב הונא: הנכנס לבית הכנסת ומצא צבור שמתפללין, אם יכול להתחיל ולגמור עד שלא יגיע שליח צבור ל"מודים" – יתפלל, ואם לאו – אל יתפלל; רבי יהושע בן לוי אמר: אם יכול להתחיל ולגמור עד שלא יגיע שליח צבור לקדושה – יתפלל, ואם לאו – אל יתפלל.

Rav Huna said: One who did not yet pray and **enters a synagogue and found that the congregation is** in the midst of **reciting** the *Amida* **prayer,**[H] **if he is able to begin and complete** his own prayer **before the prayer leader reaches** the blessing of **thanksgiving** [***modim***], **he should** begin to **pray, and, if not, he should not** begin to **pray. Rabbi Yehoshua ben Levi said: If he is able to begin and complete** his prayer **before the prayer leader reaches sanctification** [***kedusha***],[N] **then he should** begin to **pray. If not, then he should not** begin to **pray.**

HALAKHA

One who was standing in prayer and remembered that he already prayed – היה עומד בתפלה ונזכר שהתפלל: One who began praying under the mistaken assumption that he had not yet prayed, and then realized that he had, stops praying immediately, even if he is in the middle of a blessing and even if he is able to introduce a new element to his prayer. The *halakha* is in accordance with the opinion of Rav Yehuda because Rabbi Yoḥanan's statement refers only to situations where one is aware that he is praying an added, rather than a mandatory prayer. One is certainly not permitted to recite two mandatory prayers (*Shulḥan Arukh, Oraḥ Ḥayyim* 107:1).

Who mistakenly recited a blessing from the weekday *Amida* on Shabbat – דטעו ומדכרי דחול בשבת: One who was reciting the morning, afternoon, or evening prayer on Shabbat and mistakenly began to recite a blessing from the corresponding weekday *Amida*, completes the blessing that he began and then continues with the Shabbat prayer, in accordance with the opinion of Rabba bar Avuh. If one began to recite a weekday blessing during the additional prayer, some say that he does the same as he does in the rest of the Shabbat prayers. Others say that he stops immediately and continues with the additional prayer. The later decisors of *halakha* ruled in accordance with the latter opinion to avoid a possible blessing in vain (*Mishna Berura*; Rambam *Sefer Ahava, Hilkhot Tefilla* 10:7; *Shulḥan Arukh, Oraḥ Ḥayyim* 268:2).

One who already prayed and then enters a synagogue to find a congregation standing and praying – התפלל ונכנס לבית הכנסת ומצא צבור שמתפללין: One who already prayed, enters a synagogue and finds the congregation praying, is permitted to recite another prayer with them if he is able to introduce a new element to it, in accordance with the opinion of Rabbi Yehuda (see Rambam *Sefer Ahava, Hilkhot Tefilla* 1:9, and *Shulḥan Arukh, Oraḥ Ḥayyim* 107:1).

NOTES

And it is the Sages who did not impose upon him – ורבנן הוא דלא אטרחוהו: According to this opinion, Shabbat prayer is an abbreviated version of the weekday prayer, and therefore one who recites the weekday *Amida* on Shabbat and includes mention of Shabbat therein, has, for all intents and purposes, arrived at the essence of the prayer. Consequently, some hold that one who mistakenly begins a weekday blessing in the additional prayer on Shabbat stops immediately, as there is no connection between weekday blessings and the additional prayer (Ra'avad).

HALAKHA

One who enters a synagogue and found the congregation reciting the *Amida* prayer – 'הנכנס לבית הכנסת ומצא צבור שמתפללין וכו: One who enters a synagogue and finds the congregation reciting the *Amida* prayer, if he is able to conclude his prayer before the prayer leader recites *kedusha* or *kaddish*, he may begin to pray. If not, he should wait until after the prayer leader recites *kedusha* or *kaddish* before beginning his prayer, as long as by doing so, the deadline for reciting that prayer does not pass. The *halakha* was ruled in accordance with the opinion of Rabbi Yehoshua ben Levi, who was greater than Rav Huna. In addition, the statement of Rav Adda bar Ahava and the talmudic discussion support his opinion. However, if he entered the synagogue after *kedusha*, if he is able to conclude his prayer before the prayer leader begins the blessing of thanksgiving, he may begin to pray, as, with regard to that case, there is no dispute between Rabbi Yehoshua ben Levi and Rav Huna (Rambam *Sefer Ahava, Hilkhot Tefilla* 10:16, *Shulḥan Arukh, Oraḥ Ḥayyim* 109:1).

NOTES

***Kedusha* – קדושה:** Generally, the term *kedusha* refers to the sanctification recited in the prayer leader's repetition of the *Amida* prayer. However, there are additional passages that fall under that rubric, e.g., the sanctification recited in the first blessing accompanying *Shema* in the morning as well as the sanctification included in the prayer: "A Redeemer will come to Zion [*uva leTziyyon*]," recited at the conclusion of the service. The *ge'onim* debated whether an individual is permitted to recite those passages. Furthermore, there were those who asserted that the *kedusha* in the *Amida* prayer, since it is merely a series of verses, is not considered a sacred matter and may be recited by an individual (*Tosefot Rabbi Yehuda HaḤasid*, *Tosefot HaRosh*).

בְּמַאי קָא מִפַּלְגִי? מָר סָבַר: יָחִיד אוֹמֵר קְדוּשָּׁה; וּמָר סָבַר: אֵין יָחִיד אוֹמֵר קְדוּשָּׁה.

The Gemara clarifies: **With regard to what do they disagree?** The basis for their dispute is that one **Sage,** Rav Huna, **holds: An individual** is permitted to **recite *kedusha*** on his own, so he need not insist on reciting it along with the prayer leader; **and the other Sage,** Rabbi Yehoshua ben Levi, **holds** that **an individual may not recite *kedusha*** alone, and, therefore he is required to complete his prayer before the communal prayer leader reaches *kedusha*.

וְכֵן אָמַר רַב אַדָּא בַּר אַהֲבָה: מִנַּיִן שֶׁאֵין הַיָּחִיד אוֹמֵר קְדוּשָּׁה – שֶׁנֶּאֱמַר: ״וְנִקְדַּשְׁתִּי בְּתוֹךְ בְּנֵי יִשְׂרָאֵל״ – כָּל דָּבָר שֶׁבִּקְדוּשָּׁה לֹא יְהֵא פָּחוֹת מֵעֲשָׂרָה.

Similarly, Rav Adda bar Ahava stated, in accordance with the second opinion: **From where is it derived that an individual may not recite *kedusha*** alone? **As it is stated: "And I shall be hallowed among the children of Israel"** (Leviticus 22:32), **any expression of sanctity may not be** recited in a quorum of **fewer than ten** men.[H]

מַאי מַשְׁמַע? דְּתָנֵי רַבְּנַאי אֲחוּהּ דְּרַבִּי חִיָּיא בַּר אַבָּא: אַתְיָא ״תּוֹךְ״ ״תּוֹךְ״. כְּתִיב הָכָא: ״וְנִקְדַּשְׁתִּי בְּתוֹךְ בְּנֵי יִשְׂרָאֵל״ וּכְתִיב הָתָם: ״הִבָּדְלוּ מִתּוֹךְ הָעֵדָה הַזֹּאת״, מַה לְּהַלָּן עֲשָׂרָה, אַף כָּאן עֲשָׂרָה.

The Gemara asks: **How is this inferred** from that verse? The Gemara responds: This must be understood in light of a *baraita*, **which was taught by Rabbenai, the brother of** Rabbi **Ḥiyya bar Abba: It is inferred** by means of a verbal analogy [*gezera shava*] between the words **among, among.**[N] **Here it is written: "And I shall be hallowed among the children of Israel," and there,** regarding Korah's congregation, **it is written "Separate yourselves from among this congregation"** (Numbers 16:21). **Just as there** among connotes **ten, so too here,** among connotes **ten.** The connotation of ten associated with the word among written in the portion of Korah is, in turn, derived by means of another verbal analogy between the word congregation written there and the word congregation written in reference to the ten spies who slandered Eretz Yisrael: "How long shall I bear with this evil congregation?" (Numbers 14:27). Consequently, among the congregation there must be at least ten.

וּדְכוּלֵּי עָלְמָא מִיהַת מִפְסַק לָא פָּסֵיק.

And, in any case, everyone agrees that **one may not interrupt** his prayer in order to respond to *kedusha*.

אִיבַּעְיָא לְהוּ: מַהוּ לְהַפְסִיק לִ״יהֵא שְׁמוֹ הַגָּדוֹל מְבוֹרָךְ״? כִּי אֲתָא רַב דִּימִי אָמַר, רַבִּי יְהוּדָה וְרַבִּי שִׁמְעוֹן תַּלְמִידֵי דְּרַבִּי יוֹחָנָן אָמְרִי: לַכֹּל אֵין מַפְסִיקִין, חוּץ מִן ״יְהֵא שְׁמוֹ הַגָּדוֹל מְבוֹרָךְ״, שֶׁאֲפִילּוּ עוֹסֵק בְּמַעֲשֵׂה מֶרְכָּבָה – פּוֹסֵק. וְלֵית הִלְכְתָא כְּוָתֵיהּ.

However, **a dilemma was raised** before the Sages of the yeshiva: **What is** the ruling? Is one permitted **to interrupt**[H] his prayer in order **to** recite: **"May His great name be blessed"** in *kaddish*? **When Rav Dimi came** from Eretz Yisrael to Babylonia, **he said: Rabbi Yehuda and Rabbi Shimon, disciples of Rabbi Yoḥanan, said: One may not interrupt** his prayer **for anything, except for: "May His great name be blessed," as even** if one was **engaged in** the exalted study of the **Act of the** Divine **Chariot** [*Ma'aseh Merkava*] (see Ezekiel 1) **he stops** to recite it. However, the Gemara concludes: **The *halakha* is not in accordance with his opinion.**[N]

״רַבִּי יְהוּדָה אוֹמֵר, מְבָרֵךְ לִפְנֵיהֶם וּלְאַחֲרֵיהֶם״. לְמֵימְרָא דְּקָסָבַר רַבִּי יְהוּדָה בַּעַל קֶרִי מוּתָּר בְּדִבְרֵי תוֹרָה? וְהָאָמַר רַבִּי יְהוֹשֻׁעַ בֶּן לֵוִי: מִנַּיִן לְבַעַל קֶרִי שֶׁאָסוּר בְּדִבְרֵי תוֹרָה – שֶׁנֶּאֱמַר: ״וְהוֹדַעְתָּם לְבָנֶיךָ וְלִבְנֵי בָנֶיךָ״, וְסָמֵיךְ לֵיהּ: ״יוֹם אֲשֶׁר עָמַדְתָּ וגו׳״ – מַה לְּהַלָּן בַּעֲלֵי קְרָיִין אֲסוּרִין, אַף כָּאן – בַּעֲלֵי קְרָיִין אֲסוּרִין!

We learned in the mishna that **Rabbi Yehuda says** with regard to one who experiences a seminal emission; **he recites a blessing beforehand and afterward** in both the case of *Shema* and in the case of food. The Gemara asks: **Is that to say that Rabbi Yehuda holds that one who experienced a seminal emission is permitted** to engage **in matters of Torah? Didn't Rabbi Yehoshua ben Levi say: From where** in the Torah is it derived **that one who experiences a seminal emission is prohibited from** engaging **in matters of Torah?**[N] **As it is stated:** "Just take heed and guard your soul diligently lest you forget the things your eyes have seen, and lest they depart from your heart, for all the days of your life, **and you shall impart them to your children and your children's children"** (Deuteronomy 4:9), from which we derive, among other things, the obligation to study Torah. **And, juxtaposed to it,** is the verse: **"The day that you stood** before the Lord your God at Horeb" (Deuteronomy 4:10). This juxtaposition teaches us that **just as below,** at the revelation at Mount Sinai, **those who experienced a seminal emission were prohibited** and were commanded to refrain from relations with their wives and immerse themselves, **so too here,** throughout the generations, **those who experience a seminal emission are prohibited** from engaging in Torah study.

וְכִי תֵּימָא: רַבִּי יְהוּדָה לָא דָּרֵישׁ סְמוּכִים, וְהָאָמַר רַב יוֹסֵף: אֲפִילּוּ מַאן דְּלָא דָּרֵישׁ סְמוּכִים בְּכָל הַתּוֹרָה – בְּמִשְׁנֵה תוֹרָה דָּרֵישׁ. דְּהָא רַבִּי יְהוּדָה לָא דָּרֵישׁ סְמוּכִין בְּכָל הַתּוֹרָה כּוּלָּהּ, וּבְמִשְׁנֵה תוֹרָה דָּרֵישׁ.

And if you **say that Rabbi Yehuda does not derive homiletic interpretations from juxtaposed** verses, **didn't Rav Yosef** already **say: Even one who does not derive homiletic interpretations from juxtaposed** verses throughout **the entire Torah,** nevertheless, **derives them in Deuteronomy** [*Mishne Torah*],[N] **as Rabbi Yehuda does not derive homiletic interpretations from juxtaposed** verses **throughout the entire Torah and he does derive them in *Mishne Torah*.**

HALAKHA

Any expression of sanctity may not be recited in a quorum of fewer than ten men – כָּל דָּבָר שֶׁבִּקְדוּשָּׁה לֹא יְהֵא פָּחוֹת מֵעֲשָׂרָה: All matters of sanctity, e.g., *barekhu*, *kaddish*, and *kedusha* are only recited in the presence of ten men who have reached majority (Rambam *Sefer Ahava, Hilkhot Tefilla* 8:6, *Shulḥan Arukh, Oraḥ Ḥayyim* 55:1).

What is the ruling? Is one permitted to interrupt, etc. – מַהוּ לְהַפְסִיק וכו׳: It is prohibited to interrupt the *Amida* prayer for any sacred matter. However, if one hears *kaddish* he must remain silent during the recitation of the passage: May His great name be blessed for ever and time, as well as during the *barekhu* and *kedusha* prayers and he must focus his heart on the communal prayer leader as he recites them (*Shulḥan Arukh, Oraḥ Ḥayyim* 104:7).

NOTES

Among, among – ״תּוֹךְ״ ״תּוֹךְ״: This verbal analogy appears in greater detail in parallel sources, while here, the essence of the proof is cited. Nevertheless, the question is: What is the meaning of among? How many people must be present in order for one of them to be characterized as being among them? It is derived indirectly from the verses until the conclusion is reached that even ten people are enough for that purpose.

The *halakha* is not in accordance with his opinion – וְלֵית הִלְכְתָא כְּוָתֵיהּ: From here it was derived that one who is engaged in prayer does not respond with any other praise or sanctification. This is illustrated by the following parable: A king ordered two people to perform different tasks, each must engage in performing his own task and neither should neglect his own task to perform the task of the other (*Ba'al Halakhot Gedolot, ge'onim*).

From where in the Torah is it derived that one who experiences a seminal emission is prohibited from engaging in matters of Torah? – מִנַּיִן לְבַעַל קֶרִי שֶׁאָסוּר בְּדִבְרֵי תוֹרָה: The question was posed: The immersion of one who experienced a seminal emission is a rabbinic ordinance instituted by Ezra. Why is the Gemara challenging Rabbi Yehuda's opinion from Rabbi Yehoshua ben Levi's statement as if it was by Torah law? The answer is: Since, based on Ezra's ordinance, the question is legitimate, the Gemara was not insistent on phrasing it with precision and posed the question utilizing the allusion of Rabbi Yehoshua ben Levi (*Shitta Mekubbetzet*). Furthermore, the Gemara below explains the entire matter differently (*Tosefot Rabbi Yehuda HaḤasid*).

He derives them in Deuteronomy [*Mishne Torah*] – בְּמִשְׁנֵה תוֹרָה דָּרֵישׁ: The reason is: Although the sanctity of Deuteronomy is equal to the sanctity of the other books of the Torah, it consists of Moses recapitulating that which was previously stated. Certainly, it was not repeated in vain. Moses' juxtapositions and combinations are significant and *halakha* may be derived from them (*Shitta Mekubbetzet*).

וּבְכׇל הַתּוֹרָה כּוּלָּהּ מְנָא לָן דְּלָא דָּרֵישׁ – דְּתַנְיָא, בֶּן עַזַּאי אוֹמֵר: נֶאֱמַר ״מְכַשֵּׁפָה לֹא תְחַיֶּה״ וְנֶאֱמַר ״כׇּל שׁוֹכֵב עִם בְּהֵמָה מוֹת יוּמָת״, סְמָכוֹ עִנְיָן לוֹ, לוֹמַר: מָה שׁוֹכֵב עִם בְּהֵמָה בִּסְקִילָה – אַף מְכַשֵּׁפָה נַמִּי בִּסְקִילָה;

And from where do we derive that Rabbi Yehuda **does not derive homiletic interpretations** from juxtaposed verses **throughout the entire Torah? As it was taught** in a *baraita* with regard to the punishment of a sorceress, **ben Azzai**[P] **says: It is stated: "You shall not allow a sorceress to live"** (Exodus 22:17), although the manner of her execution is not specified, **and it is stated: "Whoever lies with a beast shall surely be put to death"** (Exodus 22:18). The fact that the Torah **juxtaposed this matter to that** was **to say: Just as one who lies with a beast** is executed **by stoning** (see Leviticus 20), **so too a sorceress** is executed **by stoning.**

אֲמַר לֵיהּ רַבִּי יְהוּדָה: וְכִי מִפְּנֵי שֶׁסְּמָכוֹ עִנְיָן לוֹ נוֹצִיא לָזֶה לִסְקִילָה? אֶלָּא: אוֹב וְיִדְּעוֹנִי בִּכְלָל כׇּל הַמְכַשְּׁפִים הָיוּ, וְלָמָּה יָצְאוּ – לְהַקִּישׁ לָהֶן, וְלוֹמַר לָךְ: מָה אוֹב וְיִדְּעוֹנִי בִּסְקִילָה – אַף מְכַשֵּׁפָה בִּסְקִילָה.

With regard to this proof **Rabbi Yehuda said to him: And does** the fact **that** the Torah **juxtaposed this matter to that warrant taking** this person **out to be stoned?** Should he be sentenced to the most severe of the death penalties on that basis **Rather,** the source is: **Mediums and wizards were included among all sorcerers. And why were they singled out**[B] from the rest, in the verse: "And a man or a woman who is a medium or a wizard shall surely be put to death; they shall stone them with stones, their blood is upon them" (Leviticus 20:27)? In order to **draw an analogy to them and say to you: Just as a medium and a wizard** are executed **by stoning, so too is a sorceress**[H] executed **by stoning.**

וּבְמִשְׁנֵה תוֹרָה מְנָא לָן דְּדָרֵישׁ – דְּתַנְיָא, רַבִּי אֱלִיעֶזֶר אוֹמֵר: נוֹשֵׂא אָדָם אֲנוּסַת אָבִיו וּמְפוּתַּת אָבִיו, אֲנוּסַת בְּנוֹ וּמְפוּתַּת בְּנוֹ.

And from where do we derive that Rabbi Yehuda **derives homiletic interpretations** from juxtaposed verses **in *Mishne Torah*? As it was taught** in another *baraita*: **Rabbi Eliezer said that a man** may **wed** a woman **raped by his father and** one **seduced by his father;** a woman **raped by his son and** one **seduced by his son.**[H] Though one is prohibited by Torah law from marrying the wife of his father or the wife of his son, this prohibition does not apply to a woman raped or seduced by them.

רַבִּי יְהוּדָה אוֹסֵר בַּאֲנוּסַת אָבִיו וּבִמְפוּתַּת אָבִיו. וְאָמַר רַב גִּידֵּל אָמַר רַב: מַאי טַעְמָא דְּרַבִּי יְהוּדָה, דִּכְתִיב: ״לֹא יִקַּח אִישׁ אֶת אֵשֶׁת אָבִיו וְלֹא יְגַלֶּה (אֶת) כְּנַף אָבִיו״ – כָּנָף שֶׁרָאָה אָבִיו לֹא יְגַלֶּה.

And Rabbi Yehuda prohibits him from marrying **a woman raped by his father and a woman seduced by his father. And Rav Giddel said** that **Rav said: What is the reason for Rabbi Yehuda's** opinion? **As it is written: "A man shall not take his father's wife, and shall not uncover his father's skirt"** (Deuteronomy 23:1). The last expression, "and shall not uncover his father's skirt," implies that: **A skirt that has been seen by his father,** i.e., any woman who has had sexual relations with his father, **may not be uncovered** by his son, i.e., his son may not marry her.

וּמִמַּאי דְּבַאֲנוּסַת אָבִיו כְּתִיב – דִּסְמִיךְ לֵיהּ: ״וְנָתַן הָאִישׁ הַשֹּׁכֵב עִמָּהּ וגו׳״!

And from where do we know **that** the verse **is written with regard to a woman raped by his father? As** the previous section, **juxtaposed to it,** deals with the laws of rape: **"And the man who lay with her must give** her father fifty shekels…because he has violated her" (Deuteronomy 22:29).

אָמְרִי: אִין, בְּמִשְׁנֵה תוֹרָה דָּרֵישׁ. וְהָנֵי סְמוּכִין מִבְּעֵי לֵיהּ לְאִידַּךְ דְּרַבִּי יְהוֹשֻׁעַ בֶּן לֵוִי, דְּאָמַר רַבִּי יְהוֹשֻׁעַ בֶּן לֵוִי: כׇּל הַמְלַמֵּד לִבְנוֹ תּוֹרָה – מַעֲלֶה עָלָיו הַכָּתוּב כְּאִילּוּ קִבְּלָהּ מֵהַר חוֹרֵב, שֶׁנֶּאֱמַר ״וְהוֹדַעְתָּם לְבָנֶיךָ וְלִבְנֵי בָנֶיךָ״, וּכְתִיב בָּתְרֵיהּ: ״יוֹם אֲשֶׁר עָמַדְתָּ לִפְנֵי ה׳ אֱלֹהֶיךָ בְּחוֹרֵב״.

At any rate, we see that in Deuteronomy, Rabbi Yehuda derives homiletic interpretations from juxtaposed verses. Why does he fail to derive that one who experiences a seminal emission is prohibited from engaging in matters of Torah from the juxtaposition of the verses? **They replied: Indeed, in *Mishne Torah*** Rabbi Yehuda **does derive homiletic interpretations** from the juxtaposition of verses, **but** he requires **these juxtaposed verses** in order **to** derive **another** statement **of Rabbi Yehoshua ben Levi, as Rabbi Yehoshua ben Levi said: One who teaches his son Torah, the verse ascribes to him** credit **as if he received** the Torah **from Mount Horeb. As it is stated: "And you shall impart them to your children and your children's children"** (Deuteronomy 4:9) **after which it is written: "The day that you stood before the Lord your God at Horeb."** Therefore, Rabbi Yehuda cannot derive from that same juxtaposition a prohibition banning one who experienced a seminal emission from engaging in matters of Torah.

תְּנַן: זָב שֶׁרָאָה קֶרִי, וְנִדָּה שֶׁפָּלְטָה שִׁכְבַת זֶרַע, הַמְשַׁמֶּשֶׁת וְרָאֲתָה דָּם צְרִיכִין טְבִילָה; וְרַבִּי יְהוּדָה פּוֹטֵר.

We learned in a mishna that **a *zav* who experienced a seminal emission, and a menstruating woman who discharged semen, and a woman who engaged in intercourse** with her husband **and she saw** menstrual **blood,** all of whom are ritually impure for at least seven days due to the severity of their impurity, nevertheless **require ritual immersion** in order to purify themselves from the impurity of the seminal emission before they may engage in matters of Torah. **And Rabbi Yehuda exempts** them from immersion.

PERSONALITIES

Ben Azzai – בֶּן עַזַּאי: Ben Azzai is Shimon ben Azzai, one of the *tanna'im* in Yavne. Shimon ben Azzai was never ordained, which is why he is called by his name alone, without a title. He is usually referred to simply as ben Azzai. He was considered one of the outstanding Sages and his wisdom was celebrated for many generations. Apparently, he did not study Torah in his youth until he met Rabbi Akiva's daughter. She promised to marry him if he studied Torah. Consequently, he went to study with Rabbi Yehoshua and Rabbi Yishmael and was the primary student and even a disciple-colleague of Rabbi Akiva, whom he considered to be the preeminent Sage of his generation in Israel. It is unclear whether he never married, or whether he married Rabbi Akiva's daughter and left her a short time later due to his overwhelming desire to study Torah. He completely devoted himself to the study of Torah, as can be seen in the mishna in *Sota*, which says: Since ben Azzai died, there are no more diligent people. His statements can be found in the Mishna, in *baraitot* and in the Gemara dealing with both *halakha* and *aggada*. Apparently, he had several disciples in Tiberias, his city of residence. Ben Azzai engaged in the study of esoterica and is one of the four who entered the mystical orchard. The *baraita* in tractate *Ḥagiga* says that he peeked and died. The verse: "Precious in the sight of the Lord is the death of His saints" (Psalms 116:15), was quoted in reference to his death.

BACKGROUND

Why were they singled out – לָמָּה יָצְאוּ: This is an instance of one of the thirteen hermeneutic principles through which the Torah is interpreted: When a particular case, already included in the general category, is expressly mentioned to teach something new, that special provision applies to all other cases included in the general category. Here, included in the general category are all of the various kinds of sorcerers; explicitly specified are the mediums and wizards who are mentioned in their own verse. The verse that teaches that they are punished by stoning was expressly mentioned not only to teach about their punishment, but rather to illuminate the general category, i.e., the punishment for all sorcerers.

HALAKHA

The legal status of a sorceress – דִּין מְכַשֵּׁפָה: A sorcerer who performed actual sorcery is executed by stoning. One who merely creates the impression of sorcery is punished with lashes of rebellion (Rambam *Sefer HaMadda, Hilkhot Avodat Kokhavim* 11:15).

A man may wed a woman raped by his father and one seduced by his father; a woman raped by his son and one seduced by his son – נוֹשֵׂא אָדָם אֲנוּסַת אָבִיו וּמְפוּתַּת אָבִיו אֲנוּסַת בְּנוֹ וּמְפוּתַּת בְּנוֹ: This is because the Torah only prohibited a woman married to his father or his son and not a woman with whom they had promiscuous relations (Rambam), as per the opinion of the Rabbis in their dispute with the individual opinion of Rabbi Yehuda (Rambam *Sefer Kedusha, Hilkhot Issurei Bia* 2:13; *Shulḥan Arukh, Even HaEzer* 15:5).

BACKGROUND

In order to convey the far-reaching nature of the opinion of the Rabbis – לְהוֹדִיעָךְ כֹּחָן דְּרַבָּנַן: Since the statements of the Sages are deemed to be as concise and precise as possible, the expectation is that a dispute will be framed in a manner that will facilitate a more profound understanding of the different opinions. Therefore, one may not ascribe a broader scope to a given opinion beyond that which was expressed. At times, however, the disagreement is framed in a manner that does not, in fact, elucidate the entire scope of possibilities in the position of one of the parties to the dispute. That is the case when it is framed in a manner that demonstrates the far-reaching nature of the position of the other party to the dispute. In our case, that is the opinion of the Rabbis, who are stringent.

עַד כָּאן לֹא פָּטַר רַבִּי יְהוּדָה אֶלָּא בְּזָב שֶׁרָאָה קֶרִי – דְּמֵעִיקָּרָא לָאו בַּר טְבִילָה הוּא, אֲבָל בַּעַל קֶרִי גְּרֵידָא מְחַיֵּיב!

However, **Rabbi Yehuda only exempted** from immersion in the case **of a *zav* who experienced a seminal emission, who was unfit to immerse himself from the outset,** as even after immersion he would remain impure with the seven-day impurity of the *zav*. **But,** in the case of **one who experienced a seminal emission alone,** with no concurrent impurity, even Rabbi Yehuda **requires** immersion before he may engage in Torah matters.

וְכִי תֵּימָא, הוּא הַדִּין דַּאֲפִילּוּ בַּעַל קֶרִי גְּרֵידָא נַמִי פָּטַר רַבִּי יְהוּדָה; וְהַאי דְּקָא מִפַּלְגִי בְּזָב שֶׁרָאָה קֶרִי – לְהוֹדִיעָךְ כֹּחָן דְּרַבָּנַן, אֵימָא סֵיפָא: הַמְשַׁמֶּשֶׁת וְרָאֲתָה דָּם צְרִיכָה טְבִילָה,

And if you say: The same is true even in the case of **one who experienced a seminal emission alone,** that **Rabbi Yehuda also exempts** him from immersion, **and the fact that they disagree** in the case of **a *zav* who experienced a seminal emission** and not in the case of a person who experienced a seminal emission alone **is in order to convey the far-reaching** nature of the opinion **of the Rabbis,**[B] who require immersion even in this case. If so, **say the last case** of that same mishna: **A woman who was engaged in intercourse and she saw** menstrual **blood requires immersion.**

לְמַאן קָתָנֵי לַהּ? אִילֵימָא לְרַבָּנַן – פְּשִׁיטָא! הַשְׁתָּא וּמַה זָב שֶׁרָאָה קֶרִי דְּמֵעִיקָּרָא לָאו בַּר טְבִילָה הוּא – מְחַיְּיבִי רַבָּנַן, הַמְשַׁמֶּשֶׁת וְרָאֲתָה דָּם, דְּמֵעִיקָּרָא בַּת טְבִילָה הִיא – לֹא כׇּל שֶׁכֵּן! אֶלָּא לָאו רַבִּי יְהוּדָה הִיא, וְדַוְקָא קָתָנֵי לַהּ

The Gemara seeks to clarify: **In accordance with whose** opinion **was this** case in the mishna **taught? If you say** that it is in accordance with the opinion of **the Rabbis, that is obvious;** if in the case of **a *zav* who experienced a seminal emission who was unfit to immerse himself from the outset,** when he experienced the seminal emission, **the Rabbis** nevertheless **require immersion, all the more so** wouldn't they require immersion for **a woman who engaged in intercourse and** only then **saw blood,** who **was fit to immerse herself from the outset,** when she came into contact with the seminal emission of her husband? **Rather, isn't this Rabbi Yehuda's** opinion, **and** this case **was taught specifically** in order to teach

Perek **III**
Daf **22** Amud **a**

מְשַׁמֶּשֶׁת וְרָאֲתָה נִדָּה אֵינָהּ צְרִיכָה טְבִילָה, אֲבָל בַּעַל קֶרִי גְּרֵידָא – מְחַיֵּיב! לָא תֵּימָא 'מְבָרֵךְ' אֶלָּא 'מְהַרְהֵר'.

that **a woman who engaged in intercourse and saw menstrual** blood **is not required to immerse herself, but one who experienced a seminal emission alone,** with no concurrent impurity, **is required to do so?** If so, we must interpret Rabbi Yehuda's statement in the mishna that one recites a blessing both beforehand and thereafter as follows: **Do not say** that one **recites a blessing** orally, but rather he means that **one contemplates** those blessings in his heart.

וּמִי אִית לֵיהּ לְרַבִּי יְהוּדָה הִרְהוּר?! וְהָתַנְיָא: בַּעַל קֶרִי שֶׁאֵין לוֹ מַיִם לִטְבּוֹל – קוֹרֵא קְרִיאַת שְׁמַע, וְאֵינוֹ מְבָרֵךְ לֹא לְפָנֶיהָ וְלֹא לְאַחֲרֶיהָ, וְאוֹכֵל פִּתּוֹ וּמְבָרֵךְ לְאַחֲרֶיהָ וְאֵינוֹ מְבָרֵךְ לְפָנֶיהָ, אֲבָל מְהַרְהֵר בְּלִבּוֹ וְאֵינוֹ מוֹצִיא בִּשְׂפָתָיו, דִּבְרֵי רַבִּי מֵאִיר. רַבִּי יְהוּדָה אוֹמֵר: בֵּין כָּךְ וּבֵין כָּךְ מוֹצִיא בִּשְׂפָתָיו.

The Gemara challenges this explanation: **And does Rabbi Yehuda maintain that** there is validity to **contemplating** in his heart? **Wasn't it taught** in a *baraita*: **One who experienced a seminal emission and who has no water to immerse** and purify himself **recites *Shema* and neither recites the blessings** of *Shema* **beforehand nor thereafter? And** when **he eats his bread, he recites the blessing thereafter,** Grace after Meals, **but does not recite the blessing:** Who brings forth bread from the earth, **beforehand. However,** in the instances where he may not recite the blessing, **he contemplates** it **in his heart rather than utter** it **with his lips,** this is **the statement of Rabbi Meir.** However **Rabbi Yehuda says: In either case, he utters** all of the blessings **with his lips.** Rabbi Yehuda does not consider contemplating the blessings in his heart a solution and permits them to be recited.

אָמַר רַב נַחְמָן בַּר יִצְחָק: עֲשָׂאָן רַבִּי יְהוּדָה כְּהִלְכוֹת דֶּרֶךְ אֶרֶץ.

Rav Naḥman bar Yitzḥak said: Rabbi Yehuda's statement in the mishna should be interpreted in another way. **Rabbi Yehuda rendered** the blessings **like *Hilkhot Derekh Eretz,*** which according to some Sages were not considered to be in the same category as all other matters of Torah and therefore, one is permitted to engage in their study even after having experienced a seminal emission.

דְּתַנְיָא: "וְהוֹדַעְתָּם לְבָנֶיךָ וְלִבְנֵי בָנֶיךָ", וּכְתִיב בָּתְרֵיהּ "יוֹם אֲשֶׁר עָמַדְתָּ לִפְנֵי ה' אֱלֹהֶיךָ בְּחוֹרֵב", מָה לְהַלָּן בְּאֵימָה וּבְיִרְאָה וּבִרְתֵת וּבְזִיעַ אַף כָּאן בְּאֵימָה וּבְיִרְאָה וּבִרְתֵת וּבְזִיעַ;

As it was taught in a *baraita*: It is written: **"And you shall impart them to your children and your children's children"** (Deuteronomy 4:9), **and it is written thereafter: "The day that you stood before the Lord your God at Horeb"** (Deuteronomy 4:10). **Just as below,** the Revelation at Sinai was **in reverence, fear, quaking, and trembling, so too here,** in every generation, Torah must be studied with a sense of **reverence, fear, quaking, and trembling.**

מִכָּאן אָמְרוּ: הַזָּבִים וְהַמְּצוֹרָעִים וּבָאִין עַל נִדּוֹת – מוּתָּרִים לִקְרוֹת בַּתּוֹרָה וּבַנְּבִיאִים וּבַכְּתוּבִים, לִשְׁנוֹת בְּמִשְׁנָה וּגְמָרָא וּבַהֲלָכוֹת וּבָאַגָּדוֹת, אֲבָל בַּעֲלֵי קְרָיִין אֲסוּרִים;

From here the Sages **stated: *Zavim*, lepers, and those who engaged in intercourse with menstruating women**, despite their severe impurity, **are permitted to read the Torah, Prophets, and Writings, and to study Mishna and Gemara and *halakhot* and *aggada*. However, those who experienced a seminal emission are prohibited** from doing so.[H] The reason for this distinction is that the cases of severe impurity are caused by ailment or other circumstances beyond his control and, as a result, they do not necessarily preclude a sense of reverence and awe as he studies Torah. This, however, is not the case with regard to impurity resulting from a seminal emission, which usually comes about due to frivolity and a lack of reverence and awe. Therefore, it is inappropriate for one who experiences a seminal emission to engage in matters of in Torah.

רַבִּי יוֹסֵי אוֹמֵר: שׁוֹנֶה הוּא בִּרְגִילִיּוֹת וּבִלְבַד שֶׁלֹּא יַצִּיעַ אֶת הַמִּשְׁנָה; רַבִּי יוֹנָתָן בֶּן יוֹסֵף אוֹמֵר: מַצִּיעַ הוּא אֶת הַמִּשְׁנָה וְאֵינוֹ מַצִּיעַ אֶת הַגְּמָרָא; רַבִּי נָתָן בֶּן אֲבִישָׁלוֹם אוֹמֵר: אַף מַצִּיעַ אֶת הַגְּמָרָא וּבִלְבַד שֶׁלֹּא יֹאמַר אַזְכָּרוֹת שֶׁבּוֹ; רַבִּי יוֹחָנָן הַסַּנְדְּלָר תַּלְמִידוֹ שֶׁל רַבִּי עֲקִיבָא מִשּׁוּם רַבִּי עֲקִיבָא אוֹמֵר: לֹא יִכָּנֵס לַמִּדְרָשׁ כָּל עִיקָּר, וְאָמְרִי לַהּ: לֹא יִכָּנֵס לְבֵית הַמִּדְרָשׁ כָּל עִיקָּר; רַבִּי יְהוּדָה אוֹמֵר: שׁוֹנֶה הוּא בְּהִלְכוֹת דֶּרֶךְ אֶרֶץ.

However, there are many opinions concerning the precise parameters of the Torah matters prohibited by this decree. **Rabbi Yosei says:** One who experiences a seminal emission **studies *mishnayot*** that he is **accustomed** to study,[N] **as long as he does not expound upon** a new **mishna** to study it in depth. **Rabbi Yonatan ben Yosef says: He expounds upon the mishna but he does not expound upon the Gemara,** which is the in-depth analysis of the Torah. **Rabbi Natan ben Avishalom says: He may even expound upon the Gemara, as long as he does not utter the mentions** of God's name **therein. Rabbi Yoḥanan the Cobbler, Rabbi Akiva's student, says in the name of Rabbi Akiva:** One who experiences a seminal emission **may not enter into homiletic interpretation** [*midrash*] of verses **at all. Some say** that he says: **He may not enter the study hall** [*beit hamidrash*] **at all. Rabbi Yehuda says: He may study** only ***Hilkhot Derekh Eretz***. In terms of the problem raised above, apparently Rabbi Yehuda considers the legal status of the blessings to be parallel to the legal status of *Hilkhot Derekh Eretz*, and therefore one may utter them orally.

מַעֲשֶׂה בְּרַבִּי יְהוּדָה שֶׁרָאָה קֶרִי וְהָיָה מְהַלֵּךְ עַל גַּב הַנָּהָר. אָמְרוּ לוֹ תַּלְמִידָיו: רַבֵּינוּ, שְׁנֵה לָנוּ פֶּרֶק אֶחָד בְּהִלְכוֹת דֶּרֶךְ אֶרֶץ! יָרַד וְטָבַל וְשָׁנָה לָהֶם. אָמְרוּ לוֹ: לֹא כָּךְ לִמַּדְתָּנוּ רַבֵּינוּ: שׁוֹנֶה הוּא בְּהִלְכוֹת דֶּרֶךְ אֶרֶץ? אָמַר לָהֶם: אַף עַל פִּי שֶׁמֵּיקֵל אֲנִי עַל אֲחֵרִים, מַחְמִיר אֲנִי עַל עַצְמִי.

The Gemara relates **an incident involving Rabbi Yehuda** himself, who **experienced a seminal emission and was walking along the riverbank** with his disciples. **His disciples said to him: Rabbi, teach us a chapter from *Hilkhot Derekh Eretz*,** as he maintained that even in a state of impurity, it is permitted. **He descended and immersed himself** in the river **and taught them** *Hilkhot Derekh Eretz*. **They said to him: Did you not teach us, our teacher, that he may study *Hilkhot Derekh Eretz*? He said to them: Although I am lenient with others,** and allow them to study it without immersion, **I am stringent with myself.**[N]

תַּנְיָא, רַבִּי יְהוּדָה בֶּן בְּתֵירָא הָיָה אוֹמֵר: אֵין דִּבְרֵי תוֹרָה מְקַבְּלִין טוּמְאָה. מַעֲשֶׂה בְּתַלְמִיד אֶחָד שֶׁהָיָה מְגַמְגֵּם לְמַעְלָה מֵרַבִּי יְהוּדָה בֶּן בְּתֵירָא. אָמַר לֵיהּ: בְּנִי, פְּתַח פִּיךָ וְיָאִירוּ דְּבָרֶיךָ; שֶׁאֵין דִּבְרֵי תוֹרָה מְקַבְּלִין טוּמְאָה שֶׁנֶּאֱמַר "הֲלֹא כֹה דְבָרִי כָּאֵשׁ נְאֻם ה'" מָה אֵשׁ אֵינוֹ מְקַבֵּל טוּמְאָה אַף דִּבְרֵי תוֹרָה אֵינָן מְקַבְּלִין טוּמְאָה.

Further elaborating on the issue of Torah study while in a state of impurity, **it was taught** in a *baraita* that **Rabbi Yehuda ben Beteira**[P] **would say: Matters of Torah do not become ritually impure**[N] and therefore one who is impure is permitted to engage in Torah study. He implemented this *halakha* in practice. The Gemara relates **an incident involving a student who was** reciting *mishnayot* and *baraitot* **hesitantly before** the study hall of **Rabbi Yehuda ben Beteira.** The student experienced a seminal emission, and when he was asked to recite he did so in a rushed, uneven manner, as he did not want to utter the words of Torah explicitly. Rabbi Yehuda **said to him: My son, open your mouth and let your words illuminate, as matters of Torah do not become ritually impure, as it is stated: "Is not my word like fire, says the Lord"** (Jeremiah 23:29). **Just as fire does not become ritually impure, so too matters of Torah do not become ritually impure.**

אָמַר מָר: מַצִּיעַ אֶת הַמִּשְׁנָה וְאֵינוֹ מַצִּיעַ אֶת הַגְּמָרָא. מְסַיַּיע לֵיהּ לְרַבִּי אֶלְעַאי; דְּאָמַר רַבִּי אֶלְעַאי אָמַר רַבִּי אַחָא בַּר יַעֲקֹב מִשּׁוּם רַבֵּינוּ: הֲלָכָה, מַצִּיעַ אֶת הַמִּשְׁנָה וְאֵינוֹ מַצִּיעַ אֶת הַגְּמָרָא. כְּתַנָּאֵי: מַצִּיעַ אֶת הַמִּשְׁנָה וְאֵינוֹ מַצִּיעַ אֶת הַגְּמָרָא, דִּבְרֵי רַבִּי מֵאִיר; רַבִּי יְהוּדָה בֶּן גַּמְלִיאֵל אוֹמֵר מִשּׁוּם רַבִּי חֲנִינָא בֶּן גַּמְלִיאֵל: זֶה וָזֶה אָסוּר; וְאָמְרִי לַהּ: זֶה וָזֶה מוּתָּר.

In this *baraita* **the Master said** that one who is impure because of a seminal emission **expounds upon the mishna but does not expound upon the Gemara.** The Gemara notes: This statement **supports** the opinion of **Rabbi El'ai,**[P] as **Rabbi El'ai said** that **Rabbi Aḥa bar Ya'akov said in the name of Rabbeinu,** Rav: **The *halakha*** is that one who experienced a seminal emission **may expound upon the mishna but may not expound upon the Gemara.** This dispute **is parallel a tannaitic** dispute, as it was taught: One who experienced a seminal emission **expounds upon the mishna but does not expound upon the Gemara;** that is **the statement of Rabbi Meir. Rabbi Yehuda ben Gamliel says in the name of Rabbi Ḥanina ben Gamliel: Both this and that are prohibited. And some say** that he said: Both **this and that are permitted.**

HALAKHA

Zavim and lepers…are permitted to read the Torah…But those who experienced a seminal emission are prohibited from doing so – הַזָּבִים וְהַמְּצוֹרָעִים...מוּתָּרִים לִקְרוֹת בַּתּוֹרָה...אֲבָל בַּעֲלֵי קְרָיִין אֲסוּרִים: Everyone who is ritually impure is permitted to read the Torah, recite *Shema*, and pray, except for those who experienced a seminal emission, as Ezra decreed that they are prohibited to do so until they immerse in a ritual bath. However, in subsequent generations that ordinance was repealed and one who experienced a seminal emission was permitted to engage in all those activities without immersion or bathing in nine *kav* of water. That remains the prevalent custom (Rambam *Sefer Ahava, Hilkhot Keriat Shema* 4:8; *Shulḥan Arukh, Oraḥ Hayyim* 88).

NOTES

He studies the *mishnayot* that he is accustomed to study – שׁוֹנֶה הוּא בִּרְגִילִיּוֹת: Some interpret this to refer to those *misnnayot* with which everyone is familiar, such as Ethics of the Fathers or those recited as part of the portion of the daily offering (Rav Sa'adia Gaon), and expound a mishna means that he may not explain it to others (*Arukh*).

I am stringent with myself – מַחְמִיר אֲנִי עַל עַצְמִי: Rabbi Yehuda followed the path of those Sages, who, although they ruled leniently with regard to a particular *halakha* and instructed the public accordingly, they did not rely upon that leniency themselves and, in doing so, at times, placed themselves in danger. They did so because they held their colleagues and their opinions in such high regard.

Matters of Torah do not become ritually impure – אֵין דִּבְרֵי תוֹרָה מְקַבְּלִין טוּמְאָה: This statement does not contradict the prohibition against reciting matters of Torah in a filthy place. The distinction is that ritual impurity is intangible and is experienced intellectually. Since the words of God are like fire, they do not become ritually impure. However, filth offends the senses and creates a clear impression that one is in a despicable place. Uttering matters of Torah there would fall under the rubric of: "For he has shown contempt for the word of the Lord" (Numbers 15:31; *Kesef Mishne*).

PERSONALITIES

Rabbi Yehuda ben Beteira – רַבִּי יְהוּדָה בֶּן בְּתֵירָא: The Benei Beteira family produced renowned Sages over several generations. Some members of the family served as *Nasi* during the time of Hillel, but transferred the position to him.

It is almost certain that there were two Sages named Yehuda ben Beteira. The second may have been the grandson of the first. Both lived in the city of Netzivin in Babylonia: one, while the Temple was still standing, and the second at the end of the tannaitic period. The Rabbi Yehuda ben Beteira whose teaching is cited here is most likely the second one. He was one of the greatest Torah scholars of his age and organized the study of Torah throughout Babylonia before the great yeshivas were established. He was venerated by the Sages of Eretz Yisrael.

Rabbi El'ai – רַבִּי אֶלְעַאי: This page cites two Sages named Rabbi El'ai. The first, the Rabbi El'ai who makes a statement in the name of Rabbi Aḥa bar Ya'akov, was an *amora* in Eretz Yisrael during the generation of Rabbi Yoḥanan's students. The Rabbi El'ai who makes a statement with regard to the first shearing is the *tanna* Rabbi El'ai the Elder, a student of Rabbi Eliezer the Great, ben Hyrcanus, and father of the famous *tanna* Rabbi Yehuda ben El'ai.

Comparing these opinions: **The one who said** that both **this and that are prohibited** holds **in accordance with** the opinion of **Rabbi Yoḥanan the Cobbler; the one who said** that both **this and that are permitted** holds **in accordance with** the opinion of **Rabbi Yehuda ben Beteira.**

מַאן דְּאָמַר זֶה וָזֶה אָסוּר – כְּרַבִּי יוֹחָנָן הַסַּנְדְּלָר, מַאן דְּאָמַר זֶה וָזֶה מוּתָּר – כְּרַבִּי יְהוּדָה בֶּן בְּתֵירָא.

Summarizing the *halakha*, **Rav Naḥman bar Yitzḥak said: The universally** accepted **practice is in accordance with** the opinions of **these three elders: In accordance with** the opinion of **Rabbi El'ai with regard to** the *halakhot* of **the first shearing,**[H] **in accordance with** the opinion of **Rabbi Yoshiya with regard to** the laws of prohibited **diverse kinds,** and **in accordance with** the opinion of **Rabbi Yehuda ben Beteira with regard to matters of Torah.**

אָמַר רַב נַחְמָן בַּר יִצְחָק נָהוּג עָלְמָא כְּהָנֵי תְּלָת סָבֵי: כְּרַבִּי אֶלְעַאי בְּרֵאשִׁית הַגֵּז, כְּרַבִּי יֹאשִׁיָּה בְּכִלְאַיִם, כְּרַבִּי יְהוּדָה בֶּן בְּתֵירָא בְּדִבְרֵי תוֹרָה.

The Gemara elaborates: **In accordance with** the opinion of **Rabbi El'ai with regard to the first shearing, as it was taught** in a *baraita* that **Rabbi El'ai says:** The obligation to set aside **the first shearing** from the sheep for the priest **is only practiced in Eretz** Yisrael and not in the Diaspora, and that is the accepted practice.

כְּרַבִּי אֶלְעַאי בְּרֵאשִׁית הַגֵּז – דְּתַנְיָא, רַבִּי אֶלְעַאי אוֹמֵר: רֵאשִׁית הַגֵּז אֵינוֹ נוֹהֵג אֶלָּא בָּאָרֶץ.

In accordance with the opinion of **Rabbi Yoshiya with regard to diverse kinds, as it is written: "You shall not sow your vineyard with diverse kinds"** (Deuteronomy 22:9).[H] **Rabbi Yoshiya says:** This means that **one** who sows diverse kinds **is not liable** by Torah law **until he sows wheat and barley and a grape pit with a single hand motion,** meaning that while sowing in the vineyard he violates the prohibition of diverse kinds that applies to seeds and to the vineyard simultaneously.

כְּרַבִּי יֹאשִׁיָּה בְּכִלְאַיִם – כִּדְכְתִיב: "לֹא תִזְרַע [כַּרְמְךָ] כִּלְאָיִם", רַבִּי יֹאשִׁיָּה אוֹמֵר: לְעוֹלָם אֵינוֹ חַיָּיב עַד שֶׁיִּזְרַע חִטָּה וּשְׂעוֹרָה וְחַרְצָן בְּמַפּוֹלֶת יָד.

In accordance with Rabbi Yehuda ben Beteira with regard to one who experiences a seminal emission is permitted to engage in **matters of Torah, as it was taught** in a *baraita* that **Rabbi Yehuda ben Beteira says: Matters of Torah do not become ritually impure.**[H]

כְּרַבִּי יְהוּדָה בֶּן בְּתֵירָא בְּדִבְרֵי תוֹרָה, דְּתַנְיָא, רַבִּי יְהוּדָה בֶּן בְּתֵירָא אוֹמֵר: אֵין דִּבְרֵי תוֹרָה מְקַבְּלִין טוּמְאָה.

And the Gemara relates: **When Ze'iri came** from Eretz Yisrael to Babylonia, **he** succinctly capsulated this *halakha* and **said: They abolished ritual immersion,**[N] **and some say that** he said: **They abolished ritual washing of the hands.** The Gemara explains: **The one who says** that **they abolished immersion** holds in accordance with the opinion of **Rabbi Yehuda ben Beteira** that one who experienced a seminal emission is not required to immerse. **And the one who says** that **they abolished washing of the hands** holds **in accordance with that which Rav Ḥisda cursed one who** goes out of his way **to seek water at the time of prayer.**

כִּי אֲתָא זְעִירִי, אָמַר: בַּטְּלוּהָ לִטְבִילוּתָא, וְאָמְרִי לַהּ: בַּטְּלוּהָ לִנְטִילוּתָא. מַאן דְּאָמַר "בַּטְּלוּהָ לִטְבִילוּתָא" – כְּרַבִּי יְהוּדָה בֶּן בְּתֵירָא. מַאן דְּאָמַר "בַּטְּלוּהָ לִנְטִילוּתָא" – כִּי הָא דְּרַב חִסְדָּא לָיֵיט אַמַּאן דִּמְהַדַּר אַמַּיָּא בְּעִידָּן צְלוֹתָא.

The Sages taught in a *baraita*: **One who experienced a seminal emission who had nine *kav*** of drawn water **poured over him,** that is sufficient to render him **ritually pure** and he need not immerse himself in a ritual bath. The Gemara relates: **Naḥum of Gam Zo whispered** this *halakha* to **Rabbi Akiva, and Rabbi Akiva whispered it**[N] to his student **ben Azzai, and ben Azzai went out and taught it to his students** publicly **in the marketplace. Two *amora'im* in Eretz Yisrael, Rabbi Yosei bar Avin and Rabbi Yosei bar Zevida, disagreed** as to the correct version of the conclusion of the incident. **One taught:** Ben Azzai **taught it** to his students in the market. **And the other taught: Ben Azzai** also **whispered it** to his students.

תָּנוּ רַבָּנַן: בַּעַל קֶרִי שֶׁנָּתְנוּ עָלָיו תִּשְׁעָה קַבִּין מַיִם – טָהוֹר; נַחוּם אִישׁ גַּם זוֹ לְחָשָׁהּ לְרַבִּי עֲקִיבָא, וְרַבִּי עֲקִיבָא לְחָשָׁהּ לְבֶן עַזַּאי, וּבֶן עַזַּאי יָצָא וּשְׁנָאָהּ לְתַלְמִידָיו בַּשּׁוּק. פְּלִיגִי בָּהּ תְּרֵי אָמוֹרָאֵי בְּמַעְרְבָא, רַבִּי יוֹסֵי בַּר אָבִין וְרַבִּי יוֹסֵי בַּר זְבִידָא: חַד תָּנֵי 'שְׁנָאָהּ' וְחַד תָּנֵי 'לְחָשָׁהּ'.

The Gemara explains the rationale behind the two versions of this incident. **The** Sage **who taught** that ben Azzai **taught** the law openly in the market held that the leniency was **due to** concern that the *halakhot* requiring ritual immersion would promote **dereliction** in the study **of Torah.** The ruling of Rabbi Yehuda ben Beteira eases the way for an individual who experienced a seminal emission to study Torah. This was **also due to** concern that the *halakhot* requiring ritual immersion would promote **the suspension of procreation,** as one might abstain from marital relations to avoid the immersion required thereafter. **And the** Sage, **who taught** that ben Azzai only **whispered** this *halakha* to his students, held that he did so **in order that Torah scholars would not be with their wives like roosters.**[H] If the purification process was that simple, Torah scholars would engage in sexual activity constantly, which would distract them from their studies.

מַאן דְּתָנֵי 'שְׁנָאָהּ' מִשּׁוּם בִּטּוּל תּוֹרָה, וּמִשּׁוּם בִּטּוּל פְּרִיָּה וּרְבִיָּה. וּמַאן דְּתָנֵי 'לְחָשָׁהּ' – שֶׁלֹּא יְהוּ תַּלְמִידֵי חֲכָמִים מְצוּיִים אֵצֶל נְשׁוֹתֵיהֶם כְּתַרְנְגוֹלִים.

HALAKHA

The first shearing – רֵאשִׁית הַגֵּז: The mitzva of the first shearing is in effect in all generations, whether or not the Temple is intact. However, it is only in effect in Eretz Yisrael as per the opinion of Rabbi El'ai. Some say that, by Torah law, it is in effect outside of Eretz Yisrael as well, but the custom is not in accordance with that opinion (Rema; Rambam *Sefer Zera'im, Hilkhot Bikkurim* 10:1; *Shulḥan Arukh, Yoreh De'a* 333:1).

Diverse kinds in a vineyard – כִּלְאַיִם בְּכֶרֶם: One is liable for lashes for sowing diverse kinds in a vineyard only if he sowed wheat, barley, and a grape seed, or two species of vegetable and a grape seed, or a vegetable, a grain, and a grape seed, in a single motion. Sowing other diverse kinds of seeds together is prohibited only by rabbinic law, in accordance with the opinion of Rabbi Yoshiya (Rambam *Sefer Zera'im, Hilkhot Kilayim* 5:2, *Hilkhot Bikkurim* 8:13; *Shulḥan Arukh, Yoreh De'a* 296:1–2).

Matters of Torah do not become ritually impure – אֵין דִּבְרֵי תוֹרָה מְקַבְּלִין טוּמְאָה: Matters of Torah do not become ritually impure and nowadays everyone is permitted to study Torah and touch sacred objects even if he is ritually impure, in accordance with the opinion of Rabbi Yehuda ben Beteira (Rambam *Sefer Ahava, Hilkhot Keriat Shema* 4:8, *Hilkhot Tefilla* 4:5, *Hilkhot Tefillin Sefer Torah UMezuza* 10:8; *Shulḥan Arukh, Oraḥ Ḥayyim* 88, *Yoreh De'a* 282:9).

So that Torah scholars would not be with their wives constantly, like roosters – שֶׁלֹּא יְהוּ תַּלְמִידֵי חֲכָמִים מְצוּיִים אֵצֶל נְשׁוֹתֵיהֶם כְּתַרְנְגוֹלִים: It is inappropriate for a Torah scholar to overindulge in conjugal relations with his wife. The conjugal rights of the wife of a Torah scholar are once a week, on Shabbat eve (Rambam *Sefer HaMadda, Hilkhot De'ot* 5:4, *Sefer Ahava, Hilkhot Tefilla* 4:4; *Shulḥan Arukh, Oraḥ Ḥayyim* 240:1, *Even HaEzer* 25:2).

NOTES

They abolished ritual immersion – בַּטְּלוּהָ לִטְבִילוּתָא: According to most commentaries, (Rambam, Ra'avad, *Shitta Mekubbetzet, Talmidei Rabbeinu Yona*), they could do so because Ezra's ordinance did not gain acceptance throughout Israel. The principle is that any ordinance that did not gain acceptance, even if it was instituted by Torah giants, may be overturned by later generations; even by a court of lower stature than the one that instituted it in the first place. Indeed, the ordinance was repealed for several reasons. It led to dereliction in the study of Torah and it discouraged procreation. Therefore, it only remained as a custom to enhance sanctity (*Me'iri*).

Whispered it – לְחָשָׁהּ: With regard to several *halakhot*, the Gemara says: This is the *halakha*, but a public ruling is not issued. If an individual poses the question, he is answered in accordance with the *halakha*. There are other *halakhot* which are not shared with individuals either and they remain the exclusive purview of the Torah scholars familiar with it.

אמר רבי ינאי: שמעתי שמקילין בה ושמעתי שמחמירין בה, וכל המחמיר בה על עצמו מאריכין לו ימיו ושנותיו.

With regard to this ritual immersion, **Rabbi Yannai said: I heard that there are those who are lenient with regard to it and I have heard that there are those who are stringent with regard to it.**[N] The *halakha* in this matter was never conclusively established **and** anyone who accepts **upon himself to be stringent with regard to it, they prolong for him his days and years.**[H]

אמר רבי יהושע בן לוי: מה טיבן של טובלי שחרין? – מה טיבן? הא איהו דאמר: בעל קרי אסור בדברי תורה! – הכי קאמר: מה טיבן בארבעים סאה? אפשר בתשעה קבין, מה טיבן בטבילה? אפשר בנתינה!

The Gemara relates that **Rabbi Yehoshua ben Levi said: What is the essence of those who immerse themselves in the morning?**[B] The Gemara retorts: How can one ask **what is their essence? Isn't he** the one **who said** that **one who experiences a seminal emission is prohibited from** engaging in **matters of Torah** and is required to immerse himself in the morning? Rather, **this is** what **he** meant to **say: What is the essence of** immersion in a ritual bath of **forty** ***se'a*** of water when **it is possible** to purify oneself **with nine** ***kav***? Furthermore, **what is the essence of immersion** when **it is** also **possible** to purify oneself by **pouring** water?

אמר רבי חנינא: גדר גדול גדרו בה, דתניא: מעשה באחד שתבע אשה לדבר עבירה. אמרה לו: ריקא! יש לך ארבעים סאה שאתה טובל בהן? מיד פירש.

Regarding this, **Rabbi Ḥanina said: They established a massive fence** protecting one from sinning with their decree that one must immerse himself in forty *se'a* of water. **As it was taught** in a *baraita*: There was **an incident involving one who solicited a woman to** commit **a sinful act. She said to him: Good-for-nothing. Do you have forty** ***se'a*** **in which to immerse** and purify **yourself** afterwards? He **immediately desisted.** The obligation to immerse oneself caused individuals to refrain from transgression.

אמר להו רב הונא לרבנן: רבותי, מפני מה אתם מזלזלין בטבילה זו? אי משום צינה, אפשר במרחצאות!

Rav Huna said to the Sages: Gentlemen, why do you disdain this immersion? If it is because it is difficult for you to immerse in the **cold** waters of the ritual bath, **it is possible** to purify oneself by immersing oneself in the heated **bathhouses,** which are unfit for immersion for other forms of ritual impurity but are fit for immersion in this case.

אמר ליה רב חסדא: וכי יש טבילה בחמין? אמר ליה: רב אדא בר אהבה קאי כוותך.

Rabbi Ḥisda said to him: Is there ritual immersion in hot water?[N] Rav Huna **said to him:** Indeed, doubts with regard to the fitness of baths have been raised, and **Rav Adda bar Ahava holds in accordance with your** opinion. Nevertheless, I remain convinced that it is permitted.

רבי זירא הוה יתיב באגנא דמיא בי מסותא. אמר ליה לשמעיה: זיל ואייתי לי תשעה קבין ושדי עלאי. אמר ליה רבי חייא בר אבא: למה ליה למר כולי האי? והא יתיב בגווייהו! אמר ליה: כארבעים סאה; מה ארבעים סאה בטבילה ולא בנתינה אף תשעה קבין בנתינה ולא בטבילה.

The Gemara relates: **Rabbi Zeira was sitting in a tub of water in the bathhouse. He said to his attendant: Go and get nine** ***kav*** of water **and pour it over me** so that I may purify myself from the impurity caused by a seminal emission. **Rabbi Ḥiyya bar Abba said to him: Why does my master** require **all of this? Aren't you seated in** at least nine *kav* of water in the tub. **He said to him:** The law of nine *kav* **parallels** the law of **forty** ***se'a,*** in that their *halakhot* are exclusive. **Just as forty** ***se'a*** can only purify an individual through **immersion and not through pouring, so too nine** ***kav*** can only purify one who experienced a seminal emission **through pouring**[H] **and not through immersion.**

רב נחמן תקן חצבא בת תשעה קבין. כי אתא רב דימי אמר, רבי עקיבא ורבי יהודה גלוסטרא אמרו: לא שנו אלא לחולה לאונסו, אבל לחולה המרגיל ארבעים סאה.

The Gemara relates that **Rav Naḥman prepared a jug** with a capacity **of nine** ***kav*** so that his students could pour water over themselves and become pure. **When Rav Dimi came** from Eretz Yisrael to Babylonia, **he said: Rabbi Akiva and Rabbi Yehuda Gelostera**[L] **said:** The *halakha* that one who experienced a seminal emission can be purified by pouring nine *kav* **was only taught for a sick person** who experienced the emission **involuntarily. However, a sick person** who experienced a **normal** seminal emission[N] in the course of marital relations, is required to immerse himself in **forty** ***se'a.***

אמר רב יוסף: אתבר חצביה דרב נחמן. כי אתא רבין אמר: באושא הוה עובדא

Rav Yosef said: In that case, **Rav Naḥman's jug is broken,** meaning it is no longer of any use, as few people fall into the category of sick people who experienced seminal emissions. Nevertheless, **when Ravin came** from Eretz Yisrael to Babylonia **he said: In Usha there was an incident**

NOTES

I heard that there are those who are lenient with regard to it and I have heard that there are those who are stringent with regard to it – שמעתי שמקילין בה ושמעתי שמחמירין בה: There are several interpretations of this statement. Some explained that lenient means that they do not require immersion but suffice with pouring nine *kav* of water and stringent means that they require immersion (*Shitta Mekubbetzet*). Others explained that lenient means immersion in a bath containing forty *se'a* and stringent means immersion in a full-fledged ritual bath (*Ba'al Halakhot Gedolot*).

Immersion in hot water – טבילה בחמין: The problem with bathhouses is not with the issue of immersion in hot water, as there are numerous methods to heat the water of the ritual bath while keeping it fit for immersion. The problem is that the water in bathhouses is drawn water, which is not fit for immersion at all. Therefore, they wondered whether or not immersion in hot water is appropriate (*Penei Yehoshua*).

One who experienced a normal seminal emission – המרגיל: Some interpret this expression as a euphemism for conjugal relations with a woman based on the verse: "And she uncovered his feet [*margelotav*] and laid herself down" (Ruth 3:7; see Rav Sa'adia Gaon).

HALAKHA

Anyone who accepts upon himself to be stringent with regard to this, they prolong for him his days and years – כל המחמיר בה על עצמו מאריכין לו ימיו ושנותיו: Even though the basic *halakha* is that one who experiences a seminal emission is not required to immerse himself, nevertheless, one who is stringent is praiseworthy as per the statement of Rabbi Yannai (*Tur, Oraḥ Ḥayyim* 241).

Nine ***kav*** **only through pouring** – תשעה קבין בנתינה: One who seeks to purify himself from the ritual impurity of a seminal emission by pouring nine *kav* of water must pour it on his back all at once as per the opinion of Rav Ḥisda (*Beit Yosef* on *Tur Oraḥ Ḥayyim* 88).

BACKGROUND

Those who immerse themselves in the morning – טובלי שחרית: Those mentioned here as immersing in the morning may have once comprised a clearly defined group who deviated from the path established by the Sages in different ways.

At the end of the *Tosefta* for tractate *Yadayim* we find the following: Those who immerse in the morning said: We rail against you Pharisees, for you recite the Name of God in a state of impurity. They replied: We rail against you who immerse in the morning, for you recite the Name in an impure body. Apparently, those who immersed in the morning considered themselves separate from the Pharisee Sages of Israel. Indeed, some theorize that this refers to an Essene cult that was particularly strict with regard to the laws of purity and whose members stringently purified themselves after seminal emissions by immersing in an actual ritual bath.

LANGUAGE

Gelostera – גלוסטרא: The source of this word is from the Greek κλεῖστρον, *kleistron*, or from the Latin claustrum, both of which mean bolt or lock. The Sages used it to refer to a specific type of bolt. It seems here that it should be read *gelustara'a*, which is how it appears in other versions and manuscripts. In Aramaic, this refers to the individual who fashions bolts and the nickname was thus given to this Sage who worked as a locksmith. Many nicknames were similarly given to Sages based on their unique professions.

HALAKHA

The immersion of one who is impure because of a seminal emission – טְבִילַת בַּעַל קֶרִי: Although Ezra's ordinance was annulled, there are many communities where the custom remains for one who experienced a seminal emission to immerse himself before prayer. They hold that Ezra's ordinance was only repealed with regard to Torah study, not prayer (See Rambam *Sefer Ahava, Hilkhot Tefilla* 4:5–6).

BACKGROUND

***Kav* – קַב:** This is a basic unit of measurement from which many other small units are derived. It is equivalent to one-sixth of a *se'a* or 24 egg-bulks.

Forty *se'a* – אַרְבָּעִים סְאָה: A *se'a* is one-thirtieth of a *kor* or the equivalent of 144 egg-bulks. Forty *se'a* are the equivalent of 80 *hin* or 5,760 egg-bulks. This is the minimum amount of water required for a ritual bath. A container large enough to hold 40 *se'a* or more is no longer considered to be a utensil, but rather, a building of sorts. This has ramifications in areas of *halakha* like ritual impurity and prohibited labor on Shabbat. The 40 *se'a* measure is the basis of all modern calculations of the various measures of volume. The Talmud tells us that the dimensions of a ritual bath must be 3 cubits by 1 cubit, and that its volume must be 40 *se'a*. Consequently, according to the Na'e scale, a ritual bath must contain 332 ℓ of water (87 US gal), and, according to the Ḥazon Ish, 573 ℓ (151 US gal).

בְּקִילְעָא דְּרַב אוֹשַׁעְיָא, אָתוּ וּשְׁאַלוּ לְרַב אַסִי, אֲמַר לְהוּ: לֹא שָׁנוּ אֶלָּא לַחוֹלֶה הַמַּרְגִּיל, אֲבָל לַחוֹלֶה לְאוֹנְסוֹ פָּטוּר מִכְּלוּם. אֲמַר רַב יוֹסֵף: אִצְטְמִיד חַצְבֵיהּ דְּרַב נַחְמָן.

that this problem was raised **in Rav Oshaya's chamber,** and **they came and asked Rav Asi. He said to them: They only stated** the obligation to pour water over one who is impure because of a seminal emission **with regard to a sick person who experienced a normal** seminal emission, **but a sick person who experienced an involuntary** seminal emission is clearly **exempt from anything** and requires no immersion whatsoever. **Rav Yosef said:** In that case, **Rav Naḥman's jug is rejoined,** meaning that it is effective with regard to purification.

מִכְּדִי כּוּלְּהוּ אֲמוֹרָאֵי וְתַנָּאֵי בְּדְעֶזְרָא קָמִיפַּלְגִי, וְנֶחְזֵי עֶזְרָא הֵיכִי תַּקֵּין!

Up to now, discussion has focused on various problems pertaining to the laws of immersion as they concern one whose impurity is due to seminal emission. The Gemara asks: **Since all of the *amora'im* and *tanna'im* disagree with regard to** the decree of **Ezra, let us examine how Ezra instituted** this ordinance, as this is not an uncommon circumstance and we can see how they conducted themselves.

אֲמַר אַבַּיֵי: עֶזְרָא תַּקֵּין לְבָרִיא הַמַּרְגִּיל אַרְבָּעִים סְאָה, וּבָרִיא לְאוֹנְסוֹ – תִּשְׁעָה קַבִּין. וְאָתוּ אֲמוֹרָאֵי וּפְלִיגִי בְּחוֹלֶה; מָר סְבַר: חוֹלֶה הַמַּרְגִּיל כְּבָרִיא הַמַּרְגִּיל, וְחוֹלֶה לְאוֹנְסוֹ כְּבָרִיא לְאוֹנְסוֹ; וּמָר סְבַר: חוֹלֶה הַמַּרְגִּיל כְּבָרִיא לְאוֹנְסוֹ, וְחוֹלֶה לְאוֹנְסוֹ פָּטוּר מִכְּלוּם.

Abaye said: Ezra did not institute a sweeping ordinance concerning every case of one who experienced a seminal emission; rather, he **instituted** only that **a healthy person who experienced a normal** seminal emission is required to immerse himself in **forty *se'a*, while for a healthy person** who experienced an **involuntary** seminal emission, **nine *kav*** are sufficient.[H] **And the *amora'im* came and disagreed with regard to a sick person. One Sage held** that **a sick person who experienced a normal** seminal emission is considered **like a healthy person who experienced a normal** seminal emission, **while a sick person** who experienced an **involuntary** seminal emission is considered **like a healthy person** who experienced an **involuntary** seminal emission. **However, another Sage maintained** that **a sick person who experienced a normal** seminal emission is considered **like a healthy person** who experienced an **involuntary** seminal emission, and consequently requires only that nine *kav* be poured over him, **while a sick person** who experienced an **involuntary** seminal emission **is exempt from any** form of immersion or purification.

אֲמַר רָבָא: נְהִי דְּתַקֵּין עֶזְרָא טְבִילָה, נְתִינָה מִי תַּקֵּין? וְהָאָמַר מָר: עֶזְרָא תַּקֵּין טְבִילָה לְבַעֲלֵי קְרָיִין! אֶלָּא אָמַר רָבָא: עֶזְרָא תַּקֵּין טְבִילָה לְבָרִיא הַמַּרְגִּיל אַרְבָּעִים סְאָה. וְאָתוּ רַבָּנַן וְהִתְקִינוּ לְבָרִיא לְאוֹנְסוֹ תִּשְׁעָה קַבִּין. וְאָתוּ אֲמוֹרָאֵי וְקָא מִיפַּלְגִי בְּחוֹלֶה; מָר סְבַר: חוֹלֶה הַמַּרְגִּיל כְּבָרִיא הַמַּרְגִּיל, וְחוֹלֶה לְאוֹנְסוֹ כְּבָרִיא לְאוֹנְסוֹ; וּמָר סְבַר: לְבָרִיא הַמַּרְגִּיל אַרְבָּעִים סְאָה וְחוֹלֶה הַמַּרְגִּיל כְּבָרִיא לְאוֹנְסוֹ, תִּשְׁעָה קַבִּין, אֲבָל לַחוֹלֶה לְאוֹנְסוֹ – פָּטוּר מִכְּלוּם.

Rava said: Although Ezra instituted immersion for one who experienced a seminal emission, **did he institute the pouring** of nine *kav*?[B] **Didn't the Master say** that we have a tradition that **Ezra** only **instituted immersion for those who experienced a seminal emission? Rather, Rava said:** We must explain that the diverse opinions developed after Ezra's decree. **Ezra** himself **instituted immersion in forty *se'a*[B]** only **for a healthy person who experienced a normal** seminal emission. **And the Sages came and instituted that a healthy person who experienced an involuntary** seminal emission should have **nine *kav*** poured over him. And then **the *amora'im* came and disagreed** with regard to **a sick person; one Sage held** that **a sick person who experienced a normal** seminal emission is considered **like a healthy person who experienced a normal** seminal emission, **while a sick person** who experienced an **involuntary** seminal emission is considered **like a healthy person** who experienced an **involuntary** seminal emission, **another Sage maintained** that only **a healthy person who experienced a normal** seminal emission is required to immerse himself in **forty *se'a* while a sick person who experienced a normal** seminal emission is considered **like a healthy person** who experienced an **involuntary** seminal emission, requiring only **nine *kav*. But a sick person** who experienced an **involuntary** seminal emission **is exempt from any** form of immersion or purification.

אֲמַר רָבָא: הִלְכְתָא, בָּרִיא הַמַּרְגִּיל וְחוֹלֶה הַמַּרְגִּיל – אַרְבָּעִים סְאָה, וּבָרִיא לְאוֹנְסוֹ – תִּשְׁעָה קַבִּין, אֲבָל לַחוֹלֶה לְאוֹנְסוֹ – פָּטוּר מִכְּלוּם.

Rava stated that **the** halakhic ruling is in accordance with the first opinion: **A healthy person** who experienced **a normal** seminal emission **and a sick person** who experienced **a normal** seminal emission require **forty *se'a*, while a healthy person** who experienced **an involuntary** seminal emission suffices with **nine *kav*. But a sick person** who experienced **an involuntary** seminal emission **is exempt from** undergoing **any** rite of purification.

תָּנוּ רַבָּנַן: בַּעַל קֶרִי שֶׁנָּתְנוּ עָלָיו תִּשְׁעָה קַבִּין מַיִם – טָהוֹר; בַּמֶּה דְּבָרִים אֲמוּרִים – לְעַצְמוֹ, אֲבָל לַאֲחֵרִים – אַרְבָּעִים סְאָה; רַבִּי יְהוּדָה אוֹמֵר: אַרְבָּעִים סְאָה מִכָּל מָקוֹם.

The Sages taught in a *Tosefta*: **One who experienced a seminal emission and had nine *kav* of** drawn **water poured over him is ritually pure. In what** case **is this statement said?** In a case involving Torah study **for himself, but** in order to purify himself that he may teach Torah **to others,** he must immerse himself in **forty *se'a*. Rabbi Yehuda says: Forty *se'a*** is required for purification **in any case.**

רַבִּי יוֹחָנָן וְרַבִּי יְהוֹשֻׁעַ בֶּן לֵוִי וְרַבִּי אֶלְעָזָר וְרַבִּי יוֹסֵי בְּרַבִּי חֲנִינָא, חַד מֵהַאי זוּגָא וְחַד מֵהַאי זוּגָא אַרֵישָׁא. חַד אָמַר: הָא דְּאָמְרַתְּ "בַּמֶּה דְּבָרִים אֲמוּרִים לְעַצְמוֹ אֲבָל לַאֲחֵרִים אַרְבָּעִים סְאָה" – לֹא שָׁנוּ אֶלָּא לַחוֹלֶה הַמַּרְגִּיל, אֲבָל לַחוֹלֶה לְאוֹנְסוֹ – תִּשְׁעָה קַבִּין; וְחַד אָמַר: כֹּל לַאֲחֵרִים – אֲפִילּוּ חוֹלֶה לְאוֹנְסוֹ – עַד דְּאִיכָּא אַרְבָּעִים סְאָה.

With regard to this issue, a dispute arose between **Rabbi Yoḥanan and Rabbi Yehoshua ben Levi, and Rabbi Elazar and Rabbi Yosei, son of Rabbi Ḥanina. One** member **of this pair**[N] **and one** member **of that pair** disagreed **with regard to the first clause** of the *Tosefta*. **One said: That which you said: In what** case **is this statement said?** In a case involving Torah study **for himself, but** in order to purify himself that he may teach Torah **to others,** he must immerse himself in **forty *se'a*,** was **only taught regarding a sick person who experienced a normal** seminal emission, **but for a sick person** who experienced an **involuntary** seminal emission, **nine *kav*** is sufficient even for teaching others. **And one said** that **anyone** who teaches **others, even** if he was **sick** and experienced an **involuntary** seminal emission, is not considered pure **until there are forty *se'a*.**

וְחַד מֵהַאי זוּגָא וְחַד מֵהַאי זוּגָא אַסֵּיפָא. חַד אָמַר: הָא דְּאָמַר רַבִּי יְהוּדָה "אַרְבָּעִים סְאָה מִכָּל מָקוֹם" – לֹא שָׁנוּ אֶלָּא בְּקַרְקַע, אֲבָל בְּכֵלִים – לֹא; וְחַד אָמַר: אֲפִילּוּ בְּכֵלִים נַמִי.

And one member **of this pair and one** member **of that pair** disagreed **with regard to the latter clause** of the *Tosefta*. **One said: That which Rabbi Yehuda said: Forty *se'a* in any case, was only taught when** the water is in **the ground,** in accordance with the Torah law of ritual bath,[N] **but not** if it was collected **in vessels. And one said: Even** forty *se'a* collected **in vessels** are sufficient for purification.

בִּשְׁלָמָא לְמַאן דַּאֲמַר אֲפִילּוּ בְּכֵלִים – הַיְינוּ דְּקָתָנֵי: "רַבִּי יְהוּדָה אוֹמֵר אַרְבָּעִים סְאָה מִכָּל מָקוֹם". אֶלָּא לְמַאן דַּאֲמַר "בְּקַרְקַע – אִין, בְּכֵלִים – לָא" "מִכָּל מָקוֹם" לְאַתּוֹיֵי מַאי?

The Gemara clarifies this problem: **Granted, according to the one who said** that forty *se'a* purifies **even in vessels. That is** why the *Tosefta* **taught: Rabbi Yehuda says: Forty *se'a* in any case. However,** according to **the one who said** that Rabbi Yehuda's opinion is that forty *se'a* **in the ground, yes,** it purifies, but **in vessels, no,** it does not purify, **what** does the expression **in any case** come **to include?**

לְאַתּוֹיֵי מַיִם שְׁאוּבִין.

The Gemara explains: In any case comes **to include drawn water,**[N] as Rabbi Yehuda permits immersion in forty *se'a* of water collected in the ground even if the water was drawn by human hand.

רַב פַּפָּא וְרַב הוּנָא בְּרֵיהּ דְּרַב יְהוֹשֻׁעַ וְרָבָא (בְּרַבִּי) בַּר שְׁמוּאֵל כְּרִיכוּ רִיפְתָּא בַּהֲדֵי הֲדָדֵי. אֲמַר לְהוּ רַב פַּפָּא: הֲבוּ לִי לְדִידִי לְבָרוֹךְ, דִּנְפוּל עִילָּוַאי תִּשְׁעָה קַבִּין. אֲמַר לְהוּ רָבָא (בְּרַבִּי) [בַּר] שְׁמוּאֵל, תָּנֵינָא: בַּמֶּה דְּבָרִים אֲמוּרִים – לְעַצְמוֹ, אֲבָל לַאֲחֵרִים – אַרְבָּעִים סְאָה; אֶלָּא, הֲבוּ לִי לְדִידִי לְבָרוֹךְ, דִּנְפוּל עִילָּוַאי אַרְבָּעִים סְאָה. אֲמַר לְהוּ רַב הוּנָא: הֲבוּ לִי לְדִידִי לְבָרוֹךְ, דְּלֵיכָּא עִילָּוַאי לָא הַאי וְלָא הַאי.

The Gemara relates that **Rav Pappa and Rav Huna, son of Rav Yehoshua, and Rava bar Shmuel ate bread together. Rav Pappa said to them: Allow me to recite** Grace after Meals for the group, **as I** am ritually pure because **nine *kav*** of water **fell upon me;** in other words, he poured it over himself. **Rava bar Shmuel said to them: We learned, in what** case **is this statement** that nine *kav* purify, **said?** In a case involving Torah study **for himself. But,** in order to purify himself that he may teach Torah **to others,** and by extension to fulfill the obligation of others, he must immerse himself in **forty *se'a*.**[N] **Rather, allow me to recite** Grace after Meals for the group, **as forty *se'a*** of water **fell upon me;** in other words, I immersed myself in a ritual bath. **Rav Huna said to them: Allow me to recite** Grace after Meals for the group, **as I have** had **neither this nor that upon me** because I remained ritually pure.

רַב חָמָא טָבֵיל בְּמַעֲלֵי יוֹמָא דְּפִסְחָא לְהוֹצִיא רַבִּים יְדֵי חוֹבָתָן. וְלֵית הִלְכְתָא כְּוָותֵיהּ.

It is also said that **Rav Ḥama would immerse himself on Passover eve in order to fulfill the obligations of the masses.** However the Gemara concludes: **The *halakha* is not in accordance with his** opinion that distinguishes between the purification for oneself and purification for the sake of others.

מתני׳ הָיָה עוֹמֵד בַּתְּפִלָּה וְנִזְכַּר שֶׁהוּא בַּעַל קֶרִי – לֹא יַפְסִיק, אֶלָּא יְקַצֵּר.

MISHNA This mishna contains various statements with regard to individuals with different types of ritual impurity as well as the need to distance oneself from filth and impurity. **One who was standing in prayer and he recalled that he experienced a seminal emission,** and according to this opinion he is prohibited from praying, should **not interrupt** his prayer, **rather he should abridge** each individual blessing.

NOTES

One member of this pair – חַד מֵהַאי זוּגָא: In other words, Rabbi Yoḥanan and Rabbi Yehoshua ben Levi constitute one pair. Although they were not members of the same generation, there was a personal connection between them and there are numerous disputes between them. The second pair is Rabbi Elazar and Rabbi Yosei son of Rabbi Ḥanina, who were both students of Rabbi Yoḥanan. In these matters, it was specifically the Sages from different pairs that disagreed with each other (*Arukh* based on Rabbeinu Ḥananel).

Ritual bath – מִקְוֶה: Regarding that which purifies an individual, the Torah states: "Only a spring or a pit wherein water collects [*mikve mayyim*] will be pure" (Leviticus 11:36). The Sages established the minimum quantity of water in a ritual bath capable of purifying an individual at forty *se'a*. The water must gather by itself. Not only does water drawn by hand fail to purify, in certain circumstances it can disqualify a ritual bath previously fit to purify. The Sages only permitted immersion in drawn water in certain cases where one is impure by rabbinic law.

To include drawn water – לְאַתּוֹיֵי מַיִם שְׁאוּבִין: Immersion in drawn water was permitted only to enable those who experienced a seminal emission to engage in matters of Torah. Since their impurity is not very severe, the Sages were lenient as to their purification. This is explicitly stated in the mishna (*Mikvaot* 5:1).

To others, forty *se'a* – לַאֲחֵרִים – אַרְבָּעִים סְאָה: The reason for the stringency with regard to teaching Torah to others is due to the fact that the prohibition for those who experienced a seminal emission to engage in Torah matters is derived by means of allusion from the revelation at Sinai, where the Torah was transmitted to the masses (*Tosefot HaRosh*, *Shitta Mekubbetzet*). That was why Rav Ḥama immersed himself in order to fulfill the obligations of the many at the Passover seder. Although he was not teaching them Torah, many people were there (Rav Natronai).

יָרַד לִטְבּוֹל, אִם יָכוֹל לַעֲלוֹת וּלְהִתְכַּסּוֹת וְלִקְרוֹת עַד שֶׁלֹּא תְּהֵא הָנֵץ הַחַמָּה – יַעֲלֶה וְיִתְכַּסֶּה וְיִקְרָא, וְאִם לָאו – יִתְכַּסֶּה בַּמַּיִם וְיִקְרָא; וְלֹא יִתְכַּסֶּה לֹא בַּמַּיִם הָרָעִים וְלֹא בְּמֵי הַמִּשְׁרָה, עַד שֶׁיַּטִּיל לְתוֹכָן מַיִם. וְכַמָּה יַרְחִיק מֵהֶן וּמִן הַצּוֹאָה – אַרְבַּע אַמּוֹת.

They stated a general principle: **One who descended to immerse himself,**[H] **if he is able to ascend, cover himself** with a garment, **and recite** the morning *Shema* **before sunrise,** he **should ascend, cover himself, and recite** *Shema*, **and if not,** he should **cover himself in the water and recite** *Shema* there. **He may not, however, cover himself in either foul water, or water** in which flax was **soaked,**[B] **until he pours** other **water into it. And** in general, **how far must one distance** himself **from urine and feces** in order to recite *Shema*? At least **four cubits.**

גמ׳ תָּנוּ רַבָּנַן: הָיָה עוֹמֵד בַּתְּפִלָּה וְנִזְכַּר שֶׁהוּא בַּעַל קֶרִי – לֹא יַפְסִיק אֶלָּא יְקַצֵּר. הָיָה קוֹרֵא בַּתּוֹרָה וְנִזְכַּר שֶׁהוּא בַּעַל קֶרִי – אֵינוֹ מַפְסִיק וְעוֹלֶה, אֶלָּא מְגַמְגֵּם וְקוֹרֵא; רַבִּי מֵאִיר אוֹמֵר: אֵין בַּעַל קֶרִי רַשַּׁאי לִקְרוֹת בַּתּוֹרָה יוֹתֵר מִשְּׁלֹשָׁה פְּסוּקִים.

GEMARA A *baraita* further elaborates on the first *halakha* in the mishna. **The Sages taught: One who was standing in prayer and he recalled that he** had **experienced a seminal emission,** should **not interrupt** his prayer. **Rather, he should abridge. One who was reading the Torah and recalled that he experienced a seminal emission, does not interrupt** his reading, **but rather reads quickly** with less than perfect diction. **Rabbi Meir** disagrees and **says: One who experienced a seminal emission is not permitted to read more than three verses in the Torah,** as one may read no fewer than three verses in the Torah. After he completes three verses, he must stop and let someone else continue.

תַּנְיָא אִידָךְ: הָיָה עוֹמֵד בַּתְּפִלָּה וְרָאָה צוֹאָה כְּנֶגְדּוֹ – מְהַלֵּךְ לְפָנָיו עַד שֶׁיִּזְרְקֶנָּה לַאֲחוֹרָיו אַרְבַּע אַמּוֹת. וְהָתַנְיָא: לִצְדָדִין! – לָא קַשְׁיָא: הָא – דְּאֶפְשָׁר, הָא – דְּלָא אֶפְשָׁר.

It was taught in another *baraita*: **One who was standing in prayer and he saw feces before him**[H] **must walk forward until he has placed it four cubits behind him.** The Gemara challenges this: **Wasn't it taught** in another *baraita* that it is sufficient if he distances himself four cubits **to the side?** The Gemara resolves this contradiction: **This is not difficult,** as **that** *baraita* which taught that it must be four cubits behind him, is referring to a case **where it is possible** for him to advance that distance, **while that** *baraita* which taught that he may distance himself four cubits to the side, is referring to a case **where it is not possible** to advance four cubits, in which case he must at least step to the side.

הָיָה מִתְפַּלֵּל וּמָצָא צוֹאָה בִּמְקוֹמוֹ. אָמַר רַבָּה: אַף עַל פִּי שֶׁחָטָא – תְּפִלָּתוֹ תְּפִלָּה. מַתְקִיף לַהּ רָבָא: וְהָא ״זֶבַח רְשָׁעִים תּוֹעֵבָה״! אֶלָּא אָמַר רָבָא: הוֹאִיל וְחָטָא, אַף עַל פִּי שֶׁהִתְפַּלֵּל – תְּפִלָּתוֹ תּוֹעֵבָה.

The Gemara cites another *halakha*: **One who was praying** and later **found feces in the place** where he prayed,[H] **Rabba said: Although he committed a transgression** in his failure to examine that venue to determine if it was worthy of prayer (*Tosafot*), **his prayer is a** valid **prayer** and he fulfilled his obligation. **Rava strongly objects to his** statement: **Isn't** it stated: **"The sacrifice of the wicked is an abomination,**[N] the more so as he offers it in depravity" (Proverbs 21:27), from which we derive that a mitzva performed inappropriately is no mitzva at all? Consequently, the fact that he did not pay proper attention invalidates his prayer. **Rather, Rava said: Because** this person **committed a transgression, although he prayed, his prayer is an abomination** and he must pray again.

תָּנוּ רַבָּנַן: הָיָה עוֹמֵד בַּתְּפִלָּה וּמַיִם שׁוֹתְתִין עַל בִּרְכָּיו – פּוֹסֵק עַד שֶׁיִּכְלוּ הַמַּיִם, וְחוֹזֵר וּמִתְפַּלֵּל. לְהֵיכָן חוֹזֵר? רַב חִסְדָּא וְרַב הַמְנוּנָא, חַד אָמַר: חוֹזֵר לָרֹאשׁ; וְחַד אָמַר: לַמָּקוֹם שֶׁפָּסַק.

The Sages taught in a *baraita*: **One who was standing in prayer when,** for some reason, **urine is flowing on his knees,**[BH] **he must interrupt** his prayer **until the urine ceases, and then resume praying.** The Gemara, asks: **To where** in the prayer **does he return** when he resumes his prayer? **Rav Ḥisda and Rav Hamnuna** disagreed; **one said: He must return to the beginning** of the prayer, **and the other said:** He must return **to the point where he stopped.**

לֵימָא בְּהָא קָמִיפַּלְגִי,

The Gemara notes: **Let us say that they disagree about this:**

BACKGROUND

Soaking water – מֵי הַמִּשְׁרָה: Flax cultivation was widespread throughout Israel at the time of the Mishna, and nearly every household would process the flax necessary to meet its own needs. The linen fiber was extracted from the flax by breaking it up and retting it in vats or pools of water and allowing it to soak until the outer husks would rot away revealing the fibers ready to be processed. This is why soaking water is often cited as an example of foul-smelling, stagnant water present in many homes.

Urine flowing on his knees – מַיִם שׁוֹתְתִין עַל בִּרְכָּיו: Both the anus and the urethra are controlled by muscles, which, in the course of the maturation process, one learns to control and relax when necessary. At the same time, there are situations of sudden fear or pain that can cause one to lose control over those muscles and lead to a spontaneous release of urine or excrement.

NOTES

The sacrifice of the wicked is an abomination – זֶבַח רְשָׁעִים תּוֹעֵבָה: Some explain that this is an excerpt from a different verse in Proverbs: "The sacrifice of the wicked is an abomination to the Lord; but the prayer of the upright is His delight" (Proverbs 15:8; see *Siftei Ḥakhamim*).

HALAKHA

One who was standing in prayer and he recalled that he experienced a seminal emission…one who descended to immerse himself, etc. – ...הָיָה עוֹמֵד בַּתְּפִלָּה וְנִזְכַּר שֶׁהוּא בַּעַל קֶרִי יָרַד לִטְבּוֹל וכו׳: One who is in the ritual bath immersing himself when the time to recite *Shema* arrives, covers himself in the water and recites *Shema*. This applies only when the water is at least slightly murky and obscures view of his nakedness; however, not when the water is foul, in accordance with the mishna (Rambam *Sefer Ahava, Hilkhot Keriat Shema* 2:7).

One who was standing in prayer when he saw feces before him – הָיָה מִתְפַּלֵּל וְרָאָה צוֹאָה כְּנֶגְדּוֹ: One who is reciting *Shema* or praying and sees feces before him must walk forward until it is four cubits behind him. If he is unable to walk forward four cubits, he moves to the side. If he is in the middle of the *Amida* prayer, turns his head aside (*Magen Avraham*), and then continues where he interrupted his reciting of *Shema* or his prayer, in accordance with the *baraita* (Rambam *Sefer Ahava, Hilkhot Tefilla* 4:9; *Shulḥan Arukh, Oraḥ Ḥayyim* 81:2).

One who was praying and later found feces in the place where he prayed – הָיָה מִתְפַּלֵּל וּמָצָא צוֹאָה בִּמְקוֹמוֹ: One who prayed or recited *Shema* in a place where there was room for concern that feces were present, and indeed later discovered feces there, distances himself from that area and repeats the entire prayer in accordance with the opinion of Rava, who challenged Rabba's ruling and whose opinion was adopted (Rambam *Sefer Ahava, Hilkhot Tefilla* 4:9; *Shulḥan Arukh, Oraḥ Ḥayyim* 76:8).

One who was standing in prayer when, for some reason, urine is flowing on his knees – הָיָה עוֹמֵד בַּתְּפִלָּה וּמַיִם שׁוֹתְתִין עַל בִּרְכָּיו: One who recites *Shema*, and the same is true with regard to the *Amida* prayer (*Peri Megadim*), and his urine began to flow, must suspend his recitation until the flow stops and then start his prayer again, as per the opinion of Rava (Rambam *Sefer Ahava, Hilkhot Tefilla* 4:13; *Shulḥan Arukh, Oraḥ Ḥayyim* 76, 78).

מַר סָבַר: אִם שָׁהָה כְּדֵי לִגְמוֹר אֶת כּוּלָּהּ – חוֹזֵר לָרֹאשׁ; וּמָר סָבַר: לְמָקוֹם שֶׁפָּסַק.

One **Sage held** that, as a rule, **if** one interrupted his prayer and **delayed** continuing his prayer for an interval **sufficient to complete the entire** prayer,[H] **he returns to the beginning** of the prayer. **And** one **Sage held:** He returns **to the place** in the prayer **where he stopped.**

אָמַר רַב אָשֵׁי: הַאי "אִם שָׁהָה"? "אִם לֹא שָׁהָה" מִיבְּעֵי לֵיהּ! – אֶלָּא, דְּכוּלֵּי עָלְמָא אִם שָׁהָה כְּדֵי לִגְמוֹר אֶת כּוּלָּהּ – חוֹזֵר לָרֹאשׁ, וְהָתָם בִּדְלָא שָׁהָה קָמִיפַּלְגִי; דְּמָר סָבַר: גַּבְרָא דְּחוּיָא הוּא, וְאֵין רָאוּי, וְאֵין תְּפִלָּתוֹ תְּפִלָּה; וּמָר סָבַר: גַּבְרָא חֲזְיָא הוּא, וּתְפִלָּתוֹ תְּפִלָּה.

Rejecting this possibility, **Rav Ashi said:** If that was the point of their dispute, they should not have simply issued a ruling in a case: **If he delayed.** They **should have** also addressed a case **if he did not delay** as well as discussing the length of the delay. **Rather, everyone,** both Rav Ḥisda and Rav Hamnuna, **agrees that if one delayed** continuing his prayer for an interval **sufficient to complete the entire** prayer, **he returns to the beginning** of the prayer. **And there,** in the dispute under discussion, **they disagreed with regard to one who did not delay** that long. The dispute deals with his particular predicament. **As one Sage held: He is a man** who is **disqualified and unfit, and his prayer is not a** valid **prayer;** therefore he must repeat it in its entirety. **And** one **Sage held: He is a man who is fit and his prayer is a** valid **prayer.**

תָּנוּ רַבָּנַן: הַנִּצְרָךְ לִנְקָבָיו – אַל יִתְפַּלֵּל, וְאִם הִתְפַּלֵּל – תְּפִלָּתוֹ תּוֹעֵבָה. אָמַר רַב זְבִיד וְאִיתֵּימָא רַב יְהוּדָה: לֹא שָׁנוּ אֶלָּא שֶׁאֵינוֹ יָכוֹל לִשְׁהוֹת בְּעַצְמוֹ, אֲבָל אִם יָכוֹל לִשְׁהוֹת בְּעַצְמוֹ – תְּפִלָּתוֹ תְּפִלָּה.

The Sages taught in a *baraita*: **One who needs to relieve himself may not pray,**[HN] **and if he prayed, his prayer is an abomination. Rav Zevid and some say Rav Yehuda said** in qualifying this statement: **They only taught** this *halakha* in a case where **one cannot restrain himself. But, if he can restrain himself, his prayer is a** valid **prayer** as he is not tarnished by his need to relieve himself.

וְעַד כַּמָּה? – אָמַר רַב שֵׁשֶׁת: עַד פַּרְסָה. אִיכָּא דְּמַתְנֵי לַהּ אַמַּתְנִיתָא: בַּמֶּה דְּבָרִים אֲמוּרִים – כְּשֶׁאֵין יָכוֹל לַעֲמוֹד עַל עַצְמוֹ, אֲבָל אִם יָכוֹל לַעֲמוֹד עַל עַצְמוֹ – תְּפִלָּתוֹ תְּפִלָּה. וְעַד כַּמָּה? אָמַר רַב זְבִיד: עַד פַּרְסָה.

The Gemara asks: **And** for **how long** must he be able to restrain himself? **Rav Sheshet said:** For **as long as** it takes to walk **one parasang.**[B] **Some teach this** *halakha* directly **on** what was taught in **the** *baraita*: **In what** case **is this statement said? Where he is unable to restrain himself, but if he is able to restrain himself, his prayer is a valid prayer. And for how long? Rav Zevid said:** For as **long as** it takes to walk **one parasang.**

אָמַר רַבִּי שְׁמוּאֵל בַּר נַחְמָנִי אָמַר רַבִּי יוֹנָתָן: הַנִּצְרָךְ לִנְקָבָיו הֲרֵי זֶה לֹא יִתְפַּלֵּל, מִשּׁוּם שֶׁנֶּאֱמַר: "הִכּוֹן לִקְרַאת אֱלֹהֶיךָ יִשְׂרָאֵל".

Rabbi Shmuel bar Naḥmani said that **Rabbi Yonatan said: One who needs to relieve himself may not pray, because it is stated: "Prepare to greet your God, O Israel"** (Amos 4:12), and one must clear his mind of all distractions to prepare to receive the Lord during prayer.

וְאָמַר רַבִּי שְׁמוּאֵל בַּר נַחְמָנִי אָמַר רַבִּי יוֹנָתָן: מַאי דִּכְתִיב "שְׁמוֹר רַגְלְךָ כַּאֲשֶׁר תֵּלֵךְ אֶל בֵּית הָאֱלֹהִים", שְׁמוֹר עַצְמְךָ שֶׁלֹּא תֶּחֱטָא, וְאִם תֶּחֱטָא – הָבֵא קָרְבָּן לְפָנַי. "וְקָרוֹב לִשְׁמֹעַ דִּבְרֵי חֲכָמִים", אָמַר רָבָא: הֱוֵי קָרוֹב לִשְׁמוֹעַ דִּבְרֵי חֲכָמִים שֶׁאִם חוֹטְאִים מְבִיאִים קָרְבָּן וְעוֹשִׂים תְּשׁוּבָה. "מִתֵּת הַכְּסִילִים זָבַח" – אַל תְּהִי כַּכְּסִילִים שֶׁחוֹטְאִים וּמְבִיאִים קָרְבָּן וְאֵין עוֹשִׂים תְּשׁוּבָה.

In this context, the Gemara cites an additional statement, which **Rabbi Shmuel bar Naḥmani said** that **Rabbi Yonatan said: What is the meaning of that which is written: "Guard your foot**[N] **when you go to the house of God,** and prepare to listen; it is better than when fools offer sacrifices, as they know not to do evil" (Ecclesiastes 4:17)? It means: When you enter the house of the Lord, **guard yourself from transgression, and if you commit a transgression, bring a sacrifice before Me** in atonement. The verse continues: **"And draw near and listen to the words of the wise." Rava said: Be prepared to hearken to the words of the wise, who, if they commit a transgression, they bring a sacrifice and repent.** He interprets the next part of the verse: **"It is better than when fools give sacrifices,"** that **one should not act like the fools who commit a transgression and bring a sacrifice but do not repent.**

"כִּי אֵינָם יוֹדְעִים לַעֲשׂוֹת רָע", אִי הָכִי, צַדִּיקִים נִינְהוּ! אֶלָּא, אַל תְּהִי כַּכְּסִילִים שֶׁחוֹטְאִים וּמְבִיאִים קָרְבָּן, וְאֵינָם יוֹדְעִים אִם עַל הַטּוֹבָה הֵם מְבִיאִים אִם עַל הָרָעָה הֵם מְבִיאִים. אָמַר הַקָּדוֹשׁ בָּרוּךְ הוּא: בֵּין טוֹב לָרַע אֵינָן מַבְחִינִים, וְהֵם מְבִיאִים קָרְבָּן לְפָנַי?

Regarding the end of the verse: **"As they know not to do evil,"**[N] the Gemara asks: **If so, they are righteous. Rather** it must be understood: **Do not be like the fools who commit a transgression and bring a sacrifice, but are unaware whether they are bringing it** as a thanks-offering **for the good,** or as an offering of atonement **for the evil.** This is the meaning of the verse: "As they know not to do evil"; they know not if and when their actions are evil. With regard to those individuals, **the Holy One, Blessed be He, said: They cannot distinguish between good and evil and yet they bring a sacrifice before me?**

HALAKHA

If one delayed for an interval sufficient to complete the entire prayer – אִם שָׁהָה כְּדֵי לִגְמוֹר אֶת כּוּלָּהּ וכו׳: One who interrupted his prayer or recitation of *Shema* long enough to have completed the entire prayer, even if the interval passed in silence, must repeat the prayer or *Shema* from the beginning. One who interrupted for a shorter period must return to the point in the prayer where he paused, in accordance with the opinion of Rav Ashi. In the case of prayer, that interval is defined as the beginning of that particular blessing. However, the first three and last three blessings are each considered one indivisible unit. Consequently, one who paused during any of the first three blessings must return to the beginning of the *Amida* prayer and one who paused during any of the three final blessings must return to the blessing of the Temple service [*retze*] (Rambam *Sefer Ahava, Hilkhot Tefilla* 4:13; *Shulḥan Arukh, Oraḥ Ḥayyim* 104:5).

One who needs to relieve himself may not pray – הַנִּצְרָךְ לִנְקָבָיו אַל יִתְפַּלֵּל: If he did pray, his prayer is an abomination and he is required repeat his prayer. However, if he is capable of restraining himself for the time it takes to walk a parasang, he fulfilled his obligation. If the end of the period when that prayer may be recited is imminent, he is permitted to pray under those circumstances (*Magen Avraham*, in accordance with the conclusion of Rav Zevid; Rambam *Sefer Ahava, Hilkhot Tefilla* 4:10; *Shulḥan Arukh, Oraḥ Ḥayyim* 92:1, 3).

NOTES

One who needs to relieve himself may not pray – הַנִּצְרָךְ לִנְקָבָיו אַל יִתְפַּלֵּל: He may not pray for two reasons: First, he is distracted and unable to concentrate on his prayer; and because one who needs to relieve himself is considered filthy and unfit to pray.

Guard your foot – שְׁמוֹר רַגְלְךָ: The word foot is used here as a euphemism for defecating as in the verse: "He is covering his feet" (Judges 3:24).

As they know not to do evil – כִּי אֵינָם יוֹדְעִים לַעֲשׂוֹת רָע: Here, the word to do [*la'asot*] is interpreted as it appears in the verse: "Nor did he trim [*asa*] his beard" (II Samuel 19:25), where it means to fix or arrange. Here too, *la'asot* evil means to reform it and make it better (Rav Ya'akov Emden). And the phrase: They are unaware whether they are bringing it as a thanks-offering for the good, or as an offering of atonement for the evil, means that, although they are bringing an offering, they believe that the sin had no effect, as the sacrifice fixes everything (*Tosefot Rabbi Yehuda HaḤasid*).

BACKGROUND

As long as it takes to walk one parasang – הִילּוּךְ פַּרְסָה: The determination of the length of time necessary to walk a parasang is connected to the disagreement with regard to the basic unit of measurement, the time necessary to walk a talmudic *mil*. The talmudic *mil* is a unit of distance related to, but not identical with, the Roman mile, from which it received its name. One *mil* is equal to 2,000 cubits, 960 m (1,049 yd) according to Na'e, or 1,150 m (1,258 yd) according to the Ḥazon Ish. The fundamental problem lies in the method used to determine a person's regular walking pace. According to the various opinions, the time it takes to walk a parasang is either one hour and twelve minutes or one hour and thirty-six minutes.

רַב אַשִׁי וְאִיתֵימָא רַבִּי חֲנִינָא בַּר פַּפָּא אָמַר: שְׁמוֹר נְקָבֶיךָ בְּשָׁעָה שֶׁאַתָּה עוֹמֵד בִּתְפִלָּה לְפָנַי.

Rav Ashi and some say Rabbi Ḥanina bar Pappa said: Mind your orifices when you stand before me in prayer.

תָּנוּ רַבָּנַן: הַנִּכְנָס לְבֵית הַכִּסֵּא – חוֹלֵץ תְּפִילָּיו בְּרִחוּק אַרְבַּע אַמּוֹת, וְנִכְנָס. אָמַר רַב אַחָא בַּר רַב הוּנָא אָמַר רַב שֵׁשֶׁת: לֹא שָׁנוּ אֶלָּא בֵּית הַכִּסֵּא קָבוּעַ, אֲבָל בֵּית הַכִּסֵּא עֲרַאי – חוֹלֵץ וְנִפְנֶה לְאַלְתַּר. וּכְשֶׁהוּא יוֹצֵא – מַרְחִיק אַרְבַּע אַמּוֹת וּמַנִּיחָן, מִפְּנֵי שֶׁעֲשָׂאוֹ בֵּית הַכִּסֵּא קָבוּעַ.

The Sages taught: One who enters a bathroom[H] **must remove his phylacteries**[H] **at a distance of four cubits and enter. Rav Aḥa bar Rav Huna said that Rav Sheshet said: This was only taught** with regard to one entering **a regular bathroom, but** one who enters **a makeshift bathroom may remove** his phylacteries and **defecate immediately. But when one exits** from a makeshift bathroom, **he must distance himself four cubits** before **donning** his phylacteries because **he has** now **rendered** that place **a regular bathroom.**

אִיבַּעְיָא לְהוּ: מַהוּ שֶׁיִּכָּנֵס אָדָם בִּתְפִילִּין לְבֵית הַכִּסֵּא קָבוּעַ לְהַשְׁתִּין מַיִם? רָבִינָא שָׁרֵי, רַב אַדָּא בַּר מַתְּנָא אָסַר. אֲתוֹ שַׁיְילוּהּ לְרָבָא, אֲמַר לְהוּ: אָסוּר, חָיְישִׁינַן שֶׁמָּא יִפָּנֶה בָּהֶן; וְאָמְרִי לָהּ: שֶׁמָּא יָפִיחַ בָּהֶן.

A dilemma was raised before the Sages in the yeshiva: **What is** the *halakha*; may **one enter a regular bathroom wearing his phylacteries in order to urinate?** The Sages disagreed: **Ravina permitted** to do so while **Rav Adda bar Mattana prohibited** it. **They came and asked this of Rava. He said to them: It is forbidden** because **we are concerned lest he will** come to **defecate with them** still on. **Others say** that this *halakha* is because we are concerned that, since he is already in the bathroom, he **might** forget that his phylacteries are on his head and **will break wind with them** still on him.

תַּנְיָא אִידָךְ: הַנִּכְנָס לְבֵית הַכִּסֵּא קָבוּעַ – חוֹלֵץ תְּפִילָּיו בְּרִחוּק אַרְבַּע אַמּוֹת, וּמַנִּיחָן בַּחַלּוֹן הַסָּמוּךְ לִרְשׁוּת הָרַבִּים וְנִכְנָס, וּכְשֶׁהוּא יוֹצֵא – מַרְחִיק אַרְבַּע אַמּוֹת וּמַנִּיחָן, דִּבְרֵי בֵּית שַׁמַּאי. וּבֵית הִלֵּל אוֹמְרִים: אוֹחֲזָן בְּיָדוֹ וְנִכְנָס; רַבִּי עֲקִיבָא אוֹמֵר: אוֹחֲזָן בְּבִגְדוֹ וְנִכְנָס.

It was taught in another *baraita*: **One who enters a regular bathroom must remove his phylacteries at a distance of four cubits, place them in the window** in the wall of the bathroom **adjacent to the public domain, and then enter. And when he exits, he must distance** himself **four cubits before donning them.** This is **the statement of Beit Shammai. Beit Hillel say:** He must remove his phylacteries but **he holds them in his hand and enters. Rabbi Akiva says: He holds them in his garment and enters.**

בְּבִגְדוֹ סָלְקָא דַּעְתָּךְ? זִימְנִין מִישְׁתְּלֵי לְהוּ וְנָפְלִי! אֶלָּא אֵימָא: אוֹחֲזָן בְּבִגְדוֹ וּבְיָדוֹ וְנִכְנָס,

The Gemara wonders: **Does it enter your mind** to say **in his garment?** There is room for concern because **sometimes he forgets them and** they **fall. Rather, say: He holds them with his garment and in his hand and enters** the bathroom. He holds the phylacteries in his hand and covers it with the garment.

וּמַנִּיחָם בַּחוֹרִין הַסְּמוּכִים לְבֵית הַכִּסֵּא; וְלֹא יַנִּיחֵם בַּחוֹרִין הַסְּמוּכִים לִרְשׁוּת הָרַבִּים, שֶׁמָּא יִטְּלוּ אוֹתָם עוֹבְרֵי דְרָכִים וְיָבֹא לִידֵי חֲשָׁד.

It was established in the *baraita*: **And** if there is room to place them, **he places them in the holes adjacent to the bathroom, but he does not place them in the holes adjacent to the public domain, lest** the phylacteries **will be taken by passersby and he will come to be suspect.**

וּמַעֲשֶׂה בְּתַלְמִיד אֶחָד שֶׁהִנִּיחַ תְּפִילָּיו בַּחוֹרִין הַסְּמוּכִים לִרְשׁוּת הָרַבִּים, וּבָאת זוֹנָה אַחַת וּנְטָלָתַן, וּבָאת לְבֵית הַמִּדְרָשׁ וְאָמְרָה: רְאוּ מַה נָּתַן לִי פְּלוֹנִי בִּשְׂכָרִי! כֵּיוָן שֶׁשָּׁמַע אוֹתוֹ תַּלְמִיד כָּךְ, עָלָה לְרֹאשׁ הַגַּג וְנָפַל וּמֵת. בְּאוֹתָהּ שָׁעָה הִתְקִינוּ שֶׁיְּהֵא אוֹחֲזָן בְּבִגְדוֹ וּבְיָדוֹ וְנִכְנָס.

And an incident occurred **involving a student who placed his phylacteries in the holes adjacent to the public domain, and a prostitute passed by and took** the phylacteries. **She came to the study hall and said: See what so-and-so gave me as my payment.**[N] **When that student heard this, he ascended to the rooftop and fell and died. At that moment they instituted that one should hold them with his garment and in his hand and enter** to avoid situations of that kind.

תָּנוּ רַבָּנַן: בָּרִאשׁוֹנָה הָיוּ מַנִּיחִין תְּפִילִּין בַּחוֹרִין הַסְּמוּכִים לְבֵית הַכִּסֵּא, וּבָאִין עַכְבָּרִים וְנוֹטְלִין אוֹתָן. הִתְקִינוּ שֶׁיְּהוּ מַנִּיחִין אוֹתָן בַּחַלּוֹנוֹת הַסְּמוּכוֹת לִרְשׁוּת הָרַבִּים, וּבָאִין עוֹבְרֵי דְרָכִים וְנוֹטְלִין אוֹתָן; הִתְקִינוּ שֶׁיְּהֵא אוֹחֲזָן בְּיָדוֹ וְנִכְנָס.

The Sages taught in a *baraita* on this topic: **At first, they would place the phylacteries in the holes adjacent to the bathroom, and mice would come and take them** or gnaw upon them. Therefore, **they instituted that they should place them in the holes adjacent to the public domain,** where there were no mice. However, **passersby would come and take the** phylacteries. Ultimately, **they instituted that one should hold** the phylacteries **in his hand and enter.**

אָמַר רַבִּי מְיָאשָׁא בְּרֵיהּ דְּרַבִּי יְהוֹשֻׁעַ בֶּן לֵוִי: הֲלָכָה, גּוֹלְלָן כְּמִין סֵפֶר וְאוֹחֲזָן בִּימִינוֹ כְּנֶגֶד לִבּוֹ. אָמַר רַב יוֹסֵף בַּר מַנְיוּמִי אָמַר רַב נַחְמָן: וּבִלְבַד שֶׁלֹּא תְּהֵא רְצוּעָה יוֹצֵאת מִתַּחַת יָדוֹ טֶפַח.

On this topic, **Rabbi Meyasha, son of Rabbi Yehoshua ben Levi, said: The** ***halakha*** in this case **is that one rolls up** the phylacteries in their straps **like a scroll,**[B] **and holds them in his hand opposite his heart. Rav Yosef bar Manyumi said that Rav Naḥman said:** This is **provided that the strap** of the phylacteries **does not emerge** more than **a handbreadth below his hand.**

HALAKHA

One who enters a bathroom, etc. – הַנִּכְנָס לְבֵית הַכִּסֵּא וכו׳: One who wishes to enter a bathroom but has no safe place to leave his phylacteries, should remove them at a distance of four cubits from the bathroom, wind their straps, cover them with his garment, hold them opposite his heart, and only then enter. He should make certain that the straps are not dangling from his hand. When he emerges, he should distance himself four cubits before donning them again (Rambam *Sefer Ahava, Hilkhot Tefillin UMezuza VeSefer Torah* 4:17; *Shulḥan Arukh, Oraḥ Ḥayyim* 43:5).

Phylacteries in the bathroom – תְּפִילִּין בְּבֵית הַכִּסֵּא: One may not defecate while phylacteries are on his head, nor may he enter a bathroom under those circumstances. As per the conclusion of Rava (Rambam *Sefer Ahava, Hilkhot Tefillin UMezuza VeSefer Torah* 4:17; *Shulḥan Arukh, Oraḥ Ḥayyim* 43:1).

NOTES

See what so-and-so gave me as my payment – רְאוּ מַה נָּתַן לִי פְּלוֹנִי בִּשְׂכָרִי: Apparently, the student was searching everywhere for his phylacteries. The prostitute who took them did not want to be accused of theft, so she brought them to the study hall and claimed that he gave them to her as her payment (Rav Ya'akov Emden).

BACKGROUND

Rolls up the phylacteries in their straps like a scroll – גּוֹלְלָן כְּמִין סֵפֶר: One of the manners in which the head phylacteries are rolled, probably the method called in the Gemara: Like a scroll.

Phylacteries of the head

אָמַר רַבִּי יַעֲקֹב בַּר אַחָא אָמַר רַבִּי זֵירָא: לֹא שָׁנוּ אֶלָּא שֶׁיֵּשׁ שָׁהוּת בַּיּוֹם לְלׇבְשָׁן, אֲבָל אֵין שָׁהוּת בַּיּוֹם לְלׇבְשָׁן – עוֹשֶׂה לָהֶן כְּמִין כִּיס טֶפַח, וּמַנִּיחָן.

Rabbi Ya'akov bar Aḥa said that **Rabbi Zeira said: It was only taught** that one rolls up his phylacteries when there is still **time** left **in the day to don them. If there is not time** left **in the day to don them** before nightfall, when phylacteries are not donned, **he makes a one-handbreadth pouch of sorts for them and he places them** in it.

אָמַר רַבָּה בַּר בַּר חָנָה אָמַר רַבִּי יוֹחָנָן: בַּיּוֹם – גּוֹלְלָן כְּמִין סֵפֶר וּמַנִּיחָן בְּיָדוֹ כְּנֶגֶד לִבּוֹ, וּבַלַּיְלָה – עוֹשֶׂה לָהֶן כְּמִין כִּיס טֶפַח, וּמַנִּיחָן.

Similarly, **Rabba bar bar Ḥana said** that **Rabbi Yoḥanan said: During the day one rolls up** the phylacteries **like a scroll and places them in his hand opposite his heart, and at night he makes a one-handbreadth pouch of sorts for them and he places them** in it.

אָמַר אַבָּיֵי: לֹא שָׁנוּ אֶלָּא בִּכְלִי שֶׁהוּא כְּלִיָין, אֲבָל בִּכְלִי שֶׁאֵינוֹ כְּלִיָין – אֲפִילּוּ פָּחוֹת מִטֶּפַח.

Abaye said: They only taught that it must be a one-handbreadth pouch **with regard to a vessel that is** the phylacteries' regular **vessel,**[NH] **but in a vessel that is not their** regular **vessel,** he may place the phylacteries in it, **even** if it is **less than a handbreadth.**

אָמַר מָר זוּטְרָא וְאִיתֵּימָא רַב אָשֵׁי: תֵּדַע, שֶׁהֲרֵי פַּכִּין קְטַנִּים מַצִּילִין בְּאֹהֶל הַמֵּת.

Mar Zutra and, some say, Rav Ashi, said as proof for that distinction: The laws of impurity state that only a space of at least a handbreadth can serve as a barrier to prevent the spread of impurity imparted by a corpse. Nevertheless, **small** sealed **vessels** less than a handbreadth in size **protect** their contents from ritual impurity even if they are inside **a tent over a corpse.** This proves that even a space smaller than a handbreadth can serve as a barrier before impurity.

אָמַר רַבָּה בַּר בַּר חָנָה: כִּי הֲוָה אָזְלִינַן בָּתְרֵיהּ דְּרַבִּי יוֹחָנָן, כִּי הֲוָה בָּעֵי לְמֵיעַל לְבֵית הַכִּסֵּא, כִּי הֲוָה נְקִיט סִפְרָא דְּאַגַּדְתָּא – הֲוָה יָהֵיב לַן, כִּי הֲוָה נְקִיט תְּפִילִּין – לָא הֲוָה יָהֵיב לַן, אָמַר: הוֹאִיל וְשָׁרוּנְהוּ רַבָּנַן –

Rabba bar bar Ḥana said: When we would walk after Rabbi Yoḥanan, we would see **that when he sought to enter the bathroom while holding a book of *aggada*,**[B] **he would give** it **to us. When he was holding phylacteries, he would not give** them **to us,** as **he said: Since the Sages permitted** to hold **them,**

NOTES

A vessel that is their regular vessel – בִּכְלִי שֶׁהוּא כְּלִיָין: The basis for this distinction is that a vessel that is designated for phylacteries is no longer considered a separate entity, but rather as ancillary to the phylacteries. Consequently, a small vessel designated for use with phylacteries is subsumed and does not constitute a barrier. However, if the vessel is larger than a handbreadth, since the space of a handbreadth is considered a substantial area in and of itself, it is not considered ancillary to the object inside it (*Shitta Mekubbetzet*).

HALAKHA

They only taught this with regard to a vessel that is the phylacteries' regular vessel – לֹא שָׁנוּ אֶלָּא בִּכְלִי שֶׁהוּא כְּלִיָין: The pouch in which he places his phylacteries, if it was designed for that purpose, must be at least one handbreadth in size in order to permit him to enter the bathroom carrying it. For other purposes, even a smaller pouch is sufficient, as per the opinion of Abaye (Rambam *Sefer Ahava, Hilkhot Tefillin UMezuza VeSefer Torah* 4:19; *Shulḥan Arukh, Oraḥ Ḥayyim* 43:6).

BACKGROUND

Book of *aggada* – סִפְרָא דְּאַגַּדְתָּא: While the prohibition against committing the Oral Torah to writing was still in force several generations after the codification of the Mishna, the Sages would write down various notes for themselves. They were especially lenient with regard to aggadic books. The Gemara tells of several *amora'im* who would carry aggadic books which they frequently perused, while halakhic books were not common at all.

Perek **III**
Daf **23** Amud **b**

נִינְטְרָן. אָמַר רָבָא: כִּי הֲוָה אָזְלִינַן בָּתְרֵיהּ דְּרַב נַחְמָן, כִּי הֲוָה נְקִיט סִפְרָא דְּאַגַּדְתָּא – יָהֵיב לַן, כִּי הֲוָה נְקִיט תְּפִילִּין – לָא יָהֵיב לַן, אָמַר: הוֹאִיל וְשָׁרוּנְהוּ רַבָּנַן – נִינְטְרָן.

they will protect me. Although there were people on hand to whom he could have handed the phylacteries, he kept them to protect himself from danger. **Rava said: When we would walk after Rabbi Naḥman,** we would see that **when he was holding a book of *aggada*, he would give it to us. When he was holding phylacteries, he would not give** them **to us,** as **he said: Since the Sages permitted** to hold **them, they will protect me.**

תָּנוּ רַבָּנַן: לֹא יֹאחֵז אָדָם תְּפִילִּין בְּיָדוֹ וְסֵפֶר תּוֹרָה בִּזְרוֹעוֹ וְיִתְפַּלֵּל, וְלֹא יַשְׁתִּין בָּהֶן מַיִם, וְלֹא יִישַׁן בָּהֶן לֹא שֵׁינַת קֶבַע וְלֹא שֵׁינַת עֲרַאי. אָמַר שְׁמוּאֵל: סַכִּין, וּמָעוֹת, וּקְעָרָה, וְכִכָּר הֲרֵי אֵלּוּ כַּיּוֹצֵא בָּהֶן.

The Sages taught: One may not hold phylacteries in his hand or **a Torah scroll in his arm and pray,**[H] because his concern that the phylacteries or Torah scroll might fall will distract him from his prayer. **And** so too, with regard to sacred objects, **one may not urinate with them** in his hands **and may not sleep with them**[N] in his hands, **neither a deep sleep nor** even **a brief nap. Shmuel said:** Not only should one holding phylacteries refrain from prayer, but one holding **a knife, money, a bowl,** or a **loaf** of bread **have a similar** status in that his concern that they might fall will distract him from his prayer.

אָמַר רָבָא אָמַר רַב שֵׁשֶׁת: לֵית הִלְכְתָא כִּי הָא מַתְנִיתָא – דְּבֵית שַׁמַּאי הִיא. דְּאִי בֵּית הִלֵּל – הַשְׁתָּא בֵּית הַכִּסֵּא קָבוּעַ שָׁרֵי, בֵּית הַכִּסֵּא עֲרַאי מִיבַּעְיָא?!

Rava said that **Rav Sheshet said: The *halakha* is not in accordance with this *baraita*, because it** in accordance with the opinion of **Beit Shammai. As if** it was in accordance with the opinion of **Beit Hillel, now** Beit Hillel **permitted** to hold phylacteries in his hand when he defecates in a regular bathroom, **is it necessary** to say that it is permitted when he urinates in **a makeshift bathroom?**

HALAKHA

One may not hold phylacteries in his hand or a Torah scroll in his arm and pray – לֹא יֹאחֵז אָדָם תְּפִילִּין בְּיָדוֹ וְסֵפֶר תּוֹרָה בִּזְרוֹעוֹ וְיִתְפַּלֵּל: One is prohibited from holding phylacteries or a Torah scroll in his hand while praying. The same is true when reciting *Shema* and *Pesukei DeZimra* (*Peri Megadim*). One must also refrain from holding a bowl or money or any other object of value, as his concern lest they fall and be damaged will distract him from praying properly (Rambam *Sefer Ahava, Hilkhot Tefilla* 5:5; *Shulḥan Arukh, Oraḥ Ḥayyim* 96:1).

NOTES

And may not sleep with them – וְלֹא יִישַׁן בָּהֶן: The reason is that they might fall off in his sleep (Rabbi Akiva Eiger and see *Sukka* 26b). The Vilna Gaon assumed that Rashi understood it that way.

מֵיתִיבֵי: ״דְּבָרִים שֶׁהִתַּרְתִּי לְךָ כָּאן, אָסַרְתִּי לְךָ כָּאן״, מַאי לָאו תְּפִילִּין? אִי אָמְרַתְּ בִּשְׁלָמָא בֵּית הִלֵּל – ״הִתַּרְתִּי לְךָ כָּאן״ – קָבוּעַ, ״אָסַרְתִּי לְךָ כָּאן״ – בֵּית הַכִּסֵּא עֲרַאי. אֶלָּא אִי אָמְרַתְּ בֵּית שַׁמַּאי – הָא לֹא שָׁרוּ וְלֹא מִידִּי!

The Gemara **raised an objection** based on the second part of the *baraita*, where it was taught: **Matters which I permitted you** to do **here, I prohibited you** from doing **there.** In other words, there are matters that were permitted in a regular bathroom and not in a makeshift bathroom. **What, is it not** referring to **phylacteries? Granted, if you say** that the prohibition against urinating while wearing phylacteries is in accordance with the opinion of **Beit Hillel,** then we would understand the *baraita* as follows: Matters which **I permitted you** to do **here,** to hold phylacteries in a regular bathroom, **I have prohibited you** from doing **there,** in the **makeshift bathroom. But if you hold** that this *baraita* is in accordance with the opinion of **Beit Shammai, they did not permit anything** in a regular bathroom. What, then, is the meaning of matters which I permitted you to do here?

כִּי תַּנְיָא הַהִיא לְעִנְיַן טֶפַח וּטְפָחַיִים. דְּתָנֵי חֲדָא: כְּשֶׁהוּא נִפְנֶה – מְגַלֶּה לַאֲחֲרָיו טֶפַח וּלְפָנָיו טְפָחַיִים. וְתַנְיָא אִידָּךְ: לַאֲחֲרָיו טֶפַח, וּלְפָנָיו וְלֹא כְּלוּם!

This challenge is rejected by the Gemara, which explains: **When that *baraita* was taught** it was not in reference to phylacteries, but **with regard to the matter of one handbreadth and two handbreadths.** As is **it was taught in one** *baraita*: **When one relieves himself, he** must maintain modesty and **bare a single handbreadth** of his flesh **behind him and two handbreadths before him. And it was taught in another** *baraita*: One may only bare **a single handbreadth behind him and nothing before him.**

מַאי לָאו אִידִי וְאִידִי בְּאִישׁ, וְלֹא קַשְׁיָא: כָּאן לִגְדוֹלִים, כָּאן לִקְטַנִּים.

What, are not both **this** *baraita* **and that** one referring to **a male, and** the apparent contradiction between the two *baraitot* **is not difficult,** as **here** the *baraita* that states that one may bare a handbreadth behind him and nothing before him is referring to **defecation, while here,** the other *baraita* that states that one may bare a handbreadth behind him and two handbreadths before him is referring to **urination.** Accordingly, despite the fact that one may bare two handbreadths before him when urinating in a makeshift bathroom, matters that I have permitted you to do here, one may bare nothing before him when defecating in an established bathroom, I have prohibited you from doing there.

וְתִסְבְּרָא?! אִי בִּקְטַנִּים לַאֲחֲרָיו טֶפַח לָמָּה לִי! אֶלָּא, אִידִי וְאִידִי בִּגְדוֹלִים, וְלֹא קַשְׁיָא: הָא בְּאִישׁ, הָא בְּאִשָּׁה.

The Gemara immediately rejects this explanation: **And** how **can you understand** it that way? Can you accept that explanation? **If** that *baraita* is referring to **urination, why do I need to** bare **a handbreadth behind him? Rather,** both **this** *baraita* **and that** one are referring to **defecation and** the apparent contradiction between the two *baraitot* **is not difficult,** as **this** *baraita* that states that one may bare two handbreadths before him is referring **to a man,** who must bare before him to facilitate urination, while **this** other *baraita* that states that one may bare nothing before him is referring **to a woman,** who need not bare anything before her in order to urinate.

אִי הָכִי, הָא דְּקָתָנֵי עֲלָהּ: ״זֶהוּ קַל וָחוֹמֶר שֶׁאֵין עָלָיו תְּשׁוּבָה״, מַאי ״אֵין עָלָיו תְּשׁוּבָה״? דַּרְכָּא דְּמִלְּתָא הָכִי אִיתָא! אֶלָּא לָאו – תְּפִילִּין, וּתְיוּבְתָּא דְּרָבָא אָמַר רַב שֵׁשֶׁת,

The Gemara challenges this: **If so, then that which was taught with regard to** this *halakha* in the *baraita*: **This is an *a fortiori* inference that cannot be rebutted,** meaning that even though logically it would have been appropriate to be stricter in the case of defecating in a regular bathroom than in the case of urinating in a makeshift bathroom, that is not the ruling. According to the distinction suggested above, **what** is **cannot be rebutted? That is the nature of the matter;** men and women need to bare themselves differently. **Rather,** is the *baraita* which states: Matters which I permitted you to do here, I prohibited you from doing there, **not** referring to **phylacteries?** And the *a fortiori* inference that cannot be rebutted is similarly referring to phylacteries. This is a **conclusive refutation** of that which **Rava said** that **Rav Sheshet said** that the *baraita* is not referring to phylacteries.

תְּיוּבְתָּא.

The Gemara concludes: Indeed, it is a **conclusive refutation.**[B]

מִכָּל מָקוֹם קַשְׁיָא: הַשְׁתָּא בֵּית הַכִּסֵּא קָבוּעַ שָׁרֵי, בֵּית הַכִּסֵּא עֲרַאי לֹא כָּל שֶׁכֵּן?!

The Gemara asks: **Nevertheless, it** remains **difficult: Now,** holding phylacteries in his hand when he defecates in a **regular bathroom**[B] **is permitted, all the more so** that it is permitted when he urinates in **a makeshift bathroom.**

הָכִי קָאָמַר: בֵּית הַכִּסֵּא קָבוּעַ דְּלֵיכָּא נִיצוֹצוֹת – שָׁרֵי, בֵּית הַכִּסֵּא עֲרַאי דְּאִיכָּא נִיצוֹצוֹת – אָסְרִי.

The Gemara explains: **It says as follows:** When defecating in **a regular bathroom, where** one sits **there are no drops** of urine on one's clothes or shoes, he need not dirty his hands to clean his garment, and therefore one is **permitted** to hold phylacteries in his hand. However, in **a makeshift bathroom, where** one stands, and **there are** ricocheting **drops** which he may touch with his hand, **it is prohibited.**

BACKGROUND

Refutation and *halakha* – תְּיוּבְתָּא וְהִלְכְתָא: The difference between *kashya*, a difficulty or contradiction, and *teyuvta*, a conclusive refutation, is that *kashya* with regard to a particular opinion does not disqualify that opinion; it merely poses a difficulty. *Teyuvta*, however, conclusively refutes and disqualifies that opinion. This is the case particularly where we encounter the phrase: This is a conclusive refutation…Indeed, this is a conclusive refutation. However, there do exist rare cases in which a particular *halakha* remains in place despite the existence of a conclusive refutation contradicting it. From here we learn that when there is an explanation in support of an *amora*, a refutation from a *baraita* does not necessarily prove it incorrect (Rabbi Betzalel Ronsburg).

Bathroom – בֵּית הַכִּסֵּא: There were very few places where bathrooms were actually indoors. In most places, people relieved themselves in empty lots, e.g., the municipal garbage dump. At night, it was possible to find a closer place for that purpose. However, during the day, because of numerous passersby, one was forced to find a spot that was a considerable distance beyond the city limits.

אִי הָכִי, אַמַּאי "אֵין עָלָיו תְּשׁוּבָה"? תְּשׁוּבָה מְעַלְּיְתָא הִיא!

The Gemara challenges: **If so, then why** was it referred to as an *a fortiori* inference that **"cannot be refuted"?** This seems **an excellent refutation** that explains the distinction.

הָכִי קָאָמַר: הָא מִילְּתָא תֵּיתֵי לַהּ בְּתוֹרַת טַעְמָא וְלָא תֵּיתֵי לַהּ בְּקַל וָחוֹמֶר, דְּאִי אָתְיָא לַהּ בְּתוֹרַת קַל וָחוֹמֶר – זֶהוּ קַל וָחוֹמֶר שֶׁאֵין עָלָיו תְּשׁוּבָה.

The Gemara explains that **it says as follows: Derive this matter based on the reason** mentioned above that due to different circumstances the ruling is different. **Do not derive it by means of an *a fortiori* inference, as** if you were **to derive it by means of an *a fortiori* inference, it would** certainly **be an *a fortiori* inference that cannot be rebutted.**

תָּנוּ רַבָּנַן: הָרוֹצֶה לִיכָּנֵס לִסְעוּדַת קֶבַע – מְהַלֵּךְ עֲשָׂרָה פְּעָמִים אַרְבַּע אַמּוֹת, אוֹ אַרְבָּעָה פְּעָמִים עֶשֶׂר אַמּוֹת וְיִפָּנֶה, וְאַחַר כָּךְ נִכְנָס.

The Sages taught: One who wishes to enter and partake of **a regular meal**[H] that will last for some time, **paces** a distance of **four cubits ten times, or ten cubits four times,** in order to expedite the movement of the bowels, and **defecates.** Only **then may he enter** and partake of the meal. That way he spares himself the unpleasantness of being forced to leave in the middle of the meal.

אָמַר רַבִּי יִצְחָק: הַנִּכְנָס לִסְעוּדַת קֶבַע – חוֹלֵץ תְּפִילָּיו וְאַחַר כָּךְ נִכְנָס. וּפְלִיגָא דְּרַבִּי חִיָּיא, דְּאָמַר רַבִּי חִיָּיא: מַנִּיחָן עַל שֻׁלְחָנוֹ, וְכֵן הָדוּר לוֹ.

On this same subject, **Rabbi Yitzḥak said: One who partakes of a regular meal removes his phylacteries and then enters,** as it is inappropriate to partake in a meal where there is frivolity while wearing phylacteries. **And** this statement **disputes** the statement **of Rabbi Ḥiyya, as Rabbi Ḥiyya said:** During a formal meal **one places** his phylacteries **on his table, and it is admirable for him** to do **so** in order that they will be available to don immediately if he so desires.

וְעַד אֵימַת? אָמַר רַב נַחְמָן בַּר יִצְחָק: עַד זְמַן בְּרָכָה.

The Gemara asks: **And until when** in the meal must he refrain from wearing phylacteries? **Rav Naḥman bar Yitzḥak said: Until the time of the recitation of the blessing** of Grace after Meals.

תָּנֵי חֲדָא: צוֹרֵר אָדָם תְּפִילָּיו עִם מְעוֹתָיו בְּאַפַּרְקְסוּתוֹ, וְתַנְיָא אִידָּךְ: לֹא יָצוּר!

It was taught in one *baraita*: **One may bundle his phylacteries with his money in his head covering** [*apraksuto*],[L] **and it was taught in another** *baraita*: **One may not bundle** phylacteries and money together.

לָא קַשְׁיָא: הָא – דְּאַזְמְנֵיהּ, הָא – דְּלָא אַזְמְנֵיהּ. דְּאָמַר רַב חִסְדָּא: הַאי סוּדָרָא תְּפִילִּין דְּאַזְמְנֵיהּ לְמֵיצַר בֵּיהּ תְּפִילִּין, צַר בֵּיהּ תְּפִילִּין – אָסוּר לְמֵיצַר בֵּיהּ פְּשִׁיטֵי, אַזְמְנֵיהּ וְלָא צַר בֵּיהּ, צַר בֵּיהּ וְלָא אַזְמְנֵיהּ – שָׁרֵי לְמֵיצַר בֵּיהּ זוּזֵי.

The Gemara explains: **This is not difficult,** as one must distinguish and say that **this** *baraita*, which prohibits bundling phylacteries and money together, refers to a case where the vessel **was designated** for use with phylacteries, while **this** *baraita*, which permits one to do so, refers to a case where the vessel **was not designated** for that purpose. As **Rav Ḥisda said:** With regard to **this cloth** used with **phylacteries that one designated to bundle phylacteries in it,** if one already **bundled phylacteries in it then it is prohibited to bundle coins**[B] **in it,** but if he only **designated it** for that purpose, **but did not yet bundle** phylacteries **in it,** or **if he bundled** phylacteries **in it** but did **not** originally **designate it** for that purpose, then **it is permitted to bundle money in it.**

וּלְאַבָּיֵי, דְּאָמַר הַזְמָנָה מִילְּתָא הִיא, אַזְמְנֵיהּ אַף עַל גַּב דְּלָא צַר בֵּיהּ. צַר בֵּיהּ, אִי אַזְמְנֵיהּ – אֲסִיר, אִי לָא אַזְמְנֵיהּ – לָא.

And according to Abaye, who said that **designation is significant,** as Abaye holds that all relevant *halakhot* apply to an object designated for a specific purpose, whether or not it has been already used for that purpose, the *halakha* is: **If he designated** the cloth, **even if he did not bundle** phylacteries **in it,** he is prohibited from bundling money in it. However, **if he bundled** phylacteries **in it, if he designated** the cloth for that particular use, **it is prohibited** to bundle money in it, but **if he did not designate it, no,** it is not prohibited.

בְּעָא מִינֵּיהּ רַב יוֹסֵף בְּרֵיהּ דְּרַב נְחוּנְיָא מֵרַב יְהוּדָה: מַהוּ שֶׁיַּנִּיחַ אָדָם תְּפִילָּיו תַּחַת מְרַאֲשׁוֹתָיו? תַּחַת מַרְגְּלוֹתָיו לָא קָא מִבַּעְיָא לִי – שֶׁנּוֹהֵג בָּהֶן מִנְהַג בִּזָּיוֹן, כִּי קָא מִבַּעְיָא לִי – תַּחַת מְרַאֲשׁוֹתָיו, מַאי? – אָמַר לֵיהּ, הָכִי אָמַר שְׁמוּאֵל: מוּתָּר, אֲפִילּוּ אִשְׁתּוֹ עִמּוֹ.

Rav Yosef, son of Rav Neḥunya, raised a dilemma before Rav Yehuda: What is the *halakha*; may **a man place his phylacteries** in his bed, **under his head** while he sleeps? He himself explains: With regard to whether or not one may place them **under his feet, I have no dilemma, as that would be treating them in a deprecating manner** and is certainly prohibited. **My dilemma is** whether or not one may place them **under his head; what is** the *halakha* in that case? Rav Yehuda **said to him, Shmuel said as follows: It is permitted, even** if his **wife is with him** in his bed.

מֵיתִיבֵי: לֹא יַנִּיחַ אָדָם תְּפִילָּיו תַּחַת מַרְגְּלוֹתָיו מִפְּנֵי שֶׁנּוֹהֵג בָּהֶם דֶּרֶךְ בִּזָּיוֹן, אֲבָל מַנִּיחָם תַּחַת מְרַאֲשׁוֹתָיו. וְאִם הָיְתָה אִשְׁתּוֹ עִמּוֹ – אָסוּר. הָיָה מָקוֹם שֶׁגָּבוֹהַּ שְׁלֹשָׁה טְפָחִים אוֹ נָמוּךְ שְׁלֹשָׁה טְפָחִים – מוּתָּר.

The Gemara **raises an objection** based on what was taught in a *baraita*: **A man may not place his phylacteries under his feet, as** in doing so, **he treats them in a deprecating manner, but he may place them under his head. And if his wife was with him, it is prohibited** even to place it under his head. **If there was a place** where he could place the phylacteries **three handbreadths above or three handbreadths below** his head **it is permissible,** as that space is sufficient for the phylacteries to be considered in a separate place.

תְּיוּבְתָּא דִּשְׁמוּאֵל! תְּיוּבְתָּא.

This is a conclusive refutation of Shmuel's statement. The Gemara concludes: Indeed, it is **a conclusive refutation.**

אָמַר רָבָא: אַף עַל גַּב דְּתַנְיָא תְּיוּבְתָּא דִּשְׁמוּאֵל – הִלְכְתָא כְּוָותֵיהּ. מַאי טַעְמָא?

Rava said: Although a *baraita* **was taught** that constitutes **a conclusive refutation of Shmuel, the *halakha* is in accordance with his** opinion in this matter. **What is the reason** for this?

HALAKHA

One who wishes to partake of a regular meal – הָרוֹצֶה לִיכָּנֵס לִסְעוּדַת קֶבַע מְהַלֵּךְ וכו׳: It is common courtesy that before beginning a meal one should ascertain whether or not he needs to relieve himself. If he does, he should see to it beforehand, as per the *baraita* (Rambam *Sefer HaMadda, Hilkhot De'ot* 4:2).

LANGUAGE

Head covering [*apraksuto*] – אַפַּרְקְסוּתוֹ: The commentators disagree over the exact meaning of *apraksuto*. Some say that it is a type of scarf that covers the head with fringes dangling down on both sides in which objects might sometimes be wrapped (Rashi). However, according to the *ge'onim*, *apraksuto* refers to a broad, shawl-like undergarment generally worn beneath an outer cloak, and in which it was possible to fold pockets for storage.

The source of the word is most likely the Greek **ἐπικάρσιον**, *epikarsion*, meaning a gown or garment. Indeed, it is often written as it would sound in Greek or Syrian *afkaresot*.

BACKGROUND

Coins – פְּשִׁיטֵי: Some explain this term literally as referring to simple copper coins. Others tied this word to the Middle Persian *pišiz*, meaning small coin, *peruta*.

כל לנטורינהו טפי עדיף. והיכא מנח להו? – אמר רבי ירמיה: בין כר לכסת, שלא כנגד ראשו.

Because **whatever** offers more **protection is preferable**[N] even at the cost of deprecation. **And where** under his head **does he place them? Rabbi Yirmeya said:** He places them **between the pillow and the mattress, not** directly **aligned with his head** but rather a bit to the side.

והא תני רבי חייא: מניחן בכובע תחת מראשותיו! דמפיק ליה למורשא כובע לבר.

The Gemara asks: **Didn't Rabbi Ḥiyya teach a** *baraita* that in that case **he places them in a pouch** used for phylacteries, directly **under his head?** The Gemara replies: He does so in a manner **that the bulge** in the **pouch,** where the phylacteries are, **protrudes out** and is not beneath his head.

בר קפרא צייר להו בכילתא ומפיק למורשהון לבר. רב שישא בריה דרב אידי מנח להו אשרשיפא ופריס סודרא עילוייהו.

On this note, the Gemara relates that **Bar Kappara would tie them in his bed curtain and project their bulge outward. Rav Sheisha, son of Rav Idi, would place them on a bench and spread a cloth over them.**[H]

אמר רב המנונא בריה דרב יוסף: זימנא חדא הוה קאימנא קמיה דרבא ואמר לי: זיל אייתי לי תפילין. ואשכחתינהו בין כר לכסת, שלא כנגד ראשו, והוה ידענא דיום טבילה הוה, ולאגמורן הלכה למעשה הוא דעבד.

Rav Hamnuna, son of Rav Yosef, said: I was once standing before Rava and he told me: Go and **bring me** my **phylacteries. And I found them** in his bed, **between the mattress and the pillow, not aligned with his head. And I knew** that **it was the day** of his wife's **immersion** in the ritual bath for purification from the ritual impurity of a menstruating woman, and he certainly engaged in marital relations in order to fulfill the mitzva, **and he did so,** he sent me to bring him his phylacteries, **to teach us the practical** ***halakha***[N] in that case.

בעי מיניה רב יוסף בריה דרב נחוניא מרב יהודה: שנים שישנים במטה אחת, מהו שזה יחזיר פניו ויקרא קריאת שמע, וזה יחזיר פניו ויקרא קריאת שמע? אמר ליה הכי אמר שמואל: ואפילו אשתו עמו.

Rav Yosef, son of Rav Neḥunya, who raised a dilemma above, **raised a dilemma before Rav Yehuda: Two individuals sleeping in a single bed,**[H] given that it was standard practice to sleep without clothing, **what is the** ***halakha***; is it permissible **for this one to turn his head** aside **and recite** ***Shema*** **and for that** one **turns his head and recites** ***Shema***; or is it prohibited because they are unclothed and are considered unfit to recite *Shema* even though they are covered with a blanket? **He said to him: Shmuel said as follows:** This is permitted **even if his wife** is in bed **with him.**[H]

מתקיף לה רב יוסף: אשתו ולא מיבעיא אחר?! אדרבה! אשתו כגופו, אחר לאו כגופו!

Rav Yosef strongly objects to this response: You say that he is permitted to recite *Shema* in bed with **his wife, and needless to say** he is permitted to do so when in bed with **another. On the contrary,** since **his wife is like his own flesh,** and he will not have lustful thoughts of her, it is permitted; **another is not like his own flesh** and it is prohibited.

מיתיבי: שנים שישנים במטה אחת – זה מחזיר פניו וקורא, וזה מחזיר פניו וקורא. ותניא אחריתי: הישן במטה, ובניו ובני ביתו בצדו – הרי זה לא יקרא קריאת שמע אלא אם כן היתה טלית מפסקת ביניהן. ואם היו בניו ובני ביתו קטנים – מותר.

The Gemara **raises an objection** to this from the resolution of an apparent contradiction between two *baraitot*. It was taught in one *baraita*: **Two** unclothed **individuals who are sleeping in a single bed, this** one **turns his head** aside **and recites** *Shema* **and that** one **turns his head** aside **and recites** *Shema*. **And it was taught in another** *baraita*: **One who is sleeping in bed and his** unclothed **children and members of his household are beside him, may not recite** ***Shema*** **unless a garment separates between them. If his children and the members of his household were minors, it is permitted** to recite *Shema* even without a garment separating between them.

בשלמא לרב יוסף לא קשיא: הא – אשתו, והא – באחר. אלא לשמואל קשיא!

Granted, according to Rav Yosef, the apparent contradiction between the two *baraitot* **is not difficult,** as **this** *baraita* is referring to a case **where his wife** is in the bed with him, **while this** other *baraita* is referring to a case **where another** person is in bed with him and there is concern lest he will have lustful thoughts. **However, according to Shmuel,** who permits one to recite *Shema* regardless of who is in bed with him, **it is** indeed **difficult.** How would he interpret the *baraita* that prohibits?

NOTES

Whatever offers more protection is preferable – כל לנטורינהו טפי עדיף: This reason, in and of itself, would not be sufficient to allow Shmuel to dispute the ruling of the *baraita*. Rather, Shmuel relied on a different *baraita* in which it was taught that phylacteries may be brought into a regular bathroom. The priority placed on protecting the phylacteries led the Gemara to adopt Shmuel's opinion in this matter (*Penei Yehoshua*).

To teach us the practical *halakha* – ולאגמורן הלכה למעשה: The general principle taught in the Gemara (*Bava Batra* 130b) is that practical *halakha* can neither be determined based on teaching alone nor based on observing the action of an authority. It can only be determined based on teaching applied to a practical situation. Therefore, it would not have been sufficient for Rava to teach this ruling in the classroom. He needed to illustrate to his students that this teaching was also put into practice.

HALAKHA

He would place them on a bench and spread a cloth over them – מנח להו אשרשיפא ופריס סודרא עילוייהו: One may not engage in conjugal relations with phylacteries in the room. If they are in the room, he must cover them with two vessels, the outermost of which must not be its regular container. One is permitted to place the phylacteries in a box and spread a garment over it, as that is considered to be two vessels (*Shulḥan Arukh, Oraḥ Ḥayyim* 240:6).

Two individuals sleeping in a single bed – שנים שישנים במטה אחת: In order to recite *Shema,* two unclothed individuals sharing a single blanket must have a garment from the waist down to serve as a barrier between them (Rambam *Sefer Ahava, Hilkhot Keriat Shema* 3:18; *Shulḥan Arukh, Oraḥ Ḥayyim* 73:1).

Even if his wife is with him – אשתו עמו: One whose wife is in bed with him may turn his head and recite *Shema* in accordance with the opinions of Shmuel and Rav Yosef. Some require a garment to serve as a barrier between them, and it is proper to do so (Rambam *Sefer Ahava, Hilkhot Keriat Shema* 3:18; *Shulḥan Arukh, Oraḥ Ḥayyim* 73:2).

אָמַר לָךְ שְׁמוּאֵל: לְרַב יוֹסֵף מִי נִיחָא?! וְהָתַנְיָא: הָיָה יָשֵׁן בְּמִטָּה, וּבָנָיו וּבְנֵי בֵיתוֹ בְּמִטָּה – לֹא יִקְרָא קְרִיאַת שְׁמַע אֶלָּא אִם כֵּן הָיְתָה טַלִּיתוֹ מַפְסֶקֶת בֵּינֵיהֶן! אֶלָּא מַאי אִית לָךְ לְמֵימַר – אִשְׁתּוֹ לְרַב יוֹסֵף תַּנָּאֵי הִיא, לְדִידִי נַמִּי תַּנָּאֵי הִיא.

The Gemara replies: **Shmuel** could have **said to you: And according to Rav Yosef's** opinion, **does it** work out **well? Wasn't it taught** in that same *baraita* that **one who is sleeping in bed and his children and members of his household are beside him, may not recite *Shema* unless a garment separates between them?** Doesn't Rav Yosef hold that his wife is like his own flesh and no separation is necessary? **Rather, what have you to say** in response? **Rav Yosef holds that there is a tannaitic** dispute in the case of **one's wife; I, too, hold that it is a tannaitic** dispute, and I accept the ruling of one of the *baraitot*.

אָמַר מָר: ״זֶה מַחֲזִיר פָּנָיו וְקוֹרֵא קְרִיאַת שְׁמַע״. וְהָא אִיכָּא עֲגָבוֹת! מְסַיַּיע לֵיהּ לְרַב הוּנָא, דְּאָמַר רַב הוּנָא: עֲגָבוֹת אֵין בָּהֶם מִשּׁוּם עֶרְוָה. לֵימָא מְסַיַּיע לֵיהּ לְרַב הוּנָא: הָאִשָּׁה יוֹשֶׁבֶת וְקוֹצָה לָהּ חַלָּתָהּ עֲרוּמָּה מִפְּנֵי שֶׁיְּכוֹלָה לְכַסּוֹת פָּנֶיהָ בַּקַּרְקַע, אֲבָל לֹא הָאִישׁ.

The Gemara reverts to clarify something mentioned above. **The Master said** in a *baraita*: **This** one **turns his head** aside **and recites *Shema*.** The Gemara notes a difficulty: **Aren't there** bare **buttocks?** This **supports** the opinion of **Rav Huna, as Rav Huna said: Buttocks do not constitute nakedness.**[H] **Let us say** that the following mishna **supports Rav Huna's** opinion: **A woman sits and separates her *ḥalla* naked,** despite the fact that she must recite a blessing over the separation of the *ḥalla*, **because she can cover her face,** a euphemism for her genitals, **in the ground, but a male,** whose genitals are not covered when he sits, may **not** do so. The mishna teaches that exposed buttocks do not constitute nakedness.

תַּרְגְּמָהּ רַב נַחְמָן בַּר יִצְחָק: כְּגוֹן שֶׁהָיוּ פָּנֶיהָ טוּחוֹת בַּקַּרְקַע.

Rav Naḥman bar Yitzḥak interpreted the mishna as referring to **a case where her face,** genitals, **was completely covered in the ground** such that her posterior was covered by the ground. Therefore, proof for Rav Huna's opinion cannot be brought from this mishna.

אָמַר מָר: ״אִם הָיוּ בָּנָיו וּבְנֵי בֵיתוֹ קְטַנִּים – מוּתָּר״. וְעַד כַּמָּה? – אָמַר רַב חִסְדָּא: תִּינוֹקֶת בַּת שָׁלֹשׁ שָׁנִים וְיוֹם אֶחָד, וְתִינוֹק בֶּן תֵּשַׁע שָׁנִים וְיוֹם אֶחָד. אִיכָּא דְּאָמְרִי: תִּינוֹקֶת בַּת אַחַת עֶשְׂרֵה שָׁנָה וְיוֹם אֶחָד, וְתִינוֹק בֶּן שְׁתֵּים עֶשְׂרֵה שָׁנָה וְיוֹם אֶחָד, אִידִי וְאִידִי עַד כְּדֵי ״שָׁדַיִם נָכֹנוּ וּשְׂעָרֵךְ צִמֵּחַ״.

The Master said in a *baraita*: **If his children and the members of his household were minors,**[H] even though they are unclothed, **it is permitted** to recite *Shema* even without a garment separating between them. The Gemara asks: **Until what** age is one still considered a minor? **Rav Ḥisda said: A girl** until she is **three years and one day old, and a boy** until **he is nine years and one day old,** for these are the ages from which a sexual act in which they participate is considered a sexual act. **Some say: A girl eleven years and one day old and a boy of twelve years and one day old,** as that is the age at which they are considered adults in this regard. This age is only approximate, as the age of majority for both **this,** the boy, **and that,** the girl, is **at** the onset of puberty in accordance with the verse: **"Your breasts were formed and your hair was grown"** (Ezekiel 16:7).

אֲמַר לֵיהּ רַב כָּהֲנָא לְרַב אָשֵׁי: הָתָם אָמַר רָבָא: אַף עַל גַּב דִּתְיוּבְתָּא דִּשְׁמוּאֵל, הִלְכְתָא כְּוָותֵיהּ דִּשְׁמוּאֵל. הָכָא מַאי? אֲמַר לֵיהּ: אַטּוּ כּוּלְּהוּ בַּחֲדָא מַחְתָּא מַחְתִינְהוּ?! אֶלָּא: הֵיכָא דְּאִיתְּמַר אִיתְּמַר, וְהֵיכָא דְּלָא אִיתְּמַר לָא אִיתְּמַר.

Rav Kahana said to Rav Ashi: There, with regard to the law of phylacteries, **Rava said: Despite a conclusive refutation** of the opinion **of Shmuel, the *halakha* is in accordance with** the opinion **of Shmuel. Here, what** is the ruling?[N] **He said to him: Were all of them woven in the same** act of **weaving?** Are there no distinctions between different cases? **Rather, where it is stated, it is stated, and where it is not stated, it is not stated,** and there is no comparison.

אֲמַר לֵיהּ רַב מָרִי לְרַב פַּפָּא: שֵׂעָר יוֹצֵא בְּבִגְדוֹ מַהוּ? קָרָא עֲלֵיהּ: שֵׂעָר, שֵׂעָר.

Rav Mari said to Rav Pappa: Does it constitute nakedness **if one's** pubic **hair protruded from his garment?** Rav Pappa said **about him: A hair, a hair.**[N] You are splitting hairs and being pedantic over trivialities.

אָמַר ר׳ יִצְחָק: טֶפַח בְּאִשָּׁה עֶרְוָה. לְמַאי? אִילֵימָא לְאִסְתַּכּוֹלֵי בַּהּ, וְהָא אָמַר רַב שֵׁשֶׁת: לָמָּה מָנָה הַכָּתוּב תַּכְשִׁיטִין שֶׁבַּחוּץ עִם תַּכְשִׁיטִין שֶׁבִּפְנִים? לוֹמַר לָךְ: כָּל הַמִּסְתַּכֵּל בְּאֶצְבַּע קְטַנָּה שֶׁל אִשָּׁה, כְּאִילּוּ מִסְתַּכֵּל בִּמְקוֹם הַתּוֹרֶף!

Rabbi Yitzḥak stated: An exposed **handbreadth in a woman** constitutes **nakedness.** The Gemara asks: Regarding **which** *halakha* was this said? **If you say** that it comes to prohibit **looking at** an exposed handbreadth in **her, didn't Rav Sheshet say: Why did the verse enumerate** "anklets and bracelets, rings, earrings and girdles" (Numbers 31:50), **jewelry that is worn externally,** over her clothing, e.g., bracelets, **together with jewelry** worn **internally,** beneath her clothing, near her nakedness, e.g., girdles? This was **to tell you: Anyone who gazes upon a woman's little finger**[H] is considered **as if he gazed upon her** naked **genitals,** for if his intentions are impure, it makes no difference where he looks or how much is exposed; even less than a handbreadth.

אֶלָּא: בְּאִשְׁתּוֹ, וְלִקְרִיאַת שְׁמַע.

Rather, it is referring even to **his wife, with regard to** the **recitation of *Shema*.** One may not recite *Shema* before an exposed handbreadth of his wife.

HALAKHA

Buttocks do not constitute nakedness – עֲגָבוֹת אֵין בָּהֶם מִשּׁוּם עֶרְוָה: The halakhic decisors disagree whether or not to adopt Rav Huna's opinion that exposed buttocks do not constitute nakedness. Some accept his opinion (Rashba, *Magen Avraham*), while others reject it because it is not corroborated by the *baraita* (*Beit Yosef*, Vilna Gaon; see *Magen Avraham* on *Shulḥan Arukh*, *Oraḥ Ḥayyim* 73:2).

If his children and members of his household were minors – אִם הָיוּ בָּנָיו וּבְנֵי בֵיתוֹ קְטַנִּים: Regarding the recitation of *Shema* by one who was sleeping on the same bed with his unclothed children; if the boys were under the age of twelve and the girls under the age of eleven, it is permitted. If the boys were between twelve and thirteen and the girls between eleven and twelve, if they have two pubic hairs it is prohibited, and if not, it is permitted. Beyond those ages, it is prohibited. The *halakha* is ruled in accordance with the second version of Rav Ḥisda's statement (Rambam *Sefer Ahava*, *Hilkhot Keriat Shema* 3:19; *Shulḥan Arukh*, *Oraḥ Ḥayyim* 73:4).

Anyone who gazes upon a woman's little finger – הַמִּסְתַּכֵּל בְּאֶצְבַּע קְטַנָּה שֶׁל אִשָּׁה: One is prohibited from gazing for sensual pleasure upon a woman to whom he is not married. Even gazing upon her finger is prohibited. One who does so for his enjoyment is liable to receive rabbinically ordained lashes for rebelliousness (Rambam *Sefer Kedusha*, *Hilkhot Issurei Bia* 21:2; *Shulḥan Arukh*, *Even HaEzer* 21:1).

NOTES

Despite a conclusive refutation of Shmuel, the law is in accordance with him…Here, what is the ruling – אַף עַל גַּב דִּתְיוּבְתָּא דִּשְׁמוּאֵל, הִלְכְתָא כְּוָותֵיהּ...הָכָא מַאי: The question of whether the *halakha* will be ruled in accordance with Shmuel even after he was refuted seems odd. However, since the nature of the *halakhot* regarding phylacteries and the recitation of *Shema* are similar, one might have presumed that since it was ruled in accordance with Shmuel with regard to *tefillin*, the same would be true here (*Tosefot Rabbeinu Yehuda HaḤasid*).

A hair, a hair – שֵׂעָר, שֵׂעָר: Meaning, ultimately it is hair and not flesh (*Rabbeinu Tam*).

אמר רב חסדא: שוק באשה ערוה, שנאמר: "גלי שוק עברי נהרות", וכתיב "תגל ערותך וגם תראה חרפתך". אמר שמואל: קול באשה ערוה, שנאמר: "כי קולך ערב ומראך נאוה". אמר רב ששת: שער באשה ערוה, שנאמר: "שערך כעדר העזים".

Along these lines, **Rav Ḥisda said:** Even **a woman's** exposed **leg is** considered **nakedness, as it is stated: "Uncover the leg and pass through the rivers"** (Isaiah 47:2), **and it is written** in the following verse: **"Your nakedness shall be revealed and your shame shall be seen"** (Isaiah 47:3). **Shmuel** further **stated: A woman's** singing **voice is** considered **nakedness,**[NH] which he derives from the praise accorded a woman's voice, **as it is stated: "Sweet is your voice and your countenance is alluring"** (Song of Songs 2:14). Similarly, **Rav Sheshet stated:** Even **a woman's hair is** considered **nakedness,**[H] for it too is praised, **as it is written: "Your hair is like a flock of goats,** trailing down from Mount Gilead" (Song of Songs 4:1).

אמר רבי חנינא: אני ראיתי את רבי שתלה תפיליו. מיתיבי: התולה תפיליו יתלו לו חייו!

The Gemara resumes its discussion of phylacteries. **Rabbi Ḥanina said: I saw Rabbi** Yehuda HaNasi **hang his phylacteries.** The Gemara **raises an objection:** It was taught in a *baraita* that **one who hangs his phylacteries**[H] **will have his life hang** in the balance.

דורשי חמורות אמרו: "והיו חייך תלאים לך מנגד" – זה התולה תפיליו!

Moreover, **the Symbolic Interpreters** of the Torah **said** that the verse: **"And your life shall hang in doubt before you** [*minneged*]**"** (Deuteronomy 28:66),[N] that is the punishment of **one who hangs his phylacteries.**

לא קשיא, הא – ברצועה, הא – בקציצה.

The Gemara replies: This apparent contradiction **is not difficult, as this** *baraita*, which condemns one who hangs his phylacteries, refers to one who hangs them **by the strap,** allowing the leather boxes into which the parchment is placed to dangle in a deprecating way, which is certainly prohibited. **That** *baraita*, which relates that Rabbi Yehuda HaNasi would hang his phylacteries and that it is clearly permitted, refers to when one hangs them **from the box** with the straps dangling.

ואיבעית אימא: לא שנא רצועה ולא שנא קציצה – אסור, וכי תלה רבי – בכיסתא תלה.

And if you wish, say another explanation instead: **There is no difference** whether he hangs the phylacteries from the **strap and there is no difference** whether he hangs the phylacteries from **the box;** both **are prohibited. And when Rabbi** Yehuda HaNasi **hung** his phylacteries, **he hung them in** their **pouch.**

אי הכי, מאי למימרא? – מהו דתימא: תיבעי הנחה כספר תורה, קא משמע לן.

The Gemara asks: **If so, what** is the purpose **to relate** that incident? The Gemara replies: **Lest you say** that phylacteries **would require placement** atop a surface, **as** is the custom with **a Torah scroll.** Therefore, **it teaches us** that this is unnecessary.

ואמר רבי חנינא: אני ראיתי את רבי שגיהק ופיהק, ונתעטש, ורק

Since Rabbi Ḥanina related a story involving Rabbi Yehuda HaNasi, the Gemara cites another such story. **Rabbi Ḥanina said: I saw Rabbi** Yehuda HaNasi, while he was praying, **belch, yawn, sneeze, spit,**

NOTES

A woman's singing voice is considered nakedness – קול באשה ערוה: The commentators and *poskim* delve into the specifics of this issue to determine the practical application of this statement. Some argue that it merely warns us to act modestly, and that it is inappropriate for a woman to expose certain parts of her body or to sing publicly. Others maintain that "nakedness" refers here strictly to the context of the recitation of the *Shema* and prayer, meaning that this is included in the category of "nakedness" regarding settings where one is forbidden to recite the *Shema* (see *Tosefot Rabbeinu Yehuda HaḤasid* and *Tosefot HaRosh*).

"And your life shall hang in doubt [*minneged*]" – והיו חייך תלאים לך מנגד: Some commentators emphasize the homiletic interpretation of the phrase "And your life shall hang in doubt" by reading *minneged* to mean "from afar," and thus the sustenance of one who makes light of phylacteries will be kept at a distance from him (*Talmidei Rabbeinu Yona*). Alternately, *minneged* can mean measure-for-measure (*midda keneged midda*), such that one who hangs his phylacteries will suffer correspondingly, and his life will be hung in doubt (Rabbi Elazar Moshe Horowitz).

HALAKHA

A woman's singing voice is considered nakedness – קול באשה ערוה: The sound of a woman's singing voice is considered nakedness, and a man may not hear the voice of a woman singing while reciting *Shema*, even the voice of his own wife. However, he is permitted to hear a voice to which he is accustomed and which he knows will not arouse in him lustful thoughts, even while reciting *Shema* (Rema; Rambam *Sefer Kedusha, Hilkhot Issurei Bia* 21:2; *Shulḥan Arukh, Oraḥ Ḥayyim* 75:3, *Even HaEzer* 21:1).

A woman's hair is considered nakedness – שער באשה ערוה: Hair that a woman (in most Jewish communities this applies only to a married woman) would normally cover is considered nakedness when exposed, and one is prohibited from reciting *Shema* with it in his sight, whether it is the hair of his wife or that of another woman (Rema; Rambam *Sefer Kedusha, Hilkhot Issurei Bia* 21:2; *Shulḥan Arukh, Oraḥ Ḥayyim* 75:1–2).

One who hangs his phylacteries – התולה תפיליו: One is prohibited from hanging phylacteries, whether he suspends them by their boxes with the straps hanging down or by their straps with the boxes hanging down. One is permitted to hang the pouch in which they are stored, in accordance with both versions of the statement in the Gemara (Rambam *Sefer Ahava, Hilkhot Tefillin Mezuza VeSefer Torah* 4:9; *Shulḥan Arukh, Oraḥ Ḥayyim* 40:1).

Perek **III**
Daf **24** Amud **b**

וממשמש בבגדו, אבל לא היה מתעטף, וכשהוא מפהק – היה מניח ידו על סנטרו.

and if he was stung by a louse, he may **feel** for it and remove it **with his garment,**[H] **but he would not wrap himself** in his prayer shawl[H] if it fell during prayer. **And when he would yawn he would place his hand on his chin**[L] so that his open mouth would not be visible.

מיתיבי: המשמיע קולו בתפלתו – הרי זה מקטני אמנה. המגביה קולו בתפלתו – הרי זה מנביאי השקר,

The Gemara **raises an objection** based on a *baraita*: **One who sounds his voice during his** *Amida* **prayer is among those of little faith,** as he seems to believe that the Lord cannot hear his prayer when it is uttered silently. **One who raises his voice during prayer** is considered to be **among the false prophets,** as they too were wont to cry out and shout to their gods.

מגהק ומפהק – הרי זה מגסי הרוח. המתעטש בתפלתו – סימן רע לו, ויש אומרים: ניכר שהוא מכוער. הרק בתפלתו – כאילו רק בפני המלך!

Furthermore, one who **belches and yawns** while praying **is** surely **among the uncouth. One who sneezes during his prayer, for him it is a bad omen. And some say: It is clear that he is repulsive.** Also, **one who spits during prayer, it is tantamount to spitting in the face of the king.** In light of all this, how could Rabbi Yehuda HaNasi have done all that while praying?

HALAKHA

And feel and remove it with his garment – וממשמש בבגדו: One who has a louse on his garment while reciting the *Amida* prayer may use his garment to remove it; however, he may not remove it with his hand (*Shulḥan Arukh, Oraḥ Ḥayyim* 97:3).

But he would not wrap himself in his prayer shawl – אבל לא היה מתעטף: If one's prayer shawl fell entirely off of him, he may not lift it and wrap himself in it during the *Amida* prayer, as that would constitute an interruption. If it fell partially off of him, he is permitted to adjust it (*Tosafot*; *Shulḥan Arukh, Oraḥ Ḥayyim* 97:4).

LANGUAGE

Chin [*santer*] – סנטר: In this context, there are two possible explanations of this word. According to the standard translation it is from the Greek ἀνθερεών *anthereon*, meaning chin. However, the *ge'onim*, Rabbeinu Ḥananel and, apparently, the Rambam explain that it means hips, from the Aramaic *satar*, meaning side. It is inappropriate to stand that way in prayer as it conveys levity and arrogance.

בִּשְׁלָמָא מְגַהֵק וּמְפַהֵק לָא קַשְׁיָא: כָּאן – לְאוֹנְסוֹ, כָּאן – לִרְצוֹנוֹ, אֶלָּא מִתְעַטֵּשׁ אַמִּתְעַטֵּשׁ קַשְׁיָא!

The Gemara explains: **Granted,** with regard to **one who belches and yawns, it is not difficult: Here,** in the case where Rabbi Yehuda HaNasi did so, **it was involuntary** and therefore permissible; **here,** where it is considered uncouth, is in a case where **it is deliberate.** However, the contradiction **between sneezing** in the case where Rabbi Yehuda HaNasi did so **and sneezing** where it is considered a bad omen **is difficult.**

מִתְעַטֵּשׁ אַמִּתְעַטֵּשׁ נַמִּי לָא קַשְׁיָא: כָּאן – מִלְמַעְלָה, כָּאן – מִלְּמַטָּה; דַּאֲמַר רַב זֵירָא: הָא מִילְּתָא אִבְלְעָא לִי בֵּי רַב הַמְנוּנָא, וּתְקִילָא לִי כִּי כּוּלֵּי תַּלְמוּדַאי: הַמִּתְעַטֵּשׁ בִּתְפִלָּתוֹ – סִימָן יָפֶה לוֹ, כְּשֵׁם שֶׁעוֹשִׂים לוֹ נַחַת רוּחַ מִלְּמַטָּה, כָּךְ עוֹשִׂים לוֹ נַחַת רוּחַ מִלְמַעְלָה.

The Gemara responds: The contradiction **between sneezing** in one case **and sneezing** in the other case **is also not difficult: Here,** in the case of Rabbi Yehuda HaNasi, it is referring to sneezing **from above,** his nose; **here,** where it is a bad omen, is referring to sneezing **from below,** flatulence. **As Rav Zeira said: In the school of Rav Hamnuna I absorbed this matter** in passing, **and it is equal** in significance **to all the rest of my learning: One who sneezes in the midst of prayer, it is a good omen for him. Just as** the sneeze soothes his irritation, **giving him pleasure below,** it is a sign that **they are similarly giving him pleasure above.** Since Rav Zeira sneezed often, he was extremely pleased to hear this.

אֶלָּא רַק אַרַק קַשְׁיָא! – רַק אַרַק נַמִּי לָא קַשְׁיָא: אֶפְשָׁר כִּדְרַב יְהוּדָה; דְּאָמַר רַב יְהוּדָה: הָיָה עוֹמֵד בַּתְּפִילָּה וְנִזְדַּמֵּן לוֹ רוֹק – מַבְלִיעוֹ בְּטַלִּיתוֹ, וְאִם טַלִּית נָאָה הוּא – מַבְלִיעוֹ בְּאַפַּרְקָסוּתוֹ. רָבִינָא הֲוָה קָאֵי אֲחוֹרֵי רַב אַשִׁי, נִזְדַּמֵּן לוֹ רוֹק, פְּתַקֵיהּ לַאֲחוֹרֵיהּ. אֲמַר לֵיהּ: לָא סְבַר לָהּ מָר לְהָא דְּרַב יְהוּדָה "מַבְלִיעוֹ בְּאַפַּרְקָסוּתוֹ"?! – אֲמַר לֵיהּ: אֲנָא אֲנִינָא דַּעֲתַאי.

However, The contradiction **between spitting** in the case where Rabbi Yehuda HaNasi did so **and spitting** where it is deemed tantamount to spitting in the face of the king **is difficult.** The Gemara replies: The contradiction **between spitting** in one case **and spitting** in the other case **is also not difficult,** as **it is possible** to resolve it **in accordance with** the opinion of **Rav Yehuda,** as **Rav Yehuda said: One who was standing in prayer, and saliva happened** to accumulate in **his mouth,**[H] **he absorbs it in his garment. And if it was a fine garment** and he does not want it to become sullied, **he may cover it up in his head covering.** That way, one is permitted to spit. The Gemara relates: **Ravina was standing behind Rav Ashi** during prayer when **saliva happened** to accumulate in **his mouth, so he discharged it behind him.** Rav Ashi **said to him:** And **does the Master not hold** in accordance with **that** statement of **Rav Yehuda, who said** that **one absorbs it in his head covering? He said to him: I am delicate,** and the mere knowledge that there is spittle in my head covering disturbs my prayer.

הַמַּשְׁמִיעַ קוֹלוֹ בִּתְפִלָּתוֹ הֲרֵי זֶה מִקְּטַנֵּי אֲמָנָה. אָמַר רַב הוּנָא: לֹא שָׁנוּ אֶלָּא שֶׁיָּכוֹל לְכַוֵּין אֶת לִבּוֹ בְּלַחַשׁ, אֲבָל אֵין יָכוֹל לְכַוֵּין אֶת לִבּוֹ בְּלַחַשׁ – מוּתָּר; וְהָנֵי מִילֵּי – בְּיָחִיד, אֲבָל בְּצִיבּוּר – אָתֵי לְמִיטְרַד צִיבּוּרָא.

It was taught in a *baraita*: **One who sounds his voice during his** *Amida* **prayer is among those of little faith. Rav Huna said: This was only taught** in a case **where one is able to focus his heart** while praying silently, **but** if he **is unable to focus his heart** while praying silently, **he is permitted** to sound his voice. **This applies only to** one praying **alone,** but when he is praying **in a congregation** his voice **will come to disturb the congregation** and it is prohibited.

רַבִּי אַבָּא הֲוָה קָא מִשְׁתַּמֵּיט מִינֵּיהּ דְּרַב יְהוּדָה, דַּהֲוָה קָא בָּעֵי לְמֵיסַק לְאַרְעָא דְיִשְׂרָאֵל, דְּאָמַר רַב יְהוּדָה: כָּל הָעוֹלֶה מִבָּבֶל לְאֶרֶץ יִשְׂרָאֵל עוֹבֵר בַּעֲשֵׂה, שֶׁנֶּאֱמַר: "בָּבֶלָה יוּבָאוּ וְשָׁמָּה יִהְיוּ עַד יוֹם פָּקְדִי אוֹתָם נְאֻם ה'". אֲמַר: אֵיזִיל וְאֶשְׁמַע מִינֵּיהּ מִילְּתָא מִבֵּית וַעֲדָא, וַהֲדַר אֵפּוֹק.

The Gemara relates that **Rabbi Abba was avoiding** being seen **by** his teacher **Rav Yehuda,** as Rabbi Abba **sought to ascend to Eretz Yisrael** and his teacher disapproved, **as Rav Yehuda said: Anyone who ascends from Babylonia to Eretz Yisrael**[N] **transgresses a positive commandment, as it is stated: "They shall be taken to Babylonia and there they shall remain until the day that I recall them, said the Lord"** (Jeremiah 27:22). Rabbi Abba did not want to discuss his desire to emigrate with Rav Yehuda. Nevertheless **he said: I will go and hear something from him at the hall** where the Sages **assemble,** without being seen, **and afterwards I will leave** Babylonia.

אֲזַל אַשְׁכְּחֵיהּ לְתַנָּא דְּקָתָנֵי קַמֵּיהּ דְּרַב יְהוּדָה: הָיָה עוֹמֵד בִּתְפִלָּה וְנִתְעַטֵּשׁ – מַמְתִּין עַד שֶׁיִּכְלֶה הָרוּחַ וְחוֹזֵר וּמִתְפַּלֵּל; אִיכָּא דְּאָמְרִי: הָיָה עוֹמֵד בִּתְפִלָּה וּבִיקֵּשׁ לְהִתְעַטֵּשׁ – מַרְחִיק לַאֲחֲרָיו אַרְבַּע אַמּוֹת וּמִתְעַטֵּשׁ, וּמַמְתִּין עַד שֶׁיִּכְלֶה הָרוּחַ, וְחוֹזֵר וּמִתְפַּלֵּל; וְאוֹמֵר: "רִבּוֹנוֹ שֶׁל עוֹלָם, יְצַרְתָּנוּ נְקָבִים נְקָבִים חֲלוּלִים חֲלוּלִים, גָּלוּי וְיָדוּעַ לְפָנֶיךָ חֶרְפָּתֵנוּ וּכְלִימָּתֵנוּ בְּחַיֵּינוּ, וּבְאַחֲרִיתֵנוּ רִמָּה וְתוֹלֵעָה"; וּמַתְחִיל מִמָּקוֹם שֶׁפָּסַק.

He went and found the *tanna,* who recites the tannaitic sources before the study hall, **reciting** the following *baraita* **before Rav Yehuda: One who was standing in prayer and sneezed** from below[H] **waits until the odor dissipates and resumes praying. Some say: One who was standing in prayer when he felt the need to sneeze** from below, **retreats four cubits, sneezes, waits until the odor dissipates and resumes praying. And** before resuming his prayer, **he says: Master of the universe, You have formed us with many orifices and cavities; our disgrace and shame in life are clear and evident before You, as is our destiny with maggots and worms,** and so we should not be judged harshly. **And he resumes** his prayer **from where he stopped.**[H]

HALAKHA

One who was standing in prayer, and saliva happened to accumulate in his mouth – הָיָה עוֹמֵד בַּתְּפִילָּה וְנִזְדַּמֵּן לוֹ רוֹק: It is prohibited to spit while praying. If saliva nevertheless accumulates, he should absorb it in his garment. If he is delicate, he should spit it behind him in accordance with the custom of Ravina (Rambam *Sefer Ahava, Hilkhot Tefilla* 4:11; *Shulḥan Arukh, Oraḥ Ḥayyim* 97:2).

One who was standing in prayer and sneezed from below – הָיָה עוֹמֵד בִּתְפִלָּה וְנִתְעַטֵּשׁ: One who was standing in prayer and broke wind must wait until the odor dissipates and only then resume his prayer from the point that he stopped. If one feels that he is about to break wind, he distances himself four cubits from where he was standing, and after breaking wind waits until the odor dissipates before reciting: Master of the universe, You have formed us with many orifices and cavities; our disgrace and shame in life are clear and evident before You, as is our destiny with maggots and worms. Only then does he return to the place that he had been standing and resume his prayer. The Rema notes that this applies specifically to one who is praying at home; however, one praying in public need neither distance himself nor recite Master of the universe, etc., as that would exacerbate his embarrassment. Rather, the custom is that he waits until the odor dissipates and resumes his prayer (Rambam *Sefer Ahava, Hilkhot Tefilla* 4:11–12; *Shulḥan Arukh, Oraḥ Ḥayyim* 103:1–2 and in the comment of the Rema).

Manners during prayer – נִימוּס בִּשְׁעַת הַתְּפִילָּה: It is prohibited to belch or yawn while praying. If one yawns involuntarily, he covers his mouth with his hand. He should not place his hand on his chin as that is the conceit of the arrogant (in accordance with the Rif's explanation of the Gemara; *Shulḥan Arukh, Oraḥ Ḥayyim* 97:1 and the comment of the Rema).

NOTES

Anyone who ascends from Babylonia to Eretz Yisrael – כָּל הָעוֹלֶה מִבָּבֶל לְאֶרֶץ יִשְׂרָאֵל: Apparently even according to Rav Yehuda this prohibition, which is unique to Babylonia, does not apply while the Temple is standing, for then there is clearly a mitzva to immigrate to the land of Israel and fulfill the mitzvot that are connected with the land of Israel, as did Hillel the Elder. However, Rav Yehuda maintained that after the destruction of the Temple it was forbidden to leave Babylonia (Rabbi Yosef Ḥanina Meizlish).

אָמַר לֵיהּ: אִילּוּ לֹא בָּאתִי אֶלָּא לִשְׁמוֹעַ דָּבָר זֶה – דַּיִּי.

Rabbi Abba **said to him: Had I only come** to the assembly of the Sages **to hear this teaching, it would have been sufficient for me.**

תָּנוּ רַבָּנַן: הָיָה יָשֵׁן בְּטַלִּיתוֹ וְאֵינוֹ יָכוֹל לְהוֹצִיא אֶת רֹאשׁוֹ מִפְּנֵי הַצִּנָּה – חוֹצֵץ בְּטַלִּיתוֹ עַל צַוָּארוֹ וְקוֹרֵא קְרִיאַת שְׁמַע. וְיֵשׁ אוֹמְרִים: עַל לִבּוֹ.

The Sages taught: One who **was sleeping** unclothed, but was covered **with his garment, and he is unable to stick his head out** from under the garment **because of the cold,** may **form a barrier with his garment at his neck and recite *Shema*** in bed. **And some say:** He must form a barrier with his garment **at his heart.**

וְתַנָּא קַמָּא – הֲרֵי לִבּוֹ רוֹאֶה אֶת הָעֶרְוָה! קָסָבַר: לִבּוֹ רוֹאֶה אֶת הָעֶרְוָה מוּתָּר.

The Gemara asks: **And** according to **the first *tanna*,** shouldn't he be prohibited from reciting *Shema* because **his heart sees** his **nakedness,** as there is no barrier between them? The Gemara responds: Indeed, the first *tanna* **holds that** when **one's heart sees** his **nakedness, it is permitted** to recite *Shema*, and a barrier is only necessary to separate between his mouth and his nakedness.

אָמַר רַב הוּנָא אָמַר רַבִּי יוֹחָנָן: הָיָה מְהַלֵּךְ בַּמְּבוֹאוֹת הַמְטוּנָּפוֹת – מַנִּיחַ יָדוֹ עַל פִּיו וְקוֹרֵא קְרִיאַת שְׁמַע. אָמַר לֵיהּ רַב חִסְדָּא: הָאֱלֹהִים! אִם אֲמַרָהּ לִי רַבִּי יוֹחָנָן בְּפוּמֵּיהּ – לֹא צַיֵּיתְנָא לֵיהּ.

Rav Huna said that **Rabbi Yoḥanan said: One who was walking in alleyways filthy** with human excrement and he must recite *Shema*, **he places his hand over his mouth and recites *Shema*. Rav Ḥisda said to him: By God!** Even **if Rabbi Yoḥanan had said it to me** directly, **with his own mouth, I would not have obeyed him.**[N]

אִיכָּא דְּאָמְרִי, אָמַר רַבָּה בַּר בַּר חָנָה אָמַר רַבִּי יְהוֹשֻׁעַ בֶּן לֵוִי: הָיָה מְהַלֵּךְ בַּמְּבוֹאוֹת הַמְטוּנָּפוֹת – מַנִּיחַ יָדוֹ עַל פִּיו וְקוֹרֵא קְרִיאַת שְׁמַע. אָמַר לֵיהּ רַב חִסְדָּא: הָאֱלֹהִים! אִם אֲמָרָהּ לִי רַבִּי יְהוֹשֻׁעַ בֶּן לֵוִי בְּפוּמֵּיהּ – לֹא צַיֵּיתְנָא לֵיהּ.

Some say this *halakha*: **Rabba bar bar Ḥana said** that **Rabbi Yehoshua ben Levi said: One who was walking in alleyways filthy** with human excrement and he must recite *Shema*, **he places his hand over his mouth and recites *Shema*. Rav Ḥisda said to him: By God!** Even **if Rabbi Yehoshua ben Levi had said it to me** directly, **with his own mouth, I would not have obeyed him.**

וּמִי אָמַר רַב הוּנָא הָכִי? וְהָאָמַר רַב הוּנָא: תַּלְמִיד חָכָם אָסוּר לוֹ לַעֲמוֹד בִּמְקוֹם הַטִּנּוֹפֶת – לְפִי שֶׁאִי אֶפְשָׁר לוֹ לַעֲמוֹד בְּלִי הִרְהוּר תּוֹרָה! לָא קַשְׁיָא, כָּאן – בְּעוֹמֵד, כָּאן – בִּמְהַלֵּךְ.

The Gemara challenges this: **Did Rav Huna** really **say that? Didn't Rav Huna say: A Torah scholar is prohibited from standing in a place of filth,**[H] **as he is unable to stand without contemplating Torah,** and uttering *Shema* orally is graver than mere contemplation. The Gemara responds: This **is not difficult; here,** Rav Huna prohibited contemplating Torah **in** a case where one is **standing** in a place of filth, while **here** he permitted to recite *Shema* **in** a case where one is **walking** through a place of filth.

וּמִי אָמַר רַבִּי יוֹחָנָן הָכִי? וְהָאָמַר רַבָּה בַּר בַּר חָנָה אָמַר רַבִּי יוֹחָנָן: בְּכָל מָקוֹם מוּתָּר לְהַרְהֵר בְּדִבְרֵי תוֹרָה – חוּץ מִבֵּית הַמֶּרְחָץ וּמִבֵּית הַכִּסֵּא. וְכִי תֵּימָא, הָכָא נַמִי, כָּאן בְּעוֹמֵד כָּאן בִּמְהַלֵּךְ; אִינִי?! וְהָא רַבִּי אַבָּהוּ הֲוָה קָא אָזֵיל בַּתְרֵיהּ דְּרַבִּי יוֹחָנָן, וַהֲוָה קָא קָרֵי קְרִיאַת שְׁמַע, כִּי מְטָא בַּמְּבוֹאוֹת הַמְטוּנָּפוֹת אִשְׁתִּיק. אָמַר לֵיהּ לְרַבִּי יוֹחָנָן: לְהֵיכָן אַהֲדַר? אָמַר לֵיהּ: אִם שָׁהִיתָ כְּדֵי לִגְמוֹר אֶת כּוּלָּהּ – חֲזוֹר לָרֹאשׁ!

The Gemara asks: **Did Rabbi Yoḥanan** really **say that? Didn't Rabba bar bar Ḥana say** that **Rabbi Yoḥanan said: One is permitted to contemplate matters of Torah everywhere, except**[H] **the bathhouse**[B] **and the bathroom?** Consequently, it is prohibited to even contemplate Torah in a place of filth. **And if you say: Here, too,** there is a distinction between the two cases, **here,** Rabbi Yoḥanan prohibited contemplating Torah **in** a case where one is **standing; here,** Rabbi Yoḥanan permitted to recite *Shema* **in** a case where one is **walking, is that so? Wasn't Rabbi Abbahu walking after Rabbi Yoḥanan and reciting *Shema*,** and **when he reached a filthy alleyway he fell silent** and stopped reciting *Shema*. When they emerged, Rabbi Abbahu **said to Rabbi Yoḥanan: To where** in *Shema* **should I return** and resume reciting it? Rabbi Yoḥanan **said to him: If you delayed** continuing *Shema* for an interval **sufficient to complete the entire** *Shema*, **return to the beginning** and recite it from there. From the fact that Rabbi Yoḥanan did not admonish him for interrupting his recitation, apparently he, too, prohibits reciting *Shema* while walking through a filthy alleyway.

הָכִי קָאָמַר לֵיהּ: לְדִידִי – לָא סְבִירָא לִי, לְדִידָךְ דִּסְבִירָא לָךְ – אִם שָׁהִיתָ כְּדֵי לִגְמוֹר אֶת כּוּלָּהּ חֲזוֹר לָרֹאשׁ.

The Gemara responds: This is not a proof, as **he says to him as follows: I do not hold** that one must interrupt the recitation of *Shema* in this case, but **for you, who holds** that one must, **if you delayed** *Shema* for an interval **sufficient to complete the entire** *Shema*, **return to the beginning** and recite it from there.

תַּנְיָא כְּוָתֵיהּ דְּרַב הוּנָא, תַּנְיָא כְּוָתֵיהּ דְּרַב חִסְדָּא. תַּנְיָא כְּוָתֵיהּ דְּרַב הוּנָא: הַמְהַלֵּךְ בַּמְּבוֹאוֹת הַמְטוּנָּפוֹת – מַנִּיחַ יָדוֹ עַל פִּיו וְיִקְרָא קְרִיאַת שְׁמַע. תַּנְיָא כְּוָתֵיהּ דְּרַב חִסְדָּא: הָיָה מְהַלֵּךְ בַּמְּבוֹאוֹת הַמְטוּנָּפוֹת – לֹא יִקְרָא קְרִיאַת שְׁמַע; וְלֹא עוֹד אֶלָּא שֶׁאִם הָיָה קוֹרֵא וּבָא – פּוֹסֵק.

The Gemara cites tannaitic sources to corroborate both the lenient and the stringent opinions. **It was taught** in a *baraita* **in accordance with** the opinion of **Rav Huna: One who was walking in filthy alleyways places his hand over his mouth and recites *Shema*. It was taught** in a *baraita* **in accordance with** the opinion of **Rav Ḥisda: One who was walking in filthy alleyways may not recite *Shema*.**[H] **Furthermore, if he was in the course of reciting** *Shema* when he reached a filthy alleyway, **he stops** his recitation at that point.

NOTES

The approaches of Rav Huna and Rav Ḥisda – שִׁיטַת רַב הוּנָא וְרַב חִסְדָּא: The differences in approach between Rav Huna and Rav Ḥisda appear to parallel those that were stated above with regard to their disagreement about prayer in the place of nakedness or filth. According to Rav Huna, cleanliness of the mouth is paramount. As a result, if one's mouth is covered it is acceptable. Rav Ḥisda, however, citing the verse: "All of my bones shall say," prohibits reciting *Shema* when the body is in a filthy place (*Kehillat Ya'akov*).

HALAKHA

A Torah scholar is prohibited from standing in a place of filth – תַּלְמִיד חָכָם אָסוּר לוֹ לַעֲמוֹד בִּמְקוֹם הַטִּנּוֹפֶת: One may not engage in matters of Torah in a filthy place. Therefore, a Torah scholar, whose mind is always contemplating matters of Torah, may not stand there (*Shulḥan Arukh, Yoreh De'a* 246:26 in the comment of the Rema).

One is permitted to contemplate matters of Torah everywhere, except… – בְּכָל מָקוֹם מוּתָּר לְהַרְהֵר בְּדִבְרֵי תוֹרָה חוּץ וכו׳: One is prohibited from even contemplating matters of Torah in the bathroom or bathhouse, or in any filthy place in which there is feces and the like (Rambam *Sefer Ahava, Hilkhot Keriat Shema* 3:4; *Shulḥan Arukh, Oraḥ Ḥayyim* 85:2).

One who was walking in filthy alleyways may not recite *Shema* – הָיָה מְהַלֵּךְ בַּמְּבוֹאוֹת הַמְטוּנָּפוֹת לֹא יִקְרָא קְרִיאַת שְׁמַע: One is prohibited from reciting *Shema* in a filthy alleyway. If one must pass through a place of that sort while reciting *Shema*, he pauses and only resumes reciting it after emerging from the alleyway. Some say that when he emerges, he must recite it from the beginning (Rema). Even though Rav Huna was more prominent than Rav Ḥisda, the *halakha* is ruled in accordance with Rav Ḥisda's more stringent opinion since most of the amoraic statements cited in the Gemara were based upon it (Rambam *Sefer Ahava, Hilkhot Keriat Shema* 3:14; *Shulḥan Arukh, Oraḥ Ḥayyim* 85:1).

BACKGROUND

Bathhouse – בֵּית הַמֶּרְחָץ:

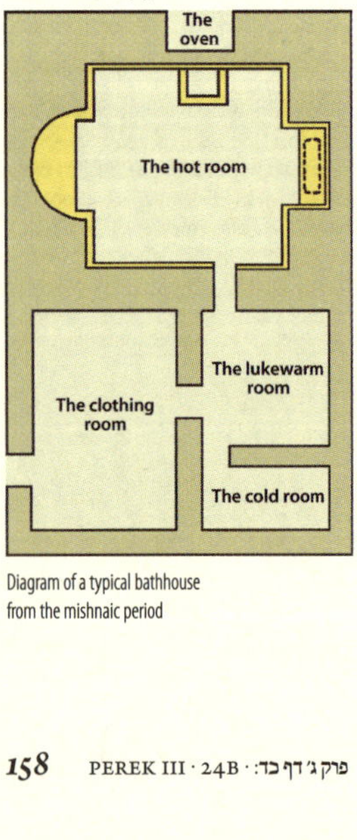

Diagram of a typical bathhouse from the mishnaic period

לא פסק מאי? – אמר רבי מיאשה בר בריה דרבי יהושע בן לוי: עליו הכתוב אומר "וגם אני נתתי להם חקים לא טובים ומשפטים לא יחיו בהם".

The Gemara asks: If **one did not stop, what** is his status? **Rabbi Meyasha, son of the son of Rabbi Yehoshua ben Levi,**[P] **said: Of him the verse says: "Moreover, I gave them statutes that were not good and laws by which they could not live"** (Ezekiel 20:25), as in this case following these statutes and laws led to sin, not to mitzva.

רב אסי אמר: "הוי מושכי העון בחבלי השוא". רב אדא בר אהבה אמר מהכא: "כי דבר ה' בזה".

Rav Asi said that this is derived from the verse: **"Woe to those who draw iniquity with cords of vanity"** (Isaiah 5:18), meaning that this man brings sin upon himself for naught. **Rav Adda bar Ahava said** it is derived **from here: "For he has shown contempt for the word of the Lord"** (Numbers 15:31), meaning that uttering God's word in a place of filth shows contempt for the Lord.

ואם פסק מה שכרו? אמר רבי אבהו עליו הכתוב אומר: "ובדבר הזה תאריכו ימים".

The Gemara asks: **And if he stopped** his recitation, **what is his reward? Rabbi Abbahu said: Of him the verse says: "And it is through this matter that you will prolong your days"** (Deuteronomy 32:47), meaning that by being careful with one's speech one merits longevity.

אמר רב הונא: היתה טליתו חגורה לו על מתניו – מותר לקרות קריאת שמע. תניא נמי הכי: היתה טליתו, של בגד ושל עור ושל שק, חגורה על מתניו – מותר לקרות קריאת שמע;

Rav Huna said: One whose **garment was tied around his waist,** even if he was bare above the waist, **is permitted to recite *Shema*.** Indeed, **that** opinion **was also taught** in a *baraita*: **One** whose **garment** made **of cloth, of leather, of sack**[N] or of any other material **was strapped around his waist, he is permitted to recite *Shema*.**

PERSONALITIES

Rabbi Meyasha, son of the son of Rabbi Yehoshua ben Levi – רבי מיאשה בר בריה דרבי יהושע בן לוי: Based on his age and the Sages with whom he associated, apparently, Rabbi Meyasha was among the students of Rabbi Yoḥanan; however, he clearly learned most of his Torah from his grandfather, in whose name he often cites his teachings. Rabbi Meyasha did not live a long life, as he died during his grandfather's lifetime after a protracted illness. It is precisely the fact that so young a scholar was privileged to have halakhic statements cited in his name in both the Babylonian and the Jerusalem Talmuds as well as in midrashic literature that underscores his greatness.

NOTES

A garment of cloth, of leather, of sack – של בגד ושל עור ושל שק: This list begins with an ordinary garment, moves on to leather which is also appropriate, and ends with sackcloth, which is only barely considered suitable human clothing, in which, nevertheless, one is permitted to recite *Shema* (*Adderet Eliyahu*).

Perek **III**
Daf **25** Amud **a**

אבל לתפלה – עד שיכסה את לבו.

However, for prayer, one may not recite it **until he covers his heart,** because in prayer he addresses God directly and he must dress accordingly.[H]

ואמר רב הונא: שכח ונכנס בתפילין לבית הכסא – מניח ידו עליהן עד שיגמור. עד שיגמור סלקא דעתך?! – אלא כדאמר רב נחמן בר יצחק: עד שיגמור עמוד ראשון. ולפסוק לאלתר וליקום! – משום דרבן שמעון בן גמליאל. דתניא, רבן שמעון בן גמליאל אומר: עמוד החוזר מביא את האדם לידי הדרוקן, סילון החוזר – מביא את האדם לידי ירקון.

And Rav Huna said: One who **forgot and entered the bathroom while donning phylacteries**[H] **places his hand on them until he finishes.** The Gemara wonders: **Does it enter your mind** that he can do so **until he is finished? Rather, as Rav Naḥman bar Yitzḥak said: Until he finishes** discharging **the first mass** of feces, at which point he can step out and remove his phylacteries. The Gemara asks: **Let him stop immediately** when he realizes that he is donning phylacteries **and stand** and step out. The Gemara replies: He cannot do so **because of** the statement of **Rabban Shimon ben Gamliel. As it was taught** in a *baraita*: **A mass** of feces **that is held back** without having been discharged **causes a person** to suffer **from dropsy** [*hidrokan*], **while a stream** of urine **that is held back causes a person** to suffer **from jaundice** [*yerakon*]. Since there is potential danger, the Sages did not require him to step out.

איתמר: צואה על בשרו, או ידו מונחת בבית הכסא; רב הונא אמר: מותר לקרות קריאת שמע; רב חסדא אמר: אסור לקרות קריאת שמע. אמר רבא: מאי טעמא דרב הונא – דכתיב "כל הנשמה תהלל יה הללויה".

It was stated that the Sages disagreed with regard to one who had **fecal matter on his skin**[H] **or** whose **hand,** but not the rest of his body, **was placed inside the bathroom.** Under those circumstances, **Rav Huna said:** He is **permitted to recite *Shema*. Rav Ḥisda said: He is prohibited from reciting *Shema*. Rava said: What is the reason for Rav Huna's** opinion? **As it is written: "Let every soul [*neshama*] praise the Lord; Halleluya"** (Psalms 150:6), which he interprets as "Let everything that has breath" [*neshima*]. As long as the mouth with which one recites praise is in a place of purity, the location of the other limbs of his body is irrelevant.

ורב חסדא אמר: אסור לקרות קריאת שמע. מאי טעמא דרב חסדא – דכתיב "כל עצמותי תאמרנה ה' מי כמוך".

And Rav Ḥisda said: He is prohibited from reciting *Shema*. What is the reason for Rav Ḥisda's opinion? **As it is written: "All of my bones shall say: Lord, who is like You"** (Psalms 35:10). Since this praise is undertaken with one's entire body, he may not recite *Shema* even if just one limb is not appropriately clean.

HALAKHA

For prayer until he covers his heart – לתפלה עד שיכסה את לבו: One who has a garment strapped around his waist, even if it covers his nakedness and serves as a barrier between his nakedness and his heart, is prohibited from praying until he covers his entire body (*Mishna Berura*). If he failed to cover himself or, due to circumstances beyond his control, he had nothing with which to cover himself, and he nevertheless prayed, he fulfilled his obligation because his nakedness was covered (Rambam *Sefer Ahava, Hilkhot Tefilla* 4:7; *Shulḥan Arukh, Oraḥ Ḥayyim* 74:6, 91:1).

One who forgot and entered the bathroom while donning phylacteries – שכח ונכנס בתפילין לבית הכסא: One who forgot that his phylacteries were on his head and began to defecate, covers them with his hand until he has passed the first mass of feces, after which he must emerge and remove them before returning to the bathroom. He dons his phylacteries only after cleaning himself (Rambam *Sefer Ahava, Hilkhot Tefillin Mezuza VeSefer Torah* 4:20; *Shulḥan Arukh, Oraḥ Ḥayyim* 43:8).

One who had fecal matter on his skin – צואה על בשרו: With regard to one who has fecal matter on his skin and seeks to recite *Shema*, there is a dispute between the authorities. Some ruled that he is permitted to do so as per the opinion of Rav Huna (Rif, Rosh, Rabbeinu Yona) and some ruled that it is prohibited as per the opinion of Rav Ḥisda (Rambam, *Or Zarua*). Even those who ruled leniently only did so if the fecal matter was covered and gave off no foul odor. One should adopt the more stringent ruling in all but exigent circumstances (Rambam *Sefer Ahava, Hilkhot Keriat Shema* 3:11; *Shulḥan Arukh, Oraḥ Ḥayyim* 76:4).

אִתְּמַר: רֵיחַ רַע שֶׁיֵּשׁ לוֹ עִיקָּר, רַב הוּנָא אָמַר: מַרְחִיק אַרְבַּע אַמּוֹת וְקוֹרֵא קְרִיאַת שְׁמַע; וְרַב חִסְדָּא אָמַר: מַרְחִיק אַרְבַּע אַמּוֹת מִמָּקוֹם שֶׁפָּסַק הָרֵיחַ, וְקוֹרֵא קְרִיאַת שְׁמַע.

It was said that the Sages disagreed over a similar issue: What is the legal status of **a foul odor that** emanates from a visible **source?**[H] **Rav Huna said: He distances himself four cubits** from the source of the odor **and recites *Shema*. And Rav Ḥisda said:** The source is irrelevant; **he distances himself four cubits from the place that the odor ceased and recites *Shema*.**

תַּנְיָא כְּוָתֵיהּ דְּרַב חִסְדָּא: לֹא יִקְרָא אָדָם קְרִיאַת שְׁמַע, לֹא כְּנֶגֶד צוֹאַת אָדָם וְלֹא כְּנֶגֶד צוֹאַת כְּלָבִים, וְלֹא כְּנֶגֶד צוֹאַת חֲזִירִים, וְלֹא כְּנֶגֶד צוֹאַת תַּרְנְגוֹלִים, וְלֹא כְּנֶגֶד צוֹאַת אַשְׁפָּה שֶׁרֵיחָהּ רַע; וְאִם הָיָה מָקוֹם גָּבוֹהַּ עֲשָׂרָה טְפָחִים אוֹ נָמוּךְ עֲשָׂרָה טְפָחִים – יוֹשֵׁב בְּצִדּוֹ וְקוֹרֵא קְרִיאַת שְׁמַע, וְאִם לָאו – מַרְחִיק מִמֶּנּוּ מְלוֹא עֵינָיו; וְכֵן לִתְפִלָּה. רֵיחַ רַע שֶׁיֵּשׁ לוֹ עִיקָּר – מַרְחִיק אַרְבַּע אַמּוֹת מִמְּקוֹם הָרֵיחַ, וְקוֹרֵא קְרִיאַת שְׁמַע.

The Gemara notes that **it was taught in** a *baraita* **in accordance with** the opinion of **Rav Ḥisda: A person may not recite *Shema* opposite human excrement, dog excrement, pig excrement,**[H] **chicken excrement, a foul-smelling dung-heap**[H] or anything repulsive. **However, if** the filth **were in a place ten handbreadths above**[H] **or ten handbreadths below** him, **he may sit alongside it and recite *Shema*,** as a height disparity of ten handbreadths renders it a separate domain. **And if** the filth were **not** ten handbreadths above or below him, **he must distance himself** until it remains beyond **his range of vision. And the same is true of prayer.**[H] However, from **a foul odor with** a visible **source, he distances himself four cubits from the place** that **the odor** ceased **and recites *Shema*.**

אָמַר רָבָא, לֵית הִלְכְתָא כִּי הָא מַתְנִיתָא בְּכָל הָנֵי שְׁמַעְתָּתָא אֶלָּא כִּי הָא דְּתַנְיָא: לֹא יִקְרָא אָדָם קְרִיאַת שְׁמַע לֹא כְּנֶגֶד צוֹאַת אָדָם וְלֹא כְּנֶגֶד צוֹאַת חֲזִירִים וְלֹא כְּנֶגֶד צוֹאַת כְּלָבִים בִּזְמַן שֶׁנָּתַן עוֹרוֹת לְתוֹכָן.

Rava said: The *halakha* is not in accordance with this *baraita* in all of these rulings, but **rather in accordance with that which** was **taught** in another *baraita*: **One may neither recite *Shema* opposite human excrement** under all circumstances, **nor opposite pig excrement, nor opposite dog excrement into which skins had been placed** for tanning, but other materials do not defile the venue of prayer.

בְּעוֹ מִינֵּיהּ מֵרַב שֵׁשֶׁת: רֵיחַ רַע שֶׁאֵין לוֹ עִיקָּר מַהוּ? אָמַר לְהוּ: אֲתוֹ חֲזוֹ הָנֵי צִיפֵּי דְּבֵי רַב, דְּהָנֵי גָּנוּ וְהָנֵי גָּרְסִי. וְהָנֵי מִילֵּי – בְּדִבְרֵי תוֹרָה, אֲבָל בִּקְרִיאַת שְׁמַע – לֹא; וְדִבְרֵי תוֹרָה נַמִּי לֹא אֲמַרַן אֶלָּא דְּחַבְרֵיהּ, אֲבָל דִּידֵיהּ – לֹא.

They raised a dilemma before Rav Sheshet: What is the legal status of **a foul odor that has no** visible **source,**[H] e.g., flatulence? **He said to them: Come and see these mats in the study hall, as these** students **are sleeping** on them **and these** other students **are studying,** and they are not concerned about foul odors. **However, this only applies to Torah study** because there is no alternative, **but not to the recitation of *Shema*. And** with regard **to Torah study we said** that it is permitted **only** when the odor originated **with another, but not** when it originated **with himself.**

אִתְּמַר, צוֹאָה עוֹבֶרֶת; אַבַּיֵי אָמַר: מוּתָּר לִקְרוֹת קְרִיאַת שְׁמַע; רָבָא אָמַר: אָסוּר לִקְרוֹת קְרִיאַת שְׁמַע.

It was stated that the Sages disagreed over a parallel issue: What is the law with regard to **feces passing**[H] before him, being moved from place to place? **Abaye stated: One is permitted to recite *Shema*** opposite it, **while Rava said: One is forbidden to recite *Shema*** opposite it.

אָמַר אַבַּיֵי: מְנָא אָמִינָא לַהּ – דִּתְנַן: הַטָּמֵא עוֹמֵד תַּחַת הָאִילָן וְהַטָּהוֹר עוֹבֵר – טָמֵא, טָהוֹר עוֹמֵד תַּחַת הָאִילָן וְטָמֵא עוֹבֵר – טָהוֹר, וְאִם עָמַד – טָמֵא; וְכֵן בְּאֶבֶן הַמְנוּגַּעַת.

Abaye said: From where do I say this *halakha*? I say this on the basis of what **we learned** in a mishna: One who is afflicted with biblical leprosy renders the area beneath any covering under which he is located ritually impure. In a case where **the ritually impure** leper **is standing under** the branches of **a tree and a ritually pure** person **passes** under the branches of that same tree, the pure person **is** rendered **impure,** as the entire area under that covering is impure. However, if the **pure person is standing under the tree and the impure** leper **passes,**[HN] **he** remains **pure. And if** the leper **stopped** under the tree, the pure person is immediately rendered **impure. The same is true with regard to a stone afflicted** with biblical leprosy (see Leviticus 14), in that if it is merely being moved from place to place, it does not cause impurity. The upshot is that impurity is only disseminated in all directions when the source of the impurity is stationary.

וְרָבָא אָמַר לָךְ: הָתָם – בִּקְבִיעוּתָא תַּלְיָא מִילְּתָא, דִּכְתִיב: ״בָּדָד יֵשֵׁב מִחוּץ לַמַּחֲנֶה מוֹשָׁבוֹ״, הָכָא: ״וְהָיָה מַחֲנֶיךָ קָדוֹשׁ״ אָמַר רַחֲמָנָא, וְהָא לֵיכָּא.

And Rava could have **said to you: There,** in the case of leprosy, **it is contingent upon the permanence** of the place, **as** with regard to the leper **it is written: "He shall dwell alone; outside the camp shall his dwelling be"** (Leviticus 13:46). His impurity is in his permanent dwelling-place. **Here,** with regard to the obligation to distance oneself from something repulsive, **the Torah stated** the principle: **"And your camp shall be holy"** (Deuteronomy 23:15), **and there is no** holiness in those circumstances.

HALAKHA

A foul odor that has a source – רֵיחַ רַע שֶׁיֵּשׁ לוֹ עִיקָּר: One who seeks to recite *Shema* must distance himself four cubits from the source of a foul odor. If he is still able to smell the odor, he must distance himself until he can no longer smell the foul odor, in accordance with the opinion of Rav Ḥisda, which is supported by the *baraita* (Rambam *Sefer Ahava, Hilkhot Keriat Shema* 3:12 and in the comment of the Ra'avad, who cites Rav Hai Gaon and disagrees with the Rambam).

Dog excrement, pig excrement – צוֹאַת כְּלָבִים...חֲזִירִים: The excrement of dogs and pigs; if one used them in processing animal skins or if they give off a foul odor, one must distance himself from them as he does from human excrement. If not, it is unnecessary, as per the *baraita* cited by Rava (Rambam *Sefer Ahava, Hilkhot Keriat Shema* 3:6; *Shulḥan Arukh, Oraḥ Ḥayyim* 79:4).

A foul-smelling dung-heap – צוֹאַת אַשְׁפָּה שֶׁרֵיחָהּ רַע: One is prohibited from reciting *Shema* opposite a foul-smelling dung-heap, in accordance with the *baraita* (*Shulḥan Arukh, Oraḥ Ḥayyim* 76:7).

If the filth were in a place ten handbreadths above – הָיָה מָקוֹם גָּבוֹהַּ עֲשָׂרָה טְפָחִים: If the excrement was ten handbreadths above or below the place where one was located, if it gave off no odor, according to the *Tur* who disagrees with Rabbeinu Yona, he is permitted to recite *Shema* there; as per the *baraita*. Some say that it is permitted even if it gave off a foul odor as the ten handbreadths are significant in terms of the odor as well. There are disputes with regard to other details as well; some say that in addition to being ten handbreadths above or below, it must rest on a surface that is four square handbreadths, which constitutes an independent domain (Rambam, *Eliyahu Rabba, Baḥ, Magen Avraham*) and others are lenient in that regard (Taz). There is also a dispute whether or not he is permitted to recite *Shema* in a case where the excrement is visible. Some hold that he may do so only in a case where it is not visible (Rashba; Rambam *Sefer Ahava, Hilkhot Keriat Shema* 3:9; *Shulḥan Arukh, Oraḥ Ḥayyim* 79:2).

And the same is true of prayer – וְכֵן לִתְפִלָּה: A place where one may not recite *Shema* one is also prohibited from reciting the *Amida* prayer (Rambam *Sefer Ahava, Hilkhot Tefilla* 4:8; *Shulḥan Arukh, Oraḥ Ḥayyim* 90:26).

A foul odor that has no visible source – רֵיחַ רַע שֶׁאֵין לוֹ עִיקָּר: One who broke wind and emitted a foul odor is prohibited from reciting *Shema* and studying Torah until the odor has dissipated. If the odor was emitted by another person, he is permitted to study Torah but prohibited to recite *Shema*, in accordance with the opinion of Rav Sheshet (Rambam *Sefer Ahava, Hilkhot Keriat Shema* 3:14).

Feces passing – צוֹאָה עוֹבֶרֶת: If excrement or a pig, even if it emerged from a river, was passing before him, one may not recite *Shema*. Some say that as long as it passes at a distance of four cubits, he may recite *Shema* (Rambam *Sefer Ahava, Hilkhot Keriat Shema* 3:13; *Shulḥan Arukh, Oraḥ Ḥayyim* 76:3).

Ritual impurity passing – טוּמְאָה עוֹבֶרֶת: If there was ritual impurity imparted by a leper under a tree and a ritually pure person passed under the tree, he becomes ritually impure. If a person was standing under a tree and the ritual impurity passed under that tree, he does not become ritually impure. If the ritual impurity came to a stop under the tree, he becomes ritually impure (Rambam, *Sefer Tahara, Hilkhot Tumat Tzara'at* 10:12).

NOTES

Ritual impurity passing – טוּמְאָה עוֹבֶרֶת: The laws concerning this type of ritual impurity are relevant to the impurity of the dead and the impurity of the leper as well. With regard to those impurities, in addition to being imparted by touch, it is also spread by means of a tent, i.e., a corpse or leper that is underneath an awning or a tent, the impurity fills that space. The related *halakhot* are quite detailed, in tractate *Oholot* and elsewhere, and include the requirement that the impurity is stable. If the source of impurity is not standing in one place, it does not impart impurity of the tent (see Rashi).

אָמַר רַב פַּפָּא: פִּי חֲזִיר כְּצוֹאָה עוֹבֶרֶת דָּמֵי. פְּשִׁיטָא! – לָא צְרִיכָא, אַף עַל גַּב דִּסְלֵיק מִנַּהֲרָא.

On this topic **Rav Pappa said: The mouth of a pig is like passing feces.** The Gemara asks: **That is obvious.** The Gemara replies: **No,** this *halakha* is only **necessary** to teach that **even though** the pig **emerged from the river** and one might assume that its mouth was thereby cleansed, it never becomes completely clean.

אָמַר רַב יְהוּדָה: סָפֵק צוֹאָה – אֲסוּרָה; סָפֵק מֵי רַגְלַיִם – מוּתָּרִים. אִיכָּא דְּאָמְרִי, אָמַר רַב יְהוּדָה: סָפֵק צוֹאָה, בַּבַּיִת – מוּתֶּרֶת, בָּאַשְׁפָּה – אֲסוּרָה; סָפֵק מֵי רַגְלַיִם – אֲפִילּוּ בָּאַשְׁפָּה נַמִי מוּתָּרִין.

Rav Yehuda said: If there is **uncertainty** as to the presence of **feces,** e.g., whether something is or is not feces, and therefore whether or not one is permitted to utter sacred matters in its presence, **it is prohibited** to do so. However, if there is **uncertainty** as to the presence of **urine,**[H] **it is permitted** to do so. **Some say** an alternative version of this. **Rav Yehuda said:** If there is **uncertainty** as to the presence of **feces, in the home** one may assume that there is no feces present and **it is permitted** to speak sacred matters, but if there is doubt as to the presences of feces **in the dung-heap** it is **forbidden** to do so. If there is **uncertainty** as to the presence of **urine,** however, **even in the dung-heap it is permitted** to do so.

סָבַר לָהּ כִּי הָא דְּרַב הַמְנוּנָא, דְּאָמַר רַב הַמְנוּנָא: לֹא אָסְרָה תּוֹרָה אֶלָּא כְּנֶגֶד עַמּוּד בִּלְבַד,

He holds in accordance with that which Rav Hamnuna said, **as Rav Hamnuna said: The Torah prohibited** the utterance of sacred matters **only opposite the stream** of urine.

וְכִדְרַבִּי יוֹנָתָן. דְּרַבִּי יוֹנָתָן רָמֵי: כְּתִיב ״וְיָד תִּהְיֶה לְךָ מִחוּץ לַמַּחֲנֶה וְיָצָאתָ שָׁמָּה חוּץ״, וּכְתִיב: ״וְיָתֵד תִּהְיֶה לְךָ וגו׳ וְכִסִּיתָ אֶת צֵאָתֶךָ״!

And in accordance with the opinion of **Rabbi Yonatan, as Rabbi Yonatan** raised a **contradiction** between two verses: On the one hand **it is written: "You shall also have a place outside the camp, to which you will go"** (Deuteronomy 23:13), meaning that one must exit the camp before attending to his bodily needs but there is no obligation to cover it; **and it is written** in another verse: **"And you shall have a spade** among your weapons; and when you ease yourself outside, you shall dig with it, and turn back **and cover your excrement"** (Deuteronomy 23:14), indicating a clear obligation to conceal one's excrement.

הָא כֵּיצַד – כָּאן בִּגְדוֹלִים, כָּאן בִּקְטַנִּים; אַלְמָא: קְטַנִּים לֹא אָסְרָה תּוֹרָה אֶלָּא כְּנֶגֶד עַמּוּד בִּלְבַד. הָא נְפוּל לְאַרְעָא – שְׁרֵי, וְרַבָּנַן הוּא דִּגְזַרוּ בְּהוּ, וְכִי גְּזַרוּ בְּהוּ רַבָּנַן – בְּוַדָּאָן, אֲבָל בִּסְפֵקָן לֹא גְּזַר.

He resolves this contradiction: **How is this** resolved? **Here,** where one is required to conceal his bodily needs, **it refers to feces; here,** where there is no requirement to conceal his bodily needs, **it refers to urine. Consequently,** with regard to **urine,** reciting *Shema* **was only prohibited by Torah law opposite the stream** of urine, **but once it has fallen to the ground, it is permitted. And the Sages are those who issued a decree with regard to** urine. **And when they issued a decree, it was only** in a case of **their certain** presence, **but** in a case of **their uncertain** presence, **they did not issue a decree.**

וּבְוַדָּאָן עַד כַּמָּה? אָמַר רַב יְהוּדָה אָמַר שְׁמוּאֵל: כָּל זְמַן שֶׁמְּטַפְּחִין; וְכֵן אָמַר רַבָּה בַּר בַּר חָנָה אָמַר רַבִּי יוֹחָנָן: כָּל זְמַן שֶׁמְּטַפְּחִין; וְכֵן אָמַר עוּלָּא: כָּל זְמַן שֶׁמְּטַפְּחִין. גְּנִיבָא מִשְּׁמֵיהּ דְּרַב אָמַר: כָּל זְמַן שֶׁרִשּׁוּמָן נִיכָּר.

The Gemara asks: **In a case of the certain** presence of urine, **until when** and in what state does its presence preclude one from uttering sacred matters? **Rav Yehuda said** that **Shmuel said: As long as** it is wet enough **to moisten** the hands of one who touches it. **And so too Rabba bar bar Ḥana said** that **Rabbi Yoḥanan said: As long as it moistens. And so too Ulla said: As long as it moistens. Geniva**[P] **in the name of Rav said:** It is forbidden **as long as its mark is apparent** on the ground.

אָמַר רַב יוֹסֵף: שָׁרֵא לֵיהּ מָרֵיהּ לִגְנִיבָא! הַשְׁתָּא צוֹאָה, אָמַר רַב יְהוּדָה אָמַר רַב: כֵּיוָן שֶׁקָּרְמוּ פָּנֶיהָ מוּתָּר, מֵי רַגְלַיִם מִיבַּעְיָא?!

Rav Yosef said: May God, **his Master, forgive Geniva,**[B] as Rav could have said no such thing. **Now,** in the case of **feces, Rav Yehuda said** that **Rav said: Once its surface has** dried sufficiently to form a **crust, one is permitted** to utter sacred matters opposite it; **is it necessary** to say that opposite **urine** it is permitted once it dries?

אָמַר לֵיהּ אַבָּיֵי: מַאי חָזֵית דְּסָמְכַתְּ אַהָא – סְמוֹךְ אַהָא! דְּאָמַר רַבָּה בַּר רַב הוּנָא אָמַר רַב: צוֹאָה, אֲפִילּוּ כְּחֶרֶס – אֲסוּרָה.

Abaye said to him: What did you see that led you to rely on that *halakha*? **Rely on this** *halakha*; **as Rabba bar Rav Huna said** that **Rav said:** Uttering sacred matters opposite **feces, even** if it is as dry **as earthenware, is prohibited.**

וְהֵיכִי דָּמֵי צוֹאָה כְּחֶרֶס? אָמַר רַבָּה בַּר בַּר חָנָה אָמַר רַבִּי יוֹחָנָן: כָּל זְמַן שֶׁזּוֹרְקָהּ וְאֵינָהּ נִפְרֶכֶת; וְאִיכָּא דְּאָמְרִי: כָּל זְמַן שֶׁגּוֹלְלָהּ וְאֵינָהּ נִפְרֶכֶת.

The Gemara asks: **What are the circumstances** of **feces like earthenware? Rabba bar bar Ḥana said** that **Rabbi Yoḥanan said: As long as one throws it and it does not crumble,** it is still considered moist. **And some say: As long as one** can **roll it** from place to place **and it does not crumble.**

אָמַר רָבִינָא: הֲוָה קָאֵימְנָא קַמֵּיהּ דְּרַב יְהוּדָה מִדִּיפְתִּי, חֲזָא צוֹאָה, אָמַר לִי: עַיֵּין אִי קָרְמוּ פָּנֶיהָ אִי לָא. אִיכָּא דְּאָמְרִי, הָכִי אָמַר לֵיהּ: עַיֵּין אִי מִפְּלְאֵי אִפְּלוּיֵי.

Ravina said: I was standing before Rav Yehuda of Difti when **he saw feces. He said to me: Examine** it and see **whether or not its surface** has dried sufficiently to form a **crust. Some say** that **he said to him as follows: Examine** it and see **if it is cracked,** as only then is it considered dry.

HALAKHA

Uncertainty as to the presence of feces…uncertainty as to the presence of urine – סָפֵק צוֹאָה...סָפֵק מֵי רַגְלַיִם: If there is uncertainty with regard to the presence of feces, if he is in the house, he may recite *Shema*, if he is in the dung-heap, he may not recite *Shema*. If there is uncertainty with regard to the presence of urine, he may recite *Shema* everywhere, as the Sages did not issue a decree in that case (Rambam *Sefer Ahava, Hilkhot Keriat Shema* 3:15; *Shulḥan Arukh, Oraḥ Ḥayyim* 76:7).

PERSONALITIES

Geniva – גְּנִיבָא: A member of the first and second generations of *amora'im* in Babylonia, Geniva was one of the more colorful characters of the era. A Sage of great stature, he was often visited in his home by the *amora*, Rav, in whose name he cited many of his Torah statements. The second generation of *amora'im* treated his teachings with respect. While Geniva was a wealthy and powerful man, at the same time he was quarrelsome and contentious. Though the details of the incident are unclear, it is known that he had a serious dispute with the Exilarch at the time, Mar Ukva, and it was only by virtue of Mar Ukva's moderation and judiciousness that the affair did not come before the Persian authorities. Ultimately, Geniva was charged with another offense, perhaps plotting against the crown, and was sentenced to death by the authorities. The Sages of the following (third) generation cite his teachings, always appreciating his Torah while disapproving of his conduct.

BACKGROUND

May his Master forgive him – שָׁרֵא לֵיהּ מָרֵיהּ: Though this expression does not outwardly convey an element of condemnation, it still hints to the serious reprobation of a Sage whose statements or actions are inappropriate. It has been said that when God's name is desecrated through a Sage's actions, it is said of that Sage: May his Master forgive him.

HALAKHA

Feces as dry as earthenware – צוֹאָה כְּחֶרֶס: Excrement that dried to the extent that it crumbles when it is rolled, assumes the legal status of dust. Some say that it assumes that legal status only if it crumbles when it is thrown, as per the second, more stringent, version of Rabbi Yoḥanan's statement (Rambam *Sefer Ahava, Hilkhot Keriat Shema* 3:7; *Shulḥan Arukh, Oraḥ Ḥayyim* 82:1).

And urine, as long as it moistens – וּמֵי רַגְלַיִם כָּל זְמַן שֶׁמַּטְפִּיחִין: It is prohibited to recite *Shema* opposite urine that was absorbed into the ground but remained moist. This is only true if it remained moist enough to moisten another object (Rema; Rambam *Sefer Ahava, Hilkhot Keriat Shema* 3:7; *Shulḥan Arukh, Oraḥ Ḥayyim* 82:2).

BACKGROUND

No inference can be deduced from this – מֵהָא לֵיכָּא לְמִשְׁמַע מִינָּהּ: This expression, found throughout the Gemara, concludes the refutation of an inference [*diyuk*]. Inference in the Gemara is a method of interpretation used to draw conclusions from tannaitic sources. According to this method, inferences may be drawn not only from what is explicitly stated in a mishna or *baraita*, but also from what is left unsaid. The rejection of the inference is effected by illustrating that another part of the same mishna or *baraita* can lead to the opposite conclusion. In that case the Gemara concludes: No inference can be deduced from this, indicating that this mishna or *baraita* was not composed in a manner that lends itself to drawing conclusions by means of inference. Rather, it is to be accepted as written, without reading anything further into it.

מאי הוי עלה? איתמר: צואה כחרס; אמימר אמר: אסורה; ומר זוטרא אמר: מותרת. אמר רבא, הלכתא: צואה כחרס אסורה, ומי רגלים כל זמן שמטפיחין.

Since several opinions were expressed on the subject, the Gemara asks: **What** halakhic conclusion was reached **about this? It was stated** that the *halakha* is subject to dispute: Reciting sacred matters opposite **feces** as dry **as earthenware;**[H] **Ameimar said: It is prohibited, and Mar Zutra said: It is permitted. Rava said that the *halakha* is:** Opposite **feces** as dry **as earthenware it is prohibited, and** opposite **urine,** it is prohibited **as long as it moistens.**[H]

מיתיבי: מי רגלים כל זמן שמטפיחין – אסורין, נבלעו או יבשו – מותרים; מאי לאו "נבלעו" דומיא "דיבשו", מה יבשו – דאין רשומן ניכר, אף נבלעו – דאין רשומן ניכר, הא רשומן ניכר – אסור, אף על גב דאין מטפיחין!

The Gemara **raises an objection** based on what was taught in a *baraita*: **Urine, as long as it moistens it is prohibited. If it was absorbed** into the ground **or dried** in place, **it is permitted. What, is** urine that was **absorbed not similar** to urine that **dried? Just as when it dries its mark is no** longer **apparent, so too when it is absorbed, its mark is no** longer **apparent** and then it is permissible. **But** when **its mark is apparent, it is prohibited, even though it no longer moistens.**

ולטעמיך, אימא רישא: כל זמן שמטפיחין הוא דאסור, הא רשומן ניכר – שרי! – אלא: מהא ליכא למשמע מינה.

The Gemara raises a difficulty to counter this: **And according to your reasoning, say the first clause: As long as it moistens it is prohibited,** from which one can infer: **But if** it does not moisten, but **its mark is apparent, it is permitted. Rather, no** inference beyond its basic meaning **can be deduced from this**[B] *baraita*, as the inferences are contradictory.

לימא כתנאי: כלי שנשפכו ממנו מי רגלים – אסור לקרות קריאת שמע כנגדו, ומי רגלים עצמן שנשפכו, נבלעו – מותר, לא נבלעו – אסור. רבי יוסי אומר: כל זמן שמטפיחין.

The Gemara notes: **Let us say** that this is **parallel to a** dispute between **the *tanna'im*,** as it was taught a *baraita*: **It is forbidden to recite *Shema* opposite a vessel from which urine was poured. However, the urine itself that was poured,** if it **was absorbed it is permitted;** if it **was not absorbed, it is prohibited. Rabbi Yosei** disagrees and **says:** It is prohibited **as long as it moistens.**

מאי "נבלעו" ומאי "לא נבלעו" דקאמר תנא קמא? אילימא נבלעו – דאין מטפיחין, לא נבלעו – דמטפיחין, ואתא רבי יוסי למימר: כל זמן שמטפיחין הוא דאסור, הא רשומן ניכר שרי – היינו תנא קמא! אלא "נבלעו" – דאין רשומן ניכר, "לא נבלעו" – דרשומן ניכר. ואתא רבי יוסי למימר: כל זמן שמטפיחין הוא דאסור, הא רשומן ניכר – שרי!

The Gemara clarifies this dispute: **What is** the meaning of **absorbed and not absorbed in what the first *tanna* says? If you say** that **absorbed** means that it **does not moisten and not absorbed** means that it **moistens, and Rabbi Yosei came to say: As long as it moistens it is prohibited, but** if there is no moisture but its **mark is apparent, it is permitted.** If so, **that is** identical to the opinion of the **first *tanna*** and there is no dispute at all. **Rather, absorbed** means that **its mark is not apparent** and **not absorbed** means that **its mark is apparent. And Rabbi Yosei came to say: As long as it moistens, it is prohibited, but** if there is no moisture but its **mark is apparent, it is permitted,** in which case the dispute in our Gemara is parallel to this tannaitic dispute.

לא, דכולי עלמא כל זמן שמטפיחין הוא דאסור, הא רשומן ניכר – שרי

The Gemara states that it is not necessarily parallel: **No, everyone,** both *tanna'im*, agrees that **as long as it moistens, it is prohibited,** and if there is no moisture but its **mark is apparent, it is permitted.**

Perek **III**
Daf **25** Amud **b**

והכא, בטופח על מנת להטפיח איכא בינייהו.

And here, the difference between them is in a case **where it is moist enough to moisten** other things. According to the first *tanna* the prohibition is only in effect when the urine is moist enough to moisten other objects, while according to Rabbi Yosei it applies as long as the urine itself is moist, even if it is not moist enough to moisten other objects.

"ירד לטבול אם יכול לעלות כו'". לימא תנא סתמא כרבי אליעזר, דאמר: עד הנץ החמה!

We learned in a mishna that **one who descended to immerse himself** due to a seminal emission must calculate, **whether or not he is able to ascend,** cover himself with a garment and recite the morning *Shema* before sunrise. The Gemara asks: **Let us say** that Rabbi Yehuda HaNasi **taught** this in the **unattributed** mishna **in accordance with** the opinion of **Rabbi Eliezer, who said:** One may recite *Shema* **until sunrise.**

אֲפִילּוּ תֵּימָא רַבִּי יְהוֹשֻׁעַ, וְדִלְמָא כְּוָתִיקִין; דְּאָמַר רַבִּי יוֹחָנָן: וָתִיקִין הָיוּ גּוֹמְרִין אוֹתָהּ עִם הָנֵץ הַחַמָּה.

The Gemara immediately rejects this assumption: **Even if you say** that the mishna is in accordance with the opinion of **Rabbi Yehoshua,** who disagrees with Rabbi Eliezer and holds that one may recite the morning *Shema* until the third hour of the day, **and perhaps** the *halakha* in the mishna was directed toward those whose practice was **in accordance with** the custom of the ***vatikin***,[L] pious individuals who were scrupulous in their performance of mitzvot, with regard to whom **Rabbi Yoḥanan said: The *vatikin* would conclude** the recitation of *Shema* **with sunrise.**

״וְאִם לָאו יִתְכַּסֶּה בַּמַּיִם וְיִקְרָא״. וַהֲרֵי לִבּוֹ רוֹאֶה אֶת הָעֶרְוָה!

We learned in the mishna: **And if** one calculates that he will **not** be able to ascend and cover himself with a garment in time to recite *Shema*, he should **cover himself in the water and recite** *Shema* there. The Gemara asks: How can one recite *Shema* with his head above water? **His heart sees** his **nakedness** as there is no barrier between them.

אָמַר רַבִּי אֶלְעָזָר, וְאִי תֵּימָא רַבִּי אַחָא בַּר אַבָּא בַּר אַחָא מִשּׁוּם רַבֵּינוּ: בְּמַיִם עֲכוּרִין שָׁנוּ, דְּדָמוּ כְּאַרְעָא סְמִיכְתָּא, שֶׁלֹּא יִרְאֶה לִבּוֹ עֶרְוָתוֹ.

Regarding this **Rabbi Elazar said, and some say** it was **Rabbi Aḥa bar Abba bar Aḥa in the name of Rabbeinu,** Rav: **This was taught with regard to murky water,**[H] which is considered to be **like solid earth.** Therefore, it constitutes a barrier so that **his heart does not see** his **nakedness.**

תָּנוּ רַבָּנַן: מַיִם צְלוּלִין – יֵשֵׁב בָּהֶן עַד צַוָּארוֹ וְקוֹרֵא; וְיֵשׁ אוֹמְרִים: עוֹכְרָן בְּרַגְלוֹ.

On this same topic, **the Sages taught** in a *baraita*: If one was in **clear water, he should sit in it up to his neck and recite *Shema*. And some say: He sullies** the water **with his foot.**

וְתַנָּא קַמָּא – וַהֲרֵי לִבּוֹ רוֹאֶה אֶת הָעֶרְוָה! – קָסָבַר: לִבּוֹ רוֹאֶה אֶת הָעֶרְוָה – מוּתָּר. וַהֲרֵי עֲקֵבוֹ רוֹאֶה אֶת הָעֶרְוָה! – קָסָבַר: עֲקֵבוֹ רוֹאֶה אֶת הָעֶרְוָה – מוּתָּר.

The Gemara asks: **And** according to **the first *tanna* doesn't his heart see** his **nakedness** through the clear water? The Gemara replies: **He holds** that even if **his heart sees** his **nakedness, it is permitted** to recite *Shema*. The Gemara continues and asks: **But** in the clear water, **doesn't his heel see** his **nakedness?** The Gemara replies: Here too, the first *tanna* **holds** that in a case where **his heel sees** his **nakedness**[H] it is **permitted.**

אִתְּמַר: עֲקֵבוֹ רוֹאֶה אֶת הָעֶרְוָה – מוּתָּר. נוֹגֵעַ, אַבָּיֵי אָמַר: אָסוּר, וְרָבָא אָמַר: מוּתָּר. רַב זְבִיד מַתְנֵי לַהּ לְהָא שְׁמַעְתָּא הָכִי. רַב חִינְנָא בְּרֵיהּ דְּרַב אִיקָא מַתְנֵי לַהּ הָכִי: נוֹגֵעַ – דִּבְרֵי הַכֹּל אָסוּר; רוֹאֶה, אַבָּיֵי אָמַר: אָסוּר, רָבָא אָמַר: מוּתָּר, לֹא נִתְּנָה תּוֹרָה לְמַלְאֲכֵי הַשָּׁרֵת. וְהִלְכְתָא: נוֹגֵעַ – אָסוּר, רוֹאֶה – מוּתָּר.

The Gemara notes, **it was stated:** If **one's heel sees** his **nakedness it is permitted.** However, what is the *halakha* in a case where his heel **touches** his nakedness? May one in that circumstance recite *Shema* or not? **Abaye said: It is prohibited, and Rava said: It is permitted.** The Gemara notes: **Rav Zevid taught this *halakha* in that manner. Rav Ḥinnana, son of Rav Ika, taught it as follows:** In a case where his heel **touches** his nakedness, **everyone agrees that it is prohibited.** Their dispute is with regard to a case where his heel **sees** his nakedness. **Abaye said: It is prohibited, and Rava said: It is permitted; the Torah was not given to the ministering angels,** and a person, who, as opposed to a ministering angel, has genitals, cannot avoid this. **And the *halakha*** is that if his heel **touches** his nakedness **it is prohibited,** but if it merely **sees** his nakedness, **it is permitted.**

אָמַר רָבָא: צוֹאָה בַּעֲשָׁשִׁית – מוּתָּר לִקְרוֹת קְרִיאַת שְׁמַע כְּנֶגְדָּהּ, עֶרְוָה בַּעֲשָׁשִׁית – אָסוּר לִקְרוֹת קְרִיאַת שְׁמַע כְּנֶגְדָּהּ. צוֹאָה בַּעֲשָׁשִׁית מוּתָּר לִקְרוֹת קְרִיאַת שְׁמַע כְּנֶגְדָּהּ – דְּצוֹאָה בְּכִיסּוּי תַּלְיָא מִילְּתָא, וְהָא מִיכַּסְיָא; עֶרְוָה בַּעֲשָׁשִׁית אָסוּר לִקְרוֹת קְרִיאַת שְׁמַע כְּנֶגְדָּהּ ״וְלֹא יֵרָאֶה בְךָ עֶרְוַת דָּבָר״ אָמַר רַחֲמָנָא, וְהָא קָמִיתַחְזְיָא.

Rava said: Opposite feces covered only **by** a **lantern**-like covering,[H] which is transparent, **it is permitted to recite *Shema*.** But **opposite nakedness** covered only **by** a **lantern**-like covering,[H] **it is prohibited to recite *Shema*. Opposite feces in a lantern, it is permitted to recite *Shema*** because with regard to **feces,** the ability to recite *Shema* **is contingent upon covering,** as it is said: "And cover your excrement" (Deuteronomy 23:14), **and** although it is visible, **it is covered.** On the other hand, **opposite nakedness** covered only **by** a **lantern**-like covering, **it is prohibited to recite *Shema*; the Torah said: "And no indecent thing shall be seen in you"** (Deuteronomy 23:15), **and** here **it is seen.**

אָמַר אַבָּיֵי: צוֹאָה כָּל שֶׁהוּ – מְבַטְּלָהּ בְּרוֹק; אָמַר רָבָא: וּבְרוֹק עָבֶה. אָמַר רָבָא: צוֹאָה בְּגוּמָּא – מַנִּיחַ סַנְדָּלוֹ עָלֶיהָ וְקוֹרֵא קְרִיאַת שְׁמַע. בָּעֵא מָר בְּרֵיהּ דְּרָבִינָא: צוֹאָה דְּבוּקָה בְּסַנְדָּלוֹ מַאי? תֵּיקוּ.

Abaye said: A small amount of feces may be nullified with spittle, and as long as it is covered, it is permitted to recite *Shema*. **Rava said:** This applies specifically when it is **thick spittle. Rava said: Feces in a hole** in the ground, **he places his sandal over** the hole to cover **it and recites *Shema*. Mar, son of Ravina, raised a dilemma: What** is the *halakha* in a case where **feces is stuck to his sandal?**[H] Perhaps he would be considered filthy in that case? **Let** this dilemma **stand** unresolved.

LANGUAGE

Vatikin – וָתִיקִין: The origin of this word, used often by the Sages, is unknown and its meaning is unclear. Some say that the word is of Semitic origin while others maintain that it is from Greek. If it is indeed from Greek, then it likely comes from the word ἠθικός, *ethikos*, meaning ethics, in the sense of God-fearing. Some argue that it comes from the Arabic وثيق, *wathīq*, meaning strong or brave, or alternatively, hidden, in which case *vatikin* would mean modest ones. Based on the translation of the word in the book of Ben Sira, apparently, the word meant wise or experienced.

HALAKHA

This was taught with regard to murky water – בְּמַיִם עֲכוּרִין שָׁנוּ: One is permitted to recite *Shema* when his body is submerged in murky water, in accordance with the Gemara's interpretation of the mishna (Rambam *Sefer Ahava, Hilkhot Keriat Shema* 2:7; *Shulḥan Arukh, Oraḥ Ḥayyim* 74:2).

His heel sees his nakedness – עֲקֵבוֹ רוֹאֶה אֶת הָעֶרְוָה: If any of one's limbs, the heel being only one example (Rabbeinu Yona, Rosh), is exposed to his nakedness, one is permitted to recite the *Shema*. If it is in contact with his or another's nakedness, it is prohibited (Rambam *Sefer Ahava, Hilkhot Keriat Shema* 3:17; *Shulḥan Arukh, Oraḥ Ḥayyim* 74:5).

Feces covered by a lantern-like covering – צוֹאָה בַּעֲשָׁשִׁית: One may recite *Shema* opposite covered fecal matter, even if the covering is transparent, as long as it emits no foul odor. Opposite fecal matter that emits a foul odor, even if it is covered, it is prohibited to recite *Shema* (Rambam *Sefer Ahava, Hilkhot Keriat Shema* 3:10; *Shulḥan Arukh, Oraḥ Ḥayyim* 76:1).

Nakedness covered by a lantern-like covering – עֶרְוָה בַּעֲשָׁשִׁית: It is prohibited to recite *Shema* opposite anything considered nakedness with a transparent covering (Rambam *Sefer Ahava, Hilkhot Keriat Shema* 3:16; *Shulḥan Arukh, Oraḥ Ḥayyim* 75:5).

Feces stuck to his sandal – צוֹאָה דְּבוּקָה בְּסַנְדָּלוֹ: It is prohibited to recite *Shema* opposite someone with fecal matter stuck to his sandal. This dilemma was not resolved in the Gemara and the *halakha* is in accordance with the stringent opinion (Rambam *Sefer Ahava, Hilkhot Keriat Shema* 3:11; *Shulḥan Arukh, Oraḥ Ḥayyim* 76:2).

אמר רב יהודה: גוי ערום – אסור לקרות קריאת שמע כנגדו. מאי איריא גוי, אפילו ישראל נמי! – ישראל – פשיטא ליה דאסור, אלא גוי איצטריכא ליה; מהו דתימא: הואיל וכתיב בהו "אשר בשר חמורים בשרם", אימא כחמור בעלמא הוא – קא משמע לן: דאינהו נמי איקרו ערוה, דכתיב "וערות אביהם לא ראו".

Rav Yehuda said: Opposite a naked gentile,[NH] **it is forbidden to recite** ***Shema.*** The Gemara asks: **Why did** the Gemara discuss **particularly** the case of **a gentile? Even with regard to a Jew** it is **also** prohibited. The Gemara replies: Opposite the nakedness of **a Jew, it is obvious** that it is **prohibited; however,** opposite the nakedness of **a gentile, it was necessary for him** to say. **Lest you say** that **since it is written about** gentiles: **"Their flesh is the flesh of donkeys"** (Ezekiel 23:20), **say** that his nakedness **is like** that of **a mere donkey** and does not constitute nakedness. The Gemara **taught us that their** nakedness **is also considered nakedness, as it is written** regarding the sons of Noah: **"And their father's nakedness they did not see"** (Genesis 9:23). Although Noah predated Abraham and was consequently not Jewish, his nakedness is mentioned.

"ולא יתכסה לא במים הרעים ולא במי המשרה עד שיטיל לתוכן מים". וכמה מיא רמי ואזיל? אלא הכי קאמר: לא יתכסה לא במים הרעים ולא במי המשרה כלל; ומי רגלים – עד שיטיל לתוכן מים, ויקרא.

And we learned in the mishna: **And** one who needs to recite *Shema* **may not cover himself with either foul water or water** in which flax was **soaked until he pours** other **water into it.** The Gemara asks: **How much water does he continue to pour** in order to render them a permissible covering. If he is covering himself in water in which flax was soaked, it must be a considerable amount of water, requiring at least an equally considerable amount of water to neutralize it. **Rather, this what it says: One may neither cover himself with foul water nor water** in which flax was **soaked at all; and urine,** which is considered repugnant, **until he adds** clean **water to it, and** only then **he may** recite *Shema.*

תנו רבנן: כמה יטיל לתוכן מים – כל שהוא; רבי זכאי אומר: רביעית.

The Sages taught a related disagreement in a *baraita*: **How much water must one add** in order **to** nullify urine? **Any quantity** is sufficient. **Rabbi Zakkai says:** One must add **a quarter** of a *log.*

אמר רב נחמן: מחלוקת – לבסוף, אבל בתחילה – כל שהן;

Rav Naḥman said: This **dispute** is with regard to a case where the urine is already in a vessel, and **afterward** one seeks to nullify it. **However,** if the clean water was in a vessel **at the beginning,** before the urine, each drop of urine is nullified as it enters the vessel and therefore **any amount** of clean water in the vessel is sufficient.

ורב יוסף אמר: מחלוקת – לכתחילה, אבל לבסוף – דברי הכל רביעית. אמר ליה רב יוסף לשמעיה: אייתי לי רביעיתא דמיא, כרבי זכאי.

And Rav Yosef said: This **dispute** is with regard to the amount of water necessary to have in the vessel **at the beginning,** before the urine. **However, afterward, everyone agrees** that **a quarter** of a *log* is required. The Gemara relates: **Rav Yosef said to his servant** at the beginning: **Bring me a quarter** of a *log* **of water, in accordance with** the opinion of **Rabbi Zakkai.**

תנו רבנן: גרף של רעי ועביט של מי רגלים – אסור לקרות קריאת שמע כנגדן, ואף על פי שאין בהן כלום, ומי רגלים עצמן – עד שיטיל לתוכן מים. וכמה יטיל לתוכן מים? כל שהוא; רבי זכאי אומר: רביעית. בין לפני המטה בין לאחר המטה; רבן שמעון בן גמליאל אומר: לאחר המטה – קורא, לפני המטה – אינו קורא, אבל מרחיק הוא ארבע אמות וקורא; רבי שמעון בן אלעזר אומר: אפילו בית מאה אמה – לא יקרא עד שיוציאם, או שיניחם תחת המטה.

The Sages taught an elaboration of this point in the *Tosefta*: **Opposite a chamber pot** used for **excrement or urine,**[H] **it is prohibited to recite** ***Shema,*** **even if there is nothing in it,** as it is always considered filthy. **Opposite urine itself,** one may not recite *Shema* **until he pours water into it. And how much water must he pour into it? Any quantity. Rabbi Zakkai says: A quarter** of a *log.* That is the ruling **both** when it is **before the bed** and when it is **behind the bed. Rabban Shimon ben Gamliel says:** When it is **behind the bed, one may recite** *Shema,* but when it is **before the bed, one may not recite** *Shema,* **but he** must **distance himself four cubits and** only then **recite** ***Shema.*** **Rabbi Shimon ben Elazar** is even more strict, **saying: Even in a house one hundred cubits** in size, **one may not recite** *Shema* **until he removes it or places it beneath the bed.**

איבעיא להו: היכי קאמר אחר המטה – קורא מיד, לפני המטה – מרחיק ארבע אמות וקורא; או דילמא הכי קאמר: לאחר המטה – מרחיק ארבע אמות וקורא, לפני המטה – אינו קורא כלל?

A dilemma was raised before students at the yeshiva: **How does** Rabban Shimon ben Gamliel **state** this *halakha*? What did he mean? Did he mean that if the chamber pot is **behind the bed, he recites** ***Shema*** **immediately; before the bed, he distances himself four cubits and recites? Or perhaps he states the following:** If the chamber pot is **behind the bed, he distances himself four cubits and then recites** *Shema,* but if it is **before the bed he may not recite** *Shema* **at all?**

NOTES

A naked gentile – גוי ערום: This problem stems from uncertainty regarding the basis of the prohibition of nakedness itself. Is the indecency of nakedness associated specifically with the holiness of Israel, just as, biblically, most laws of ritual impurity, leprosy, *zav,* and the like apply only to Jews, or is it associated with the very image of the human being? Consequently, it was necessary to specify that an unclothed gentile, too, is considered nakedness.

HALAKHA

A naked gentile – גוי ערום: One may not recite *Shema* opposite the nakedness of a gentile, which constitutes full-fledged nakedness in every sense, in accordance with the opinion of Rabbi Yehuda (Rambam *Sefer Ahava, Hilkhot Keriat Shema* 3:16; *Shulḥan Arukh, Oraḥ Ḥayyim* 75:4).

A chamber pot used for excrement or urine – גרף של רעי ועביט של מי רגלים: One must distance himself from a chamber pot of excrement or urine just as he distances himself from fecal matter, i.e., until it is beyond his range of vision before him and four cubits beyond the point where the odor ceases behind him (*Mishna Berura*). This applies even if it is empty and even if it was cleaned inside and out (*Mishna Berura*), and even if it was filled with water. This applies specifically to chamber pots made of wood or clay, but with regard to those made of metal or glass, if they were washed it is permitted, as long as it produces no odor (Rambam *Sefer Ahava, Hilkhot Keriat Shema* 3:12; *Shulḥan Arukh, Oraḥ Ḥayyim* 87:1).

תָּא שְׁמַע, דְּתַנְיָא רַבִּי שִׁמְעוֹן בֶּן אֶלְעָזָר אוֹמֵר: אַחַר הַמִּטָּה – קוֹרֵא מִיָּד, לִפְנֵי הַמִּטָּה – מַרְחִיק אַרְבַּע אַמּוֹת; רַבָּן שִׁמְעוֹן בֶּן גַּמְלִיאֵל אוֹמֵר: אֲפִילּוּ בַּיִת מֵאָה אַמָּה – לֹא יִקְרָא עַד שֶׁיּוֹצִיאֵם אוֹ שֶׁיַּנִּיחֵם תַּחַת הַמִּטָּה.

In order to resolve this dilemma, the Gemara cites proof. **Come** and **hear** that **it was taught** in a *baraita*: **Rabbi Shimon ben Elazar says:** If it is **behind the bed he recites** *Shema* **immediately; before the bed, he distances himself four cubits. Rabban Shimon ben Gamliel says: Even** in a large **house of one hundred cubits one may not recite** *Shema* **until he removes it or places it beneath the bed.** Thus we see from this *baraita* that if the vessel is obstructed by the bed he may recite *Shema* immediately.

בְּעַיִין אִיפְּשִׁיטָא לָן, מַתְנְיָיתָא קַשְׁיָין אַהֲדָדֵי! – אֵיפוֹךְ בַּתְרַיְיתָא.

The Gemara notes: **Our dilemma has been resolved,** but **the** *baraitot* **contradict each other.** The statements made in the name of Rabban Shimon ben Gamliel in one *baraita* were made in the name of Rabbi Shimon ben Elazar in the other. The Gemara resolves the contradiction: **Reverse** the **latter** *baraita* and say that the names of the *tanna'im* were attached to the wrong opinions.

מַה חֲזֵית דְּאַפַּכְתְּ בַּתְרַיְיתָא? אֵיפוֹךְ קַמַּיְיתָא!

This solution is difficult: **What did you see** that led you to **reverse** the **latter** *baraita*? **Reverse the first** one.

מַאן שָׁמְעַתְּ לֵיהּ דַּאֲמַר: כּוּלֵּיהּ בַּיִת כְּאַרְבַּע אַמּוֹת דָּמֵי – רַבִּי שִׁמְעוֹן בֶּן אֶלְעָזָר הִיא.

The Gemara proves that the latter *baraita* should be reversed in accordance with the opinions expressed by these Sages in general. **Who did you hear** that **said that an entire house is considered like four cubits? It is Rabbi Shimon ben Elazar,** who expressed that opinion in the *halakhot* of *eiruv* (Rav Nissim). Consequently, it is reasonable to posit that this would also be his opinion with regard to these *halakhot*, and the *baraita* was reversed accordingly.

אָמַר רַב יוֹסֵף, בְּעַאי מִינֵּיהּ מֵרַב הוּנָא: מִטָּה פָּחוֹת מִשְּׁלֹשָׁה – פְּשִׁיטָא לִי דִּכְלָבוּד – דָּמֵי; שְׁלֹשָׁה אַרְבָּעָה, חֲמִשָּׁה, שִׁשָּׁה, שִׁבְעָה, שְׁמֹנָה, תִּשְׁעָה, מַהוּ? אָמַר לֵיהּ: לָא יָדַעְנָא. עֲשָׂרָה, וַדַּאי לֹא מִיבָּעֲיָא לִי. אָמַר אַבַּיֵי: שַׁפִּיר עֲבַדְתְּ לֹא אִיבַּעְיָא לָךְ, כָּל עֲשָׂרָה רְשׁוּתָא אַחֲרִיתִי הִיא.

Rav Yosef said: I raised a dilemma before Rav Huna: It is obvious to me that a bed under which there is a space of **less than three** handbreadths **is considered connected** [*lavud*][B] to the ground as if the void beneath it does not exist, as *halakha* considers a void of less than three handbreadths as sealed. What, then, is the dilemma? **What is** the *halakha* if that space is **three, four, five, six, seven, eight** or **nine** handbreadths? **He said to him: I do not know.** However, with regard to a space greater than **ten** handbreadths **I certainly have no dilemma,** as it is clear that this space is considered a separate domain. **Abaye said** to him: **You did well that you did not have a dilemma,** as the *halakha* is that **any** space **ten**[N] handbreadths high **is a separate domain.**

אָמַר רָבָא, הִלְכְתָא: פָּחוֹת מִשְּׁלֹשָׁה – כְּלָבוּד דָּמֵי, עֲשָׂרָה – רְשׁוּתָא אַחֲרִיתִי הִיא, מִשְּׁלֹשָׁה עַד עֲשָׂרָה – הַיְינוּ דִּבְעָא מִינֵּיהּ רַב יוֹסֵף מֵרַב הוּנָא וְלֹא פְּשַׁט לֵיהּ. אָמַר רַב: הֲלָכָה כְּרַבִּי שִׁמְעוֹן בֶּן אֶלְעָזָר; וְכֵן אָמַר בָּאלִי אָמַר רַב יַעֲקֹב בְּרָהּ בַּת שְׁמוּאֵל: הֲלָכָה כְּרַבִּי שִׁמְעוֹן בֶּן אֶלְעָזָר; וְרָבָא אָמַר: אֵין הֲלָכָה כְּרַבִּי שִׁמְעוֹן בֶּן אֶלְעָזָר.

Rava summarized and **said: The** ***halakha*** **is that less than three** handbreadths **is considered connected** and it is permitted to recite *Shema*. **Ten** handbreadths **is a separate domain. Three to ten** handbreadths is the case with regard to which **Rav Yosef raised a dilemma before Rav Huna,** and Rav Huna **did not resolve it for him. Rav said: The** ***halakha*** **is in accordance with** the opinion of **Rabbi Shimon ben Elazar. And,** so too, the Sage **Bali said** that **Rav Ya'akov, son of Shmuel's daughter, said: The** ***halakha*** **is in accordance with** the opinion of **Rabbi Shimon ben Elazar. And Rava said: The** ***halakha*** **is not** is in accordance with the opinion of **Rabbi Shimon ben Elazar.**

רַב אַחַאי אִיעֲסַק לֵיהּ לִבְרֵיהּ בֵּי רַב יִצְחָק בַּר שְׁמוּאֵל בַּר מָרְתָא, עַיְילֵיהּ לַחוּפָּה וְלֹא הֲוָה מִסְתַּיְיעָא מִילְּתָא. אֲזַל בַּתְרֵיהּ לְעַיּוּנֵי, חֲזָא סֵפֶר תּוֹרָה דְּמַנְּחָא. אָמַר לְהוּ: אִיכּוּ הָשְׁתָּא לֹא אֲתַאי סַכַּנְתּוּן לִבְרִי! דְּתַנְיָא: בַּיִת שֶׁיֵּשׁ בּוֹ סֵפֶר תּוֹרָה אוֹ תְּפִילִּין – אָסוּר לְשַׁמֵּשׁ בּוֹ אֶת הַמִּטָּה עַד שֶׁיּוֹצִיאֵם אוֹ שֶׁיַּנִּיחֵם כְּלִי בְּתוֹךְ כְּלִי.

The Gemara relates: **Rav Aḥai arranged for his son** to marry into **the family of Rav Yitzḥak bar Shmuel bar Marta. He led him to enter the wedding canopy** for the wedding ceremony, **but he was unsuccessful** in his attempts to consummate the marriage. Rav Aḥai **followed him to examine** possible causes of the problem and **he saw a Torah scroll placed** there. **He said to them: Had I not come now, you would have endangered** the life of **my son. As it was taught** in a *baraita*: **In a room in which there is a Torah scroll or phylacteries, it is forbidden to engage in conjugal relations**[H] **until he takes them out** of the room **or places them in a vessel inside a** second **vessel.**

אָמַר אַבַּיֵי: לֹא שָׁנוּ אֶלָּא בִּכְלִי שֶׁאֵינוֹ כְּלְיָין, אֲבָל בִּכְלִי שֶׁהוּא כְּלְיָין – אֲפִילּוּ עֲשָׂרָה מָאנֵי כְּחַד מָאנָא דָּמֵי. אָמַר רָבָא: גְּלִימָא

Abaye said: They only taught that a vessel inside a second vessel is sufficient **when the vessel is not their,** the Torah scroll's or the phylacteries', regular **vessel. But a vessel that is their** regular **vessel, even ten vessels are considered as one vessel,** and the Torah or phylacteries must be covered in another vessel not typically used for that purpose. **Rava said: A cloak**

BACKGROUND

Connected [*lavud*] – לָבוּד: A *halakha* transmitted to Moses from Sinai stating that two solid surfaces are considered as connected if the gap between them is less than three handbreadths. This *halakha* is applicable with regard to the establishment of Shabbat boundaries and the construction of a *sukka*.

NOTES

Less than three…ten – פָּחוֹת מִשְּׁלֹשָׁה...עֲשָׂרָה וכו׳: Two basic measurements are established here: A space of less than three handbreadths is considered as if it were connected, so any void smaller than this is not considered a separate domain with regard to practical demarcation of limits and boundaries. Ten handbreadths, however, establishes not only a significant separation, but a separate domain in and of itself. Since their beds were covered along the sides, anything less than three handbreadths is considered connected, while more than ten is considered a separate room (*Tosefot Rabbeinu Yitzḥak* based on the *ge'onim*).

HALAKHA

In a room in which there is a Torah scroll or phylacteries, it is forbidden to engage in conjugal relations – **בַּיִת שֶׁיֵּשׁ בּוֹ סֵפֶר תּוֹרָה אוֹ תְּפִילִּין אָסוּר לְשַׁמֵּשׁ בּוֹ אֶת הַמִּטָּה:** One is prohibited from engaging in conjugal relations in a room in which there is a Torah scroll, phylacteries, or other sacred objects or holy books until one covers them in one vessel inside another vessel (Rambam *Sefer Ahava, Hilkhot Tefillin Mezuza VeSefer Torah* 4:24; *Shulḥan Arukh, Oraḥ Ḥayyim* 40:2; 240:6).

אַקְמַטְרָא – כִּכְלִי בְּתוֹךְ כְּלִי דָּמֵי. אָמַר רַבִּי יְהוֹשֻׁעַ בֶּן לֵוִי: סֵפֶר תּוֹרָה – צָרִיךְ לַעֲשׂוֹת לוֹ מְחִיצָה עֲשָׂרָה. מָר זוּטְרָא אִיקְלַע לְבֵי רַב אַשִׁי, חַזְיֵיהּ לְדוּכְתֵּיהּ דְּמָר בַּר רַב אַשִׁי דְּמַנַּח בֵּיהּ סֵפֶר תּוֹרָה וְעָבֵיד לֵיהּ מְחִיצָה עֲשָׂרָה. אָמַר לֵיהּ: כְּמַאן – כְּרַבִּי יְהוֹשֻׁעַ בֶּן לֵוִי? אֵימַר דַּאֲמַר רַבִּי יְהוֹשֻׁעַ בֶּן לֵוִי – דְּלֵית לֵיהּ בֵּיתָא אַחֲרִינָא, מָר הָא אִית לֵיהּ בֵּיתָא אַחֲרִינָא! אָמַר לֵיהּ: לָאו אַדַּעְתַּאי.

atop a chest is like a vessel within a vessel. On a similar note, **Rabbi Yehoshua ben Levi said:** One who wishes to engage in marital relations in a room in which there is **a Torah scroll, must erect a partition**[H] **ten** handbreadths high. The Gemara relates: **Mar Zutra happened** to come **to the house of Rav Ashi and he saw** that **in the** bed **chamber of** his son **Mar bar Rav Ashi, there was a Torah scroll, and a partition of ten** handbreadths **had been erected for it. He said to him: In accordance with whose** opinion did you do this? Is it **in accordance with** the opinion of **Rabbi Yehoshua ben Levi? Say** that **Rabbi Yehoshua ben Levi said** this only as a makeshift solution in exigent situations, when **he has no other room** in which to place it, but **don't** you, **Master, have another room** where you could place the Torah scroll? **He said to him:** Indeed, **that** did **not** enter **my mind.**

"כַּמָּה יַרְחִיק מֵהֶן וּמִן הַצּוֹאָה – אַרְבַּע אַמּוֹת". אָמַר רָבָא אָמַר רַב סְחוֹרָה אָמַר רַב הוּנָא: לֹא שָׁנוּ אֶלָּא לַאֲחוֹרָיו, אֲבָל לְפָנָיו – מַרְחִיק מְלֹא עֵינָיו, וְכֵן לִתְפִלָּה.

We learned in the mishna: **And, how far must one distance himself from urine and from feces**[H] in order to recite *Shema*? **Four cubits. Rava said** that **Rav Seḥora said** that **Rav Huna said: They only taught** that it is sufficient to distance oneself four cubits when the feces are **behind him, but** if they are **before him he must distance himself** to the point that it is **no longer within his range of vision;** and the *halakha* **is the same** for **prayer.**

אִינִי?! וְהָא אָמַר רַפְרָם בַּר פַּפָּא אָמַר רַב חִסְדָּא: עוֹמֵד אָדָם כְּנֶגֶד בֵּית הַכִּסֵּא וּמִתְפַּלֵּל! – הָכָא בְּמַאי עָסְקִינַן – בְּבֵית הַכִּסֵּא שֶׁאֵין בּוֹ צוֹאָה.

The Gemara challenges this: **Is that so? Didn't Rafram bar Pappa say** that **Rav Ḥisda said: One may stand opposite a bathroom**[H] **and pray.** The Gemara resolves this contradiction: **With what are we dealing here? With a bathroom that has no feces,** and therefore there is no need to distance himself to that extent.

אִינִי?! וְהָאָמַר רַב יוֹסֵף בַּר חֲנִינָא: בֵּית הַכִּסֵּא שֶׁאָמְרוּ – אַף עַל פִּי שֶׁאֵין בּוֹ צוֹאָה, וּבֵית הַמֶּרְחָץ שֶׁאָמְרוּ – אַף עַל פִּי שֶׁאֵין בּוֹ אָדָם! אֶלָּא, הָכָא בְּמַאי עָסְקִינַן: בַּחֲדַתִּי.

The Gemara asks again: **Is that so? Didn't Rav Yosef bar Ḥanina say: The bathroom to which** the Sages **referred** in all of the *halakhot* of distancing oneself was **even** one **in which there were no feces, and the bathhouse to which** the Sages **referred** in all of the *halakhot* of uttering sacred matters, was **even** one **in which there was no** naked **person. Rather, with what are we dealing here?** We are dealing **with a new** structure, built as a bathroom but not yet used for that purpose.

וְהָא מִיבַּעְיָא לֵיהּ לְרָבִינָא: הִזְמִינוֹ לְבֵית הַכִּסֵּא מַהוּ, יֵשׁ זִימּוּן אוֹ אֵין זִימּוּן? – כִּי קָא מִיבַּעְיָא לֵיהּ לְרָבִינָא – לְמֵיקַם עֲלֵיהּ לְצַלּוֹיֵי בְּגַוֵּיהּ, אֲבָל כְּנֶגְדּוֹ – לֹא.

The Gemara asks: **Wasn't this** already **raised as a dilemma** by **Ravina: One who designated** the structure for use **as a bathroom,**[H] **what is its** legal status? Is **designation** effective **or is designation not** effective? The Gemara replies: **When Ravina raised the dilemma,** it was whether or not one may **stand and pray inside it, but** he had **no** dilemma whether or **not one may pray opposite it.**

אָמַר רָבָא: הָנֵי בָּתֵּי כִסְאֵי דְּפָרְסָאֵי, אַף עַל גַּב דְּאִית בְּהוּ צוֹאָה – כִּסְתוּמִין דָּמוּ.

Rava said: These Persian bathrooms, even though they contain feces, they are considered as sealed,[H] as they are constructed on an incline so the feces will roll out of the bathroom underground.

מתני׳ זָב שֶׁרָאָה קֶרִי, וְנִדָּה שֶׁפָּלְטָה שִׁכְבַת זֶרַע, וְהַמְשַׁמֶּשֶׁת שֶׁרָאֲתָה נִדָּה – צְרִיכִין טְבִילָה, וְרַבִּי יְהוּדָה פּוֹטֵר.

MISHNA Continuing the earlier discussion of the *halakhot* of immersion for Torah study and prayer for one who experienced a seminal emission, the mishna discusses a case where individuals who were already impure with a severe form of ritual impurity are exposed to the impurity of a seminal emission as well. They are required to immerse themselves and purify themselves of the impurity of the seminal emission even though they remain impure due to the more severe impurity. Consequently, even a ***zav***, whose impurity lasts at least seven days, **who experienced a seminal emission,** for which, were he not a *zav*, he would be impure for only one day; **a menstruating woman who discharged semen,** despite the fact that she is already impure with a severe impurity unaffected by her immersion; **and** a woman **who engaged in conjugal relations** with her husband **and later saw menstrual blood,** all **require immersion. And Rabbi Yehuda exempts** them from immersion.

HALAKHA

For a Torah scroll, one must erect a partition – סֵפֶר תּוֹרָה צָרִיךְ לַעֲשׂוֹת לוֹ מְחִיצָה: One who wishes to engage in conjugal relations must erect a partition ten handbreadths high between his bed and Torah scrolls or Bibles. If there is another room, he should move the sacred items there (Rambam *Sefer Ahava, Hilkhot Tefillin Mezuza VeSefer Torah* 10:7; *Shulḥan Arukh, Oraḥ Ḥayyim* 240:6).

How far must one distance himself from urine and from feces… – כַּמָּה יַרְחִיק מֵהֶן וּמִן הַצּוֹאָה: A person standing alongside excrement or foul water and wishes to recite *Shema*, if they are before him, he must distance himself until they are out of his sight. If they are behind him, he must distance himself four cubits beyond the point where the odor can no longer be sensed. Only then may he recite *Shema* (Rambam *Sefer Ahava, Hilkhot Keriat Shema* 3:8; *Shulḥan Arukh, Oraḥ Ḥayyim* 79:1).

Distancing oneself from the bathroom – הַרְחָקָה מִבֵּית הַכִּסֵּא: One may not recite *Shema* opposite a bathroom that has already been used, even if it is clean. He must distance himself from it as he would from excrement. If there are walls and it does not give off a foul odor, one may recite *Shema* adjacent to it (Rambam *Sefer Ahava, Hilkhot Keriat Shema* 3:2; *Shulḥan Arukh, Oraḥ Ḥayyim* 83:1).

One who designated the structure for use as a bathroom – הִזְמִינוֹ לְבֵית הַכִּסֵּא: It is prohibited to recite *Shema* inside a place that was designated for use as a bathroom even if it has not yet been used for that purpose. However, one may recite *Shema* opposite it, as mere designation does not disqualify the site to that extent (Rambam *Sefer Ahava, Hilkhot Keriat Shema* 3:3; *Shulḥan Arukh, Oraḥ Ḥayyim* 83:2).

These Persian bathrooms…are considered as sealed – הָנֵי בָּתֵּי כִסְאֵי דְּפָרְסָאֵי...כִּסְתוּמִין דָּמוּ: A bathroom from which the excrement and the urine reach a distance of four cubits by means of a pipe or a canal has the legal status of a sealed bathroom and if there is no foul odor, one may recite *Shema* opposite it (*Shulḥan Arukh, Oraḥ Ḥayyim* 83:4).

גמ׳ אִיבַּעְיָא לְהוּ: בַּעַל קֶרִי שֶׁרָאָה זִיבָה, לְרַבִּי יְהוּדָה מַהוּ? כִּי פְּטַר רַבִּי יְהוּדָה הָתָם בְּזָב שֶׁרָאָה קֶרִי – דְּמֵעִיקָּרָא לָאו בַּר טְבִילָה הוּא, אֲבָל בַּעַל קֶרִי שֶׁרָאָה זִיבָה, דְּמֵעִיקָּרָא בַּר טְבִילָה הוּא – מְחַיֵּיב, אוֹ דִּילְמָא לָא שְׁנָא?

GEMARA **A dilemma was raised before** the students of the yeshiva: **One who experienced a seminal emission** and was therefore required to immerse himself, who later **saw a discharge** that rendered him a *zav*; **according to Rabbi Yehuda, what is the his legal status?** The Gemara explains the sides of the dilemma: **When,** in our mishna, **Rabbi Yehuda exempted a *zav* who saw a seminal emission** from immersion, that **was because from the outset he was not fit for immersion,** as the immersion would not be effective in purifying him from the impurity of a *zav*; **however, one who experienced a seminal emission,** who later **saw a discharge** that rendered him a *zav*, who **was fit for immersion** and only later became impure with the severe impurity of a *zav*, would Rabbi Yehuda **require** immersion? **Or perhaps there is no difference** and he is exempt from immersion in both cases?

תָּא שְׁמַע: הַמְשַׁמֶּשֶׁת וְרָאֲתָה נִדָּה צְרִיכָה טְבִילָה, וְרַבִּי יְהוּדָה פּוֹטֵר. וְהָא מְשַׁמֶּשֶׁת וְרָאֲתָה נִדָּה כְּבַעַל קֶרִי שֶׁרָאָה זִיבָה דָּמְיָא, וְקָא פָּטַר רַבִּי יְהוּדָה – שְׁמַע מִינָּהּ. תָּנֵי רַבִּי חִיָּיא בְּהֶדְיָא: בַּעַל קֶרִי שֶׁרָאָה זִיבָה – צָרִיךְ טְבִילָה, וְרַבִּי יְהוּדָה פּוֹטֵר.

In order to resolve this dilemma, **come** and **hear** the last case of the mishna: A woman **who engaged in conjugal relations** with her husband **and** later **saw menstrual blood requires immersion. And Rabbi Yehuda exempts** them from immersion. **Isn't the** woman **who engaged in conjugal relations** with her husband **and** later **saw menstrual blood like one who experienced a seminal emission,** who later **saw a discharge** that rendered him a ***zav***, as in both cases there is a less severe ritual impurity followed by a more severe impurity; **and** nevertheless, **Rabbi Yehuda exempts. Conclude from this** that Rabbi Yehuda does not distinguish between the cases. And indeed, **Rabbi Ḥiyya explicitly taught: One who experienced a seminal emission** who later **saw a discharge** that rendered him a ***zav*** **requires immersion, and Rabbi Yehuda exempts.**

הדרן עלך מי שמתו

Summary of **Perek III**

Several problems were addressed in this chapter. Primary among them is how the recitation of *Shema* requires one to distance himself from anything disgusting, filthy, or ritually impure. However, other related halakhic and aggadic matters were also cited.

In this chapter, *halakhot* were articulated with regard to the extent that dealing with burial of the dead exempts one from the obligation to recite *Shema*, and the guiding principles were clarified. It became clear that the basis of the myriad *halakhot* regarding respect for the dead is the comprehensive principle of maintaining human dignity. Due to that principle, several mitzvot are superseded due to both respect for the dead and human dignity. Several times in this chapter it was emphasized that the deceased should be treated like a person, and that his body is inexorably tied to his eternal soul.

Another fundamental discussion in this chapter dealt with the ordinance of Ezra, which prohibits one who experienced a seminal emission from engaging in Torah study and prayer until he immerses himself and becomes ritually pure. This ordinance had considerable influence on the life of the Jewish people for several generations, and many of the Sages sought to clarify its practical ramifications. It never achieved widespread acceptance among the Jewish people, and the Sages agreed to abrogate it. Nevertheless, the ordinance remains in effect, even today, as a custom of the pious.

In addition, there was considerable discussion devoted to the need to distance oneself from exposed nakedness while reciting *Shema* and praying. In this case, the reference is to exposed nakedness in its broadest sense, which includes not only exposure of the specific parts of the body usually associated with that term, but also all body parts that are usually covered. In practice, one must avoid exposure to any potentially alluring sights while reciting *Shema* and praying.

With regard to that issue, as well as with regard to avoiding exposure to filth, some of the Sages expressed stringent opinions that called for extreme measures to ensure total separation. However the guiding principle is: The Torah was not given to ministering angels. Exaggerated caution is difficult to implement and is even liable to cause people to distance themselves from Torah. Consequently, the *halakha* adopted moderate standards of cleanliness and modesty.

Introduction to **Perek IV**

Now his windows were open in his upper chamber toward Jerusalem and he kneeled upon his knees three times a day, and prayed, and gave thanks before his God, as he had done before.

(Daniel 6:11)

The primary focus of this chapter is the *Amida* prayer, also called *Shemoneh Esreh* (Eighteen), which was the number of blessings originally instituted in the weekday prayer. It is recited on weekdays, on Shabbat, and on Festivals. The fundamental question is: What is the source of the *Amida* prayer? Is it tied to *Shema*, the course of a person's daily life, the days that turn into night and vice-versa? Or is the primary element its connection to the sacred service performed in the Temple, serving as a substitute form of worship since its destruction? This dilemma, manifest in the dispute amongst the Sages whether prayer was instituted by the Patriarchs or established parallel to the daily offerings in the Temple, touches upon the different characteristics of prayer and serves as a basis for the halakhic questions discussed in this chapter.

Clearly, there is a consensus that beyond the essential obligation to pray, the source of which was subject to dispute, the various prayers must be recited at fixed times. It is, then, necessary to ascertain the parameters of those times: When is the earliest and latest time that each prayer can be recited? This is relevant to the morning prayer, which is parallel to the daily offering sacrificed early in the morning when the Temple stood, and to the afternoon prayer, which is parallel to the daily offering sacrificed in the afternoon.

This close connection between the prayers and the communal offerings was already observed in practice when the Temple stood, as the people would recite a communal prayer together with the sacrifice of the offering. Consequently, there are two prayers that enjoy unique status in the context of this discussion: The additional prayer and the evening prayer.

The additional prayer was clearly instituted parallel to the offering; there is no other possible explanation. Therefore, its status and the parameters of the time that it may be recited are clearer. Yet specifically for that reason, there is room to consider whether or not this prayer, like the sacrifice after which it was modeled, is a matter exclusively for the community. The question is: May it only be recited in the framework of communal prayer; or, perhaps, may the additional prayer be recited even individually?

The opposite problem exists with regard to the evening prayer. Since this prayer is not directly parallel to a specific offering, it does not have a set time like the other prayers. On the other hand, in terms of its essence as a prayer recited at night, tied to the changes from day to night and to *Shema* of the day and the night, there is room to stipulate a set time and a fixed obligation as in the case of the other prayers.

The dispute between the Sages regarding this issue, whose far-reaching consequences will be related in this chapter, constitutes a manifestation of another aspect of the fundamental question: What is the obligation of prayer? Is the primary obligation to recite the prayer communally, with the devotional aspect of prayer secondary in importance? Or, perhaps, the essence of prayer is turning to God, and the primary obligation is in its devotional aspect and the desire to draw closer to God.

Between these two approaches, which differ with regard to the fundamental understanding of communal prayer, the more specific questions raised in this chapter are resolved.

מתני׳ תְּפִלַּת הַשַּׁחַר עַד חֲצוֹת, רַבִּי יְהוּדָה אוֹמֵר: עַד אַרְבַּע שָׁעוֹת. תְּפִלַּת הַמִּנְחָה עַד הָעֶרֶב; רַבִּי יְהוּדָה אוֹמֵר: עַד פְּלַג הַמִּנְחָה.

MISHNA This mishna determines the times beyond which the different prayers may not be recited. According to the Rabbis, **the morning prayer** may be recited **until noon. Rabbi Yehuda says:** It may be recited only **until four hours** after sunrise.[NH] According to the Rabbis, **the afternoon prayer** may be recited **until the evening. Rabbi Yehuda says:** It may be recited only **until the midpoint of the afternoon** [*pelag haminḥa*],[L] i.e., the midpoint of the period that begins with the sacrifice of the daily afternoon offering and ends at nightfall, which is the end of the afternoon.

תְּפִלַּת הָעֶרֶב אֵין לָהּ קֶבַע; וְשֶׁל מוּסָפִים כָּל הַיּוֹם, רַבִּי יְהוּדָה אוֹמֵר: עַד שֶׁבַע שָׁעוֹת.

The evening prayer may be recited throughout the night and **is not fixed** to a specific hour. According to the Rabbis, **the additional prayer** may be recited **all day. Rabbi Yehuda says:** It may be recited only **until seven hours** after sunrise.

גמ׳ וּרְמִינְהוּ: מִצְוָתָהּ עִם הָנֵץ הַחַמָּה, כְּדֵי שֶׁיִּסְמוֹךְ גְּאוּלָּה לִתְפִלָּה וְנִמְצָא מִתְפַּלֵּל בַּיּוֹם!

GEMARA We learned in the mishna that the morning prayer may be recited only until a few hours into the day. The Gemara **raises a contradiction** based on what was taught in a *baraita*: **The mitzva is** to recite the morning *Shema* **with sunrise** so that **he will juxtapose redemption,** which is mentioned in the blessings following *Shema*, **to the** *Amida* **prayer,** which is recited immediately after sunrise, and **find** himself **praying in the daytime.** Clearly, the time to recite the morning prayer is immediately after sunrise.

כִּי תַּנְיָא הַהִיא – לְוָתִיקִין, דְּאָמַר רַבִּי יוֹחָנָן: וָתִיקִין הָיוּ גּוֹמְרִים אוֹתָהּ עִם הָנֵץ הַחַמָּה.

The Gemara responds: This *baraita* does not establish a binding *halakha*. Rather, it **taught that** rule specifically **with regard to those who are scrupulous in fulfillment of mitzvot** [*vatikin*]. **As Rabbi Yoḥanan said:** ***Vatikin*** **would finish** reciting the morning *Shema* **with sunrise,** but those who are not *vatikin* may recite their prayers later.

וְכוּלֵּי עָלְמָא עַד חֲצוֹת וְתוּ לָא?! וְהָאָמַר רַב מָרִי בְּרֵיהּ דְּרַב הוּנָא בְּרֵיהּ דְּרַבִּי יִרְמְיָה בַּר אַבָּא אָמַר רַבִּי יוֹחָנָן: טָעָה וְלֹא הִתְפַּלֵּל עַרְבִית – מִתְפַּלֵּל בְּשַׁחֲרִית שְׁתַּיִם, שַׁחֲרִית – מִתְפַּלֵּל בְּמִנְחָה שְׁתַּיִם!

The Gemara asks: **Does everyone** hold that one may recite the morning prayer only **until noon and no later? Didn't Rav Mari, son of Rav Huna, son of Rabbi Yirmeya bar Abba, say** that **Rabbi Yoḥanan said: One who erred and did not recite the evening prayer,**[H] **prays in the morning prayer two** *Amida* prayers; one who erred and did not recite **the morning prayer, prays in the afternoon prayer two** *Amida* prayers? Apparently, the morning prayer may be recited until the evening, at least in the event that he forgot to recite it in the morning.

כּוּלֵּי יוֹמָא מְצַלֵּי וְאָזֵיל, עַד חֲצוֹת – יָהֲבִי לֵיהּ שְׂכַר תְּפִלָּה בִּזְמַנָּהּ, מִכָּאן וְאֵילָךְ – שְׂכַר תְּפִלָּה יָהֲבִי לֵיהּ, שְׂכַר תְּפִלָּה בִּזְמַנָּהּ – לָא יָהֲבִי לֵיהּ.

The Gemara answers: Indeed, **one may continue praying for the entire day.** However, if he prayed **until noon, they give him a reward for** reciting the **prayer at its** appointed **time.** If he prayed **from there on, they give him a reward for** reciting the **prayer. They do not give him a reward for** reciting the **prayer at its** appointed **time.**

אִיבַּעְיָא לְהוּ: טָעָה וְלֹא הִתְפַּלֵּל מִנְחָה, מַהוּ שֶׁיִּתְפַּלֵּל עַרְבִית שְׁתַּיִם? אִם תִּמְצָא לוֹמַר טָעָה וְלֹא הִתְפַּלֵּל עַרְבִית מִתְפַּלֵּל שַׁחֲרִית שְׁתַּיִם – מִשּׁוּם דְּחַד יוֹמָא הוּא, דִּכְתִיב ״וַיְהִי עֶרֶב וַיְהִי בֹקֶר יוֹם אֶחָד,״ אֲבָל הָכָא – תְּפִלָּה בִּמְקוֹם קׇרְבָּן הִיא, וְכֵיוָן דַּעֲבַר יוֹמוֹ בָּטֵל קׇרְבָּנוֹ; אוֹ דִּילְמָא, כֵּיוָן דִּצְלוֹתָא רַחֲמֵי הִיא – כׇּל אֵימַת דְּבָעֵי מְצַלֵּי וְאָזֵיל?

On the topic of one who forgot to pray and seeks to compensate for the prayer that he missed, **a dilemma was raised before them** in the study hall: **One who erred and did not recite the afternoon prayer, what is** the ruling? May he **recite** in **the evening prayer two** *Amida* prayers? The Gemara articulates the sides of the dilemma: **If you say** that **one who erred and did not pray the evening prayer prays in the morning prayer two** *Amida* prayers, perhaps that is **because** the evening and the morning are both part of **one day, as it is written: "And there was evening and there was morning, one day"** (Genesis 1:5); the evening and the following morning constitute a single unit. **But here,** in the case under discussion, perhaps **prayer is in place of sacrifice.** Since in the case of sacrifice we say, **since its day passed, his sacrifice is invalid**[N] and there is no way to compensate for the missed opportunity, the same should be true for prayer. **Or, perhaps, since prayer is supplication, any time that one wishes, he may continue to pray?**

NOTES

The time for the morning prayer – זְמַן תְּפִלַּת הַשַּׁחַר: Based on an allusion from the verse: "Evening and morning and at noon will I pray and cry aloud" (Psalms 55:18), it is derived that one is obligated to pray three times daily. The dispute with regard to the morning prayer is: Until what time is it considered morning (*She'iltot*)?

And since its day passed, his sacrifice is invalid – וְכֵיוָן דַּעֲבַר יוֹמוֹ בָּטֵל קׇרְבָּנוֹ: From the verse: "To bring forth a fire-offering to the Lord, a burnt-offering and a meal-offering, a slaughtered sacrifice and libations, that of each day on its day" (Leviticus 23:37), it is derived that a particular day's offering is not acceptable on another day (Maharshal).

HALAKHA

The end of the time for the morning prayer – סוֹף זְמַן תְּפִלַּת הַשַּׁחַר: The period during which the morning prayer may be recited lasts until the end of the fourth hour or one-third of the day, as per the opinion of Rabbi Yehuda, since the Gemara ruled in accordance with his opinion. Nevertheless, some of the authorities (Rif, Rosh) established that one who failed to pray before that time may, after the fact, pray until midday. The fact that one is not yet permitted to recite the afternoon prayer at that time proves that there is still room to recite the morning prayer (Rambam *Sefer Ahava, Hilkhot Tefilla* 3:1; *Shulḥan Arukh, Oraḥ Ḥayyim* 89:1).

One who erred and did not recite the evening prayer – טָעָה וְלֹא הִתְפַּלֵּל עַרְבִית: One who erred or one who, due to circumstances beyond his control, failed to recite the *Amida* prayer at the appropriate time, may compensate for his failure after reciting the following prayer. However, one may not recite the compensatory prayer on its own, as per the Rashba. This *halakha* is in accordance with the statement of Rabbi Yoḥanan, which was universally accepted. There is no distinction between the various prayers. Even if the prayer that he missed was the afternoon prayer, he may compensate for it by reciting the evening prayer twice. The principle: Since its day passed, his sacrifice is invalid, does not apply here (Rambam *Sefer Ahava, Hilkhot Tefilla* 3:8–9; *Shulḥan Arukh, Oraḥ Ḥayyim* 108:1, 2, 4).

LANGUAGE

The midpoint of the afternoon [*pelag haminḥa*] – פְּלַג הַמִּנְחָה: This is based on the biblical term *bein ha'arbayim*. In rabbinic literature, this refers to the time between two definitions of evening. One definition of evening is the time that the sun begins to tend westward, which begins a half-hour after noon, six-and-a-half hours into the day. Absolute evening is sunset. *Bein ha'arbayim* is the midpoint between these two evenings. Here there is another sense of evening, the time when the daily evening offering is sacrificed. This is approximately halfway between noon and sunset, nine-and-a-half hours into the day. Based on that definition of evening, *bein ha'arbayim* is the midpoint between that time and sunset. The Gemara refers to this as the second midpoint of *minḥa*.

תא שמע: דאמר רב הונא בר יהודה אמר רבי יצחק אמר רבי יוחנן: טעה ולא התפלל מנחה – מתפלל ערבית שתים, ואין בזה משום "דעבר יומו בטל קרבנו."

Come and hear a resolution to this dilemma from that **which Rav Huna bar Yehuda said that Rabbi Yitzḥak said that Rabbi Yoḥanan said: One who erred and did not recite the afternoon prayer, prays in the evening prayer two** *Amida* prayers **and there is no element of: Its day passed, his sacrifice is invalid.**

מיתיבי: "מעוות לא יוכל לתקן וחסרון לא יוכל להמנות"; "מעוות לא יוכל לתקן" – זה שבטל קריאת שמע של ערבית וקריאת שמע של שחרית, או תפלה של ערבית, או תפלה של שחרית; "וחסרון לא יוכל להמנות" – זה שנמנו חביריו לדבר מצוה ולא נמנה עמהם!

With regard to the possibility to compensate for a prayer that he failed to recite at its appointed time, the Gemara **raises an objection** based on what was taught in a *baraita*. The meaning of the verse: **"That which is crooked cannot be made straight; and that which is wanting cannot be numbered"** (Ecclesiastes 1:15), is as follows: **That which is crooked cannot be made straight** refers to **one who omitted the evening** ***Shema*** **and the morning** ***Shema*****, or the evening prayer, or the morning prayer. And that which is wanting cannot be numbered** [*lehimanot*] refers to **one whose friends reached a consensus** [***nimnu***] to perform **a mitzva and he was not part of their consensus** [***nimnu***] and, consequently, he missed his opportunity to join them in performance of the mitzva. This *baraita* clearly states that there is no way to compensate for a missed prayer.

אמר רבי יצחק אמר רבי יוחנן: הכא במאי עסקינן – שבטל במזיד

To resolve this difficulty, **Rabbi Yitzḥak said that Rabbi Yoḥanan said: With what are we dealing here** in this *baraita*? We are dealing with a case where one **intentionally failed** to recite the prayer.[H] Only then he has no remedy. However, one who failed to pray due to error can compensate for the missed prayer by reciting the next prayer twice.

HALAKHA

One intentionally failed to recite the prayer – שבטל במזיד: One who intentionally did not pray may not compensate for the missed prayer. If he wishes to recite a voluntary prayer he may do so, even without introducing a novel element to his prayer (Rambam *Sefer Ahava, Hilkhot Tefilla* 3:8; *Shulḥan Arukh, Oraḥ Ḥayyim* 108:7).

אמר רב אשי: דיקא נמי דקתני "בטל," ולא קתני "טעה" – שמע מינה.

Rav Ashi said: The language of the *baraita* **is also precise as it teaches omitted and did not teach erred.** This indicates that the *halakha* is different in the case of error. The Gemara concludes: Indeed, **learn from this.**

Perek **IV**
Daf **26** Amud **b**

תנו רבנן: טעה ולא התפלל מנחה בערב שבת – מתפלל בליל שבת שתים, טעה ולא התפלל מנחה בשבת – מתפלל במוצאי שבת שתים. מבדיל בראשונה ואינו מבדיל בשניה, ואם הבדיל בשניה ולא הבדיל בראשונה – שניה עלתה לו, ראשונה לא עלתה לו.

On a similar note, **the Sages taught** in a *baraita*: **One who erred and did not recite the afternoon prayer on the eve of Shabbat,**[H] **prays in** the evening prayer **two** *Amida* prayers **on Shabbat evening. One who erred and did not recite the afternoon prayer on Shabbat,**[H] **recites two** *Amida* prayers in the evening prayer **at the conclusion of Shabbat. He recites** ***havdala*** [the prayer of **distinction**] between the sanctity of Shabbat and the profanity of the week by reciting: You have graced us, etc., in the fourth blessing of the *Amida,* which is: Who graciously grants knowledge, **in the first** prayer, as it is the actual evening prayer, **but he does not recite** ***havdala*** **in the second** prayer, which is in place of the afternoon prayer. Moreover, **if he recited** ***havdala*** **in the second** prayer **and did not recite** ***havdala*** **in the first, the second prayer fulfilled his** obligation, the **first one did not fulfill his** obligation.

למימרא, דכיון דלא אבדיל בקמייתא כמאן דלא צלי דמי ומהדרינן ליה?

The Gemara comments: **Is that to say** that **since he did not recite** ***havdala*** **in the first** prayer, he is **as one who did not pray and we require him to return** to the beginning of the prayer and repeat it? If so, the conclusion is that one who fails to recite *havdala* in the prayer must repeat that prayer.

HALAKHA

One who erred and did not recite the afternoon prayer on the eve of Shabbat – טעה ולא התפלל מנחה בערב שבת: One who erred and did not recite the afternoon prayer on Shabbat eve recites the Shabbat evening prayer twice; the first, to fulfill his obligation to recite the Shabbat evening prayer and the second to compensate for the afternoon prayer (Rambam *Sefer Ahava, Hilkhot Tefilla* 10:15; *Shulḥan Arukh, Oraḥ Ḥayyim* 108:9).

One who erred and did not recite the afternoon prayer on Shabbat – טעה ולא התפלל מנחה בשבת: One who erred and did not recite the afternoon prayer on Shabbat recites the weekday evening prayer twice at the conclusion of Shabbat; the first to fulfill his obligation to recite the weekday evening prayer and the second to compensate for the Shabbat afternoon prayer. He recites *havdala* during the first evening prayer, in the fourth blessing: Who graciously grants knowledge. He may not recite *havdala* in the compensatory prayer. If he recites *havdala* in the second prayer and not the first, he did not fulfill his obligation to compensate for his missed prayer and must pray again (Rambam *Sefer Ahava, Hilkhot Tefilla* 10:15; *Shulḥan Arukh, Oraḥ Ḥayyim* 108:10).

וּרְמִינְהוּ: טָעָה וְלֹא הִזְכִּיר גְּבוּרוֹת גְּשָׁמִים בִּתְחִיַּית הַמֵּתִים וּשְׁאֵלָה בְּבִרְכַּת הַשָּׁנִים – מַחֲזִירִין אוֹתוֹ, הַבְדָּלָה בְּחוֹנֵן הַדַּעַת – אֵין מַחֲזִירִין אוֹתוֹ, מִפְּנֵי שֶׁיָּכוֹל לְאוֹמְרָהּ עַל הַכּוֹס! – קַשְׁיָא.

The Gemara **raises a contradiction** to the above conclusion from the *Tosefta*: **One who erred and did not mention the might of the rains:**[H] He makes the wind blow and rain fall **in** the second blessing of the *Amida*, the blessing on **the revival of the dead, and** one who erred and failed to recite **the request** for rain **in** the ninth blessing of the *Amida*, **the blessing of the years,**[H] **we require him to return** to the beginning of the prayer and repeat it. However, one who erred and failed to recite ***havdala*** **in** the blessing: **Who graciously grants knowledge,**[H] **we do not require him to return** to the beginning of the prayer and repeat it, **as he can recite** *havdala* **over the cup** of wine, independent of his prayer. This contradiction was not resolved and remains **difficult.**

אִיתְּמַר, רַבִּי יוֹסֵי בְּרַבִּי חֲנִינָא אָמַר: תְּפִלּוֹת אָבוֹת תִּקְּנוּם; רַבִּי יְהוֹשֻׁעַ בֶּן לֵוִי אָמַר: תְּפִלּוֹת כְּנֶגֶד תְּמִידִין תִּקְּנוּם.

The dispute between the Rabbis and Rabbi Yehuda with regard to the times beyond which the different prayers may not be recited is rooted in a profound disagreement, also manifest in a later amoraic dispute. **It was stated: Rabbi Yosei, son of Rabbi Ḥanina, said:** The practice of praying three times daily is ancient, albeit not in its present form; **prayers were instituted by the Patriarchs.** However, **Rabbi Yehoshua ben Levi said** that the **prayers were instituted based on the daily offerings**[HB] sacrificed in the Holy Temple, and the prayers parallel the offerings, in terms of both time and characteristics.

תַּנְיָא כְּוָותֵיהּ דְּרַבִּי יוֹסֵי בְּרַבִּי חֲנִינָא, וְתַנְיָא כְּוָותֵיהּ דְּרַבִּי יְהוֹשֻׁעַ בֶּן לֵוִי. תַּנְיָא כְּוָותֵיהּ דְּרַבִּי יוֹסֵי בְּרַבִּי חֲנִינָא: אַבְרָהָם תִּקֵּן תְּפִלַּת שַׁחֲרִית – שֶׁנֶּאֱמַר ״וַיַּשְׁכֵּם אַבְרָהָם בַּבֹּקֶר אֶל הַמָּקוֹם אֲשֶׁר עָמַד שָׁם,״ וְאֵין עֲמִידָה אֶלָּא תְּפִלָּה, שֶׁנֶּאֱמַר ״וַיַּעֲמֹד פִּינְחָס וַיְפַלֵּל״;

The Gemara comments: **It was taught** in a *baraita* **in accordance with** the opinion of **Rabbi Yosei, son of Rabbi Ḥanina, and it was taught** in a *baraita* **in accordance with** the opinion of **Rabbi Yehoshua ben Levi.** The Gemara elaborates: **It was taught** in a *baraita* **in accordance with** the opinion of **Rabbi Yosei, son of Rabbi Ḥanina: Abraham instituted the morning prayer, as it is stated** when Abraham came to look out over Sodom the day after he had prayed on its behalf: **"And Abraham rose early in the morning to the place where he had stood** before the Lord" (Genesis 19:27), **and** from the context as well as the language utilized in the verse, the verb **standing** means **nothing other than prayer,** as this language is used to describe Pinehas' prayer after the plague, **as it is stated: "And Pinehas stood up and prayed** and the plague ended" (Psalms 106:30). Clearly, Abraham was accustomed to stand in prayer in the morning.

יִצְחָק תִּקֵּן תְּפִלַּת מִנְחָה – שֶׁנֶּאֱמַר ״וַיֵּצֵא יִצְחָק לָשׂוּחַ בַּשָּׂדֶה לִפְנוֹת עָרֶב,״ וְאֵין שִׂיחָה אֶלָּא תְּפִלָּה, שֶׁנֶּאֱמַר ״תְּפִלָּה לְעָנִי כִי יַעֲטֹף וְלִפְנֵי ה׳ יִשְׁפֹּךְ שִׂיחוֹ״;

Isaac instituted the afternoon prayer, as it is stated: "And Isaac went out to converse [*lasuaḥ*] **in the field toward evening"** (Genesis 24:63), **and conversation** means **nothing other than prayer, as it is stated: "A prayer of the afflicted when he is faint and pours out his complaint** [*siḥo*] **before the Lord"** (Psalms 102:1). Obviously, Isaac was the first to pray as evening approached, at the time of the afternoon prayer.

יַעֲקֹב תִּקֵּן תְּפִלַּת עַרְבִית – שֶׁנֶּאֱמַר: ״וַיִּפְגַּע בַּמָּקוֹם וַיָּלֶן שָׁם,״ וְאֵין פְּגִיעָה אֶלָּא תְּפִלָּה, שֶׁנֶּאֱמַר ״וְאַתָּה אַל תִּתְפַּלֵּל בְּעַד הָעָם הַזֶּה וְאַל תִּשָּׂא בַעֲדָם רִנָּה וּתְפִלָּה וְאַל תִּפְגַּע בִּי.״

Jacob instituted the evening prayer, as it is stated: "And he encountered [*vayifga*] **the place and he slept there** for the sun had set" (Genesis 28:11). The word **encounter** means **nothing other than prayer, as it is stated** when God spoke to Jeremiah: **"And you, do not pray on behalf of this nation and do not raise on their behalf song and prayer, and do not encounter** [*tifga*] **Me** for I do not hear you" (Jeremiah 7:16). Jacob prayed during the evening, after the sun had set.

וְתַנְיָא כְּוָותֵיהּ דְּרַבִּי יְהוֹשֻׁעַ בֶּן לֵוִי: מִפְּנֵי מָה אָמְרוּ תְּפִלַּת הַשַּׁחַר עַד חֲצוֹת – שֶׁהֲרֵי תָּמִיד שֶׁל שַׁחַר קָרֵב וְהוֹלֵךְ עַד חֲצוֹת; וְרַבִּי יְהוּדָה אוֹמֵר: עַד אַרְבַּע שָׁעוֹת, שֶׁהֲרֵי תָּמִיד שֶׁל שַׁחַר קָרֵב וְהוֹלֵךְ עַד אַרְבַּע שָׁעוֹת.

And it was taught in a *baraita* **in accordance with** the opinion of **Rabbi Yehoshua ben Levi** that the laws of prayer are based on the laws of the daily offerings: **Why did** the Rabbis **say** that **the morning prayer** may be recited **until noon? Because,** although the **daily morning offering** is typically brought early in the morning, it may be **sacrificed until noon. And Rabbi Yehuda says:** My opinion, that the morning prayer may be recited **until four hours** into the day, is **because the daily morning offering is sacrificed until four hours.**

וּמִפְּנֵי מָה אָמְרוּ תְּפִלַּת הַמִּנְחָה עַד הָעֶרֶב – שֶׁהֲרֵי תָּמִיד שֶׁל בֵּין הָעַרְבַּיִם קָרֵב וְהוֹלֵךְ עַד הָעֶרֶב; רַבִּי יְהוּדָה אוֹמֵר: עַד פְּלַג הַמִּנְחָה, שֶׁהֲרֵי תָּמִיד שֶׁל בֵּין הָעַרְבַּיִם קָרֵב וְהוֹלֵךְ עַד פְּלַג הַמִּנְחָה.

And why did the Rabbis **say** that **the afternoon prayer** may be recited **until the evening? Because the daily afternoon offering is sacrificed until the evening. Rabbi Yehuda says** that **the afternoon prayer** may be recited only **until the midpoint of the afternoon because,** according to his opinion, **the daily afternoon offering is sacrificed until the midpoint of the afternoon.**

וּמִפְּנֵי מָה אָמְרוּ תְּפִלַּת הָעֶרֶב אֵין לָהּ קֶבַע – שֶׁהֲרֵי אֵבָרִים וּפְדָרִים שֶׁלֹּא נִתְעַכְּלוּ מִבָּעֶרֶב קְרֵבִים וְהוֹלְכִים כָּל הַלַּיְלָה;

And why did they say that **the evening prayer is not fixed? Because** the burning of the **limbs and fats** of the offerings that were **not consumed** by the fire on the altar **until the evening.** They remained on the altar and were **offered continuously** throughout **the entire night.**

HALAKHA

One who erred and did not mention the might of the rains – **טָעָה וְלֹא הִזְכִּיר גְּבוּרוֹת גְּשָׁמִים:** One who neglected to recite: He makes the winds blow and the rain fall, in the blessing: Who revives the dead; in the winter, he is required to repeat the *Amida* prayer, in accordance with the uncontested *Tosefta*. However, if he mentioned: He causes the dew to fall, he is not required to repeat the *Amida* prayer (Rambam *Sefer Ahava, Hilkhot Tefilla* 10:8; *Shulḥan Arukh, Oraḥ Ḥayyim* 114:5).

One who erred and did not mention the request for rain in the blessing of the years – **טָעָה וְלֹא הִזְכִּיר...וּשְׁאֵלָה בְּבִרְכַּת הַשָּׁנִים:** One who erroneously did not recite the request for rain in the blessing of the years during the winter, is required to repeat the *Amida* prayer even if he recited a request for dew (Rambam *Sefer Ahava, Hilkhot Tefilla* 10:9; *Shulḥan Arukh, Oraḥ Ḥayyim* 117:4).

One who erred and failed to recite *havdala* in the blessing: Who graciously grants knowledge – **טָעָה וְלֹא הִזְכִּיר...הַבְדָּלָה בְּחוֹנֵן הַדַּעַת:** Hne who neglected to recite *havdala* in the blessing: Who graciously grants knowledge, in the evening prayer at the conclusion of Shabbat, need not repeat the *Amida* prayer because he has the opportunity to recite it on a cup of wine (Rambam *Sefer Ahava, Hilkhot Tefilla* 10:14; *Shulḥan Arukh, Oraḥ Ḥayyim* 294:1).

Prayers were instituted based on the daily offerings – **תְּפִלּוֹת כְּנֶגֶד תְּמִידִין תִּקְּנוּם:** Ultimately, it was determined that the Sages instituted prayer based on the daily offerings. Consequently, several elements that apply to the *halakhot* of offerings apply to prayer as well, i.e., establishing a fixed place to pray, the capacity of improper thought to invalidate prayer, etc. Although the Talmud cites proof in support of both amoraic opinions, since the Gemara raised a challenge to the opinion of Rabbi Yosei son of Rabbi Ḥanina from the *baraita* supporting the opinion of Rabbi Yehoshua ben Levi, apparently that is the preferred opinion (*Kesef Mishne*, who disagrees with *Leḥem Mishne*; Rambam *Sefer Ahava, Hilkhot Tefilla* 1:5–6).

BACKGROUND

Prayers were instituted based on the daily offerings – **תְּפִלּוֹת כְּנֶגֶד תְּמִידִין תִּקְּנוּם:** Some explain that this means that prayers were instituted by the Sages after the destruction of the Temple to replace the offerings. However, these prayers were already extant throughout the Second Temple era with virtually the same formula that was instituted later, with certain known differences. Furthermore, there were already synagogues at that time, some even in close proximity to the Temple. The dispute in this case is whether the prayers were instituted to parallel the offerings, or whether the prayers have an independent source, unrelated to the Temple Service.

HALAKHA

Minḥa gedola – מִנְחָה גְּדוֹלָה: The period of *minḥa gedola* begins six-and-a-half hours into the day, half an hour after midday. The authorities disagree whether one may only recite the afternoon prayer at that point after the fact (Rambam) or whether even *ab initio* one is permitted to pray then (*Tur*). The conclusion is that, when the need arises, one is permitted to pray during the *minḥa gedola* period even though the ideal time to recite the afternoon prayer is during the period of *minḥa ketana*, which lasts from nine-and-a-half hours into the day until sunset (Rambam *Sefer Ahava, Hilkhot Tefilla* 3:3–4; *Shulḥan Arukh, Oraḥ Ḥayyim* 234:1).

BACKGROUNDS

Until and including – עַד וְעַד בִּכְלָל: The dilemma raised here is a fundamental problem in delineating halakhic parameters. Parallel dilemmas are raised in other cases to determine the application of halakhic parameters and to establish whether there is a set principle with regard to their application or whether each instance is handled individually.

וּמִפְּנֵי מָה אָמְרוּ שֶׁל מוּסָפִין כָּל הַיּוֹם – שֶׁהֲרֵי קָרְבָּן שֶׁל מוּסָפִין קָרֵב כָּל הַיּוֹם; רַבִּי יְהוּדָה אוֹמֵר: עַד שֶׁבַע שָׁעוֹת, שֶׁהֲרֵי קָרְבַּן מוּסָף קָרֵב וְהוֹלֵךְ עַד שֶׁבַע שָׁעוֹת.

And why did the Rabbis **say that the additional prayer** may be recited **all day? Because the additional offering is brought** throughout **the entire day.** However, **Rabbi Yehuda says** that **the additional prayer** may be recited **until the seventh hour** of the day, **because the additional offering is sacrificed until the seventh hour.**

וְאֵיזוֹ הִיא מִנְחָה גְּדוֹלָה – מִשֵּׁשׁ שָׁעוֹת וּמֶחֱצָה וּלְמַעְלָה; וְאֵיזוֹ הִיא מִנְחָה קְטַנָּה – מִתֵּשַׁע שָׁעוֹת וּמֶחֱצָה וּלְמַעְלָה.

The *baraita* continues and states that there are two times for the afternoon prayer. Greater, earlier *minḥa* [*minḥa gedola*] and lesser, later *minḥa* [*minḥa ketana*]. The Gemara clarifies the difference between them: **Which is *minḥa gedola*?**[H] **From six-and-a-half hours** after sunrise **and on,** which is a half an hour after noon and on. It is the earliest time that the daily afternoon offering may be sacrificed, as in the case on the eve of Passover that occurs on Shabbat. **Which is *minḥa ketana*? From nine-and-a-half hours and on,** which is the standard time that the daily afternoon offering is sacrificed.

אִיבַּעְיָא לְהוּ: רַבִּי יְהוּדָה פְּלַג מִנְחָה קַמָּא קָאָמַר, אוֹ פְּלַג מִנְחָה אַחֲרוֹנָה קָאָמַר? תָּא שְׁמַע: דְּתַנְיָא, רַבִּי יְהוּדָה אוֹמֵר: פְּלַג הַמִּנְחָה אַחֲרוֹנָה אָמְרוּ, וְהִיא אַחַת עֶשְׂרֵה שָׁעוֹת חָסֵר רְבִיעַ.

On that note, **a dilemma was raised before them: Rabbi Yehuda,** who holds that the afternoon prayer may be recited only until the midpoint of the afternoon, does **he say the midpoint of the first *minḥa*,** *minḥa gedola*? **Or,** does **he say the midpoint of the last *minḥa*? Come and hear** an explicit resolution to this dilemma: **As it was taught** in a *baraita*, **Rabbi Yehuda says: They said the midpoint of the last *minḥa*, and that is eleven hours minus a quarter** of an hour after sunrise, i.e., an hour-and-a-quarter hours before sunset.

נֵימָא תֶּיהֱוֵי תְּיוּבְתֵּיהּ דְּרַבִּי יוֹסֵי בְּרַבִּי חֲנִינָא! אָמַר לָךְ רַבִּי יוֹסֵי בְּרַבִּי חֲנִינָא: לְעוֹלָם אֵימָא לָךְ תְּפִלּוֹת אָבוֹת תִּקְנוּם, וְאַסְמְכִינְהוּ רַבָּנַן אַקָּרְבָּנוֹת. דְּאִי לָא תֵּימָא הָכִי – תְּפִלַּת מוּסָף לְרַבִּי יוֹסֵי בְּרַבִּי חֲנִינָא מַאן תִּקְנָהּ? אֶלָּא: תְּפִלּוֹת אָבוֹת תִּקְנוּם, וְאַסְמְכִינְהוּ רַבָּנַן אַקָּרְבָּנוֹת.

In any case, it is clear that according to this *baraita* the *halakhot* of prayer are based on the Temple offerings. The Gemara suggests: **Let us say that this is a conclusive refutation of** the opinion of **Rabbi Yosei, son of Rabbi Ḥanina,** who held that the forefathers instituted the prayers. **Rabbi Yosei, son of Rabbi Ḥanina,** could have **said to you: Actually, I will say to you that the Patriarchs instituted the prayers and the Sages based** the times and characteristics of prayer **on the Temple offerings,** even though they do not stem from the same source. **As, if you do not say so,** that even Rabbi Yosei, son of Rabbi Ḥanina, would agree that the laws of offerings and those of prayers are related, **then, according to Rabbi Yosei, son of Rabbi Ḥanina, who instituted the additional prayer?** It is not one of the prayers instituted by the forefathers. **Rather,** even according to Rabbi Yosei, son of Rabbi Ḥanina, **the prayers were instituted by the Patriarchs and the Sages based them** on the laws of the **offerings.**

רַבִּי יְהוּדָה אוֹמֵר: עַד אַרְבַּע שָׁעוֹת. אִיבַּעְיָא לְהוּ: עַד וְעַד בִּכְלָל, אוֹ דִּילְמָא, עַד וְלֹא עַד בִּכְלָל? תָּא שְׁמַע, רַבִּי יְהוּדָה אוֹמֵר: עַד פְּלַג הַמִּנְחָה. אִי אָמְרַתְּ בִּשְׁלָמָא עַד וְלֹא עַד בִּכְלָל – הַיְינוּ דְּאִיכָּא בֵּין רַבִּי יְהוּדָה לְרַבָּנַן, אֶלָּא אִי אָמְרַתְּ עַד וְעַד בִּכְלָל – רַבִּי יְהוּדָה

We learned in the mishna that **Rabbi Yehuda says:** The morning prayer may be recited **until four hours** of the day. **A dilemma was raised before** the yeshiva students: When Rabbi Yehuda says **until,** does he mean **until and including**[B] the fourth hour, **or, perhaps** when he says **"until"** he means **until and not including,** in which case one may not pray during the fourth hour? **Come and hear** a resolution to this dilemma based on the mishna. **Rabbi Yehuda says:** The afternoon prayer may be recited only **until the midpoint of the afternoon.** Now, **granted, if you say** that **until** means **until and not including, then there is** a difference **between** the opinion of **Rabbi Yehuda and** the opinion of **the Rabbis. However, if you say** that **until** means **until and including,** then the opinion of **Rabbi Yehuda**

Perek **IV**
Daf **27** Amud **a**

הַיְינוּ רַבָּנַן!

is identical to the opinion of **the Rabbis,** as the end of the period that begins with the midpoint of the afternoon is sunset.

אֶלָּא מַאי? עַד וְלֹא עַד בִּכְלָל – אֵימָא סֵיפָא: וְשֶׁל מוּסָפִין כָּל הַיּוֹם, רַבִּי יְהוּדָה אוֹמֵר: עַד שֶׁבַע שָׁעוֹת; וְתַנְיָא: הָיוּ לְפָנָיו שְׁתֵּי תְּפִלּוֹת, אַחַת שֶׁל מוּסָף, וְאַחַת שֶׁל מִנְחָה – מִתְפַּלֵּל שֶׁל מִנְחָה וְאַחַר כָּךְ שֶׁל מוּסָף, שֶׁזּוֹ תְּדִירָה וְזוֹ אֵינָהּ תְּדִירָה; רַבִּי יְהוּדָה אוֹמֵר: מִתְפַּלֵּל שֶׁל מוּסָף וְאַחַר כָּךְ שֶׁל מִנְחָה, שֶׁזּוֹ עוֹבֶרֶת וְזוֹ אֵינָהּ עוֹבֶרֶת.

The Gemara immediately rejects this proof: **Rather, what** is the alternative? That **until** means **until and not including?** It remains problematic. **Say the latter clause** of the mishna: **The additional prayer** may be recited **all day. Rabbi Yehuda says:** It may be recited **until the seven hours. And it was taught** in a *baraita*: **If** the obligation to recite **two prayers was before him, one the additional prayer and one the afternoon prayer, he prays the afternoon prayer** first **and the additional prayer thereafter,** because **this,** the afternoon prayer, **is** recited on a **frequent** basis, **and that,** the additional prayer, **is** recited on a relatively **infrequent** basis as it is only recited on Shabbat, the New Moon, and Festivals. The principle states: When a frequent practice and an infrequent practice clash, the frequent practice takes precedence over the infrequent practice. **Rabbi Yehuda says: He recites the additional prayer** first **and the afternoon prayer thereafter,** because the time to recite **this, the additional prayer,** will soon **elapse, and this,** the time to recite **the afternoon prayer,** will **not** soon **elapse,** as one may recite it until the midpoint of the afternoon.

אִי אָמְרַתְּ בִּשְׁלָמָא עַד וְעַד בִּכְלָל – הַיְינוּ דְּמַשְׁכַּחַתְּ לְהוּ שְׁתֵּי תְּפִלּוֹת בַּהֲדֵי הֲדָדֵי, אֶלָּא אִי אָמְרַתְּ עַד וְלֹא עַד בִּכְלָל – הֵיכִי מַשְׁכַּחַתְּ לְהוּ שְׁתֵּי תְּפִלּוֹת בַּהֲדֵי הֲדָדֵי? כֵּיוָן דְּאָתְיָא לַהּ שֶׁל מִנְחָה אָזְלָא לַהּ שֶׁל מוּסָפִין!

The relevant point is: **Granted, if you say** that **until** means **until and including, that is how you can find** a situation where the times to recite **two prayers,** the afternoon prayer and the additional prayer, **overlap. But if you say** that **until** means **until and not including,** and that until seven hours means until the beginning of the seventh hour, noon, then **how can you find** a situation where the times to recite **two prayers overlap? Once** the time to recite **the afternoon prayer,** a half hour past noon, **has arrived,** the time to recite **the additional prayer** is already **gone?**

אֶלָּא מַאי, עַד וְעַד בִּכְלָל? קַשְׁיָא רֵישָׁא: מַאי אִיכָּא בֵּין רַבִּי יְהוּדָה לְרַבָּנַן? – מִי סָבְרַתְּ דְּהַאי ״פְּלַג מִנְחָה״ פְּלַג אַחֲרוֹנָה קָאָמַר? פְּלַג רִאשׁוֹנָה קָאָמַר, וְהָכִי קָאָמַר: אֵימַת נָפֵיק פְּלַג רִאשׁוֹנָה וְעָיֵיל פְּלַג אַחֲרוֹנָה? מִכִּי נָפְקֵי אַחַת עֶשְׂרֵה שָׁעוֹת חָסֵר רְבִיעַ.

Rather, what is the alternative? That **until** means **until and including?** Then **the first clause** of the mishna **is difficult,** as explained above with regard to the midpoint of the afternoon: **What is** the halakhic difference **between** the opinion of **Rabbi Yehuda and** the opinion of **the Rabbis?** The Gemara answers: **Do you think that** when **this midpoint of the afternoon** was mentioned it was **speaking of** the period following **the midpoint, the last** part of the afternoon, from an hour-and-a-quarter before sunset until sunset? This was not the intention. Rather, it was **speaking of** the period prior to **the midpoint, the first** part of the afternoon, which, as explained above, is from nine-and-a-half hours after sunrise until an hour-and-a-quarter before sunset. Consequently, until the midpoint of the afternoon means until the end of the first half of that afternoon period. **And this is what he is saying: When does the first half leave and the second half enter? From when eleven hours minus a quarter have passed** since sunrise. Rabbi Yehuda's use of the term until always means until and including.

אָמַר רַב נַחְמָן: אַף אֲנַן נַמִי תְּנֵינָא,

Practically speaking, this means that, according to Rabbi Yehuda, it is permissible to recite the morning prayer until the end of the fourth hour. In support of this **Rav Naḥman said: We, too, learned** this in a mishna:

רַבִּי יְהוּדָה בֶּן בָּבָא הֵעִיד חֲמִשָּׁה דְּבָרִים: שֶׁמְּמָאֲנִין אֶת הַקְּטַנָּה, וְשֶׁמַּשִּׂיאִין אֶת הָאִשָּׁה עַל פִּי עֵד אֶחָד, וְעַל תַּרְנְגוֹל שֶׁנִּסְקַל בִּירוּשָׁלַיִם עַל שֶׁהָרַג אֶת הַנֶּפֶשׁ, וְעַל יַיִן בֶּן אַרְבָּעִים יוֹם שֶׁנִּתְנַסֵּךְ עַל גַּבֵּי הַמִּזְבֵּחַ, וְעַל תָּמִיד שֶׁל שַׁחַר שֶׁקָּרַב בְּאַרְבַּע שָׁעוֹת;

Rabbi Yehuda ben Bava testified about **five matters of** *halakha*:

When an orphan girl, who was married off by her mother or brother before reaching the age of majority, reaches the age of majority, she may refuse to continue living with her husband and thereby retroactively annul their marriage. Normally, marriage refusals are discouraged. However, in specific instances where it is clear that if the marriage were to remain in effect it would engender problems related to levirate marriage and *ḥalitza*, Rabbi Yehuda ben Bava testified that **one may persuade the minor girl to refuse**[H] to continue living with her husband, thereby resolving the complications involved in this case.

And he testified **that one may** allow **a woman** who, after hearing of her husband's death, seeks to remarry, **to marry based on** the testimony **one witness,**[H] as opposed to the two witnesses required for other testimonies of the Torah.

And he testified **about a rooster that was stoned**[H] to death **in Jerusalem for killing a person,** in order to teach that the Torah law (Exodus 21:28) which requires the stoning of an ox that killed a person, applies to other animals as well.

And he testified **about forty-day-old wine that was** used for **libation on the altar.**[H]

And he testified **about** the **daily morning offering that was sacrificed at four hours**[H] of the day.

שְׁמַע מִינַּהּ: ״עַד״ וְ״עַד״ בִּכְלָל, שְׁמַע מִינַּהּ.

Learn from this final testimony, which is in accordance with the opinion of Rabbi Yehuda, that **until** means **until and including.** The Gemara concludes: Indeed, **learn from this.**

אָמַר רַב כָּהֲנָא: הֲלָכָה כְּרַבִּי יְהוּדָה, הוֹאִיל וּתְנַן בִּבְחִירְתָּא כְּוָותֵיהּ.

Based on this mishna, **Rav Kahana said: The** *halakha* **is in accordance with** the opinion of **Rabbi Yehuda since we learned** in a mishna in the **preferred** tractate, *Eduyyot*,[N] **in accordance with his** opinion. Since the *halakha* is ruled in accordance with all of the *mishnayot* in *Eduyyot*, the opinion of a *tanna* who rules in accordance with the opinion of Rabbi Yehuda in that mishna means that the *halakha* is in accordance with that opinion.

״וְעַל תָּמִיד שֶׁל שַׁחַר שֶׁקָּרַב בְּאַרְבַּע שָׁעוֹת.״ מַאן תַּנָּא לְהָא, דִּתְנַן: ״וְחַם הַשֶּׁמֶשׁ וְנָמָס״ – בְּאַרְבַּע שָׁעוֹת.

And about the **daily morning offering that was sacrificed at four hours.** Based on this, the Gemara attempts to identify **the** ***tanna*** **who taught that which we learned** in the mishna about the manna that fell for the children of Israel in the desert: "And they gathered it morning by morning, each according to what he eats, **and when the sun grew hot it melted**" (Exodus 16:21); that took place **four hours** into the day.

HALAKHA

One may persuade the minor girl to refuse – שֶׁמְּמָאֲנִין אֶת הַקְּטַנָּה: Two brothers were married to two sisters who were orphaned from their father. One of the sisters, who passed the age of majority, was betrothed to her husband of her own volition, and her marriage was by Torah law. The other sister was a minor and her brother agreed to her betrothal *in loco parentis*, and, consequently, her marriage was by rabbinic law. If the husband of the older sister died, his brother would be obligated to enter into a levirate marriage with the older sister. However, he would be forbidden to do so by the prohibition of marrying two sisters. In this case, based on the testimony of Rabbi Yehuda ben Bava, they persuade the younger sister to opt out of her marriage by means of the rite of refusal, enabling her husband to enter into a levirate marriage with the older sister (Rambam *Sefer Nashim, Hilkhot Yibbum VeḤalitza* 7:15; *Shulḥan Arukh, Even HaEzer* 175:11).

One may allow a woman to marry based on one witness – וְשֶׁמַּשִּׂיאִין אֶת הָאִשָּׁה עַל פִּי עֵד אֶחָד: If a woman's husband traveled to a distant venue, and one witness from that venue came and testified that he died, she may remarry based on that testimony. In all cases, the requirement is to have the testimony of two witnesses. However, since the information in this case is likely to be confirmed or contradicted, the assumption is that the woman would not remarry unless she was certain that the testimony was true. The Sages were lenient and accepted the testimony in order to save the woman from the never-ending status of a deserted wife (Rambam *Sefer Nashim, Hilkhot Gerushin* 12:15; *Shulḥan Arukh, Even HaEzer* 17:3).

And about a rooster that was stoned – וְעַל תַּרְנְגוֹל שֶׁנִּסְקַל: Any animal or bird that kills a person is put to death by stoning (Rambam *Sefer Nezikin, Hilkhot Nizkei Mamon* 10:2).

Forty-day-old wine that was used for libation on the altar – יַיִן בֶּן אַרְבָּעִים יוֹם שֶׁנִּתְנַסֵּךְ עַל גַּבֵּי הַמִּזְבֵּחַ: When forty days pass from the time the wine emerged from the wine press, it may be offered on the altar as a libation (Rambam *Sefer Avoda, Hilkhot Issurei Mizbe'aḥ* 6:9).

The daily morning offering that was sacrificed at four hours – תָּמִיד שֶׁל שַׁחַר שֶׁקָּרַב בְּאַרְבַּע שָׁעוֹת: Although the daily morning offering was sacrificed before sunrise, in exigent circumstances, it may be sacrificed until the end of the fourth hour of the day (Rambam *Sefer Avoda, Hilkhot Temidin UMusafin* 1:2).

NOTES

We also learned this in the preferred tractate, *Eduyyot* – וּתְנַן בִּבְחִירְתָּא (מַסֶּכֶת עֵדֻיּוֹת): This tractate includes numerous testimonies attested to by the Sages before their colleagues with regard to established *halakhot* that they heard and unique situations that they witnessed. In addition, this tractate contains other accepted *halakhot*. Apparently, there is an additional meaning of the name of the tractate, a variation on the word *idit*, which is the term used in *halakha* for the highest quality land. This tractate is the highest quality tractate in terms of its halakhic authority.

אַתָּה אוֹמֵר בְּאַרְבַּע שָׁעוֹת, אוֹ אֵינוֹ אֶלָּא בְּשֵׁשׁ שָׁעוֹת?! כְּשֶׁהוּא אוֹמֵר: ״כְּחֹם הַיּוֹם״ – הֲרֵי שֵׁשׁ שָׁעוֹת אָמוּר, הָא מָה אֲנִי מְקַיֵּים ״וְחַם הַשֶּׁמֶשׁ וְנָמָס״ – בְּאַרְבַּע שָׁעוֹת. מַנִּי? לָא רַבִּי יְהוּדָה וְלָא רַבָּנַן! אִי רַבִּי יְהוּדָה עַד אַרְבַּע שָׁעוֹת נַמִּי צַפְרָא הוּא, אִי רַבָּנַן – עַד חֲצוֹת נַמִּי צַפְרָא הוּא!

The Gemara asks: Do **you say** that the time when the sun grew hot was **at four hours, or** perhaps **it was only at six hours** of the day? **When** the verse **says: "In the heat of the day"** (Genesis 18:1), **six hours is** already **mentioned** in the Torah as the heat of the day. **How, then, do I establish** the verse: **"And when the sun grew hot it melted"?** This must refer to an earlier time, **at four hours. Who is the** ***tanna*** of this mishna? It is **neither Rabbi Yehuda nor the Sages. If** it was in accordance with the opinion of **Rabbi Yehuda, until four hours is also** considered **morning,** as he holds that the daily morning offering may still be sacrificed then, while here it says that in the morning the manna was gathered and it melted after the morning. **If** it was in accordance with the opinion of **the Rabbis, until noon is also** considered **morning,** since, according to the Sages, the daily morning offering could be sacrificed until noon. Apparently, this is an entirely new position.

אִי בָּעֵית אֵימָא: רַבִּי יְהוּדָה, אִי בָּעֵית אֵימָא: רַבָּנַן. אִי בָּעֵית אֵימָא רַבָּנַן – אָמַר קְרָא: ״בַּבֹּקֶר בַּבֹּקֶר״ – חַלְּקֵהוּ לִשְׁנֵי בְקָרִים; וְאִי בָּעֵית אֵימָא רַבִּי יְהוּדָה, הַאי בֹּקֶר יְתֵירָא – לְהַקְדִּים לוֹ שָׁעָה אַחַת. דְּכוּלֵּי עָלְמָא מִיהָא ״וְחַם הַשֶּׁמֶשׁ וְנָמָס״ בְּאַרְבַּע שָׁעוֹת,

The Gemara responds: **If you wish, say** that the mishna is in accordance with the opinion of **Rabbi Yehuda,** and **if you wish, say** instead that the mishna is in accordance with the opinion of **the Rabbis.** The Gemara explains: **If you wish, say** in accordance with the opinion of **the Rabbis. The verse states: Morning by morning, divide it into two mornings.** Morning, according to the Rabbis, lasts until noon. The repetition of the term morning in the Torah indicates that the period when the manna was gathered ended at the conclusion of the first half of the morning, i.e., the end of the third hour. **And if you wish, say** instead in accordance with the opinion of **Rabbi Yehuda,** who would say that: **This extra morning** in the phrase morning by morning comes to **make** the end of the period when the manna was gathered **an hour earlier.** In any event, **everyone agrees** that the verse, **And when the sun grew hot it melted,** refers to **four hours** of the day.

מַאי מַשְׁמַע? אָמַר רַבִּי אַחָא בַּר יַעֲקֹב, אָמַר קְרָא: ״וְחַם הַשֶּׁמֶשׁ וְנָמָס,״ אֵיזוֹ הִיא שָׁעָה שֶׁהַשֶּׁמֶשׁ חַם וְהַצֵּל צוֹנֵן? הֱוֵי אוֹמֵר בְּאַרְבַּע שָׁעוֹת.

The Gemara asks: **From where is the inference** drawn that this is the meaning of the verse? **Rabbi Aḥa bar Ya'akov said: The verse states: "When the sun grew hot it melted." Which is the hour that the sun is hot but the shade remains cool,** before the heat of the day, when even the shade is hot? **You must say at four hours.**

״תְּפִלַּת הַמִּנְחָה עַד הָעֶרֶב וכו׳.״ אָמַר לֵיהּ רַב חִסְדָּא לְרַב יִצְחָק: הָתָם אָמַר רַב כָּהֲנָא ״הֲלָכָה כְּרַבִּי יְהוּדָה הוֹאִיל וּתְנַן בִּבְחִירָתָא כְּוָותֵיהּ,״ הָכָא מַאי? אִישְׁתֵּיק וְלָא אָמַר לֵיהּ וְלָא מִידֵּי. אָמַר רַב חִסְדָּא: נֶחֱזֵי אֲנַן, מִדְּרַב מְצַלֵּי שֶׁל שַׁבָּת בְּעֶרֶב שַׁבָּת מִבְּעוֹד יוֹם – שְׁמַע מִינָּהּ הֲלָכָה כְּרַבִּי יְהוּדָה.

We learned in the mishna: The Rabbis hold that **the afternoon prayer** may be recited **until the evening.** Rabbi Yehuda says: It may be recited only until the midpoint of the afternoon. **Rav Ḥisda said to Rav Yitzḥak: There,** with regard to the morning prayer, **Rav Kahana said: The** ***halakha*** **is in accordance with** the opinion of **Rabbi Yehuda, since we learned** in a mishna in the **preferred** tractate, *Eduyyot*, **in accordance with his** opinion. **Here, what** is the ruling? **He was silent and said nothing to him,** as he was familiar with no established ruling in this matter. **Rav Ḥisda said: Let us see** and try to resolve this ourselves **from** the fact **that Rav prayed** the **Shabbat** prayers on the eve of Shabbat **while it was still day. Learn from this** that **the** ***halakha*** **is in accordance with** the opinion of **Rabbi Yehuda,** and the time for the afternoon prayer ends at the midpoint of the afternoon, after which time one may recite the evening prayer.

אַדְּרַבָּה, מִדְּרַב הוּנָא וְרַבָּנַן לָא הֲווּ מְצַלּוּ עַד אוּרְתָּא, שְׁמַע מִינָּהּ אֵין הֲלָכָה כְּרַבִּי יְהוּדָה! הָשְׁתָּא דְּלָא אִתְּמַר הִלְכְתָא לָא כְּמָר וְלָא כְּמָר, דַּעֲבַד כְּמָר – עֲבַד, וּדַעֲבַד כְּמָר – עֲבַד.

The Gemara immediately rejects the proof based on Rav's practice: **On the contrary,** from the fact **that Rav Huna and the Sages,** students of Rav, **would not pray until evening, learn from that** that **the** ***halakha*** **is not in accordance with** the opinion of **Rabbi Yehuda.** The Gemara concludes: **Now that the** ***halakha*** **was stated neither in accordance with** the opinion of this **Sage nor in accordance with** the opinion of that **Sage, one who acted in accordance with** the opinion of this **Sage has acted** legitimately, **and one who acted in accordance with** the opinion of that **Sage has acted** legitimately,[H] as this *halakha* is left to the decision of each individual.

רַב אִיקְלַע לְבֵי גְּנִיבָא וְצַלֵּי שֶׁל שַׁבָּת בְּעֶרֶב שַׁבָּת, וַהֲוָה מְצַלֵּי רַבִּי יִרְמְיָה בַּר אַבָּא לַאֲחוֹרֵי דְּרַב, וְסַיֵּים רַב וְלָא פַּסְקֵיהּ לִצְלוֹתֵיהּ דְּרַבִּי יִרְמְיָה. שְׁמַע מִינָּהּ תְּלָת: שְׁמַע מִינָּהּ מִתְפַּלֵּל אָדָם שֶׁל שַׁבָּת בְּעֶרֶב שַׁבָּת, וּשְׁמַע מִינָּהּ מִתְפַּלֵּל תַּלְמִיד אֲחוֹרֵי רַבּוֹ, וּשְׁמַע מִינָּהּ אָסוּר לַעֲבוֹר כְּנֶגֶד הַמִּתְפַּלְּלִין.

The Gemara relates: **Rav happened by the house of** the Sage, **Geniva, and he prayed the Shabbat** prayer **on the eve of Shabbat** before nightfall.[H] **Rabbi Yirmeya bar Abba**[P] **was praying behind Rav, and Rav finished** his prayer **but did not** take three steps back and **interrupt the prayer** of **Rabbi Yirmeya. Derive from this** incident **three** ***halakhot*****: Derive from this** that **one may pray the Shabbat** prayer **on the eve of Shabbat** before nightfall. **And derive from this that a student** may **pray behind his rabbi. And derive from this** that it is **prohibited to pass before those who are praying.**[H]

HALAKHA

One who acted in accordance with the opinion of this Sage has acted legitimately, and one who acted in accordance with the opinion of that Sage has acted legitimately – דַּעֲבַד כְּמָר עֲבַד, וּדַעֲבַד כְּמָר עֲבַד: In the Gemara, the dispute between Rabbi Yehuda and the Rabbis with regard to the time beyond which one may not recite the afternoon prayer, until the evening or until the midpoint of *minḥa*, was not resolved. Therefore, the Gemara concluded that each individual has license to conduct himself as he pleases, and whichever option he chooses, he fulfills his obligation. However, once he chooses, he is required to continue conducting himself in accordance with that choice. Therefore, if he recites the afternoon prayer after the midpoint of *minḥa*, he may not recite the evening prayer until the evening. If he plans on reciting the evening prayer after the midpoint of *minḥa* before sunset, he must recite the afternoon prayer before the midpoint of *minḥa*. The generally accepted custom is that the afternoon prayer may be recited until sunset (Rambam *Sefer Ahava, Hilkhot Tefilla* 3:4; *Shulḥan Arukh, Oraḥ Ḥayyim* 233:1).

One may recite the Shabbat prayer on the eve of Shabbat before nightfall – מִתְפַּלֵּל אָדָם שֶׁל שַׁבָּת בְּעֶרֶב שַׁבָּת: One is permitted to pray the Shabbat evening prayer before nightfall and assume all of the customs of Shabbat, i.e., *kiddush* and the Shabbat meal, at that time. This is based on the opinion of Rabbi Yehuda with regard to the afternoon prayer, that one may always recite the evening prayer before nightfall. Even if one does not always conduct himself in accordance with this opinion, in deference to Shabbat the Sages were lenient and allowed him to do so on Shabbat eve (Rambam *Sefer Ahava, Hilkhot Tefilla* 3:7; *Shulḥan Arukh, Oraḥ Ḥayyim* 267:2).

It is prohibited to pass before those who are praying – אָסוּר לַעֲבוֹר כְּנֶגֶד הַמִּתְפַּלְּלִין: One may not pass within four cubits before another who is praying. However, one may pass adjacent to one who is praying if he is alongside and not before him. The *Zohar* on the portion of *Ḥayyei Sara* makes no distinction and prohibits passing within four cubits on all sides of one who is praying (Rambam *Sefer Ahava, Hilkhot Tefilla* 5:6; *Shulḥan Arukh, Oraḥ Ḥayyim* 102:4).

PERSONALITIES

Rabbi Yirmeya bar Abba – רַבִּי יִרְמְיָה בַּר אַבָּא: A first and second generation Babylonian *amora*, Rabbi Yirmeya bar Abba was one of the first Sages to study under Rav after the latter's arrival in Babylonia. As Rabbi Yirmeya bar Abba was already a scholar in his own right, he came to Rav primarily to learn the Torah of Eretz Yisrael. Rav knew Rabbi Yirmeya bar Abba's family and considered his father, Abba, among the greatest penitents of all time. Rabbi Yirmeya bar Abba is among the most prominent promulgators of Rav's teachings, and many Sages from both Babylonia and Eretz Yisrael studied with him. His son, Rav Huna, was one of the Sages, as were his son-in-law, Rav Huna bar Ḥiyya, and his daughter's son, Levi ben Rav Huna bar Ḥiyya.

מְסַיֵּיע לֵיהּ לְרַבִּי יְהוֹשֻׁעַ בֶּן לֵוִי, דְּאָמַר רַבִּי יְהוֹשֻׁעַ בֶּן לֵוִי: אָסוּר לַעֲבוֹר כְּנֶגֶד הַמִּתְפַּלְּלִין. – אִינִי?! וְהָא רַבִּי אַמִי וְרַבִּי אַסִּי חָלְפִי! – רַבִּי אַמִי וְרַבִּי אַסִּי חוּץ לְאַרְבַּע אַמּוֹת הוּא דְּחָלְפִי.

The Gemara responds: This **supports** the opinion of **Rabbi Yehoshua ben Levi, as Rabbi Yehoshua ben Levi said: It is prohibited to pass before those who are praying.** The Gemara asks: **Is that so? Didn't Rabbi Ami and Rabbi Asi pass** before those who were praying? The Gemara responds: **Rabbi Ami and Rabbi Asi** were **beyond four cubits** from those who were praying **when they passed.**

וְרַבִּי יִרְמְיָה הֵיכִי עָבֵיד הָכִי? וְהָא אָמַר רַב יְהוּדָה אָמַר רַב: לְעוֹלָם אַל יִתְפַּלֵּל אָדָם

One particular detail was surprising: **How did Rabbi Yirmeya act that way** and pray behind Rav? **Didn't Rav Yehuda say** that **Rav said: A person should never pray**

Perek **IV**
Daf **27** Amud **b**

לֹא כְּנֶגֶד רַבּוֹ וְלֹא אֲחוֹרֵי רַבּוֹ;

directly **next to his rabbi,** presumptuously indicating that he is his rabbi's equal, **and behind his rabbi**[H] as it creates the impression that he is bowing to him (*Tosafot*)?

וְתַנְיָא, רַבִּי אֱלִיעֶזֶר אוֹמֵר: הַמִּתְפַּלֵּל אֲחוֹרֵי רַבּוֹ, וְהַנּוֹתֵן שָׁלוֹם לְרַבּוֹ, וְהַמַּחֲזִיר שָׁלוֹם לְרַבּוֹ, וְהַחוֹלֵק עַל יְשִׁיבָתוֹ שֶׁל רַבּוֹ, וְהָאוֹמֵר דָּבָר שֶׁלֹּא שָׁמַע מִפִּי רַבּוֹ – גּוֹרֵם לַשְּׁכִינָה שֶׁתִּסְתַּלֵּק מִיִּשְׂרָאֵל!

And it was taught in a *baraita*, in a more extreme manner, as **Rabbi Eliezer says: One who prays behind his rabbi and one who greets his rabbi**[HN] without waiting for his rabbi to greet him first, **one who returns his rabbi's greeting** without saying: Greetings to you, rabbi, **one who rivals his rabbi's yeshiva,**[H] i.e., establishes a yeshiva of his own and teaches during his rabbi's lifetime without his consent (Rambam), **and one who says something** in the name of his rabbi **which he did not hear directly from his rabbi,**[HN] **causes the Divine Presence to withdraw from Israel.**

שָׁאנֵי רַבִּי יִרְמְיָה בַּר אַבָּא, דְּתַלְמִיד חָבֵר הֲוָה. וְהַיְינוּ דְּקָאָמַר לֵיהּ רַבִּי יִרְמְיָה בַּר אַבָּא לְרַב: "מִי בַּדְלַתְּ?" אָמַר לֵיהּ: אִין, בְּדֵילְנָא, וְלֹא אָמַר, "מִי בָּדֵיל מָר."

With regard to Rabbi Yirmeya's conduct, the Gemara explains that **Rabbi Yirmeya bar Abba is different,** as he was not a mere student of Rav. Rather, he **was a disciple-colleague**[HN] and was, therefore, permitted to act that way. **And that is why** on one occasion, when Rav prayed the Shabbat prayer early, **Rabbi Yirmeya bar Abba asked him: Did you distance yourself** from labor and accept the sanctity of Shabbat? **Rav said to him: Yes, I distanced myself. And** Rabbi Yirmeya **did not say to him: Did the Master distance himself,** as would have been appropriate had he merely been Rav's student.

וּמִי בָּדֵיל?! וְהָאָמַר רַבִּי אָבִין: פַּעַם אַחַת הִתְפַּלֵּל רַבִּי שֶׁל שַׁבָּת בְּעֶרֶב שַׁבָּת, וְנִכְנַס לַמֶּרְחָץ וְיָצָא וְשָׁנָה לָן פִּרְקִין וַעֲדַיִין לֹא חֲשֵׁכָה! אָמַר רָבָא: הַהוּא דְּנִכְנַס לְהַזִּיעַ, וְקוֹדֶם גְּזֵירָה הֲוָה.

Although Rav replied that he distanced himself from labor, **did he** indeed need to **distance himself** from labor? **Didn't Rabbi Avin say: Once Rabbi** Yehuda HaNasi **prayed** the **Shabbat** prayer **on the eve of Shabbat** before nightfall. **He** then **entered the bathhouse and emerged and taught us our chapters** that we had learned, **and it was not yet dark. Rava said: That** is a case where he had **entered** the bathhouse **to perspire, and it was before the** Sages issued a **decree** prohibiting perspiring in a bathhouse on Shabbat.

אִינִי?! וְהָא אַבַּיֵי שְׁרָא לֵיהּ לְרַב דִּימִי בַּר לִיוָאֵי לְכַבְרוּיֵי סַלֵּי!

The Gemara asks: **Is that so,** that he was required to refrain from labor? **Didn't Abaye permit Rav Dimi bar Liva'ei to fumigate baskets with sulfur** even though he had already recited the Shabbat prayer, indicating that it is permitted to perform labor even after the Shabbat prayer?

הַהוּא טָעוּתָא הֲוַאי.

The Gemara responds: **That was an error,**[H] as Rav Dimi did not intend to begin Shabbat early. It was a cloudy day and he mistakenly thought that the sun had set and that was why he prayed. Consequently, even though he prayed, the Shabbat prayer did not obligate him to conduct himself in accordance with the sanctity of Shabbat and he was allowed to perform labor even after his prayer.

HALAKHA

A person should never pray…and behind his rabbi – אַל יִתְפַּלֵּל אָדָם...וְלֹא אֲחוֹרֵי רַבּוֹ: A student may not pray directly behind his rabbi, before him, or alongside him, within four cubits. Beyond four cubits, it is considered a separate domain and, therefore, is permitted. Some say that this applies only when they are praying as individuals, but when praying with a congregation, if that is the regular seating arrangement, it is not a problem. Even though it is preferable to avoid doing so, the custom is to allow it (Rambam *Sefer HaMadda, Hilkhot Talmud Torah* 5:6; *Shulḥan Arukh, Oraḥ Ḥayyim* 90:24 and in the comment of the Rema).

One who greets his rabbi – וְהַנּוֹתֵן שָׁלוֹם לְרַבּוֹ: A student may not greet his rabbi in the manner that he greets others. He must bow before him and say: Greetings to you, my rabbi. If the rabbi greeted him, he should reply: Greetings to you, my rabbi, my teacher, as per the statement of Rabbi Eliezer here, as the prohibition to greet his rabbi is limited to when he does not greet him with the requisite respect. Some say that a student may not greet his rabbi at all (Jerusalem Talmud; Rambam *Sefer HaMadda, Hilkhot Talmud Torah* 5:5; *Shulḥan Arukh, Yoreh De'a* 242:16 and in the comment of the Rema).

One who rivals his rabbi's yeshiva – וְהַחוֹלֵק עַל יְשִׁיבָתוֹ שֶׁל רַבּוֹ: Entering into a dispute with one's rabbi is tantamount to entering into a dispute with the Divine Presence. What is the definition of one who enters into a dispute with his rabbi? It is one who establishes, in his rabbi's lifetime, a rival study hall where he teaches without the permission of his rabbi (Rambam *Sefer HaMadda, Hilkhot Talmud Torah* 5:1–2; *Shulḥan Arukh, Yoreh De'a* 242:2).

One who says something which he did not hear directly from his rabbi – וְהָאוֹמֵר דָּבָר שֶׁלֹּא שָׁמַע מִפִּי רַבּוֹ: A student may not make an unattributed statement that he did not hear from his rabbi, as others are liable to mistakenly assume that he heard it from his rabbi. When making a statement from another source, he must attribute it to that source (Rambam *Sefer HaMadda, Hilkhot Talmud Torah* 5:9; *Shulḥan Arukh, Yoreh De'a* 242:24, see the comment of the *Shakh*).

He was a disciple-colleague – דְּתַלְמִיד חָבֵר הֲוָה: A disciple-colleague may pray behind his rabbi. However, even a disciple-colleague may not pray before him (Rambam *Sefer HaMadda, Hilkhot Talmud Torah* 5:9; *Shulḥan Arukh, Oraḥ Ḥayyim* 90:25).

Accepting Shabbat by mistake – קַבָּלַת שַׁבָּת בְּטָעוּת: An individual who inadvertently began Shabbat before its designated time and lit candles and recited the Shabbat evening prayer before realizing his error, may perform labor that is prohibited on Shabbat until Shabbat begins. At that time, he must repeat the evening prayer. However, a community that inadvertently began Shabbat before its designated time, and prayed after the midpoint of *minḥa*, need not pray again. With regard to performance of labor prohibited on Shabbat, some permit it as their acceptance of Shabbat was inadvertent. Others distinguish between those members of the community who lit Shabbat candles, for whom labor is prohibited, and those who did not light candles, for whom it is permitted (*Magen Avraham*). Others rule in accordance with this opinion *ab initio*, but not after the fact (*Shulḥan Arukh HaRav; Shulḥan Arukh, Oraḥ Ḥayyim* 263:14).

NOTES

One who greets his rabbi – וְהַנּוֹתֵן שָׁלוֹם לְרַבּוֹ: Various explanations were suggested for this *halakha*. According to Rashi, it prohibits a student from greeting his rabbi in the same manner in which he greets others. He should address his rabbi with greater deference. Others say that this prohibits a student from addressing his rabbi at all; he must wait until the rabbi addresses him (*Talmidei Rabbeinu Yona*). Apparently, the practice in Babylonia was different from the practice in Eretz Yisrael (see tractate *Shekalim*).

One who says something which he did not hear directly from his rabbi – וְהָאוֹמֵר דָּבָר שֶׁלֹּא שָׁמַע מִפִּי רַבּוֹ: In certain cases, Sages allowed themselves to make statements that they did not hear from their rabbi. They saw an educational need to place emphasis on different aspects, which superseded any concern with regard to precision in quoting their mentors.

He was a disciple-colleague – דְּתַלְמִיד חָבֵר הֲוָה: This refers to a student whose growth in Torah stature ultimately rendered him his teacher's colleague. Nevertheless, he continued to treat him with the deference accorded to a mentor. Sometimes this term refers to a younger individual who, due to his lack of experience, still relies on his teacher's oral traditions, but does not require his teacher's explanations of those traditions.

וְטָעוּתָא מִי הָדְרָא?! וְהָא אָמַר אַבִידָן: פַּעַם אַחַת נִתְקַשְּׁרוּ שָׁמַיִם בֶּעָבִים, כִּסְבוּרִים הָעָם לוֹמַר חֲשֵׁכָה הוּא, נִכְנְסוּ לְבֵית הַכְּנֶסֶת וְהִתְפַּלְּלוּ שֶׁל מוֹצָאֵי שַׁבָּת בְּשַׁבָּת, וְנִתְפַּזְּרוּ הֶעָבִים וְזָרְחָה הַחַמָּה,

The Gemara goes on to ask: **Can a mistake be reversed,** enabling one to conduct himself as if he had not prayed? **Didn't Avidan,**[P] a student of Rabbi Yehuda HaNasi, **say: Once the sky became overcast,** leading **the people to think that it was** the **dark** of night; **they entered the synagogue and recited the** evening **prayer of the conclusion of Shabbat on Shabbat. And** later, **the clouds cleared and the sun shone,** indicating that it was still day.

וּבָאוּ וְשָׁאֲלוּ אֶת רַבִּי, וְאָמַר: הוֹאִיל וְהִתְפַּלְּלוּ – הִתְפַּלְּלוּ! – שָׁאנֵי צִבּוּר, דְּלָא מַטְרְחִינַן לְהוּ.

And they came and asked Rabbi Yehuda HaNasi what they should do, **and he said: Since they have prayed, they have prayed,** and they need not pray again. Although they prayed erroneously, their mistake is not reversible and what was done remains. The Gemara responds: **A community is different** in **that we do not burden them** to pray again.

אָמַר רַבִּי חִיָּיא בַּר אָבִין: רַב צַלֵּי שֶׁל שַׁבָּת בְּעֶרֶב שַׁבָּת, רַבִּי יֹאשִׁיָּה מְצַלֵּי שֶׁל מוֹצָאֵי שַׁבָּת בְּשַׁבָּת. רַב צַלֵּי שֶׁל שַׁבָּת בְּעֶרֶב שַׁבָּת. אוֹמֵר קְדוּשָּׁה עַל הַכּוֹס, אוֹ אֵינוֹ אוֹמֵר קְדוּשָּׁה עַל הַכּוֹס? תָּא שְׁמַע: דְּאָמַר רַב נַחְמָן אָמַר שְׁמוּאֵל: מִתְפַּלֵּל אָדָם שֶׁל שַׁבָּת בְּעֶרֶב שַׁבָּת וְאוֹמֵר קְדוּשָּׁה עַל הַכּוֹס. וְהִלְכְתָא כְּוָותֵיהּ.

The Gemara continues to discuss the possibility of reciting the evening prayer early, even on Shabbat. **Rabbi Ḥiyya bar Avin said: Rav prayed** the **Shabbat** prayer **on the eve of Shabbat** before nightfall. **Rabbi Yoshiya would pray the** evening **prayer of the conclusion of Shabbat on Shabbat.** With regard to the fact that **Rav prayed** the **Shabbat** prayer **on the eve of Shabbat** before nightfall, the dilemma is raised: In those cases, did **he recite *kiddush* over the cup** of wine, **or did he not recite *kiddush* over the cup** of wine before the stars emerged? **Come and hear** a resolution to this, as **Rav Naḥman said** that **Shmuel said: One prays** the **Shabbat** prayer **on the eve of Shabbat** before nightfall **and recites *kiddush* over the cup** of wine.[H] **And the *halakha* is in accordance with his** ruling.

רַבִּי יֹאשִׁיָּה מְצַלֵּי שֶׁל מוֹצָאֵי שַׁבָּת בְּשַׁבָּת. אוֹמֵר הַבְדָּלָה עַל הַכּוֹס אוֹ אֵינוֹ אוֹמֵר הַבְדָּלָה עַל הַכּוֹס? תָּא שְׁמַע דְּאָמַר רַב יְהוּדָה אָמַר שְׁמוּאֵל: מִתְפַּלֵּל אָדָם שֶׁל מוֹצָאֵי שַׁבָּת בְּשַׁבָּת, וְאוֹמֵר הַבְדָּלָה עַל הַכּוֹס.

A similar dilemma was raised concerning the fact that **Rabbi Yoshiya would pray the** evening **prayer of the conclusion of Shabbat on Shabbat:** After praying, while it is still Shabbat, **does he recite *havdala* over the cup** of wine **or does one not recite *havdala* over the cup** of wine? **Come and hear** a resolution to this, as **Rav Yehuda said** that **Shmuel said: One prays the** evening **prayer of the conclusion of Shabbat on Shabbat and recites *havdala* over the cup** of wine.[H]

אָמַר רַבִּי זֵירָא אָמַר רַבִּי אַסִּי אָמַר רַבִּי אֶלְעָזָר אָמַר רַבִּי חֲנִינָא אָמַר רַב: בְּצַד עַמּוּד זֶה הִתְפַּלֵּל רַבִּי יִשְׁמָעֵאל בְּרַבִּי יוֹסֵי שֶׁל שַׁבָּת בְּעֶרֶב שַׁבָּת.

Rabbi Zeira said that **Rabbi Asi said** that **Rabbi Elazar said** that **Rabbi Ḥanina said** that **Rav said: Alongside this** specific **pillar** before me, **Rabbi Yishmael, son of Rabbi Yosei, prayed** the **Shabbat** prayer **on the eve of Shabbat** before nightfall.

כִּי אֲתָא עוּלָּא, אָמַר: בְּצַד תְּמָרָה הֲוָה וְלֹא בְּצַד עַמּוּד הֲוָה, וְלֹא רַבִּי יִשְׁמָעֵאל בְּרַבִּי יוֹסֵי הֲוָה אֶלָּא רַבִּי אֶלְעָזָר בְּרַבִּי יוֹסֵי הֲוָה, וְלֹא שֶׁל שַׁבָּת בְּעֶרֶב שַׁבָּת הֲוָה אֶלָּא שֶׁל מוֹצָאֵי שַׁבָּת בְּשַׁבָּת הֲוָה.

But when Ulla came from the Eretz Yisrael to Babylonia, he related a different version of this story. **He said** that he had heard: This transpired **beside a palm tree, not beside a pillar, and it was not Rabbi Yishmael, son of Rabbi Yosei, but** it was **Rabbi Elazar, son of Rabbi Yosei, and it was not** the **Shabbat** prayer **on Shabbat** eve before nightfall, **rather** it was the **prayer of the conclusion of Shabbat on Shabbat.**

״תְּפִלַּת הָעֶרֶב אֵין לָהּ קֶבַע.״ מַאי ״אֵין לָהּ קֶבַע?״ אִילֵימָא דְּאִי בָּעֵי מְצַלֵּי כּוּלֵּיהּ לֵילְיָא – לִיתְנֵי תְּפִלַּת הָעֶרֶב כָּל הַלַּיְלָה! אֶלָּא מַאי ״אֵין לָהּ קֶבַע?״

We learned in the mishna: **The evening prayer** may be recited throughout the night and **is not fixed** to a specific hour. The Gemara asks: **What is the meaning of is not fixed? If you say that if** one **wishes, he may pray throughout the night,** then **let** the mishna **teach: The evening prayer** may be recited **throughout the night. Rather, what is** the meaning of **not fixed?**

כְּמַאן דְּאָמַר: תְּפִלַּת עַרְבִית רְשׁוּת. דְּאָמַר רַב יְהוּדָה אָמַר שְׁמוּאֵל: תְּפִלַּת עַרְבִית, רַבָּן גַּמְלִיאֵל אוֹמֵר: חוֹבָה, רַבִּי יְהוֹשֻׁעַ אוֹמֵר: רְשׁוּת. אָמַר אַבַּיֵי: הֲלָכָה כְּדִבְרֵי הָאוֹמֵר חוֹבָה. וְרָבָא אָמַר: הֲלָכָה כְּדִבְרֵי הָאוֹמֵר רְשׁוּת.

It is **in accordance with** the opinion of **the one who said: The evening prayer is optional.** As **Rav Yehuda said** that **Shmuel said** with regard to **the evening prayer. Rabban Gamliel says:** It is **obligatory. Rabbi Yehoshua says:** It is **optional. Abaye said: The *halakha* is in accordance with the statement of the one who said:** The evening prayer is **obligatory. Rava said: The *halakha* is in accordance with the statement of the one who said:** The evening prayer is **optional.**[H]

תָּנוּ רַבָּנַן: מַעֲשֶׂה בְּתַלְמִיד אֶחָד שֶׁבָּא לִפְנֵי רַבִּי יְהוֹשֻׁעַ, אָמַר לוֹ: תְּפִלַּת עַרְבִית רְשׁוּת אוֹ חוֹבָה? אָמַר לֵיהּ: רְשׁוּת.

The Sages taught: There was **an incident involving a student,** who came before **Rabbi Yehoshua.** The student **said to him: Is the evening prayer optional or obligatory?** Rabbi Yehoshua **said to him: Optional.**

PERSONALITIES

Avidan – אַבִידָן: Also referred to as Avdan, his name is an abbreviated version of the name Abba Yudan. He was a student of Rabbi Yehuda HaNasi, with whom he had a close relationship and he often served as the one who repeated and disseminated Rabbi Yehuda HaNasi's lectures. Therefore, he was able to transmit many teachings in the name of Rabbi Yehuda HaNasi of which other Sages were unaware. Considered to be one of the last *tanna'im*, Avidan was widely recognized as a wise and pious man. A series of tragic events befell him near the end of his life, when he was afflicted with leprosy and his two sons drowned. The Sages saw this as divine punishment for insulting Rabbi Yishmael son of Rabbi Yosei, although that, too, was performed in his zeal to defend his rabbi's honor. Isolated statements are cited in his name in the Talmud and midrash.

HALAKHA

***Kiddush* while it is still day – קִדּוּשׁ מִבְּעוֹד יוֹם:** One who began Shabbat before its designated time may recite *kiddush* and eat the Shabbat meal before dark, as per the statement that Rav Naḥman said that Shmuel said, in accordance with which the Gemara ruled. Some say that he must extend the meal until after dark and make certain to eat at least an olive-bulk past dark, so that it will be considered a meal eaten on Shabbat, as it is stated: "Eat that today; for today is Shabbat unto the Lord" (Exodus 16:25). *Ab initio*, one should adopt that stringency (*Mishna Berura*; Rambam *Sefer Ahava, Hilkhot Tefilla* 3:7, *Sefer Zemanim, Hilkhot Shabbat* 29:11; *Shulḥan Arukh, Oraḥ Ḥayyim* 267:2).

One prays the evening prayer of the conclusion of Shabbat on Shabbat and recites *havdala* over the cup of wine – מִתְפַּלֵּל אָדָם שֶׁל מוֹצָאֵי שַׁבָּת בְּשַׁבָּת, וְאוֹמֵר הַבְדָּלָה עַל הַכּוֹס: This is only done in exigent circumstances or when it is necessary to facilitate the performance of a mitzva. Then one is permitted to recite the evening prayer of the conclusion of Shabbat on Shabbat and to recite *havdala* over a cup of wine. However, one does not recite the blessing over the candle or perform prohibited labor until nightfall. In regular circumstances, there is no need to end Shabbat hastily, especially because many hold in accordance with the ruling of the *Tur* that one may not recite the evening prayer, *Arvit*, until dark (Rambam *Sefer Ahava, Hilkhot Tefilla* 3:7, *Sefer Zemanim, Hilkhot Shabbat* 29:11; *Shulḥan Arukh, Oraḥ Ḥayyim* 293:3).

The evening prayer is optional – תְּפִלַּת עַרְבִית רְשׁוּת: The evening prayer is optional, as per the opinion of Rabbi Yehoshua in his dispute with Rabban Gamliel; and the opinion of Rava in his dispute with Abaye. This is in accordance with the accepted halakhic principle. Although it is optional, there is still a mitzva to recite this prayer and it should not be missed. The Rif writes that now that all of Israel has accepted upon themselves to recite the evening prayer, it has become obligatory like the morning and afternoon prayers (Rambam *Sefer Ahava, Hilkhot Tefilla* 1:6, 3:6–7, 9:9; *Tur, Oraḥ Ḥayyim* 235).

בא לפני רבן גמליאל, אמר לו: תפלת ערבית רשות או חובה? אמר לו: חובה. אמר לו: והלא רבי יהושע אמר לי רשות! אמר לו: המתן עד שיכנסו בעלי תריסין לבית המדרש.

The same student **came before Rabban Gamliel and said to him: Is the evening prayer optional or obligatory?** Rabban Gamliel **said to him: Obligatory.** The student **said to** Rabban Gamliel: **But didn't Rabbi Yehoshua tell me** that the evening prayer is **optional?** Rabban Gamliel **said to** the student: **Wait until the "masters of the shields,"**[L] a reference to the Torah scholars who battle in the war of Torah, **enter the study hall,** at which point we will discuss this issue.

כשנכנסו בעלי תריסין, עמד השואל ושאל: תפלת ערבית רשות או חובה? אמר לו רבן גמליאל: חובה. אמר להם רבן גמליאל לחכמים: כלום יש אדם שחולק בדבר זה? אמר ליה רבי יהושע: לאו. אמר לו: והלא משמך אמרו לי רשות!

When the masters of the shields entered, the questioner stood before everyone present **and asked: Is the evening prayer optional or obligatory? Rabban Gamliel said to him: Obligatory.** In order to ascertain whether or not Rabbi Yehoshua still maintained his opinion, **Rabban Gamliel said to** the Sages: **Is there any person who disputes this matter? Rabbi Yehoshua said to him: No,** no one disagrees. In deference to the *Nasi*, he did not wish to argue with him publicly (*Tziyyun LeNefesh Ḥayya*). Rabban Gamliel **said to** Rabbi Yehoshua: **But was it not in your name that they told me** that the evening prayer is **optional?**

אמר ליה: יהושע, עמוד על רגליך ויעידו בך! עמד רבי יהושע על רגליו ואמר: אלמלא אני חי והוא מת – יכול החי להכחיש את המת, ועכשיו שאני חי והוא חי – היאך יכול החי להכחיש את החי?

Rabban Gamliel **said to** Rabbi Yehoshua: **Yehoshua, stand on your feet and they will testify against you. Rabbi Yehoshua stood on his feet and said: If I were alive and** the student **were dead, the living can contradict the dead,** and I could deny issuing that ruling. **Now that I am alive and he is alive, how can the living contradict the living?** I have no choice but to admit that I said it.

היה רבן גמליאל יושב ודורש, ורבי יהושע עומד על רגליו, עד שרננו כל העם ואמרו לחוצפית התורגמן: עמוד! ועמד.

In the meantime, **Rabban Gamliel,** as the *Nasi*, **was sitting and lecturing, and Rabbi Yehoshua** all the while **was standing on his feet,** because Rabban Gamliel did not instruct him to sit. He remained standing in deference to the *Nasi*. This continued for some time, **until** it aroused great resentment against Rabban Gamliel, and **all of the people** assembled began **murmuring and said to Ḥutzpit the disseminator:**[P] **Stop** conveying Rabban Gamliel's lecture. **And he stopped.**

אמרי: עד כמה נצעריה וניזיל? בראש השנה אשתקד צעריה, בבכורות במעשה דרבי צדוק צעריה, הכא נמי צעריה, תא ונעבריה!

The Gemara relates that in their murmuring **they said: How long will Rabban Gamliel continue afflicting him? Last year on Rosh HaShana, he afflicted him;** Rabban Gamliel ordered Rabbi Yehoshua to come to him carrying his staff and bag, on the day on which Yom Kippur occurred, according to Rabbi Yehoshua's calculations. **Regarding the firstborn, in the incident** involving the question **of Rabbi Tzadok, he afflicted him** just as he did now, and forced him to remain standing as punishment for his failure to defend his differing opinion. **Here too, he is afflicting him. Let us remove him** from his position as *Nasi*.

מאן נוקים ליה? נוקמיה לרבי יהושע? בעל מעשה הוא; נוקמיה לרבי עקיבא? דילמא עניש ליה, דלית ליה זכות אבות;

It was so agreed, but the question arose: **Who shall we establish** in his place? Shall we **establish Rabbi Yehoshua** in his place? The Sages rejected that option because Rabbi Yehoshua **was party to the incident**[N] for which Rabban Gamliel was deposed. Appointing him would be extremely upsetting for Rabban Gamliel. Shall we **establish Rabbi Akiva** in his place? The Sages rejected that option because Rabbi Akiva, who descended from a family of converts, would be vulnerable. **Perhaps** due to Rabban Gamliel's resentment he **would** cause **him** to be divinely **punished as he lacks the merit of his ancestors** to protect him.

אלא נוקמיה לרבי אלעזר בן עזריה, דהוא חכם והוא עשיר והוא עשירי לעזרא. הוא חכם – דאי מקשי ליה מפרק ליה, והוא עשיר – דאי אית ליה לפלוחי לבי קיסר אף הוא איזיל ופלח, והוא עשירי לעזרא – דאית ליה זכות אבות ולא מצי עניש ליה. אתו ואמרו ליה: ניחא ליה למר דליהוי ריש מתיבתא? אמר להו: איזיל ואימליך באינשי ביתי. אזל ואמליך בדביתהו. אמרה ליה:

Rather, suggested the Sages, **let us establish Rabbi Elazar ben Azarya** in his place, his outstanding characteristics set him apart from the other candidates. **He is wise, rich, and a tenth** generation descendant **of Ezra.** The Gemara explains: **He is wise, so if** Rabban Gamliel raises a **challenge** in matters of Torah, **he will answer it** and not be embarrassed. **And he is rich, so if the need** arises **to pay homage to the Caesar's court** and serve as a representative of Israel to lobby and negotiate, he has sufficient wealth to cover the costs of the long journeys, taxes, and gifts, so **he too is able to go and pay homage. And he is** a **tenth** generation descendant **of Ezra, so he has the merit of his ancestors, and** Rabban Gamliel **will be unable to** cause **him** to be **punished. They came and said to him: Would the Master consent to being the Head of the Yeshiva? He said to them: I will go and consult with my household. He went and consulted with his wife. She said to him:**

LANGUAGE

Shields [*terisin*] – תריסין: From the Greek θυρεός, *thureos*, meaning large shield. Keepers of the shield are the ones who hold those shields, i.e., warriors.

PERSONALITIES

Ḥutzpit the disseminator – חוצפית התורגמן: Rabbi Ḥutzpit, one of the Sages of the Mishna (see *Shevi'it* ch. 10) is known as Rabban Gamliel's *turgeman*. That position entailed more than merely repeating the Sage's lecture aloud. He also expanded upon the concise, cryptic statements made by that Sage in the course of the lecture. Because of his skill in explaining Rabban Gamliel's lectures, Rabbi Ḥutzpit was called: The mouth that produced pearls. We know nothing else about him, except that he died as one of the ten martyrs at the hands of the Roman empire.

NOTES

Rabbi Yehoshua was party to the incident – רבי יהושע בעל מעשה הוא: Some explained that Rabbi Yehoshua was not appointed because that would have created the impression that he initiated the dispute as a ploy to be appointed *Nasi* (Maharsha).

דלמא מעברין לך? אמר לה: לשתמש איניש יומא חדא בכסא דמוקרא, ולמחר ליתבר. אמרה ליה: לית לך חיורתא. ההוא יומא בר תמני סרי שני הוה, אתרחיש ליה ניסא ואהדרו ליה תמני סרי דרי חיורתא. היינו דקאמר רבי אלעזר בן עזריה: הרי אני ״כבן״ שבעים שנה, ולא ״בן״ שבעים שנה.

There is room for concern. **Perhaps they will remove you** from office just as they removed Rabban Gamliel. **He said to her,** based on the folk saying: **Let a person use an expensive goblet one day and let it break tomorrow.** In other words, one should take advantage of an opportunity that presents itself and he need not concern himself whether or not it will last. **She said to him: You have no white** hair, and it is inappropriate for one so young to head the Sages. The Gemara relates: **That day, he was eighteen years old, a miracle transpired for him and eighteen rows of hair turned white.** The Gemara comments: **That** explains **that which Rabbi Elazar ben Azarya**[P] **said: I am as one who is seventy years old and he did not say: I am seventy years old,** because he looked older than he actually was.

תנא; אותו היום סלקוהו לשומר הפתח ונתנה להם רשות לתלמידים ליכנס. שהיה רבן גמליאל מכריז ואומר: כל תלמיד שאין תוכו כברו – לא יכנס לבית המדרש.

It was taught: On that day that they removed Rabban Gamliel from his position and appointed Rabbi Elazar ben Azarya in his place, there was also a fundamental change in the general approach of the study hall as **they dismissed the guard at the door and permission was granted to the students to enter.** Instead of Rabban Gamliel's selective approach that asserted that the students must be screened before accepting them into the study hall, the new approach asserted that anyone who seeks to study should be given opportunity to do so. **As Rabban Gamliel would proclaim and say: Any student whose inside,** his thoughts and feelings, **are not like his outside,** i.e., his conduct and his character traits are lacking, **will not enter the study hall.**

ההוא יומא אתוספו כמה ספסלי. אמר רבי יוחנן: פליגי בה אבא יוסף בן דוסתאי ורבנן, חד אמר: אתוספו ארבע מאה ספסלי; וחד אמר: שבע מאה ספסלי. הוה קא חלשה דעתיה דרבן גמליאל, אמר: דלמא חס ושלום מנעתי תורה מישראל. אחזו ליה בחלמיה חצבי חיורי דמליין קטמא. ולא היא, ההיא ליתובי דעתיה הוא דאחזו ליה.

The Gemara relates: **On that day several benches were added** to the study hall to accommodate the numerous students. **Rabbi Yoḥanan said: Abba Yosef ben Dostai and the Rabbis disputed this** matter. **One said: Four hundred benches were added** to the study hall. **And one said: Seven hundred benches were added** to the study hall. When he saw the tremendous growth in the number of students, **Rabban Gamliel was disheartened. He said: Perhaps, Heaven forbid, I prevented Israel from** engaging in **Torah** study. **They showed him in his dream white jugs filled with ashes** alluding to the fact that the additional students were worthless idlers. The Gemara comments: **That is not** the case, but **that** dream **was shown to him to ease his mind** so that he would not feel bad.

תנא: עדיות בו ביום נשנית, וכל היכא דאמרינן ״בו ביום״ – ההוא יומא הוה. ולא היתה הלכה שהיתה תלויה בבית המדרש שלא פירשוה. ואף רבן גמליאל לא מנע עצמו מבית המדרש אפילו שעה אחת,

It was taught: There is a tradition that tractate *Eduyyot* **was taught that day. And everywhere** in the Mishna or in a *baraita* **that they say: On that day,** it is referring to **that day. There was no** ***halakha*** **whose ruling was pending in the study hall that they did not explain** and arrive at a practical halakhic conclusion. **And even Rabban Gamliel did not avoid the study hall for even one moment,** as he held no grudge against those who removed him from office and he participated in the halakhic discourse in the study hall as one of the Sages.

דתנן: בו ביום בא יהודה גר עמוני לפניהם בבית המדרש, אמר להם: מה אני לבא בקהל?

As we learned in a mishna: **On that day, Yehuda, the Ammonite convert, came before** the students in the study hall **and he said to them: What is my** legal status in terms of **entering into the congregation** of Israel, i.e., to marry a Jewish woman?

אמר לו רבן גמליאל: אסור אתה לבא בקהל; אמר לו רבי יהושע: מותר אתה לבא בקהל. אמר לו רבן גמליאל: והלא כבר נאמר: ״לא יבא עמוני ומואבי בקהל ה׳״! אמר לו רבי יהושע: וכי עמון ומואב במקומן הן יושבין?! כבר עלה סנחריב מלך אשור ובלבל את כל האומות, שנאמר: ״ואסיר גבלות עמים ועתודותיהם שושתי ואוריד כביר יושבים,״ וכל דפריש – מרובא פריש.

Rabban Gamliel said to him: You are forbidden to enter into the congregation. Rabbi Yehoshua[P] **said to him: You are permitted to enter into the congregation. Rabban Gamliel said to** Rabbi Yehoshua: **Wasn't it already stated: "An Ammonite and a Moabite**[H] **shall not enter into the congregation of the Lord;** even to the tenth generation shall none of them enter into the congregation of the Lord forever" (Deuteronomy 23:4)? How can you permit him to enter the congregation? **Rabbi Yehoshua said to** Rabban Gamliel: **Do Ammon and Moab reside in their place? Sennacherib already came and,** through his policy of population transfer, **scrambled all the nations** and settled other nations in place of Ammon. Consequently, the current residents of Ammon and Moab are not ethnic Ammonites and Moabites, **as it is stated in** reference to Sennacherib: **"I have removed the bounds of the peoples, and have robbed their treasures, and have brought down as one mighty the inhabitants"** (Isaiah 10:13). **And** although it is conceivable that this particular convert is an ethnic Ammonite, nevertheless, there is no need for concern due to the halakhic principle: **Anything that parts** from a group **parts from the majority,**[B] and the assumption is that he is from the majority of nations whose members are permitted to enter the congregation.

PERSONALITIES

Rabbi Elazar ben Azarya – רבי אלעזר בן עזריה: One of the most significant *tanna'im* in the generation following the destruction of the Temple, Rabbi Elazar ben Azarya descended from a family of great wisdom, distinguished lineage, and wealth. His father, Azarya, was also a Torah scholar and an extremely wealthy man. He supported his brother Shimon, one of the Sages, who is, therefore, referred to as Shimon brother of Azarya. Rabbi Elazar ben Azarya's family were priests, descended from Ezra the Scribe, and there are traditions that tell of similarities between them. Some conjecture that Rabbi Eliezer was Rabbi Elazar ben Azarya's mentor.

Rabbi Yehoshua – רבי יהושע: This is Rabbi Yehoshua ben Ḥananya the Levite, one of the leading Sages in the generation following the destruction of the Second Temple. He had served as one of the Levite singers in the Temple. After its destruction, he was among the students who went with their primary teacher, Rabban Yoḥanan ben Zakkai, to Yavne. Unlike his colleague Rabbi Eliezer, Rabbi Yehoshua completely adhered to the approach of his teacher and of Beit Hillel.

HALAKHA

An Ammonite and a Moabite – עמוני ומואבי: Those who dwell in contemporary lands of Ammon and Moab, i.e., Jordan, do not have the legal status of Ammonites and Moabites, and converts from those areas may enter the congregation of Israel in accordance with the opinion of Rabbi Yehoshua (Rambam *Sefer Kedusha, Hilkhot Issurei Bia* 12:25; *Shulḥan Arukh, Even HaEzer* 4:10).

BACKGROUND

Everything that parts from a group parts from the majority – כל דפריש מרובא פריש: This principle applies to many dilemmas with regard to the laws of prohibited and permitted mixtures. One may only rely on this principle in specific cases. In other words, the object must have spontaneously emerged from a mixture whose proportions are known. That is not the case when the object remains in the mixture. In that case, the sample is flawed and there is room for concern that the object in question is not really from the majority component. Then the principle is: Anything that is fixed, i.e., remains in the mixture, is considered an evenly balanced uncertainty and the object is not attributed to the majority.

אָמַר לוֹ רַבָּן גַּמְלִיאֵל: וַהֲלֹא כְּבַר נֶאֱמַר: "וְאַחֲרֵי כֵן אָשִׁיב אֶת שְׁבוּת בְּנֵי עַמּוֹן נְאֻם ה'" – וּכְבָר שָׁבוּ.

Rabban Gamliel said to Rabbi Yehoshua: **But wasn't it already stated: "But afterward I will bring back the captivity of the children of Ammon, says the Lord"** (Jeremiah 49:6) **and they have already returned** to their land? Therefore, he is an ethnic Ammonite and he may not convert.

אָמַר לוֹ רַבִּי יְהוֹשֻׁעַ: וַהֲלֹא כְּבָר נֶאֱמַר: "וְשַׁבְתִּי אֶת שְׁבוּת עַמִּי יִשְׂרָאֵל" – וַעֲדַיִין לֹא שָׁבוּ. מִיָּד הִתִּירוּהוּ לָבֹא בַּקָּהָל.

Rabbi Yehoshua said to Rabban Gamliel: That is no proof. **Wasn't it already stated** in another prophecy: **"And I will turn the captivity of My people Israel** and they shall build the waste cities, and inhabit them; and they shall plant vineyards, and drink the wine thereof; they shall also make gardens, and eat the fruit of them" (Amos 9:14), **and they have not yet returned?** In rendering the ruling, only proven facts may be taken into consideration. **They immediately permitted him to enter the congregation.** This proves that Rabban Gamliel did not absent himself from the study hall that day and participated in the halakhic discourse.

אָמַר רַבָּן גַּמְלִיאֵל: הוֹאִיל וְהָכִי הֲוָה, אֵיזִיל וַאֲפַיְּיסֵיהּ לְרַבִּי יְהוֹשֻׁעַ. כִּי מְטָא לְבֵיתֵיהּ, חֲזֵינְהוּ לְאֻשְׁיָתָא דְּבֵיתֵיהּ דִּמְשַׁחֲרָן. אֲמַר לֵיהּ: מִכּוֹתְלֵי בֵיתְךָ אַתָּה נִיכָּר שֶׁפֶּחָמִי אַתָּה. אָמַר לוֹ: אוֹי לוֹ לַדּוֹר שֶׁאַתָּה פַּרְנָסוֹ, שֶׁאִי אַתָּה יוֹדֵעַ בְּצַעֲרָן שֶׁל תַּלְמִידֵי חֲכָמִים בַּמָּה הֵם מִתְפַּרְנְסִים וּבַמָּה הֵם נִזּוֹנִים.

Rabban Gamliel said to himself: **Since this is** the situation,[N] that the people are following Rabbi Yehoshua, apparently he was right. Therefore, it would be appropriate for me to **go and appease Rabbi Yehoshua. When he reached** Rabbi Yehoshua's **house, he saw** that **the walls of his house were black.** Rabban Gamliel **said to** Rabbi Yehoshua in wonderment: **From the walls of your house it is apparent that you are a blacksmith,**[N] as until then he had no idea that Rabbi Yehoshua was forced to engage in that arduous trade in order to make a living. Rabbi Yehoshua **said to him: Woe unto a generation that you are its leader as you are unaware of the difficulties of Torah scholars, how they make a living and how they feed themselves.**

אָמַר לוֹ: נַעֲנֵיתִי לָךְ, מְחוֹל לִי! לֹא אַשְׁגַּח בֵּיהּ. עֲשֵׂה בִּשְׁבִיל כְּבוֹד אַבָּא! פַּיֵּיס.

Rabban Gamliel **said to him: I insulted you, forgive me.** Rabbi Yehoshua **paid him no attention** and did not forgive him. He asked him again: **Do it in deference to my father,** Rabban Shimon ben Gamliel, who was one of the leaders of Israel at the time of the destruction of the Temple. **He was appeased.**

אֲמַרוּ: מַאן נֵיזִיל וְלֵימָא לְהוּ לְרַבָּנַן? אָמַר לְהוּ הַהוּא כּוֹבֵס: אֲנָא אֵזִילְנָא. שְׁלַח לְהוּ רַבִּי יְהוֹשֻׁעַ לְבֵי מִדְרְשָׁא: מַאן דְּלָבֵישׁ מַדָּא יִלְבַּשׁ מַדָּא, וּמַאן דְּלָא לָבֵישׁ מַדָּא יֵימָר לֵיהּ לְמַאן דְּלָבֵישׁ מַדָּא "שְׁלַח מַדָּךְ וַאֲנָא אֶלְבְּשֵׁיהּ"? אָמַר לְהוּ רַבִּי עֲקִיבָא לְרַבָּנַן: טְרוֹקוּ גַּלֵּי, דְּלָא לֵיתוּ עַבְדֵי דְּרַבָּן גַּמְלִיאֵל וּלְצַעֲרוּ לְרַבָּנַן.

Now that Rabbi Yehoshua was no longer offended, it was only natural that Rabban Gamliel would be restored to his position. **They said: Who will go and inform the Sages?** Apparently, they were not eager to carry out the mission that would undo the previous actions and remove Rabbi Elazar ben Azarya from his position as *Nasi*. **This launderer said to them: I will go. Rabbi Yehoshua sent to the Sages to the study hall: The one who wears the uniform will** continue to **wear the uniform,** the original *Nasi* will remain in his position so that **the one who did not wear the uniform will** not **say to the one who wears the uniform, remove your uniform and I will wear it.** Apparently, the Sages believed that this emissary was dispatched at the initiative of Rabban Gamliel and they ignored him. **Rabbi Akiva said to the Sages: Lock the gates so that Rabban Gamliel's servants will not come and disturb the Sages.**

אָמַר רַבִּי יְהוֹשֻׁעַ: מוּטָב דְּאֵיקוּם וְאֵיזִיל אֲנָא לְגַבַּיְיהוּ. אֲתָא, טְרַף אַבָּבָא. אֲמַר לְהוּ: מַזֶּה בֶּן מַזֶּה יַזֶּה, וְשֶׁאֵינוֹ לֹא מַזֶּה וְלֹא בֶּן מַזֶּה יֹאמַר לְמַזֶּה בֶּן מַזֶּה: מֵימֶיךָ מֵי מְעָרָה וְאֶפְרְךָ אֵפֶר מִקְלֶה? אָמַר לוֹ רַבִּי עֲקִיבָא: רַבִּי יְהוֹשֻׁעַ, נִתְפַּיַּיסְתָּ? כְּלוּם עָשִׂינוּ אֶלָּא בִּשְׁבִיל כְּבוֹדֶךָ! לְמָחָר אֲנִי וְאַתָּה נַשְׁכִּים לְפִתְחוֹ.

When he heard what happened, **Rabbi Yehoshua said: It is best if I go to them. He came and knocked on the door. He said to them** with a slight variation: **One who sprinkles** pure water on those who are ritually impure, **son of one who sprinkles** water **shall** continue **to sprinkle** water. And it is inappropriate that he who is **neither one who sprinkles nor son of one who sprinkles will say to one who sprinkles son of one who sprinkles: Your water is cave water** and not the running water required to purify one exposed to ritual impurity imparted by a corpse **and your ashes are burnt ashes** and not the ashes of a red heifer. **Rabbi Akiva said to him: Rabbi Yehoshua, have you been appeased? Everything we did was to** defend **your honor.** If you have forgiven him, none of us is opposed. **Early tomorrow you and I will go to** Rabban Gamliel's **doorway** and offer to restore him to his position as *Nasi*.

NOTES

Since this is the situation – הוֹאִיל וְהָכִי הֲוָה: Rabban Gamliel's reaction is based on the premise that until a *halakha* was voted on in the study hall and adopted as final, the extent to which it represents the truth cannot be determined. Once the Sages arrive at a decision with regard to a specific issue, it is deemed to be absolute truth. The fact that Rabbi Yehoshua was right became clear by means of the conclusive determination of the *halakha*.

From the walls of your house it is apparent that you are a blacksmith – מִכּוֹתְלֵי בֵיתְךָ אַתָּה נִיכָּר שֶׁפֶּחָמִי אַתָּה: Rabbi Yehoshua's actual profession is unclear. Some interpret the word *peḥami* as coal worker, i.e., one who makes charcoal from wood. Others interpret it as blacksmith, a conclusion supported by the Jerusalem Talmud which states that Rabbi Yehoshua manufactured needles.

HALAKHA

And the additional prayer all day – וְשֶׁל מוּסָפִין כָּל הַיּוֹם: *Ab initio*, the time to recite the additional prayer extends through the end of the seventh hour. One who recites it later than that is called negligent. Nevertheless, one who recites the additional prayer later fulfills his obligation, as the time to recite it is all day, as per the opinion of the Rabbis (Rambam *Sefer Ahava, Hilkhot Tefilla* 3:5; *Shulḥan Arukh, Oraḥ Ḥayyim* 286:1).

NOTES

Is called negligent – נִקְרָא פּוֹשֵׁעַ: The Hebrew word *poshe'a* can refer either to a transgressor, who commits a *pesha, a transgression*, or to one who is negligent, who is guilty of *peshia*, negligence. As one is within his rights to recite the additional prayer all day, referring to him as a transgressor is a bit extreme. Rabbi Akiva Eiger in *Gilyon HaShas* refers to the Gemara below on 43b where one who arrives last to the study hall is similarly called a *poshe'a*. Rashi there defines it as one who is lazy, which seems more in line with negligence than transgression. It is conceivable that the determination whether it is negligence or transgression depends on the definition of the term, is called. If it refers to an objective pronouncement, he has certainly not transgressed any *halakha*. On the other hand, if it refers to the subjective judgment of onlookers, it is certainly possible that they would conclude that one who postpones reciting the additional prayer and comes last to the study hall is also a transgressor.

אָמְרִי: הֵיכִי נַעֲבֵיד? נַעַבְרֵיהּ – גְּמִירִי: מַעֲלִין בַּקֹּדֶשׁ וְאֵין מוֹרִידִין! נִדְרוֹשׁ מָר חֲדָא שַׁבְּתָא וּמָר חֲדָא שַׁבְּתָא – אָתֵי לְקַנְאוּיֵי! אֶלָּא: לִדְרוֹשׁ רַבָּן גַּמְלִיאֵל תְּלָתָא שַׁבָּתֵי, וְרַבִּי אֶלְעָזָר בֶּן עֲזַרְיָה חֲדָא שַׁבְּתָא. וְהַיְינוּ דְּאָמַר מָר: שַׁבָּת שֶׁל מִי הָיְתָה – שֶׁל רַבִּי אֶלְעָזָר בֶּן עֲזַרְיָה הָיְתָה. וְאוֹתוֹ תַּלְמִיד – רַבִּי שִׁמְעוֹן בֶּן יוֹחַאי הֲוָה.

The question arose what to do with Rabbi Elazar ben Azarya? **They said: What shall we do? Remove him** from his position. That is inappropriate as we **learned** a *halakha* through tradition: One **elevates** to a higher level of **sanctity and does not downgrade.** Therefore, one who was the *Nasi* of the Sanhedrin cannot be demoted. **Let** one **Sage lecture one week and** the other **Sage one week, they will come to be jealous** of one another, as they will be forced to appoint one as the acting head of the Sanhedrin. **Rather, Rabban Gamliel will lecture three weeks and Rabbi Elazar ben Azarya** will lecture as head of the yeshiva **one week.** That arrangement was adopted **and that is** the explanation of the exchange in tractate *Ḥagiga*: **Whose week was it? It was the week of Rabbi Elazar ben Azarya.** One final detail: **That student** who asked the original question that sparked this entire incident **was Rabbi Shimon ben Yoḥai.**

״וְשֶׁל מוּסָפִין כָּל הַיּוֹם.״ אָמַר רַבִּי יוֹחָנָן: וְנִקְרָא פּוֹשֵׁעַ.

We learned in the mishna: **And the additional prayer** may be recited **all day.**[H] **Rabbi Yoḥanan said:** Nevertheless, **one** who postpones his prayer excessively **is called negligent.**[N]

תָּנוּ רַבָּנַן: הָיוּ לְפָנָיו שְׁתֵּי תְפִלּוֹת, אַחַת שֶׁל מִנְחָה וְאַחַת שֶׁל מוּסָף – מִתְפַּלֵּל שֶׁל מִנְחָה וְאַחַר כָּךְ מִתְפַּלֵּל שֶׁל מוּסָף, שֶׁזּוֹ תְּדִירָה וְזוֹ אֵינָהּ תְּדִירָה. רַבִּי יְהוּדָה אוֹמֵר: מִתְפַּלֵּל שֶׁל מוּסָף וְאַחַר כָּךְ מִתְפַּלֵּל שֶׁל מִנְחָה, שֶׁזּוֹ מִצְוָה עוֹבֶרֶת וְזוֹ מִצְוָה שֶׁאֵינָהּ עוֹבֶרֶת. אָמַר רַבִּי יוֹחָנָן, הֲלָכָה: מִתְפַּלֵּל שֶׁל מִנְחָה וְאַחַר כָּךְ מִתְפַּלֵּל שֶׁל מוּסָף.

The Rabbis taught in a *baraita*: If the obligation to recite **two prayers was before him, one, the additional prayer and one, the afternoon prayer, he recites the afternoon prayer** first **and the additional prayer thereafter,** because **this,** the afternoon prayer, is recited on a **frequent** basis, **and this one,** the additional prayer, is recited on a relatively **infrequent** basis. **Rabbi Yehuda says: He recites the additional prayer** first **and the afternoon prayer thereafter,** because **this, the additional prayer, is a mitzva** whose time soon **elapses,** as it may only be recited until the seventh hour **and this, the afternoon prayer, is a mitzva** whose time does **not** soon **elapse** as one may recite it until the midpoint of the afternoon. **Rabbi Yoḥanan said: The** *halakha* is that **he recites the afternoon prayer** first **and the additional prayer thereafter,** in accordance with the opinion of the Rabbis.

רַבִּי זֵירָא כִּי הֲוָה חָלֵישׁ מִגִּירְסֵיהּ, הֲוָה אָזֵיל וְיָתֵיב אַפִּתְחָא דְּבֵי רַבִּי נָתָן בַּר טוֹבִי, אָמַר: כִּי חָלְפִי רַבָּנַן אָז אֵיקוּם מִקַּמַּיְיהוּ וַאֲקַבֵּל אַגְרָא. נְפַק אֲתָא רַבִּי נָתָן בַּר טוֹבִי, אָמַר לֵיהּ: מַאן אָמַר הֲלָכָה בֵּי מִדְרָשָׁא? אָמַר לֵיהּ, הָכִי אָמַר רַבִּי יוֹחָנָן: אֵין הֲלָכָה כְּרַבִּי יְהוּדָה דְּאָמַר: מִתְפַּלֵּל אָדָם שֶׁל מוּסָף וְאַחַר כָּךְ מִתְפַּלֵּל שֶׁל מִנְחָה.

The Gemara cites additional sources relating to this issue: **When Rabbi Zeira would tire of his studies, he would go and sit in the doorway of Rabbi Natan bar Tovi's study hall. He said** to himself: **When the** entering and exiting **Sages pass, I will rise before them and be rewarded** for the mitzva of honoring Torah scholars. **Rabbi Natan bar Tovi** himself **emerged and came** to where Rabbi Zeira was seated. Rabbi Zeira **said to him: Who just stated a** ***halakha*** **in the study hall?** Rabbi Natan bar Tovi **said to him: Rabbi Yoḥanan** just **said as follows: The** ***halakha*** **is not in accordance with** the opinion of **Rabbi Yehuda who said: He recites the additional prayer** first **and the afternoon prayer thereafter.**

אָמַר לֵיהּ: רַבִּי יוֹחָנָן אֲמָרַהּ?! אָמַר לֵיהּ: אִין. תְּנָא מִינֵּיהּ אַרְבְּעִין זִמְנִין. אָמַר לֵיהּ: חֲדָא הִיא לָךְ, אוֹ חֲדַת הִיא לָךְ? אָמַר לֵיהּ: חֲדַת הִיא לִי, מִשּׁוּם דִּמְסַפְּקָא לִי בְּרַבִּי יְהוֹשֻׁעַ בֶּן לֵוִי.

Rabbi Zeira **said to him:** Did **Rabbi Yoḥanan** himself **say** this *halakha*? Rabbi Natan **said to him: Yes. He learned** this statement **from him forty times,** etching it into his memory. Rabbi Natan **said to him:** Is this *halakha* so dear to you because **it is singular for you,** as it is the only *halakha* that you learned in the name of Rabbi Yoḥanan, **or is it new to you,** as you were previously unaware of this ruling? Rabbi Zeira **said to him:** It is somewhat **new to me, as I was uncertain** whether this *halakha* was said in the name of Rabbi Yoḥanan or in the name of **Rabbi Yehoshua ben Levi.** Now it is clear to me that this *halakha* is in the name of Rabbi Yoḥanan.

אָמַר רַבִּי יְהוֹשֻׁעַ בֶּן לֵוִי: כָּל הַמִּתְפַּלֵּל תְּפִלָּה שֶׁל מוּסָפִין לְאַחַר שֶׁבַע שָׁעוֹת לְרַבִּי יְהוּדָה, עָלָיו הַכָּתוּב אוֹמֵר: ״נוּגֵי מִמּוֹעֵד אָסַפְתִּי מִמֵּךְ הָיוּ.״ מַאי מַשְׁמַע דְּהַאי ״נוּגֵי״ לִישָּׁנָא דְּתַבְרָא הוּא? כִּדְמְתַרְגֵּם רַב יוֹסֵף: ״תַּבְרָא אָתֵי עַל שַׂנְאֵיהוֹן דְּבֵית יִשְׂרָאֵל עַל דְּאַחֲרוּ זִמְנֵי מוֹעֲדַיָּא דְּבִירוּשְׁלֵים.״

Rabbi Yehoshua ben Levi said: With regard to **anyone who recites the additional prayer after seven hours** of the day, **according to Rabbi Yehuda, the verse states: "Those who are destroyed [*nugei*] far from the Festivals, I shall gather from you,** they who carried for you the burden of insult" (Zephaniah 3:18). **From where** may it **be inferred that** ***nugei*** **is an expression of destruction? As Rav Yosef translated** the verse into Aramaic: **Destruction comes upon the enemies of the house of Israel,** a euphemism for Israel itself, **for they have delayed the times of the Festivals in Jerusalem.** This proves both that *nugei* means destruction and that destruction comes upon those who fail to fulfill a mitzva at its appointed time.

אָמַר רַבִּי אֶלְעָזָר: כָּל הַמִּתְפַּלֵּל תְּפִלָּה שֶׁל שַׁחֲרִית לְאַחַר אַרְבַּע שָׁעוֹת לְרַבִּי יְהוּדָה, עָלָיו הַכָּתוּב אוֹמֵר: ״נוּגֵי מִמּוֹעֵד אָסַפְתִּי מִמֵּךְ הָיוּ.״ מַאי מַשְׁמַע דְּהַאי ״נוּגֵי״ לִישָּׁנָא דְּצַעֲרָא הוּא? דִּכְתִיב: ״דָּלְפָה נַפְשִׁי מִתּוּגָה.״ רַב נַחְמָן בַּר יִצְחָק אָמַר, מֵהָכָא: ״בְּתוּלוֹתֶיהָ נּוּגוֹת וְהִיא מַר לָהּ.״

Similarly, **Rabbi Elazar said: Regarding anyone who recites the morning prayer after four hours** of the day, **according to Rabbi Yehuda, the verse states: "Those who are in sorrow [*nugei*] far from the Festivals, I shall gather from you,** they who carried for you the burden of insult" (Zephaniah 3:18). **From where** may it **be inferred that** ***nugei*** **is an expression of sorrow? As it is written: "My soul drips in sorrow [*tuga*]"** (Psalms 119:28). **Rav Naḥman bar Yitzḥak said:** The proof that *nugei* indicates suffering is **from here: "Her virgins are sorrowed [*nugot*] and she is embittered"** (Lamentations 1:4).

רַב אָוְיָא חֲלַשׁ וְלָא אֲתָא לְפִרְקָא דְּרַב יוֹסֵף. לְמָחָר כִּי אֲתָא, בְּעָא אַבָּיֵי לְאַנּוֹחֵי דַּעְתֵּיהּ דְּרַב יוֹסֵף. אֲמַר לֵיהּ: מַאי טַעְמָא לָא אֲתָא מָר לְפִרְקָא? אֲמַר לֵיהּ: דַּהֲוָה חֲלִישׁ לִבַּאי וְלָא מָצֵינָא. אֲמַר לֵיהּ: אַמַּאי לָא טְעַמְתְּ מִידֵּי וְאָתֵית? אֲמַר לֵיהּ: לָא סְבַר לַהּ מָר לְהָא דְּרַב הוּנָא? דְּאָמַר רַב הוּנָא: אָסוּר לוֹ לְאָדָם שֶׁיִּטְעוֹם כְּלוּם קוֹדֶם שֶׁיִּתְפַּלֵּל תְּפִלַּת הַמּוּסָפִין! – אֲמַר לֵיהּ: אִיבְּעִי לֵיהּ לְמָר לְצַלּוֹיֵי צְלוֹתָא דְּמוּסְפִין בְּיָחִיד, וְלִטְעוֹם מִידֵּי וּלְמֵיתֵי! – אֲמַר לֵיהּ: וְלָא סְבַר לַהּ מָר לְהָא דְּאָמַר רַבִּי יוֹחָנָן: אָסוּר לוֹ לְאָדָם שֶׁיַּקְדִּים תְּפִלָּתוֹ לִתְפִלַּת הַצִּבּוּר?! – אֲמַר לֵיהּ: לָאו אִתְּמַר עֲלַהּ: אָמַר רַבִּי אַבָּא: בְּצִבּוּר שָׁנוּ?!

After mentioning until when the additional prayer may be recited, the Gemara relates: **Rav Avya was ill and did not come to Rav Yosef's Shabbat lecture. When** Rav Avya **came the following day, Abaye sought to placate Rav Yosef,** and through a series of questions and answers sought to make clear to him that Rav Avya's failure to attend the lecture was not a display of contempt for Rav Yosef.

To this end, he asked him: **Why did the Master not attend the Shabbat lecture?**

Rav Avya **said to him: Because my heart was faint and I was unable** to attend.

Abaye **said to him: Why did you not eat something and come?**

Rav Avya **said to him:** Does **the Master not hold** in accordance with that statement **of Rav Huna? As Rav Huna said: A person may not taste anything before he recites the additional prayer.**[H]

Abaye **said to him: My Master should have recited the additional prayer individually, eaten something, and** then **come** to the lecture.

Rav Avya **said to him:** Does **my Master not hold** in accordance with that statement **of Rabbi Yoḥanan: A person may not recite his** individual **prayer prior to the communal prayer?**[H]

Abaye **said to him:** Was **it not stated regarding this** *halakha*, **Rabbi Abba said: They taught** this **in a communal** setting?

In other words, only one who is part of a congregation is prohibited from praying alone prior to the prayer of the congregation. Even though Rav Avya was incorrect, the reason for his failure to attend the lecture was clarified through this discussion.

וְלֵית הִלְכְתָא; לָא כְּרַב הוּנָא וְלָא כְּרַבִּי יְהוֹשֻׁעַ בֶּן לֵוִי; כְּרַב הוּנָא – הָא דַּאֲמָרַן, כְּרַבִּי יְהוֹשֻׁעַ בֶּן לֵוִי – דְּאָמַר רַבִּי יְהוֹשֻׁעַ בֶּן לֵוִי: כֵּיוָן שֶׁהִגִּיעַ זְמַן תְּפִלַּת מִנְחָה, אָסוּר לוֹ לְאָדָם שֶׁיִּטְעוֹם כְּלוּם קוֹדֶם שֶׁיִּתְפַּלֵּל תְּפִלַּת הַמִּנְחָה.

And the Gemara summarizes: **The *halakha* is neither in accordance with** the statement of **Rav Huna nor in accordance with** the statement of **Rabbi Yehoshua ben Levi.** The Gemara explains: It is not **in accordance with** the statement of **Rav Huna, as we said** above with regard to the prohibition to eat prior to the additional prayer. It is not **in accordance with** the statement of **Rabbi Yehoshua ben Levi, as Rabbi Yehoshua ben Levi said: Once the time** to recite **the afternoon prayer has arrived, a person may not taste anything before he recites the afternoon prayer.**[H]

מתני׳ רַבִּי נְחוּנְיָא בֶּן הַקָּנָה הָיָה מִתְפַּלֵּל בִּכְנִיסָתוֹ לְבֵית הַמִּדְרָשׁ וּבִיצִיאָתוֹ תְּפִלָּה קְצָרָה. אָמְרוּ לוֹ: מַה מָּקוֹם לִתְפִלָּה זוֹ? אָמַר לָהֶם: בִּכְנִיסָתִי אֲנִי מִתְפַּלֵּל שֶׁלֹּא יֶאֱרַע דְּבַר תַּקָּלָה עַל יָדִי, וּבִיצִיאָתִי אֲנִי נוֹתֵן הוֹדָאָה עַל חֶלְקִי.

MISHNA

In addition to the *halakhot* relating to the fixed prayers, the Gemara relates: **Rabbi Neḥunya ben Hakana would recite a brief prayer upon his entrance into the study hall and upon his exit. They said to him:** The study hall is not a dangerous place that would warrant a prayer when entering and exiting, so **what room is there for this prayer? He said to them: Upon my entrance, I pray that no mishap will transpire** caused by **me** in the study hall. **And upon my exit, I give thanks for my portion.**

גמ׳ תָּנוּ רַבָּנַן: בִּכְנִיסָתוֹ מַהוּ אוֹמֵר? יְהִי רָצוֹן מִלְּפָנֶיךָ ה׳ אֱלֹהַי שֶׁלֹּא יֶאֱרַע דְּבַר תַּקָּלָה עַל יָדִי, וְלֹא אֶכָּשֵׁל בִּדְבַר הֲלָכָה וְיִשְׂמְחוּ בִּי חֲבֵרַי, וְלֹא אוֹמַר עַל טָמֵא טָהוֹר וְלֹא עַל טָהוֹר טָמֵא, וְלֹא יִכָּשְׁלוּ חֲבֵרַי בִּדְבַר הֲלָכָה וְאֶשְׂמַח בָּהֶם.

GEMARA

The Sages taught in a *baraita* the complete formula of Rabbi Neḥunya ben Hakana's prayer: **Upon his entrance, what does he say? May it be Your will, Lord my God, that no mishap** in determining the *halakha* **transpires caused by me, and that I not fail in any matter of *halakha*, and that my colleagues,** who together with me engage in clarifying the *halakha*, **will rejoice in me.** He specified: **And that I will neither declare pure that which is impure, nor declare impure that which is pure and that my colleagues will not fail in any matter of *halakha*, and that I will rejoice in them.**

בִּיצִיאָתוֹ מַהוּ אוֹמֵר? מוֹדֶה אֲנִי לְפָנֶיךָ ה׳ אֱלֹהַי שֶׁשַּׂמְתָּ חֶלְקִי מִיּוֹשְׁבֵי בֵּית הַמִּדְרָשׁ וְלֹא שַׂמְתָּ חֶלְקִי מִיּוֹשְׁבֵי קְרָנוֹת, שֶׁאֲנִי מַשְׁכִּים וְהֵם מַשְׁכִּימִים – אֲנִי מַשְׁכִּים לְדִבְרֵי תוֹרָה וְהֵם מַשְׁכִּימִים לִדְבָרִים בְּטֵלִים, אֲנִי עָמֵל וְהֵם עֲמֵלִים – אֲנִי עָמֵל וּמְקַבֵּל שָׂכָר וְהֵם עֲמֵלִים וְאֵינָם מְקַבְּלִים שָׂכָר, אֲנִי רָץ וְהֵם רָצִים – אֲנִי רָץ לְחַיֵּי הָעוֹלָם הַבָּא וְהֵם רָצִים לִבְאֵר שַׁחַת.

Upon his exit, what did he say? I give thanks before You, Lord my God, that You have placed my lot among those who sit in the study hall, and that you have not given me my portion among those who sit idly **on street corners. I rise early, and they rise early. I rise early** to pursue **matters of Torah, and they rise early to pursue frivolous matters. I toil and they toil. I toil and receive a reward, and they toil and do not receive a reward. I run and they run.**[N] **I run to the life of the World-to-Come and they run to the pit of destruction.**

HALAKHA

Tasting before the additional prayer – טְעִימָה קוֹדֶם מוּסָף: One is permitted to taste a small amount of food, such as fruit or even bread, before the additional prayer, provided it is less than an egg-bulk. An actual meal, though, is prohibited. Some hold that this is prohibited by law (*Taz* according to medieval commentaries), while others hold that it is merely custom (*Baḥ* and *Magen Avraham*; *Shulḥan Arukh, Oraḥ Ḥayyim* 286:3).

A person may not recite his individual prayer prior to the communal prayer – אָסוּר לוֹ לְאָדָם שֶׁיַּקְדִּים תְּפִלָּתוֹ לִתְפִלַּת הַצִּבּוּר: One praying as part of a congregation may not recite his individual prayer before the rest of the congregation begins to pray, unless the designated time for prayer is passing and the congregation is extending the service by adding liturgy or for some other reason. This is in accordance with the conclusion in our Gemara based on the statement by Rabbi Yoḥanan (Rambam *Sefer Ahava, Hilkhot Tefilla* 10:16; *Shulḥan Arukh, Oraḥ Ḥayyim* 90:10).

Tasting before the afternoon prayer – טְעִימָה קוֹדֶם מִנְחָה: One is permitted to eat fruit or even bread prior to the afternoon prayer, provided it is less than a egg-bulk. An actual meal, however, is prohibited (*Shulḥan Arukh, Oraḥ Ḥayyim* 232:2–3).

NOTES

I run and they run – אֲנִי רָץ וְהֵם רָצִים: In the course of one's life, everyone moves rapidly towards death. One engaged in Torah study runs toward life in the World-to-Come, while those engaged in idle pursuits run to the pit of destruction (*Talmidei Rabbeinu Yona*).

תָּנוּ רַבָּנַן: כְּשֶׁחָלָה רַבִּי אֱלִיעֶזֶר, נִכְנְסוּ תַּלְמִידָיו לְבַקְּרוֹ. אָמְרוּ לוֹ: רַבֵּינוּ, לַמְּדֵנוּ אוֹרְחוֹת חַיִּים וְנִזְכֶּה בָּהֶן לְחַיֵּי הָעוֹלָם הַבָּא.

On a similar note, the Gemara recounts related stories with different approaches. **The Sages taught: When Rabbi Eliezer fell ill, his students entered to visit him. They said to him: Teach us paths of life,** guidelines by which to live, **and we will thereby merit the life of the World-to-Come.**

אָמַר לָהֶם: הִזָּהֲרוּ בִּכְבוֹד חַבְרֵיכֶם, וּמִנְעוּ בְּנֵיכֶם מִן הַהִגָּיוֹן, וְהוֹשִׁיבוּם בֵּין בִּרְכֵּי תַלְמִידֵי חֲכָמִים, וּכְשֶׁאַתֶּם מִתְפַּלְּלִים – דְּעוּ לִפְנֵי מִי אַתֶּם עוֹמְדִים, וּבִשְׁבִיל כָּךְ תִּזְכּוּ לְחַיֵּי הָעוֹלָם הַבָּא.

He said to them: Be vigilant in the honor of your counterparts, and prevent your children from logic when studying verses that tend toward heresy (*ge'onim*),[N] **and place** your children, while they are still young, **between the knees of Torah scholars, and when you pray, know before Whom you stand. For** doing **that, you will merit the life of the World-to-Come.**

וּכְשֶׁחָלָה רַבִּי יוֹחָנָן בֶּן זַכַּאי, נִכְנְסוּ תַּלְמִידָיו לְבַקְּרוֹ. כֵּיוָן שֶׁרָאָה אוֹתָם הִתְחִיל לִבְכּוֹת. אָמְרוּ לוֹ תַּלְמִידָיו: נֵר יִשְׂרָאֵל, עַמּוּד הַיְמִינִי, פַּטִּישׁ הֶחָזָק, מִפְּנֵי מָה אַתָּה בוֹכֶה?

A similar story is told about Rabbi Eliezer's mentor, Rabban Yoḥanan ben Zakkai:[P] When **Rabbi Yoḥanan ben Zakkai fell ill his students entered to visit him. When he saw them, he began to cry.**[N] **His students said to him: Lamp of Israel, the right pillar, the mighty hammer,** the man whose life's work is the foundation of the future of the Jewish people, **for what** reason **are you crying?** With a life as complete as yours, what is upsetting you?

אָמַר לָהֶם: אִילּוּ לִפְנֵי מֶלֶךְ בָּשָׂר וָדָם הָיוּ מוֹלִיכִין אוֹתִי, שֶׁהַיּוֹם כָּאן וּמָחָר בַּקֶּבֶר, שֶׁאִם כּוֹעֵס עָלַי – אֵין כַּעֲסוֹ כַּעַס עוֹלָם, וְאִם אוֹסְרֵנִי – אֵין אִיסּוּרוֹ אִיסּוּר עוֹלָם, וְאִם מְמִיתֵנִי – אֵין מִיתָתוֹ מִיתַת עוֹלָם, וַאֲנִי יָכוֹל לְפַיְּיסוֹ בִּדְבָרִים וּלְשַׁחֲדוֹ בְּמָמוֹן – אַף עַל פִּי כֵן הָיִיתִי בוֹכֶה; וְעַכְשָׁיו שֶׁמּוֹלִיכִים אוֹתִי לִפְנֵי מֶלֶךְ מַלְכֵי הַמְּלָכִים הַקָּדוֹשׁ בָּרוּךְ הוּא, שֶׁהוּא חַי וְקַיָּים לְעוֹלָם וּלְעוֹלְמֵי עוֹלָמִים, שֶׁאִם כּוֹעֵס עָלַי – כַּעֲסוֹ כַּעַס עוֹלָם, וְאִם אוֹסְרֵנִי – אִיסּוּרוֹ אִיסּוּר עוֹלָם, וְאִם מְמִיתֵנִי – מִיתָתוֹ מִיתַת עוֹלָם, וְאֵינִי יָכוֹל לְפַיְּיסוֹ בִּדְבָרִים וְלֹא לְשַׁחֲדוֹ בְּמָמוֹן; וְלֹא עוֹד, אֶלָּא שֶׁיֵּשׁ לְפָנַי שְׁנֵי דְרָכִים, אַחַת שֶׁל גַּן עֵדֶן וְאַחַת שֶׁל גֵּיהִנָּם, וְאֵינִי יוֹדֵעַ בְּאֵיזוֹ מוֹלִיכִים אוֹתִי – וְלֹא אֶבְכֶּה?!

He said to them: I cry in fear of heavenly judgment, as the judgment of the heavenly court is unlike the judgment of man. **If they were leading me before a flesh and blood king** whose life is temporal, **who is here today and dead in the grave tomorrow; if he is angry with me, his anger is not eternal** and, consequently, his punishment is not eternal; **if he incarcerates me, his incarceration is not an eternal incarceration,** as I might maintain my hope that I would ultimately be freed. **If he kills me, his killing is not for eternity,** as there is life after any death that he might decree. Moreover, **I am able to appease him with words and** even **bribe him with money,** and **even so I would cry** when standing before royal judgment. **Now that they are leading me before the supreme King of Kings, the Holy One, Blessed be He, Who lives and endures forever and all time; if He is angry with me, His anger is eternal; if He incarcerates me, His incarceration is an eternal incarceration; and if He kills me, His killing is for eternity. I am unable to appease Him with words and bribe him with money. Moreover, but I have two paths before me, one of the Garden of Eden and one of Gehenna, and I do not know on which they are leading me; and will I not cry?**

אָמְרוּ לוֹ: רַבֵּינוּ, בָּרְכֵנוּ! אָמַר לָהֶם: יְהִי רָצוֹן שֶׁתְּהֵא מוֹרָא שָׁמַיִם עֲלֵיכֶם כְּמוֹרָא בָּשָׂר וָדָם. אָמְרוּ לוֹ תַּלְמִידָיו: עַד כָּאן?! – אָמַר לָהֶם: וּלְוַאי! תֵּדְעוּ, כְּשֶׁאָדָם עוֹבֵר עֲבֵירָה אוֹמֵר: "שֶׁלֹּא יִרְאֵנִי אָדָם."

His students **said to him: Our teacher, bless us. He said to them: May it be** His **will that the fear of Heaven shall be upon you like the fear of flesh and blood. His students** were puzzled **and said: To that point** and not beyond? Shouldn't one fear God more? **He said to them: Would that** a person achieve that level of fear. **Know that when one commits a transgression, he says** to himself: I hope **that no man will see me.** If one was as concerned about avoiding shame before God as he is before man, he would never sin.

בִּשְׁעַת פְּטִירָתוֹ, אָמַר לָהֶם: פַּנּוּ כֵּלִים מִפְּנֵי הַטּוּמְאָה, וְהָכִינוּ כִּסֵּא לְחִזְקִיָּהוּ מֶלֶךְ יְהוּדָה שֶׁבָּא.

The Gemara relates that **at the time of his death,** immediately beforehand, **he said to them: Remove the vessels** from the house and take them outside **due to the ritual impurity** that will be imparted by my corpse, which they would otherwise contract. **And prepare a chair for Hezekiah, the King of Judea, who is coming**[N] from the upper world to accompany me.

מתני׳ רַבָּן גַּמְלִיאֵל אוֹמֵר: בְּכָל יוֹם וָיוֹם מִתְפַּלֵּל אָדָם שְׁמוֹנֶה עֶשְׂרֵה. רַבִּי יְהוֹשֻׁעַ אוֹמֵר: מֵעֵין שְׁמוֹנֶה עֶשְׂרֵה. רַבִּי עֲקִיבָא אוֹמֵר: אִם שְׁגוּרָה תְּפִלָּתוֹ בְּפִיו – מִתְפַּלֵּל שְׁמוֹנֶה עֶשְׂרֵה, וְאִם לָאו – מֵעֵין שְׁמוֹנֶה עֶשְׂרֵה.

MISHNA The mishna cites a dispute with regard to the obligation to recite the *Amida* prayer, also known as *Shemoneh Esreh*, the prayer of eighteen blessings, or simply as *tefilla*, prayer. **Rabban Gamliel says: Each and every day a person recites the** prayer of **eighteen blessings. Rabbi Yehoshua says:** A short prayer is sufficient, and one only recites **an abridged** version of the prayer of **eighteen blessings. Rabbi Akiva says** an intermediate opinion: **If he is fluent in his prayer, he recites the** prayer of **eighteen blessings, and if not,** he need only recite **an abridged** version of the prayer of **eighteen blessings.**[H]

רַבִּי אֱלִיעֶזֶר אוֹמֵר: הָעוֹשֶׂה תְּפִלָּתוֹ קֶבַע אֵין תְּפִלָּתוֹ תַּחֲנוּנִים.

Rabbi Eliezer says: One whose prayer is fixed, his prayer is not supplication and is flawed. The Gemara will clarify the halakhic implications of this flaw.

NOTES

And prevent your children from logic when studying verses that tend toward heresy – וּמִנְעוּ בְּנֵיכֶם מִן הַהִגָּיוֹן: Many explanations were suggested for this phrase. According to Rashi, it means that one should prevent his children from studying Bible in general. Some say that it refers specifically to when the children merely study the Bible without understanding it. For this reason, they should be seated at the knee of a Torah scholar who will teach them the meaning of the text (*HaKotev*). Others explained that one should prevent children from studying the philosophical discipline of logic (Rav Hai Gaon). Yet others held that it means that one should prevent them from studying the Bible in a way that is not in accordance with the interpretation of the Sages (*Arukh*).

He began to cry – הִתְחִיל לִבְכּוֹת: Some say that he cried in order to enhance his students' fear of divine judgment and to spur them on to engage more fervently in Torah and mitzvot (*HaKotev*, *Ḥefetz Hashem*).

Prepare a chair for Hezekiah, the King of Judea, who is coming – וְהָכִינוּ כִּסֵּא לְחִזְקִיָּהוּ מֶלֶךְ יְהוּדָה שֶׁבָּא: Some say that it was specifically Hezekiah who appeared to Rabban Yoḥanan because he was one of his descendants (Rav Sa'adia Gaon). Others say that Hezekiah appeared because Rabban Yoḥanan, like Hezekiah before him, brought about an increase in the Torah study among the Jews (see Proverbs 25:1). This may also be interpreted symbolically. Hezekiah, as the representative of the royal House of David, was declaring that there is no anger over the fact that Rabbi Yoḥanan filled the position of *Nasi* in place of the descendants of Beit Hillel who were descendants of the House of David. It was also an allusion to the fact that the position of *Nasi*, the throne represented by the chair, would be restored to a descendant of the House of David, Rabban Gamliel (*Tziyyun LeNefesh Ḥayya*). Others interpret the appearance of King Hezekiah as a message that, although Hezekiah did not surrender when Assyria laid siege to Jerusalem, he approved of Rabban Yoḥanan's concessions to Roman rule as timely, and that is why he came to accompany him (Rabbi Y. A. Herzog).

PERSONALITIES

Rabban Yoḥanan ben Zakkai – רַבָּן יוֹחָנָן בֶּן זַכַּאי: *Nasi* of the Sanhedrin following the destruction of the Temple, Rabban Yoḥanan ben Zakkai was among the greatest leaders of Israel of any generation. A priest, Rabban Yoḥanan ben Zakkai was one of the youngest students of Hillel the Elder. He led Israel for many years of his long life. Prior to the destruction of the Temple he lived in Beror Ḥayil, afterwards he moved to the city of Arev.

HALAKHA

If he is fluent in his prayer, he recites the prayer of eighteen blessings, and if not, he need only recite an abridged version of the prayer of eighteen blessings – אִם שְׁגוּרָה תְּפִלָּתוֹ בְּפִיו – מִתְפַּלֵּל שְׁמוֹנֶה עֶשְׂרֵה וְאִם לָאו מֵעֵין שְׁמוֹנֶה עֶשְׂרֵה: One who stands in prayer and is fluent in the prayer is required to recite the entire *Amida* prayer. This is in accordance with Rabbi Akiva, who adopts the compromise position between the other two opinions. The *halakha* is generally ruled in accordance with his opinion. Only in exigent circumstances, i.e., when the time is passing or when traveling, may one recite the first three blessings of the *Amida* prayer, followed by *havinenu*, followed by the final three blessings. Even if it turns out that he does have time later to recite the entire *Amida* prayer, he need not do so (Rambam *Sefer Ahava, Hilkhot Tefilla* 2:2; *Shulḥan Arukh, Oraḥ Ḥayyim* 110:1).

רַבִּי יְהוֹשֻׁעַ אוֹמֵר: הַהוֹלֵךְ בִּמְקוֹם סַכָּנָה מִתְפַּלֵּל תְּפִלָּה קְצָרָה, וְאוֹמֵר: "הוֹשַׁע ה' אֶת עַמְּךָ אֶת שְׁאֵרִית יִשְׂרָאֵל, בְּכָל פָּרָשַׁת הָעִבּוּר יִהְיוּ צָרְכֵיהֶם לְפָנֶיךָ, בָּרוּךְ אַתָּה ה' שׁוֹמֵעַ תְּפִלָּה.

Rabbi Yehoshua says: One who cannot recite a complete prayer because he **is walking in a place of danger, recites a brief prayer and says: Redeem, Lord, Your people, the remnant of Israel, at every transition** [*parashat ha'ibur*], the meaning of which will be discussed in the Gemara. **May their needs be before You. Blessed are You, Lord, Who listens to prayer.**

הָיָה רוֹכֵב עַל הַחֲמוֹר – יֵרֵד וְיִתְפַּלֵּל, וְאִם אֵינוֹ יָכוֹל לֵירֵד – יַחֲזִיר אֶת פָּנָיו, וְאִם אֵינוֹ יָכוֹל לְהַחֲזִיר אֶת פָּנָיו – יְכַוֵּין אֶת לִבּוֹ כְּנֶגֶד בֵּית קָדְשֵׁי הַקֳּדָשִׁים. הָיָה מְהַלֵּךְ בִּסְפִינָה אוֹ בְּאַסְדָּא – יְכַוֵּין אֶת לִבּוֹ כְּנֶגֶד בֵּית קָדְשֵׁי הַקֳּדָשִׁים.

While praying, one must face toward the direction of the Holy Temple. **One who was riding on a donkey should dismount and pray** calmly. **If he is unable to dismount, he should turn his face** toward the direction of the Temple. **If he is unable to turn his face,** it is sufficient that **he focus his heart opposite the Holy of Holies.** Similarly, **one who was traveling in a ship or on a raft** [*asda*][B] and is unable to turn and face in the direction of Jerusalem, **should focus his heart opposite the Holy of Holies.**

גמ' הָנֵי שְׁמוֹנֶה עֶשְׂרֵה כְּנֶגֶד מִי?

GEMARA

Since the mishna deals with the fundamental obligation to recite the *Amida* prayer, the Gemara seeks to resolve fundamental problems pertaining to this prayer. **Corresponding to what were these eighteen** blessings instituted?[N] When the *Shemoneh Esreh* was instituted by the Sages, on what did they base the number of blessings?

אָמַר רַבִּי הִלֵּל בְּרֵיהּ דְּרַבִּי שְׁמוּאֵל בַּר נַחְמָנִי: כְּנֶגֶד שְׁמוֹנֶה עֶשְׂרֵה אַזְכָּרוֹת שֶׁאָמַר דָּוִד בְּ"הָבוּ לַה' בְּנֵי אֵלִים." רַב יוֹסֵף אָמַר: כְּנֶגֶד שְׁמוֹנֶה עֶשְׂרֵה אַזְכָּרוֹת שֶׁבִּקְרִיאַת שְׁמַע. אָמַר רַבִּי תַּנְחוּם אָמַר רַבִּי יְהוֹשֻׁעַ בֶּן לֵוִי: כְּנֶגֶד שְׁמוֹנֶה עֶשְׂרֵה חוּלְיוֹת שֶׁבַּשִּׁדְרָה.

Rabbi Hillel, son of Rabbi Shmuel bar Naḥmani, said: Corresponding to the eighteen mentions of God's name that King **David said** in the psalm: **"Give unto the Lord, O you sons of might"** (Psalms 29). **Rav Yosef said: Corresponding to the eighteen mentions of God's name in *Shema*. Rabbi Tanḥum said** that **Rabbi Yehoshua ben Levi said: Corresponding to the eighteen vertebrae in the spine** beneath the ribs.

וְאָמַר רַבִּי תַּנְחוּם אָמַר רַבִּי יְהוֹשֻׁעַ בֶּן לֵוִי: הַמִּתְפַּלֵּל צָרִיךְ שֶׁיִּכְרַע עַד שֶׁיִּתְפַּקְקוּ כׇּל חוּלְיוֹת שֶׁבַּשִּׁדְרָה;

Since Rabbi Yehoshua ben Levi's opinion based the *Amida* prayer on the spinal vertebrae, the Gemara cites another statement of his that connects the two: **Rabbi Tanḥum said** that **Rabbi Yehoshua ben Levi said:** In those blessings where one is required to bow, **one who prays must bow**[H] **until all the vertebrae in the spine protrude.**

עוּלָּא אָמַר: עַד כְּדֵי שֶׁיִּרְאֶה אִיסָּר כְּנֶגֶד לִבּוֹ; רַבִּי חֲנִינָא אָמַר: כֵּיוָן שֶׁנִּעְנַע רֹאשׁוֹ שׁוּב אֵינוֹ צָרִיךְ. אָמַר רָבָא: וְהוּא – דְּמִצְטַעֵר נַפְשֵׁיהּ וּמֶחְזֵי כְּמַאן דְּכָרַע.

Establishing a different indicator to determine when he has bowed sufficiently, **Ulla said:** Until **he can see a small coin** [*issar*],[B] on the ground before him **opposite his heart**[N] (Rav Hai Gaon). **Rabbi Ḥanina said:** There is room for leniency; **once he moves his head** forward, **he need not** bow any further. **Rava said: But that** applies only if **he is exerting himself** when doing so, **and he appears like one who is bowing.** However, if he is able, he should bow further.

הָנֵי תַּמְנֵי סְרֵי, תְּשַׁסְרֵי הָוְיָין!

Until now, the prayer of eighteen blessings has been discussed as if it was axiomatic. The Gemara wonders: Are **these eighteen** blessings? **They are nineteen.**

אָמַר רַבִּי לֵוִי: בִּרְכַּת הַמִּינִים בְּיַבְנֶה תִּקְנוּהָ. כְּנֶגֶד מִי תִּקְנוּהָ?

Rabbi Levi said: The blessing of the heretics, which curses informers, **was instituted in Yavne** and is not included in the original tally of blessings. Nevertheless, since the number of blessings corresponds to various allusions, the Gemara attempts to clarify: **Corresponding to what was** this nineteenth blessing **instituted?**

אָמַר רַבִּי לֵוִי: לְרַבִּי הִלֵּל בְּרֵיהּ דְּרַבִּי שְׁמוּאֵל בַּר נַחְמָנִי – כְּנֶגֶד "אֵל הַכָּבוֹד הִרְעִים," לְרַב יוֹסֵף – כְּנֶגֶד "אֶחָד" שֶׁבִּקְרִיאַת שְׁמַע; לְרַבִּי תַּנְחוּם אָמַר רַבִּי יְהוֹשֻׁעַ בֶּן לֵוִי – כְּנֶגֶד חוּלְיָא קְטַנָּה שֶׁבַּשִּׁדְרָה.

Rabbi Levi said: According to Rabbi Hillel, son of Rabbi Shmuel bar Naḥmani, who said that the eighteen blessings correspond to the eighteen mentions of God's name that King David said in the psalm, the nineteenth blessing **corresponds to** a reference to God in that psalm, where a name other than the tetragrammaton was used: **"The God of glory thunders"** (Psalms 29:3). **According to Rav Yosef,** who said that the eighteen blessings correspond to the eighteen mentions of God's name in *Shema*, the additional blessing **corresponds to** the word **one that is in *Shema*.** Although it is not the tetragrammaton, it expresses the essence of faith in God. According to what **Rabbi Tanḥum** said that **Rabbi Yehoshua ben Levi said,** that the eighteen blessings correspond to the eighteen vertebrae in the spine, the additional blessing **corresponds to the small vertebra that is** at the bottom **of the spine.**

BACKGROUND

Raft [*asda*] – אַסְדָּא:

Babylonian raft from the First Temple period

***Issar* – אִיסָּר:** The *issar* was one of the smallest coins, although a *peruta* was worth only an eighth of an *issar*, and was typically made of copper. The size of an *issar* is often used as a gauge of measurement in the Talmud.

Two sides of an *issar*

NOTES

Corresponding to what were these eighteen blessings instituted – הָנֵי שְׁמוֹנֶה עֶשְׂרֵה כְּנֶגֶד מִי: The Gemara was impelled to search for a source for eighteen blessings, as it elsewhere condemned excessive praise of God. Therefore, it cites an allusion to show that there is a solid foundation for this practice (*Penei Yehoshua*). The Jerusalem Talmud added: These blessings correspond to the eighteen times that Abraham, Isaac, and Jacob are mentioned in a single verse, and the eighteen mitzvot commanded in the construction of the Sanctuary.

Until he can see an *issar* opposite his heart – כְּדֵי שֶׁיִּרְאֶה אִיסָּר כְּנֶגֶד לִבּוֹ: There are several interpretations of this phrase. Rashi explains that when one bends over, there will be a wrinkle of flesh the size of an *issar* near his heart. Others explained that one standing opposite an individual who is bowing will be able to see no more than the size of an *issar* next to his heart (Rashi as quoted by *Talmidei Rabbeinu Yona*).

HALAKHA

One who prays must bow, etc. – הַמִּתְפַּלֵּל צָרִיךְ שֶׁיִּכְרַע וכו': In those blessings of the *Amida* prayer in which one is required to bow, he must do so until the vertebrae in the spine protrude. He should not bend so low that his head is level with his belt, as that appears arrogant. One who is sick or elderly may lower his head in a manner that makes it obvious that he wishes to bow (Rambam *Sefer Ahava*, *Hilkhot Tefilla* 5:12; *Shulḥan Arukh*, *Oraḥ Ḥayyim* 113:4–5).

תָּנוּ רַבָּנַן: שִׁמְעוֹן הַפָּקוּלִי הִסְדִּיר שְׁמוֹנֶה עֶשְׂרֵה בְּרָכוֹת לִפְנֵי רַבָּן גַּמְלִיאֵל עַל הַסֵּדֶר בְּיַבְנֶה. אָמַר לָהֶם רַבָּן גַּמְלִיאֵל לַחֲכָמִים: כְּלוּם יֵשׁ אָדָם שֶׁיּוֹדֵעַ לְתַקֵּן בִּרְכַּת הַמִּינִים? עָמַד שְׁמוּאֵל הַקָּטָן וְתִקְּנָהּ,

In light of the previous mention of the blessing of the heretics, the Gemara explains how this blessing was instituted: **The Sages taught: Shimon HaPakuli**[L] **arranged** the **eighteen blessings,** already extant during the period of the Great Assembly, **before Rabban Gamliel,** the *Nasi* of the Sanhedrin, **in order**[N] **in Yavne.** Due to prevailing circumstances, there was a need to institute a new blessing directed against the heretics. **Rabban Gamliel said to the Sages: Is there any person who knows to institute the blessing of the heretics,** a blessing directed against the Sadducees? **Shmuel HaKatan,** who was one of the most pious men of that generation, **stood and instituted it.**

לְשָׁנָה אַחֶרֶת שְׁכָחָהּ.

The Gemara relates: **The next year,** when Shmuel HaKatan served as the prayer leader, **he forgot** that blessing,

LANGUAGE

HaPakuli – הַפָּקוּלִי: Shimon HaPakuli was referred to as such because of his profession, for he worked with bundles. φάκελος, *fakelos,* is Greek for a bundle of wood.

NOTES

Arranged…in order – הִסְדִּיר...עַל הַסֵּדֶר: Although the members of the Great Assembly instituted the formulas of the individual blessings, each individual recited only those blessings relevant to him (*Talmidei Rabbeinu Yona*). Alternatively, perhaps there was no definite order to the blessings (*Ḥefetz Hashem*), and Shimon HaPakuli came and established a definite order. "Arranged…in order," indicates that one who failed to recite the *Amida* prayer in that order did not fulfill his obligation (*Alfasi Zuta*).

Perek **IV**
Daf **29** Amud **a**

וְהִשְׁקִיף בָּהּ שְׁתַּיִם וְשָׁלֹשׁ שָׁעוֹת וְלֹא הֶעֱלוּהוּ.

and scrutinized it, in an attempt to remember the blessing for **two or three hours, and they did not remove him** from serving as prayer leader.

אַמַּאי לֹא הֶעֱלוּהוּ? וְהָאָמַר רַב יְהוּדָה אָמַר רַב: טָעָה בְּכׇל הַבְּרָכוֹת כּוּלָּן – אֵין מַעֲלִין אוֹתוֹ, בְּבִרְכַּת הַמִּינִים – מַעֲלִין אוֹתוֹ, חָיְישִׁינַן שֶׁמָּא מִין הוּא!

The Gemara asks: **Why did they not remove him? Didn't Rav Yehuda say** that **Rav said:** One who was serving as the prayer leader before the congregation and **erred in** reciting **any of the blessings,**[H] **they do not remove him** from serving as the prayer leader. However, one who erred while reciting **the blessing of the heretics they remove him,** as **we suspect that perhaps he is a heretic** and intentionally omitted the blessing to avoid cursing himself. Why, then, did they not remove Shmuel HaKatan?[P]

שָׁאנֵי שְׁמוּאֵל הַקָּטָן, דְּאִיהוּ תִּקְּנָהּ.

The Gemara answers: **Shmuel HaKatan is different because he instituted** this blessing and there is no suspicion of him.

וְנֵיחוּשׁ דִּלְמָא הָדַר בֵּיהּ! אָמַר אַבָּיֵי, גְּמִירִי: טָבָא לָא הָוֵי בִּישָׁא.

The Gemara continues: **Let us suspect** that **perhaps he reconsidered** and, although he had been righteous, he had a change of heart? **Abaye said: We learned** through tradition that a **good** person **does not become wicked.**

וְלָא?! וְהָכְתִיב ״וּבְשׁוּב צַדִּיק מִצִּדְקָתוֹ וְעָשָׂה עָוֶל״! הַהוּא רָשָׁע מֵעִיקָּרוֹ, אֲבָל צַדִּיק מֵעִיקָּרוֹ – לָא.

The Gemara challenges this: **And does he not** become wicked? **Isn't it** explicitly **written: "And when the righteous one returns from his righteousness and does wicked** like all of the abominations that the wicked one has done, will he live? All of the righteous deeds that he has done will not be remembered given the treachery that he has carried out, and in his sin that he has transgressed, for these he shall die" (Ezekiel 18:24)? Abaye responds: **That** verse refers to a righteous individual who was **initially wicked**[N] and repented, but ultimately returned to his evil ways. **However, one who is initially righteous** does **not** become wicked.

וְלָא?! וְהָא תְּנַן: אַל תַּאֲמִין בְּעַצְמְךָ עַד יוֹם מוֹתְךָ, שֶׁהֲרֵי יוֹחָנָן כֹּהֵן גָּדוֹל שִׁמֵּשׁ בִּכְהוּנָּה גְּדוֹלָה שְׁמוֹנִים שָׁנָה וּלְבַסּוֹף נַעֲשָׂה צְדוֹקִי!

The Gemara asks: **And** does he **not** become wicked? **Didn't we learn** in a mishna: **Do not be sure of yourself until the day you die, as Yoḥanan the High Priest served in the High Priesthood for eighty years and ultimately became a Sadducee.** Even one who is outstanding in his righteousness can become a heretic.

אָמַר אַבָּיֵי: הוּא יַנַּאי הוּא יוֹחָנָן. רָבָא אָמַר: יַנַּאי לְחוּד וְיוֹחָנָן לְחוּד, יַנַּאי – רָשָׁע מֵעִיקָּרוֹ, וְיוֹחָנָן – צַדִּיק מֵעִיקָּרוֹ. הָנִיחָא לְאַבָּיֵי, אֶלָּא לְרָבָא קַשְׁיָא!

Abaye responded: He is Yannai he is Yoḥanan.[N] In other words, from its inception, the entire Hasmonean dynasty had the same positive attitude toward the Sadducees, and there was no distinction between Yoḥanan Hyrcanus and Alexander Yannai. Yoḥanan the High Priest had Sadducee leanings from the outset. **Rava said: Yannai is distinct and Yoḥanan is distinct.** They did not share the same position in this regard. **Yannai was wicked from the outset and Yoḥanan was righteous from the outset.** If so, **it works out well according to Abaye's** opinion; **however, according to Rava's** opinion, **it is difficult.** How could Yoḥanan, a righteous individual, have changed and turned wicked?

HALAKHA

One who erred in reciting any of the blessings – טָעָה בְּכׇל הַבְּרָכוֹת: A communal prayer leader who inadvertently omits a blessing, or even several blessings (*Taz*, *Perisha*) in the *Amida* prayer, is not replaced. Rather, they wait a while and jog his memory, and he then he resumes his prayer from the blessing that he omitted. One who skips the blessing of the heretics is replaced immediately. However, if he began reciting that blessing and only then erred, he need not be replaced. With regard to other blessings, if he omitted them intentionally, he is immediately replaced (*Mishna Berura*; Rambam *Sefer Ahava*, *Hilkhot Tefilla* 10:3; *Shulḥan Arukh*, *Oraḥ Ḥayyim* 126:1).

PERSONALITIES

Shmuel HaKatan – שְׁמוּאֵל הַקָּטָן: One of the *tanna'im* from the era of the destruction of the Temple, Shmuel HaKatan [The Small] was among the outstanding pious men of his generation and was well known for his humility and love of humanity. The Gemara relates that a Divine Voice emerged and proclaimed that he was among those worthy of divine inspiration, though his generation was not worthy. Indeed, the Gemara also relates prophecies that he uttered at the time of his death.

NOTES

Righteous individual who was initially wicked – רָשָׁע מֵעִיקָּרוֹ: Some find evidence for this interpretation from the language of the verse: "And when the righteous one returns from his righteousness." In other words, he is reverting to his previous condition (Mahari).

He is Yannai he is Yoḥanan – הוּא יַנַּאי הוּא יוֹחָנָן: This dispute with regard to Yannai and Yoḥanan alludes to the general assessment of the entire royal house of the Hasmoneans. In this passage, Yoḥanan the High Priest symbolizes all the Hasmonean kings who served as High Priests for approximately eighty years. Ultimately, the degree to which they distanced themselves from the Pharisee tradition and drew closer to the Sadducee tradition became more and more evident, culminating in the reign of Alexander Yannai. The dispute here focuses on whether their dynasty was flawed from its inception or whether it deteriorated over time.

אָמַר לָךְ רָבָא: צַדִּיק מֵעִיקָּרוֹ נַמִי, דִּלְמָא הֲדַר בֵּיהּ. אִי הָכִי, אַמַּאי לֹא אַסְּקוּהוּ?

The Gemara responds: **Rava** could have **said to you:** There is **also** room for concern **that one who is righteous from the outset will perhaps reconsider** and turn wicked, as was the case with Yoḥanan the High Priest. **If so,** the original question is difficult: **Why did they not remove** Shmuel HaKatan from serving as the prayer leader?

שָׁאנֵי שְׁמוּאֵל הַקָּטָן דְּאַתְחֵיל בָּהּ. דְּאָמַר רַב יְהוּדָה אָמַר רַב, וְאִיתֵּימָא רַבִּי יְהוֹשֻׁעַ בֶּן לֵוִי: לֹא שָׁנוּ אֶלָּא שֶׁלֹּא הִתְחִיל בָּהּ, אֲבָל הִתְחִיל בָּהּ – גּוֹמְרָהּ.

The Gemara answers: The case of **Shmuel HaKatan is different, as he began** reciting the blessing of the heretics and while reciting it he became confused and forgot the end of the blessing. Consequently, he was not suspected of heretical leanings. Indeed, **Rav Yehuda said** that **Rav, and some say** that **Rabbi Yehoshua ben Levi, said: They only taught** that one who errs while reciting the blessing of the heretics is removed in a case **where he did not begin** reciting **it. But** if he **began** reciting **it,** then we allow him to collect his thoughts **and finish** reciting **it.**

הָנֵי שֶׁבַע דְּשַׁבְּתָא כְּנֶגֶד מִי? אָמַר רַבִּי חֲלַפְתָּא בֶּן שָׁאוּל: כְּנֶגֶד שִׁבְעָה קוֹלוֹת שֶׁאָמַר דָּוִד עַל הַמַּיִם.

To this point, the Gemara discussed allusions to the nineteen blessings that constitute the weekday *Amida* prayer. The Gemara asks: **Corresponding to what** were **these seven** blessings **of the Shabbat** *Amida* prayer instituted? The Gemara answers: **Rabbi Ḥalafta ben Shaul said: Corresponding to the seven "voices" which David mentioned on the waters;** in other words, the seven times that "the voice of God" is mentioned in Psalms 29, which served as the source for the weekday prayer.

הָנֵי תֵּשַׁע דְּרֹאשׁ הַשָּׁנָה כְּנֶגֶד מִי? אָמַר רַבִּי יִצְחָק דְּמִן קַרְטִיגְנִין: כְּנֶגֶד תִּשְׁעָה אַזְכָּרוֹת שֶׁאָמְרָה חַנָּה בִּתְפִלָּתָהּ, דְּאָמַר מָר: בְּרֹאשׁ הַשָּׁנָה נִפְקְדָה שָׂרָה רָחֵל וְחַנָּה.

The Gemara asks further: **Corresponding to what** were **these nine** blessings **of the Rosh HaShana** additional prayer instituted? **Rabbi Yitzḥak of Kartignin said:** They **correspond to the nine mentions of God's name that Hannah said in her prayer** (1 Samuel 2:10). The connection between Hannah's prayer and Rosh HaShana is based on what **the Master said: On Rosh HaShana, Sarah, Rachel, and Hannah were remembered** and the divine decree that they would conceive their sons was issued.

הָנֵי עֶשְׂרִים וְאַרְבַּע דְּתַעֲנִיתָא כְּנֶגֶד מִי? אָמַר רַבִּי חֶלְבּוֹ: כְּנֶגֶד עֶשְׂרִים וְאַרְבַּע רְנָנוֹת שֶׁאָמַר שְׁלֹמֹה בְּשָׁעָה שֶׁהִכְנִיס אָרוֹן לְבֵית קָדְשֵׁי הַקֳּדָשִׁים. אִי הָכִי, כָּל יוֹמָא נַמִי נֵימְרִינְהוּ! אֵימַת אָמְרִינְהוּ שְׁלֹמֹה – בְּיוֹמָא דְּרַחֲמֵי, אֲנַן נַמִי בְּיוֹמָא דְּרַחֲמֵי אָמְרִי לְהוּ.

The Gemara continues: **Corresponding to what** were **these twenty-four** blessings **of the** *Amida* prayer of **the fast** days instituted? **Rabbi Ḥelbo said:** They **correspond to the twenty-four "songs" that Solomon said when he brought the ark into the Holy of Holies** during the dedication of the Temple, as there are twenty-four expressions of song, prayer, and supplication there (1 Kings 8). The Gemara asks: **If so, then let us say these** twenty-four blessing **every day.** The Gemara answers: **When did Solomon say them? On a day of** supplication for **mercy. We, too, say them on a day of** supplication for **mercy.**

"רַבִּי יְהוֹשֻׁעַ אוֹמֵר מֵעֵין שְׁמוֹנֶה עֶשְׂרֵה." מַאי מֵעֵין שְׁמוֹנֶה עֶשְׂרֵה? רַב אָמַר: מֵעֵין כָּל בְּרָכָה וּבְרָכָה, וּשְׁמוּאֵל אָמַר: "הֲבִינֵנוּ ה׳ אֱלֹהֵינוּ לָדַעַת דְּרָכֶיךָ, וּמוֹל אֶת לְבָבֵנוּ לְיִרְאָתֶךָ, וְתִסְלַח לָנוּ לִהְיוֹת גְּאוּלִים, וְרַחֲקֵנוּ מִמַּכְאוֹבֵינוּ, וְדַשְּׁנֵנוּ בִּנְאוֹת אַרְצֶךָ, וּנְפוּצוֹתֵינוּ מֵאַרְבַּע תְּקַבֵּץ, וְהַתּוֹעִים עַל דַּעְתְּךָ יִשָּׁפֵטוּ, וְעַל הָרְשָׁעִים תָּנִיף יָדֶיךָ, וְיִשְׂמְחוּ צַדִּיקִים בְּבִנְיַן עִירֶךָ וּבְתִקּוּן הֵיכָלֶךָ וּבִצְמִיחַת קֶרֶן לְדָוִד עַבְדֶּךָ וּבַעֲרִיכַת נֵר לְבֶן יִשַׁי מְשִׁיחֶךָ, טֶרֶם נִקְרָא אַתָּה תַעֲנֶה, בָּרוּךְ אַתָּה ה׳ שׁוֹמֵעַ תְּפִלָּה."

We learned in the mishna that **Rabbi Yehoshua says** that each day one recites **an abridged** version of the prayer of **eighteen blessings.** The Gemara asks: **What** is the **abridged** version of the prayer of **eighteen blessings?** There are different opinions. **Rav said:** One recites **an abridged** version **of each and every blessing. Shmuel said:** An abridged version of the prayer of eighteen blessings refers to a blessing composed specifically to be recited in place of the thirteen middle blessings. It contains references to each of the thirteen middle blessings. The formula for that blessing is: **Grant us understanding, Lord our God, to know Your ways, and sensitize our hearts so that we may revere You, and forgive us so that we may be redeemed, and keep us far from our suffering, and satisfy us with the pastures of Your land, and gather our scattered** people **from the four** corners of the earth, **and those who go astray shall be judged according to Your will, and raise Your hand against the wicked, and may the righteous rejoice in the rebuilding of Your city, and the restoration of Your Sanctuary, and in the flourishing of Your servant David, and in establishing a light for Your Messiah, son of Yishai. Before we call, may You answer. Blessed are You, Lord, Who listens to prayer."**

לָיֵיט עֲלָהּ אַבַּיֵי אַמַּאן דִּמְצַלֵּי "הֲבִינֵנוּ."

Although Shmuel mentioned this abridged prayer, **Abaye would curse anyone**[N] **who recited** the prayer: **Grant us understanding,** as he held that one may recite it only in exigent circumstances (Rabbi Ḥananel, *Me'iri*).

NOTES

Would curse anyone – לָיֵיט עֲלָהּ: This means that Abaye disapproved of this custom and would harshly criticize those who followed it. This is the meaning of this phrase throughout the Talmud.

אמר רב נחמן אמר שמואל: כל השנה כולה מתפלל אדם "הביננו," חוץ ממוצאי שבת וממוצאי ימים טובים, מפני שצריך לומר הבדלה ב"חונן הדעת."

The Gemara further restricts the occasions when one may recite the abridged prayer. **Rav Naḥman said that Shmuel said: One may recite: Grant us understanding throughout the entire year, except for**[H] in the **evening** prayer **at the conclusion of Shabbat and at the conclusion of Festivals, because he must recite** the prayer of **distinction** [*havdala*] **in the blessing: Who graciously grants knowledge.**

מתקיף לה רבה בר שמואל: ונימרה ברכה רביעית בפני עצמה! מי לא תנן, רבי עקיבא אומר: אומרה ברכה רביעית בפני עצמה; רבי אליעזר אומר: בהודאה!

Rabba bar Shmuel strongly objects to this: After reciting the three initial blessings, **let us say** *havdala* **as an independent fourth blessing,** and afterwards recite the prayer of **Grant us understanding.** This is feasible. **Didn't we learn** in a mishna that **Rabbi Akiva says: He says** *havdala* **as an independent fourth blessing? Rabbi Eliezer says:** He says *havdala* **in** the blessing of **thanksgiving.**

אטו כל השנה כולה מי עבדינן כרבי עקיבא, דהשתא נמי נעביד?! כל השנה כולה מאי טעמא לא עבדינן כרבי עקיבא – תמני סרי תקון, תשסרי לא תקון; הכא נמי – שבע תקון, תמני לא תקון.

The Gemara responds: **Do we practice in accordance with** the opinion of **Rabbi Akiva throughout the entire year** regarding this issue, **that we will also practice** this way **now? Throughout the entire year, what is the reason that we do not practice in accordance with** the opinion of **Rabbi Akiva?** Because **they instituted eighteen** blessings, **they did not institute nineteen. Here too, they instituted seven** blessings, **they did not institute eight.** Therefore, the possibility to recite *havdala* as an independent fourth blessing is rejected.

מתקיף לה מר זוטרא: ונכללה מכלל "הביננו ה' אלהינו המבדיל בין קדש לחול"! קשיא.

Mar Zutra strongly objects to this: Let us include *havdala* in the **framework** of the abridged blessing: **Grant us understanding, Lord our God, Who distinguishes between sacred and profane.** No response was offered to this objection, and it remains **difficult.**

אמר רב ביבי בר אביי: כל השנה כולה מתפלל אדם "הביננו" חוץ מימות הגשמים, מפני שצריך לומר שאלה בברכת השנים. מתקיף לה מר זוטרא: ונכללה מכלל "ודשננו בנאות ארצך ותן טל ומטר"!

Rav Beivai bar Abaye[P] **said:** There is an additional restriction that applies to the abridged prayer. **One may recite Grant us understanding throughout the entire year, except during the rainy season, because he must recite the request** for rain **in the blessing of the years. Mar Zutra strongly objects to this: Let us include** the request for rain in the **framework** of the abridged blessing: **And satisfy us with the pastures of Your land, and grant dew and rain.**

אתי לאטרודי. אי הכי, הבדלה ב"חונן הדעת" נמי אתי לאטרודי!

The Gemara responds: That is unfeasible, as he will **become confused** by introducing a new element to the standard formula of the blessing. The Gemara asks: **If so,** by introducing ***havdala*** **in** the framework of the abridged blessing in the section alluding to the blessing, **Who graciously grants knowledge,** he will **also become confused.** Why did the Gemara fail to respond to Mar Zutra's strong objection with regard to *havdala* in that manner?

אמרי: התם כיון דאתיא בתחלת צלותא – לא מטריד, הכא כיון דאתיא באמצע צלותא – מטריד.

The Gemara answers: **They say** that these cases are different: **There,** regarding *havdala*, **since** the introduction of the new element **comes at the beginning of the prayer, he will not** become **confused. Here, since** the request for rain **comes in the middle of the prayer, he will** become **confused.**

מתקיף לה רב אשי: ונימרה ב"שומע תפלה"! דאמר רבי תנחום אמר רב אסי: טעה ולא הזכיר גבורות גשמים בתחיית המתים – מחזירין אותו, שאלה בברכת השנים – אין מחזירין אותו, מפני שיכול לאומרה ב"שומע תפלה," והבדלה ב"חונן הדעת" – אין מחזירין אותו, מפני שיכול לאומרה על הכוס! – טעה שאני.

Rav Ashi strongly objects to this: If so, **let us say** the request for rain **in** the framework of the abridged blessing in the section alluding to the blessing **Who listens to prayer. As Rabbi Tanḥum said** that **Rav Asi said: One who erred and did not mention the might of the rains** in the blessing on **the revival of the dead, we require him to return** to the beginning of the prayer and repeat it. However, one who erred and failed to recite **the request** for rain **in** the ninth blessing of the *Amida*, **the blessing of the years,**[H] **we do not require him to return** to the beginning of the prayer and repeat it **because he can recite it in the blessing Who listens to prayer. And** one who erred and failed to recite ***havdala*** **in the blessing Who graciously grants knowledge, we do not require him to return** to the beginning of the prayer and repeat it, **as he can recite** *havdala* **over the cup** of wine. One can ask for rain in the blessing Who listens to prayer, and, consequently, can introduce it at the end of the abridged blessing without becoming confused. The Gemara responds: **One who erred is different,** and only then does he have the option to ask for rain in the blessing Who listens to prayer. *Ab initio*, the request for rain may not be inserted there.

HALAKHA

One may recite: Grant us understanding throughout the entire year, except for – כל השנה כולה מתפלל אדם הביננו חוץ: One does not recite: Grant us understanding, during the rainy season because one must include the request for rain, which does not appear in the formula of the blessing. Similarly, one does not recite: Grant us understanding at the conclusion of Shabbat, because *havdala* does not appear in the formula of the blessing. Others explain that it may not be recited at the conclusion of Shabbat because it is liable to create the mistaken impression that the *halakha* is in accordance with the opinion of Rabbi Akiva. Some are uncertain whether or not, in exigent circumstances, i.e., if the time to recite the prayer is passing, one would be permitted to recite: Grant us understanding at the conclusion of Shabbat, even though it does not include *havdala* (Rabbi Akiva Eiger). The *Biur Halakha* rules that it is permitted (Rambam *Sefer Ahava, Hilkhot Tefilla* 2:4; *Shulḥan Arukh, Oraḥ Ḥayyim* 110:1).

One who erred and did not recite the request for rain in the blessing of the years – טעה...שאלה בברכת השנים: If he failed to request rain in the blessing of the years, he recites the request in the blessing: Who listens to prayer. If he only realized his omission after completing that blessing, but prior to beginning the blessing of Temple service: Find favor, he immediately recites the request for rain and then continues with the following blessing. If he began the next blessing but has not yet completed the *Amida* prayer, he returns to the blessing of the years and continues from there. However, if he completed the *Amida* prayer, he must repeat the prayer from the beginning. That is the conclusion of the Gemara according to the Rif and the Rambam (Rambam *Sefer Ahava, Hilkhot Tefilla* 10:9; *Shulḥan Arukh, Oraḥ Ḥayyim* 117:5).

PERSONALITIES

Rav Beivai bar Abaye – רב ביבי בר אביי: Rav Beivai was a fifth generation Babylonian *amora* and apparently the son of Abaye, Rava's friend and colleague. There is no available information with regard to the identity of his teachers. Presumably, he studied with his father and the other Sages of the previous generation. He engaged in halakhic discussions primarily with Rav Pappa and Rav Huna, son of Rav Yehoshua. Apparently, he lived in Pumbedita and worked with his father as a farmer. His statements appear throughout the Talmud, although he never headed his own yeshiva. Rav Beivai engaged in the study of esoterica and many of his statements in that area are found in the Talmud.

גּוּפָא, אָמַר רַבִּי תַּנְחוּם אָמַר רַב אַסִּי: טָעָה וְלֹא הִזְכִּיר גְּבוּרוֹת גְּשָׁמִים בִּתְחִיַּית הַמֵּתִים – מַחֲזִירִין אוֹתוֹ, שְׁאֵלָה בְּבִרְכַּת הַשָּׁנִים – אֵין מַחֲזִירִין אוֹתוֹ, מִפְּנֵי שֶׁיָּכוֹל לְאוֹמְרָהּ בְּ״שׁוֹמֵעַ תְּפִלָּה,״ וְהַבְדָּלָה בְּ״חוֹנֵן הַדַּעַת״ – אֵין מַחֲזִירִין אוֹתוֹ, מִפְּנֵי שֶׁיָּכוֹל לְאוֹמְרָהּ עַל הַכּוֹס.

The statement that Rabbi Tanḥum said that Rav Asi said was incidental to the previous discussion. The Gemara attempts to understand **the matter itself. Rabbi Tanḥum said** that **Rav Asi said: One who erred and did not mention the might of the rains** in the blessing on **the revival of the dead, we require him to return** to the beginning of the prayer and repeat it. However, one who erred and failed to recite **the request** for rain **in the blessing of the years, we do not require him to return** to the beginning of the prayer and repeat it **because he can recite it in** the blessing **Who listens to prayer. And** one who erred and failed to recite ***havdala* in** the blessing **Who graciously grants knowledge, we do not require him to return** to the beginning of the prayer and repeat it, **as he can recite** *havdala* **over the cup** of wine.

מֵיתִיבֵי: טָעָה וְלֹא הִזְכִּיר גְּבוּרוֹת גְּשָׁמִים בִּתְחִיַּית הַמֵּתִים – מַחֲזִירִין אוֹתוֹ, שְׁאֵלָה בְּבִרְכַּת הַשָּׁנִים – מַחֲזִירִין אוֹתוֹ, וְהַבְדָּלָה בְּ״חוֹנֵן הַדַּעַת״ – אֵין מַחֲזִירִין אוֹתוֹ, מִפְּנֵי שֶׁיָּכוֹל לְאוֹמְרָהּ עַל הַכּוֹס!

The Gemara **raised an objection** based on what was taught in the *Tosefta*: **One who erred and did not mention the might of the rains** in the blessing on **the revival of the dead, we require him to return** to the beginning of the prayer and repeat it. One who erred and failed to recite **the request** for rain **in the blessing of the years, we require him to return** to the beginning of the prayer and repeat it. However, one who erred and failed to recite ***havdala* in** the blessing **Who graciously grants knowledge, we do not require him to return** to the beginning of the prayer and repeat it, **as he can recite** *havdala* **over the cup** of wine. The *Tosefta* contradicts the statement of Rabbi Tanḥum with regard to one who erred and failed to recite the request for rain in the blessing of the years.

לָא קַשְׁיָא: הָא בְּיָחִיד, הָא בְּצִבּוּר.

The Gemara responds: **This is not difficult. This** case, where we require him to return to the beginning of the prayer and repeat it, refers to a situation where he is praying **as an individual.** While **that** case, where we do not require him to return to the beginning of the prayer and repeat it, refers to a situation where he is praying **as** part of **a congregation.**

בְּצִבּוּר מַאי טַעְמָא לֹא – מִשּׁוּם דְּשַׁמְעָהּ מִשְּׁלִיחַ צִבּוּר, אִי הָכִי, הַאי ״מִפְּנֵי שֶׁיָּכוֹל לְאוֹמְרָהּ בְּשׁוֹמֵעַ תְּפִילָּה״ – ״מִפְּנֵי שֶׁשּׁוֹמֵעַ מִשְּׁלִיחַ צִיבּוּר״ מִיבָּעֵי לֵיהּ!

The Gemara raises a difficulty: When praying **as** part of **a congregation, what is the reason** that he need **not** need return to the beginning of the prayer and repeat it? **Because** he can fulfill his obligation **when he hears it from the communal prayer leader** in the repetition of the *Amida* prayer. **If so,** Rabbi Tanḥum's formulation is imprecise. **That** which he said that he need not return to the beginning of the prayer and repeat it **because he can recite it in** the blessing: **Who listens to prayer, should have been: Because he hears it from the communal prayer leader.** This proves that the attempt to rebuff the challenge from the *Tosefta* to Rabbi Tanḥum was incorrect.

אֶלָּא, אִידִי וְאִידִי בְּיָחִיד, וְלָא קַשְׁיָא: הָא – דְּאִדְּכַר קוֹדֶם ״שׁוֹמֵעַ תְּפִלָּה,״

Rather, both **this** statement of Rabbi Tanḥum **and that** statement in the *Tosefta* refer to one praying **as an individual, and it is,** nevertheless, **not difficult. This** case, where we do not require him to return to the beginning of the prayer and repeat it, refers to a case where **he recalls** his error **before** he reaches the blessing: **Who listens to prayer,** in which case he can ask for rain in that blessing.

Perek **IV**
Daf **29** Amud **b**

הָא – דְּאִדְּכַר בָּתַר ״שׁוֹמֵעַ תְּפִלָּה.״

This case, where we require him to return to the beginning of the prayer and repeat it, refers to a situation where **he recalls his error after** he reaches the blessing: **Who listens to prayer,** in which case the option of asking for rain in that blessing no longer exists and he must return to the beginning of the prayer.

אָמַר רַבִּי תַּנְחוּם אָמַר רַב אַסִי אָמַר רַבִּי יְהוֹשֻׁעַ בֶּן לֵוִי: טָעָה וְלֹא הִזְכִּיר שֶׁל רֹאשׁ חֹדֶשׁ בַּעֲבוֹדָה – חוֹזֵר לָעֲבוֹדָה, נִזְכַּר בְּהוֹדָאָה – חוֹזֵר לָעֲבוֹדָה. בְּ״שִׂים שָׁלוֹם״ – חוֹזֵר לָעֲבוֹדָה, וְאִם סִיֵּים – חוֹזֵר לָרֹאשׁ.

On a similar note, the Gemara cites an additional statement of Rabbi Tanḥum. **Rabbi Tanḥum said that Rav Asi said that Rabbi Yehoshua ben Levi said: One who erred and did not mention the New Moon,**[H] the addition: May there rise and come [*ya'aleh veyavo*] **in the** blessing of Temple **service,** the seventeenth blessing in the *Amida* prayer, **he returns to the** blessing of Temple **service.** So too, if he **remembers during** the blessing of **thanksgiving, he returns to the** blessing of Temple **service. If** he remembers in the blessing: **Grant peace, he returns to the** blessing of Temple **service. If** he remembers after he **completed** the *Amida* prayer, **he returns to the beginning** of the prayer.

אָמַר רַב פַּפָּא בְּרֵיהּ דְּרַב אַחָא בַּר אַדָּא: הָא דַּאֲמַרַן ״סִיֵּים חוֹזֵר לָרֹאשׁ״ – לֹא אֲמַרַן אֶלָּא שֶׁעָקַר רַגְלָיו, אֲבָל לֹא עָקַר רַגְלָיו – חוֹזֵר לָעֲבוֹדָה.

Rav Pappa son of Rav Aḥa bar Adda said: That which we said that if he already **finished** the *Amida* prayer **he returns to the beginning, we only said** that in a case **where he** already **moved his feet** from where he stood in prayer. **However,** if he **did not** yet **move his feet, he** need only **return to the** blessing of Temple **service,** and include the addition for the New Moon therein.

אֲמַר לֵיהּ: מְנָא לָךְ הָא? אֲמַר לֵיהּ: מֵאַבָּא מָרִי שְׁמִיעַ לִי, וְאַבָּא מָרִי מֵרַב.

He said to him: From where do you derive **this** *halakha*? **He said to him: My father my teacher told** it **to me and my father my teacher** heard it **from Rav.**

אָמַר רַב נַחְמָן בַּר יִצְחָק: הָא דַּאֲמַרַן ״עָקַר רַגְלָיו חוֹזֵר לָרֹאשׁ״ – לֹא אֲמַרַן אֶלָּא שֶׁאֵינוֹ רָגִיל לוֹמַר תַּחֲנוּנִים אַחַר תְּפִלָּתוֹ, אֲבָל רָגִיל לוֹמַר תַּחֲנוּנִים אַחַר תְּפִלָּתוֹ – חוֹזֵר לָעֲבוֹדָה.

On a similar note, **Rav Naḥman bar Yitzḥak said: That which we** said that if he already **moved his feet he returns to the beginning, we only said** that in a case **where he is unaccustomed to reciting** additional **supplications after his prayer. However, if he is accustomed to reciting supplications after his prayer,** and while reciting them he remembers that he omitted mention of the New Moon from his prayer, **he** need only **return to the** blessing of Temple **service,** and he includes the addition for the New Moon therein.

אִיכָּא דְּאָמְרִי, אָמַר רַב נַחְמָן בַּר יִצְחָק: הָא דַּאֲמַרַן כִּי לֹא עָקַר רַגְלָיו חוֹזֵר לָעֲבוֹדָה – לָא אֲמַרַן אֶלָּא שֶׁרָגִיל לוֹמַר תַּחֲנוּנִים אַחַר תְּפִלָּתוֹ, אֲבָל אִם אֵינוֹ רָגִיל לוֹמַר תַּחֲנוּנִים אַחַר תְּפִלָּתוֹ – חוֹזֵר לָרֹאשׁ.

Some say, Rav Naḥman bar Yitzḥak said: That which we said that if he **did not** yet **move his feet, he** need only **return to the** blessing of Temple **service, we only said** that in a case **where he is accustomed to reciting** additional **supplications after his prayer. However,** if **he is unaccustomed to reciting supplications after his prayer, he must return to the beginning of the prayer,** as it is considered as if he already completed it.

״רַבִּי אֱלִיעֶזֶר אוֹמֵר: כָּל הָעוֹשֶׂה תְּפִלָּתוֹ קֶבַע״ וכו׳. מַאי ״קֶבַע?״ אָמַר רַבִּי יַעֲקֹב בַּר אִידִי אָמַר רַבִּי אוֹשַׁעְיָא: כָּל שֶׁתְּפִלָּתוֹ דּוֹמָה עָלָיו כְּמַשּׂוֹי; וְרַבָּנַן אָמְרִי: כָּל מִי שֶׁאֵינוֹ אוֹמְרָהּ בִּלְשׁוֹן תַּחֲנוּנִים; רַבָּה וְרַב יוֹסֵף דְּאָמְרִי תַּרְוַיְיהוּ: כָּל שֶׁאֵינוֹ יָכוֹל לְחַדֵּשׁ בָּהּ דָּבָר.

We learned in the mishna that **Rabbi Eliezer says: One whose prayer is fixed, his prayer is not supplication.** The Gemara asks: **What is** the meaning of **fixed** in this context? **Rabbi Ya'akov bar Idi said** that **Rabbi Oshaya said:** It means **anyone for whom his prayer is like a burden upon him,** from which he seeks to be quickly unburdened. **The Rabbis say:** This refers to **anyone who does not recite** prayer **in the language of supplication,** but as a standardized recitation without emotion. **Rabba and Rav Yosef both said:** It refers to **anyone unable to introduce** a novel **element,** i.e., something personal reflecting his personal needs, to his prayer, and only recites the standard formula.[N]

אָמַר רַבִּי זֵירָא: אֲנָא יָכֵילְנָא לְחַדּוּשֵׁי בָּהּ מִילְּתָא, וּמִסְתְּפֵינָא דִּלְמָא מִטְּרִידְנָא.

Rabbi Zeira said: I could introduce a novel **element** in every prayer, but **I am afraid that perhaps I will** become **confused.** Consequently, there is no room to require the masses to introduce a novel element into their prayers.

אַבַּיֵי בַּר אָבִין וְרַבִּי חֲנִינָא בַּר אָבִין דְּאָמְרִי תַּרְוַיְיהוּ: כָּל שֶׁאֵין מִתְפַּלֵּל עִם דִּמְדּוּמֵי חַמָּה, דְּאָמַר רַבִּי חִיָּיא בַּר אַבָּא אָמַר רַבִּי יוֹחָנָן: מִצְוָה לְהִתְפַּלֵּל עִם דִּמְדּוּמֵי חַמָּה; וְאָמַר רַבִּי זֵירָא: מַאי קְרָאָה – ״יִירָאוּךָ עִם שָׁמֶשׁ וְלִפְנֵי יָרֵחַ דּוֹר דּוֹרִים.״ לַיְיטִי עֲלַהּ בְּמַעְרְבָא אַמַּאן דִּמְצַלֵּי עִם דִּמְדּוּמֵי חַמָּה, מַאי טַעְמָא? דִּלְמָא מִיטְּרְפָא לֵיהּ שַׁעְתָּא.

The brothers, **Abaye bar Avin and Rabbi Ḥanina bar Avin, both said:** One whose prayer is fixed refers to **anyone who does not** make the effort to **pray with the reddening of the sun,** just after sunrise and just before sunset, which are auspicious times for prayer. As **Rabbi Ḥiyya bar Abba said that Rabbi Yoḥanan said: It is a mitzva to pray with the reddening of the sun. And Rabbi Zeira said: What is the verse** that alludes to this? **"Let them fear You with the sun and before the moon, generation after generation"** (Psalms 72:5). Prayer, the manifestation of the fear of God, should be undertaken adjacent to sunrise and sunset. Nevertheless, **in the West,** Eretz Yisrael, **they cursed one who prays with the reddening of the sun,** adjacent to sunset. **What is the reason? Perhaps,** due to preoccupation, he will become **confused about the hour** and the time for prayer will pass.

HALAKHA

One who erred and did not mention the New Moon – טָעָה וְלֹא הִזְכִּיר שֶׁל רֹאשׁ חֹדֶשׁ: If one forgot to recite: May there rise and come, in the morning or afternoon prayers on the New Moon, he does the following: If he realized his omission before beginning the following blessing of thanksgiving, even if he concluded the blessing of Temple service: And may our eyes witness, he recites it there. If he began the blessing of thanksgiving but did not yet complete the *Amida* prayer, he returns to the blessing of Temple service. If he realizes his omission only after concluding the *Amida* prayer, he repeats the *Amida* from the beginning. If he completed the *Amida* prayer but has not yet moved his feet, or has not yet completed the supplications that he always recites at the end of his prayer, he returns to the blessing of Temple service. If one forgot to recite: May there rise and come, in the evening prayer, whether it is a one-day or two-day New Moon, he need not repeat the *Amida* prayer (Rambam *Sefer Ahava, Hilkhot Tefilla* 10:10; *Shulḥan Arukh, Oraḥ Ḥayyim* 422:1).

NOTES

Prayer which is fixed and prayer which is supplication – קֶבַע וְתַחֲנוּנִים: The difference between the opinions of Rabbi Ya'akov bar Idi and the Rabbis is as follows. According to Rabbi Ya'akov bar Idi, the emphasis is on one's intent and inner devotion. According to the Sages, the demand is merely that one turn to God with an expression of supplication (Rabbi Ḥananel).

"רַבִּי יְהוֹשֻׁעַ אוֹמֵר: הַמְהַלֵּךְ בִּמְקוֹם סַכָּנָה מִתְפַּלֵּל תְּפִלָּה קְצָרָה וכו׳ בְּכׇל פָּרָשַׁת הָעִבּוּר." מַאי "פָּרָשַׁת הָעִבּוּר"? אָמַר רַב חִסְדָּא אָמַר מָר עוּקְבָא: אֲפִילּוּ בְּשָׁעָה שֶׁאַתָּה מִתְמַלֵּא עֲלֵיהֶם עֶבְרָה כְּאִשָּׁה עוּבָּרָה – יִהְיוּ כׇּל צׇרְכֵיהֶם לְפָנֶיךָ. אִיכָּא דְּאָמְרִי, אָמַר רַב חִסְדָּא אָמַר מָר עוּקְבָא: אֲפִילּוּ בְּשָׁעָה שֶׁהֵם עוֹבְרִים עַל דִּבְרֵי תוֹרָה – יִהְיוּ כׇּל צׇרְכֵיהֶם לְפָנֶיךָ.

We learned in the mishna that **Rabbi Yehoshua says: One who is walking in a place of danger, recites a brief prayer…at *parashat ha'ibur*.** The Gemara asks: **What is the meaning of *parashat ha'ibur*? Rav Ḥisda**[P] **said that Mar Ukva said:** This can be interpreted in a manner underscoring two connotations of the term *ibur*: **Even at a time when You are as filled with anger [*evra*], towards them, as a pregnant woman [*ubara*], may all of their needs be before You. Some say** a different version of what **Rav Ḥisda said that Mar Ukva said: Even when they violate [*ovrim*] the commandments of the Torah, may all of their needs be before You.**

תָּנוּ רַבָּנַן: הַמְהַלֵּךְ בִּמְקוֹם גְּדוּדֵי חַיָּה וְלִסְטִים מִתְפַּלֵּל תְּפִלָּה קְצָרָה. וְאֵיזֶה הִיא תְּפִלָּה קְצָרָה? רַבִּי אֱלִיעֶזֶר אוֹמֵר: "עֲשֵׂה רְצוֹנְךָ בַּשָּׁמַיִם מִמַּעַל, וְתֵן נַחַת רוּחַ לִירֵאֶיךָ מִתַּחַת, וְהַטּוֹב בְּעֵינֶיךָ עֲשֵׂה, בָּרוּךְ אַתָּה ה׳ שׁוֹמֵעַ תְּפִלָּה".

One formula for the prayer recited in places of danger is cited in the mishna. Additional formulas are cited in the *Tosefta*. **The Sages taught: One who walks in a place where there are groups of wild beasts and robbers recites an abbreviated prayer.**[H] **Which is an abbreviated prayer? Rabbi Eliezer says, "Carry out Your will in the heavens above, and give peace of mind to those who fear You below, and perform that which is good in Your eyes. Blessed are You, Lord, Who listens to prayer."**

רַבִּי יְהוֹשֻׁעַ אוֹמֵר: "שְׁמַע שַׁוְעַת עַמְּךָ יִשְׂרָאֵל וַעֲשֵׂה מְהֵרָה בַּקָּשָׁתָם, בָּרוּךְ אַתָּה ה׳ שׁוֹמֵעַ תְּפִלָּה".

Rabbi Yehoshua says that he recites: **Hear the cry of Your nation, Israel, and quickly fulfill their request. Blessed are You, Lord, Who listens to prayer.**

רַבִּי אֶלְעָזָר בְּרַבִּי צָדוֹק אוֹמֵר: "שְׁמַע צַעֲקַת עַמְּךָ יִשְׂרָאֵל וַעֲשֵׂה מְהֵרָה בַּקָּשָׁתָם, בָּרוּךְ אַתָּה ה׳ שׁוֹמֵעַ תְּפִלָּה".

Rabbi Eliezer, son of Rabbi Tzadok says that he recites: **Hear the shout of Your nation, Israel, and quickly fulfill their request. Blessed are You, Lord, Who listens to prayer.**

אֲחֵרִים אוֹמְרִים: "צׇרְכֵי עַמְּךָ יִשְׂרָאֵל מְרוּבִּין וְדַעְתָּם קְצָרָה, יְהִי רָצוֹן מִלְּפָנֶיךָ ה׳ אֱלֹהֵינוּ שֶׁתִּתֵּן לְכׇל אֶחָד וְאֶחָד כְּדֵי פַּרְנָסָתוֹ וּלְכׇל גְּוִיָּה וּגְוִיָּה דֵּי מַחְסוֹרָהּ, בָּרוּךְ אַתָּה ה׳ שׁוֹמֵעַ תְּפִלָּה".

Aḥerim **say** that he recites: **The needs of Your nation, Israel, are many and their intelligence is limited,** and, consequently, they are unable to effectively articulate their thoughts in prayer (Maharsha). So **may it be Your will, Lord our God, to provide each and every one with his necessary sustenance, and to each and every body all that it lacks. Blessed are You, Lord, Who listens to prayer.**

אָמַר רַב הוּנָא: הֲלָכָה כַּאֲחֵרִים.

Rav Huna said: The *halakha* with regard to the version of the prayer recited in a place of danger **is in accordance with** the opinion of *Aḥerim*.

אָמַר לֵיהּ אֵלִיָּהוּ לְרַב יְהוּדָה אֲחוּהּ דְּרַב סַלָּא חֲסִידָא: לָא תִּרְתַּח וְלָא תֶּחֱטֵי, לָא תִּרְוֵי וְלָא תֶּחֱטֵי, וּכְשֶׁאַתָּה יוֹצֵא לַדֶּרֶךְ – הִמָּלֵךְ בְּקוֹנְךָ וָצֵא. מַאי "הִמָּלֵךְ בְּקוֹנְךָ וָצֵא"? אָמַר רַבִּי יַעֲקֹב אָמַר רַב חִסְדָּא: זוֹ תְּפִלַּת הַדֶּרֶךְ. וְאָמַר רַבִּי יַעֲקֹב אָמַר רַב חִסְדָּא: כׇּל הַיּוֹצֵא לַדֶּרֶךְ צָרִיךְ לְהִתְפַּלֵּל תְּפִלַּת הַדֶּרֶךְ.

On the topic of prayers recited while traveling and in times of danger, the Gemara discusses the traveler's prayer. When he appeared to him, **Elijah** the Prophet **said to Rav Yehuda brother of Rav Sala Ḥasida: Do not get angry and you will not sin. Do not get drunk and you will not sin. And when you set out on a journey, consult with your Creator, and then set out. Rabbi Ya'akov said** that **Rav Ḥisda said: That is the traveler's prayer.**[H] **And Rabbi Ya'akov said** that **Rav Ḥisda said:** It is not only good advice, but established *halakha* that **anyone who sets out on a journey must recite the traveler's prayer** prior to embarking on his journey.

מַאי תְּפִלַּת הַדֶּרֶךְ? "יְהִי רָצוֹן מִלְּפָנֶיךָ ה׳ אֱלֹהַי, שֶׁתּוֹלִיכֵנִי לְשָׁלוֹם וְתַצְעִידֵנִי לְשָׁלוֹם וְתִסְמְכֵנִי לְשָׁלוֹם, וְתַצִּילֵנִי מִכַּף כׇּל אוֹיֵב וְאוֹרֵב בַּדֶּרֶךְ, וְתִשְׁלַח בְּרָכָה בְּמַעֲשֵׂי יָדַי, וְתִתְּנֵנִי לְחֵן לְחֶסֶד וּלְרַחֲמִים בְּעֵינֶיךָ וּבְעֵינֵי כׇל רוֹאַי, בָּרוּךְ אַתָּה ה׳ שׁוֹמֵעַ תְּפִלָּה".

The Gemara asks: **What is** the formula for **the traveler's prayer?** The Gemara answers: **May it be Your will, Lord my God, to lead me to peace, direct my steps to peace, and guide me to peace, and rescue me from the hands of any enemy or ambush along the way, and send blessing to the work of my hands, and let me find grace, kindness, and compassion in Your eyes and in the eyes of all who see me. Blessed are You, Lord, Who hears prayer.**

אָמַר אַבַּיֵי: לְעוֹלָם

Abaye said: At all times

Perek **IV**
Daf **30** Amud **a**

לִישַׁתֵּף אִינִישׁ נַפְשֵׁיהּ בַּהֲדֵי צִבּוּרָא. הֵיכִי נֵימָא? – "יְהִי רָצוֹן מִלְּפָנֶיךָ ה׳ אֱלֹהֵינוּ שֶׁתּוֹלִיכֵנוּ לְשָׁלוֹם וכו׳".

a person should associate himself with the congregation and should not pray for himself alone. **How should he say** it? **May it be Your will, Lord our God, that You lead us to peace, etc.,** in the plural.

PERSONALITIES

Rav Ḥisda – רַב חִסְדָּא: One of the greatest second generation Babylonian *amora'im*, Rav Ḥisda, a priest, was one of Rav's younger students. After Rav's death, he remained a disciple-colleague of Rav's student, Rav Huna. Throughout his life, Rav Ḥisda showed great affection for the teachings of Rav, and constantly tried to learn additional matters of Torah in his name. Although he was poor as a youth, he became wealthy and lived most of his life in comfort. He was very generous toward his fellow man. He was devoted to his students, his sons, and his daughters, guiding them along the straight and narrow in both spiritual and worldly matters.

HALAKHA

One who walks in a place where there are groups of wild beasts and robbers recites an abbreviated prayer – הַמְהַלֵּךְ בִּמְקוֹם גְּדוּדֵי חַיָּה וְלִסְטִים מִתְפַּלֵּל תְּפִלָּה קְצָרָה: When walking in a dangerous place, one recites an abbreviated prayer. The formula is in accordance with the opinion of *Aḥerim: The needs of Your nation, Israel, are many, etc.*, as per the ruling of Rav Huna. However, if one arrives at a safe haven before the time for prayer has passed, he recites the standard *Amida* prayer. If he was unable to recite the standard *Amida* prayer, his legal status is equal to one who forgot to pray and he compensates for the missed prayer after completing the next *Amida* prayer (Rambam *Sefer Ahava, Hilkhot Tefilla* 4:19; *Shulḥan Arukh, Oraḥ Ḥayyim* 110:4 in the comment of the Rema).

The traveler's prayer – תְּפִלַּת הַדֶּרֶךְ: One who sets out on a journey recites May it be Your will, as formulated in the Gemara. It is recited in the plural as per the ruling of Abaye (see *Beit Yosef*; Rambam *Sefer Ahava, Hilkhot Berakhot* 10:25; *Shulḥan Arukh, Oraḥ Ḥayyim* 110:4).

אֵימַת מְצַלֵּי? – אָמַר רַבִּי יַעֲקֹב אָמַר רַב חִסְדָּא: מִשָּׁעָה שֶׁמְּהַלֵּךְ בַּדֶּרֶךְ. עַד כַּמָּה? – אָמַר רַבִּי יַעֲקֹב אָמַר רַב חִסְדָּא: עַד פַּרְסָה. וְהֵיכִי מְצַלֵּי לָהּ? – רַב חִסְדָּא אָמַר: מְעוּמָּד; רַב שֵׁשֶׁת אָמַר: אֲפִילּוּ מְהַלֵּךְ.

The Gemara discusses specific details pertaining to this prayer. **When does one pray? Rabbi Ya'akov said** that **Rav Ḥisda said: From when one sets out on his journey,**[H] and not before. **How long** must one's planned journey be in order to require him to recite this prayer (*Ba'al Halakhot Gedolot*)? **Rabbi Ya'akov said** that **Rav Ḥisda said: At least a parasang.**[H] **How does he recite** this prayer? **Rav Ḥisda said:** Only while **standing** in one place. **Rav Sheshet said: Even walking**[H] or sitting.

רַב חִסְדָּא וְרַב שֵׁשֶׁת הֲווּ קָאָזְלִי בְּאוֹרְחָא, קָם רַב חִסְדָּא וְקָא מְצַלֵּי. אָמַר לֵיהּ רַב שֵׁשֶׁת לְשַׁמָּעֵיהּ: מַאי קָא עָבֵיד רַב חִסְדָּא? אָמַר לֵיהּ: קָאֵי וּמְצַלֵּי. אָמַר לֵיהּ: אוֹקְמָן נַמִי לְדִידִי וַאֲצַלֵּי, מִהְיוֹת טוֹב אַל תִּקָּרֵא רַע.

The Gemara relates: **Rav Ḥisda and Rav Sheshet were walking along the path, Rav Ḥisda stood and recited** the traveler's prayer. Since he was blind and did not see his colleague, **Rav Sheshet asked his servant: What is Rav Ḥisda doing** now? His servant **said to him: He is standing and praying.** Rav Sheshet **said to** his servant: **Stand me up as well and I will pray.** Even though Rav Sheshet held that there is no need to stand during this prayer, nevertheless: **From being good, do not be called wicked.** In other words, one should do better if he is able. Rav Sheshet said that one is not required to stop and stand. He did not say that it is preferable to walk or sit. Since standing in this case required no special effort on his part, as Rav Ḥisda had stopped to stand and pray anyway, why insist on sitting?

מַאי אִיכָּא בֵּין ״הֲבִינֵנוּ״ לִתְפִלָּה קְצָרָה? – הֲבִינֵנוּ – בָּעֵי לְצַלּוֹיֵי שָׁלֹשׁ קַמַּיָּיתָא וְשָׁלֹשׁ בַּתְרַיְיתָא, וְכִי מָטֵי לְבֵיתֵיהּ לָא בָּעֵי לְמֶהְדַּר לְצַלּוֹיֵי; בִּתְפִלָּה קְצָרָה – לָא בָּעֵי לְצַלּוֹיֵי לֹא שָׁלֹשׁ קַמַּיָּיתָא וְלֹא שָׁלֹשׁ בַּתְרַיְיתָא, וְכִי מָטֵי לְבֵיתֵיהּ בָּעֵי לְמֶהְדַּר לְצַלּוֹיֵי.

The mishna mentioned both a brief prayer recited in times of danger and an abridged prayer, with regard to which there was a dispute between the *tanna'im*. The Gemara asks: **What is** the practical halakhic difference between the abridged prayer: **Grant us understanding and the brief prayer** recited in times of danger? The Gemara answers: One who recites: **Grant us understanding is required to recite the first three** blessings **and the last three** blessings of the *Amida* prayer, **and when he reaches his home, he need not pray again.** One who recites **the brief prayer,** however, **need recite neither the first three** blessings **nor the last three** blessings of the *Amida* prayer. **However, when he reaches his home, he must pray again.** Grant us understanding has the legal status of the *Amida* prayer, despite its brevity, while the brief prayer is merely recited in place of the *Amida* prayer in exigent circumstances.

וְהִלְכְתָא: הֲבִינֵנוּ – מְעוּמָּד, תְּפִלָּה קְצָרָה – בֵּין מְעוּמָּד בֵּין מְהַלֵּךְ.

The *halakha* is: Grant us understanding, as mentioned above, has the legal status of the *Amida* prayer, and must therefore be recited while **standing.**[H] **The brief prayer,** since it does not have that status, may be recited **whether** one is **standing or whether** one is **walking.**[H]

״הָיָה רוֹכֵב עַל הַחֲמוֹר״ וכו׳. תָּנוּ רַבָּנַן: הָיָה רוֹכֵב עַל הַחֲמוֹר וְהִגִּיעַ זְמַן תְּפִלָּה, אִם יֵשׁ לוֹ מִי שֶׁיֹּאחַז אֶת חֲמוֹרוֹ – יֵרֵד לְמַטָּה וְיִתְפַּלֵּל, וְאִם לָאו – יֵשֵׁב בִּמְקוֹמוֹ וְיִתְפַּלֵּל; רַבִּי אוֹמֵר: בֵּין כָּךְ וּבֵין כָּךְ – יֵשֵׁב בִּמְקוֹמוֹ וְיִתְפַּלֵּל, לְפִי שֶׁאֵין דַּעְתּוֹ מְיוּשֶּׁבֶת עָלָיו.

We learned in the mishna: **One who was riding on a donkey**[H] should dismount and pray. Only in exigent circumstances may he pray while riding, focusing his heart toward Jerusalem and the Holy of Holies. **The Sages taught** in a *Tosefta*: **One who was riding on a donkey and the time for prayer arrived, if he has someone to hold** onto **the donkey, he should dismount and pray. If not, he should sit in his place** atop the donkey **and pray. Rabbi** Yehuda HaNasi **says: In any case,** whether or not there is someone to hold onto the donkey, **he should sit in his place** atop the donkey **and pray, as his mind will not be calm.** Since he is hurrying to arrive at his destination, the need to dismount the donkey, stand in prayer, and remount the donkey would delay his journey, and the delay is likely to interfere with his concentration during prayer.

אָמַר רָבָא וְאִיתֵימָא רַבִּי יְהוֹשֻׁעַ בֶּן לֵוִי: הֲלָכָה כְּרַבִּי.

Rava, and some say Rabbi Yehoshua ben Levi, said: The ***halakha*** here **is in accordance with** the opinion of **Rabbi** Yehuda HaNasi.

תָּנוּ רַבָּנַן: סוּמָא וּמִי שֶׁאֵינוֹ יָכוֹל לְכַוֵּין אֶת הָרוּחוֹת – יְכַוֵּין לִבּוֹ כְּנֶגֶד אָבִיו שֶׁבַּשָּׁמַיִם, שֶׁנֶּאֱמַר: ״וְהִתְפַּלְלוּ אֶל ה׳״;

The Sages taught in a *Tosefta*: **A blind person and one who is unable to approximate the directions** and, therefore, is unable to face Jerusalem in order to pray, **may focus his heart towards his Father in Heaven, as it is stated: "And they shall pray to the Lord"** (I Kings 8:44).

HALAKHA

From when one sets out on his journey – מִשָּׁעָה שֶׁמְּהַלֵּךְ בַּדֶּרֶךְ: The traveler's prayer is recited as soon as one sets out on his journey, i.e., when he leaves the city (*Eliyahu Rabba*, *Peri Megadim*). Some say that it is recited when one decides to set out on the journey (*Taz*). *Ab initio*, one should conduct oneself in accordance with the opinion of *Eliyahu Rabba* (*Shulḥan Arukh HaRav*, *Mishna Berura*; *Shulḥan Arukh*, *Oraḥ Ḥayyim* 110:7).

At least a parasang – עַד פַּרְסָה: One does not recite the traveler's prayer unless he plans on traveling at least a parasang. If his plan is to travel a shorter distance, he should recite the prayer without a blessing. *Ab initio*, he should recite the prayer in the first parasang of his journey (*Shulḥan Arukh*, *Oraḥ Ḥayyim* 110:7 and in the comment of the Rema).

The traveler's prayer while walking – תְּפִלַּת הַדֶּרֶךְ בִּמְהַלֵּךְ: In this case, Rav Sheshet conducted himself according to the opinion of Rav Ḥisda. Because of this, the medieval commentaries disagreed whether to rule in accordance with the opinion of Rav Sheshet, which is the general rule in his dispute with Rav Ḥisda, or in accordance with the opinion of Rav Ḥisda. Ultimately, the ruling was as follows: *Ab initio*, one should stand in one place and recite the traveler's prayer. However, if one is riding an animal, he need not dismount. If possible, though, he should stop the animal and then recite the prayer (*Shulḥan Arukh*, *Oraḥ Ḥayyim* 110:4).

Grant us understanding while standing – הֲבִינֵנוּ מְעוּמָּד: One recites the abridged version of the *Amida* prayer: Grant us understanding, in the same manner that he recites the standard *Amida* prayer, standing (*Shulḥan Arukh*, *Oraḥ Ḥayyim* 110:1).

The brief prayer whether one is standing or whether one is walking – תְּפִלָּה קְצָרָה בֵּין מְעוּמָּד בֵּין מְהַלֵּךְ: When one is allowed to recite a brief prayer because he is walking in a place where he is threatened by bands of wild animals or highwaymen, he may continue walking as he recites it (Rambam *Sefer Ahava*, *Hilkhot Tefilla* 4:19; *Shulḥan Arukh*, *Oraḥ Ḥayyim* 110:3).

One who was riding on a donkey – הָיָה רוֹכֵב עַל הַחֲמוֹר: One who is riding on a donkey need not dismount in order to pray, even if there is someone available to hold the donkey, as per the opinion of Rabbi Yehoshua ben Levi and the conclusion of the Gemara (Rambam *Sefer Ahava*, *Hilkhot Tefilla* 5:2; *Shulḥan Arukh*, *Oraḥ Ḥayyim* 94:4).

הָיָה עוֹמֵד בְּחוּץ לָאָרֶץ – יְכַוֵּין אֶת לִבּוֹ כְּנֶגֶד אֶרֶץ יִשְׂרָאֵל, שֶׁנֶּאֱמַר: ״וְהִתְפַּלְלוּ אֵלֶיךָ דֶּרֶךְ אַרְצָם״; הָיָה עוֹמֵד בְּאֶרֶץ יִשְׂרָאֵל – יְכַוֵּין אֶת לִבּוֹ כְּנֶגֶד יְרוּשָׁלַיִם, שֶׁנֶּאֱמַר: ״וְהִתְפַּלְלוּ אֶל ה׳ דֶּרֶךְ הָעִיר אֲשֶׁר בָּחַרְתָּ״; הָיָה עוֹמֵד בִּירוּשָׁלַיִם – יְכַוֵּין אֶת לִבּוֹ כְּנֶגֶד בֵּית הַמִּקְדָּשׁ, שֶׁנֶּאֱמַר: ״וְהִתְפַּלְלוּ אֶל הַבַּיִת הַזֶּה״; הָיָה עוֹמֵד בְּבֵית הַמִּקְדָּשׁ – יְכַוֵּין אֶת לִבּוֹ כְּנֶגֶד בֵּית קָדְשֵׁי הַקֳּדָשִׁים, שֶׁנֶּאֱמַר: ״וְהִתְפַּלְלוּ אֶל הַמָּקוֹם הַזֶּה״; הָיָה עוֹמֵד בְּבֵית קָדְשֵׁי הַקֳּדָשִׁים – יְכַוֵּין אֶת לִבּוֹ כְּנֶגֶד בֵּית הַכַּפּוֹרֶת; הָיָה עוֹמֵד אֲחוֹרֵי בֵּית הַכַּפּוֹרֶת – יֵרָאֶה עַצְמוֹ כְּאִילּוּ לִפְנֵי הַכַּפּוֹרֶת; נִמְצָא: עוֹמֵד בַּמִּזְרָח – מַחֲזִיר פָּנָיו לַמַּעֲרָב, בַּמַּעֲרָב – מַחֲזִיר פָּנָיו לַמִּזְרָח, בַּדָּרוֹם – מַחֲזִיר פָּנָיו לַצָּפוֹן, בַּצָּפוֹן – מַחֲזִיר פָּנָיו לַדָּרוֹם; נִמְצְאוּ כׇּל יִשְׂרָאֵל מְכַוְּונִין אֶת לִבָּם לְמָקוֹם אֶחָד.

One who was standing in prayer **in the Diaspora, should focus his heart toward Eretz Yisrael, as it is stated: "And they shall pray to You by way of their land** which You have given to their fathers" (I Kings 8:48).

One who was standing in Eretz Yisrael, should focus his heart toward Jerusalem, as it is stated: "And they shall pray to the Lord by way of the city that You have chosen" (I Kings 8:44).

One who was standing in Jerusalem, should focus his heart toward the Temple, as it is stated: "And they shall pray toward this house" (II Chronicles 6:32).

One who was standing in the Temple, should focus his heart toward the Holy of Holies, as it is stated: "And they shall pray toward this place" (I Kings 8:35).

One who was standing in the Holy of Holies, should focus his heart toward the seat of the ark-cover [*kapporet*], atop the ark, the dwelling place of God's glory.

One who was standing behind the seat of the ark-cover, should visualize himself as if standing before the ark-cover and turn toward it.

Consequently, one **standing** in prayer **in the East turns to face west,** and one standing **in the West, turns to face east.** One standing **in the South, turns to face north,** and one standing **in the North, turns to face south; all of** the people of **Israel find** themselves **focusing their hearts toward one place,** the Holy of Holies in the Temple.[H]

אָמַר רַבִּי אָבִין, וְאִיתֵּימָא רַבִּי אָבִינָא: מַאי קְרָאָה – ״כְּמִגְדַּל דָּוִיד צַוָּארֵךְ בָּנוּי לְתַלְפִּיּוֹת״, תֵּל שֶׁכׇּל פִּיּוֹת פּוֹנִים בּוֹ.

An allusion to this is found in what **Rabbi Avin, and some say Rabbi Avina, said: What verse** alludes to **this? "Your neck is like the Tower of David, built with turrets** [*talpiyyot*], one thousand shields hang from it, all of the armor of the mighty" (Song of Songs 4:4). He interprets the word *talpiyyot* as the **hill** [*tel*] **toward which all mouths** [*piyyot*] **turn,** i.e., the Temple Mount.

אֲבוּהּ דִּשְׁמוּאֵל וְלֵוִי, כִּי הָווּ בָּעוּ לְמִיפַּק לְאוֹרְחָא הָווּ מַקְדְּמִי וּמְצַלּוּ, וְכִי הֲוָה מָטֵי זְמַן קְרִיאַת שְׁמַע קָרוּ.

With regard to prayer while traveling, the Gemara relates: **When Shmuel's father and Levi wanted to set out on a journey** in the morning, **they would pray early** before sunrise. **When,** during their journey, **the time to recite *Shema* would arrive, they recited it.**

כְּמַאן; כִּי הַאי תַּנָּא – דְּתַנְיָא: הַשְׁכִּים לָצֵאת לַדֶּרֶךְ – מְבִיאִין לוֹ שׁוֹפָר וְתוֹקֵעַ, לוּלָב וּמְנַעְנֵעַ, מְגִילָּה וְקוֹרֵא בָּהּ, וּכְשֶׁיַּגִּיעַ זְמַן קְרִיאַת שְׁמַע קוֹרֵא. הִשְׁכִּים לֵישֵׁב בְּקָרוֹן אוֹ בִּסְפִינָה – מִתְפַּלֵּל, וּכְשֶׁיַּגִּיעַ זְמַן קְרִיאַת שְׁמַע קוֹרֵא;

The Gemara asks: **In accordance with whose** opinion did they do this? **In accordance with this *tanna*, as it was taught** in the *Tosefta*: **One who rose early to set out on** his **path**[H] before the time to recite *Shema* arrives, **they bring him a *shofar* and he sounds** it, if it was Rosh HaShana; **a *lulav* and he takes** it on *Sukkot*; **a megilla,** the Scroll of Esther, **and he reads it** on Purim; **and when the time comes to recite *Shema*, he recites** it. So too, **one who rose early to sit in a wagon or in a boat prays, and when the time comes to recite *Shema*, he recites it.**

רַבִּי שִׁמְעוֹן בֶּן אֶלְעָזָר אוֹמֵר: בֵּין כָּךְ וּבֵין כָּךְ קוֹרֵא קְרִיאַת שְׁמַע וּמִתְפַּלֵּל, כְּדֵי שֶׁיִּסְמוֹךְ גְּאוּלָּה לִתְפִלָּה.

Rabbi Shimon ben Elazar, says: In either case, it is preferable to **recite *Shema* and** then **pray** the *Amida* prayer in the wagon **so that he will juxtapose redemption and prayer.**

בְּמַאי קָמִיפַּלְגִי? – מָר סָבַר: תְּפִלָּה מְעוּמָּד עָדִיף; וּמָר סָבַר: מִסְמַךְ גְּאוּלָּה לִתְפִלָּה עָדִיף.

The Gemara explains: **Regarding what do they disagree?** The Gemara answers: **This Sage,** the first *tanna*, **holds** that **prayer** while **standing is preferable.** Therefore, one should pray earlier, at home, while standing. **This Sage,** Rabbi Shimon ben Elazar, **holds** that the **juxtaposition of redemption and prayer is preferable,** even if in doing so one is unable to stand while praying.

מָרֵימָר וּמָר זוּטְרָא הָווּ מְכַנְּפִי בֵּי עַשְׂרָה בְּשַׁבְּתָא דְּרִגְלָא וּמְצַלּוּ, וַהֲדַר נָפְקִי לְפִרְקָא.

On a similar note, the Gemara cites additional circumstances where Sages were forced to make exceptional arrangements to pray. **Mareimar and Mar Zutra would gather ten** people **on the Shabbat of the festival and pray, and set out to deliver their lecture** [*pirka*]. Due to the crowds that gathered to hear the lectures of the Sages on the festival, they were unable to pray at the proper time, so they were forced to pray earlier.

רַב אַשִׁי מְצַלֵּי בַּהֲדֵי צִבּוּרָא בְּיָחִיד מְיוּשָּׁב, כִּי הֲוָה אָתֵי לְבֵיתֵיהּ הֲדַר וּמְצַלֵּי מְעוּמָּד. אָמְרִי לֵיהּ רַבָּנַן: וְלַעֲבִיד מָר כְּמָרֵימָר וּמָר זוּטְרָא! – אֲמַר לְהוּ: טְרִיחָא לִי מִלְּתָא. – וְלַעֲבִיד מָר כַּאֲבוּהּ דִּשְׁמוּאֵל וְלֵוִי! – אֲמַר לְהוּ: לָא חֲזֵינָא לְהוּ לְרַבָּנַן קַשִּׁישֵׁי מִינַּן דְּעָבְדִי הָכִי.

In similar circumstances, **Rav Ashi would pray with the congregation individually** while **seated,** so that they would not notice that he was praying. Afterwards, **when he would come to his house, he would pray again** while **standing** in order to pray without distraction. **The Sages said to him: The Master should do as Mareimar and Mar Zutra** do, i.e., gather a prayer quorum at home to pray before the lecture. **He said to them: It is burdensome to me** to delay the lecture so much. The Sages **said to him: The Master should do as Shmuel's father and Levi** did and pray before sunrise. **He said to them: I have not seen Sages older than us do that,** indicating that this is not the accepted *halakha*.

HALAKHA

Turning in prayer – הַפְּנִיָּה בִּתְפִלָּה: Everyone faces the Holy of Holies in Jerusalem while praying, i.e., those west of Jerusalem turn east, etc. If one cannot determine the direction of Jerusalem, it does not prevent him from praying, and he may suffice with focusing his heart toward heaven (Rambam *Sefer Ahava, Hilkhot Tefilla* 5:3; *Shulḥan Arukh, Oraḥ Ḥayyim* 94:1, 3).

One who rose early to set out on his path – הַמְמַהֵר לְדַרְכּוֹ: In exigent circumstances, e.g., one needs to set out on a journey early, he may pray any time after dawn at home, standing. When the time to recite *Shema* arrives, he recites it in the course of the journey, as per the opinion of the first *tanna*, even though he does not juxtapose redemption with prayer. These days, the custom is to wait and recite both *Shema* and the *Amida* prayer in the course of the journey (*Mishna Berura*). Since, as a rule, we are unable to muster proper intent while praying, it is preferable to juxtapose redemption and prayer (*Shulḥan Arukh HaRav*; *Shulḥan Arukh, Oraḥ Ḥayyim* 89:8).

NOTES

The additional prayer is only recited in a city where there is a quorum of ten [*hever ir*] – אֵין תְּפִלַּת הַמּוּסָפִין אֶלָּא בְּחֶבֶר עִיר: This is because the additional prayer is not one of personal requests and supplication. Rather, it is praise of God modeled after the sacrificial offerings. It is only appropriate to recite this communal praise in the framework of a congregation (*Talmidei Rabbeinu Yona*).

BACKGROUND

***Ḥever ir* – חֶבֶר עִיר:** According to most commentaries, the *ḥever ir* is a type of city council on which the leading Sages sat, either in official capacities or just as religious leaders. The *ge'onim*, and Rashi in certain places, translate the word *ḥaver* as outstanding Torah scholar. The *ḥaver* was the leader or chief rabbi of the city and the congregation generally prayed with him. According to this interpretation, the additional prayer was only recited in the leader's presence.

HALAKHA

The additional prayer is recited…with a *ḥever ir* or without a *ḥever ir* – תְּפִלַּת הַמּוּסָפִין...בְּחֶבֶר עִיר וְשֶׁלֹּא בְּחֶבֶר עִיר: Each individual is required to recite the additional prayer, whether or not there is a quorum of ten in the city, as per the opinion of the Rabbis in their dispute with Rabbi Elazar ben Azarya (*Shulḥan Arukh, Oraḥ Ḥayyim* 286:2).

מתני׳ רַבִּי אֶלְעָזָר בֶּן עֲזַרְיָה אוֹמֵר: אֵין תְּפִלַּת הַמּוּסָפִין אֶלָּא בְּחֶבֶר עִיר, וַחֲכָמִים אוֹמְרִים: בְּחֶבֶר עִיר וְשֶׁלֹּא בְּחֶבֶר עִיר; רַבִּי יְהוּדָה אוֹמֵר מִשְּׁמוֹ: כׇּל מָקוֹם שֶׁיֵּשׁ שָׁם חֶבֶר עִיר – יָחִיד פָּטוּר מִתְּפִלַּת הַמּוּסָפִין.

MISHNA **Rabbi Elazar ben Azarya says: The additional prayer is only** recited **in a city where there is a quorum of ten [*ḥever ir*].**[NB] **The Rabbis say:** One may recite the additional prayer **with a *ḥever ir* or without a *ḥever ir*.**[H] **Rabbi Yehuda says** another opinion **in his name,** the name of Rabbi Elazar ben Azarya: **Any place where there is a *ḥever ir*, an individual is** completely **exempt from** reciting **the additional prayer.**

גמ׳ רַבִּי יְהוּדָה הַיְינוּ תַּנָּא קַמָּא! אִיכָּא בֵּינַיְיהוּ: יָחִיד שֶׁלֹּא בְּחֶבֶר עִיר; תַּנָּא קַמָּא סָבַר: פָּטוּר, וְרַבִּי יְהוּדָה סָבַר: חַיָּיב.

GEMARA There is no apparent difference between the opinion of Rabbi Elazar ben Azarya and the opinion cited in his name by Rabbi Yehuda. The Gemara asks: **Rabbi Yehuda's** opinion **is** identical to the opinion of Rabbi Elazar ben Azarya cited by **the first *tanna*.** The Gemara answers: **There is a** practical halakhic difference **between them:** The case of **an individual who is not in** a place where there is a ***ḥever ir*.** In other words, in a place where there is not a prayer quorum of ten people, the **first *tanna* holds** that Rabbi Elazar ben Azarya's opinion is that the **individual is exempt** from reciting the additional prayer, as it was only instituted to be recited with a quorum. **And Rabbi Yehuda holds** that Rabbi Elazar ben Azarya's opinion is that the individual is **obligated** to recite the additional prayer, as he is only exempt in a place where there is a prayer quorum, and, therefore, a communal prayer leader fulfills his obligation.

אָמַר רַב הוּנָא בַּר חִינָּנָא אָמַר רַב חִיָּיא בַּר רַב: הֲלָכָה כְּרַבִּי יְהוּדָה שֶׁאָמַר מִשּׁוּם רַבִּי אֶלְעָזָר בֶּן עֲזַרְיָה. אָמַר לֵיהּ רַב חִיָּיא בַּר אָבִין: שַׁפִּיר קָאָמְרַתְּ, דַּאֲמַר שְׁמוּאֵל: מִיָּמַי לֹא מְצַלֵּינָא צְלוֹתָא דְמוּסָפִין בְּיָחִיד

Rav Huna bar Ḥinnana said that **Ḥiyya bar Rav said: The *halakha* is in accordance with** the opinion of **Rabbi Yehuda, who said** it **in the name of** his mentor, **Rabbi Elazar ben Azarya. Rav Ḥiyya bar Avin said to him: You have spoken well,** as proven by what **Shmuel said: In all my days I have never prayed the additional prayer as an individual**

Perek **IV**
Daf **30** Amud **b**

LANGUAGE

Army [*pulmusa*] – פּוּלְמוּסָא: From the Greek πόλεμος, *polemos*, meaning war.

PERSONALITIES

Rabbi Ḥanina Kara, the Bible expert – רַבִּי חֲנִינָא קָרָא: A second generation *amora* in Eretz Yisrael, Rabbi Ḥanina was a disciple of Rabbi Ḥanina bar Ḥama, Rabbi Ḥanina the Great, and Rabbi Yannai. Apparently, Rabbi Ḥanina not only taught young children, but was also a Bible expert, which is why he was called *Kara*. He is mentioned in the Talmud and the midrash in discussions with his two teachers, both on matters relating to his work and also on other halakhic matters.

בִּנְהַרְדְּעָא, לְבַר מֵהַהוּא יוֹמָא דַּאֲתָא פּוּלְמוּסָא דְמַלְכָּא לְמָתָא וְאִטְרִידוּ רַבָּנַן וְלָא צַלּוּ, וְצַלַּי לִי בְּיָחִיד, וַהֲוָאי יָחִיד שֶׁלֹּא בְּחֶבֶר עִיר.

in Neharde'a, where there is always a prayer quorum, **except for the day when the king's army [*pulmusa*]**[L] **came to the city, and the Sages were preoccupied and did not pray** communally, **and I prayed as an individual, and I was an individual** who was **not** praying **in a prayer quorum.** Shmuel's conduct was in accordance with the opinion of Rabbi Yehuda in this matter.

יָתֵיב רַבִּי חֲנִינָא קָרָא קַמֵּיהּ דְּרַבִּי יַנַּאי, וְיָתֵיב וְקָאָמַר: הֲלָכָה כְּרַבִּי יְהוּדָה שֶׁאָמַר מִשּׁוּם רַבִּי אֶלְעָזָר בֶּן עֲזַרְיָה. אָמַר לֵיהּ: פּוּק קְרָא קְרָאֵיךְ לְבָרָא! דְּאֵין הֲלָכָה כְּרַבִּי יְהוּדָה שֶׁאָמַר מִשּׁוּם רַבִּי אֶלְעָזָר בֶּן עֲזַרְיָה.

Yet this opinion was not universally accepted. The Gemara relates: **Rabbi Ḥanina Kara,** the Bible expert,[P] **sat before Rabbi Yannai, and he sat and he said: The *halakha* is in accordance with** the opinion of **Rabbi Yehuda who said** it **in the name of Rabbi Elazar ben Azarya.** Rabbi Yannai **said to him: Go and read your verses outside,** as that *halakha* is not accepted by the Sages in the study hall, and it belongs outside, **as the *halakha* is not in accordance with** the opinion of **Rabbi Yehuda who said** it **in the name of Rabbi Elazar ben Azarya.**

אָמַר רַבִּי יוֹחָנָן: אֲנִי רָאִיתִי אֶת רַבִּי יַנַּאי דְּצַלֵּי וַהֲדַר צַלֵּי. אָמַר לֵיהּ רַבִּי יִרְמְיָה לְרַבִּי זֵירָא: וְדִילְמָא מֵעִיקָּרָא לֹא כַּוֵּין דַּעְתֵּיהּ, וּלְבַסּוֹף כַּוֵּין דַּעְתֵּיהּ? אָמַר לֵיהּ: חֲזִי מַאן גַּבְרָא רַבָּה דְּקָמַסְהֵיד עֲלֵיהּ!

Rabbi Yoḥanan said: I saw Rabbi Yannai, who prayed and then prayed again. Presumably, his first prayer was the morning prayer and his second prayer was the additional prayer. Apparently, he does not hold in accordance with the opinion of Rabbi Elazar ben Azarya. Rather, he holds that even when not part of a prayer quorum, an individual must recite the additional prayer. Later on, when this story was related in the study hall, **Rabbi Yirmeya said to** his teacher, **Rabbi Zeira:** What proof is there that the second prayer was the additional prayer? **Perhaps initially he did not focus his mind** on his prayer **and ultimately he focused his mind,** i.e., he repeated the morning prayer in order to do so with proper concentration. Rabbi Zeira **said to him: Look at who the great man is who is testifying about him.** Rabbi Yoḥanan certainly observed carefully before relating what he witnessed.

רַבִּי אַמִי וְרַבִּי אַסִי אַף עַל גַּב דַּהֲווּ לְהוּ תְּלֵיסַר בֵּי כְּנִישְׁתָּא בִּטְבֶרְיָא, לָא הָווּ מְצַלּוּ אֶלָּא בֵּינֵי עַמּוּדֵי הֵיכָא דַּהֲווּ גָּרְסִי.

Regarding prayers of the Sages, the Gemara further relates that, **although there were thirteen synagogues in Tiberias, Rabbi Ami and Rabbi Asi would only pray between the columns**[N] **where they studied,**[H] as prayer is beloved in the eyes of God, specifically in a place of Torah.

אִיתְּמַר, רַב יִצְחָק בַּר אַבְדִּימִי מִשּׁוּם רַבֵּינוּ אָמַר: הֲלָכָה כְּרַבִּי יְהוּדָה שֶׁאָמַר מִשּׁוּם רַבִּי אֶלְעָזָר בֶּן עֲזַרְיָה. רַבִּי חִיָּיא בַּר אַבָּא צַלֵּי וַהֲדַר צַלֵּי. אֲמַר לֵיהּ רַבִּי זֵירָא: מַאי טַעְמָא עָבֵיד מָר הָכִי? אִילֵימָא מִשּׁוּם דְּלָא כַּוֵּין מָר דַּעְתֵּיהּ – וְהָאָמַר רַבִּי אֱלִיעֶזֶר: לְעוֹלָם יָמוֹד אָדָם אֶת עַצְמוֹ, אִם יָכוֹל לְכַוֵּין אֶת לִבּוֹ – יִתְפַּלֵּל, וְאִם לָאו – אַל יִתְפַּלֵּל! – אֶלָּא דְּלָא אַדְכַּר מָר דְּרֵישׁ יַרְחָא.

It was stated: Rav Yitzḥak bar Avdimi in the name of Rabbeinu, Rav, **said: The** ***halakha*** **is in accordance with** the opinion of **Rabbi Yehuda who said it in the name of Rabbi Elazar ben Azarya.** The Gemara relates: **Rabbi Ḥiyya bar Abba prayed** and then **prayed again. Rav Zeira said to him: Why did the Master do this? If you say because the Master did not focus his mind** the first time, **didn't Rabbi Eliezer say: One must always evaluate himself** before he prays? **If he is able to focus his heart** on prayer, **he should pray, but if not,** if he is unable to do so, **he should not pray.**[H] Apparently, that was not the reason that he prayed twice. **Rather,** because **my Master did not mention the New Moon** in his prayer, so he prayed again.

וְהָתַנְיָא: טָעָה וְלֹא הִזְכִּיר שֶׁל רֹאשׁ חֹדֶשׁ בְּעַרְבִית – אֵין מַחֲזִירִין אוֹתוֹ מִפְּנֵי שֶׁיָּכוֹל לְאוֹמְרָהּ בְּשַׁחֲרִית, בְּשַׁחֲרִית – אֵין מַחֲזִירִין אוֹתוֹ מִפְּנֵי שֶׁיָּכוֹל לְאוֹמְרָהּ בְּמוּסָפִין, בְּמוּסָפִין – אֵין מַחֲזִירִין אוֹתוֹ מִפְּנֵי שֶׁיָּכוֹל לְאוֹמְרָהּ בְּמִנְחָה!

The Gemara asks: **Wasn't it taught** in a *baraita*: **One who erred and did not mention the New Moon in the evening prayer,**[H] **we do not require him to return** to the beginning of the prayer and repeat it, **because he can recite it in the morning prayer.** One who erred and did not mention the New Moon **in the morning prayer, we do not require him to return** to the beginning of the prayer and repeat it, **because he can recite it in the additional prayer.** One who erred and did not mention the New Moon **in the additional prayer, we do not require him to return** to the beginning of the prayer and repeat it, **because he can recite it in the afternoon prayer?** Omitting mention of the New Moon does not require one to repeat the *Amida* prayer. Consequently, that was not the reason that Rabbi Ḥiyya bar Abba prayed a second time.

אֲמַר לֵיהּ: לָאו אִיתְּמַר עֲלָהּ, אָמַר רַבִּי יוֹחָנָן, בְּצִבּוּר שָׁנוּ.

Rabbi Ḥiyya bar Abba **said to him: Wasn't it stated about that** *baraita* that **Rabbi Yoḥanan said: They taught** this *baraita* specifically with regard to prayer **in a communal** framework?[H] However, an individual who fails to mention the New Moon is required to pray again? That is why Rabbi Ḥiyya bar Abba prayed twice.

כַּמָּה יִשְׁהֶה בֵּין תְּפִלָּה לִתְפִלָּה? רַב הוּנָא וְרַב חִסְדָּא, חַד אָמַר: כְּדֵי שֶׁתִּתְחוֹנֵן דַּעְתּוֹ עָלָיו; וְחַד אָמַר: כְּדֵי שֶׁתִּתְחוֹלֵל דַּעְתּוֹ עָלָיו.

Stemming from the discussion about individuals who recite two prayers consecutively, the Gemara asks: **How long should one wait between the first prayer and the second prayer?**[H] **Rav Huna and Rav Ḥisda** agreed about this in principle, but they formulated their opinions differently (Rashi). **One said** that an individual must wait long enough **so that his mind will be in a pleading** mode [***tit̄honen***], enabling him to recite the second prayer as a plea. **One** of them **said:** Long enough **so that his mind will be in a beseeching** mode [***titḥolel***], enabling him to beseech God in his second prayer.

מַאן דְּאָמַר כְּדֵי שֶׁתִּתְחוֹנֵן דַּעְתּוֹ עָלָיו – דִּכְתִיב: ״וָאֶתְחַנַּן אֶל ה׳״; וּמַאן דְּאָמַר כְּדֵי שֶׁתִּתְחוֹלֵל דַּעְתּוֹ עָלָיו – דִּכְתִיב: ״וַיְחַל מֹשֶׁה״.

The Gemara points out that both Rav Huna and Rav Ḥisda based their positions on the prayers of Moses. **The one who said: So that his mind will be in a pleading** mode [***titḥonen***], **as it is written: "And I pleaded** [***va'etḥanan***] **before the Lord"** (Deuteronomy 3:23). **And the one who said: So that his mind will be in a beseeching** mode [***titḥolel***] **as it is written: "And Moses besought** [***vayeḥal***] **the Lord"** (Exodus 32:11).

אָמַר רַב עָנָן אָמַר רַב: טָעָה וְלֹא הִזְכִּיר שֶׁל רֹאשׁ חֹדֶשׁ עַרְבִית – אֵין מַחֲזִירִין אוֹתוֹ, לְפִי שֶׁאֵין בֵּית דִּין מְקַדְּשִׁין אֶת הַחֹדֶשׁ אֶלָּא בַּיּוֹם.

The Gemara resumes the above discussion with regard to omission of the mention of the New Moon in the *Amida* prayer. **Rav Anan said that Rav said: One who erred and did not mention the New Moon in the evening prayer, we do not require him to return** to the beginning of the prayer and repeat it, **because the court only sanctifies the new month by day,** and the prayer of the New Moon, which parallels the court's sanctification of the new month, belongs in the daytime prayer.

NOTES

Between the columns – בֵּינֵי עַמּוּדֵי: Some say that this is repeated here to teach us that they would even recite the additional prayer between the columns, as they held that there is no need for a quorum of ten (*Penei Yehoshua*).

HALAKHA

Would only pray…where they studied – לָא הָווּ מְצַלּוּ אֶלָּא...הֵיכָא דַּהֲווּ גָּרְסִי: A permanent study hall is more sacred than a synagogue. Therefore, assuming that one prays with a prayer quorum, it is a greater mitzva to pray in the study hall than in the synagogue, as per the custom of Rabbi Ami and Rabbi Asi. Some say that, even without a prayer quorum, it is preferable to pray in the study hall (Rambam *Sefer Ahava, Hilkhot Tefilla* 8:3; *Shulḥan Arukh, Oraḥ Ḥayyim* 90:18; and in the comment of the Rema).

Intent during prayer – כַּוָּונָה בִּתְפִלָּה: While praying, one must focus his heart on the meaning of the words (*Mishna Berura*), at least during the first blessing of the *Amida* prayer, the blessing of the Patriarchs. If he was unable to muster the proper intent, he is required to repeat the prayer. However, these days, one does not repeat the *Amida* prayer for lack of proper intent, as it is safe to assume that he will not muster the requisite intent the second time either (Rambam *Sefer Ahava, Hilkhot Tefilla* 4:15; *Shulḥan Arukh, Oraḥ Ḥayyim* 101:1 and in the comment of the Rema).

One who erred and did not mention the New Moon in the evening prayer – טָעָה וְלֹא הִזְכִּיר שֶׁל רֹאשׁ חֹדֶשׁ עַרְבִית: One who erred and did not say: May there rise and come, in the evening prayer on the New Moon, whether it is a one-day or two-day New Moon, is not required to repeat the prayer, as per the opinion of Rav Ashi and the conclusion of the Gemara (Rambam *Sefer Ahava, Hilkhot Tefilla* 10:11; *Shulḥan Arukh, Oraḥ Ḥayyim* 422:1).

A prayer leader who did not mention: May there rise and come – שְׁלִיחַ צִיבּוּר שֶׁלֹּא הִזְכִּיר יַעֲלֶה וְיָבוֹא: If a prayer leader forgot to recite may there rise and come in the repetition of the morning prayer and already completed his prayer, he need not repeat the prayer because he is going to mention the New Moon in the additional prayer, as per the opinion of Rabbi Yoḥanan. If he realizes the omission before completing his prayer, he returns to the blessing of Temple service and recites: May there rise and come (*Shulḥan Arukh, Oraḥ Ḥayyim* 126:3).

How long should one wait between the first prayer and the second prayer – כַּמָּה יִשְׁהֶה בֵּין תְּפִלָּה לִתְפִלָּה: If one must recite two prayers at the same time, e.g., the morning prayer and the additional prayer, or the a prayer along with a compensatory prayer, one must wait a period of time sufficient to walk four cubits (Jerusalem Talmud) between the two prayers in order to settle his mind so that he may focus on pleading before God, as there is no halakhic difference between the two expressions in the Gemara: *titḥonen* and *titḥolel* (Rambam *Sefer Ahava, Hilkhot Tefilla* 10:15; *Shulḥan Arukh, Oraḥ Ḥayyim* 105).

אָמַר אַמֵימָר: מִסְתַּבְּרָא מִילְּתָא דְּרַב בְּחֹדֶשׁ מָלֵא, אֲבָל בְּחֹדֶשׁ חָסֵר – מַחֲזִירִין אוֹתוֹ.

Ameimar said: Rav's statement is reasonable in a full month, i.e., a month in which there are two potential days of the New Moon, the thirtieth day of the previous month and the first day of the new month. If one neglected to mention the New Moon on the night of the thirtieth, we do not require him to return to the beginning of the prayer and repeat it, because he can mention it the next night, which is the night of the first of the new month, which is the primary day of the New Moon. **But in a short month** of twenty-nine days, followed by one day of the New Moon, **we require him to return** to the beginning of the prayer and repeat it, even in the evening prayer.

אָמַר לֵיהּ רַב אַשִׁי לְאַמֵימָר: מִכְּדִי רַב טַעְמָא קָאָמַר, מַה לִּי חָסֵר וּמַה לִּי מָלֵא! אֶלָּא, לָא שְׁנָא.

Rav Ashi said to Ameimar: Since Rav states a reason for his statement, **what** difference **is** there **to me** if the month is **short, and what** difference **is** there **to me** if it is **full? Rather, there is no difference.** Rav based his opinion on the parallel drawn between the sanctification of the month and the mention of the New Moon in the *Amida* prayer; the sanctification of the month is not relevant at night.

הדרן עלך תפלת השחר

Summary of **Perek IV**

Many of the fundamental dilemmas raised in this chapter remained unresolved in the Gemara. Even where the Gemara did reach a conclusion, the conclusion did not always remain throughout the generations, as rulings in favor of one opinion were changed to favor the other. Consequently, many of the *halakhot* remain unresolved even today.

A decision was reached with regard to the time of the morning prayer; this lasts until the end of the fourth hour of the day. However, with regard to the time of the afternoon prayer, the *tanna'im* disagreed whether it extends until the evening or until the midpoint of *minḥa,* an hour and a quarter before the evening. No clear halakhic ruling was reached regarding this issue. The Gemara's conclusion is: One who practices in accordance with this Sage has fulfilled his obligation, and one who practices in accordance with that Sage has fulfilled his obligation. In other words, the decision remains in the hands of each individual. This lack of clarity blurs the distinction between the times of the afternoon and evening prayers as well as the boundary between the weekday and Shabbat prayers, which are recited during this time frame.

Another problem resolved in the Gemara concerns the evening prayer. In the dispute over this issue, which led to the temporary dismissal of the *Nasi,* the ruling was that the evening prayer is optional. Nevertheless, the custom adopted by the Jewish people throughout the generations was to treat the evening prayer as an obligation.

On a similar note, there were two conflicting approaches to the obligation to recite the *Amida* prayer. One approach favored a fixed daily prayer, while the other advocated a prayer whose essence was primarily devotional; any time that a person was unable to pray with all his heart, he would pray an abridged prayer or even not pray at all. The halakhic conclusion took the middle ground. However, fundamentally, even Rabbi Akiva's opinion, which was adopted, accepts the principle that prayer and the language of the prayer are not a fixed obligation; rather, prayer reflects the individual's circumstances and state of mind at the time.

Sages throughout Jewish history conducted themselves in this manner. Nevertheless, here too the custom adopted by the Jewish people corresponds with the first opinion that one must always recite the complete *Amida* prayer, even when he is incapable of praying with all his heart.

With regard to the additional prayer, the ruling was that the obligation to recite this prayer is incumbent even upon an individual praying alone, separate from the community.

Ultimately, it seems that the ruling accepted throughout the Jewish people is based on the approach that "the prayers were instituted parallel to the daily offerings in the Temple." At the same time, there is room for individual devotional prayer, which is not included in the framework of communal prayer.

Introduction to **Perek V**

Chapter Four dealt primarily with clarifying the framework for prayer, i.e., establishing the times of the fixed prayers and defining the circumstances in which an individual is exempt from prayer. The primary focus of Chapter Five is the content of the prayer, the details within this framework. While the previous chapter discussed the individual's obligation to engage in the act of prayer, this chapter focuses on elucidating the spiritual demands, namely, the requisite and desired approach to prayer. In particular, the chapter deals with how one approaches prayer; what elements are required, permitted, or prohibited to introduce into the prayer formula; and what prayer is capable of accomplishing. Despite the legalistic manner in which the Gemara deals with issues, the *halakha* is very closely tied to the philosophical questions involved.

There are various methods of preparation for prayer, such as adopting an approach of gravity, studying Torah, or engaging in performance of a mitzva and experiencing the joy associated with that performance. More than an expression of difference of opinion, these constitute a variety of complementary approaches to different aspects of prayer: Petition and submission, the joy of thanksgiving and the gravity of contemplation. The many aggadic passages in this chapter shed light on these different aspects of prayer.

Even the additions to the daily prayers hold significance. Prayer is a specific framework that expresses particular approaches to supplication and perspectives on faith. A person may not introduce elements to prayer indiscriminately. This was especially significant at a time when there were various deviant sects very close to traditional Judaism, who secretly sought to introduce their deviant ideas into the accepted prayer formula. On the other hand, there are specific elements that one must emphasize and include in his requests. It was vital to determine the most significant, general needs that may and even must be incorporated into the various blessings, such as the request for rain, emphasis of the sanctity of the Festivals, and recitation of *havdala* between the sacred and the profane.

Although at times one is required to include additions to the standard prayer formula, it is incumbent upon the individual to ensure that he is not swept away in a wave of enthusiasm that might lead him to introduce elements to his prayer that deviate from the fundamental tenets of Judaism.

Prayer places numerous demands upon one engaged in it. Primary among them is the requirement that one achieve a sense of absolute self-negation as he stands before his Maker. Nevertheless, the Gemara also alludes to and elaborates upon the reward of one who prays and God's response to those who call out to Him with all their heart.

מתני׳ אֵין עוֹמְדִין לְהִתְפַּלֵּל אֶלָּא מִתּוֹךְ כּוֹבֶד רֹאשׁ. חֲסִידִים הָרִאשׁוֹנִים הָיוּ שׁוֹהִין שָׁעָה אַחַת וּמִתְפַּלְּלִין, כְּדֵי שֶׁיְּכַוְּונוּ לִבָּם לַאֲבִיהֶם שֶׁבַּשָּׁמַיִם. אֲפִילּוּ הַמֶּלֶךְ שׁוֹאֵל בִּשְׁלוֹמוֹ לֹא יְשִׁיבֶנּוּ, וַאֲפִילּוּ נָחָשׁ כָּרוּךְ עַל עֲקֵבוֹ לֹא יַפְסִיק.

MISHNA **One** may **only stand** and begin to pray **from** an approach of **gravity** and submission.[H] There is a tradition that **the early** generations of **pious** men **would wait one hour,** in order to reach the solemn frame of mind appropriate for prayer, **and** then **pray, so that they would focus their hearts toward their Father in Heaven.** Standing in prayer is standing before God and, as such, **even** if **the king greets him, he should not respond to him; and even if a snake is wrapped on his heel, he should not interrupt** his prayer.

גמ׳ מְנָא הָנֵי מִילֵּי? אָמַר רַבִּי אֶלְעָזָר; דְּאָמַר קְרָא: ״וְהִיא מָרַת נָפֶשׁ״.

GEMARA We learned in the mishna that prayer should be undertaken in an atmosphere of gravity. The Gemara asks: **From where are these matters** derived? Rabbi Elazar said: They are derived from the verses describing the prayer of Hannah, mother of Samuel, **as the verse states: "And she felt bitterness of soul,** and she prayed to the Lord and she wept and wept" (I Samuel 1:10).

מִמַּאי? דִּילְמָא חַנָּה שָׁאנֵי, דַּהֲוַת מְרִירָא לִבָּא טוּבָא!

The Gemara rejects this proof: **From what** does that conclusion ensue? **Perhaps Hannah is different,** as her **heart was extremely embittered,** her prayer was embittered as well. This does not prove that everyone must pray in that frame of mind.

אֶלָּא אָמַר רַבִּי יוֹסֵי בְּרַבִּי חֲנִינָא מֵהָכָא: ״וַאֲנִי בְּרֹב חַסְדְּךָ אָבוֹא בֵיתֶךָ אֶשְׁתַּחֲוֶה אֶל הֵיכַל קָדְשְׁךָ בְּיִרְאָתֶךָ״.

Rather, Rabbi Yosei, son of Rabbi Ḥanina, said, it can be proved **from here,** as David said: **"But as for me, by Your abundant loving-kindness I will enter Your house, at Your Holy Temple I will bow in reverence for You"** (Psalms 5:8). Entering into prayer like entering the Holy Temple must be performed reverentially.

מִמַּאי, דִּילְמָא דָּוִד שָׁאנֵי, דַּהֲוָה מְצַעֵר נַפְשֵׁיהּ בְּרַחֲמֵי טוּבָא! – אֶלָּא אָמַר רַבִּי יְהוֹשֻׁעַ בֶּן לֵוִי מֵהָכָא: ״הִשְׁתַּחֲווּ לַה׳ בְּהַדְרַת קֹדֶשׁ״, אַל תִּקְרֵי ״בְּהַדְרַת״ אֶלָּא ״בְּחֶרְדַּת״.

The Gemara rejects this proof as well: **From what** does that conclusion ensue? **Perhaps David is different, as he would excessively afflict himself in prayer** in order to atone for his transgression with Bathsheba. Consequently, his cannot serve as a paradigm for proper conduct in prayer. **Rather, Rabbi Yehoshua ben Levi said,** it can be derived **from here,** from this verse that David said, not about his own worship, but about worship of God in general: "Give, unto the Lord, the honor of His name, **bow to the Lord in the beauty of holiness** [***behadrat kodesh***]" (Psalms 29:2). **Do not read: In the beauty of** [***behadrat***] holiness. **Rather** read: **In trembling of** [***beḥerdat***] holiness; one must enter into prayer from an atmosphere of gravity engendered by sanctity.

מִמַּאי? דִּילְמָא לְעוֹלָם אֵימָא לָךְ, הַדְרַת מַמָּשׁ, כִּי הָא דְּרַב יְהוּדָה הֲוָה מְצַיֵּין נַפְשֵׁיהּ וַהֲדַר מְצַלֵּי! – אֶלָּא אָמַר רַב נַחְמָן בַּר יִצְחָק מֵהָכָא: ״עִבְדוּ אֶת ה׳ בְּיִרְאָה וְגִילוּ בִּרְעָדָה״.

The Gemara rejects this too: **From what** does that conclusion ensue? **Perhaps, actually I would say to you** that it should be read as it is written: **Specifically, "in the beauty,"** and it means that one should pray in beautiful clothing, **as** in the case **of Rav Yehuda who would adorn himself and then pray.**[H] Rav Yehuda believed that one who comes before the King must wear his most beautiful clothing. The Gemara has yet to find a source for the *halakha* that one must approach prayer from an atmosphere of gravity. **Rather, Rav Naḥman bar Yitzḥak said** it can be derived **from here,** from this verse: **"Serve the Lord in fear and rejoice with trembling"** (Psalms 2:11).

מַאי ״וְגִילוּ בִּרְעָדָה״? אָמַר רַב אַדָּא בַּר מַתְנָא אָמַר רַבָּה: בִּמְקוֹם גִּילָה שָׁם תְּהֵא רְעָדָה.

Having cited this verse from Psalms, the Gemara asks: **What is** the meaning of **rejoice with trembling? Rav Adda bar Mattana said** that **Rabba said:** One may not experience unbridled joy; even **where there is rejoicing, there should be trembling.**

אַבָּיֵי הֲוָה יָתֵיב קַמֵּיהּ דְּרַבָּה, חַזְיֵיהּ דַּהֲוָה קָא בָדַח טוּבָא, אָמַר: ״וְגִילוּ בִּרְעָדָה״ כְּתִיב!

On that note, the Gemara relates: **Abaye was sitting before** his teacher **Rabba,** and Rabba **saw that he was excessively joyful. He said** to Abaye: **It is written: Rejoice with trembling,** one's joy should not be unrestrained.

HALAKHA

One may only stand and begin to pray from an approach of gravity and submission – אֵין עוֹמְדִין אֶלָּא מִתּוֹךְ כּוֹבֶד רֹאשׁ: One may stand to pray only from an atmosphere of awe and submission. He must not pray from a mood of laughter or lightheartedness, idle chatter or anger, but from a feeling of joy (Rambam *Sefer Ahava, Hilkhot Tefilla* 4:16, 18; *Shulḥan Arukh, Oraḥ Ḥayyim* 93:2).

Who would adorn himself and then pray – הֲוָה מְצַיֵּין נַפְשֵׁיהּ וַהֲדַר מְצַלֵּי: The Sages and their students only prayed when clothed appropriately. The Rema writes that in periods of calm, one should dress in fine clothing while praying; in wrathful times one should clasp one hand in the other while praying, like a servant standing before his master (Rambam *Sefer Ahava, Hilkhot Tefilla* 5:5; *Shulḥan Arukh, Oraḥ Ḥayyim* 91:6).

אָמַר לֵיהּ: אֲנָא תְּפִילִּין מַנַּחְנָא.

Abaye **said to him:** It is permissible for me because **I am donning phylacteries**[N] now and as long as they are upon me they ensure that the fear of God is upon me.

רַבִּי יִרְמְיָה הֲוָה יָתֵיב קַמֵּיהּ דְּרַבִּי זֵירָא, חַזְיֵיהּ דַּהֲוָה קָא בָּדַח טוּבָא, אָמַר לֵיהּ, ״בְּכָל עֶצֶב יִהְיֶה מוֹתָר״ כְּתִיב!

Similarly, the Gemara relates that **Rabbi Yirmeya was sitting before Rabbi Zeira. He saw that Rabbi Yirmeya was excessively joyful. He said to him: It is written: "In all sorrow there is profit"** (Proverbs 14:23); sorrow is appropriate, not excessive joy.

אָמַר לֵיהּ: אֲנָא תְּפִילִּין מַנַּחְנָא.

Rabbi Yirmeya **said to him:** It is permissible for me because **I am donning phylacteries.**

מָר בְּרֵיהּ דְּרָבִינָא עֲבַד הִילּוּלָא לִבְרֵיהּ, חֲזָנְהוּ לְרַבָּנַן דַּהֲווֹ קָבָדְחִי טוּבָא,

On a similar note, the Gemara relates: **Mar, son of Ravina, made a wedding** feast **for his son and he saw the Sages, who were excessively joyous.**

Perek **V**
Daf **31** Amud **a**

אַיְיתֵי כָּסָא דְּמוֹקְרָא, בַּת אַרְבַּע מְאָה זוּזֵי, וּתְבַר קַמַּיְהוּ, וְאַעֲצִיבוּ.

He brought a valuable cup worth four hundred ***zuz*** **and broke it before them and they became sad.**

רַב אַשִׁי עֲבַד הִילּוּלָא לִבְרֵיהּ, חֲזָנְהוּ לְרַבָּנַן דַּהֲווֹ קָא בָּדְחִי טוּבָא, אַיְיתֵי כָּסָא דְּזוּגִיתָא חִיוַּרְתָּא וּתְבַר קַמַּיְהוּ, וְאַעֲצִיבוּ.

The Gemara also relates: **Rav Ashi made a wedding** feast **for his son and he saw the Sages, who were excessively joyous. He brought a cup of** extremely valuable **white glass**[B] **and broke it before them, and they became sad.**

אֲמַרוּ לֵיהּ רַבָּנַן לְרַב הַמְנוּנָא זוּטִי בְּהִלּוּלָא דְּמָר בְּרֵיהּ דְּרָבִינָא: לִישְׁרֵי לָן מָר! – אֲמַר לְהוּ: וַי לָן דְּמִיתְנַן, וַי לָן דְּמִיתְנַן! אָמְרִי לֵיהּ: אֲנַן מַה נַּעֲנֵי בַּתְרָךְ? – אֲמַר לְהוּ: הֵי תּוֹרָה וְהֵי מִצְוָה דְּמַגְנוּ עֲלַן?

Similarly, the Gemara relates: **The Sages said to Rav Hamnuna Zuti at the wedding** feast **of Mar, son of Ravina: Let the Master sing for us.** Since he believed that the merriment had become excessive, **he said to them,** singing: **Woe unto us, for we shall die, woe unto us, for we shall die.**[N] **They said to him: What shall we respond after you?** What is the chorus of the song? **He said to them,** you should respond: **Where is Torah and where is mitzva that protect us?**

אָמַר רַבִּי יוֹחָנָן מִשּׁוּם רַבִּי שִׁמְעוֹן בֶּן יוֹחַאי: אָסוּר לְאָדָם שֶׁיְּמַלֵּא שְׂחוֹק פִּיו בָּעוֹלָם הַזֶּה, שֶׁנֶּאֱמַר: ״אָז יִמָּלֵא שְׂחוֹק פִּינוּ וּלְשׁוֹנֵנוּ רִנָּה״, אֵימָתַי – בִּזְמַן שֶׁ״יֹּאמְרוּ בַגּוֹיִם הִגְדִּיל ה׳ לַעֲשׂוֹת עִם אֵלֶּה״. אָמְרוּ עָלָיו עַל רֵישׁ לָקִישׁ, שֶׁמִּיָּמָיו לֹא מִלֵּא שְׂחוֹק פִּיו בָּעוֹלָם הַזֶּה מִכִּי שְׁמָעָהּ מֵרַבִּי יוֹחָנָן רַבֵּיהּ.

In a similar vein, **Rabbi Yoḥanan said in the name of Rabbi Shimon ben Yoḥai: One is forbidden to fill his mouth with mirth in this world,**[NH] as long as we are in exile (*ge'onim*), **as it is stated:** "When the Lord returns the captivity of Zion we will be as dreamers" (Psalms 126:1). Only **"then will our mouths fill with laughter and our lips with song"** (Psalms 126:2). **When** will that joyous era arrive? When **"they will say among nations, the Lord has done great things with these"** (Psalms 126:2). **They said about Reish Lakish that throughout his life he did not fill his mouth with laughter in this world once he heard this** statement **from his teacher, Rabbi Yoḥanan.**

תָּנוּ רַבָּנַן: אֵין עוֹמְדִין לְהִתְפַּלֵּל לֹא מִתּוֹךְ דִּין, וְלֹא מִתּוֹךְ דְּבַר הֲלָכָה, אֶלָּא מִתּוֹךְ הֲלָכָה פְּסוּקָה.

We learned in the mishna that it is appropriate to stand and begin to pray from an atmosphere of gravity. Regarding this, **the Sages taught: One** may **neither stand** and begin **to pray,** directly **from** involvement in **judgment nor** directly **from** deliberation over the ruling in a **matter of** ***halakha*****,**[H] as his preoccupation with the judgment or the halakhic ruling will distract him from prayer. **Rather** it is appropriate to pray directly **from** involvement in the study of a universally accepted **conclusive** ***halakha*** that leaves no room for further deliberation and will not distract him during prayer.

וְהֵיכִי דָּמֵי הֲלָכָה פְּסוּקָה?

And the Gemara asks: **What is an example** of a **conclusive** ***halakha*****?**

NOTES

I am donning phylacteries – אֲנָא תְּפִילִּין מַנַּחְנָא: Some explain this response to mean that he is joyful because he is wearing phylacteries, and therefore joy is permitted (*HaKotev*). Others interpret this based on a tradition that due to an illness, Rabba was unable to don phylacteries earlier, and he was overjoyed to finally be privileged to perform this mitzva (*Talmidei Rabbeinu Yona*).

BACKGROUND

A cup of valuable white glass – כָּסָא דְּזוּגִיתָא:

Glass vessels from the talmudic period

NOTES

Woe unto us, for we shall die – וַי לָן דְּמִיתְנַן: Some explain the relevance of this to a wedding as follows: As a person is destined to die and does not exist eternally as an individual, he must bring offspring into the world and perpetuate the existence of humankind (*Yoḥasin*).

One is forbidden to fill his mouth with mirth in this world – אָסוּר לְאָדָם שֶׁיְּמַלֵּא שְׂחוֹק פִּיו בָּעוֹלָם הַזֶּה: Some explain that this prohibition is not due to mourning over the destruction of the Temple; rather, it is prohibited because excessive frivolity leads one to become insensitive to transgression and distracts him from pursuing the fulfillment of the will of God (*Talmidei Rabbeinu Yona, Shitta Mekubbetzet*).

HALAKHA

One is forbidden to fill his mouth with mirth in this world – אָסוּר לְאָדָם שֶׁיְּמַלֵּא שְׂחוֹק פִּיו בָּעוֹלָם הַזֶּה: One may not fill his mouth with laughter in this world. Some say that it is because it will lead him to fail to fulfill the mitzvot. Others say that frivolity leads to sin (see *Magen Avraham* and *Taz*; *Shulḥan Arukh, Oraḥ Ḥayyim* 560:5).

One may neither stand and begin to pray from judgment nor from a matter of *halakha* – אֵין עוֹמְדִין לְהִתְפַּלֵּל לֹא מִתּוֹךְ דִּין, וְלֹא מִתּוֹךְ דְּבַר הֲלָכָה: One may not stand to pray immediately following a trial or an involved halakhic discourse (Rambam *Sefer Ahava, Hilkhot Tefilla* 4:18; *Shulḥan Arukh, Oraḥ Ḥayyim* 93:3).

אָמַר אַבַּיֵי: כִּי הָא דְּרַבִּי זֵירָא, דְּאָמַר רַבִּי זֵירָא: בְּנוֹת יִשְׂרָאֵל הֶחְמִירוּ עַל עַצְמָן, שֶׁאֲפִילּוּ רוֹאוֹת טִיפַּת דָּם כְּחַרְדָּל – יוֹשְׁבוֹת עָלֶיהָ שִׁבְעָה נְקִיִּים.

The Gemara offers several examples: **Abaye said:** One **like this** *halakha* **of Rabbi Zeira, as Rabbi Zeira said: The daughters of Israel were stringent with themselves;** to the extent **that even if they see a drop of blood corresponding to** the size of **a mustard** seed **she sits seven clean** days **for it.**[H] By Torah law, a woman who witnesses the emission of blood during the eleven days following her fixed menstrual period is not considered a menstruating woman;[B] rather she immerses herself and is purified the next day. However, the women of Israel accepted the stringency upon themselves that if they see any blood whatsoever, they act as it if were the blood of a *zava*,[B] which obligates her to count seven more clean days before becoming ritually pure (see Leviticus 15:25).

רָבָא אָמַר: כִּי הָא דְּרַב הוֹשַׁעְיָא, דְּאָמַר רַב הוֹשַׁעְיָא: מַעֲרִים אָדָם עַל תְּבוּאָתוֹ וּמַכְנִיסָהּ בְּמוֹץ שֶׁלָּהּ, כְּדֵי שֶׁתְּהֵא בְּהֶמְתּוֹ אוֹכֶלֶת וּפְטוּרָה מִן הַמַּעֲשֵׂר.

Citing an additional example of a conclusive *halakha*, **Rava said:** One **like this** *halakha* **of Rav Hoshaya, as Rav Hoshaya said: A person may employ artifice** to circumvent obligations[N] incumbent **upon** him in dealing with **his grain and bring it into** the courtyard **in its chaff**[H] **so that his animal will eat** from it, **and** the grain **is exempt** from **tithes.** *Halakha* dictates that one is obligated to tithe grain that has been threshed and piled, regardless of the ultimate purpose for which the grain was intended. By Torah law, one is exempt from tithing grain that was not threshed and is therefore still in its chaff. By rabbinic law, one is prohibited from eating this grain in the framework of a meal. Feeding animals is permitted without first tithing that grain.

וְאִיבָּעֵית אֵימָא: כִּי הָא דְּרַב הוּנָא, דְּאָמַר רַב הוּנָא אָמַר רַבִּי זְעֵירָא: הַמַּקִּיז דָּם בְּבֶהֱמַת קָדָשִׁים – אָסוּר בַּהֲנָאָה, וּמוֹעֲלִין בּוֹ.

And if you wish, say instead yet another example of a conclusive *halakha*, which is the recommended prelude to prayer. One **like this** *halakha* **of Rav Huna, as Rav Huna said** that **Rabbi Zeira said: One who lets blood from a consecrated animal**[H] that was consecrated as a sacrifice; deriving **benefit** from that blood **is prohibited.** Although blood of an offering that was sprinkled on the altar is not considered Temple property, nevertheless, deriving benefit from the blood of a living, consecrated animal is considered prohibited use of Temple property. In so doing, **one misuses** property consecrated to the Temple, and as in any other case of misusing Temple property, if he did so unwittingly, he is liable to bring a guilt-offering.

רַבָּנַן עָבְדִי כְּמַתְנִיתִין, רַב אַשִׁי עָבֵיד כְּבָרַיְיתָא.

It is related that **the Sages acted in accordance with** the opinion of **our mishna** and rose to pray from an atmosphere of gravity; **Rav Ashi acted in accordance with** the opinion of **the** ***baraita*** and preceded his prayer with a conclusive *halakha*.

תָּנוּ רַבָּנַן: אֵין עוֹמְדִין לְהִתְפַּלֵּל לֹא מִתּוֹךְ עַצְבוּת, וְלֹא מִתּוֹךְ עַצְלוּת, וְלֹא מִתּוֹךְ שְׂחוֹק, וְלֹא מִתּוֹךְ שִׂיחָה, וְלֹא מִתּוֹךְ קַלּוּת רֹאשׁ, וְלֹא מִתּוֹךְ דְּבָרִים בְּטֵלִים – אֶלָּא מִתּוֹךְ שִׂמְחָה שֶׁל מִצְוָה.

On the topic of proper preparation for prayer, **the Sages taught: One may neither stand to pray from** an atmosphere of **sorrow**[H] **nor from** an atmosphere of **laziness, nor from** an atmosphere of **laughter, nor from** an atmosphere of **conversation, nor from** an atmosphere of **frivolity, nor from** an atmosphere of **purposeless matters. Rather,** one should approach prayer **from** an atmosphere imbued with **the joy of a mitzva.**

HALAKHA

Even if they see a drop of blood corresponding to the size of a mustard seed, she sits seven clean days for it – שֶׁאֲפִילּוּ רוֹאוֹת טִיפַּת דָּם כְּחַרְדָּל יוֹשֶׁבֶת עָלֶיהָ שִׁבְעָה נְקִיִּים: If a woman discovers that a drop of blood emerged from her womb, even if she did not feel it emerge, based on this rabbinic decree, she must wait seven clean days before purifying herself (Rambam *Sefer Kedusha, Hilkhot Issurei Bia* 11:4; *Shulḥan Arukh, Yoreh De'a* 183).

A person may employ artifice in dealing with his grain and bring it into the courtyard in its chaff – מַעֲרִים אָדָם עַל תְּבוּאָתוֹ וּמַכְנִיסָהּ בְּמוֹץ שֶׁלָּהּ: One is permitted to bring grain into his courtyard while it is still mixed with chaff, in order to feed it to his animal. He is then exempt from tithing it, even if he subsequently winnows it a little bit at a time for personal use (Rambam *Sefer Zera'im, Hilkhot Ma'aser* 3:6; *Shulḥan Arukh, Yoreh De'a* 331:84).

One who lets blood from a consecrated animal – הַמַּקִּיז דָּם בְּבֶהֱמַת קָדָשִׁים: It is forbidden to benefit from blood let from an animal that has been consecrated. One who does so is guilty of misuse of property consecrated to the Temple (Rambam *Sefer Avoda, Hilkhot Me'ila* 2:11).

One may neither stand to pray from an atmosphere of sorrow, etc. – אֵין עוֹמְדִין לְהִתְפַּלֵּל לֹא מִתּוֹךְ עַצְבוּת וכו׳: One may only stand to pray from an atmosphere of reverence and subservience; not one of laughter, frivolity, idle conversation, or anger. He must also approach his prayer with joy (Rambam *Sefer Ahava, Hilkhot Tefilla* 4:16; *Shulḥan Arukh, Oraḥ Ḥayyim* 93:2). This is in accordance with Rav Ashi and the *baraita* (see the *Baḥ*; Rambam *Sefer Ahava, Hilkhot Tefilla* 4:18; *Shulḥan Arukh, Oraḥ Ḥayyim* 93:2–3).

NOTES

A person may employ artifice to circumvent obligations – מַעֲרִים אָדָם: Several examples exist in *halakha* where one is permitted to employ artifice in this manner. The common denominator in all of these cases is that the artifice is not an attempt to circumvent the essence of the halakhic ruling by Torah law, but rather to prevent a derivative prohibition. In this case, essentially, animal food is exempt from tithing. However, once it has been threshed, technically, *halakha* requires it to be tithed. Therefore, the artifice here is a permitted action undertaken to resolve a technical difficulty that arose.

BACKGROUND

A menstruating woman – נִדָּה: By Torah law, a woman is ritually impure for seven days after the onset of her menstrual bleeding. On the eve of the eighth day, she immerses herself in a spring or ritual bath to purify herself. According to Torah law, a menstruating woman may purify herself on the eighth day, even if she had been bleeding for the entire seven-day period. The Talmud, however, states that women themselves adopted a stringency, and consequently, any woman who experiences uterine bleeding is required to wait seven days without any bleeding before immersion in the ritual bath. From the beginning of her period, until she immerses herself, she renders both people and objects with which she comes into contact, or people who carry her even without making contact, ritually impure. Similarly, a man who has sexual intercourse with a menstruating woman becomes ritually impure for seven days.

***Zava* – זָבָה:** A woman who experiences a flow of menstrual-type blood on three consecutive days during a time of the month when she is not due to experience menstrual bleeding. The first secretion makes her ritually impure, but until the third secretion her status is that of a woman who keeps watch a day for a day, and she is not subject to all the halakhic rulings of a *zava*. After experiencing bleeding on the third day, the woman is considered a *zava* and is obligated to bring a sacrifice as part of her purification process. A *zava* imparts ritual impurity in the same way as a *zav*. In addition, a man who engages in sexual relations with her becomes a primary source of ritual impurity and imparts ritual impurity to others.

וכן לא יפטר אדם מחברו לא מתוך שיחה, ולא מתוך שחוק, ולא מתוך קלות ראש, ולא מתוך דברים בטלים – אלא מתוך דבר הלכה, שכן מצינו בנביאים הראשונים שסיימו דבריהם בדברי שבח ותנחומים.

Similarly, a person should neither take leave of another from an atmosphere of conversation, nor from an atmosphere of laughter, nor from an atmosphere of frivolity, nor from an atmosphere of purposeless matters. Rather, one should take leave of another from involvement in a matter of *halakha*.[N] As we found in the books of the Bible dealing with the early prophets, that they would conclude their talks with words of praise and consolation.

וכן תנא מרי בר בריה דרב הונא בריה דרבי ירמיה בר אבא: אל יפטר אדם מחבירו אלא מתוך דבר הלכה, שמתוך כך זוכרהו.

And so Mari, the grandson of Rav Huna, son of Rabbi Yirmeya bar Abba, taught in a *baraita*: One should only take leave of another from involvement in a **matter of *halakha*, so that, consequently, he will remember him;**[N] whenever he recalls the one from whom he took leave, he will think well of him because of the new *halakha* that he taught him (*Eliyahu Zuta*).

כי הא דרב כהנא אלוייה לרב שימי בר אשי מפום נהרא עד בי צניתא דבבל; כי מטא להתם, אמר ליה: מר, ודאי דאמרי אינשי: הני צניתא דבבל איתנהו מאדם הראשון ועד השתא?

As in the incident related by the Gemara **that Rav Kahana accompanied Rav Shimi bar Ashi from** the town of **Pum Nahara to the palm grove in Babylonia. When he arrived there,** Rav Kahana **said to** Rav Shimi bar Ashi: **Master, what is meant by that which people say: These palm trees** of **Babylonia have been** in this place from the time of **Adam the first** man **until now?**

אמר ליה: אדכרתן מילתא דרבי יוסי ברבי חנינא, דאמר רבי יוסי ברבי חנינא: מאי דכתיב "בארץ אשר לא עבר בה איש ולא ישב אדם שם", וכי מאחר דלא עבר היאך ישב? אלא לומר לך: כל ארץ שגזר עליה אדם הראשון לישוב – נתישבה, וכל ארץ שלא גזר עליה אדם הראשון לישוב – לא נתישבה.

Rav Shimi bar Ashi **said to him: You reminded me of something that Rabbi Yosei, son of Rabbi Ḥanina,** said, **as Rabbi Yosei, son of Rabbi Ḥanina, said: What is** the meaning **of that which is written: "In a land through which no man has passed and where no person [*adam*] has settled"** (Jeremiah 2:6)? This verse is difficult; **since it is** a land through which **no** person **has passed, how** could anyone **have settled** there permanently? The statement that "no person has settled there" is redundant. **Rather,** this verse comes **to teach** that **every land** through **which Adam the first** man passed and **decreed that it would be settled was settled, and every land** through **which** Adam passed and **decreed that it would not be settled was not settled.** Based on this, what people is say is true, and the palm trees of Babylonia are from the time of Adam, meaning that from the time of Adam this land was decreed to be suitable for growing palm trees (*Me'iri*). The Gemara cited an example of how one who parts from another with Torah learns something new.

רב מרדכי אלוייה לרב שימי בר אשי מהגרוניא ועד בי כיפי, ואמרי לה: עד בי דורא.

Having mentioned the mitzva for a student to accompany his Rabbi, the Gemara relates that **Rav Mordekhai accompanied** his mentor, **Rav Shimi bar Ashi,** a great distance, **from** the city of **Hagronya to Bei Keifei; and some say** that he accompanied from Hagronya **to Bei Dura.**

תנו רבנן: המתפלל צריך שיכוין את לבו לשמים. אבא שאול אומר, סימן לדבר: "תכין לבם תקשיב אזנך".

Returning to the topic of preparation for prayer, **the Sages taught** in the *Tosefta*: **One who prays must focus his heart toward Heaven. Abba Shaul says: An indication of** the importance of this **matter**[N] is stated in the verse: "The desire of the humble You have heard, Lord; **direct their hearts, Your ear will listen"** (Psalms 10:17). In other words, if one focuses his heart in prayer as a result of God directing his heart, his prayer will be accepted as God's ear will listen.

תניא, אמר רבי יהודה: כך היה מנהגו של רבי עקיבא, כשהיה מתפלל עם הציבור – היה מקצר ועולה, מפני טורח צבור, וכשהיה מתפלל בינו לבין עצמו – אדם מניחו בזוית זו ומוצאו בזוית אחרת, וכל כך למה – מפני כריעות והשתחויות.

With regard to one's intent during prayer, **it was taught** in a *baraita* that **Rabbi Yehuda said: This was the custom of Rabbi Akiva, when he would pray with the congregation he would shorten** his prayer **and go up,**[H] **due to** his desire to avoid being an **encumbrance on the congregation** by making them wait for him to finish his prayer. **But when he prayed by himself** he would extend his prayers to an extent that a **person would leave** Rabbi Akiva alone **in one corner** of the study hall **and** later **find him** still praying **in another corner. And why** would Rabbi Akiva move about **so much? Because of his bows and prostrations.**[N] Rabbi Akiva's enthusiasm in prayer was so great, that as a result of his bows and prostrations, he would unwittingly move from one corner to the other (Rav Hai Gaon).

אמר רבי חייא בר אבא: לעולם יתפלל אדם בבית שיש בו חלונות, שנאמר: "וכוין פתיחן ליה" וגו'.

Many *halakhot* are derived from evoking the prayers of biblical characters. **Rabbi Ḥiyya bar Abba said: One should always pray in a house with windows,**[NH] **as it is stated** regarding Daniel: "And when Daniel knew that the writing was signed, he went to his house. In his attic **there were open windows** facing Jerusalem, and three times a day he knelt upon his knees and prayed and gave thanks before his God, just as he had done before" (Daniel 6:11).

NOTES

From involvement in a matter of *halakha* – מתוך דבר הלכה: The parallel passage in the Jerusalem Talmud adds that one who engages in tending to communal needs before prayer has the same legal status as one who is involved in a matter of *halakha*.

So that, consequently, he will remember him – שמתוך כך זוכרהו: Some explain this as: So that he will remember it. When remembering parting from his colleague, he will always be reminded of this *halakha* (*Alfasi Zuta*).

An indication of this matter – סימן לדבר: The Gemara does not say: A proof for this, but rather: An indication, because in the verse it is not phrased as a command or instruction, but merely as a statement; if one focuses his heart, his prayer is accepted (*Shitta Mekubbetzet*).

Bows and prostrations – כריעות והשתחויות: The commentaries dispute whether these bows and prostrations were part of his *Amida* prayer, or whether they were an addition to that prayer. Some explain that he bowed after completing the standard prayer (Rashba, *Me'iri*, HaRav Rabbeinu Yosef), so that this would not contradict the *halakhot* requiring one to stand while praying. Others explained that, in fact, all this took place during the *Amida* prayer itself, as per the simple understanding of the Gemara (*Tosafot*, *Tosefot Rabbeinu Yehuda HaḤasid*).

A house with windows – בית שיש בו חלונות: Some explain that this is so one will be able to see the expanses and the sky (Rashi), and others say that the windows were necessary to further illuminate the synagogue as light has a salutary effect and facilitates one's focus on his prayer (*Talmidei Rabbeinu Yona*).

HALAKHA

When he would pray with the congregation he would shorten his prayer and go up – כשהיה מתפלל עם הציבור היה מקצר ועולה: It is inappropriate for a communal prayer leader to prolong his prayer and thereby burden the congregation. He should conduct himself in accordance with the conduct of Rabbi Akiva (Rambam *Sefer Ahava*, *Hilkhot Tefilla* 6:2; *Shulḥan Arukh*, *Oraḥ Ḥayyim* 53:11).

One should always pray in a house with windows – לעולם יתפלל אדם בבית שיש בו חלונות: It is appropriate for a synagogue to have windows facing Jerusalem, so that congregants will face them while praying. It is preferable for a synagogue to have twelve windows (*Zohar*, *Vayak-hel*; Rambam *Sefer Ahava*, *Hilkhot Tefilla* 5:6; *Shulḥan Arukh*, *Oraḥ Ḥayyim* 90:4).

יָכוֹל יִתְפַּלֵּל אָדָם כׇּל הַיּוֹם כּוּלּוֹ – כְּבָר מְפוֹרָשׁ עַל יְדֵי דָנִיֵּאל: ״וְזִמְנִין תְּלָתָא״ וגו׳.

In the *Tosefta*, additional *halakhot* were derived from Daniel's prayer. I **might have** thought **that one could pray** as many times as he wishes **throughout the entire day; it has already been articulated by Daniel,** with regard to whom it is stated: **"And three times** a day he knelt upon his knees and prayed." This teaches that there are fixed prayers.

יָכוֹל מִשֶּׁבָּא לַגּוֹלָה הוּחְלָה? – כְּבָר נֶאֱמַר: ״דִּי הוּא עָבֵד מִן קַדְמַת דְּנָא״.

I might have thought that this practice of fixed prayer **began** only **when he came to** the Babylonian **exile;**[N] **it was stated:** "Just **as he had done before."**

יָכוֹל יִתְפַּלֵּל אָדָם לְכׇל רוּחַ שֶׁיִּרְצֶה? – תַּלְמוּד לוֹמַר ״(לָקֳבֵל) נֶגֶד יְרוּשְׁלֶם״.

Further, I **might have** thought **that one may pray** facing **any direction he wishes; the verse states:** The appropriate direction for prayer is **"facing Jerusalem."**

יָכוֹל יְהֵא כּוֹלְלָן בְּבַת אַחַת – כְּבָר מְפוֹרָשׁ עַל יְדֵי דָוִד, דִּכְתִיב: ״עֶרֶב וָבֹקֶר וְצׇהֳרַיִם״ וגו׳.

Daniel does not describe how these three prayers are distributed during the day. I **might have** thought **that one may include all** three prayers **at one time; it has already been articulated by David** that one may not do so, **as it is written: "Evening and morning and noon,** I pray and cry aloud and He hears my voice" (Psalms 55:18).

יָכוֹל יַשְׁמִיעַ קוֹלוֹ בִּתְפִלָּתוֹ? – כְּבָר מְפוֹרָשׁ עַל יְדֵי חַנָּה, שֶׁנֶּאֱמַר: ״וְקוֹלָהּ לֹא יִשָּׁמֵעַ״.

Furthermore, **I might have** thought **that one may make his voice heard in his** *Amida* **prayer; it has already been articulated by Hannah** in her prayer, **as it is stated:** "And Hannah spoke in her heart, only her lips moved **and her voice could not be heard"** (I Samuel 1:13).

יָכוֹל יִשְׁאַל אָדָם צְרָכָיו וְאַחַר כָּךְ יִתְפַּלֵּל? – כְּבָר מְפוֹרָשׁ עַל יְדֵי שְׁלֹמֹה, שֶׁנֶּאֱמַר: ״לִשְׁמֹעַ אֶל הָרִנָּה וְאֶל הַתְּפִלָּה״, ״רִנָּה״ – זוֹ תְּפִלָּה, ״תְּפִלָּה״ – זוֹ בַּקָּשָׁה. אֵין אוֹמֵר דְּבַר בַּקָּשָׁה אַחַר אֱמֶת וְיַצִּיב, אֲבָל אַחַר הַתְּפִלָּה – אֲפִילּוּ כְּסֵדֶר וִדּוּי שֶׁל יוֹם הַכִּפּוּרִים אוֹמֵר.

Halakhot regarding the order of the prayers were also learned from the prayers of biblical characters. I **might have** thought **that one should request his own needs first, and afterwards recite prayers** of thanksgiving and praise; **it has already been articulated by Solomon** that this is not so, as in Solomon's prayer at the dedication of the Holy Temple **it is stated: "To hear the song and the prayer** that Your servant prays before You today" (I Kings 8:28). In this verse, **song is prayer** in the sense of thanks and praise, and **prayer is** one's **request** of his personal needs. Therefore, one who is praying **does not speak matters of request after** he began to recite ***emet veyatziv*** prior to the *Amida* prayer, which is the essence of prayer. Rather, he begins with praise in the first three blessings of the *Amida* prayer, and only thereafter does he include requests for his needs. **But after the** *Amida* **prayer** there is no limit. If he desires to recite **even the equivalent of the order of the confession**[B] **of Yom Kippur,** he may **recite** it.

אִיתְּמַר נַמִי, אָמַר רַב חִיָּיא בַּר אַשִׁי אָמַר רַב: אַף עַל פִּי שֶׁאָמְרוּ שׁוֹאֵל אָדָם צְרָכָיו בְּ״שׁוֹמֵעַ תְּפִלָּה״, אִם בָּא לוֹמַר אַחַר תְּפִלָּתוֹ אֲפִילּוּ כְּסֵדֶר שֶׁל יוֹם הַכִּפּוּרִים – אוֹמֵר.

This **was also stated** by an *amora*; **Rav Ḥiyya bar Ashi said** that **Rav said: Although** the Sages **said** that **one requests his** personal **needs** in the blessing: **Who listens to prayer,** that is with regard to one who wishes to do so as part of the *Amida* prayer. **If he comes** to add **and recite** additional requests **after** completing **his** *Amida* **prayer, even** if his personal requests are **the equivalent of the order of the confession of Yom Kippur,** he may **recite** them.[H]

אָמַר רַב הַמְנוּנָא: כַּמָּה הִלְכְתָא גַּבְרְוָותָא אִיכָּא לְמִשְׁמַע מֵהָנֵי קְרָאֵי דְּחַנָּה: ״וְחַנָּה הִיא מְדַבֶּרֶת עַל לִבָּהּ״ – מִכָּאן לַמִּתְפַּלֵּל צָרִיךְ שֶׁיְּכַוֵּין לִבּוֹ. ״רַק שְׂפָתֶיהָ נָעוֹת״ – מִכָּאן לַמִּתְפַּלֵּל שֶׁיַּחְתּוֹךְ בִּשְׂפָתָיו. ״וְקוֹלָהּ לֹא יִשָּׁמֵעַ״ – מִכָּאן, שֶׁאָסוּר לְהַגְבִּיהַּ קוֹלוֹ בִּתְפִלָּתוֹ. ״וַיַּחְשְׁבֶהָ עֵלִי לְשִׁכֹּרָה״ – מִכָּאן, שֶׁשִּׁכּוֹר אָסוּר לְהִתְפַּלֵּל.

Rav Hamnuna said: How many significant *halakhot* **can be derived from these verses** of the prayer **of Hannah?** As it says: "And Hannah spoke in her heart, only her lips moved and her voice could not be heard, so Eli thought her to be drunk" (I Samuel 1:13). The Gemara elaborates: **From** that which is stated **here: "And Hannah spoke in her heart,"** the *halakha* that **one who prays must focus his heart** on his prayer is derived. And **from** that which is stated **here: "Only her lips moved,"** the *halakha* that **one who prays must enunciate** the words **with his lips,** not only contemplate them in his heart, is derived.[H] **From** that which is written **here: "And her voice could not be heard,"** the *halakha* that **one is forbidden to raise his voice in his** *Amida* **prayer** as it must be recited silently. **From** the continuation of the verse **here: "So Eli thought her to be drunk,"** the *halakha* that **a drunk person is forbidden to pray.**[H] That is why he rebuked her.

״וַיֹּאמֶר אֵלֶיהָ עֵלִי עַד מָתַי תִּשְׁתַּכָּרִין״ וגו׳ – אָמַר רַבִּי אֶלְעָזָר: מִכָּאן, לָרוֹאֶה בַּחֲבֵרוֹ

On the subject of Eli's rebuke of Hannah, as it is stated: **"And Eli said to her: How long will you remain drunk?** Remove your wine from yourself" (I Samuel 1:14); **Rabbi Elazar said: From here** the *halakha* that **one who sees in another**

NOTES

This began when he came to exile – מִשֶּׁבָּא לַגּוֹלָה הוּחְלָה: Some interpret the word *huḥala* not as began but rather as fell ill. In other words, lest you say that before he was exiled, Daniel prayed more and only in exile did he fall ill and was forced to curtail his prayer (Maharshal).

BACKGROUND

Confession – וִידּוּי: This is an essential part of the process of repentance. The Torah obligates a person who has sinned to confess his sin (see Numbers 5:6–7). This confession, in which the sinner acknowledges and expresses regret for his sin, is made by him alone in private. In certain circumstances, however, where the sin involved has become public knowledge, a public confession is required. In many communities, the confessional prayer is recited every weekday. The Yom Kippur service includes many prayers and petitions for atonement, and the extended confessional prayer: For the sin…is recited several times during the course of the day. The confessional prayer was also recited by a person bringing a sin-offering, a guilt-offering, or a free-will burnt-offering as he placed his hands on the head of the sacrifice.

HALAKHA

Request during prayer – בַּקָּשָׁה בִּתְפִלָּה: One may add personal requests related to the topic of the blessing in the thirteen middle blessings of request and may add any request in the final blessing of the thirteen: Who listens to prayer. At the end of the *Amida* prayer, one may introduce any prayer he chooses, both before and after he recites the verse: May…find favor (Rambam *Sefer Ahava, Hilkhot Tefilla* 6:2; *Shulḥan Arukh, Oraḥ Ḥayyim* 119:1).

From here the *halakha* that one who prays must enunciate the words with his lips is derived – מִכָּאן לַמִּתְפַּלֵּל שֶׁיַּחְתּוֹךְ בִּשְׂפָתָיו: One may not merely contemplate his prayer; he must mouth the words. However, one may not pray out loud unless he is alone and is unable otherwise to concentrate on his prayer. When praying with a congregation, one may not pray audibly in order to avoid distracting those praying beside him (Rambam *Sefer Ahava, Hilkhot Tefilla* 5:9; *Shulḥan Arukh, Oraḥ Ḥayyim* 101:2).

From here the *halakha* that a drunk person is forbidden to pray – מִכָּאן שֶׁשִּׁכּוֹר אָסוּר לְהִתְפַּלֵּל: One who drank a quarter of a *log* of wine may not pray until he becomes sober. One who drank more than a quarter of a *log* and already prayed, if he is sufficiently sober to be capable of speaking before a king, his prayer is valid. If not, his prayer is an abomination and he must repeat it when sober. There are distinctions between various levels of intoxication explicated elsewhere in the Talmud (Rambam *Sefer Ahava, Hilkhot Tefilla* 4:17; *Shulḥan Arukh, Oraḥ Ḥayyim* 99:1).

דָּבָר שֶׁאֵינוֹ הָגוּן צָרִיךְ לְהוֹכִיחוֹ. ״וַתַּעַן חַנָּה וַתֹּאמֶר לֹא אֲדוֹנִי״ אָמַר עוּלָּא וְאִיתֵּימָא רַבִּי יוֹסֵי בְּרַבִּי חֲנִינָא, אָמְרָה לֵיהּ: לֹא אָדוֹן אַתָּה בְּדָבָר זֶה, וְלֹא רוּחַ הַקּוֹדֶשׁ שׁוֹרָה עָלֶיךָ, שֶׁאַתָּה חוֹשְׁדֵנִי בְּדָבָר זֶה.

an unseemly matter, he must reprimand him, is derived.[H] **"And Hannah answered and she said no, my master,** I am a woman of sorrowful spirit, and I have drunk neither wine nor liquor, but I pour out my soul before the Lord" (I Samuel 1:15). Regarding the words: "No, my master," **Ulla, and some say Rabbi Yosei, son of Rabbi Ḥanina, said** that **she said to him,** in an allusion: **With regard to this matter, you are not a master, and the Divine Spirit does not rest upon you, as you** falsely **suspect me of this.**

אִיכָּא דְּאָמְרִי, הָכִי אָמְרָה לֵיהּ: לֹא אָדוֹן אַתָּה, לָאו אִיכָּא שְׁכִינָה וְרוּחַ הַקּוֹדֶשׁ גַּבָּךְ, שֶׁדַּנְתַּנִי לְכַף חוֹבָה וְלֹא דַּנְתַּנִי לְכַף זְכוּת, מִי לָא יָדְעַתְּ דְּאִשָּׁה קְשַׁת רוּחַ אָנוֹכִי?!

Some say another version of her response. **She said to him,** questioning: **Aren't you a master? Aren't the Divine Presence and Divine Spirit with you that you judged me to be guilty, and you did not judge me to be innocent? Didn't you know that I am a woman of distressed spirit?**

״וְיַיִן וְשֵׁכָר לֹא שָׁתִיתִי״ – אָמַר רַבִּי אֶלְעָזָר: מִכָּאן, לַנֶּחְשָׁד בְּדָבָר שֶׁאֵין בּוֹ שֶׁצָּרִיךְ לְהוֹדִיעוֹ.

With regard to Hannah's explanation that **"I have drunk neither wine nor liquor," Rabbi Elazar**[P] **said: From here** the *halakha* is derived **that one who is suspected of something of which he is not** guilty cannot suffice merely with the personal knowledge of his innocence, but **must inform** the one who suspects him that he is innocent and clear himself of suspicion.

״אַל תִּתֵּן אֶת אֲמָתְךָ לִפְנֵי בַּת בְּלִיָּעַל״ – אָמַר רַבִּי אֶלְעָזָר: מִכָּאן, לְשִׁכּוֹר שֶׁמִּתְפַּלֵּל כְּאִילּוּ עוֹבֵד עֲבוֹדָה זָרָה, כְּתִיב הָכָא ״לִפְנֵי בַּת בְּלִיָּעַל״, וּכְתִיב הָתָם ״יָצְאוּ אֲנָשִׁים בְּנֵי בְלִיַּעַל מִקִּרְבֶּךָ״, מַה לְּהַלָּן עֲבוֹדָה זָרָה, אַף כָּאן – עֲבוֹדָה זָרָה.

"Do not take your maidservant as a wicked woman [*bat beliya'al*] for out of the abundance of my complaint and anger have I spoken until now" (I Samuel 1:16). **Rabbi Elazar said: From here** the *halakha* **that when a drunk person prays it is as if he engaged in idol worship** is derived[N] as **it is written here** that Hannah, suspected of praying while drunk, defends herself and says: "Do not take your maidservant **as a *bat beliya'al*"**; and **it is written there,** with regard to a city that has been instigated to engage in idol worship: ***"Benei beliya'al* have gone out from your midst** and have lured the inhabitants of their city, saying let us go and serve other gods which we have not known" (Deuteronomy 13:14). By means of this verbal analogy it is derived: **Just as there,** in the case of the idolatrous city, the term *beliya'al* indicates **idol worship, so too here,** in the case of one who prays drunk, *beliya'al* indicates **idol worship.**

״וַיַּעַן עֵלִי וַיֹּאמֶר לְכִי לְשָׁלוֹם״ – אָמַר רַבִּי אֶלְעָזָר: מִכָּאן, לַחוֹשֵׁד אֶת חֲבֵרוֹ בְּדָבָר שֶׁאֵין בּוֹ שֶׁצָּרִיךְ לְפַיְּיסוֹ; וְלֹא עוֹד, אֶלָּא שֶׁצָּרִיךְ לְבָרְכוֹ, שֶׁנֶּאֱמַר: ״וֵאלֹהֵי יִשְׂרָאֵל יִתֵּן אֶת שֵׁלָתֵךְ״.

The verse continues: **"And Eli answered and said: May you go in peace"** (I Samuel 1:17). **Rabbi Elazar said: From here** the *halakha* is derived **that one who suspects another of something that he has not done, he must appease him. Moreover,** the one who suspected him **must bless him,** as Eli continued and offered Hannah a blessing, **as it is stated: "And may the God of Israel grant your request** that you have asked of Him" (I Samuel 1:17).

״וַתִּדֹּר נֶדֶר וַתֹּאמַר ה׳ צְבָאוֹת״, אָמַר רַבִּי אֶלְעָזָר: מִיּוֹם שֶׁבָּרָא הַקָּדוֹשׁ בָּרוּךְ הוּא אֶת עוֹלָמוֹ, לֹא הָיָה אָדָם שֶׁקְּרָאוֹ לְהַקָּדוֹשׁ בָּרוּךְ הוּא ״צְבָאוֹת״, עַד שֶׁבָּאתָה חַנָּה וּקְרָאָתוֹ ״צְבָאוֹת״;

Incidental to this discussion of Hannah's prayer, the Gemara explores related topics. In her prayer, Hannah said: **"And she swore an oath and said, Lord of Hosts [*Tzeva'ot*]** if You will indeed look upon the affliction of Your maidservant and remember me, and not forget Your maidservant and will give Your maidservant a male child, I will give him to the Lord all the days of his life, and there shall be no razor come upon his head" (I Samuel 1:11). **Rabbi Elazar said: From the day that the Holy One, Blessed be He, created His world, there was no person who called the Holy One, Blessed be He, Lord of Hosts until Hannah came and called Him Lord of Hosts.** This is the first time in the Bible that God is referred to by this name.

אָמְרָה חַנָּה לִפְנֵי הַקָּדוֹשׁ בָּרוּךְ הוּא: רִבּוֹנוֹ שֶׁל עוֹלָם, מִכׇּל צִבְאֵי צְבָאוֹת שֶׁבָּרָאתָ בְּעוֹלָמְךָ קָשֶׁה בְּעֵינֶיךָ שֶׁתִּתֵּן לִי בֵּן אֶחָד?!

Rabbi Elazar explains that **Hannah said before the Holy One, Blessed be He: Master of the Universe,** are You not the Lord of the Hosts, and **of all of the hosts and hosts** of creations **that You created in Your world, is it difficult in Your eyes to grant me one son?**

HALAKHA

From here the *halakha* that one who sees in another an unseemly matter, he must reprimand him, is derived – מִכָּאן, לָרוֹאֶה בַּחֲבֵרוֹ דָּבָר שֶׁאֵינוֹ הָגוּן צָרִיךְ לְהוֹכִיחוֹ: One who sees that another has sinned or is heading in that direction, it is a mitzva to direct him back to the straight and narrow and inform him that he is hurting himself with his wicked actions, even if he did not explicitly violate a Torah prohibition (Rambam *Sefer HaMadda, Hilkhot De'ot* 6:7).

PERSONALITIES

Rabbi Elazar – רַבִּי אֶלְעָזָר: In the Gemara, citations of Rabbi Elazar, with no patronymic, refer to Rabbi Elazar ben Pedat, a second-generation, Eretz Yisrael *amora*. He was born in Babylonia, where he was a student of both Rav and Shmuel. In his youth, he immigrated to Eretz Yisrael, where he married. In Eretz Yisrael, he became the primary student of Rabbi Yoḥanan. The connection between them was so close that at times, the Gemara raises a contradiction between the statement of one and the statement of the other, under the assumption that it was unlikely that they would hold different opinions in matters of *halakha*.

NOTES

From here the *halakha* that when a drunk person prays it is as if he engaged in idol worship is derived – מִכָּאן, לְשִׁכּוֹר שֶׁמִּתְפַּלֵּל כְּאִילּוּ עוֹבֵד עֲבוֹדָה זָרָה: Drunkenness causes confusion. One who stands in prayer drunk is liable to conjure false images in his conception of the Divine. That is the essence of idolatry (Rashba).

מָשָׁל לְמָה הַדָּבָר דּוֹמֶה – לְמֶלֶךְ בָּשָׂר וָדָם שֶׁעָשָׂה סְעוּדָה לַעֲבָדָיו, בָּא עָנִי אֶחָד וְעָמַד עַל הַפֶּתַח, אָמַר לָהֶם: תְּנוּ לִי פְּרוּסָה אַחַת! וְלֹא הִשְׁגִּיחוּ עָלָיו; דָּחַק וְנִכְנַס אֵצֶל הַמֶּלֶךְ. אָמַר לוֹ: אֲדוֹנִי הַמֶּלֶךְ, מִכׇּל סְעוּדָה שֶׁעָשִׂיתָ קָשֶׁה בְּעֵינֶיךָ לִיתֵּן לִי פְּרוּסָה אַחַת?!

The Gemara suggests **a parable: To what is this similar?** It is similar to **a flesh and blood king who made a feast for his servants. A poor person came and stood at the door. He said to them: Give me one slice** of bread! **And they paid him no attention. He pushed and entered before the king. He said to him: My lord, the King, from this entire feast that you have prepared, is it so difficult in your eyes to give me a single slice** of bread?

״אִם רָאֹה תִרְאֶה״, אָמַר רַבִּי אֶלְעָזָר: אָמְרָה חַנָּה לִפְנֵי הַקָּדוֹשׁ בָּרוּךְ הוּא: רִבּוֹנוֹ שֶׁל עוֹלָם, אִם ״רָאֹה״ – מוּטָב, וְאִם לָאו – ״תִּרְאֶה״,

As for the double language in the verse, **"if you will look upon** [*im ra'o tireh*]," **Rabbi Elazar said: Hannah said before the Holy One, Blessed be He: Master of the Universe, if You will look upon** [*ra'o*] me now, **fine, and if not,** in any case **You will see** [*tireh*].

אֵלֵךְ וְאֶסְתַּתֵּר בִּפְנֵי אֶלְקָנָה בַּעְלִי, וְכֵיוָן דְּמִסְתַּתַּרְנָא מַשְׁקוּ לִי מֵי סוֹטָה, וְאִי אַתָּה עוֹשֶׂה תּוֹרָתְךָ פַּלַסְתֵּר, שֶׁנֶּאֱמַר: ״וְנִקְּתָה וְנִזְרְעָה זָרַע״.

What was Hannah threatening? She said: **I will go and seclude myself** with another man **before Elkana, my husband. Since I secluded myself, they will force me to drink the *sota*[B] water** to determine whether or not I have committed adultery. I will be found innocent, **and** since **You will not make Your Torah false** [*pelaster*],[L] I will bear children. With regards to a woman who is falsely suspected of adultery and drank the *sota* water, the Torah **says:** "And if the woman was not defiled, but was pure, then **she shall be acquitted and she shall conceive**" (Numbers 5:28).

הָנִיחָא לְמַאן דַּאֲמַר אִם הָיְתָה עֲקָרָה נִפְקֶדֶת – שַׁפִּיר, אֶלָּא לְמַאן דַּאֲמַר אִם הָיְתָה יוֹלֶדֶת בְּצַעַר – יוֹלֶדֶת בְּרֵיוַח, נְקֵבוֹת – יוֹלֶדֶת זְכָרִים, שְׁחוֹרִים – יוֹלֶדֶת לְבָנִים, קְצָרִים – יוֹלֶדֶת אֲרוּכִּים, מַאי אִיכָּא לְמֵימַר?

However, Rabbi Elazar's opinion **works out well** according **to the one who said** that the verse means: **If she were barren, she will be remembered** by God and granted children. **But** according **to the one who said** that the verse means that childbearing will be easier and more successful, i.e., **if she had** previously **given birth with pain,** she now **gives birth with ease,** or if she had previously given birth to **daughters,** she now **gives birth to sons,** or if she had previously given birth to **black** children, considered to be unattractive, she now **gives birth to fair** children, or if she had previously given birth to **short,** weak children, she **gives birth to tall,** strong children, **what can be said?**

דְּתַנְיָא: ״וְנִקְּתָה וְנִזְרְעָה זָרַע״ – מְלַמֵּד, שֶׁאִם הָיְתָה עֲקָרָה נִפְקֶדֶת, דִּבְרֵי רַבִּי יִשְׁמָעֵאל; אָמַר לֵיהּ רַבִּי עֲקִיבָא: אִם כֵּן, יֵלְכוּ כׇּל הָעֲקָרוֹת כּוּלָּן וְיִסְתַּתְּרוּ, וְזוֹ שֶׁלֹּא קִלְקְלָה נִפְקֶדֶת! אֶלָּא: מְלַמֵּד שֶׁאִם הָיְתָה יוֹלֶדֶת בְּצַעַר – יוֹלֶדֶת בְּרֵיוַח, קְצָרִים – יוֹלֶדֶת אֲרוּכִּים, שְׁחוֹרִים – יוֹלֶדֶת לְבָנִים, אֶחָד – יוֹלֶדֶת שְׁנַיִם.

As it was taught in a *baraita* that the *tanna'im* disputed the interpretation of the verse in Numbers: **"Then she shall be acquitted and she shall conceive"** teaches that **if she was barren, she will be remembered** by God and granted children; this is **the statement of Rabbi Yishmael. Rabbi Akiva said to him: If so, all barren women will go and seclude themselves** with men who are not their husbands, **and any** woman **who did not** commit the **sin** of adultery **will be remembered** by God and granted children. **Rather,** the verse **teaches** that this is merely a promise for greater ease in childbirth; **if she has** previously **given birth with pain,** she now **gives birth with ease,** if she has previously given birth to **short** children, she **gives birth to tall** children, if she has previously given birth to **black** children, she now **gives birth to fair** children, if she has previously given birth to **one** child, she now **gives birth to two** children.

מַאי ״אִם רָאֹה תִרְאֶה״ – דִּבְּרָה תּוֹרָה כִּלְשׁוֹן בְּנֵי אָדָם.

According to Rabbi Akiva's explanation, **what** is derived from the double language uttered by Hannah: ***Im ra'o tireh*? The Torah spoke in the language of men,** meaning that this double language is not extraordinary and nothing may be derived from it. It is common biblical vernacular.

״בָּעֳנִי אֲמָתֶךָ״, ״אַל תִּשְׁכַּח אֶת אֲמָתֶךָ״, ״וְנָתַתָּה לַאֲמָתְךָ״.

In the oath/prayer uttered by Hannah, she refers to herself as "Your servant" [*amatekha*] three times: **"The affliction of Your maidservant…** and **not forget Your maidservant and will give Your maidservant"** (I Samuel 1:11).

אָמַר רַבִּי יוֹסֵי בְּרַבִּי חֲנִינָא: שָׁלֹשׁ אֲמָתוֹת הַלָּלוּ לָמָּה – אָמְרָה חַנָּה לִפְנֵי הַקָּדוֹשׁ בָּרוּךְ הוּא: רִבּוֹנוֹ שֶׁל עוֹלָם, שְׁלֹשָׁה בִּדְקֵי מִיתָה בָּרָאתָ בְּאִשָּׁה, וְאָמְרִי לַהּ: שְׁלֹשָׁה דִּבְקֵי מִיתָה, וְאֵלּוּ הֵן: נִדָּה וְחַלָּה וְהַדְלָקַת הַנֵּר, כְּלוּם עָבַרְתִּי עַל אַחַת מֵהֶן?!

Rabbi Yosei, son of Rabbi Ḥanina, said: Why are **these three maidservants** [*amatot*] cited in the verse? They are cited to teach that **Hannah said before the Holy One, Blessed be He: Master of the Universe, You have created three crucibles** potentially leading to **death**[N] **in a woman,** where she is particularly vulnerable. Alternatively, **some say:** Master of the Universe, You have created **three accelerants of death** in a woman. **They are** mitzvot that, as a rule, pertain to women: Observing the *halakhot* of **a menstruating woman,** separating *ḥalla* from dough, **and lighting** Shabbat **candles. Have I ever violated one of them?** Hannah attests to her status as God's maidservant [*ama*]. The reference to these three mitzvot is drawn from the etymological similarity between *amatekha*, your maidservant, and *mita*, death.

BACKGROUND

Sota – **סוֹטָה**: The Torah describes the procedure governing such a woman (Numbers 5:11–31): First, her husband warns her in the presence of witnesses against being alone together with a specific man about whom he is suspicious. If she disobeys this warning and is observed alone with that man (even though there is no concrete evidence that she actually committed adultery), she and her husband can no longer live together as man and wife until she has undergone the following ordeal to determine whether she has committed adultery. The woman (accompanied by her husband and two Torah scholars) is taken to the Temple in Jerusalem and forced by the priests to stand in a public place while holding the special meal-offering that she is required to bring. There she is again questioned about her behavior. If she continues to protest her fidelity and takes an oath to that effect, a scroll is brought and the curses of the *sota* mentioned in the Torah passage cited above are written on it. If she does not admit that she has committed adultery, the scroll is submerged in a clay vessel filled with water taken from the Temple basin and some earth from the Temple floor, and the scroll's writing is dissolved in the water. She is then forced to drink that water. If the husband's allegation is true, in the words of the Torah, "her belly shall swell and her thigh shall fall away" (Numbers 5:27), until ultimately she dies from the water's curse. If she is innocent, the water will bring her blessing and she is permitted to resume normal marital relations with her husband.

LANGUAGE

False [*pelaster*] – **פַּלַסְתֵּר**: The source of this word is the Greek πλάστης, *plastēs*, meaning a molder, a modeler; metaphorically, in this context, it means false.

NOTES

Three crucibles potentially leading to death – שְׁלֹשָׁה בִּדְקֵי מִיתָה: The source for this is the mishna in tractate *Shabbat* (31b) that states that for failure to fulfill these mitzvot women are punished. Various explanations were suggested why these three mitzvot were particularly emphasized. Some hold that the reason is because it is women who generally have the opportunity to engage in their performance. Another explanation ties each of these mitzvot to Eve's sin with the tree of knowledge, and each alludes to and symbolizes one of the consequences of that transgression (*Shabbat* 32a).

״וְנָתַתָּה לַאֲמָתְךָ זֶרַע אֲנָשִׁים״,

Later in her prayer, Hannah says: **"And You will grant Your servant an offspring of men."**

מַאי ״זֶרַע אֲנָשִׁים״? אָמַר רַב: גַּבְרָא בְּגוּבְרִין; וּשְׁמוּאֵל אָמַר: זֶרַע שֶׁמּוֹשֵׁחַ שְׁנֵי אֲנָשִׁים, וּמַאן אִינּוּן – שָׁאוּל וְדָוִד; וְרַבִּי יוֹחָנָן אָמַר: זֶרַע שֶׁשָּׁקוּל כִּשְׁנֵי אֲנָשִׁים, וּמַאן אִינּוּן – מֹשֶׁה וְאַהֲרֹן, שֶׁנֶּאֱמַר: ״מֹשֶׁה וְאַהֲרֹן בְּכֹהֲנָיו וּשְׁמוּאֵל בְּקוֹרְאֵי שְׁמוֹ״; וְרַבָּנַן אָמְרִי: ״זֶרַע אֲנָשִׁים״ – זֶרַע שֶׁמּוּבְלָע בֵּין אֲנָשִׁים.

The Gemara asks: **What is** the meaning of **"an offspring of men"? Rav said:** Hannah prayed for **a man among men,** a son who would be outstanding and exceptional. **And Shmuel said:** This expression means **an offspring who will anoint two men** to royalty. **And who were they? Saul and David. And Rabbi Yoḥanan said:** Hannah prayed that she would bear **an offspring who** would be **the equivalent of two** of the world's greatest **men. And who were they? Moses and Aaron. As it is stated: "Moses and Aaron among His priests, and Samuel among those who call His name"** (Psalms 99:6). In this verse, Hannah's son, Samuel, is equated to Moses and Aaron. **And the Rabbis say: "An offspring of men":** Hannah prayed for **an offspring who would be inconspicuous among men,** that he would not stand out in any way.

כִּי אֲתָא רַב דִּימִי, אָמַר: לֹא אָרוֹךְ וְלֹא גּוּץ, וְלֹא קָטָן וְלֹא אַלָּם, וְלֹא צָחוֹר וְלֹא גִּיחוֹר, וְלֹא חָכָם וְלֹא טִפֵּשׁ.

The Gemara relates: **When Rav Dimi came** from Eretz Yisrael to Babylonia, **he said** in explanation: Hannah prayed that her son would not be conspicuous among men; **neither too tall nor too short; neither too small nor too fat; neither too white nor too red; neither too smart nor too stupid.**

״אֲנִי הָאִשָּׁה הַנִּצֶּבֶת עִמְּכָה בָּזֶה״ אָמַר רַבִּי יְהוֹשֻׁעַ בֶּן לֵוִי: מִכָּאן, שֶׁאָסוּר לֵישֵׁב בְּתוֹךְ אַרְבַּע אַמּוֹת שֶׁל תְּפִלָּה.

When Hannah came to the Temple with her son Samuel, she told Eli: "My lord, as your soul lives, my lord, **I am the woman who stood here with you** to pray to the Lord" (1 Samuel 1:26). **Rabbi Yehoshua ben Levi said: From here** the *halakha* **that it is forbidden to sit within four cubits of** one who is **praying** is derived.[H] As the verse says: "Who stood here with you," indicating that Eli stood alongside Hannah because she was praying.

״אֶל הַנַּעַר הַזֶּה הִתְפַּלָּלְתִּי״ – אָמַר רַבִּי אֶלְעָזָר: שְׁמוּאֵל מוֹרֶה הֲלָכָה לִפְנֵי רַבּוֹ הָיָה, שֶׁנֶּאֱמַר: ״וַיִּשְׁחֲטוּ אֶת הַפָּר וַיָּבִיאוּ אֶת הַנַּעַר אֶל עֵלִי״, מִשּׁוּם דְּ״וַיִּשְׁחֲטוּ אֶת הַפָּר״ הֵבִיאוּ הַנַּעַר אֶל עֵלִי?!

Additionally, Hannah's emphasis in speaking to Eli, **"for this youth I prayed"** (1 Samuel 1:27), indicates that she came to protect him from danger. As **Rabbi Elazar said: Samuel was** one who **taught** *halakha* **in the presence of his teacher.**[N] Hannah wanted to pray that he not be punished by death at the hand of Heaven for his transgression, **as it is stated: "And they slaughtered the cow and they brought the youth to Eli"** (1 Samuel 1:25). This verse is puzzling. **Because they slaughtered the cow,** therefore, **they brought the youth to Eli?** What does one have to do with the next?

אֶלָּא, אָמַר לָהֶן עֵלִי: קִרְאוּ כֹּהֵן, לֵיתֵי וְלִשְׁחוֹט. חָזִנְהוּ שְׁמוּאֵל דְּהָווּ מְהַדְּרִי בָּתַר כֹּהֵן לְמִישְׁחַט, אָמַר לְהוּ: לָמָּה לְכוּ לְאַהֲדוּרֵי בָּתַר כֹּהֵן לְמִישְׁחַט? שְׁחִיטָה בְּזָר כְּשֵׁרָה! אַיְיתוּהוּ לְקַמֵּיהּ דְּעֵלִי, אָמַר לֵיהּ: מְנָא לָךְ הָא? אֲמַר לֵיהּ: מִי כְּתִיב ״וְשָׁחַט הַכֹּהֵן״?! ״וְהִקְרִיבוּ הַכֹּהֲנִים״ כְּתִיב! מִקַּבָּלָה וְאֵילָךְ מִצְוַת כְּהוּנָּה; מִכָּאן לִשְׁחִיטָה שֶׁכְּשֵׁרָה בְּזָר.

Rather, this is what happened: **Eli said to** those who brought the offering: **Call a priest; he will come and slaughter** the offering. **Samuel saw them looking for a priest to slaughter** the animal. **He said to them: Why do you need to look for a priest to slaughter** it? **Slaughter** of an offering performed **by a non-priest is valid.**[H] **They brought him before Eli** to clarify his statement. Eli **said to him: How do you know this?** Samuel **said to him: Is it written** in the Torah: **And the priest shall slaughter** indicating that the offering may only be slaughtered by a priest? **It is written: "And the priests shall offer,"** only **from** the stage of **receiving** the blood in the bowls **and onward is it a mitzva** incumbent upon **priests** alone. **From here** the *halakha* that **slaughter by a non-priest is acceptable** is derived.

אָמַר לֵיהּ: מֵימַר שַׁפִּיר קָא אָמְרַתְּ, מִיהוּ, מוֹרֶה הֲלָכָה בִּפְנֵי רַבָּךְ אַתְּ – וְכָל הַמּוֹרֶה הֲלָכָה בִּפְנֵי רַבּוֹ חַיָּיב מִיתָה. אָתְיָא חַנָּה וְקָא צָוְוחָה קַמֵּיהּ: ״אֲנִי הָאִשָּׁה הַנִּצֶּבֶת עִמְּכָה בָּזֶה״ וגו׳. אָמַר לָהּ: שִׁבְקִי לִי דְּאַעַנְשֵׁיהּ, וּבָעֵינָא רַחֲמֵי וְיָהֵיב לָךְ רַבָּא מִינֵּיהּ. אָמְרָה לֵיהּ: ״אֶל הַנַּעַר הַזֶּה הִתְפַּלָּלְתִּי״.

Eli **said to** Samuel: **You have spoken well** and your statement is correct, but **nevertheless, you are** one who **issued a halakhic ruling in the presence of your teacher, and anyone who issues a halakhic ruling in the presence of his teacher,** even if the particular *halakha* is correct, **is liable for death**[H] at the hand of Heaven for showing contempt for his teacher. **Hannah came and shouted before him: "I am the woman who stood here with you** to pray to the Lord;" do not punish the child who was born of my prayers. **He said to her: Let me punish him, and I will pray** for mercy, that the Holy One, Blessed be He, **will grant you** a son who will be **greater than** this one. **She said to him: "For this youth I prayed"** and I want no other.

HALAKHA

From here the *halakha* that it is forbidden to sit within four cubits of one who is praying is derived – מִכָּאן, שֶׁאָסוּר לֵישֵׁב בְּתוֹךְ אַרְבַּע אַמּוֹת שֶׁל תְּפִלָּה: One may not sit within four cubits on any side of one who is praying, as per the opinion of Rabbi Yehoshua ben Levi cited here. If one is himself engaged in Torah study or prayer, it is permitted, as in that case he does not appear to be displaying contempt for the prayer of the person beside him (*Shulḥan Arukh HaRav*; Rambam *Sefer Ahava, Hilkhot Tefilla* 5:6; *Shulḥan Arukh, Oraḥ Ḥayyim* 102:1).

Slaughter by a non-priest is valid – שְׁחִיטָה בְּזָר כְּשֵׁרָה: Non-priests are permitted to slaughter consecrated animals and even sacrifices of the most sacred order. This is true with regard to both individual and communal offerings (Rambam *Sefer Avoda, Hilkhot Biat HaMikdash* 9:6, *Sefer Avoda, Hilkhot Ma'aseh HaKorbanot* 5:1, *Sefer Avoda, Hilkhot Pesulei HaMukdashim* 1:1).

Anyone who issues a halakhic ruling in the presence of his teacher is liable for death – הַמּוֹרֶה הֲלָכָה בִּפְנֵי רַבּוֹ חַיָּיב מִיתָה: One is always forbidden to teach *halakha* in the presence of his teacher, and one who does so is punished by death at the hand of Heaven. One who is a distance of at least twelve *mil* from his teacher, a distance derived in tractate *Sanhedrin* from the size of Israelite camp in the desert, and someone happens to ask him a question, he may answer. However, he is forbidden to establish himself as a halakhic authority until his teacher dies or has given him permission to issue halakhic rulings. If one is within three parasangs, twelve *mil*, of his teacher, even with his permission he may issue rulings (Rema). Some say that one who issues halakhic rulings within twelve *mil* of his teacher is liable to receive the death penalty. Beyond twelve *mil*, although he is prohibited from doing so, he is exempt from receiving the death penalty (Rambam *Sefer HaMadda, Hilkhot Talmud Torah* 5:2–3; *Shulḥan Arukh, Yoreh De'a* 242:4 and in the Rema).

NOTES

Samuel was one who taught *halakha* in the presence of his teacher – שְׁמוּאֵל מוֹרֶה הֲלָכָה לִפְנֵי רַבּוֹ הָיָה: This did not transpire when Samuel was first brought to the Tabernacle, but on one of the Festivals after he was already grown (*ge'onim*).

"וְחַנָּה הִיא מְדַבֶּרֶת עַל לִבָּהּ" אָמַר רַבִּי אֶלְעָזָר מִשּׁוּם רַבִּי יוֹסֵי בֶּן זִמְרָא: עַל עִסְקֵי לִבָּהּ. אָמְרָה לְפָנָיו: רִבּוֹנוֹ שֶׁל עוֹלָם, כָּל מַה שֶּׁבָּרָאתָ בְּאִשָּׁה לֹא בָּרָאתָ דָּבָר אֶחָד לְבַטָּלָה, עֵינַיִם לִרְאוֹת, וְאׇזְנַיִם לִשְׁמוֹעַ, חוֹטֶם לְהָרִיחַ, פֶּה לְדַבֵּר, יָדַיִם לַעֲשׂוֹת בָּהֶם מְלָאכָה, רַגְלַיִם לְהַלֵּךְ בָּהֶן, דַּדִּים לְהָנִיק בָּהֶן; דַּדִּים הַלָּלוּ שֶׁנָּתַתָּ עַל לִבִּי לָמָּה, לֹא לְהָנִיק בָּהֶן?! תֵּן לִי בֵּן וְאָנִיק בָּהֶן.

The Gemara continues to deal with Hannah's prayer. It is said: **"And Hannah spoke on her heart."** Several interpretations are offered to explain her use of the phrase "on her heart" instead of the common phrase to her heart (Maharsha). **Rabbi Elazar said in the name of Rabbi Yosei ben Zimra:** Hannah spoke to God **concerning matters of her heart. She said before Him: Master of the Universe,** of all the organs **You created in a woman, You have not created one in** vain. Every organ fulfills its purpose; **eyes to see, ears to hear, a nose to smell, a mouth to speak, hands with which to perform labor, feet with which to walk, breasts with which to nurse.** If so, **these breasts that You placed upon my heart, to what** purpose did You place them? Was it **not** in order **to nurse with them? Grant me a son and I will nurse with them.**

וְאָמַר רַבִּי אֶלְעָזָר מִשּׁוּם רַבִּי יוֹסֵי בֶּן זִמְרָא: כָּל הַיּוֹשֵׁב בְּתַעֲנִית בְּשַׁבָּת – קוֹרְעִים לוֹ גְּזַר דִּינוֹ שֶׁל שִׁבְעִים שָׁנָה, וְאַף עַל פִּי כֵן חוֹזְרִין וְנִפְרָעִין מִמֶּנּוּ דִּין עוֹנֶג שַׁבָּת.

Tangentially, the Gemara also cites an additional statement that **Rabbi Elazar said in the name of Rabbi Yosei ben Zimra: Anyone who sits** in observance of a **fast on Shabbat,**[NH] his merit is great and **they tear up** and repeal **his sentence of seventy years;** because everyone is enjoying himself and a feast is prepared, it is more difficult to fast on Shabbat than on any other day. **Nevertheless, they then hold him accountable** for failing to fulfill **the *halakha* of delight of Shabbat.**

מַאי תַּקַּנְתֵּיהּ? אָמַר רַב נַחְמָן בַּר יִצְחָק: לֵיתִיב תַּעֲנִיתָא לְתַעֲנִיתָא.

The Gemara asks: **What is his remedy** to atone and avoid punishment? **Rav Naḥman bar Yitzḥak said: He must sit** in observance of another **fast** on a weekday to atone **for the fast** on Shabbat.

וְאָמַר רַבִּי אֶלְעָזָר: חַנָּה הֵטִיחָה דְּבָרִים כְּלַפֵּי מַעְלָה, שֶׁנֶּאֱמַר: "וַתִּתְפַּלֵּל עַל ה'" – מְלַמֵּד, שֶׁהֵטִיחָה דְּבָרִים כְּלַפֵּי מַעְלָה.

After explaining the uncommon expression, on her heart, the Gemara cites an additional statement in the matter of Hannah. **And Rabbi Elazar said: Hannah spoke impertinently toward** God **on High. As it is stated: "And she prayed onto the Lord,"** as opposed to the common phrase: To the Lord. This **teaches that she spoke impertinently toward on High.**

וְאָמַר רַבִּי אֶלְעָזָר: אֵלִיָּהוּ הֵטִיחַ דְּבָרִים כְּלַפֵּי מַעְלָה, שֶׁנֶּאֱמַר: "וְאַתָּה הֲסִבֹּתָ אֶת לִבָּם אֲחֹרַנִּית". אָמַר רַבִּי שְׁמוּאֵל בַּר רַבִּי יִצְחָק: מִנַּיִן שֶׁחָזַר הַקָּדוֹשׁ בָּרוּךְ הוּא וְהוֹדָה לוֹ לְאֵלִיָּהוּ?

And on a similar note, **Rabbi Elazar said** that **Elijah spoke impertinently toward** God **on High** as well in his prayer at Mount Carmel, **as it is stated:** "Answer me, Lord, answer me, that this people will know that You are the Lord, God, **and You have turned their hearts backward"** (I Kings 18:37), claiming that God caused Israel to sin. On this topic, **Rabbi Shmuel bar Rabbi Yitzḥak said: From where do we know that the Holy One, Blessed be He, ultimately conceded to Elijah** that he was correct?

Perek **V**
Daf **32** Amud **a**

דִּכְתִיב: "וַאֲשֶׁר הֲרֵעֹתִי".

As it is written in a future prophecy: "In that day, says the Lord, I will assemble the lame, and I will gather those who are abandoned and **those with whom I have dealt in wickedness"** (Micah 4:6). God states that He caused Israel to act wickedly.

אָמַר רַבִּי חָמָא בְּרַבִּי חֲנִינָא: אִלְמָלֵא שָׁלֹשׁ מִקְרָאוֹת הַלָּלוּ – נִתְמוֹטְטוּ רַגְלֵיהֶם שֶׁל שׂוֹנְאֵי יִשְׂרָאֵל:

Similarly, **Rabbi Ḥama, son of Rabbi Ḥanina, said: Had it not been for these three verses, the legs of the enemies of Israel,** a euphemism for Israel itself, **would have collapsed,** as Israel would have been unable to withstand God's judgment.

חַד, דִּכְתִיב: "וַאֲשֶׁר הֲרֵעֹתִי", וְחַד, דִּכְתִיב: "הִנֵּה כַחֹמֶר בְּיַד הַיּוֹצֵר כֵּן אַתֶּם בְּיָדִי בֵּית יִשְׂרָאֵל"; וְחַד, דִּכְתִיב: "וַהֲסִרֹתִי אֶת לֵב הָאֶבֶן מִבְּשַׂרְכֶם וְנָתַתִּי לָכֶם לֵב בָּשָׂר".

One is the verse just mentioned in which **it is written: "Those whom I have dealt in wickedness." And one** is the verse in which **it is written: "Behold, like clay in the potter's hand, so are you in My hand, house of Israel"** (Jeremiah 18:6). **And one** is the verse in which **it is written:** "And I will give you a new heart and a new spirit I will place within you, **and I will remove the heart of stone from your flesh and I will give you a heart of flesh"** (Ezekiel 36:26). These three verses indicate that God influences a person's decisions, and therefore one does not have sole responsibility for his actions.

NOTES

Anyone who sits in observance of a fast on Shabbat – הַיּוֹשֵׁב בְּתַעֲנִית בְּשַׁבָּת: Opinions differ as to whether this refers specifically to a fast that one fasts after experiencing a bad dream the night before, in order to repent and thereby prevent the actualization of that dream, which, according to the *ge'onim*, is permitted on Shabbat, or whether it is saying that even in other specific cases, one is permitted to fast on Shabbat in order to repent (see Rashba).

HALAKHA

Anyone who sits in observance of a fast on Shabbat – הַיּוֹשֵׁב בְּתַעֲנִית בְּשַׁבָּת: It is generally prohibited to fast on Shabbat beyond the sixth hour of the day, noon, although one may fast on Shabbat after having a bad dream. That is because through fasting, the decree against him will be repealed and the depression caused by the dream will dissipate, contributing to his sense of enjoyment on Shabbat. Nevertheless, one who does so must fast again on a weekday to atone for fasting on Shabbat and negating the primary mitzva of enjoyment on Shabbat (Rambam *Sefer Zemanim, Hilkhot Shabbat* 30:12, *Sefer Zemanim, Hilkhot Ta'anit* 1:12; *Shulḥan Arukh, Oraḥ Ḥayyim* 288:1, 4).

רַב פַּפָּא אָמַר, מֵהָכָא: ״וְאֶת רוּחִי אֶתֵּן בְּקִרְבְּכֶם וְעָשִׂיתִי אֵת אֲשֶׁר בְּחֻקַּי תֵּלֵכוּ״.

Rav Pappa said there is a clearer proof **from here: "And I will place My spirit within you and I will cause you to walk in My statutes,** and you will observe My decrees and do them" (Ezekiel 36:27).

וְאָמַר רַבִּי אֶלְעָזָר: מֹשֶׁה הֵטִיחַ דְּבָרִים כְּלַפֵּי מַעְלָה, שֶׁנֶּאֱמַר: ״וַיִּתְפַּלֵּל מֹשֶׁה אֶל ה׳״, אַל תִּקְרֵי ״אֶל״ ה׳ אֶלָּא ״עַל״ ה׳,

And Rabbi Elazar said: Moses also **spoke impertinently toward** God **on High, as it is stated** in the verse following the sin of those who murmured against God in the desert: **"And Moses prayed to the Lord** and the fire subsided" (Numbers 11:2), and this verse is interpreted homiletically: **Do not read to** [*el*] **the Lord,** but rather **onto** [*al*] **the Lord,**[N] which indicates that he spoke impertinently.

שֶׁכֵּן דְּבֵי רַבִּי אֱלִיעֶזֶר בֶּן יַעֲקֹב קוֹרִין לְאַלְפִי״ן עַיְינִי״ן וּלְעַיְינִי״ן אַלְפִי״ן.

The Gemara explains the basis for this interpretation: **As the Sages of the school of Rabbi Eliezer ben Ya'akov would** indiscriminately **read** ***alef*** **as** ***ayin*** **and** ***ayin*** **as** ***alef*** and in this case transforming *el* into *al*.[L]

דְּבֵי רַבִּי יַנַּאי אָמְרִי, מֵהָכָא: ״וְדִי זָהָב״,

The Sages of **the school of Rabbi Yannai,** however, **say** proof that Moses spoke impertinently toward God on High is derived **from here,** Moses' rebuke at the beginning of Deuteronomy: **"And Di Zahav"** (Deuteronomy 1:1). This is an entry in a list of places where Moses had spoken to Israel. As there was no place encountered by that name, it is interpreted as an allusion to another matter.

מַאי ״וְדִי זָהָב״? אָמְרִי דְּבֵי רַבִּי יַנַּאי, כָּךְ אָמַר מֹשֶׁה לִפְנֵי הַקָּדוֹשׁ בָּרוּךְ הוּא: רִבּוֹנוֹ שֶׁל עוֹלָם, בִּשְׁבִיל כֶּסֶף וְזָהָב שֶׁהִשְׁפַּעְתָּ לָהֶם לְיִשְׂרָאֵל עַד שֶׁאָמְרוּ דַּי – הוּא גָּרַם שֶׁעָשׂוּ אֶת הָעֵגֶל.

We must clarify: **What is** the meaning of **and Di Zahav?** The Sages of **the school of Rabbi Yannai said**[B] **that Moses said the following before the Holy One, Blessed be He,** to atone for Israel after the sin of the Golden Calf: **Master of the Universe, because of the gold and silver that you lavished upon Israel** during the exodus from Egypt **until they said enough** [*dai*]; it was this wealth **that caused** Israel **to make the** Golden **Calf.**

אָמְרִי דְּבֵי רַבִּי יַנַּאי: אֵין אֲרִי נוֹהֵם מִתּוֹךְ קוּפָּה שֶׁל תֶּבֶן אֶלָּא מִתּוֹךְ קוּפָּה שֶׁל בָּשָׂר.

Establishing a general moral principle, the Sages **the school of Rabbi Yannai said: A lion does not roar** standing **over a basket of straw** from which he derives no pleasure, **but** he roars standing **over a basket of meat,** as he only roars when satiated.

אָמַר רַבִּי אוֹשַׁעְיָא: מָשָׁל, לְאָדָם שֶׁהָיְתָה לוֹ פָּרָה כְּחוּשָׁה וּבַעֲלַת אֵבָרִים, הֶאֱכִילָהּ כַּרְשִׁינִין וְהָיְתָה מְבַעֶטֶת בּוֹ. אָמַר לָהּ: מִי גָּרַם לִיךְ שֶׁתְּהֵא מְבַעֶטֶת בִּי – אֶלָּא כַּרְשִׁינִין שֶׁהֶאֱכַלְתִּיךְ.

Similarly, **Rabbi Oshaya said:** This is **comparable to a person who had a lean, but large-limbed cow.** At one point, **he fed it lupines,** a choice food, **and** soon thereafter the cow **was kicking him. He said to** the cow: **Who caused** you to begin **kicking me if not the lupines I fed you?** Here, too, the sin was caused by an abundance of good.

אָמַר רַבִּי חִיָּיא בַּר אַבָּא אָמַר רַבִּי יוֹחָנָן: מָשָׁל, לְאָדָם אֶחָד שֶׁהָיָה לוֹ בֵּן, הִרְחִיצוֹ וְסָכוֹ, וְהֶאֱכִילוֹ וְהִשְׁקָהוּ, וְתָלָה לוֹ כִּיס עַל צַוָּארוֹ, וְהוֹשִׁיבוֹ עַל פֶּתַח שֶׁל זוֹנוֹת, מַה יַּעֲשֶׂה אוֹתוֹ הַבֵּן שֶׁלֹּא יֶחֱטָא?!

The Gemara offers another analogy: **Rabbi Ḥiyya bar Abba said** that **Rabbi Yoḥanan said:** This is **comparable to a person who had a son; he bathed him and anointed him** with oil, **fed him and gave him drink, and hung a purse** of money **around his neck.** Then, he **brought** his son **to the entrance of a brothel. What could the son do to avoid sinning?**

אָמַר רַב אַחָא בְּרֵיהּ דְּרַב הוּנָא אָמַר רַב שֵׁשֶׁת: הַיְינוּ דְּאָמְרִי אֱינָשֵׁי ״מְלֵי כְּרֵסֵיהּ זְנֵי בִּישֵׁי״, שֶׁנֶּאֱמַר: ״כְּמַרְעִיתָם וַיִּשְׂבָּעוּ שָׂבְעוּ וַיָּרָם לִבָּם עַל כֵּן שְׁכֵחוּנִי״; רַב נַחְמָן אָמַר, מֵהָכָא: ״וְרָם לְבָבֶךָ וְשָׁכַחְתָּ אֶת ה׳״; וְרַבָּנַן אָמְרִי, מֵהָכָא: ״וְאָכַל וְשָׂבַע וְדָשֵׁן וּפָנָה״;

On a similar note, **Rav Aḥa, son of Rav Huna, said** that **Rav Sheshet said: That is what people say** in a popular maxim: **Filling his stomach is a type of sin, as it is stated: "When they were fed and became full they were sated, and their hearts were lifted and they have forgotten Me"** (Hosea 13:6). **Rav Naḥman said:** This principle is derived not from the verse in Hosea, but **from here: "And your heart is lifted and you forget the Lord"** (Deuteronomy 8:14). **And the Rabbis say** that this principle is derived **from here: "And they will have eaten and been sated and fattened, and they will turn** to other gods" (Deuteronomy 31:20).

וְאִי בָּעֵית אֵימָא, מֵהָכָא: ״וַיִּשְׁמַן יְשׁוּרוּן וַיִּבְעָט״. אָמַר רַבִּי שְׁמוּאֵל בַּר נַחְמָנִי אָמַר רַבִּי יוֹנָתָן: מִנַּיִן שֶׁחָזַר הַקָּדוֹשׁ בָּרוּךְ הוּא וְהוֹדָה לוֹ לְמֹשֶׁה – שֶׁנֶּאֱמַר: ״וְכֶסֶף הִרְבֵּיתִי לָהֶם וְזָהָב עָשׂוּ לַבַּעַל״.

And if you wish, say instead that it is derived **from here: "And Jeshurun grew fat and kicked"** (Deuteronomy 32:15). **Rabbi Shmuel bar Naḥmani said that Rabbi Yonatan said: From where** in the Torah is it derived that **the Holy One, Blessed be He,** ultimately **conceded to Moses** that the reason for the sin of the Golden Calf was indeed the riches lavished upon Israel? **As it is stated: "And I gave them an abundance of silver and gold, which they used for the Ba'al"** (Hosea 2:10).

NOTES

Do not read to [*el*] the Lord, but rather onto [*al*] the Lord – אַל תִּקְרֵי ״אֶל״ ה׳ אֶלָּא ״עַל״ ה׳: The verse is interpreted in this manner because of its unusual formulation. The verse states that Moses prayed to the Lord, but the content of his prayer is not mentioned. Therefore, to the Lord is interpreted as onto the Lord, i.e., Moses became angry and spoke impertinently (*Penei Yehoshua*).

LANGUAGE

***Alef* into *ayin* – אַלְפִי״ן עַיְינִי״ן:** Interchange of guttural letters was very common in the Galilee. Nearly all guttural letters were obscured and swallowed when pronounced in this region, and were all ultimately pronounced the same. Some Sages utilize these interchanges, some of which appear in the Bible in certain roots, in the homiletic interpretation of the verses. The interchange of the *heh* and *ḥet* was most common; however *alef* and *ayin* were also interchanged. This was done not only by those in the study hall of Rabbi Eliezer ben Ya'akov, but also according to the approach of Rabbi Meir.

BACKGROUND

The Sages of the school of Rabbi…said – אָמְרִי דְּבֵי רַבִּי…: This unique expression is rooted in the practice of those generations. During the lifetimes of prominent Sages, the Sages' students would bond and form a close-knit community. During the particular teacher's lifetime, and often after his death as well, the Sages of a particular school would continue studying Torah together according to the approach espoused by their teacher. In the period of the *tanna'im*, this phenomenon was expressed with the phrase: It was taught in the school of Rabbi… in the sense that the *halakha* was taught in the study hall of a particular Sage. In the period of the *amora'im* or with regard to matters not incorporated in the Mishna, the phrase: The Sages of the school of Rabbi…said, was employed.

"וַיְדַבֵּר ה׳ אֶל מֹשֶׁה לֵךְ רֵד", מַאי "לֵךְ רֵד"? אָמַר רַבִּי אֶלְעָזָר, אָמַר לוֹ הַקָּדוֹשׁ בָּרוּךְ הוּא לְמֹשֶׁה: מֹשֶׁה, רֵד מִגְּדוּלָּתְךָ! כְּלוּם נָתַתִּי לְךָ גְּדוּלָּה אֶלָּא בִּשְׁבִיל יִשְׂרָאֵל, וְעַכְשָׁיו יִשְׂרָאֵל חָטְאוּ – אַתָּה לָמָּה לִי? מִיָּד תָּשַׁשׁ כּוֹחוֹ שֶׁל מֹשֶׁה, וְלֹא הָיָה לוֹ כֹּחַ לְדַבֵּר. וְכֵיוָן שֶׁאָמַר: "הֶרֶף מִמֶּנִּי וְאַשְׁמִידֵם", אָמַר מֹשֶׁה: דָּבָר זֶה תָּלוּי בִּי – מִיָּד עָמַד וְנִתְחַזֵּק בִּתְפִלָּה וּבִקֵּשׁ רַחֲמִים.

The Gemara elaborates upon additional aspects of the sin of the Golden Calf. It is stated: **"And the Lord said to Moses: Go and descend,** for your people whom you have lifted out of the land of Egypt have been corrupted" (Exodus 32:7). **What is the meaning of "go and descend"? Rabbi Elazar said: The Holy One, Blessed be He, said to Moses: Moses, descend from your greatness.**[N] **Isn't it only for the sake of Israel,** so that you may serve as an emissary, **that I granted you prominence; and now that Israel has sinned, why do I need you?** There is no need for an emissary. **Immediately, Moses' strength waned and he was powerless to speak** in defense of Israel. **And once** God **said** to Moses: **"Leave Me be, that I may destroy them"** (Deuteronomy 9:19), **Moses said** to himself: If God is telling me to let Him be, it must be because **this matter is dependent upon me. Immediately Moses stood and was strengthened in prayer, and asked** that God have **mercy** on the nation of Israel and forgive them for their transgression.

מָשָׁל, לְמֶלֶךְ שֶׁכָּעַס עַל בְּנוֹ וְהָיָה מַכֵּהוּ מַכָּה גְּדוֹלָה, וְהָיָה אוֹהֲבוֹ יוֹשֵׁב לְפָנָיו וּמִתְיָירֵא לוֹמַר לוֹ דָּבָר. אָמַר הַמֶּלֶךְ: אִלְמָלֵא אוֹהֲבִי זֶה שֶׁיּוֹשֵׁב לְפָנַי הֲרַגְתִּיךָ! אָמַר: דָּבָר זֶה תָּלוּי בִּי – מִיָּד עָמַד וְהִצִּילוֹ.

The Gemara says: This is **comparable to a king who became angry at his son** who had sinned against him, **and beat him,** administering a **severe beating.** At that moment, **a well-wisher** of the king **was sitting before him** and witnessed the entire event, **and was afraid to say anything to** the king about the excessive beating. Meanwhile, **the king said** to his son: **Were it not for this well-wisher of mine who is sitting before me, I would have killed you.** Upon hearing this, the king's friend **said** to himself: This is clearly a sign that **this matter,** rescuing the son from the hands of his father, **is dependent upon me. Immediately he stood and rescued him** from the king.

"וְעַתָּה הַנִּיחָה לִּי וְיִחַר אַפִּי בָהֶם וַאֲכַלֵּם וְאֶעֱשֶׂה אוֹתְךָ לְגוֹי גָּדוֹל" וגו׳ – אָמַר רַבִּי אַבָּהוּ: אִלְמָלֵא מִקְרָא כָּתוּב אִי אֶפְשָׁר לְאוֹמְרוֹ; מְלַמֵּד, שֶׁתְּפָסוֹ מֹשֶׁה לְהַקָּדוֹשׁ בָּרוּךְ הוּא כְּאָדָם שֶׁהוּא תּוֹפֵס אֶת חֲבֵירוֹ בְּבִגְדוֹ, וְאָמַר לְפָנָיו: רִבּוֹנוֹ שֶׁל עוֹלָם, אֵין אֲנִי מַנִּיחֲךָ עַד שֶׁתִּמְחוֹל וְתִסְלַח לָהֶם.

In an additional aspect of the sin of the Golden Calf, God told Moses: **"Now leave Me be, that My wrath will be enraged against them and I will consume them; and I will make of you a great nation"** (Exodus 32:10). Explaining this verse, **Rabbi Abbahu said: Were the verse not written** in this manner, **it would be impossible to utter** it, in deference to God. The phrase: Leave Me be, **teaches that Moses grabbed the Holy One, Blessed be He, as a person who grabs his friend by his garment** would, **and he said before Him: Master of the Universe, I will not leave You be until You forgive and pardon them.**

"וְאֶעֱשֶׂה אוֹתְךָ לְגוֹי גָּדוֹל" וגו׳ – אָמַר רַבִּי אֶלְעָזָר, אָמַר מֹשֶׁה לִפְנֵי הַקָּדוֹשׁ בָּרוּךְ הוּא: רִבּוֹנוֹ שֶׁל עוֹלָם, וּמָה כִּסֵּא שֶׁל שָׁלֹשׁ רַגְלַיִם אֵינוֹ יָכוֹל לַעֲמוֹד לְפָנֶיךָ בִּשְׁעַת כַּעַסְךָ, כִּסֵּא שֶׁל רֶגֶל אֶחָד עַל אַחַת כַּמָּה וְכַמָּה!

In the same verse, God promised Moses: **"And I will make of you a great nation."** What was Moses' response? **Rabbi Elazar said: Moses said before the Holy One, Blessed be He: Master of the Universe, if a chair with three legs,** the collective merit of the three forefathers, **is unable to stand before You in Your moment of wrath, all the more so** that **a chair with one leg,** my merit alone, will be unable to withstand your wrath.

וְלֹא עוֹד אֶלָּא שֶׁיֵּשׁ בִּי בּוֹשֶׁת פָּנִים מֵאֲבוֹתַי. עַכְשָׁיו יֹאמְרוּ: רְאוּ פַּרְנָס שֶׁהֶעֱמִיד עֲלֵיהֶם, בִּקֵּשׁ גְּדוּלָּה לְעַצְמוֹ וְלֹא בִּקֵּשׁ עֲלֵיהֶם רַחֲמִים.

Moreover, but I have a sense of **shame before my forefathers. Now** they will **say: See** this **leader that** God **placed over** Israel. **He requested greatness for himself but did not pray for** God to have **mercy upon them** in their troubled time.

"וַיְחַל מֹשֶׁה אֶת פְּנֵי ה׳" – אָמַר רַבִּי אֶלְעָזָר: מְלַמֵּד שֶׁעָמַד מֹשֶׁה בִּתְפִלָּה לִפְנֵי הַקָּדוֹשׁ בָּרוּךְ הוּא עַד שֶׁהֶחֱלָהוּ; וְרָבָא אָמַר: עַד שֶׁהֵפֵר לוֹ נִדְרוֹ, כְּתִיב הָכָא "וַיְחַל" וּכְתִיב הָתָם "לֹא יַחֵל דְּבָרוֹ", וְאָמַר מָר: הוּא אֵינוֹ מֵיחֵל אֲבָל אֲחֵרִים מְחַלִּין לוֹ.

The Torah continues: **"And Moses beseeched [*vayḥal*] before the Lord"** (Exodus 32:11). Many interpretations were given for this uncommon term, *vayḥal*: **Rabbi Elazar said:** It **teaches that Moses stood in prayer before the Holy One, Blessed be He, until it made him ill [*heḥelahu*]** from overexertion. **And Rava said:** Moses stood in prayer **until he nullified His vow,** as the term *vayḥal* alludes to nullification of an oath. **Here it is written *vayḥal*, and there** referring to vows, **it is written: "He shall not nullify [*lo yaḥel*] his word"** (Numbers 30:3). **And** with regard to vows, **the Master said: He** who vowed **cannot nullify** his vow, **but others,** the court, **can nullify** his vow **for him.** Here, it is as if Moses nullified the Lord's vow to destroy Israel.

וּשְׁמוּאֵל אָמַר: מְלַמֵּד שֶׁמָּסַר עַצְמוֹ לְמִיתָה עֲלֵיהֶם, שֶׁנֶּאֱמַר: "וְאִם אַיִן מְחֵנִי נָא מִסִּפְרְךָ".

And Shmuel said: The term *vayḥal* **teaches that** Moses **gave his life,** from the term *ḥalal*, a dead person, **for** Israel, **as it is stated: "And if not, erase me, please, from Your book"** (Exodus 32:32).

אָמַר רָבָא אָמַר רַב יִצְחָק: מְלַמֵּד שֶׁהֶחֱלָה עֲלֵיהֶם מִדַּת רַחֲמִים.

Rava, also interpreting this verse, **said** that **Rav Yitzḥak said:** The term *vayḥal* **teaches that he caused the Divine Attribute of Mercy to take effect [*heḥela*] upon them.**

NOTES

Go and descend…descend from your greatness – לֵךְ רֵד...רֵד מִגְּדוּלָּתְךָ: The phrase, go and descend, is not interpreted as a command to literally descend the mountain, but as a symbolic expression. As God did not tell Moses what to do once he descended the mountain, apparently, this is a statement removing Moses from his position of prominence (Maharsha). Indeed, that seems to be the case, as, after commanding him to descend, God continued to speak to Moses, indicating that go and descend referred to descent from prominence, not from the mountain (*Tziyyun LeNefesh Ḥayya*).

NOTES

His strength weakened like a female – תָּשַׁשׁ כֹּחוֹ כִּנְקֵבָה: God's ability is one of the manifestations of His essence. Consequently, when it appears that God is incapable of performing a certain action, it is ostensibly due to a diminution in His power; His strength weakened like a female. Therefore, when God forgave the people in response to Moses' prayers, it was affirmation that the Lord does, in fact, maintain and rule all worlds. That is the subtext of God's reaction: You have given Me life with your words (Rav Nissim Gaon, Rashba).

וְרַבָּנַן אָמְרִי: מְלַמֵּד שֶׁאָמַר מֹשֶׁה לִפְנֵי הַקָּדוֹשׁ בָּרוּךְ הוּא: רִבּוֹנוֹ שֶׁל עוֹלָם, חוּלִּין הוּא לְךָ מֵעֲשׂוֹת כַּדָּבָר הַזֶּה.

And the Rabbis say that this term constitutes the essence of Moses' claim: **It teaches that Moses said before the Holy One Blessed be He: It is a sacrilege [*ḥullin*] for You to do something like this.**

״וַיְחַל מֹשֶׁה אֶת פְּנֵי ה׳״. תַּנְיָא, רַבִּי אֱלִיעֶזֶר הַגָּדוֹל אוֹמֵר: מְלַמֵּד שֶׁעָמַד מֹשֶׁה בִּתְפִלָּה לִפְנֵי הַקָּדוֹשׁ בָּרוּךְ הוּא עַד שֶׁאֲחָזַתּוּ אֲחִילוּ. מַאי אֲחִילוּ? אָמַר רַבִּי אֶלְעָזָר: אֵשׁ שֶׁל עֲצָמוֹת. מַאי אֵשׁ שֶׁל עֲצָמוֹת? אָמַר אַבַּיֵי: אֶשְׁתָּא דְּגַרְמֵי.

And another interpretation of the verse, **"And Moses beseeched [*vayḥal*] before the Lord." It was taught** in a *baraita*: **Rabbi Eliezer the Great says: This** term **teaches that Moses stood in prayer until he was overcome by *aḥilu*.** Even the Sages were unfamiliar with this term. Therefore, the Gemara asks: **What is** the meaning of ***aḥilu*? Rabbi Elazar,** an *amora* of Eretz Yisrael, **said** that *aḥilu* is **fire in the bones.** However, this expression was familiar in Eretz Yisrael but not in Babylonia. They asked in Babylonia: **What is** the disease that they called **fire of the bones? Abaye said** that is a disease known in Babylonia as ***eshta degarmei*,** which in Aramaic means **fire of the bones;** in other words, a fever.

״זְכֹר לְאַבְרָהָם לְיִצְחָק וּלְיִשְׂרָאֵל עֲבָדֶיךָ אֲשֶׁר נִשְׁבַּעְתָּ לָהֶם בָּךְ״. מַאי ״בָּךְ״ – אָמַר רַבִּי אֶלְעָזָר: אָמַר מֹשֶׁה לִפְנֵי הַקָּדוֹשׁ בָּרוּךְ הוּא: רִבּוֹנוֹ שֶׁל עוֹלָם, אִלְמָלֵא נִשְׁבַּעְתָּ לָהֶם בַּשָּׁמַיִם וּבָאָרֶץ הָיִיתִי אוֹמֵר: כְּשֵׁם שֶׁשָּׁמַיִם וָאָרֶץ בְּטֵלִים – כָּךְ שְׁבוּעָתְךָ בְּטֵלָה. וְעַכְשָׁו שֶׁנִּשְׁבַּעְתָּ לָהֶם בְּשִׁמְךָ הַגָּדוֹל, מַה שִּׁמְךָ הַגָּדוֹל חַי וְקַיָּים לְעוֹלָם וּלְעוֹלְמֵי עוֹלָמִים – כָּךְ שְׁבוּעָתְךָ קַיֶּימֶת לְעוֹלָם וּלְעוֹלְמֵי עוֹלָמִים.

As Moses continues his prayer, he says: **"Remember Abraham, Isaac and Israel Your servants, to whom You swore in Your name"** (Exodus 32:13). **What is** the meaning of **in Your name? Rabbi Elazar said: Moses said before the Holy One, Blessed be He: Master of the Universe, had You sworn to them by the heavens and the earth, I would say: Just as the heavens and the earth will** ultimately **be no more, so too Your oath will be null and void. Now that You swore to them by Your great name, just as Your name lives and stands for all eternity, so too does Your oath live and stand for all eternity.**

״וַתְּדַבֵּר אֲלֵיהֶם אַרְבֶּה אֶת זַרְעֲכֶם כְּכוֹכְבֵי הַשָּׁמַיִם וְכָל הָאָרֶץ הַזֹּאת אֲשֶׁר אָמַרְתִּי״. הַאי ״אֲשֶׁר אָמַרְתִּי״? ״אֲשֶׁר אָמַרְתָּ״ מִיבְּעֵי לֵיהּ!

In this verse, Moses continues: **"And You said to them: I will make your offspring as numerous as the stars of heaven, and all this land of which I have spoken** I will give to your offspring that they shall inherit it forever." The Gemara clarifies a puzzling phrase in this verse. **That** phrase **of which I have spoken, it should** have said: **Of which You have spoken,** as Moses is referring to God's promise to the forefathers.

אָמַר רַבִּי אֶלְעָזָר: עַד כָּאן דִּבְרֵי תַלְמִיד, מִכָּאן וְאֵילָךְ – דִּבְרֵי הָרַב. וְרַבִּי שְׁמוּאֵל בַּר נַחְמָנִי אָמַר: אֵלּוּ וָאֵלּוּ דִּבְרֵי תַלְמִיד, אֶלָּא כָּךְ אָמַר מֹשֶׁה לִפְנֵי הַקָּדוֹשׁ בָּרוּךְ הוּא: רִבּוֹנוֹ שֶׁל עוֹלָם, דְּבָרִים שֶׁאָמַרְתָּ לִי ״לֵךְ אֱמוֹר לָהֶם לְיִשְׂרָאֵל״ בִּשְׁמִי, הָלַכְתִּי וְאָמַרְתִּי לָהֶם בְּשִׁמְךָ, עַכְשָׁו מָה אֲנִי אוֹמֵר לָהֶם?

Rabbi Elazar said: To this point, the verse cites **the words of the student,** Moses; **from this point,** and all this land of which I have spoken, the verse cites **the words of the Master,** God. **And Rabbi Shmuel bar Naḥmani said: These and those are the words of the student;** Moses spoke the entire verse. **Rather, Moses said before the Holy One, Blessed be He: Master of the Universe, those matters which You told me to go and say to Israel in My name, I went and told** it **to them in Your name.** I have already told Israel of God's promise to the forefathers. **Now what do I say to them?**

״מִבִּלְתִּי יְכֹלֶת ה׳, ״יָכוֹל ה׳״ מִיבְּעֵי לֵיהּ!

The Gemara moves to a discussion of additional prayers offered by Moses. Moses said that if God fails to bring the Jewish people into Eretz Yisrael, the nations of the world will say: **"The Lord did not have the ability [*yekholet*]** to bring this people into the land which He swore to them, and He killed them in the desert" (Numbers 14:16). The Gemara examines this verse closely: The verse should not have utilized the term *yekholet*, an abstract feminine noun, but rather, **it should have said: "The Lord** was not **able [*yakhol*],"** a masculine verb.

אָמַר רַבִּי אֶלְעָזָר, אָמַר מֹשֶׁה לִפְנֵי הַקָּדוֹשׁ בָּרוּךְ הוּא: רִבּוֹנוֹ שֶׁל עוֹלָם, עַכְשָׁיו יֹאמְרוּ אוּמּוֹת הָעוֹלָם: תָּשַׁשׁ כֹּחוֹ כִּנְקֵבָה וְאֵינוֹ יָכוֹל לְהַצִּיל. אָמַר הַקָּדוֹשׁ בָּרוּךְ הוּא לְמֹשֶׁה: וַהֲלֹא כְּבָר רָאוּ נִסִּים וּגְבוּרוֹת שֶׁעָשִׂיתִי לָהֶם עַל הַיָּם! – אָמַר לְפָנָיו: רִבּוֹנוֹ שֶׁל עוֹלָם, עֲדַיִין יֵשׁ לָהֶם לוֹמַר: לְמֶלֶךְ אֶחָד – יָכוֹל לַעֲמוֹד, לִשְׁלֹשִׁים וְאֶחָד מְלָכִים – אֵינוֹ יָכוֹל לַעֲמוֹד.

Rabbi Elazar said: Moses phrased it that way because he **said before the Holy One, Blessed be He: Master of the Universe, now the nations of the world will say that His strength weakened like a female**[N] **and He is unable to rescue** the nation of Israel. **The Holy One, Blessed be He, said to Moses: And did** the nations of the world **not already see the miracles and the mighty acts that I performed on behalf of** Israel **at the Red Sea?** Moses **said before Him: Master of the Universe, they can still say:** The Lord **can stand up to a single king** like Pharaoh and defeat him, but **He is unable stand up to the thirty-one kings** in the land of Canaan.

אָמַר רַבִּי יוֹחָנָן: מִנַּיִן שֶׁחָזַר הַקָּדוֹשׁ בָּרוּךְ הוּא וְהוֹדָה לוֹ לְמֹשֶׁה – שֶׁנֶּאֱמַר: ״וַיֹּאמֶר ה׳ סָלַחְתִּי כִּדְבָרֶךָ״. תָּנֵי דְּבֵי רַבִּי יִשְׁמָעֵאל: כִּדְבָרֶיךָ עֲתִידִים אוּמּוֹת הָעוֹלָם לוֹמַר כֵּן.

Rabbi Yoḥanan said: From where is it derived that **the Holy One, Blessed be He, ultimately conceded to Moses? As it is said: "And the Lord said: I have forgiven according to your word"** (Numbers 14:20). The Sages **of the school of Rabbi Yishmael taught: According to your word,** it will be, as indeed **in the future the nations of the world will say this.**

אַשְׁרֵי תַּלְמִיד שֶׁרַבּוֹ מוֹדֶה לוֹ.

The Gemara concludes: **Happy is the student whose teacher concedes to him** as the Lord conceded to Moses.

״וְאוּלָם חַי אָנִי״. אָמַר רָבָא אָמַר רַב יִצְחָק: מְלַמֵּד, שֶׁאָמַר לוֹ הַקָּדוֹשׁ בָּרוּךְ הוּא לְמֹשֶׁה: מֹשֶׁה, הֶחֱיִיתַנִי בִּדְבָרֶיךָ.

Explaining the next verse, "**Nevertheless, as I live,** and the glory of the Lord fills the entire world" (Numbers 14:21), **Rava said** that **Rav Yitzḥak said:** This **teaches** that **the Holy One, Blessed be He, said to Moses: Moses, you have given Me life with your words.** I am happy that on account of your arguments, I will forgive Israel.

דָּרַשׁ רַבִּי שִׂמְלַאי: לְעוֹלָם יְסַדֵּר אָדָם שִׁבְחוֹ שֶׁל הַקָּדוֹשׁ בָּרוּךְ הוּא וְאַחַר כָּךְ יִתְפַּלֵּל. מְנָלַן – מִמֹּשֶׁה, דִּכְתִיב: ״וָאֶתְחַנַּן אֶל ה׳ בָּעֵת הַהִיא״; וּכְתִיב ״ה׳ אֱלֹהִים אַתָּה הַחִלּוֹתָ לְהַרְאוֹת אֶת עַבְדְּךָ אֶת גָּדְלְךָ וְאֶת יָדְךָ הַחֲזָקָה אֲשֶׁר מִי אֵל בַּשָּׁמַיִם וּבָאָרֶץ אֲשֶׁר יַעֲשֶׂה כְמַעֲשֶׂיךָ וְכִגְבוּרוֹתֶיךָ״, וּכְתִיב בַּתְרֵיהּ ״אֶעְבְּרָה נָּא וְאֶרְאֶה אֶת הָאָרֶץ הַטּוֹבָה וגו׳״.

Based on Moses' prayers, **Rabbi Simlai taught: One should always set forth praise of the Holy One, Blessed be He, and then pray** for his own needs.[H] **From where do we** derive that one should conduct himself in this manner? **From Moses, as it is written** in his prayer: **"And I beseeched the Lord at that time"** (Deuteronomy 3:23). **And** immediately afterward in his prayer, **it is written: "Lord, God, You have begun to show Your servant Your greatness and Your strong hand, for what God is there in the heavens or on earth who can perform deeds such as Yours and Your might"** (Deuteronomy 3:24)? Here, Moses began with praise of God, **and it is** only **thereafter** that **it is written: "Please, let me pass over and see the good land** that is beyond the Jordan, that good hill country and the Lebanon" (Deuteronomy 3:25). Only after his praise did Moses make his personal request.

סִימָן: מַעֲשִׂי״ם, צְדָקָ״ה, קָרְבָּ״ן, כֹּהֵ״ן, תַּעֲנִי״ת, מִנְעָ״ל, בַּרְזֶ״ל.

The Gemara prefaces the next discourse with **a mnemonic symbol:**[B] **Deeds, charity, offering, priest, fast, shoe, iron.**

HALAKHA

One should always set forth praise of the Holy One, Blessed be He, and then pray for his own needs – לְעוֹלָם יְסַדֵּר אָדָם שִׁבְחוֹ שֶׁל הַקָּדוֹשׁ בָּרוּךְ הוּא וְאַחַר כָּךְ יִתְפַּלֵּל: One who prays must first praise God, and only then request his own needs. All prayers are formulated in that manner (Rambam *Sefer Ahava*, *Hilkhot Tefilla* 1:2).

BACKGROUND

A mnemonic symbol – סִימָן: Because the Talmud was studied orally for many generations, mnemonic devices were necessary to remember a series of *halakhot* and the order in which they were taught.

Perek **V**
Daf **32** Amud **b**

אָמַר רַבִּי אֶלְעָזָר: גְּדוֹלָה תְּפִלָּה יוֹתֵר מִמַּעֲשִׂים טוֹבִים. שֶׁאֵין לְךָ גָּדוֹל בְּמַעֲשִׂים טוֹבִים יוֹתֵר מִמֹּשֶׁה רַבֵּינוּ, אַף עַל פִּי כֵן לֹא נַעֲנָה אֶלָּא בִּתְפִלָּה, שֶׁנֶּאֱמַר: ״אַל תּוֹסֶף דַּבֵּר אֵלַי״, וְסָמִיךְ לֵיהּ ״עֲלֵה רֹאשׁ הַפִּסְגָּה״.

Rabbi Elazar said: This story proves that **prayer is greater than good deeds** without prayer (*Tosafot*), as **there was none greater in** the performance of **good deeds than Moses our teacher; nevertheless, his request was granted,** albeit in a limited manner, in his request to enter Eretz Yisrael, **only through prayer,** when God permitted him to climb the mountain and look out over the land. **As,** initially **it is stated: "Speak no more to Me," juxtaposed to which is: "Go up to the summit of the mountain."**

וְאָמַר רַבִּי אֶלְעָזָר: גְּדוֹלָה תַּעֲנִית יוֹתֵר מִן הַצְּדָקָה. מַאי טַעְמָא – זֶה בְּגוּפוֹ וְזֶה בְּמָמוֹנוֹ.

After comparing and contrasting prayer and good deeds, the Gemara explores another comparison. **Rabbi Elazar said: A fast is greater than charity. What is the reason** that fasting is greater? Because a fast **is** a mitzva performed **with one's body** as he afflicts himself, **while** charity **is** performed only **with one's money.**

וְאָמַר רַבִּי אֶלְעָזָר: גְּדוֹלָה תְּפִלָּה יוֹתֵר מִן הַקָּרְבָּנוֹת, שֶׁנֶּאֱמַר ״לָמָּה לִּי רֹב זִבְחֵיכֶם״, וּכְתִיב ״וּבְפָרִשְׂכֶם כַּפֵּיכֶם״.

In another comparison, **Rabbi Elazar said: Prayer is greater than sacrifices, as it is stated: "To what purpose is the multitude of your sacrifices to Me,** says the Lord. I am full of the burnt-offerings of rams and the fat of fed beasts; I do not desire the blood of bulls and sheep and goats" (Isaiah 1:11). **And** several verses later **it is written: "And when you spread forth your hands** I will hide My eyes from you, and even if you increase your prayer, I will not hear; your hands are full of blood" (Isaiah 1:15). Not only Israel's sacrifices, but even their prayers, which are on a higher spiritual level, will not be accepted.

אָמַר רַבִּי יוֹחָנָן: כׇּל כֹּהֵן שֶׁהָרַג אֶת הַנֶּפֶשׁ לֹא יִשָּׂא אֶת כַּפָּיו, שֶׁנֶּאֱמַר ״יְדֵיכֶם דָּמִים מָלֵאוּ״.

Speaking of that verse in Isaiah, the Gemara cites that **Rabbi Yoḥanan said: Any priest who killed a person**[H] **may not lift his hands** in the Priestly Blessing[B] **as it is stated:** "And when you spread forth your hands I will hide My eyes from you… **your hands are full of blood."** Here we see that the Priestly Blessing, performed with hands spread forth, is not accepted when performed by priests whose "hands are full of blood."

HALAKHA

A priest who killed a person – כֹּהֵן שֶׁהָרַג אֶת הַנֶּפֶשׁ: A priest who killed a person, even unwittingly, may not recite the Priestly Blessing. If he did so under duress, he is permitted to recite it (*Be'er Heitev*). Some say that even if he repents, the prohibition remains in effect, while others are lenient and allow him to recite the Priestly Blessing after repenting (Rema; Rambam *Sefer Ahava*, *Hilkhot Tefilla* 15:3; *Shulḥan Arukh*, *Oraḥ Ḥayyim* 128:35).

BACKGROUND

The Priestly Blessing – בִּרְכַּת כֹּהֲנִים: The three verses of blessing (Numbers 6:24–26) with which the priests bless the congregation in the synagogue. The Priestly Blessing is recited between the blessings of thanksgiving and peace, the final two blessings in the repetition of the *Amida* prayer. As the priests turn to face the congregation to recite the Priestly Blessing, they first recite a blessing acknowledging the holiness of the priestly line and their responsibility to bless the people in a spirit of love. While reciting the Priestly Blessing, the priests lift their hands according to the traditional rite (known as *nesiat kappayim*). In most places in Eretz Yisrael, the Priestly Blessing is recited by the priests during the repetition of every morning and additional prayer. In the Diaspora, however, there is a long established Ashkenazi practice of reciting it only during the additional prayer on Festivals.

וְאָמַר רַבִּי אֶלְעָזָר: מִיּוֹם שֶׁחָרַב בֵּית הַמִּקְדָּשׁ נִנְעֲלוּ שַׁעֲרֵי תְפִלָּה, שֶׁנֶּאֱמַר: ״גַּם כִּי אֶזְעַק וַאֲשַׁוֵּעַ שָׂתַם תְּפִלָּתִי״, וְאַף עַל פִּי שֶׁשַּׁעֲרֵי תְפִילָּה נִנְעֲלוּ שַׁעֲרֵי דִמְעָה לֹא נִנְעֲלוּ, שֶׁנֶּאֱמַר: ״שִׁמְעָה תְפִלָּתִי ה׳ וְשַׁוְעָתִי הַאֲזִינָה אֶל דִּמְעָתִי אַל תֶּחֱרַשׁ״.

On the subject of prayer, **Rabbi Elazar also said: Since the day the Temple was destroyed the gates of prayer were locked** and prayer is not accepted as it once was, **as it is said** in lamentation of the Temple's destruction: **"Though I plead and call out, He shuts out my prayer"** (Lamentations 3:8). Yet, **despite** the fact **that the gates of prayer were locked** with the destruction of the Temple, **the gates of tears were not locked,** and one who cries before God may rest assured that his prayers will be answered, **as it is stated: "Hear my prayer, Lord, and give ear to my pleading, keep not silence at my tears"** (Psalms 39:13). Since this prayer is a request that God should pay heed to the tears of one who is praying, he is certain that at least the gates of tears are not locked.

רָבָא לֹא גָּזַר תַּעֲנִיתָא בְּיוֹמָא דְּעֵיבָא מִשּׁוּם שֶׁנֶּאֱמַר ״סַכֹּתָה בֶעָנָן לָךְ מֵעֲבוֹר תְּפִלָּה״.

With regard to the locking of the gates of prayer, the Gemara relates that **Rava did not decree a fast on a cloudy day because it is stated: "You have covered Yourself in a cloud, through which prayer cannot pass"** (Lamentations 3:44). The verse indicates that clouds are a bad omen, indicating that God has averted His face (Rav Hai Gaon).

וְאָמַר רַבִּי אֶלְעָזָר: מִיּוֹם שֶׁחָרַב בֵּית הַמִּקְדָּשׁ נִפְסְקָה חוֹמַת בַּרְזֶל בֵּין יִשְׂרָאֵל לַאֲבִיהֶם שֶׁבַּשָּׁמַיִם, שֶׁנֶּאֱמַר ״וְאַתָּה קַח לְךָ מַחֲבַת בַּרְזֶל וְנָתַתָּ אוֹתָהּ קִיר בַּרְזֶל בֵּינְךָ וּבֵין הָעִיר״.

And Rabbi Elazar said: Since the day the Temple was destroyed an iron wall separates Israel from their Father in heaven, as it is stated to the prophet Ezekiel, instructing him to symbolize that separation: **"And take for yourself an iron griddle, and set it as an iron wall between yourself and the city…** it will be a sign for the house of Israel" (Ezekiel 4:3).

אָמַר רַבִּי חָנִין אָמַר רַבִּי חֲנִינָא: כָּל הַמַּאֲרִיךְ בִּתְפִלָּתוֹ אֵין תְּפִלָּתוֹ חוֹזֶרֶת רֵיקָם. מְנָא לָן – מִמֹּשֶׁה רַבֵּינוּ, שֶׁנֶּאֱמַר: ״וָאֶתְפַּלֵּל אֶל ה׳״, וּכְתִיב בַּתְרֵיהּ: ״וַיִּשְׁמַע ה׳ אֵלַי גַּם בַּפַּעַם הַהִיא״.

The Gemara cites other statements in praise of prayer: **Rabbi Ḥanin said** that **Rabbi Ḥanina said: Anyone who prolongs his prayer is** assured that **his prayer does not return unanswered;** it will surely be accepted. **From where do we** derive this? **From Moses our teacher, as it is stated** that Moses said: "So I fell down before the Lord the forty days and forty nights that I fell down; **and I prayed to the Lord"** (Deuteronomy 9:26–27), **and it is written thereafter: "And the Lord heard me that time as well,** the Lord would not destroy you" (Deuteronomy 10:10).

אִינִי?! וְהָא אָמַר רַבִּי חִיָּיא בַּר אַבָּא אָמַר רַבִּי יוֹחָנָן: כָּל הַמַּאֲרִיךְ בִּתְפִילָּתוֹ וּמְעַיֵּין בָּהּ – סוֹף בָּא לִידֵי כְּאֵב לֵב, שֶׁנֶּאֱמַר: ״תּוֹחֶלֶת מְמֻשָּׁכָה מַחֲלָה לֵב״, מַאי תַּקַּנְתֵּיהּ – יַעֲסוֹק בַּתּוֹרָה, שֶׁנֶּאֱמַר: ״וְעֵץ חַיִּים תַּאֲוָה בָאָה״, וְאֵין עֵץ חַיִּים אֶלָּא תּוֹרָה, שֶׁנֶּאֱמַר: ״עֵץ חַיִּים הִיא לַמַּחֲזִיקִים בָּהּ״! – לָא קַשְׁיָא, הָא – דְּמַאֲרִיךְ וּמְעַיֵּין בָּהּ, הָא – דְּמַאֲרִיךְ וְלֹא מְעַיֵּין בָּהּ.

The Gemara raises an objection: **Is that so? Didn't Rabbi Ḥiyya bar Abba** say that **Rabbi Yoḥanan said: Anyone who prolongs his prayer and expects it to be answered, will ultimately come to heartache,** as it will not be answered. **As it is stated: "Hope deferred makes the heart sick"** (Proverbs 13:12). **And what is the remedy** for one afflicted with that illness? He should **engage in Torah** study, **as it is stated: "But desire fulfilled is the tree of life"** (Proverbs 13:12), **and tree of life is nothing other than Torah, as it is stated: "It is a tree of life to those who hold fast to it,** and those who support it are joyous" (Proverbs 3:18). This is **not difficult. This,** Rabbi Ḥiyya bar Abba's statement that one will suffer heartache refers to one **who prolongs** his prayer **and expects it to be answered; that,** Rabbi Ḥanin's statement that one who prolongs his prayer is praiseworthy refers to **one who prolongs his prayer and** does **not expect it to be answered.**

אָמַר רַבִּי חָמָא בְּרַבִּי חֲנִינָא: אִם רָאָה אָדָם שֶׁהִתְפַּלֵּל וְלֹא נַעֲנָה יַחֲזוֹר וְיִתְפַּלֵּל, שֶׁנֶּאֱמַר: ״קַוֵּה אֶל ה׳ חֲזַק וְיַאֲמֵץ לִבֶּךָ וְקַוֵּה אֶל ה׳״.

On a similar note, **Rabbi Ḥama, son of Rabbi Ḥanina, said: A person who prayed and saw that he was not answered,** should **pray again, as it is stated: "Hope in the Lord, strengthen yourself, let your heart take courage, and hope in the Lord"** (Psalms 27:14). One should turn to God with hope, and if necessary turn to God again with hope.

תָּנוּ רַבָּנַן, אַרְבָּעָה צְרִיכִין חִזּוּק, וְאֵלּוּ הֵן: תּוֹרָה, וּמַעֲשִׂים טוֹבִים, תְּפִלָּה וְדֶרֶךְ אֶרֶץ.

Connected to the emphasis on the need to bolster one's effort in prayer, the Gemara notes that **the Sages taught** in a *baraita*: **Four** things **require bolstering,** constant effort to improve, **and they are: Torah, good deeds, prayer, and occupation.**

תּוֹרָה וּמַעֲשִׂים טוֹבִים מִנַּיִן – שֶׁנֶּאֱמַר ״רַק חֲזַק וֶאֱמַץ מְאֹד לִשְׁמֹר וְלַעֲשׂוֹת כְּכָל הַתּוֹרָה״. ״חֲזַק״ – בַּתּוֹרָה, ״וֶאֱמַץ״ – בְּמַעֲשִׂים טוֹבִים.

For each of these, a biblical proof is cited: **From where** is it derived that **Torah and good deeds** require bolstering? **As it is stated** in the instruction to Joshua: **"Only be strong and be extremely courageous, observe and do all of the Torah** that Moses My servant commanded you; do not deviate to the right or to the left, that you may succeed wherever you go" (Joshua 1:7). In this verse, observe refers to Torah study and do refers to good deeds (Maharsha); the apparently repetitive language is not extraneous. The Gemara derives: **Be strong in Torah and be courageous in good deeds.**

תפלה מנין – שנאמר "קוה אל ה' חזק ויאמץ לבך וקוה אל ה'";

From where is it derived that **prayer** requires bolstering? **As it is said: "Hope in the Lord, strengthen yourself, let your heart take courage, and hope in the Lord."**

דרך ארץ מנין – שנאמר "חזק ונתחזק בעד עמנו" וגו'.

From where is it derived that **occupation** requires bolstering? **As it is stated: "Be strong and we will be strong for the sake of our nation** and for the cities of our God" (II Samuel 10:12). All of one's labor requires bolstering.

"ותאמר ציון עזבני ה' וה' שכחני". היינו עזובה היינו שכוחה! אמר ריש לקיש, אמרה כנסת ישראל לפני הקדוש ברוך הוא: רבונו של עולם, אדם נושא אשה על אשתו ראשונה – זוכר מעשה הראשונה, אתה עזבתני ושכחתני.

The Gemara cites a midrash on the following verse from Isaiah, relating to the sin of the Golden Calf and Moses' supplication for forgiveness: **"But Zion said: The Lord has forsaken me and the Lord has forgotten me.** Can a woman forget her suckling baby, that she would not have compassion for the child of her womb? These may forget, but you I will not forget" (Isaiah 49:14–15). The Gemara seeks to clarify: **Forsaken is the same as forgotten.** They are synonymous; why repeat the same idea twice? **Reish Lakish said: The community of Israel said before the Holy One, Blessed be He: Master of the Universe,** even when **a man marries** a second **wife after his first wife, he** certainly **recalls the deeds of his first** wife. Yet **You have** not only **forsaken me,** but You have **forgotten me** as well.

אמר לה הקדוש ברוך הוא: בתי, שנים עשר מזלות בראתי ברקיע ועל כל מזל ומזל בראתי לו שלשים חיל ועל כל חיל וחיל בראתי לו שלשים לגיון, ועל כל לגיון ולגיון בראתי לו שלשים רהטון, ועל כל רהטון ורהטון בראתי לו שלשים קרטון, ועל כל קרטון וקרטון בראתי לו שלשים גסטרא, ועל כל גסטרא וגסטרא תליתי בו שלש מאות וששים וחמשה אלפי רבוא כוכבים כנגד ימות החמה – וכולן לא בראתי אלא בשבילך, ואת אמרת עזבתני ושכחתני?!

The Holy One, Blessed be He, said to Israel: **My daughter, I created twelve constellations in the firmament,**[B] **and for each and every constellation I have created thirty armies, and for each and every army I have created thirty legions** [*ligyon*],[L] **and for each and every legion I have created thirty infantry division leaders** [*rahaton*],[L] **and for each and every infantry division leader I have created thirty military camp leaders** [*karton*],[L] **and for each and every military camp leader I have created thirty leaders of forts** [*gastera*],[L] **and on each and every leader of a fort I have hung three hundred and sixty-five thousand stars corresponding to the days of the solar year. And all of them I have created only for your sake; and you said** the Lord **has forsaken me and** the Lord **has forgotten me?**

"התשכח אשה עולה", אמר הקדוש ברוך הוא: כלום אשכח עולות אילים ופטרי רחמים שהקרבת לפני במדבר?! אמרה לפניו: רבונו של עולם, הואיל ואין שכחה לפני כסא כבודך שמא לא תשכח לי מעשה העגל? – אמר לה: "גם אלה תשכחנה".

The verse goes on to say: **"Can a woman forget her suckling baby,** that she would not have compassion for the child of her womb? These may forget, but you I will not forget." The meaning of this verse is that **the Holy One, Blessed be He, said** to the community of Israel: **Have I forgotten the ram offerings and firstborn animals that you offered before Me in the desert?** The community of Israel **replied to Him: Master of the Universe, since there is no forgetfulness before the Throne of Your Glory, perhaps you will not forget my sin of the Golden Calf?** God **responded to** Israel: **"These** [*elu*] **too shall be forgotten."** "These" is a reference to the sin of the Golden Calf, regarding which Israel said: "These [*elu*] are your gods."

אמרה לפניו: רבונו של עולם, הואיל ויש שכחה לפני כסא כבודך, שמא תשכח לי מעשה סיני? – אמר לה: "ואנכי לא אשכחך".

The community of Israel **said before Him: Master of the Universe, since there is forgetfulness before the Throne of Your Glory, perhaps You will** also **forget the events** revolving around the revelation at **Sinai?** God **said to Israel: I** [*anokhi*] **will not forget you** the revelation at Sinai, which began with: "I [*anokhi*] am the Lord your God."

והיינו דאמר רבי אלעזר אמר רב אושעיא: מאי דכתיב "גם אלה תשכחנה" – זה מעשה העגל, "ואנכי לא אשכחך" – זה מעשה סיני.

The Gemara notes: **That** is what **Rabbi Elazar said** that **Rav Oshaya said: What is** the meaning of that which is **written: "These too will be forgotten"? That is the sin of the Golden Calf.** And what is the meaning of **I will not forget you? Those are the events** that transpired at **Sinai.**

"חסידים הראשונים היו שוהין שעה אחת".

We learned in the mishna that **the early** generations of **pious** men **would wait one hour** in order to achieve the solemn frame of mind appropriate for prayer.

מנא הני מילי? אמר רבי יהושע בן לוי: אמר קרא "אשרי יושבי ביתך".

The Gemara asks: **From where are these matters** derived? **Rabbi Yehoshua ben Levi said:** This is alluded to when **the verse states: "Happy are those who dwell in Your House"** (Psalms 84:5), immediately after which it is said: "They will yet praise You, Selah."

BACKGROUND

Constellations in the firmament – צבא השמים: The list of constellations and stars and their details is based on the imagery of the various units of the Roman army. One must take into account that the specific order appears differently in different versions of the Talmud, and the meaning of the various terms cannot be easily determined.

LANGUAGE

Legion [*ligyon*] **– לגיון:** Based on the Latin legio/legionis. It is a legion, the largest Roman unit.

Infantry division leader [*rahaton*] **– רהטון:** The source of this word is unclear. Some attribute it to the Greek **ἀριθμός**, *arithmos*, which is literally translated as number and refers to a military unit of indeterminate size, perhaps part of a fortification. The structure of the Roman army consisted of armies, which were divided into one or more legions and their auxiliary forces. The legion, which numbered between three and six thousand soldiers, was divided into ten divisions, which were further divided into up to six camps. The Gemara's description of the heavenly hosts is influenced by the division of the large armies at the time.

Military camp leader [*karton*] **– קרטון:** This word is based on the Latin cohors/cohortis, meaning a military unit.

Leaders of forts [*gastera*] **– גסטרא:** This term is based on the Latin castra, meaning a (military) camp.

וְאָמַר רַבִּי יְהוֹשֻׁעַ בֶּן לֵוִי: הַמִּתְפַּלֵּל צָרִיךְ לִשְׁהוֹת שָׁעָה אַחַת אַחַר תְּפִלָּתוֹ, שֶׁנֶּאֱמַר: "אַךְ צַדִּיקִים יוֹדוּ לִשְׁמֶךָ יֵשְׁבוּ יְשָׁרִים אֶת פָּנֶיךָ".

And Rabbi Yehoshua ben Levi said: One who prays must also **wait one hour after his prayer, as it is stated: "Surely the righteous will give thanks unto Your name, the upright will sit before You"** (Psalms 140:14), meaning that after thanking God through prayer, one should stay and sit before Him.

תַּנְיָא נַמִּי הָכִי: הַמִּתְפַּלֵּל צָרִיךְ שֶׁיִּשְׁהֶא שָׁעָה אַחַת קוֹדֶם תְּפִלָּתוֹ, וְשָׁעָה אַחַת אַחַר תְּפִלָּתוֹ. קוֹדֶם תְּפִלָּתוֹ מִנַּיִן – שֶׁנֶּאֱמַר: "אַשְׁרֵי יוֹשְׁבֵי בֵיתֶךָ". לְאַחַר תְּפִלָּתוֹ מִנַּיִן – דִּכְתִיב "אַךְ צַדִּיקִים יוֹדוּ לִשְׁמֶךָ יֵשְׁבוּ יְשָׁרִים אֶת פָּנֶיךָ".

That opinion **was also taught** in a *baraita*: **One who prays must wait one hour before his prayer and one hour after his prayer.**[NH] **From where** is it derived that one must wait one hour **before his prayer? As it is stated: "Happy are those who dwell in Your House." And from where** is it derived that one must stay one hour **after his prayer? As it is written: "Surely the righteous will give thanks unto Your name, the upright will sit before You."**

תָּנוּ רַבָּנַן: חֲסִידִים הָרִאשׁוֹנִים הָיוּ שׁוֹהִין שָׁעָה אַחַת וּמִתְפַּלְּלִין שָׁעָה אַחַת וְחוֹזְרִין וְשׁוֹהִין שָׁעָה אַחַת. וְכִי מֵאַחַר שֶׁשּׁוֹהִין תֵּשַׁע שָׁעוֹת בַּיּוֹם בִּתְפִלָּה, תּוֹרָתָן הֵיאַךְ מִשְׁתַּמֶּרֶת, וּמְלַאכְתָּם הֵיאַךְ נַעֲשֵׂית?

The Sages taught in a *baraita* with regard to waiting before and after prayer: **The the early** generations of **pious** men **would wait one hour, pray one hour, then wait one hour again.** This raises the question: **Since** the early pious men **would spend nine hours per day** engaged either **in prayer** or the requisite waiting periods before and after prayer, three hours each for the morning, afternoon, and evening prayers, **how is their Torah preserved?** There was little time remaining to review their studies. **And how was their work accomplished?**

אֶלָּא מִתּוֹךְ שֶׁחֲסִידִים הֵם – תּוֹרָתָם מִשְׁתַּמֶּרֶת, וּמְלַאכְתָּן מִתְבָּרֶכֶת.

The Gemara answers: **Rather, because they were pious** they merited that **their Torah is preserved and their work is blessed.**

"אֲפִילּוּ הַמֶּלֶךְ שׁוֹאֵל בִּשְׁלוֹמוֹ לֹא יְשִׁיבֶנּוּ".

Additionally, we learned in the mishna: **Even if the king greets him** while he is praying, **he should not respond to him**[H] as one may not interrupt his prayer.

אָמַר רַב יוֹסֵף: לֹא שָׁנוּ אֶלָּא לְמַלְכֵי יִשְׂרָאֵל, אֲבָל לְמַלְכֵי אוּמּוֹת הָעוֹלָם פּוֹסֵק.

In limiting application of this principle, **Rav Yosef said: They only taught** this mishna **with regard to kings of Israel,** as a Jewish king would understand that the individual did not fail to respond to his greeting due to disrespect for the king. **However, with regard to kings of the nations of the world, he interrupts** his prayer and responds to their greeting due to the potential danger.

מֵיתִיבֵי: הַמִּתְפַּלֵּל וְרָאָה אַנָּס בָּא כְּנֶגְדּוֹ, רָאָה קָרוֹן בָּא כְּנֶגְדּוֹ – לֹא יְהֵא מַפְסִיק אֶלָּא מְקַצֵּר וְעוֹלֶה!

The Gemara **raised an objection** to Rav Yosef's statement: **One who is praying and saw a violent person,** feared by all, **coming toward him, or a carriage coming toward him**[H] and he is in the way, **he should not stop** his prayer **but rather abridge it and move** out of the way.

לָא קַשְׁיָא: הָא – דְּאֶפְשָׁר לְקַצֵּר יְקַצֵּר, וְאִם לָאו – פּוֹסֵק.

The Gemara responds: This is **not difficult.** Rather, **this** that teaches to abridge one's prayer rather than stopping, refers to a case **where it is possible to abridge** his prayer and complete it in time, in which case he **should abridge** it. **And if** it is **not** a situation where he can abridge his prayer, **he interrupts** his prayer.

תָּנוּ רַבָּנַן: מַעֲשֶׂה בְּחָסִיד אֶחָד שֶׁהָיָה מִתְפַּלֵּל בַּדֶּרֶךְ, בָּא הֶגְמוֹן אֶחָד וְנָתַן לוֹ שָׁלוֹם וְלֹא הֶחֱזִיר לוֹ שָׁלוֹם. הִמְתִּין לוֹ עַד שֶׁסִּיֵּים תְּפִלָּתוֹ. לְאַחַר שֶׁסִּיֵּים תְּפִלָּתוֹ, אָמַר לוֹ: רֵיקָא, וַהֲלֹא כָּתוּב בְּתוֹרַתְכֶם "רַק הִשָּׁמֶר לְךָ וּשְׁמֹר נַפְשְׁךָ", וּכְתִיב "וְנִשְׁמַרְתֶּם מְאֹד לְנַפְשֹׁתֵיכֶם". כְּשֶׁנָּתַתִּי לְךָ שָׁלוֹם לָמָּה לֹא הֶחֱזַרְתָּ לִי שָׁלוֹם? אִם הָיִיתִי חוֹתֵךְ רֹאשְׁךָ בְּסַיִף, מִי הָיָה תּוֹבֵעַ אֶת דָּמְךָ מִיָּדִי?!

The Sages taught: There was a related **incident, involving a particular pious man who was praying** while traveling **along his path when an officer** [*hegmon*][L] **came and greeted him.** The pious man did not pause from his prayer **and did not respond with a greeting.**[N] The officer **waited for him until he finished his prayer.**

After he finished his prayer, the officer **said him:** You **good for nothing.** You endangered yourself; I could have killed you.

Isn't it written in your Torah: "Take utmost care and guard yourself diligently" (Deuteronomy 4:9)?[N]

And it is also written: "Take therefore good heed unto yourselves" (Deuteronomy 4:15)? Why did you ignore the danger to your life?

When I greeted you, why did you not respond with a greeting?

Were I to sever your head with a sword, who would hold me accountable for your spilled blood?

אָמַר לוֹ: הַמְתֵּן לִי עַד שֶׁאֲפַיֶּיסְךָ בִּדְבָרִים. אָמַר לוֹ: אִילּוּ הָיִיתָ עוֹמֵד לִפְנֵי מֶלֶךְ בָּשָׂר וָדָם, וּבָא חֲבֵרְךָ וְנָתַן לְךָ שָׁלוֹם – הָיִיתָ

The pious man **said to him: Wait for me until I will appease you with** my **words.**

He said to him: Had you been standing before a flesh and blood king and your friend came and greeted you, would you

NOTES

One who prays must wait one hour before his prayer…after his prayer – הַמִּתְפַּלֵּל צָרִיךְ שֶׁיִּשְׁהֶא שָׁעָה אַחַת קוֹדֶם תְּפִלָּתוֹ...אַחַר תְּפִלָּתוֹ: Waiting before prayer is in order to prepare for prayer and the brief waiting period after prayer is to avoid the impression that he is eager to flee. Because the prayer of the early generations of pious men was so intense, they required a full hour of preparation beforehand and a full hour thereafter to ease their return to mundane activities.

An incident, involving a particular pious man…and did not respond with a greeting – ...מַעֲשֶׂה בְּחָסִיד אֶחָד וְלֹא הֶחֱזִיר לוֹ שָׁלוֹם: The commentaries ask why the pious man did not act in accordance with the *halakha* and interrupt his prayer and respond to the greeting due to the danger. They answer that because the officer offered his greeting and even waited for him, the pious man knew that the officer would accept his explanation and apology afterward (*Taz*, *Tziyyun LeNefesh Ḥayya*).

Take utmost care and guard yourself diligently – וְנִשְׁמַרְתֶּם מְאֹד לְנַפְשֹׁתֵיכֶם: Though this verse is often utilized as a warning to avoid danger, that is not its plain meaning. It is actually a section of a verse that warns one to stay away from idolatry. Nonetheless, as an allusion, the Sages used it for this purpose (Maharsha).

HALAKHA

One who prays must wait one hour before his prayer…after his prayer – הַמִּתְפַּלֵּל צָרִיךְ שֶׁיִּשְׁהֶא שָׁעָה אַחַת קוֹדֶם תְּפִלָּתוֹ...אַחַר תְּפִלָּתוֹ: One should wait one hour before prayer to focus his heart on the Holy One, Blessed be He, and one should also wait after prayer to avoid the impression that it is burdensome to him. The early generations of pious men would wait a full hour; however, for most people, a short time, e.g., the time that it takes to walk the length of two doorways that was taught at the beginning of this tractate, is sufficient (*Magen Avraham*; Rambam *Sefer Ahava*, *Hilkhot Tefilla* 4:16; *Shulḥan Arukh*, *Oraḥ Ḥayyim* 93:1).

Even if the king greets him, he should not respond to him – אֲפִילּוּ הַמֶּלֶךְ שׁוֹאֵל בִּשְׁלוֹמוֹ לֹא יְשִׁיבֶנּוּ: One who is in the midst of the *Amida* prayer should not interrupt his prayer to show deference to anyone; even to a king of Israel. If it is a non-Jewish king or a violent person (*Be'er Heitev*) one is permitted to interrupt his prayer. If possible, though, it is preferable to move out of the way or to abbreviate one's prayer instead (Rambam *Sefer Ahava*, *Hilkhot Tefilla* 6:9; *Shulḥan Arukh*, *Oraḥ Ḥayyim* 104:1).

One who is praying and saw a violent person, feared by all, coming toward him, or a carriage coming toward him – הַמִּתְפַּלֵּל וְרָאָה אַנָּס בָּא כְּנֶגְדּוֹ, רָאָה קָרוֹן בָּא כְּנֶגְדּוֹ: One who is standing and praying on the road and sees a carriage or some other hindrance approaching, he should move out of the way rather than interrupt his prayer (Rambam *Sefer Ahava*, *Hilkhot Tefilla* 6:9; *Shulḥan Arukh*, *Oraḥ Ḥayyim* 104:2).

LANGUAGE

Officer [*hegmon*] – הֶגְמוֹן: From the Greek ἡγεμών, *hegemon*, this term originally referred to an army commander, and was later used to refer to a governor or a minister in general. The Talmud utilizes this term in the civil, not the military sense.

מַחֲזִיר לוֹ?! – אָמַר לוֹ: לָאו. וְאִם הָיִיתָ מַחֲזִיר לוֹ, מֶה הָיוּ עוֹשִׂים לְךָ? – אָמַר לוֹ: הָיוּ חוֹתְכִים אֶת רֹאשִׁי בְּסַיִיף. – אָמַר לוֹ: וַהֲלֹא דְּבָרִים קַל וָחוֹמֶר; וּמָה אַתָּה שֶׁהָיִיתָ עוֹמֵד לִפְנֵי מֶלֶךְ בָּשָׂר וָדָם שֶׁהַיּוֹם כָּאן וּמָחָר בַּקֶּבֶר – כָּךְ; אֲנִי שֶׁהָיִיתִי עוֹמֵד לִפְנֵי מֶלֶךְ מַלְכֵי הַמְּלָכִים הַקָּדוֹשׁ בָּרוּךְ הוּא, שֶׁהוּא חַי וְקַיָּים לָעַד וּלְעוֹלְמֵי עוֹלָמִים – עַל אַחַת כַּמָּה וְכַמָּה!

return his greeting?
The officer **said to him: No.**
The pious man continued: **And if you would** greet **him, what would they do to you?**
The officer **said to him: They would cut** off **my head with a sword.**
The pious man **said to him: Isn't this matter an *a fortiori* inference?**
You who were standing before a king of flesh and blood,
of whom your fear is limited **because today he is here but tomorrow he is in the grave,**
would have reacted in **that** way;
I, who was standing and praying **before the Supreme King of kings, the Holy One, Blessed be He,**
Who lives and endures for all eternity,
all the more so that I could not pause to respond to someone's greeting.

מִיָּד נִתְפַּיֵּיס אוֹתוֹ הֶגְמוֹן, וְנִפְטַר אוֹתוֹ חָסִיד לְבֵיתוֹ לְשָׁלוֹם.

When he heard this, **the officer was immediately appeased and the pious man returned home in peace.**

"אֲפִילּוּ נָחָשׁ כָּרוּךְ עַל עֲקֵבוֹ לֹא יַפְסִיק". אָמַר רַב שֵׁשֶׁת: לֹא שָׁנוּ אֶלָּא נָחָשׁ, אֲבָל עַקְרָב – פּוֹסֵק.

We learned in the mishna that **even if a snake is wrapped around his heel, he may not interrupt** his prayer. In limiting application of this principle, **Rav Sheshet said: They only taught** this mishna **with regard to a snake,** as if one does not attack the snake it will not bite him. **But** if **a scorpion**[H] approaches an individual while he is praying, **he stops,** as the scorpion is liable to sting him even if he does not disturb it.

מֵיתִיבֵי: נָפַל לְגוֹב אֲרָיוֹת אֵין מְעִידִין עָלָיו שֶׁמֵּת, נָפַל לַחֲפִירָה מְלֵאָה נְחָשִׁים וְעַקְרַבִּים – מְעִידִין עָלָיו שֶׁמֵּת!

The Gemara **raises an objection** based on what was taught in a *Tosefta*: Those who saw one **fall into a lions' den** but did not see what happened to him thereafter, **do not testify that he died.** Their testimony is not accepted by the court as proof that he has died as it is possible that the lions did not eat him. However, those who saw one **fall into a pit of snakes and scorpions,**[H] **testify that he died** as surely the snakes bit him.

שָׁאנֵי הָתָם, דְּאַגַּב אִיצְצָא מַזְּקִי.

The Gemara responds: This is not difficult. **There,** in the case of one who falls into a pit of snakes, it **is different, as due to the pressure** of his falling on top of them, the snakes **will harm him,** but a snake who is not touched will not bite.

אָמַר רַבִּי יִצְחָק: רָאָה שְׁוָורִים פּוֹסֵק, דְּתָנֵי רַב הוֹשַׁעְיָה: מַרְחִיקִין מִשּׁוֹר תָּם חֲמִשִּׁים אַמָּה, וּמִשּׁוֹר מוּעָד – כִּמְלוֹא עֵינָיו.

The Gemara cites another *halakha* stating that he must interrupt his prayer in a case of certain danger. **Rabbi Yitzḥak said: One who saw oxen**[H] coming toward him, **he interrupts** his prayer, **as Rav Hoshaya taught: One distances himself fifty cubits from an innocuous ox** [*shor tam*],[B] an ox with no history of causing damage with the intent to injure, **and from a forewarned ox** [*shor muad*],[B] an ox whose owner was forewarned because his ox has gored three times already, one distances himself until it is beyond **eyeshot.**

תָּנָא מִשְּׁמֵיהּ דְּרַבִּי מֵאִיר: רֵישׁ תּוֹרָא בְּדִקּוּלָּא – סְלֵיק לְאִגָּרָא, וּשְׁדִי דַּרְגָּא מִתּוּתָךְ. אָמַר שְׁמוּאֵל: הָנֵי מִילֵּי – בְּשׁוֹר שָׁחוֹר וּבְיוֹמֵי נִיסָן, מִפְּנֵי שֶׁהַשָּׂטָן מְרַקֵּד לוֹ בֵּין קַרְנָיו.

It was **taught in the name of Rabbi Meir:** While **the head of the ox is** still **in the basket** and he is busy eating, **go up on the roof and kick the ladder out from underneath you. Shmuel said: This applies only with regard to a black ox,**[B] **and during the days of Nisan, because** that species of ox is particularly dangerous, and during that time of year **Satan dances between its horns.**

BACKGROUND

Innocuous ox [*shor tam*]– שׁוֹר תָּם: An animal that is not known to cause damage with the intent to injure. The first three times an animal causes damage of this nature, its owner is only required to pay half the damage it has caused. Afterwards it becomes a dangerous forewarned animal, an animal with a history of causing injury. The owner of a forewarned animal is required to pay for all the damage it causes. An animal can be considered innocuous with regard to certain kinds of damage and forewarned with regard to others. For example, an ox that has a history of goring other oxen is still considered innocuous with regard to goring humans. Similarly, if it is established that the animal causes injury only on certain days, for example, on Shabbat and Festivals, it may be considered forewarned on those days alone and innocuous during the rest of the week. An animal that is forewarned can regain status as innocuous if, on three separate occasions, animals that it was accustomed to attacking passed by and it refrained from attacking them.

Forewarned ox [*shor muad*] – שׁוֹר מוּעָד: In its more limited sense, this expression is used to refer to an ox whose owner has been forewarned, i.e., an ox that has gored three times. If an ox causes damage by goring, or, in general, any animal causes malicious damage, the first three times that it does so, the owner is liable for only half of the resulting damage. If, however, the ox gores a fourth time, and the owner was officially notified that it had gored three times previously, the animal is considered forewarned, and the owner must pay in full for the resulting damage.

HALAKHA

Even if a snake is wrapped around his heel…a scorpion – נָחָשׁ כָּרוּךְ עַל עֲקֵבוֹ...עַקְרָב: One who was standing in prayer and a snake wrapped itself around his ankle, he should not interrupt his prayer to tell someone else to remove the snake (*Mishna Berura*). If he sees that the snake is agitated and primed for attack, he stops his prayer (Jerusalem Talmud). However, in the case of a scorpion, which is deadly (*Magen Avraham*), one always stops his prayer (Rambam *Sefer Ahava, Hilkhot Tefilla* 6:9; *Shulḥan Arukh, Oraḥ Ḥayyim* 104:3).

One who fell into a lions' den…snakes and scorpions – נָפַל לְגוֹב אֲרָיוֹת...נְחָשִׁים וְעַקְרַבִּים: Based on witnessing someone fall into a lions' den, one cannot testify that he is dead, as perhaps they did not harm him. However, if he witnessed him fall into a pit of snakes and scorpions, he can testify that he is dead, as due to the pressure of his falling on top of them they certainly harmed him and he died (Rambam *Sefer Nashim, Hilkhot Gerushin* 13:17; *Shulḥan Arukh, Even HaEzer* 17:29).

One who saw oxen – רָאָה שְׁוָורִים: One who is standing in prayer and sees an ox approaching stops his prayer and distances himself from the ox. If the local oxen are known to be benign, he need not distance himself (*Shulḥan Arukh, Oraḥ Ḥayyim* 104:4).

BACKGROUND

Black ox – שׁוֹר שָׁחוֹר: The ox referenced here may be the buffalo. It is very similar to common cattle, and is distinguishable by its strength, size, dark color, the shape of its horns, and the extended period during which it remains in the water. It is indigenous to Asia, and is used primarily as a work animal. Though mild-mannered around those who tend to it, it can be very dangerous to strangers and many have died as a result of its attacks.

Black ox

תָּנוּ רַבָּנַן: מַעֲשֶׂה בְּמָקוֹם אֶחָד שֶׁהָיָה עָרוֹד וְהָיָה מַזִּיק אֶת הַבְּרִיּוֹת, בָּאוּ וְהוֹדִיעוּ לוֹ לְרַבִּי חֲנִינָא בֶּן דּוֹסָא. אָמַר לָהֶם: הַרְאוּ לִי אֶת חוֹרוֹ! הֶרְאוּהוּ אֶת חוֹרוֹ, נָתַן עֲקֵבוֹ עַל פִּי הַחוֹר, יָצָא וּנְשָׁכוֹ וּמֵת אוֹתוֹ עָרוֹד.

With regard to the praise for one who prays and need not fear even a snake, **the Sages taught:** There was **an incident in one place where an *arvad*[B] was harming the people. They came and told Rabbi Ḥanina ben Dosa** and asked for his help. **He told them: Show me the hole of the *arvad*. They showed him its hole. He placed his heel over the mouth of the hole** and the ***arvad* came out and bit him, and died.**

נְטָלוֹ עַל כְּתֵפוֹ וֶהֱבִיאוֹ לְבֵית הַמִּדְרָשׁ. אָמַר לָהֶם: רְאוּ בָּנַי, אֵין עָרוֹד מֵמִית אֶלָּא הַחֵטְא מֵמִית.

Rabbi Ḥanina ben Dosa **placed** the *arvad* **over his shoulder and brought it to the study hall. He said to** those assembled there: **See, my sons, it is not** the ***arvad* that kills** a person, **rather transgression kills** a person. The *arvad* has no power over one who is free of transgression.

בְּאוֹתָהּ שָׁעָה אָמְרוּ: אוֹי לוֹ לָאָדָם שֶׁפָּגַע בּוֹ עָרוֹד, וְאוֹי לוֹ לָעָרוֹד שֶׁפָּגַע בּוֹ רַבִּי חֲנִינָא בֶּן דּוֹסָא.

At that moment the Sages **said: Woe unto the person who was attacked by an *arvad* and woe unto the *arvad* that was attacked by Rabbi Ḥanina ben Dosa.**

מתני׳ מַזְכִּירִין גְּבוּרוֹת גְּשָׁמִים בִּתְחִיַּית הַמֵּתִים וּשְׁאֵלָה בְּבִרְכַּת הַשָּׁנִים, וְהַבְדָּלָה בְּחוֹנֵן הַדַּעַת; רַבִּי עֲקִיבָא אוֹמֵר: אוֹמְרָהּ בְּרָכָה רְבִיעִית בִּפְנֵי עַצְמָהּ; רַבִּי אֱלִיעֶזֶר אוֹמֵר: בְּהוֹדָאָה.

MISHNA This mishna speaks of additions to the standard formula of the *Amida* prayer and the blessings in which they are incorporated. **One mentions the might of the rains** and recites: He makes the wind blow and the rain fall, **in** the second blessing of the *Amida* prayer, the blessing **of the revival of the dead.**[H] **And the request** for rain: And grant dew and rain as a blessing, **in** the ninth blessing of the *Amida* prayer, **the blessing of the years.**[H] **And the prayer of distinction** [*havdala*], between the holy and the profane recited in the evening prayer following Shabbat and festivals, **in** the fourth blessing of the *Amida* prayer: **Who graciously grants knowledge.**[H] **Rabbi Akiva says:** ***Havdala* is recited** as **an independent fourth blessing. Rabbi Eliezer says** that it is recited **in** the seventeenth blessing of the *Amida* prayer, the blessing of **thanksgiving.**

גמ׳ ״מַזְכִּירִין גְּבוּרוֹת גְּשָׁמִים״. מַאי טַעְמָא?

GEMARA We learned in the mishna that **one mentions the might of the rains** in the second blessing of the *Amida* prayer, the blessing of the revival of the dead. The Gemara asks: **What is the reason** that the might of the rains is mentioned specifically in that blessing?

אָמַר רַב יוֹסֵף: מִתּוֹךְ שֶׁשְּׁקוּלָה כִּתְחִיַּית הַמֵּתִים, לְפִיכָךְ קְבָעוּהָ בִּתְחִיַּית הַמֵּתִים.

Rav Yosef said: Because the might of the rains **is equivalent to the resurrection of the dead,** as rain revives new life in the plant world (Jerusalem Talmud).

״וּשְׁאֵלָה בְּבִרְכַּת הַשָּׁנִים״. מַאי טַעְמָא?

And we also learned in the mishna that the **request** for rain is added to **the blessing of the years.** Here, too, the Gemara asks: **What is the reason** that the request for rain is recited specifically in that blessing?

אָמַר רַב יוֹסֵף: מִתּוֹךְ שֶׁהִיא פַּרְנָסָה, לְפִיכָךְ קְבָעוּהָ בְּבִרְכַּת פַּרְנָסָה.

Rav Yosef said: Because rain is a component of **sustenance, therefore it was inserted in the blessing of sustenance** as part of our request for bountiful sustenance.

״הַבְדָּלָה בְּחוֹנֵן הַדַּעַת״. מַאי טַעְמָא?

We also learned in the mishna that ***havdala,*** distinguishing between Shabbat and the weekdays, is added **in** the blessing of: **Who graciously grants knowledge.** Here too the Gemara asks: **What is the reason** that *havdala* is recited specifically in that blessing?

אָמַר רַב יוֹסֵף: מִתּוֹךְ שֶׁהִיא חָכְמָה, קְבָעוּהָ בְּבִרְכַּת חָכְמָה; וְרַבָּנַן אָמְרִי: מִתּוֹךְ שֶׁהִיא חוֹל, לְפִיכָךְ קְבָעוּהָ בְּבִרְכַּת חוֹל.

Rav Yosef said: *Havdala* is recited in that blessing **because it** requires **wisdom** to distinguish between two entities, **they established it in the blessing of wisdom. The Rabbis say** a different reason: **Because** ***havdala*** **is** the distinction between the sacred and the **profane,** the Sages **established it in the blessing of weekdays.** The first three blessings of the *Amida* prayer are recited both on weekdays and on Shabbat and Festivals. The blessing: Who graciously grants knowledge, is the first of the blessings recited exclusively during the week.

אָמַר רַב אַמִי: גְּדוֹלָה דֵּעָה שֶׁנִּתְּנָה בִּתְחִלַּת בְּרָכָה שֶׁל חוֹל.

Having mentioned the blessing of wisdom, the Gemara cites that which **Rav Ami said** with regard to knowledge: **Great is knowledge that was placed at the beginning of the weekday blessings;** an indication of its significance.

BACKGROUND

***Arvad* – עָרוֹד:** Based on the descriptions in the Gemara, apparently the *arvad* is a type of snake or perhaps a large, very dangerous reptile. In parallel discussions in the Jerusalem Talmud, the *arvad* is called a *ḥavarbar*. Some identify this as the black snake or a snake of the *coluber* genus, which, although not poisonous, is very aggressive and bites.

Caspian whipsnake

HALAKHA

One mentions the might of the rains in the blessing of the revival of the dead – מַזְכִּירִין גְּבוּרוֹת גְּשָׁמִים בִּתְחִיַּית הַמֵּתִים: During the rainy season one mentions rain in the second blessing of the *Amida* prayer, the blessing of Divine Might (Rambam *Sefer Ahava, Hilkhot Tefilla* 2:15; *Shulḥan Arukh, Oraḥ Ḥayyim* 114:1).

The request for rain is recited in the blessing of the years – וּשְׁאֵלָה בְּבִרְכַּת הַשָּׁנִים: During the rainy season, which in Eretz Yisrael begins on the seventh of Marḥeshvan and outside of Israel, sixty days after the Tishrei, or autumnal, equinox, the request for rain is inserted in the blessing of the years, the ninth blessing of the *Amida* prayer (Rambam *Sefer Ahava, Hilkhot Tefilla* 2:16; *Shulḥan Arukh, Oraḥ Ḥayyim* 117:1).

And *havdala* in the blessing: Who graciously grants knowledge – וְהַבְדָּלָה בְּחוֹנֵן הַדַּעַת: One recites *havdala* at the conclusion of Shabbat and Festivals in the blessing: Who graciously grants knowledge, in the evening prayer. This is in accordance with the unattributed opinion in the mishna and the conclusion of the Gemara (Rambam *Sefer Ahava, Hilkhot Tefilla* 2:4; *Shulḥan Arukh, Oraḥ Ḥayyim* 294:1).

וְאָמַר רַב אַמִי: גְּדוֹלָה דֵּעָה שֶׁנִּתְּנָה בֵּין שְׁתֵּי אוֹתִיּוֹת, שֶׁנֶּאֱמַר: ״כִּי אֵל דֵּעוֹת ה׳״. וְכָל מִי שֶׁאֵין בּוֹ דֵּעָה אָסוּר לְרַחֵם עָלָיו, שֶׁנֶּאֱמַר: ״כִּי לֹא עַם בִּינוֹת הוּא עַל כֵּן לֹא יְרַחֲמֶנּוּ עוֹשֵׂהוּ״.

And Rav Ami said in praise of knowledge: **Great is knowledge that was placed between two letters,** two names of God, **as it is stated: "For God of knowledge is the Lord"** (I Samuel 2:3). **And** since knowledge is regarded so highly, **anyone without knowledge,**[N] **it is forbidden to have compassion upon him, as it is stated: "For they are a people of no wisdom, so their Creator will have no compassion upon them** and their Creator will not be gracious unto them" (Isaiah 27:11). If God shows no mercy for those who lack wisdom, all the more so should people refrain from doing so.

אָמַר רַבִּי אֶלְעָזָר: גָּדוֹל מִקְדָּשׁ שֶׁנִּתַּן בֵּין שְׁתֵּי אוֹתִיּוֹת, שֶׁנֶּאֱמַר: ״פָּעַלְתָּ ה׳ מִקְּדָשׁ ה׳״.

Similarly, **Rabbi Elazar said: Great is the Holy Temple, as** it too **was placed between two letters,** two names of God, **as it is stated:** "The place in which to dwell which **You have made, Lord, the Temple, Lord,** which Your hands have prepared" (Exodus 15:17).

וְאָמַר רַבִּי אֶלְעָזָר: כָּל אָדָם שֶׁיֵּשׁ בּוֹ דֵּעָה – כְּאִילּוּ נִבְנָה בֵּית הַמִּקְדָּשׁ בְּיָמָיו; דֵּעָה נִתְּנָה בֵּין שְׁתֵּי אוֹתִיּוֹת, מִקְדָּשׁ נִתַּן בֵּין שְׁתֵּי אוֹתִיּוֹת.

Noting the parallel between these two ideas, **Rabbi Elazar** added **and said: Anyone with knowledge,** it is **as if the Holy Temple was built in his days;**[N] **knowledge was placed between two letters** and **the Temple was placed between two letters,** signifying that they stand together.

מַתְקִיף לָהּ רַב אַחָא קַרְחִינָאָה: אֶלָּא מֵעַתָּה, גְּדוֹלָה נְקָמָה שֶׁנִּתְּנָה בֵּין שְׁתֵּי אוֹתִיּוֹת, שֶׁנֶּאֱמַר: ״אֵל נְקָמוֹת ה׳״!

Rav Aḥa Karḥina'a strongly objects to this approach that being placed between two names of God accords significance: **However, if so,** the same should hold true for vengeance. **Great** is **revenge that was placed between two letters, as it is stated: "God of vengeance, Lord,** God of vengeance shine forth" (Psalms 94:1).

אָמַר לֵיהּ: אִין, בְּמִילְּתָהּ מִיהָא גְּדוֹלָה הִיא. וְהַיְינוּ דְּאָמַר עוּלָּא: שְׁתֵּי נְקָמוֹת הַלָּלוּ לָמָּה? אַחַת לְטוֹבָה וְאַחַת לְרָעָה, לְטוֹבָה – דִּכְתִיב: ״הוֹפִיעַ מֵהַר פָּארָן״, לְרָעָה – דִּכְתִיב: ״אֵל נְקָמוֹת ה׳ אֵל נְקָמוֹת הוֹפִיעַ״.

He said to him: Yes. At least in its place, in the appropriate context, **it is great.** At times it is necessary. **That is that which Ulla said:** Why are **these two vengeances** mentioned in a single verse? **One for good and one for evil.** Vengeance **for good, as it is written: "He shined forth from Mount Paran"** (Deuteronomy 33:2) with regard to God's vengeance against the wicked; vengeance **for evil, as it is written: "God of vengeance, Lord, God of vengeance shine forth"** with regard to the punishment of Israel.

״רַבִּי עֲקִיבָא אוֹמֵר אוֹמְרָהּ בְּרָכָה רְבִיעִית״ כו׳.

A tannaitic dispute is cited in the mishna with regard to the appropriate blessing in which to recite *havdala* within the *Amida* prayer. **Rabbi Akiva says:** *Havdala* **is recited** as an independent **fourth blessing.** Rabbi Eliezer says that it is recited in the seventeenth blessing of the *Amida* prayer, the blessing of thanksgiving. The first *tanna* says that it is recited in the fourth blessing of the *Amida* prayer: Who graciously grants knowledge.

אָמַר לֵיהּ רַב שֶׁמֶן בַּר אַבָּא לְרַבִּי יוֹחָנָן: מִכְּדֵי אַנְשֵׁי כְנֶסֶת הַגְּדוֹלָה תִּקְּנוּ לָהֶם לְיִשְׂרָאֵל, בְּרָכוֹת וּתְפִלּוֹת קְדוּשּׁוֹת וְהַבְדָּלוֹת, נֶחֱזֵי הֵיכָן תַּקּוּן.

Regarding this, **Rav Shemen,** Shimon, **bar Abba said to Rabbi Yoḥanan: Now, since** the eighteen blessings of the *Amida* prayer and the other prayer formulas for prayer **were instituted for Israel by the members of the Great Assembly** just like all the other **blessings and prayers, sanctifications and *havdalot*; let us see where** in the *Amida* prayer the members of the Great Assembly **instituted**[N] to recite *havdala*.

אָמַר לֵיהּ: בַּתְּחִילָּה קְבָעוּהָ בַּתְּפִלָּה, הֶעֱשִׁירוּ – קְבָעוּהָ עַל הַכּוֹס, הֶעֱנוּ – חָזְרוּ וּקְבָעוּהָ בַּתְּפִלָּה, וְהֵם אָמְרוּ: הַמַּבְדִּיל בַּתְּפִלָּה צָרִיךְ שֶׁיַּבְדִּיל עַל הַכּוֹס.

Rabbi Yoḥanan replied that that would be impossible, as the customs associated with *havdala* went through several stages. **He said to him: Initially,** during the difficult, early years of the Second Temple, **they established** that *havdala* is to be recited **in the *Amida* prayer.** Subsequently, when the people **became wealthy, they established** that *havdala* is to be recited **over the cup** of wine. When the people **became impoverished, they again established** that **it** was to be recited **in the *Amida* prayer. And they said: One who recites *havdala* in the *Amida* prayer must,** if he is able (*Shitta Mekubbetzet, Me'iri*), **recite *havdala* over the cup**[H] of wine as well. Due to all these changes, it was not clear when exactly *havdala* was to be recited.

אִיתְּמַר נַמִי, אָמַר רַבִּי חִיָּיא בַּר אַבָּא אָמַר רַבִּי יוֹחָנָן: אַנְשֵׁי כְנֶסֶת הַגְּדוֹלָה תִּקְּנוּ לָהֶם לְיִשְׂרָאֵל בְּרָכוֹת וּתְפִלּוֹת קְדוּשּׁוֹת וְהַבְדָּלוֹת. בַּתְּחִלָּה קְבָעוּהָ בַּתְּפִלָּה, הֶעֱשִׁירוּ – קְבָעוּהָ עַל הַכּוֹס, חָזְרוּ וְהֶעֱנוּ – קְבָעוּהָ בַּתְּפִלָּה, וְהֵם אָמְרוּ: הַמַּבְדִּיל בַּתְּפִלָּה צָרִיךְ שֶׁיַּבְדִּיל עַל הַכּוֹס.

It was also stated: Rabbi Ḥiyya bar Abba said that **Rabbi Yoḥanan said: The members of the Great Assembly established for Israel blessings and prayers, sanctifications and *havdalot*. Initially, they established** that *havdala* is to be recited **in the *Amida* prayer.** Subsequently, when the people **became wealthy, they established** that *havdala* is to be recited **over the cup** of wine. When the people **again became impoverished, they established** that **it** was to be recited **in the *Amida* prayer. And they said: One who recites *havdala* in the *Amida* prayer must recite *havdala* over the cup** of wine as well.

NOTES

Anyone without knowledge – מִי שֶׁאֵין בּוֹ דֵּעָה: Knowledge in this context does not refer specifically to intellectual capability, but rather to one's fundamental ability to conduct himself and live in accordance with that capability. That is why the Gemara relates so harshly to one without knowledge, as by failing to realize his potential, he negates his own essence. Every creature that maintains his fundamental essence deserves compassion; one without knowledge negates the very justification of his existence (Maharsha).

Anyone with knowledge, it is as if the Holy Temple was built in his days – כָּל אָדָם שֶׁיֵּשׁ בּוֹ דֵּעָה – כְּאִילּוּ נִבְנָה בֵּית הַמִּקְדָּשׁ בְּיָמָיו: The Sages already established that one who engages in the study of the laws of the burnt-offering it is as if he sacrificed a burnt-offering. Therefore, anyone with knowledge can achieve ultimate closeness to God, which is the purpose of the Temple and the service performed therein. Consequently, it is as if the Temple was built in his days (*Torat HaOla* of the Rema).

Let us see where the members of the Great Assembly instituted it – נֶחֱזֵי הֵיכָן תִּקּוּן: This suggestion is not raised on every occasion. It is only relevant with regard to those ordinances that everyone performs on a regular basis and there is no danger that it will be forgotten or mistaken (*Tosafot*).

HALAKHA

One who recites *havdala* in the *Amida* prayer must recite *havdala* over the cup – הַמַּבְדִּיל בַּתְּפִלָּה, צָרִיךְ שֶׁיַּבְדִּיל עַל הַכּוֹס: One who recited *havdala* in the *Amida* prayer must repeat *havdala* over a cup of wine (Rambam *Sefer Ahava, Hilkhot Tefilla* 2:12; *Shulḥan Arukh, Oraḥ Ḥayyim* 294:1).

אִיתְּמַר נַמִי, רַבָּה וְרַב יוֹסֵף דְּאָמְרִי תַּרְוַיְיהוּ: הַמַּבְדִּיל בַּתְּפִלָּה צָרִיךְ שֶׁיַּבְדִּיל עַל הַכּוֹס.

It was also stated: **Rabba and Rav Yosef who both said: One who recites *havdala* in the *Amida* prayer must recite *havdala* over the cup** of wine as well.

אָמַר רָבָא, וּמוֹתְבִינַן אַשְּׁמַעְתִּין: טָעָה וְלֹא הִזְכִּיר גְּבוּרוֹת גְּשָׁמִים בִּתְחִיַּית הַמֵּתִים וּשְׁאֵלָה בְּבִרְכַּת הַשָּׁנִים – מַחֲזִירִין אוֹתוֹ, וְהַבְדָּלָה בְּחוֹנֵן הַדַּעַת – אֵין מַחֲזִירִין אוֹתוֹ, מִפְּנֵי שֶׁיָּכוֹל לְאוֹמְרָהּ עַל הַכּוֹס!

Rava said: We raise an objection to our *halakha* based on what was taught in a *Tosefta*: **One who erred and did not mention the might of the rains in** the second blessing in the *Amida*, the blessing on **the revival of the dead,**[H] **and** one who erred and failed to recite **the request** for rain **in** the ninth blessing of the *Amida*, **the blessing of the years,**[H] **we require him to return** to the beginning of the prayer and repeat it. However, one who erred and failed to recite ***havdala*** in the blessing: **Who graciously grants knowledge,**[H] **we do not require him to return** to the beginning of the prayer and repeat it, **as he can recite *havdala* over the cup** of wine. Apparently, *havdala* over the cup of wine is optional, not obligatory, at it says because he can recite and not that he must.

לָא תֵּימָא "מִפְּנֵי שֶׁיָּכוֹל לְאוֹמְרָהּ עַל הַכּוֹס", אֶלָּא אֵימָא "מִפְּנֵי שֶׁאוֹמְרָהּ עַל הַכּוֹס".

The Gemara answers: **Do not say** as it appears in the *Tosefta*: **Because he can recite *havdala* over the cup** of wine. **Rather, say: Because he recites *havdala* over the cup** of wine.

אִיתְּמַר נַמִי, אָמַר רַבִּי בִּנְיָמִין בַּר יֶפֶת: שָׁאַל רַבִּי יוֹסֵי אֶת רַבִּי יוֹחָנָן בְּצִידָן, וְאָמְרִי לָהּ, רַבִּי שִׁמְעוֹן בֶּן יַעֲקֹב דְּמִן צוֹר אֶת רַבִּי יוֹחָנָן, וַאֲנָא שְׁמַעִית: הַמַּבְדִּיל בַּתְּפִלָּה, צָרִיךְ שֶׁיַּבְדִּיל עַל הַכּוֹס אוֹ לֹא? וְאָמַר לֵיהּ: צָרִיךְ שֶׁיַּבְדִּיל עַל הַכּוֹס.

Proof that one must recite *havdala* over the cup of wine as well as in the *Amida* prayer **was also stated: Rabbi Binyamin bar Yefet said** that **Rabbi Yosei asked Rabbi Yoḥanan in Sidon, and some say that Rabbi Shimon ben Ya'akov from** the city of **Tyre asked Rabbi Yoḥanan, and I,** Binyamin bar Yefet, **heard: One who** already **recited *havdala* in the *Amida* prayer, must he recite *havdala* over the cup** of wine **or not?** And Rabbi Yoḥanan **said to him: He must recite *havdala* over the cup.**

אִיבַּעְיָא לְהוּ: הַמַּבְדִּיל עַל הַכּוֹס, מַהוּ שֶׁיַּבְדִּיל בַּתְּפִלָּה?

Having clarified the question whether one who recited *havdala* during the *Amida* prayer must also recite *havdala* over the cup of wine, **a dilemma was raised before** the Sages: **One who** already **recited *havdala* over the cup** of wine, **what is** the ruling as far as his obligation **to recite *havdala* in the *Amida* prayer** is concerned?

אָמַר רַב נַחְמָן בַּר יִצְחָק, קַל וָחוֹמֶר מִתְּפִלָּה: וּמַה תְּפִלָּה דְּעִיקַּר תַּקַּנְתָּא הִיא – אָמְרִי: הַמַּבְדִּיל בַּתְּפִלָּה צָרִיךְ שֶׁיַּבְדִּיל עַל הַכּוֹס; הַמַּבְדִּיל עַל הַכּוֹס, דְּלָאו עִיקַּר תַּקַּנְתָּא הִיא – לֹא כָּל שֶׁכֵּן?!

Rav Naḥman bar Yitzḥak said: This can be derived ***a fortiori* from** the established *halakha* regarding *havdala* in **the *Amida* prayer. Just as** *havdala* in **the *Amida* prayer, which is** where **the principal ordinance** to recite *havdala* was instituted, the Sages **said** that it is not sufficient and **one who recited *havdala* in the *Amida* prayer must recite *havdala* over the cup** of wine as well, **all the more so** that **one who recited *havdala* over the cup** of wine, **which is not** where **the principal ordinance** to recite *havdala* was instituted, but was merely a later addition, did not fulfill his obligation and must recite *havdala* in the *Amida* prayer.

תָּנֵי רַב אַחָא אֲרִיכָא קַמֵּיהּ דְּרַב חִינָּנָא: הַמַּבְדִּיל בַּתְּפִלָּה מְשׁוּבָּח יוֹתֵר מִמִּי שֶׁיַּבְדִּיל עַל הַכּוֹס, וְאִם הִבְדִּיל בָּזוֹ וּבָזוֹ – יָנוּחוּ לוֹ בְּרָכוֹת עַל רֹאשׁוֹ.

Rabbi Aḥa Arikha, the tall, taught a *baraita* **before Rav Ḥinnana: One who recited *havdala* in the *Amida* prayer is more praiseworthy than one who recites it over the cup** of wine, **and if he recited *havdala* in this,** the *Amida* prayer, **and that,** over the cup of wine, **may blessings rest upon his head.**

הָא גּוּפָא קַשְׁיָא! אָמְרַתְּ, הַמַּבְדִּיל בַּתְּפִלָּה מְשׁוּבָּח יוֹתֵר מִמִּי שֶׁיַּבְדִּיל עַל הַכּוֹס, אַלְמָא: תְּפִלָּה לְחוּדָהּ סַגִּי, וַהֲדַר תָּנֵי: אִם הִבְדִּיל בָּזוֹ וּבָזוֹ – יָנוּחוּ לוֹ בְּרָכוֹת עַל רֹאשׁוֹ, וְכֵיוָן דְּנָפֵיק לֵיהּ בַּחֲדָא – אִפְּטַר, וְהָוְיָא בְּרָכָה שֶׁאֵינָהּ צְרִיכָה; וְאָמַר רַב וְאִיתֵּימָא רֵישׁ לָקִישׁ, וְאָמְרִי לָהּ רַבִּי יוֹחָנָן וְרֵישׁ לָקִישׁ דְּאָמְרִי תַּרְוַיְיהוּ: כָּל הַמְבָרֵךְ בְּרָכָה שֶׁאֵינָהּ צְרִיכָה – עוֹבֵר מִשּׁוּם: "לֹא תִשָּׂא"!

This *baraita* is apparently **self-contradictory.** On the one hand, **you said that one who recites *havdala* in the *Amida* prayer is more praiseworthy than one who recites *havdala* over the cup** of wine, indicating that reciting *havdala* in **the *Amida* prayer alone is sufficient. And then it is taught: If one recited *havdala* in this,** the *Amida* prayer, **and that,** over the cup of wine, **may blessings rest upon his head. And since he fulfilled** his obligation to recite *havdala* **with one,** he is **exempt, and** the additional recitation of *havdala* over the cup of wine **is an unnecessary blessing. And Rav, and some say Reish Lakish, and** still others **say Rabbi Yoḥanan and Reish Lakish both said: Anyone who recites an unnecessary blessing**[H] **violates** the biblical prohibition: **"Do not take** the name of the Lord your God in vain" (Exodus 20:6).

אֶלָּא, אֵימָא הָכִי: אִם הִבְדִּיל בָּזוֹ וְלֹא הִבְדִּיל בָּזוֹ – יָנוּחוּ לוֹ בְּרָכוֹת עַל רֹאשׁוֹ.

Rather, emend this *baraita* **and say as follows: If one recited *havdala* in this and not in that, may blessings rest upon his head.**

בְּעָא מִינֵּיהּ רַב חִסְדָּא מֵרַב שֵׁשֶׁת: טָעָה בָּזוֹ וּבָזוֹ, מַהוּ? אָמַר לֵיהּ: טָעָה בָּזוֹ וּבָזוֹ – חוֹזֵר לָרֹאשׁ.

Rav Ḥisda asked Rav Sheshet with regard to these blessings: If one **erred** in *havdala* both **in this and in that, what is** the ruling? Rav Sheshet **said to him: One who erred in this,** the *Amida* prayer, **and that,** over the cup of wine,[H] **returns to the beginning** of both the *Amida* prayer and the *havdala* over the cup of wine.

HALAKHA

One who erred and did not mention the might of the rains in the blessing on the revival of the dead – טָעָה וְלֹא הִזְכִּיר גְּבוּרוֹת גְּשָׁמִים בִּתְחִיַּית הַמֵּתִים: One who forgot to mention: He makes the wind blow and the rain fall, in the blessing of the revival of the dead during the winter, we require him to return to the beginning of the prayer and repeat it. However, if he mentioned: He causes the dew to fall, we do not require him to return to the beginning of the prayer and repeat it (Rambam *Sefer Ahava, Hilkhot Tefilla* 10:8; *Shulḥan Arukh, Oraḥ Ḥayyim* 114:5).

One who erred and did not mention…the request for rain in the blessing of the years – טָעָה וְלֹא הִזְכִּיר...וּשְׁאֵלָה בְּבִרְכַּת הַשָּׁנִים: One who erred and did not request rain in the blessing of the years during the winter, is required to return to the beginning of the prayer and repeat it, even if he requested dew, in accordance with the unattributed opinion in the Gemara (Rambam *Sefer Ahava, Hilkhot Tefilla* 10:9; *Shulḥan Arukh, Oraḥ Ḥayyim* 117:4).

One who erred and did not mention…*havdala* in the blessing: Who graciously grants knowledge – טָעָה וְלֹא הִזְכִּיר...וְהַבְדָּלָה בְּחוֹנֵן הַדַּעַת: One who failed to recite *havdala* in the blessing: Who graciously grants knowledge, in the evening prayer at the conclusion of Shabbat and Festivals need not repeat the prayer, because he is required to recite *havdala* over a cup of wine (Rambam *Sefer Ahava, Hilkhot Tefilla* 10:14; *Shulḥan Arukh, Oraḥ Ḥayyim* 294:1).

One who recites an unnecessary blessing – הַמְבָרֵךְ בְּרָכָה שֶׁאֵינָהּ צְרִיכָה: One who recites an unnecessary blessing, e.g., one who recited a blessing during a meal over food that was already exempted by the blessing: Who brings forth bread from the earth, is considered, by rabbinic law (*Magen Avraham*), as if he took God's name in vain. One must avoid reciting two blessings when one will suffice (Rambam *Sefer Ahava, Hilkhot Berakhot* 1:15; *Shulḥan Arukh, Oraḥ Ḥayyim* 215:4 and see 206:6).

One who erred in this, the *Amida* prayer, and that, over the cup of wine – טָעָה בָּזוֹ וּבָזוֹ: One who failed to recite *havdala* in the *Amida* prayer and later ate before reciting *havdala* over the cup of wine, must repeat the evening *Amida* prayer and recite *havdala* in the fourth blessing. Since eating was an action that he was not permitted to perform, he is referred to as one who erred (*Talmidei Rabbeinu Yona*; *Shulḥan Arukh, Oraḥ Ḥayyim* 294:1).

אָמַר לֵיהּ רָבִינָא לְרָבָא: הִלְכְתָא מַאי? – אָמַר לֵיהּ: כִּי קִידּוּשׁ, מַה קִידּוּשׁ אַף עַל גַּב דִּמְקַדֵּשׁ בִּצְלוֹתָא מְקַדֵּשׁ אַכָּסָא, אַף הַבְדָּלָה נַמִּי – אַף עַל גַּב דְּמַבְדִּיל בִּצְלוֹתָא מַבְדִּיל אַכָּסָא.

There are conflicting opinions with regard to reciting *havdala* over the cup of wine after reciting it in the *Amida* prayer. One opinion holds that it is appropriate to recite *havdala* a second time, while the other holds that it is prohibited. **Ravina said to Rava: What is the *halakha*?** Rava **said to him:** The *halakha* in the case of *havdala* is **like** the *halakha* in the case of **kiddush. Just as** in the case of ***kiddush*, although one recited *kiddush* in the** *Amida* **prayer** he must, nevertheless, **recite *kiddush*** again **over the cup** of wine, **so too with *havdala*, although one recited *havdala* in the** *Amida* **prayer** he must **recite *havdala*** again **over the cup** of wine.

״רַבִּי אֱלִיעֶזֶר אוֹמֵר: בְּהוֹדָאָה״.

The mishna states that **Rabbi Eliezer says:** It is recited **in** the seventeenth blessing of the *Amida* prayer, the blessing of **thanksgiving.**

רַבִּי זֵירָא הֲוָה רָכֵיב חֲמָרָא, הֲוָה קָא שָׁקֵיל וְאָזֵיל רַבִּי חִיָּיא בַּר אָבִין בַּתְרֵיהּ. אָמַר לֵיהּ, וַדַּאי דְּאָמְרִיתוּ מִשְּׁמֵיהּ דְּרַבִּי יוֹחָנָן: הֲלָכָה כְּרַבִּי אֱלִיעֶזֶר בְּיוֹם טוֹב שֶׁחָל לִהְיוֹת אַחַר הַשַּׁבָּת? – אָמַר לֵיהּ: אִין.

The Gemara cites the conclusion with regard to this *halakha* by relating a story: **Rabbi Zeira was riding a donkey** while **Rabbi Ḥiyya bar Avin was coming and walking after him. He said to him: Is** it **true that you said in the name of Rabbi Yoḥanan** that the ***halakha* is in accordance with** the opinion of **Rabbi Eliezer** in the case of **a Festival that occurs** directly **after Shabbat?** Since in that case, one cannot recite *havdala* in the blessing of Who graciously grants knowledge, as it is not included in the *Amida* prayer on the Festival, there is no alternative but to adopt Rabbi Eliezer's ruling. **He said to him: Yes.**

הֲלָכָה – מִכְּלָל דִּפְלִיגִי!

The Gemara wonders: Saying that the ***halakha*** is in accordance with the opinion of Rabbi Eliezer, **indicates that** his peers **dispute** his opinion. Where do we find that dispute?

וְלָא פְּלִיגִי?! וְהָא פְּלִיגִי רַבָּנַן!

The Gemara rejects this: **And don't they dispute** his opinion? **Don't the Rabbis dispute** his opinion, as, in their opinion the blessing of *havdala* is recited in the blessing: Who graciously grants knowledge?

אֵימַר דִּפְלִיגִי רַבָּנַן – בִּשְׁאָר יְמוֹת הַשָּׁנָה, בְּיוֹם טוֹב שֶׁחָל לִהְיוֹת אַחַר הַשַּׁבָּת מִי פְּלִיגִי?

The Gemara replies: **Say that the Rabbis dispute** Rabbi Eliezer's opinion **during the rest of the days of the year,** when the option to recite *havdala* in the blessing: Who graciously grants knowledge exists, but **in the case of a Festival that occurs** directly **after Shabbat, do they dispute** his opinion? The Rabbis would agree with him in that case.

וְהָא פָּלֵיג רַבִּי עֲקִיבָא!

The Gemara continues: **Doesn't Rabbi Akiva dispute** his opinion? He holds that *havdala* is recited as an independent fourth blessing, in which case there is a dispute.

אַטּוּ כָּל הַשָּׁנָה כּוּלָּהּ מִי עָבְדִינַן כְּרַבִּי עֲקִיבָא, דְּהָשְׁתָּא נֵיקוּ וְנַעֲבֵיד כְּוָותֵיהּ?! כָּל הַשָּׁנָה כּוּלָּהּ מַאי טַעְמָא לָא עָבְדִינַן כְּרַבִּי עֲקִיבָא? – דִּתְמָנֵי סְרֵי תַּקּוּן, תְּשַׁסְרֵי לָא תַּקּוּן, הָכָא נַמִּי – שַׁב תַּקּוּן, תְּמָנֵי לָא תַּקּוּן!

The Gemara responds: **Is that to say that throughout the entire year we act in accordance with** the opinion of **Rabbi Akiva** in this matter, **so that now,** on a Festival that occurs directly after Shabbat, **we will stand and act in accordance with** his opinion? **What is the reason that throughout the whole, entire year, we do not act in accordance with** the opinion of **Rabbi Akiva? Because** the Sages **instituted eighteen** blessings, **they did not institute nineteen** blessings. **Here, too,** the Sages **instituted seven** blessings, **they did not institute eight** blessings. Therefore, Rabbi Akiva's opinion is not taken into consideration in this case.

אָמַר לֵיהּ: לָאו ״הֲלָכָה״ אִתְּמַר, אֶלָּא ״מַטִּין״ אִתְּמַר.

In response to these questions, Rabbi Zeira **said to him** that **it was not** that **the *halakha*** is in accordance with the opinion of Rabbi Eliezer **that was stated** in the name of Rabbi Yoḥanan, from which one could infer that there was in fact a dispute; rather it was that one is **inclined**[N] to favor the opinion of Rabbi Eliezer **that was stated** in the name of Rabbi Yoḥanan.

דְּאִתְּמַר, רַבִּי יִצְחָק בַּר אַבְדִּימִי אָמַר מִשּׁוּם רַבֵּינוּ: הֲלָכָה, וְאָמְרִי לָהּ: מַטִּין.

As indeed **it was stated** that there is a dispute among the Sages in this matter. **Rav Yitzḥak bar Avdimi said in the name of Rabbeinu,** Rav: **The *halakha*** is in accordance with the opinion of Rabbi Eliezer. **And some say this** statement: One is **inclined** to favor of the opinion of Rabbi Eliezer.

NOTES

***Halakha*…inclined** – הֲלָכָה...מַטִּין: In this matter, there are various manners in which a specific opinion might be adopted as *halakha*. When it is established that the *halakha* is in accordance with a particular opinion, the *halakha* is disseminated to the public as conclusive. When it is established merely that the *halakha* is inclined in favor of a particular opinion, it is not disseminated to the general public. However, if an individual asks, the answer provided is in accordance with this ruling. A third manner in which an opinion might be adopted is by saying that the opinion of one of the Sages seems to be the *halakha*. On the one hand, the *halakha* has not been established in accordance with his opinion. On the other hand, one who conducts himself in accordance with that opinion is neither reprimanded nor encouraged.

רַבִּי יוֹחָנָן אָמַר: מוֹדִים; וְרַבִּי חִיָּיא בַּר אַבָּא אָמַר: נִרְאִין.

Rabbi Yoḥanan **said** that there is no dispute here, and the Rabbis **agree** with Rabbi Eliezer. **And Rabbi Ḥiyya bar Abba said** that it was established that Rabbi Eliezer's opinion **appears** to be correct.

אָמַר רַבִּי זֵירָא: נְקוֹט דְּרַבִּי חִיָּיא בַּר אַבָּא בִּידָךְ, דְּדַיֵּיק וּגְמַר שְׁמַעְתָּא מִפּוּמָּא דְּמָרָהּ שַׁפִּיר כְּרַחֲבָה דְּפוּמְבְּדִיתָא.

With regard to this difference of opinion **Rabbi Zeira said: Take** this statement **of Rabbi Ḥiyya bar Abba in your hand, as he is scrupulous and he learned the *halakha* well from the mouth of its originator, like** the Sage **Raḥava**[N] from the city **Pumbedita.** Raḥava was famous for the precision with which he would transmit material that he learned from his teacher.

דְּאָמַר רַחֲבָה אָמַר רַבִּי יְהוּדָה: הַר הַבַּיִת סְטָיו כָּפוּל הָיָה, וְהָיָה סְטָיו לִפְנִים מִסְּטָיו.

The Gemara cites an example: **Raḥava said** that **Rabbi Yehuda said: The Temple Mount was a double *stav*,**[L] **and there was a *stav* within a *stav*.** Here Raḥava used his Rabbi's language in describing the structure of the Temple and the rows of columns it contained, a row within a row; but he did not employ the common term *itzteba*, portico, but rather *stav*, as he heard it from his Rabbi.

אָמַר רַב יוֹסֵף: אֲנָא לָא הַאי יָדַעְנָא וְלָא הַאי יָדַעְנָא, אֶלָּא מִדְּרַב וּשְׁמוּאֵל יָדַעְנָא דְּתַקִּינוּ לַן מַרְגָּנִיתָא בְּבָבֶל:

Rav Yosef said the conclusive *halakha* on this topic: **I don't know this and I don't know that, but I do know from** the statements of **Rav and Shmuel they have instituted a pearl for us in Babylonia.** They established a version that combines the first blessing of the Festival with the formula of *havdala*, parallel to the opinion of the Rabbis who include *havdala* in the first blessing that follows the first three blessings. They instituted to recite:

וַתּוֹדִיעֵנוּ ה׳ אֱלֹהֵינוּ אֶת מִשְׁפְּטֵי צִדְקֶךָ וַתְּלַמְּדֵנוּ לַעֲשׂוֹת חֻקֵּי רְצוֹנֶךָ, וַתַּנְחִילֵנוּ זְמַנֵּי שָׂשׂוֹן וְחַגֵּי נְדָבָה וַתּוֹרִישֵׁנוּ קְדוּשַּׁת שַׁבָּת וּכְבוֹד מוֹעֵד וַחֲגִיגַת הָרֶגֶל, בֵּין קְדוּשַּׁת שַׁבָּת לִקְדוּשַּׁת יוֹם טוֹב הִבְדַּלְתָּ וְאֶת יוֹם הַשְּׁבִיעִי מִשֵּׁשֶׁת יְמֵי הַמַּעֲשֶׂה קִדַּשְׁתָּ, הִבְדַּלְתָּ וְקִדַּשְׁתָּ אֶת עַמְּךָ יִשְׂרָאֵל בִּקְדוּשָּׁתֶךָ, וַתִּתֵּן לָנוּ וכו׳.

You have made known to us,[H] **Lord our God, Your righteous laws, and taught us to perform Your will's decrees.**
You have given us as our heritage seasons of joy and Festivals of voluntary offerings.
You have given us as our heritage the holiness of Shabbat, the glory of the festival and the festive offerings of the Pilgrim Festivals.
You have distinguished between the holiness of Shabbat and the holiness of the Festival,
and have made the seventh day holy over the six days of work.
You have distinguished and sanctified Your people Israel with Your holiness,
And You have given us, etc.

מתני׳ הָאוֹמֵר ״עַל קַן צִיפּוֹר יַגִּיעוּ רַחֲמֶיךָ״ וְ״עַל טוֹב יִזָּכֵר שְׁמֶךָ״, ״מוֹדִים מוֹדִים״ – מְשַׁתְּקִין אוֹתוֹ.

MISHNA Concluding the laws of prayer in this tractate, the mishna raises several prayer-related matters. This mishna speaks of certain innovations in the prayer formula that warrant the silencing of a communal prayer leader who attempts to introduce them in his prayers, as their content tends toward heresy. **One who recites** in his supplication: Just as **Your mercy is extended to a bird's nest,**[H] as You have commanded us to send away the mother before taking her chicks or eggs (Deuteronomy 22:6–7), so too extend Your mercy to us; **and** one who recites: **May Your name be mentioned with the good** or one who recites: **We give thanks, we give thanks**[H] twice, they **silence him.**

גמ׳ בִּשְׁלָמָא ״מוֹדִים מוֹדִים״ מְשַׁתְּקִין אוֹתוֹ – מִשּׁוּם דְּמֶיחֱזֵי כְּשְׁתֵּי רְשׁוּיוֹת, וְ״עַל טוֹב יִזָּכֵר שְׁמֶךָ״ – נַמִי מַשְׁמַע עַל הַטּוֹבָה וְלֹא עַל הָרָעָה, וּתְנַן: חַיָּיב אָדָם לְבָרֵךְ עַל הָרָעָה כְּשֵׁם שֶׁמְּבָרֵךְ עַל הַטּוֹבָה. אֶלָּא ״עַל קַן צִפּוֹר יַגִּיעוּ רַחֲמֶיךָ״ מַאי טַעְמָא?

GEMARA Our mishna cited three instances where the communal prayer leader is silenced. The Gemara clarifies: **Granted,** they silence one who repeats: **We give thanks, we give thanks, as it appears like** he is acknowledging and praying to **two authorities. And** granted that **they also silence** one who says: **May Your name be mentioned with the good,** as **clearly** he is thanking God only **for the good and not for the bad, and we learned** in a mishna: **One is required to bless God for the bad**[H] **just as he blesses** Him **for the good. However,** in the case of one who recites: Just as **Your mercy is extended to a bird's nest, why** do they silence him?

פְּלִיגִי בָּהּ תְּרֵי אֲמוֹרָאֵי בְּמַעַרְבָא, רַבִּי יוֹסֵי בַּר אָבִין וְרַבִּי יוֹסֵי בַּר זְבִידָא; חַד אָמַר: מִפְּנֵי שֶׁמַּטִּיל קִנְאָה בְּמַעֲשֵׂה בְרֵאשִׁית, וְחַד אָמַר: מִפְּנֵי שֶׁעוֹשֶׂה מִדּוֹתָיו שֶׁל הַקָּדוֹשׁ בָּרוּךְ הוּא רַחֲמִים, וְאֵינָן אֶלָּא גְּזֵרוֹת.

Two *amora'im* in Eretz Yisrael disputed this question; **Rabbi Yosei bar Avin and Rabbi Yosei bar Zevida; one said** that this was **because he engenders jealousy among God's creations,** as it appears as though he is protesting the fact that the Lord favored one creature over all others. **And one said** that this was **because he transforms the attributes of the Holy One, Blessed be He, into** expressions of **mercy,**[N] **when they are nothing but decrees** of the King that must be fulfilled without inquiring into the reasons behind them.

NOTES

As he is scrupulous…like Raḥava – דְּדַיֵּיק...כְּרַחֲבָה: Various interpretations were suggested in explanation of Raḥava's unique precision. Some *ge'onim* explain that Raḥava was uncertain whether he heard the statement in the name of Rabbi Yehuda, the *tanna*, or Rav Yehuda, the *amora*, and he therefore repeated the statement in a manner that included them both. Others reject this (Rabbeinu Ḥananel, Rashi) and say that he repeated what he learned from his teacher verbatim.

He transforms the attributes of the Holy One, Blessed be He, into mercy – שֶׁעוֹשֶׂה מִדּוֹתָיו שֶׁל הַקָּדוֹשׁ בָּרוּךְ הוּא רַחֲמִים, וְאֵינָן אֶלָּא גְּזֵרוֹת: The Rambam explains that compassion is not the reason for this mitzva, as if that was the case, God would have prohibited slaughtering animals for food. Although in midrash, this mitzva is interpreted as a manifestation of compassion, it should be understood as guidance for man to act with compassion toward creatures, not as an indication of God's compassion on those creatures (Ramban on the Torah).

LANGUAGE

Colonnade [*stav*] – סְטָיו: From the Greek στοά, *stoa*, meaning a roofed row of columns, *stav* refers to a row of columns that is attached to a building. The Gemara refers to a double *stav*; two rows of columns.

Colonnade

HALAKHA

The *havdala* of: And You have made known to us, etc. – הַבְדָּלַת וַתּוֹדִיעֵנוּ: According to Rav Yosef's conclusion, the addition to the evening prayer on Festivals that occur at the conclusion of Shabbat: And You have made known to us, is the accepted formula for *havdala* on that occasion (Rambam *Sefer Ahava, Hilkhot Tefilla* 2:12; *Shulḥan Arukh, Oraḥ Ḥayyim* 491:2).

One who recites: Just as Your mercy is extended to a bird's nest… – הָאוֹמֵר עַל קַן צִיפּוֹר וכו׳: Those who hear one who recites in his prayer: Just as Your mercy is extended to a bird's nest or a similar formula, should silence him, as per our mishna (Rambam *Sefer Ahava, Hilkhot Tefilla* 9:6).

One who recites: We give thanks, we give thanks – הָאוֹמֵר מוֹדִים מוֹדִים: Those who hear one who recites: We give thanks, we give thanks, should silence him, as per our mishna (Rambam *Sefer Ahava, Hilkhot Tefilla* 9:4; *Shulḥan Arukh, Oraḥ Ḥayyim* 121:2).

One is required to bless God for the bad, etc. … – חַיָּיב אָדָם לְבָרֵךְ עַל הָרָעָה וכו׳: One is required to bless God for the bad that befalls him with devotion and enthusiasm just as he does when good befalls him (Rambam *Sefer Ahava, Hilkhot Berakhot* 10:3; *Shulḥan Arukh, Oraḥ Ḥayyim* 222:2).

הַהוּא דְּנָחֵית קַמֵּיהּ דְּרַבָּה, וַאֲמַר: אַתָּה חַסְתָּ עַל קַן צִפּוֹר, אַתָּה חוּס וְרַחֵם עָלֵינוּ. אָמַר רַבָּה: כַּמָּה יָדַע הַאי צוּרְבָא מֵרַבָּנַן לְרַצּוּיֵי לְמָרֵיהּ! – אָמַר לֵיהּ אַבָּיֵי: וְהָא ״מְשַׁתְּקִין אוֹתוֹ״ תְּנַן!

The Gemara relates that **a particular** individual **descended before the ark** as prayer leader **in the presence of Rabba, and said** in his prayers: **You have shown mercy to the bird's nest, now have mercy and pity upon us. Rabba said: How much does this Torah scholar know to appease** the Lord, **his Master. Abaye said to him: Didn't we learn** in a mishna that **they silence him?**

וְרַבָּה נַמִּי – לְחַדּוּדֵי אַבָּיֵי הוּא דְּבָעֵי.

The Gemara explains: **And Rabba too** held in accordance with this mishna but merely acted this way because **he wanted to hone Abaye's** intellect. Rabba did not make his statement to praise the scholar, but simply to test his nephew, Abaye, and to encourage him to articulate what he knows about that mishna.

הַהוּא דְּנָחֵית קַמֵּיהּ דְּרַבִּי חֲנִינָא, אָמַר: הָאֵל הַגָּדוֹל הַגִּבּוֹר וְהַנּוֹרָא וְהָאַדִּיר וְהָעִזּוּז וְהַיָּראוּי הֶחָזָק וְהָאַמִּיץ וְהַוַּדַּאי וְהַנִּכְבָּד.

With regard to additions to prayers formulated by the Sages, The Gemara relates that **a particular** individual **descended before the ark** as prayer leader **in the presence of Rabbi Ḥanina.** He extended his prayer and **said: God, the great, mighty, awesome, powerful, mighty, awe-inspiring, strong, fearless, steadfast and honored.**

הִמְתִּין לוֹ עַד דְּסַיֵּים, כִּי סַיֵּים אָמַר לֵיהּ: סַיֵּימְתִּינְהוּ לְכוּלְּהוּ שִׁבְחֵי דְּמָרָךְ?! לָמָּה לִי כּוּלֵּי הַאי? אֲנַן הָנֵי תְּלָת דְּאָמְרִינַן – אִי לָאו דְּאָמְרִינְהוּ מֹשֶׁה רַבֵּנוּ בְּאוֹרַיְיתָא, וַאֲתוֹ אַנְשֵׁי כְּנֶסֶת הַגְּדוֹלָה וְתַקְּנִינְהוּ בִּתְפִלָּה – לָא הֲוֵינַן יְכוֹלִין לְמֵימַר לְהוּ, וְאַתְּ אָמְרַתְּ כּוּלֵּי הַאי וְאָזְלַתְּ! מָשָׁל, לְמֶלֶךְ בָּשָׂר וָדָם שֶׁהָיוּ לוֹ אֶלֶף אֲלָפִים דִּינְרֵי זָהָב, וְהָיוּ מְקַלְּסִין אוֹתוֹ בְּשֶׁל כֶּסֶף, וַהֲלֹא גְּנַאי הוּא לוֹ!

Rabbi Ḥanina **waited for him until he completed** his prayer. **When he finished,** Rabbi Ḥanina **asked him: Have you concluded all of the praises of your Master? Why do I need all of this** superfluous praise?[H] **Even these three** praises **that we recite:** The great, mighty and awesome, **had Moses our teacher not said them in the Torah and had the members of the Great Assembly not come and incorporated them into the** *Amida* **prayer, we would not be permitted to recite them. And you went on and recited all of these. It is comparable to a king who possessed many thousands of golden dinars, yet they were praising him for silver ones.**[BN] **Isn't that deprecatory?** All of the praises we could possibly lavish upon the Lord are nothing but a few silver dinars relative to many thousands of gold dinars. Reciting a litany of praise does not enhance God's honor.

וְאָמַר רַבִּי חֲנִינָא: הַכֹּל בִּידֵי שָׁמַיִם – חוּץ מִיִּרְאַת שָׁמַיִם, שֶׁנֶּאֱמַר: ״וְעַתָּה יִשְׂרָאֵל מָה ה׳ אֱלֹהֶיךָ שׁוֹאֵל מֵעִמָּךְ כִּי אִם לְיִרְאָה״.

Tangentially, the Gemara cites an additional statement by Rabbi Ḥanina concerning principles of faith. **And Rabbi Ḥanina said: Everything is in the hands of Heaven, except for fear of Heaven.** Man has free will to serve God or not, **as it is stated: "And now Israel, what does the Lord your God ask of you other than to fear** the Lord your God, to walk in all of His ways, to love Him and to serve the Lord your God with all your heart and with all your soul" (Deuteronomy 10:12). The Lord asks man to perform these matters because ultimately, the choice is his hands.

אַטּוּ יִרְאַת שָׁמַיִם מִילְּתָא זוּטַרְתָּא הִיא?! וְהָאָמַר רַבִּי חֲנִינָא מִשּׁוּם רַבִּי שִׁמְעוֹן בֶּן יוֹחַי: אֵין לוֹ לְהַקָּדוֹשׁ בָּרוּךְ הוּא בְּבֵית גְּנָזָיו אֶלָּא אוֹצָר שֶׁל יִרְאַת שָׁמַיִם, שֶׁנֶּאֱמַר: ״יִרְאַת ה׳ הִיא אוֹצָרוֹ״!

The verse says: What does the Lord your God ask of you other than to fear the Lord your God. The Gemara asks: **Is fear of Heaven a minor matter** that it can be presented as if God is not asking anything significant? **Didn't Rabbi Ḥanina say in the name of Rabbi Shimon ben Yoḥai: The Holy One, Blessed be He, has nothing in his treasury other than a treasure of fear of Heaven, as it is stated: "Fear of the Lord is his treasure"** (Isaiah 33:6). The Lord values and treasures fear of Heaven over all else.

אִין, לְגַבֵּי מֹשֶׁה מִילְּתָא זוּטַרְתָּא הִיא. דְּאָמַר רַבִּי חֲנִינָא: מָשָׁל, לְאָדָם שֶׁמְּבַקְּשִׁים מִמֶּנּוּ כְּלִי גָּדוֹל וְיֵשׁ לוֹ – דּוֹמֶה עָלָיו כִּכְלִי קָטָן, קָטָן וְאֵין לוֹ – דּוֹמֶה עָלָיו כִּכְלִי גָּדוֹל.

The Gemara responds: **Indeed, for Moses** fear of Heaven **is a minor matter. As Rabbi Ḥanina stated: It is comparable to one who is asked for a large vessel and he has** one, **it seems to him like a small vessel** because he owns it. However, one who is asked for just a **small** vessel and he does not have one, **it seems to him like a large vessel.** Therefore, Moses could say: What does the Lord your God ask of you other than to fear, because in his eyes it was a minor matter.

״מוֹדִים מוֹדִים – מְשַׁתְּקִין אוֹתוֹ״.

We learned in the mishna if one repeats: **We give thanks, we give thanks, they silence him.**

אָמַר רַבִּי זֵירָא: כָּל הָאוֹמֵר ״שְׁמַע״ ״שְׁמַע״ – כְּאוֹמֵר ״מוֹדִים מוֹדִים״ דָּמֵי.

Rabbi Zeira said: One who repeats himself while reciting *Shema* and **says: Listen Israel, Listen Israel**[H] **is like one who says: We give thanks, we give thanks.**

מֵיתִיבִי: הַקּוֹרֵא אֶת שְׁמַע וְכוֹפְלָהּ – הֲרֵי זֶה מְגוּנֶּה. מְגוּנֶּה הוּא דַּהֲוֵי, שַׁתּוֹקֵי לָא מְשַׁתְּקִינַן לֵיהּ!

The Gemara **raises an objection:** It was taught in a *baraita*: **One who recites** *Shema* **and repeats it, it is reprehensible.** One may infer: **It is reprehensible, but they do not silence him.**

HALAKHA

Adding praises – מוֹסִיפִים בִּשְׁבָחִים: One may not add to the praises of God that were incorporated into the formula of the *Amida* prayer, for the reasons enumerated by Rabbi Ḥanina in the Gemara. However in personal, private pleas, one is permitted to do so (*Tur* in the name of the Tosafist, Rabbeinu Yitzḥak; Rambam *Sefer Ahava, Hilkhot Tefilla* 9:7; *Shulḥan Arukh, Oraḥ Ḥayyim* 113:9).

One who says: Listen…Listen – הָאוֹמֵר ״שְׁמַע״ ״שְׁמַע״: There is a dispute whether this prohibition applies to the repetition of the word *Shema* (*Ba'al Halakhot Gedolot*, Rabbeinu Ḥananel) or to the repetition of the entire verse (Rashi). The *halakha* ruled in accordance with both opinions, and one may not repeat the word or the verse, except in a congregation, in which case repetition is permitted in specific cases (Jerusalem Talmud, *Baḥ*; Rambam *Sefer Ahava, Hilkhot Keriat Shema* 2:11; *Shulḥan Arukh, Oraḥ Ḥayyim* 61:9).

BACKGROUND

Dinars of gold and silver – דִּינְרֵי זָהָב...כֶּסֶף: In talmudic times the average proportion between gold dinars to silver was 25:1, so the difference in their relative value was significant.

Dinars of gold (Nero)

Dinars of silver (Vespasian)

NOTES

Dinars of gold and silver – דִּינְרֵי זָהָב...כֶּסֶף: The Rambam explains that the problem was not that he brought too few dinars, but that the praise does not reach the heights of the One being praised at all, as silver dinars of are qualitatively inferior to gold dinars. Similarly, the praises that people lavish on God do not relate to His level of perfection at all. According to the Ritva's explanation, the rhetorical question: Isn't that deprecatory, refers to the person praying, whose praise indicates his lack of understanding of the King's greatness.

לָא קַשְׁיָא: הָא – דַּאֲמַר מִילְּתָא מִילְּתָא וְתָנֵי לָהּ, וְהָא – דַּאֲמַר פְּסוּקָא פְּסוּקָא וְתָנֵי לֵיהּ.

The Gemara answers: **This is not difficult; this** case, where although it is reprehensible when one repeats *Shema*, they do not silence him, is referring to **one who recites and repeats each individual word** as he says it. In so doing he ruins the recitation of *Shema*. However, **this** case, where Rabbi Zeira holds that one who repeats *Shema* they silence him, refers to **one who recites and repeats an entire verse,** as it appears that he is worshiping separate authorities.

אָמַר לֵיהּ רַב פַּפָּא לְאַבַּיֵי: וְדִילְמָא מֵעִיקָּרָא לָא כַּוֵּין דַּעְתֵּיהּ, וּלְבַסּוֹף כַּוֵּין דַּעְתֵּיהּ?

Rav Pappa said to Abaye with regard to this *halakha*: **And perhaps initially he did not focus his attention** on the recitation of *Shema*, so he repeated it **and ultimately he focused his attention** as he recited it the second time?

אָמַר לֵיהּ:

Abaye **said to him:**

Perek **V**
Daf **34** Amud **a**

חַבְרוּתָא כְּלַפֵּי שְׁמַיָּא מִי אִיכָּא?! אִי לָא כַּוֵּין דַּעְתֵּיהּ מֵעִיקָּרָא – מָחֵינַן לֵיהּ בְּמַרְזַפְתָּא דְנַפָּחָא עַד דִּמְכַוֵּין דַּעְתֵּיהּ.

Can one have that degree of **familiarity with Heaven,**[N] to the extent that he can take his words lightly and say them however he likes? **If he did not focus his attention initially, we beat him with a blacksmith's hammer**[B] **until he focuses his attention,** as conduct of that sort is unacceptable.

מתני׳ (הָאוֹמֵר: יְבָרְכוּךָ טוֹבִים – הֲרֵי זֶה דַּרְכֵי מִינוּת). הָעוֹבֵר לִפְנֵי הַתֵּיבָה וְטָעָה – יַעֲבוֹר אַחֵר תַּחְתָּיו, וְלֹא יְהֵא סַרְבָן בְּאוֹתָהּ שָׁעָה. מֵהֵיכָן הוּא מַתְחִיל? מִתְּחִלַּת הַבְּרָכָה שֶׁטָּעָה זֶה.

MISHNA This mishna and the next one deal with the communal prayer leader. (**If one says: "May the good bless You," this is a path of heresy.**)[N] **One who is passing before the ark,** as prayer leader, **and erred,**[H] **another should** immediately **pass in his place, and at that moment,** this replacement **should not refuse** in the interest of courtesy. The *Amida* prayer was interrupted and he should replace him as quickly as possible. **From where does** the replacement **commence? From the beginning of the blessing in which** the former **had erred.**

הָעוֹבֵר לִפְנֵי הַתֵּיבָה לֹא יַעֲנֶה "אָמֵן" אַחַר הַכֹּהֲנִים מִפְּנֵי הַטֵּרוּף, וְאִם אֵין שָׁם כֹּהֵן אֶלָּא הוּא – לֹא יִשָּׂא אֶת כַּפָּיו. וְאִם הַבְטָחָתוֹ שֶׁהוּא נוֹשֵׂא אֶת כַּפָּיו וְחוֹזֵר לִתְפִלָּתוֹ – רַשַּׁאי.

In order to prevent the prayer leader from erring in his prayer, it was said that **one who passes before the ark should not respond amen after the** blessing of the **priests,**[H] **because of** potential **confusion.** Since the mishna is describing a situation in which he was praying without a prayer book, responding amen would interrupt the order of the prayer and potentially lead him to begin a different blessing. For this reason, even **if there is no priest other than** the communal prayer leader,[H] **he does not lift his hands** to bless the people, lest he become confused. **And,** however, **if he is certain that he can lift his hands and resume his prayer** without becoming confused, **he is permitted** to recite the blessing.

NOTES

Can one have familiarity with Heaven – חַבְרוּתָא כְּלַפֵּי שְׁמַיָּא מִי אִיכָּא: Apparently this applies specifically to one who repeats a section of the prayer aloud, as he thereby shows that the first time that he recited it he did so with contempt and without focus. However, if one failed to muster the appropriate intent the first time, there is nothing wrong with repeating it silently (*Tal Torah*).

If one says: May the good bless You, this is a path of heresy – הָאוֹמֵר יְבָרְכוּךָ טוֹבִים הֲרֵי זֶה דַּרְכֵי מִינוּת: The heresy here lies in the fact that by saying: May the good bless You, one intimates that the wicked have a different god, indicating a belief in two entities (Rashba, based on the Jerusalem Talmud). Some explain an additional problem in that formula, as one is supposed to include both the good and the wicked in his prayers and not leave the wicked isolated (Rashba).

BACKGROUND

A blacksmith's hammer – מַרְזַפְתָּא דְנַפָּחָא:

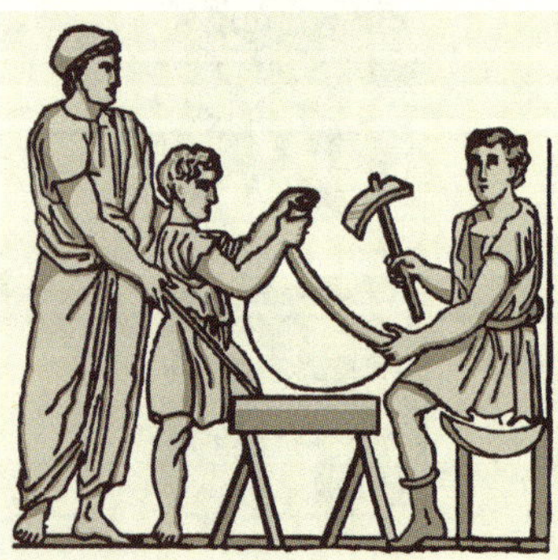

Blacksmith striking with the hammer in his hand, from a Byzantine ivory relief

HALAKHA

One who is passing before the ark, as prayer leader, and erred – הָעוֹבֵר לִפְנֵי הַתֵּיבָה וְטָעָה: If a communal prayer leader errs in his prayer and is unable to resume his prayer, another replaces him and, in that circumstance, should not refuse for reasons of propriety. He begins at the beginning of the blessing where his predecessor erred (Rambam *Sefer Ahava, Hilkhot Tefilla* 10:3; *Shulḥan Arukh, Oraḥ Ḥayyim* 126:2, *Oraḥ Ḥayyim* 53:17).

One who passes before the ark should not answer amen after the blessing of the priests – הָעוֹבֵר לִפְנֵי הַתֵּיבָה לֹא יַעֲנֶה אָמֵן אַחַר הַכֹּהֲנִים: A communal prayer leader may not answer amen after the priests. In our generation, opinions differ as to whether the concern for potential confusion applies to a prayer leader praying from a prayer book as well (*Magen Avraham*, *Taz*; Rambam *Sefer Ahava, Hilkhot Nesiat Kappayim* 14:5; *Shulḥan Arukh, Oraḥ Ḥayyim* 128:19).

If there is no priest other than him, etc. – וְאִם אֵין שָׁם כֹּהֵן אֶלָּא הוּא וכו׳: Although we learned that a prayer leader who is a priest should not recite the Priestly Blessing due to concern for potential confusion, in our generation when everyone prays from a prayer book, this is not a concern; everyone has the legal status of one who is certain that he will resume his prayer without error (*Magen Abraham*; Rambam *Sefer Ahava, Hilkhot Nesi'at Kappayim* 15:10; *Shulḥan Arukh, Oraḥ Ḥayyim* 128:20).

גמ׳ תָּנוּ רַבָּנַן: הָעוֹבֵר לִפְנֵי הַתֵּיבָה – צָרִיךְ לְסָרֵב, וְאִם אֵינוֹ מְסָרֵב – דּוֹמֶה לְתַבְשִׁיל שֶׁאֵין בּוֹ מֶלַח, וְאִם מְסָרֵב יוֹתֵר מִדַּאי – דּוֹמֶה לְתַבְשִׁיל שֶׁהִקְדִּיחַתּוּ מֶלַח. כֵּיצַד הוּא עוֹשֶׂה – פַּעַם רִאשׁוֹנָה יְסָרֵב, שְׁנִיָּה מְהַבְהֵב, שְׁלִישִׁית – פּוֹשֵׁט אֶת רַגְלָיו וְיוֹרֵד.

GEMARA The mishna teaches that one who replaces a communal prayer leader who erred in the middle of the *Amida* prayer should not refuse when approached. The Gemara cites the general *halakha* with regard to proper conduct when one is approached to serve as prayer leader. **The Sages taught** in a *baraita*: One who is approached **to pass before the ark** to serve as prayer leader, for the sake of propriety **should refuse,**[H] to avoid creating the impression that he is too eager. **And if he does not refuse,** but jumps at the opportunity, **he is like cooked food without salt,** which is to say that he acts in bad taste. **However, if he refuses too much** this is similarly inappropriate, as **he is like cooked food that was ruined by** too much **salt.** So **how should he act?** The appropriate conduct when approached to serve as communal prayer leader is as follows: When approached **the first time, one should refuse; the second** time, one should **vacillate** like a wick that has just begun to catch a flame but is not yet burning; and **the third** time, **he should stretch his legs and descend** before the ark.

תָּנוּ רַבָּנַן: שְׁלֹשָׁה רוּבָּן קָשֶׁה וּמִיעוּטָן יָפֶה, וְאֵלּוּ הֵן: שְׂאוֹר, וּמֶלַח, וְסַרְבָנוּת.

On this note, the Gemara cites that which **the Sages taught** in a *baraita*: There are **three** things that **are harmful in excess but are beneficial when used sparingly.** They are: **Leavening** in dough, **salt** in a cooked dish **and refusal** for the sake of propriety.

אָמַר רַב הוּנָא: טָעָה בְּשָׁלֹשׁ רִאשׁוֹנוֹת – חוֹזֵר לָרֹאשׁ, בָּאֶמְצָעִיּוֹת – חוֹזֵר לְ״אַתָּה חוֹנֵן״, בָּאַחֲרוֹנוֹת – חוֹזֵר לַ״עֲבוֹדָה״;

The mishna states that when one replaces the communal prayer leader, he commences from the beginning of the blessing in which the former had erred. However that is not universally true, as **Rav Huna said:** One who **erred in** any of **the first three** blessings **he must return to the beginning** of the *Amida* prayer because the first three blessing comprise a single entity. Likewise, if one **erred in** any of **the** thirteen **middle** blessings, **he returns to** the blessing of: **You grace** humanity, the first of the middle blessings. If one erred **in** any of the three **final** blessings, **he must return to the** blessing of **Temple service,** which is the first of the final blessings.[H]

וְרַב אַסִי אָמַר: אֶמְצָעִיּוֹת אֵין לָהֶן סֵדֶר.

And Rav Asi disputes one aspect of Rav Huna's opinion, as **he said: The middle** blessings **have no** set **order.** If one erred in any of them he may insert it at whatever point he becomes aware of his error.

מְתִיב רַב שֵׁשֶׁת: ״מֵהֵיכָן הוּא חוֹזֵר – מִתְּחִלַּת הַבְּרָכָה שֶׁטָּעָה זֶה״, תְּיוּבְתָּא דְּרַב הוּנָא!

Rav Sheshet raised an objection based on a *baraita*: **From where does he** commence **repetition** of the *Amida* prayer? He commences **from the beginning of the blessing in which** the former **had erred.** If so, this is **a conclusive refutation of Rav Huna's** opinion, as Rav Huna said that if one erred in one of the middle blessings, he returns to the beginning of the middle blessings, not to the beginning of that particular blessing.

אָמַר לָךְ רַב הוּנָא: אֶמְצָעִיּוֹת – כּוּלְּהוּ חֲדָא בִּרְכְתָא נִינְהוּ.

Rav Huna could have **said to you: The middle** blessings **are all** considered **one blessing;** commencing from the beginning of the blessing means returning to the beginning of the middle blessings.

אָמַר רַב יְהוּדָה: לְעוֹלָם אַל יִשְׁאַל אָדָם צְרָכָיו לֹא בְּשָׁלֹשׁ רִאשׁוֹנוֹת, וְלֹא בְּשָׁלֹשׁ אַחֲרוֹנוֹת, אֶלָּא בָּאֶמְצָעִיּוֹת. דְּאָמַר רַבִּי חֲנִינָא: רִאשׁוֹנוֹת – דּוֹמֶה לְעֶבֶד שֶׁמְּסַדֵּר שֶׁבַח לִפְנֵי רַבּוֹ, אֶמְצָעִיּוֹת – דּוֹמֶה לְעֶבֶד שֶׁמְּבַקֵּשׁ פְּרָס מֵרַבּוֹ, אַחֲרוֹנוֹת – דּוֹמֶה לְעֶבֶד שֶׁקִּבֵּל פְּרָס מֵרַבּוֹ וְנִפְטָר וְהוֹלֵךְ לוֹ.

Rav Yehuda said: There is an additional distinction between the various sections of the *Amida* prayer: **One must never request his** own **needs in the first three**[H] **or in the last three** blessings; **rather,** he should do so **in the middle** blessings. **As Rabbi Ḥanina said:** During the **first** three blessings, he **is like a servant who arranges praise before his master;** during the **middle** blessings, he **is like a servant who requests a reward from his master;** during the **final** three blessings, one **is like a servant who** already **received a reward from his master and is taking his leave and departing.**

תָּנוּ רַבָּנַן: מַעֲשֶׂה בְּתַלְמִיד אֶחָד שֶׁיָּרַד לִפְנֵי הַתֵּיבָה בִּפְנֵי רַבִּי אֱלִיעֶזֶר וְהָיָה מַאֲרִיךְ יוֹתֵר מִדַּאי. אָמְרוּ לוֹ תַּלְמִידָיו: כַּמָּה אַרְכָן הוּא זֶה! – אָמַר לָהֶם: כְּלוּם מַאֲרִיךְ יוֹתֵר מִמֹּשֶׁה רַבֵּינוּ?! דִּכְתִיב בֵּיהּ: ״אֵת אַרְבָּעִים הַיּוֹם וְאֶת אַרְבָּעִים הַלַּיְלָה״ וגו׳.

Continuing on the subject of prayer, **the Sages taught:** There was **an incident where one student descended** to serve as prayer leader **before the ark in the presence of Rabbi Eliezer, and he was excessively prolonging his prayer. His students** complained and **said to him: How long-winded he is. He said to them: Is** this student **prolonging** his prayer any more **than Moses our teacher** did? **As about Moses it is written:** "And I prostrated myself before the Lord **for the forty days and forty nights** that I prostrated myself" (Deuteronomy 9:25). There is no limit to the duration of a prayer.

HALAKHA

One who is approached to pass before the ark should refuse – הָעוֹבֵר לִפְנֵי הַתֵּיבָה – צָרִיךְ לְסָרֵב וכו׳: One who is approached to serve as prayer leader should initially refuse for reasons of propriety. This applies specifically to a case where the individual is not the regular prayer leader (*Shulḥan Arukh, Oraḥ Ḥayyim* 53:16).

One who errs in his prayer – הַטּוֹעֶה בִּתְפִלָּתוֹ: If one erred in his prayer, i.e., he skipped a blessing; if he did so in the first three blessings, he must return to the beginning of the *Amida* prayer. If he erred in the final three blessings he returns to the beginning of the blessing of Temple service. If he erred in the middle blessings, contrary to Rashi's opinion, the Rif and the Rashbam explained and the Rambam and the Ra'avad concurred that he returns to the beginning of that particular blessing and continues in order, in accordance with the opinion of Rav Asi (Rambam *Sefer Ahava, Hilkhot Tefilla* 10:1, 4; *Shulḥan Arukh, Oraḥ Ḥayyim* 119:3).

One must never request his own needs in the first three, etc. – לְעוֹלָם אַל יִשְׁאַל אָדָם צְרָכָיו לֹא בְּשָׁלֹשׁ רִאשׁוֹנוֹת וכו׳: One may only request his personal needs in the thirteen middle blessings, not during the first three or last three blessings, as per the opinion of Rav Yehuda (Rambam *Sefer Ahava, Hilkhot Tefilla* 1:4, 6:3; *Shulḥan Arukh, Oraḥ Ḥayyim* 112:1).

שׁוּב מַעֲשֶׂה בְּתַלְמִיד אֶחָד שֶׁיָּרַד לִפְנֵי הַתֵּיבָה בִּפְנֵי רַבִּי אֱלִיעֶזֶר וְהָיָה מְקַצֵּר יוֹתֵר מִדַּאי. אָמְרוּ לוֹ תַּלְמִידָיו: כַּמָּה קַצְרָן הוּא זֶה! אָמַר לָהֶם: כְּלוּם מְקַצֵּר יוֹתֵר מִמֹּשֶׁה רַבֵּינוּ?! דִּכְתִיב: ״אֵל נָא רְפָא נָא לָהּ״.

There was **again an incident where one student descended** to serve as prayer leader **before the ark in the presence of Rabbi Eliezer, and he was excessively abbreviating his praye**r. **His students** protested **and said to him: How brief is his** prayer. **He said to them: Is he abbreviating** his prayer **any more than Moses our teacher** did? **As it is written** with regard to the prayer Moses recited imploring God to cure Miriam of her leprosy: "And Moses cried out to the Lord, saying: **'Please, God, heal her, please'**" (Numbers 12:13). This student's prayer was certainly no briefer than the few words recited by Moses.

אָמַר רַבִּי יַעֲקֹב אָמַר רַב חִסְדָּא: כָּל הַמְבַקֵּשׁ רַחֲמִים עַל חֲבֵירוֹ אֵין צָרִיךְ לְהַזְכִּיר שְׁמוֹ, שֶׁנֶּאֱמַר: ״אֵל נָא רְפָא נָא לָהּ״, וְלָא קָמַדְכַּר שְׁמָהּ דְּמִרְיָם.

Having mentioned Moses' prayer for Miriam, the Gemara cites what **Rabbi Ya'akov said** that **Rav Ḥisda said: Anyone who requests mercy** on behalf **of another need not mention his name, as it is stated: "Please, God, heal her, please," and he did not mention Miriam's name.**

תָּנוּ רַבָּנַן: אֵלּוּ בְּרָכוֹת שֶׁאָדָם שׁוֹחֶה בָּהֶן: בְּאָבוֹת תְּחִלָּה וָסוֹף, בְּהוֹדָאָה תְּחִלָּה וָסוֹף, וְאִם בָּא לָשׁוּחַ בְּסוֹף כָּל בְּרָכָה וּבְרָכָה וּבִתְחִלַּת כָּל בְּרָכָה וּבְרָכָה – מְלַמְּדִין אוֹתוֹ שֶׁלֹּא יִשְׁחֶה.

The Sages taught in a *Tosefta*: **These** are the **blessings** in the *Amida* prayer **in which a person bows:**[H] **In the first blessing,** the blessing of the **Patriarchs,** one bows **at the beginning and the end; in** the blessing of **thanksgiving,** one bows **at the beginning and the end; and if one seeks to bow at the end of each and every blessing and at the beginning of each and every blessing, they teach him not to bow** so as not to go beyond the ordinance instituted by the Sages.

אָמַר רַבִּי שִׁמְעוֹן בֶּן פָּזִי אָמַר רַבִּי יְהוֹשֻׁעַ בֶּן לֵוִי מִשּׁוּם בַּר קַפָּרָא: הֶדְיוֹט – כְּמוֹ שֶׁאָמַרְנוּ.

Rabbi Shimon ben Pazi said that **Rabbi Yehoshua ben Levi said in the name of** the *tanna* **bar Kappara: An ordinary** person [*hedyot*],[L] conducts himself **as we said;** he bows at the beginning and the end of the blessings of Patriarchs and thanksgiving and is admonished if he seeks to bow at the beginning and end of the other blessings.

HALAKHA

These are the blessings in which a person bows – אֵלּוּ בְּרָכוֹת שֶׁאָדָם שׁוֹחֶה בָּהֶן: During the *Amida* prayer, one bows at the beginning and end of the blessing of Patriarchs and at the beginning and end of the blessing of thanksgiving. One who bows beyond that, we prevent him from doing so. One who bows in the middle of blessings, the custom is not to prevent him from doing so (*Magen Avraham*; Rambam *Sefer Ahava, Hilkhot Tefilla* 5:10; *Shulḥan Arukh, Oraḥ Ḥayyim* 113:1).

LANGUAGE

Ordinary person [*hedyot*] – הֶדְיוֹט: This word comes from the Greek ἰδιώτης *idiotès* and means a common person, one of the masses. The Sages use the term to refer to a typical person who has no outstanding qualities. This term refers to a commoner as opposed to a king or an ordinary priest as opposed to a High Priest. It may also refer to one who engages in labor in which he is not expert.

Perek **V**
Daf **34** Amud **b**

כֹּהֵן גָּדוֹל – בְּסוֹף כָּל בְּרָכָה וּבְרָכָה, וְהַמֶּלֶךְ – תְּחִלַּת כָּל בְּרָכָה וּבְרָכָה וְסוֹף כָּל בְּרָכָה וּבְרָכָה.

It is appropriate, though, for **a High Priest** to bow **at the end of each and every blessing; and for a king** to bow **at the beginning of each and every blessing and at the end of each and every blessing.**[H] This is because the more lofty one's status, the more important it is to demonstrate his subservience to God.

אָמַר רַבִּי יִצְחָק בַּר נַחְמָנִי, לְדִידִי מִפָּרְשָׁא לִי מִינֵּיהּ דְּרַבִּי יְהוֹשֻׁעַ בֶּן לֵוִי: הֶדְיוֹט – כְּמוֹ שֶׁאָמַרְנוּ, כֹּהֵן גָּדוֹל – תְּחִלַּת כָּל בְּרָכָה וּבְרָכָה, הַמֶּלֶךְ – כֵּיוָן שֶׁכָּרַע, שׁוּב אֵינוֹ זוֹקֵף, שֶׁנֶּאֱמַר: ״וַיְהִי כְּכַלּוֹת שְׁלֹמֹה לְהִתְפַּלֵּל וגו׳ קָם מִלִּפְנֵי מִזְבַּח ה׳ מִכְּרֹעַ עַל בִּרְכָּיו״.

Rabbi Yitzḥak bar Naḥmani said: It was explained to me directly **from Rabbi Yehoshua ben Levi** himself differently: **An ordinary** person, conducts himself **as we said; a High Priest** bows at **the beginning of each and every blessing; the king, once he has bowed** at the beginning of the first blessing, **does not rise** until he concludes the entire prayer, **as it is stated: "And it was that when Solomon finished praying** all of his prayer to the Lord, **he rose from before the altar of the Lord, from kneeling upon his knees** with his hands spread forth toward the heavens" (I Kings 8:54).

תָּנוּ רַבָּנַן: קִידָּה – עַל אַפַּיִם, שֶׁנֶּאֱמַר: ״וַתִּקֹּד בַּת שֶׁבַע אַפַּיִם אֶרֶץ״, כְּרִיעָה – עַל בִּרְכַּיִם, שֶׁנֶּאֱמַר: ״מִכְּרֹעַ עַל בִּרְכָּיו״, הִשְׁתַּחֲוָאָה – זוֹ פִּשּׁוּט יָדַיִם וְרַגְלַיִם, שֶׁנֶּאֱמַר: ״הֲבוֹא נָבוֹא אֲנִי וְאִמְּךָ וְאַחֶיךָ לְהִשְׁתַּחֲוֹת לְךָ אָרְצָה״.

Having mentioned Solomon bowing, the Gemara distinguishes between various types of bowing. **The Sages taught** in a *baraita*: The term ***kidda*** means bowing **upon** one's **face,** with his face toward the ground, **as it is stated: "Then Bathsheba bowed [*vatikod*] with her face to the ground"** (I Kings 1:31). ***Keria*** means bowing **upon one's knees,** as regarding Solomon **it is stated:** He finished praying and **"he rose from before the altar of the Lord, from kneeling [*mikkeroa*] upon his knees."** Finally, ***hishtaḥava'a,***[H] **that is** bowing with **one's hands and legs spread** in total submission, **as it is stated** in Jacob's question to Joseph in response to his dream: **"Shall we, I and your mother and your brothers, come and bow down [*lehishtaḥavot*] to you to the ground?"** (Genesis 37:10).

אָמַר רַב חִיָּיא בְּרֵיהּ דְּרַב הוּנָא: חֲזֵינָא לְהוּ לְאַבָּיֵי וְרָבָא דְּמַצְלוּ אַצְלוּיֵי.

On the topic of bowing, **Rav Ḥiyya, son of Rav Huna, said: I saw Abaye and Rava, who would lean** their heads[H] and not actually prostrate themselves on the ground.

HALAKHA

The bows of a king and a High Priest – כְּרִיעוֹת מֶלֶךְ וְכֹהֵן גָּדוֹל: A High Priest bows at the beginning and end of each blessing, according to the Rambam, based on a variant reading of the Gemara to which he had access (*Kesef Mishne*). Alternatively, that was his ruling as a compromise between the differing opinions in the Gemara (*Leḥem Mishne*). The king bows when he begins reciting the *Amida* prayer and stands upright when he concludes (Rambam *Sefer Ahava, Hilkhot Tefilla* 5:10).

Bowing [*kidda*]...kneeling [*keria*]...prostrating [*hishtaḥava'a*] – קִידָּה...כְּרִיעָה...הִשְׁתַּחֲוָאָה: Whenever *keria* is mentioned it refers to kneeling upon one's knees; *kidda* refers to bowing one's head; *hishtaḥva'a* refers to spreading out one's hands and legs (Rambam *Sefer Ahava, Hilkhot Tefilla* 5:13).

How does one lower his head – נְפִילַת אַפַּיִם כֵּיצַד: One who lowers his head leans to the side, as per the custom of Abaye and Rava. When one has phylacteries on his arm he leans to the right side and when he does not have phylacteries he leans to the left (*Baḥ*; Rambam *Sefer Ahava, Hilkhot Tefilla* 5:14, 9:5; *Shulḥan Arukh, Oraḥ Ḥayyim* 131:1).

תָּנֵי חֲדָא: הַכּוֹרֵעַ בְּהוֹדָאָה הֲרֵי זֶה מְשׁוּבָּח; וְתַנְיָא אִידָּךְ: הֲרֵי זֶה מְגוּנֶּה!

The Gemara asks: **One** *baraita* **taught: One who bows in the** blessing of **thanksgiving, it is praiseworthy. And it was taught in another** *baraita*: One who bows in the blessing of thanksgiving, **it is reprehensible.** These *baraitot* are contradictory.

לָא קַשְׁיָא: הָא – בִּתְחִלָּה, הָא – לְבַסּוֹף.

The Gemara reconciles these two *baraitot*: This is **not difficult; this** *baraita*, which praises one who bows in the blessing of thanksgiving, refers to one who bows **at the beginning** of the blessing. **This** *baraita*, which condemns one who bows in the blessing of thanksgiving, refers to one who bows **at the end** of the blessing.

רָבָא כָּרַע בְּהוֹדָאָה תְּחִלָּה וְסוֹף. אָמְרִי לֵיהּ רַבָּנַן: אַמַּאי קָא עָבֵיד מָר הָכִי? – אָמַר לְהוּ: חָזֵינָא לְרַב נַחְמָן דְּכָרַע, וַחֲזֵינָא לֵיהּ לְרַב שֵׁשֶׁת דְּקָא עָבַד הָכִי.

Rava bowed in the blessing of **thanksgiving,**[N] both **beginning and end. The Sages said to him: Why does our master do this? He said to them: I saw Rav Naḥman who bowed** in the blessing of thanksgiving, **and I saw Rav Sheshet who did so** as well.

וְהָתַנְיָא: הַכּוֹרֵעַ בְּהוֹדָאָה הֲרֵי זֶה מְגוּנֶּה!

But wasn't it taught in a *baraita* that **one who bows in thanksgiving, it is reprehensible?**

הַהִיא – בְּהוֹדָאָה שֶׁבְּהַלֵּל.

Rava explained: **That** *baraita* refers to one who bows **in the thanksgiving** that is **in** ***hallel***, when one recites: Give thanks to the Lord. Then, bowing is inappropriate.

וְהָתַנְיָא: הַכּוֹרֵעַ בְּהוֹדָאָה וּבְהוֹדָאָה שֶׁל הַלֵּל הֲרֵי זֶה מְגוּנֶּה!

The Sages continue to question Rava's conduct: **But wasn't it taught** explicitly in a *baraita*: **One who bows in thanksgiving or in thanksgiving of** ***hallel***, **it is reprehensible?** The term thanksgiving unqualified does not refer to thanksgiving of *hallel*; it obviously refers to the blessing of thanksgiving recited in the *Amida* prayer. One who bows in either, it is reprehensible.

כִּי תַּנְיָא הַהִיא – בְּהוֹדָאָה דְּבִרְכַּת הַמָּזוֹן.

The Gemara rejects this challenge as well: **When that** *baraita* **was taught,** it was in reference to the blessing of **thanksgiving,** the second blessing recited **in Grace after Meals:** We thank You.

מתני׳ הַמִּתְפַּלֵּל וְטָעָה – סִימָן רַע לוֹ, וְאִם שְׁלִיחַ צִבּוּר הוּא – סִימָן רַע לְשׁוֹלְחָיו, מִפְּנֵי שֶׁשְּׁלוּחוֹ שֶׁל אָדָם כְּמוֹתוֹ. אָמְרוּ עָלָיו עַל רַבִּי חֲנִינָא בֶּן דּוֹסָא, שֶׁהָיָה מִתְפַּלֵּל עַל הַחוֹלִים וְאוֹמֵר: ״זֶה חַי וְזֶה מֵת״. אָמְרוּ לוֹ: מִנַּיִן אַתָּה יוֹדֵעַ? אָמַר לָהֶם: אִם שְׁגוּרָה תְּפִלָּתִי בְּפִי – יוֹדֵעַ אֲנִי שֶׁהוּא מְקוּבָּל, וְאִם לָאו – יוֹדֵעַ אֲנִי שֶׁהוּא מְטוֹרָף.

MISHNA Concluding its discussion of the *halakhot* of prayer, the mishna discusses less practical aspects of prayer. **One who prays and** realizes that he **erred** in his prayer, it is **a bad omen for him;** it indicates to him that his prayer was not accepted. **And if he** who erred **is the communal prayer leader,** it is **a bad omen for those who sent him, because a person's agent** has legal status **equivalent to his own.** On a similar note, **they said about Rabbi Ḥanina ben Dosa**[P] **that he would pray on** behalf of **the sick and** immediately after his prayer he would **say: This** one shall recover from his illness and **live and this** one shall **die.** When **they said to him: From where do you know? He said to them: If my prayer is fluent in my mouth** as I recite it and there are no errors, **I know that** my prayer **is accepted. And if not, I know that** my prayer **is rejected.**

גמ׳ אַהַיָּיא?

GEMARA We learned in the mishna that if one errs in his prayer it is a bad omen. The Gemara asks: **In which blessing** is an error a bad omen?

אָמַר רַב חִיָּיא אָמַר רַב סָפְרָא מִשּׁוּם חַד דְּבֵי רַבִּי: בְּאָבוֹת.

Rabbi Ḥiyya said that **Rav Safra said in the name of one of the** Sages of the **school of Rabbi** Yehuda HaNasi: An error is a bad omen **in** the first blessing of the *Amida* prayer, the blessing of **Patriarchs.**"[N]

אִיכָּא דְּמַתְנֵי לַהּ אַבָּרַיְיתָא: הַמִּתְפַּלֵּל צָרִיךְ שֶׁיְּכַוֵּין אֶת לִבּוֹ בְּכוּלָּן, וְאִם אֵינוֹ יָכוֹל לְכַוֵּין בְּכוּלָּן – יְכַוֵּין אֶת לִבּוֹ בְּאַחַת;

Some teach that **this** statement was made **on a** ***baraita*** referring to another topic. It was taught in a *baraita*: **One who prays must focus his heart**[H] **in all** of the blessings. **And if he is unable to focus** his heart **in all of them, he should focus his heart** at least **in one.**

אָמַר רַבִּי חִיָּיא אָמַר רַב סָפְרָא מִשּׁוּם חַד דְּבֵי רַבִּי: בְּאָבוֹת.

Regarding this *baraita*, **Rabbi Ḥiyya said** that **Rav Safra said in the name of one of the** Sages of the **school of Rabbi** Yehuda HaNasi: **In** one refers to the blessing of **Patriarchs.**

NOTES

Rava bowed in the blessing of thanksgiving – רָבָא כָּרַע בְּהוֹדָאָה: Some say that this does not refer to the blessing of thanksgiving in the silent *Amida* prayer; rather, it refers to the blessing of thanksgiving recited by the congregation during the repetition of the *Amida* prayer [*modim derabbanan*]. According to this interpretation, there is no contradiction between the different sources (Ra'avad, *Tosefot HaRosh*).

In the blessing of the Patriarchs – בְּאָבוֹת: The preeminent status of this blessing stems from its juxtaposition with redemption, from the fact that it begins and ends with a blessing and that it includes mention of several of God's names (Maharsha).

PERSONALITIES

Rabbi Ḥanina ben Dosa – רַבִּי חֲנִינָא בֶּן דּוֹסָא: A *tanna* who lived at the end of the Second Temple period, Rabbi Ḥanina ben Dosa was a disciple of Rabban Yoḥanan ben Zakkai. However, he is best known as the performer of miraculous acts, a righteous man whose prayers were always heard on high. The Talmud is replete with stories of miracles that took place for him and those close to him. He was indigent and earned a very meager living. He is the paradigm of a full-fledged righteous man who received no reward in this world. In tractate *Avot*, several of his moral/ethical teachings are cited, which underscore the primacy of the fear of Heaven and the need for mutual affection in interpersonal relationships.

HALAKHA

One who prays must focus his heart, etc. – הַמִּתְפַּלֵּל צָרִיךְ שֶׁיְּכַוֵּין אֶת לִבּוֹ וכו׳: Ideally one should focus his heart throughout the entire prayer. However, after the fact, even if he failed to focus his attention, he fulfilled his obligation. Nonetheless, if one failed to have intention during the blessing of Patriarchs, he did not fulfill his obligation and must repeat the prayer. In our times, however, one does not repeat the *Amida* prayer due to lack of requisite intent (Rema; Rambam *Sefer Ahava*, *Hilkhot Tefilla* 10:1; *Shulḥan Arukh*, *Oraḥ Ḥayyim* 101:1).

״אָמְרוּ עָלָיו עַל רַבִּי חֲנִינָא״ וכו׳. מְנָא הָנֵי מִילֵּי? אָמַר רַבִּי יְהוֹשֻׁעַ בֶּן לֵוִי, דְּאָמַר קְרָא: ״בּוֹרֵא נִיב שְׂפָתַיִם שָׁלוֹם שָׁלוֹם לָרָחוֹק וְלַקָּרוֹב אָמַר ה׳ וּרְפָאתִיו״.

We learned in the mishna: **They said about Rabbi Ḥanina** ben Dosa that the indication whether or not his prayer was accepted was whether the prayer was fluent in his mouth as he recited it. The Gemara asks: **From where are these matters,** that this is an accurate indication of whether or not his prayer was accepted, derived? **Rabbi Yehoshua ben Levi said: As the verse stated: "The Lord that creates the expression of the lips**[N] **says, Peace, peace, to him that is far off and to him that is near; and I will heal him"** (Isaiah 57:19). It can be inferred from this verse that if speech of the lips, fluent speech, is granted to one who prays, it indicates that his prayer on behalf of the ill has been accepted and I will heal him, that person will be healed.

אָמַר רַבִּי חִיָּיא בַּר אַבָּא אָמַר רַבִּי יוֹחָנָן: כָּל הַנְּבִיאִים כּוּלָּן לֹא נִתְנַבְּאוּ אֶלָּא לְמַשִּׂיא בִּתּוֹ לְתַלְמִיד חָכָם וּלְעוֹשֶׂה פְּרַקְמַטְיָא לְתַלְמִיד חָכָם, וְלִמְהַנֶּה תַּלְמִיד חָכָם מִנְּכָסָיו, אֲבָל תַּלְמִידֵי חֲכָמִים עַצְמָן – ״עַיִן לֹא רָאָתָה אֱלֹהִים זוּלָתְךָ יַעֲשֶׂה לִמְחַכֵּה לוֹ״.

In conclusion of this discussion, the Gemara cites that which **Rabbi Ḥiyya bar Abba said** that **Rabbi Yoḥanan said** with regard to the reward of the righteous: **All the prophets only prophesied** in their prophecies of consolation, **with regard to one who** values wisdom and therefore **marries his daughter to a Torah scholar and to one who conducts business** [*perakmatya*][L] **on behalf of a Torah scholar as well as to one who** utilizes his wealth **to benefit a Torah scholar** in some other way. **However,** the prophets did not describe the extent of the reward for **Torah scholars themselves,** whose reward is not quantifiable as it is stated: "And from of old they have not heard, they have not lent an ear, **no eye has seen it, God, aside from You, who will do for those who await Him"** (Isaiah 64:3).

וְאָמַר רַבִּי חִיָּיא בַּר אַבָּא אָמַר רַבִּי יוֹחָנָן: כָּל הַנְּבִיאִים כּוּלָּן לֹא נִתְנַבְּאוּ אֶלָּא לִימוֹת הַמָּשִׁיחַ, אֲבָל לָעוֹלָם הַבָּא – ״עַיִן לֹא רָאָתָה אֱלֹהִים זוּלָתְךָ״.

And Rabbi Ḥiyya bar Abba said that **Rabbi Yoḥanan said: All the prophets only prophesied** with regard to the change in world order in the end of days **with regard to the days of the Messiah. However, with regard to the World-to-Come,** which exists on a higher level, it is stated: **"No eye has seen it, God, aside from You."**[H]

וּפְלִיגָא דִּשְׁמוּאֵל, דְּאָמַר שְׁמוּאֵל: אֵין בֵּין הָעוֹלָם הַזֶּה לִימוֹת הַמָּשִׁיחַ אֶלָּא שִׁעְבּוּד מַלְכֻיּוֹת בִּלְבַד. שֶׁנֶּאֱמַר: ״כִּי לֹא יֶחְדַּל אֶבְיוֹן מִקֶּרֶב הָאָרֶץ״.

And the Gemara notes that this statement **disagrees with** the opinion **of Shmuel, as Shmuel said: The only** difference **between this world and the days of the Messiah**[H] is with regard to **servitude to** foreign **kingdoms alone.** While in the days of the Messiah, Israel will be independent and free from enslavement to foreign powers, the world order will remain otherwise unchanged, **as it is stated: "For the poor shall not cease from the land"** (Deuteronomy 15:11), which indicates that the ways of the world are set and unchanging.

וְאָמַר רַבִּי חִיָּיא בַּר אַבָּא אָמַר רַבִּי יוֹחָנָן: כָּל הַנְּבִיאִים כּוּלָּן לֹא נִתְנַבְּאוּ אֶלָּא לְבַעֲלֵי תְשׁוּבָה, אֲבָל צַדִּיקִים גְּמוּרִים – ״עַיִן לֹא רָאָתָה אֱלֹהִים זוּלָתְךָ״.

And Rabbi Ḥiyya bar Abba said that **Rabbi Yoḥanan said: All of the prophets only prophesied** their prophecies of consolation **with regard to penitents but with regard to the full-fledged righteous** it is stated: **"No eye has seen it, God, aside from You."**

וּפְלִיגָא דְּרַבִּי אַבָּהוּ, דְּאָמַר רַבִּי אַבָּהוּ: מָקוֹם שֶׁבַּעֲלֵי תְשׁוּבָה עוֹמְדִין – צַדִּיקִים גְּמוּרִים אֵינָם עוֹמְדִין, שֶׁנֶּאֱמַר: ״שָׁלוֹם שָׁלוֹם לָרָחוֹק וְלַקָּרוֹב״. לָרָחוֹק בְּרֵישָׁא וַהֲדַר לַקָּרוֹב.

And the Gemara notes that **this** statement **disagrees with** the opinion of **Rabbi Abbahu** who holds that penitents are superior to the righteous. **As Rabbi Abbahu said: In the place where penitents stand, even the full-fledged righteous do not stand,**[H] **as it is stated: "Peace, peace upon him who is far and him who is near."** Peace and greeting is extended first to **him who is far,** the penitent, **and** only **thereafter** is peace extended to **him who is near,** the full-fledged righteous.

וְרַבִּי יוֹחָנָן אָמַר לָךְ: מַאי ״רָחוֹק״ – שֶׁהָיָה רָחוֹק מִדְּבַר עֲבֵירָה מֵעִיקָּרָא, וּמַאי קָרוֹב – שֶׁהָיָה קָרוֹב לִדְבַר עֲבֵירָה, וְנִתְרַחֵק מִמֶּנּוּ הַשְׁתָּא.

And Rabbi Yoḥanan could have **said to you: What is** the meaning **of him who is far?** This refers to the full-fledged righteous **who was distant from an act of transgression from the outset,** and to whom peace is extended first. **What is** meant by **him who is near?** This refers to the penitent **who was close to an act of transgression but has now distanced** himself **from it,** and to whom peace is extended only after it has been extended to him who has been righteous from the outset.

מַאי ״עַיִן לֹא רָאָתָה״? אָמַר רַבִּי יְהוֹשֻׁעַ בֶּן לֵוִי: זֶה יַיִן הַמְשׁוּמָּר בַּעֲנָבָיו מִשֵּׁשֶׁת יְמֵי בְרֵאשִׁית; רַבִּי שְׁמוּאֵל בַּר נַחְמָנִי אָמַר: זֶה עֵדֶן שֶׁלֹּא שָׁלְטָה בּוֹ עֵין כָּל בְּרִיָּה.

Earlier, Rabbi Yoḥanan said that there is a reward referred to in the verse: "No eye has seen it." The Gemara asks: **What is** this reward about which it is said: **"No eye has seen it"? Rabbi Yehoshua ben Levi said: That is the wine that has been preserved**[N] **in its grapes since the six days of creation** and which no eye has ever seen. **Rabbi Shmuel bar Naḥmani said: That is Eden, which no creature's eye has ever surveyed.**

NOTES

The Lord that creates the expression of the lips – בּוֹרֵא נִיב שְׂפָתַיִם: Several possibilities were raised with regard to how this idea is derived from this verse. Rashi interprets *borei*, creator, as *bari*, healthy or strong. When one's lips utter the prayer assertively it is a fortuitous omen for the one on whose behalf prayer is being recited. Some say that one sees that the product [*tenuva*] of his lips is being expressed with ease (Rabbeinu Ḥananel). Others interpret *borei* as deriving from the term *berirut*, clarity. When one's speech is clear, it is successful (*Shitta Mekubbetzet*). Additionally, the verse continues "The Lord that creates the expression of the lips…peace." When the speech of the lips emerges peacefully, it is successful (Maharsha).

Wine that has been preserved – יַיִן הַמְשׁוּמָּר: The metaphor chosen to symbolize the ultimate reward as wine. Just as wine causes the heart to rejoice and helps one forget his troubles, so too, the ultimate joy with which the righteous will be rewarded will be unmitigated by any suffering or worries. The Sages described this wine as having been preserved in its grapes in Eden, as, since the creation of the world there has never been a period of pure unadulterated joy. That is the reward of the righteous (Rashba).

LANGUAGE

Business [*perakmatya*] – פְּרַקְמַטְיָא: This term comes from the Greek πραγματεία, *pragmateia*, meaning conduct of business or trade.

HALAKHA

All the prophets only prophesied with regard to the days of the Messiah. However, with regard to the World-to-Come, it is stated: "No eye has seen it, God, aside from You" – כָּל הַנְּבִיאִים כּוּלָּן לֹא נִתְנַבְּאוּ אֶלָּא לִימוֹת הַמָּשִׁיחַ, אֲבָל לָעוֹלָם הַבָּא עַיִן לֹא רָאָתָה אֱלֹהִים זוּלָתְךָ: Rabbi Yoḥanan's statement is accepted as *halakha*; the goodness of the World-to-Come is beyond the purview of human comprehension, and those rewards described by the prophets refer only to the days of the Messiah in this world (Rambam *Sefer HaMadda, Hilkhot Teshuva* 8:7).

The days of the Messiah – יְמוֹת הַמָּשִׁיחַ: Although different statements appear with regard to this issue, the ruling is that Messianic times will not necessarily herald a change in the world order. Primarily, the Messianic era will feature the restoration of the kingdom of Israel in a state guided by Torah law (Rambam *Sefer HaMadda, Hilkhot Teshuva* 9:2, *Sefer Shofetim, Hilkhot Melakhim* 12:2).

In the place where penitents stand, even the full-fledged righteous do not stand – מָקוֹם שֶׁבַּעֲלֵי תְשׁוּבָה עוֹמְדִין צַדִּיקִים גְּמוּרִים אֵינָם עוֹמְדִין: The virtue of the penitent is greater than that of the full-fledged righteous, in accordance with the opinion of Rabbi Abbahu (Rambam *Sefer HaMadda, Hilkhot Teshuva* 7:4).

שֶׁמָּא תֹּאמַר, אָדָם הָרִאשׁוֹן הֵיכָן הָיָה? – בַּגַּן.

Lest you will say: Where was Adam the first man? Wasn't he there and didn't he survey Eden? The Gemara responds: Adam was only **in the Garden** of Eden, not in Eden itself.

וְשֶׁמָּא תֹּאמַר: הוּא גַּן, הוּא עֵדֶן – תַּלְמוּד לוֹמַר: "וְנָהָר יוֹצֵא מֵעֵדֶן לְהַשְׁקוֹת אֶת הַגָּן", גַּן לְחוּד וְעֵדֶן לְחוּד.

And lest you will say: It is the Garden and it is Eden; two names describing the same place. That is not the case, as **the verse states: "And a river went out from Eden to water the Garden"** (Genesis 2:10). Obviously, the **Garden** exists **on its own and Eden** exists **on its own.**

תָּנוּ רַבָּנַן: מַעֲשֶׂה שֶׁחָלָה בְּנוֹ שֶׁל רַבָּן גַּמְלִיאֵל, שִׁגֵּר שְׁנֵי תַלְמִידֵי חֲכָמִים אֵצֶל רַבִּי חֲנִינָא בֶּן דּוֹסָא לְבַקֵּשׁ עָלָיו רַחֲמִים. כֵּיוָן שֶׁרָאָה אוֹתָם עָלָה לַעֲלִיָּיה וּבִקֵּשׁ עָלָיו רַחֲמִים. בִּירִידָתוֹ, אָמַר לָהֶם: לְכוּ – שֶׁחֲלָצַתּוּ חַמָּה. אָמְרוּ לוֹ: וְכִי נָבִיא אַתָּה?! אָמַר לָהֶן: לֹא נָבִיא אָנֹכִי וְלֹא בֶּן נָבִיא אָנֹכִי, אֶלָּא כָּךְ מְקוּבְּלַנִי: אִם שְׁגוּרָה תְּפִלָּתִי בְּפִי – יוֹדֵעַ אֲנִי שֶׁהוּא מְקוּבָּל, וְאִם לָאו – יוֹדֵעַ אֲנִי שֶׁהוּא מְטוֹרָף. יָשְׁבוּ וְכָתְבוּ וְכִוְּונוּ אוֹתָהּ שָׁעָה. וּכְשֶׁבָּאוּ אֵצֶל רַבָּן גַּמְלִיאֵל, אָמַר לָהֶן: הָעֲבוֹדָה! לֹא חִסַּרְתֶּם וְלֹא הוֹתַרְתֶּם אֶלָּא כָּךְ הָיָה מַעֲשֶׂה, בְּאוֹתָהּ שָׁעָה חֲלָצַתּוּ חַמָּה וְשָׁאַל לָנוּ מַיִם לִשְׁתּוֹת.

Having mentioned Rabbi Ḥanina ben Dosa in our mishna, the Gemara proceeds to further praise the efficacy of his prayer: **The Sages taught:** There was **an incident where Rabban Gamliel's son fell ill.** Rabban Gamliel **dispatched two scholars to Rabbi Ḥanina ben Dosa to pray for mercy** and healing **on his behalf. When** Rabbi Ḥanina ben Dosa **saw them** approaching, **he went up to the attic** on the roof of his house **and prayed for mercy on his behalf. Upon his descent, he said to** the messengers: You may **go** and return to Rabban Gamliel, **as the fever has already left** his son and he has been healed. The messengers **asked him:** How do you know? **Are you a prophet? He replied to them: I am neither a prophet nor son of a prophet** (see Amos 7:14), **but I have received** a tradition with regard to **this** indication: **If my prayer is fluent in my mouth** as I recite it and there are no errors, **I know that** my prayer **is accepted. And if not, I know that** my prayer **is rejected.** The Gemara relates that these messengers **sat and wrote and approximated that** precise **moment** when Rabbi Ḥanina ben Dosa told them this. **When they came before Rabban Gamliel** and related all that had happened and showed him what they had written, Rabban Gamliel **said to them:** I swear **by the Temple service** that in the time you wrote **you were neither earlier or later; rather, this is how the event** transpired: Precisely at that moment **his fever broke and he asked us for water to drink.**

וְשׁוּב מַעֲשֶׂה בְּרַבִּי חֲנִינָא בֶּן דּוֹסָא שֶׁהָלַךְ לִלְמוֹד תּוֹרָה אֵצֶל רַבִּי יוֹחָנָן בֶּן זַכַּאי, וְחָלָה בְּנוֹ שֶׁל רַבִּי יוֹחָנָן בֶּן זַכַּאי. אָמַר לוֹ: חֲנִינָא בְּנִי, בַּקֵּשׁ עָלָיו רַחֲמִים וְיִחְיֶה. הִנִּיחַ רֹאשׁוֹ בֵּין בִּרְכָּיו וּבִקֵּשׁ עָלָיו רַחֲמִים – וְחָיָה. אָמַר רַבִּי יוֹחָנָן בֶּן זַכַּאי: אִלְמָלֵי הֵטִיחַ בֶּן זַכַּאי אֶת רֹאשׁוֹ בֵּין בִּרְכָּיו כׇּל הַיּוֹם כּוּלּוֹ – לֹא הָיוּ מַשְׁגִּיחִים עָלָיו. אָמְרָה לוֹ אִשְׁתּוֹ: וְכִי חֲנִינָא גָּדוֹל מִמְּךָ?! אָמַר לָהּ: לָאו, אֶלָּא הוּא דּוֹמֶה כְּעֶבֶד לִפְנֵי הַמֶּלֶךְ, וַאֲנִי דּוֹמֶה כְּשַׂר לִפְנֵי הַמֶּלֶךְ.

And there was **another incident** involving **Rabbi Ḥanina ben Dosa, who went to study Torah before Rabbi Yoḥanan ben Zakkai, and** Rabbi Yoḥanan's **son fell ill.** He said to him: **Ḥanina, my son, pray for mercy on behalf of** my son **so that he will live. Rabbi Ḥanina ben Dosa placed his head between his knees** in order to meditate **and prayed for mercy upon his behalf, and** Rabbi Yoḥanan ben Zakkai's son **lived. Rabbi Yoḥanan ben Zakkai said** about himself: **Had ben Zakkai stuck his head between his knees throughout the entire day, they would have paid him no attention. His wife said to him: And is Ḥanina greater than you? He replied to her: No, but** his prayer is better received than my own because **he is like a servant before the King,**[N] and as such he is able to enter before the King and make various requests at all times. **I,** on the other hand, **am like a minister before the King,** and I can enter only when invited and can make requests only with regard to especially significant matters.

וְאָמַר רַבִּי חִיָּיא בַּר אַבָּא אָמַר רַבִּי יוֹחָנָן: אַל יִתְפַּלֵּל אָדָם אֶלָּא בְּבַיִת שֶׁיֵּשׁ שָׁם חַלּוֹנוֹת, שֶׁנֶּאֱמַר: "וְכַוִּין פְּתִיחָן לֵיהּ בְּעִלִּיתֵהּ (לָקֳבֵל) נֶגֶד יְרוּשְׁלֶם."

And on the topic of prayer, **Rabbi Ḥiyya bar Abba said** that **Rabbi Yoḥanan said: One may only pray in a house with windows,**[N] as then he can see the heavens and focus his heart, **as it is stated** with regard to Daniel's prayer: "In his attic **there were open windows** facing Jerusalem" (Daniel 6:11).

אָמַר רַב כָּהֲנָא: חֲצִיף עֲלַי מַאן דִּמְצַלֵּי בְּבִקְתָּא.

With regard to the appropriate place to pray, **Rav Kahana said: I consider impudent one who prays in a field.**[H]

וְאָמַר רַב כָּהֲנָא: חֲצִיף עֲלַי מַאן דִּמְפָרֵשׁ חֶטְאֵיהּ, שֶׁנֶּאֱמַר: "אַשְׁרֵי נְשׂוּי פֶּשַׁע כְּסוּי חֲטָאָה".

Employing parallel language, **Rav Kahana also said: I consider impudent one who specifies his transgression,**[H] **as it is stated: "Happy is he whose iniquity is forgiven, whose transgression is covered over"** (Psalms 32:1); one who conceals his transgressions indicates that he is ashamed of them, and due to his shame he will be forgiven.

הדרן עלך אין עומדין

NOTES

Like a servant before the King – כְּעֶבֶד לִפְנֵי הַמֶּלֶךְ: Rabban Yoḥanan ben Zakkai sought to express that the acceptance of Rabbi Ḥanina's prayer was because his devotion to God was greater, although his Torah knowledge was not (*Or Hashem* of Rabbi Ḥisdai Crescas). The parable is explained that the minister, specifically because he is engaged in more significant undertakings, cannot raise his own personal problems or the problems of others before the king (see *HaKotev*).

One may only pray in a house with windows – אַל יִתְפַּלֵּל אָדָם אֶלָּא בְּבַיִת שֶׁיֵּשׁ שָׁם חַלּוֹנוֹת: Some say, based on the verse cited, that this was not to illuminate the room, but rather to symbolize the connection between one praying and the site of the Temple in Jerusalem (*Talmidei Rabbeinu Yona*), or to represent the direct path open to heaven (Maharsha).

HALAKHA

I consider impudent one who prays in a field – חֲצִיף עֲלַי מַאן דִּמְצַלֵּי בְּבִקְתָּא: One should not pray where there are no walls, as one experiences awe of the God in an enclosed place more than he does in an open one. Some say that this restriction applies specifically to a place where people pass regularly (*Magen Avraham*; *Shulḥan Arukh, Oraḥ Ḥayyim* 90:5).

I consider impudent one who specifies his transgression – חֲצִיף עֲלַי מַאן דִּמְפָרֵשׁ חֶטְאֵיהּ: The fundamental question whether it is appropriate to specify one's transgression appears in tractate *Yoma* (87a), and is the subject of a dispute among *tanna'im* and *amora'im*. They conclude that there is a distinction between those transgressions which are public, which may be specified (*Magen Avraham*), and those which are private. Similarly, there is a distinction between one who confesses with no one else present, in which case it is permitted (see *Beit Yosef*), and one who confesses in the presence of others (Rambam *Sefer HaMadda, Hilkhot Teshuva* 2:5; *Shulḥan Arukh, Oraḥ Ḥayyim* 607:2).

Summary of **Perek V**

Chapter Five contains discussions of ideas, mostly aggadic in nature, relating to the essence of prayer and its general role. Nevertheless, the *aggada* sections do not deal solely with the abstract and the sublime; they have practical halakhic ramifications in determining the appropriate manner of prayer.

Two discussions constitute the bulk of the chapter. The first deals with an individual's approach to prayer; the second relates to permitted and prohibited additions to the prayer formula.

Discussion of the individual's approach to prayer, which appears at the beginning and the end of the chapter, establishes the need for absolute concentration on the prayer. The mitzva of prayer, as opposed to the mitzva to recite *Shema*, is not by Torah law. However, since the essence of prayer is the intent of the heart one must concentrate on his prayer with all his might. Only a clear and present danger to one's life exempts him from this absolute demand. Because of the obligation to concentrate in this manner, any error or slip of the tongue in the course of prayer renders it seriously flawed, which is disgraceful for the prayer leader and for those who sent him.

Most of the *halakhot* in this chapter deal with additions to the established prayers. At the same time, not all of the changes are discussed in this chapter. They appear in the prayer book, which details the additions and changes introduced on Shabbat, Festivals, and other days of a unique nature. Furthermore, any of the issues that relate to changes in the prayers are discussed throughout the Talmud in different contexts: The prayers for rain in tractate *Ta'anit*; the additions on Shabbat, the New Moon, and Hanukka in tractate *Shabbat*; and so on.

However, as *Tosafot* explains, the *halakhot* here can be seen as fundamental principles that serve as the basis for more detailed discussions in other tractates. In this chapter, only the general framework is presented: These types of additions to prayer exist, and they are to be recited at the appropriate times. The discussions in this chapter do not reach a clear conclusion even with regard to inappropriate additions. These include those that undermine the style of prayer, e.g., unnecessary repetition, or those that compromise the fundamental tenets of the Torah, e.g., additions that are liable to appear heretical. These issues are discussed in greater detail in other tractates.

Image **Credits**

All images are copyright © Koren Publishers Jerusalem Ltd., except:

p123 © Clara Amit, Mariana Sulzberger, and Miki Koren, courtesy of the Antiquities Authority; **p125** 1st image © Clara Amit, Mariana Sulzberger, and Miki Koren, courtesy of the Antiquities Authority; **p131** © Clara Amit, Mariana Sulzberger, and Miki Koren, courtesy of the Antiquities Authority; **p204** © Clara Amit, Mariana Sulzberger, and Miki Koren, courtesy of the Antiquities Authority; **p220** © Kiril Kapustin.

Page numbers refer to the original Koren Talmud edition.

תלמוד בבלי

— מהדורת נאה —

ברכות · חלק ב

Steinsaltz Center

ירושלים

KOREN

תלמוד בבלי

הוצאת קוֹרֵן ירושלים

— מהדורת נאה —

ברכות

דף יז: עד דף לד:

COMMENTARY BY

Rabbi Adin Even-Israel Steinsaltz

EDITOR-IN-CHIEF

Rabbi Dr Tzvi Hersh Weinreb

SENIOR CONTENT EDITOR

Rabbi Dr Shalom Z Berger

MANAGING EDITOR

Rabbi Joshua Schreier

•

STEINSALTZ CENTER
KOREN PUBLISHERS JERUSALEM

א ג מיי' פ"ד מהלכות אבילות הלכה ו ופ"ד מהלכות ק"ש הלכה ג סמג עשין יח כ טוש"ע או"ח סימן עא סעיף א:

ב ד מיי' פ"ד מהלכות (אבל) [ק"ש] הלכה ד טור שו"ע אורח חיים סימן עב סעיף א [וביו"ד סימן שנח סעיף א]:

ג ה ו מיי' (פ"ד) [ספ"ו] מהל' תפלה ופ"ד מהלכות ק"ש הלכה א סמג עשין יח טוש"ע או"ח סימן ק"ו סעיף א:

ד ז מיי' פ"ד מהלכות אבל הלכה ו סמג עשין מד"ס ב טוש"ע יו"ד סימן שמא סעיף א וטוש"ע או"ח סימן קנט סעיף ה:

מי שמתו כו' **פטור** מלקרות ק"ש. לפי שהוא טרוד במחשבת קבורתו, והויא דומיא דחתן דפטור משום טירדא דמצוה: **וחלופיהן.** שכן דרך שמתחלפין לשאת, לפי שהכל חפצין לזכות בו: **את שלפני המטה.** שיתעסקו בו כשתגיע המטה אצלם: **ושלאחר המטה.** שנשאוהו כבר: **שלפני המטה צורך בהם פטורים.** אם צריכים לשאתו — פטורים: **ושלאחר המטה.** אף אם צורך בהם — חייבים, הואיל שכבר יצאו ידי חובתן מן המת: **ואלו ואלו פטורין מן התפלה.** דלאו דאורייתא היא. ורבותינו פירשו: לפי שיש להם עוד שהות, ולי נראה שאין זה לשון פטור: **לשורה.** שהיו מנחמין את האבל בהקף שורה סביבותיו בשובם מן הקבר: **גמ' שאינו מוטל לפניו.** כגון הוא בבית אחד והמת בבית אחר: **אוכל בבית אחר.** דנראה כלועג לרש וכו': **ואינו מיסב.** כדרך המסובים בהסיבות על צדו השמאלית ובמטה: **ואינו מברך.** אינו צריך לברך ברכת המוציא: **ואינו מזמן.** אינו צריך לברך ברכת המזון: ואין

מי שמתו מוטל לפניו. רש"י גריס "מי שמתו" אחר "תפלת השחר", אבל נראה לר"י שהוא אחר "היה קורא", דאיירי בסיפיה מק"ש, וכאן מתחיל נמי מפטור ק"ש, ובירושלמי גרים כמו כן: **פטור** מק"ש. בירושלמי מפרש טעמא: א"ר בון: כתיב "למען תזכור כו' עד כל ימי חייך" – ימים שאתה עוסק בחיים, ולא ימים שאתה עוסק במתים. הכי גרסינן: "פטור מקריאת שמע ומן התפלה ומן התפילין":

הכי גרים רש"י – שלאחר המטה אפילו המטה צריכה להם – חייבין, לפי שלעולם לא היו רגילים לשאת שכבר נשאו חלקם. ותימה קצת הלשון לפרש, מאי קאמר "אפי' צריכה להם", והלא לא היו נושאין כלל אחר המת! לכך נראה כגרסת הספרים: שלפני המטה ושלאחר המטה, את שהמטה צריכה להם – פטורין אין צריכה להם – חייבין: **אלו ואלו פטורין מן התפלה.** אבל בק"ש ובתפילין שהן מדאורייתא – חייבים ורישא דקאמר מי שמתו מוטל לפניו דפטור מן קריאת שמע ומן התפילין וכו', כל שכן דפטור מן התפלה, אלא לא בעי למיתני ברישא אלא החלוק שבין נושאי המטה למתו מוטל לפניו:

ואינו מברך. פרש"י: ואין זקוק לברך. ומשמע מתוך פירושו שאם רצה לברך – רשאי. מיהו בירושלמי קאמר: אם רצה להחמיר – אין שומעין לו. לכך נראה לומר: אינו מברך – אינו רשאי לברך. ומפרש בירושלמי למה, וקאמר מפני כבודו של מת. אי נמי – מפני שאין לו מי שישא משאו. ופריך והתניא פטור מנטילת לולב והא ס"ד דמיירי ביו"ט וגו אינו טרוד לישא משאו. ומשני: תפתר בחול. פי': בחולו של מועד.

הגהות הב"ח.

(ג) שם במשנה פטור מקריאת שמע ומן התפילין כצ"ל ותיבת ומן התפלה נמחק:

מי *שמתו מוטל לפניו – [ג]פטור מק"ש,(ג) ומן התפלה ומן התפילין, ומכל מצות האמורות בתורה. [ד]נושאי המטה וחלופיהן וחלופי חלופיהן, את שלפני המטה ואת שלאחר המטה; את שלפני המטה צורך בהם – פטורים, ואת שלאחר המטה צורך בהם – חייבין, [ה]ואלו ואלו פטורים מן התפלה. קברו את המת וחזרו, אם יכולין להתחיל ולגמור עד שלא יגיעו לשורה – יתחילו, ואם לאו – לא יתחילו. העומדים בשורה, הפנימיים – פטורים, והחיצונים – חייבים. (* [ו]נשים ועבדים וקטנים פטורים מק"ש ומן התפילין וחייבין בתפלה ובמזוזה ובברכת המזון).§ שמחות פ"י [משנה לקמן כ.]

גמ' מוטל לפניו – אין, ושאינו מוטל לפניו – לא; ורמינהי: *מי [ז]שמתו מוטל לפניו – אוכל בבית אחר, ואם אין לו בית אחר – אוכל בבית חבירו, ואם אין לו בית חבירו – עושה מחיצה ואוכל, ואם אין לו דבר לעשות מחיצה – מחזיר פניו ואוכל, ואינו מיסב ואוכל, ואינו אוכל בשר ואינו שותה יין, ואינו מברך ואינו מזמן, ואין מ"ק דף כג: שמחות פ"י

וְאֵין מְבָרְכִין עָלָיו וְאֵין מְזַמְּנִין עָלָיו, וּפָטוּר מִקְּרִיאַת שְׁמַע וּמִן הַתְּפִלָּה וּמִן הַתְּפִלִּין וּמִכָּל מִצְוֹת הָאֲמוּרוֹת בַּתּוֹרָה; וּבְשַׁבָּת – מֵיסֵב וְאוֹכֵל בָּשָׂר וְשׁוֹתֶה יַיִן, וּמְבָרֵךְ וּמְזַמֵּן, וּמְבָרְכִין עָלָיו וּמְזַמְּנִין עָלָיו, וְחַיָּיב בְּכָל הַמִּצְוֹת הָאֲמוּרוֹת בַּתּוֹרָה; *רשב"ג אוֹמֵר: מִתּוֹךְ שֶׁנִּתְחַיֵּיב בְּאֵלּוּ נִתְחַיֵּיב בְּכוּלָּן. וא"ר יוֹחָנָן: מַאי בֵּינַיְיהוּ – תַּשְׁמִישׁ הַמִּטָּה אִיכָּא בֵּינַיְיהוּ. קָתָנֵי מִיהַת "פָּטוּר מִקְּרִיאַת שְׁמַע וּמִן הַתְּפִלָּה וּמִן הַתְּפִלִּין וּמִכָּל מִצְוֹת הָאֲמוּרוֹת בַּתּוֹרָה"! אָמַר רַב פַּפָּא: תַּרְגּוּמָא אַמַּחֲזִיר פָּנָיו וְאוֹכֵל. רַב אָשֵׁי אָמַר: כֵּיוָן שֶׁמּוּטָּל עָלָיו לְקוֹבְרוֹ – כְּמוּטָּל לְפָנָיו דָּמֵי, שֶׁנֶּאֱמַר: "וַיָּקָם אַבְרָהָם מֵעַל פְּנֵי מֵתוֹ", וְנֶאֱמַר: "וְאֶקְבְּרָה מֵתִי מִלְּפָנָי" – כָּל זְמַן שֶׁמּוּטָּל עָלָיו לְקוֹבְרוֹ כְּמוּטָּל לְפָנָיו דָּמֵי. § מֵתוֹ – אִין, אֲבָל מְשַׁמְּרוֹ – לָא, וְהָתַנְיָא: הַמְשַׁמֵּר אֶת הַמֵּת אע"פ שֶׁאֵינוֹ מֵתוֹ – פָּטוּר מק"ש וּמִן הַתְּפִלָּה וּמִן הַתְּפִלִּין וּמִכָּל מִצְוֹת הָאֲמוּרוֹת בַּתּוֹרָה. מְשַׁמְּרוֹ – אע"פ שֶׁאֵינוֹ מֵתוֹ, מֵתוֹ – אע"פ שֶׁאֵינוֹ מְשַׁמְּרוֹ. מֵתוֹ וּמְשַׁמְּרוֹ – אִין, אֲבָל מְהַלֵּךְ בְּבֵית הַקְּבָרוֹת – לָא, וְהָתַנְיָא: *לֹא יְהַלֵּךְ אָדָם בְּבֵית הַקְּבָרוֹת וּתְפִלִּין בְּרֹאשׁוֹ וְסֵפֶר תּוֹרָה בִּזְרוֹעוֹ וְקוֹרֵא, וְאִם עוֹשֶׂה כֵּן עוֹבֵר מִשּׁוּם "לוֹעֵג לָרָשׁ חֵרֵף עוֹשֵׂהוּ"! הָתָם תּוֹךְ אַרְבַּע [אַמּוֹת] הוּא דְּאָסוּר, חוּץ לְאַרְבַּע אַמּוֹת חַיָּיב, דְּאָמַר מָר: *מֵת תּוֹפֵס ד' אַמּוֹת לק"ש, הָכָא – חוּץ לד' אַמּוֹת נָמֵי פָּטוּר. § גּוּפָא: "הַמְשַׁמֵּר אֶת הַמֵּת אע"פ שֶׁאֵינוֹ מֵתוֹ – פָּטוּר מִקְּרִיאַת שְׁמַע וּמִן הַתְּפִלָּה וּמִן הַתְּפִלִּין וּמִכָּל מִצְוֹת הָאֲמוּרוֹת בַּתּוֹרָה. הָיוּ שְׁנַיִם – זֶה מְשַׁמֵּר וְזֶה קוֹרֵא, וְזֶה מְשַׁמֵּר וְזֶה קוֹרֵא. בֶּן עַזַּאי אוֹמֵר: הָיוּ בָּאִים בִּסְפִינָה – מַנִּיחוֹ בְּזָוִית זוֹ וּמִתְפַּלְּלִין שְׁנֵיהֶם בְּזָוִית אַחֶרֶת. מַאי בֵּינַיְיהוּ? אָמַר רָבִינָא: "חוֹשְׁשִׁין לְעַכְבָּרִים" אִיכָּא בֵּינַיְיהוּ. מָר סָבַר: חָיְישִׁינַן, וּמָר סָבַר: לָא חָיְישִׁינַן. ת"ר: הַמּוֹלִיךְ עֲצָמוֹת מִמָּקוֹם לְמָקוֹם – הֲרֵי זֶה לֹא יִתְּנֵם בְּדִסַקַּיָּא וְיִתְּנֵם עַל גַּבֵּי חֲמוֹר וְיִרְכַּב עֲלֵיהֶם, מִפְּנֵי שֶׁנּוֹהֵג בָּהֶם מִנְהַג בִּזָּיוֹן. וְאִם הָיָה מִתְיָרֵא מִפְּנֵי גּוֹיִם וּמִפְּנֵי לִסְטִים – מוּתָּר, וּכְדֶרֶךְ שֶׁאָמְרוּ בַּעֲצָמוֹת כָּךְ אָמְרוּ [ו] בְּסֵפֶר תּוֹרָה. אַהֵייא? אִילֵימָא אַרֵישָׁא – פְּשִׁיטָא, מִי גָּרַע סֵפֶר תּוֹרָה מֵעֲצָמוֹת! אֶלָּא אַסֵּיפָא. § אָמַר רַחֲבָה *אָמַר רַב יְהוּדָה: כָּל הָרוֹאֶה הַמֵּת וְאֵינוֹ מְלַוֵּהוּ – עוֹבֵר מִשּׁוּם "לוֹעֵג לָרָשׁ חֵרֵף עוֹשֵׂהוּ". וְאִם הִלְוָהוּ מַה שְּׂכָרוֹ? אָמַר רַב אַסִּי, עָלָיו הַכָּתוּב אוֹמֵר: "מַלְוֵה ה' חוֹנֵן דָּל", "וּמְכַבְּדוֹ חוֹנֵן אֶבְיוֹן". § רַבִּי חִיָּיא וְרַבִּי יוֹנָתָן הֲווֹ שָׁקְלִי וְאָזְלִי בְּבֵית הַקְּבָרוֹת, הֲוָה קָשַׁדְיָא תְּכֵלְתָּא דְּרַבִּי יוֹנָתָן. אָמַר לֵיהּ רַבִּי חִיָּיא: [ה] דַּלְיֵיהּ, כְּדֵי שֶׁלֹּא יֹאמְרוּ "לְמָחָר בָּאִין אֶצְלֵנוּ וְעַכְשָׁיו *מְחָרְפִין אוֹתָנוּ". אָמַר לֵיהּ: וּמִי יָדְעִי כּוּלֵּי הַאי? וְהָא כְּתִיב: "וְהַמֵּתִים אֵינָם יוֹדְעִים מְאוּמָה"! אָמַר לֵיהּ: *אִם קָרִיתָ – לֹא שָׁנִיתָ, אִם שָׁנִיתָ – לֹא שִׁלַּשְׁתָּ, אִם שִׁלַּשְׁתָּ – לֹא פֵּירְשׁוּ לְךָ: "כִּי הַחַיִּים יוֹדְעִים שֶׁיָּמוּתוּ" – אֵלּוּ צַדִּיקִים שֶׁבְּמִיתָתָן נִקְרְאוּ חַיִּים, שֶׁנֶּאֱמַר: "וּבְנָיָהוּ בֶּן יְהוֹיָדָע בֶּן אִישׁ חַי רַב פְּעָלִים מִקַּבְצְאֵל הוּא הִכָּה אֵת שְׁנֵי אֲרִאֵל מוֹאָב וְהוּא יָרַד וְהִכָּה אֶת הָאֲרִי בְּתוֹךְ הַבֹּאר בְּיוֹם הַשָּׁלֶג", בֶּן

רש"י

ואין מברכין עליו. אין צריך שיברכו לו אחרים בברכת הלחם: ואין מזמנין עליו. אין מצטרף עם שלשה לזימון: תשמיש המטה איכא בינייהו. לר"ש חייב אבל בעונה בשבת: קתני מיהת פטור מק"ש ומכל ברכות. ואפילו כשהוא אוכל בבית חברו: תרגמא. למה דקתני פטור אמי שאין לו בית אחר, דקאמר מחזיר פניו ואוכל: רב אשי אמר. לעולם אכולה, ומתניתין נמי אפילו בבית אחר נמי פטר ליה, דכל שמוטל עליו לקוברו קרי מוטל לפניו: ויקם אברהם וגו' וכתיב "ואקברה מתי מלפני". והיינו שעדיין לא לפניו הוה: משמרו. אדם אחר שאינו קרובו אלא משמרו: תופס ד' אמות לק"ש. שאסור לקרות בתוך ארבע אמות שלו, משום לועג לרש: פטור מק"ש. משום דעוסק במצוה: חוששין לעכברים. תנא קמא חייש לעכברים אפילו בספינה: דסקיא. מרצוף גדול של עור: ואם היה מתירא. וצריך לרכוב על הסוס ולרוץ: אלא אסיפא. אם היה מתירא רוכב: מלוה ה' חונן דל. קרי ביה מלוה את המקום מי שחונן את הדל, ואין לך דל מן המת והמלוה אותו כאלו מלוה את המקום: דלייה. הגביהנו: לא שנית. לא חזרת עליו פעם שנית כדי שתתבונן בו: אלו צדיקים. ומאי "יודעים שימותו" – נותנים אל לבם יום המיתה ומושכים ידיהם מן העבירה, ורשעים "אינם יודעים מאומה" – שעושים עצמם כאינם יודעים וחוטאים: הוא הכה. השפיל את השנים של דורות משני מקדשים שלא היה בהם כמותו: אריאל. זה בית המקדש, שנאמר "הוי אריאל אריאל קרית חנה דוד" (ישעיה כט): מואב. על שם שבנאו דוד דאתי מרות המואביה: גזיזי:

תוספות

והתניא פטור מתקיעת שופר. אית לך למימר בחול ולא בי"ט? בתמיה, ומשני, א"ר חנינא: שהוא זקוק להכין לו ארון ותכריכין, כדתנן (שבת קנא.): מחשיכין על התחום להביא לו ארון ותכריכין, כמו שהוא נושא משאו דמי. אלמא משמע דבשבתות וי"ט אינו רשאי לברך ולהתפלל, דטרוד להחשיך לו על התחום להביא ארון ותכריכין, וקשיא מסיפא, דקתני: בשבת מברכין עליו ומזמנין עליו, וכן תניא נמי בירושלמי: בד"א – בחול, אבל בשבת מיסב ואוכל ומברך ועונים אחריו אמן. ואומר הר"י דפליגי אהדדי רישא וסיפא בירושלמי. ורבי נתנאל היה אומר דאפשר לישבו, דודאי אם דעתו להחשיך על התחום – אז יש לנו לומר דטרוד להחשיך ואינו רשאי לברך, אבל בסיפא, מיירי בשאין דעתו להחשיך על התחום, ומיהו הא טעמא לא שייך לטעמא דמשום כבודו. ומן הירושלמי דמשני דפטור מנטילת לולב, דמיירי בחול המועד דטרוד לישא משאו, למדנו בחול המועד שייך אנינות כשמתו מוטל לפניו. וכיון דכשמוטל לפניו שייך אנינות, כי מוטל עליו לקוברו כמוטל לפניו דמי. וכן איפכא, מי שמתו מוטל לפניו ואין עליו לקוברו – אינו נוהג אנינות, וכן משמע בירושלמי: נמסר לרבים – אוכל בשר ושותה יין, נמסר לכתפים – כנמסר לרבים, ועל כרחך נמסר לרבים ר"ל אפי' לפניו, דאי שלא לפניו – תיפוק ליה שמיד חל עליו אבלות משיצא מפתח ביתו, וכיון דלא חל עליה אנינות א"כ אדם שאינו יכול לקבור מתו, כגון אדם שמת בבית האסורים ואין המושל מניחו לקוברו – נראה שאין חייב לנהוג בו אנינות, שהרי אין זה מוטל עליו לקברו, מפני שאינו יכול לפדותו ולהוציאו לקברו. כדתניא במסכת שמחות (פ"ב): נתיאשו בעליו מלקוברו מתאבלין עליו, ופסיק מיניה תורת אנינות. מיהו, באותו שתפסו מושל גם אבלות אינו חייב, דלא דמי לנתיאשו מלקוברו(א) שאם אינו קוברו מת, אבל הכא הוא עדיין הוא מצפה אם יוכל לעשות פשרה עם המושל להניחו לקברו, וכן מעשה דר' אליעזר בר"ש בבבא מציעא (ד' פד:) דספק מלות אנינות. ומעשה שמתה אחותו של ר"ת בשבת והודיעו לו במוצאי שבת בעיר אחרת, ואכל בשר ושתה יין, ואמר כיון שיש לה בעל שחייב בקבורתה – אינו אסור בבשר ויין. ואפשר שגם ר"ת אם היה בעיר עצמו היה מיקל מאותו הטעם: וספר תורה בזרועו וקורא. והוא הדין דעל פה אסור לקרות: וירכב עליהם. אבל אי מפשילן לאחוריו על החמור – שפיר דמי, וכן בס"ת. ואפילו אם בדעתך לאסור ס"ת, אבל בנביאים וכתובים שפיר דמי, *מדנקט ס"ת, ולא מסתבר לומר משום שריותא דגוים ולסטים דהא פשיטא דמותר, דלמה יהיה אסור? ועוד, דבהדיא אמר בירושלמי: דסקיא מלאה ספרים או שהיו בה עצמות של מת – הרי זה מפשילן לאחוריו ורוכב עליו*: אלא אסיפא משום לסטים מותר לרכוב עליהם. וה"ה לאחוריו מותר אפילו בלא לסטים: למחר באין אצלנו ועכשיו מחרפין אותנו. ותימה: והא אמרי' בפ' "התכלת" (מנחות דף מא.): ההיא שעתא ודאי רמינן ליה. פי': נותנין ציצית בטליתותיהן(ב) משום לועג לרש! וי"ל דה"פ: הכא דמבזיון אותם במה שהחיים מצווים והמתים אינם מצווים וגדול המצווה וכו',(ג) והיינו ד"התכלת" היינו דרמו מוטים למתים ועכשיו אנו מסלקין אותן, *ומאי שנא? אומר ר"ת: דוקא הם שהיו רגילים כולם בחייהם ללבוש טלית בד' כנפות וללבוש ציצית, וגם לכל העוסקים בהם יש להם ציצית – והוה "לועג לרש" אם לא היה להם ציצית, או משום דכתיב 'לדורותם', לדור תם, אבל אנו שגם בחיינו אין מנהגינו ללבוש תמיד ציצית, אי הוי רמינן להו הוי כמו לועג לרש. וכ"ת: נשים לאותם שהיה להם בחייהם – א"כ יהיה לועג לרש לאחרים. ועוד אר"ת שמשמע מלשון לותי"ר(ד) דמסירים הציצית, דציצית עולה למנין תרי"ג עם ח' חוטין וחמשה קשרים, ואם לובש ציצית – נראה כאלו קיים כל התורה, ומיחזי כשיקרא. וזה לא נהירא, דגם חיים עתה למה לובשים? הלא לא קיימו כל התורה כולה! ומיהו, י"ל דלמו סומכים על מסכת שמחות (פי"ב) שלוה אבא שאול לבניו הטילו תכלת מטליתו, ואע"פ שהגמרא חולק עליו יש דברים שאנו מניחין הגמרא שלנו ואנו עושין כספרים החיצונים. כמו מחזון ישעיה כפסיקתא, וכמו 'ויחל' שיש בגמרא (מגילה דף לא.) דבתעניות קורין ברכות וקללות, ובמסכת סופרים (פי"ז) – מפרש ויחל. והרי"צב"א היה רגיל שלא להסירים מן הכנף, אלא לקושרם ולהדקם בתוך הכנף לאפוקי נפשיה מפלוגתא אם הם חייבין בציצית – יש להם ציצית, ואם לאו – הרי הם מכוסין*: שני אריאל מואב. על שם דוד ושלמה שבנו את הבית, ובאו מרות המואביה:

בן

עין משפט נר מצוה

ה א מיי' פ"ד מהלכות תפילין הלכה כג ופ"ד מהלכות אבל הלכה יג [ופי' מהל' ס"ת הלכה ו] סמ"ג עשין כב טוש"ע או"ח סימן מה סעיף א [וסימן עא סעיף ז] [וטור ש"ע יו"ד סימן רפב סעיף ד וסי' שמ] סעיף ג]:

ו ב מיי' פ"ד מהלכות ק"ש הלכה ב טוש"ע או"ח סימן עא סעיף ג ד וביו"ד סימן שמא סעיף ד:

ז ג מיי' פ"ד מהלכות אבל הלכה י"ד סמ"ג עשין ב טור ש"ע יו"ד סימן שסו סעיף יוד:

[ד מיי' פ"ז מהל' ס"ת הלכה יא טוש"ע י"ד סי' רפב סעיף ג']

ח ד (מיי' וסמג שם) טור ש"ע יו"ד סימן שמג סעיף ג

[ה טוש"ע או"ח סי' כג סעיף א' וביו"ד סי' שסז סעיף ד']

רב נסים גאון

פרק ג

דאמר מר מת תופש ד' אמות לקרית שמע. עיקרה במסכתא סוטה בפרק משוח מלחמה (דף מג) כי אתא רב דימי אמר ר' יוחנן משום ר' אליעזר בן יעקב מת תופש ד' אמות לקרית שמע דכתיב (משלי יז) לועג לרש חרף עושהו:

מסורת הש"ס

[כמ"ק איתא רבן גמליאל וכן איתא בשמחות]

סוטה מג:

[בשאלתות פ' חיי שרה אי' אמר רב יהודה אמר רב]

משלי יט

קהלת ט

[מ"ק כח.]

שם

שמואל ב כג

[ועיין תוספות פסחים מ: ד"ה אבל ותוס' ב"ב עד ע"א ד"ה פסקי ותוס' נדה סח. ד"ה אבל ותוס' ע"ג סה: ד"ה אבל]

הגהות הב"ח

(א) תוס' ד"ה ולוהו מבכך וכו' לנתייאשו מלקוברו שאם אינו קוברו אבל: (ב) תוס' ד"ה למחר וכו' נותנין ציצית בטליתותיהן ולוכח משום לועג. נ"ב במנחות ותראה דהגהות ל"ע: (ג) בא"ד וגדול המצווה וכו' וקשה מהסוגיא דהתכלת: (ד) בא"ד מלשון לותי"ר הא למסירים הציצית משום לציצית עולה.

נ"א מלעינין.

ומיהו נראה דאף בס"ת ש"ד מדנקט בסיפא ס"ת כצ"ל רש"א

וודקאמר אלא אסיפא כצ"ל והד"א רש"א

ומאי טעמא כצ"ל רש"א

גזיזי דברדא. חתיכות של ברד והקרח שקורין גלאנ"א בלע"ז, והיינו ביום השלג: ונחת וטבל *לקריו. כדי לעסוק בתורה: דתנא סיפרא דבי רב. תורת כהנים: חלל רשע. על צדקיהו הוא אומר, ועדיין בימי יחזקאל חי היה וקורהו 'חלל': לקריתא. להתעסק בעבודת אחוזתם: אייקר תלמודייהו. אשתכח תלמודם מגרסתם. אייקר – הוכבד עליהם מחמת שכחה: צערא דידהו. צער גופם ממש, כגון עקיצת הרימה: שתי רוחות. של שתי ילדות מתות: ונשמע. ונדע (א) מה גזרו היום פורענות בעולם, שהעולם נדון בר"ה: הפרגוד. מחיצה המבדלת בין מקום השכינה:

תורה אור

בן איש חי אטו כולי עלמא. בספרים מדויקים כתיב 'חי' וקרינן 'חיל' ומן הכתיב דייק הכי, שלא כתיב חיל אלא חי: **סיפרא** דבי רב. מ'האר"י' דריש, שהוא חמור שבספרים: **בתוך** הבור. שהוא באמצע הספרים:

אלמא ידעי. מדקאמר לעגל קא אתית. ולא מצי לשנויי כדלעיל דומה קדים ואמר להו, דהיינו דוקא לאלתר, אבל כל כך לא היה מקדים – דהוא עצמו אינו יודע: אפילו

"בן איש חי", אטו כולי עלמא בני מתי נינהו?! אלא, "בן איש חי" – שאפי' במיתתו קרוי חי; "רב פעלים מקבצאל" – שריבה וקיבץ פועלים לתורה; "והוא הכה את שני אראל מואב" – שלא הניח כמותו לא במקדש ראשון ולא במקדש שני; "והוא ירד והכה את הארי בתוך הבור ביום השלג" – איכא דאמרי: דתבר גזיזי דברדא ונחת *וטבל, איכא דאמרי דתנא סיפרא דבי רב ביומא דסיתוא. "והמתים אינם יודעים מאומה" – אלו רשעים שבחייהן קרויין מתים, שנאמר: °"ואתה חלל רשע נשיא ישראל". ואי בעית אימא, מהכא: °"על פי שנים עדים או (על פי) שלשה עדים יומת המת". חי הוא! אלא: המת מעיקרא.§ *בני ר' חייא נפוק לקרייתא אייקר להו תלמודייהו, הוו קא מצערי לאדכוריה. א"ל חד לחבריה: ידע אבון בהאי צערא? א"ל אידך: מנא ידע? והא כתיב: °"יכבדו בניו ולא ידע"! א"ל אידך: ולא ידע? והא כתיב: °"אך בשרו עליו יכאב ונפשו עליו תאבל", ואמר רבי יצחק: *קשה רמה למת *כמחט בבשר החי. אמרי: בצערא דידהו – ידעי, בצערא דאחרינא – לא ידעי. ולא? והתניא: *מעשה בחסיד אחד שנתן דינר לעני בערב ר"ה בשני בצורת והקניטתו אשתו והלך ולן בבית הקברות. ושמע שתי רוחות שמספרות זו לזו, אמרה חדא לחברתה: חברתי, בואי ונשוט בעולם ונשמע מאחורי הפרגוד מה פורענות בא לעולם. אמרה לה חברתה: איני יכולה שאני קבורה במחצלת של קנים, אלא לכי את ומה שאת שומעת אמרי לי. הלכה היא ושטה ובאה. ואמרה לה חברתה: חברתי מה שמעת מאחורי הפרגוד? אמרה לה: שמעתי, שכל הזורע ברביעה ראשונה, ברד מלקה אותו. הלך הוא וזרע ברביעה שניה. של כל העולם כולו – לקה, שלו – לא לקה. לשנה האחרת הלך ולן בבית הקברות, ושמע אותן שתי רוחות שמספרות זו עם זו. אמרה חדא לחברתה: בואי ונשוט בעולם ונשמע מאחורי הפרגוד מה פורענות בא לעולם. אמרה לה: חברתי, לא כך אמרתי לך: איני יכולה שאני קבורה במחצלת של קנים? אלא לכי את ומה שאת שומעת בואי ואמרי לי. הלכה ושטה ובאה. ואמרה לה חברתה: חברתי, מה שמעת מאחורי הפרגוד? אמרה לה: שמעתי, שכל הזורע ברביעה שניה שדפון מלקה אותו. הלך וזרע ברביעה ראשונה. של כל העולם כולו – נשדף, ושלו לא נשדף. אמרה לו אשתו: מפני מה *אשתקד של כל העולם כולו לקה ושלך לא לקה, ועכשיו של כל העולם כולו נשדף ושלך לא נשדף? סח לה כל הדברים הללו. אמרו: לא היו ימים מועטים עד שנפלה קטטה בין אשתו של אותו חסיד ובין אמה של אותה ריבה. אמרה לה: לכי ואראך בתך שהיא קבורה במחצלת של קנים. לשנה האחרת הלך ולן בבית הקברות ושמע אותן רוחות שמספרות זו עם זו. אמרה לה: חברתי, בואי ונשוט בעולם ונשמע מאחורי הפרגוד מה פורענות בא לעולם. אמרה לה: חברתי, הניחיני, דברים שביני לבינך כבר נשמעו בין החיים. אלמא ידעי! – דילמא איניש אחרינא שכיב ואזיל ואמר להו.§ ת"ש: דזעירי הוה מפקיד זוזי גבי אושפיזכתיה, עד דאתי ואזיל לבי רב, שכיבה. אזל בתרה לחצר מות. אמר לה: זוזי היכא? –אמרה ליה: זיל שקלינהו מתותי *בצנורא דדשא בדוך פלן, ואימא לה לאימא תשדר לי מסרקאי וגובתאי דכוחלא בהדי פלניתא דאתיא למחר. אלמא ידעי! – [דלמא] דומה קדים ומכריז להו. ת"ש: דאבוה דשמואל הוו קא מפקדי גביה זוזי דיתמי, כי נח נפשיה לא הוה שמואל גביה. הוו קא קרו ליה בר אכיל זוזי דיתמי. אזל אבתריה לחצר מות. אמר להו: בעינא אבא. אמרו ליה: אבא טובא איכא הכא. אמר להו: בעינא אבא בר אבא. אמרו ליה: אבא בר אבא נמי טובא איכא הכא. אמר להו: בעינא אבא בר אבא אבוה דשמואל, היכא? – אמרו ליה: סליק למתיבתא דרקיעא. אדהכי חזייה ללוי דיתיב אברא. אמר ליה: אמאי יתבת אבראי, מאי טעמא לא סלקת? אמר ליה, דאמרי לי: כל כי הנך שני דלא סליקת למתיבתא דרבי אפס ואחלישתיה לדעתיה – לא מעיילינן לך למתיבתא דרקיעא. אדהכי והכי אתא אבוה, חזייה דהוה קא בכי ואחיך. אמר ליה: מאי טעמא קא בכית? אמר ליה: דלעגל קא אתית. מאי טעמא אחיכת? – דחשיבת בהאי עלמא טובא. אמר ליה: אי חשיבנא – נעיילוה ללוי, ועיילוהו ללוי. אמר ליה: זוזי דיתמי היכא? אמר ליה: זיל שקלינהו באמתא דריחיא, עילאי ותתאי – דידן, ומיצעי – דיתמי. אמר ליה: מאי טעמא עבדת הכי? –אמר ליה: אי גנובי גנבי – מגנבו מדידן, אי אכלה ארעא – אכלה מדידן. אלמא דידעי! – דילמא שאני שמואל, כיון דחשיב – קדמי ומכרזי *"פנו מקום". °ואף ר' יונתן הדר ביה, דאמר רבי שמואל בר נחמני אמר ר' יונתן: מנין למתים שמספרים זה עם זה? שנאמר: °"ויאמר ה' אליו זאת הארץ אשר נשבעתי לאברהם ליצחק וליעקב לאמר", מאי 'לאמר' – אמר הקדוש ברוך הוא למשה: לך אמור להם לאברהם ליצחק וליעקב שבועה שנשבעתי לכם כבר קיימתיה לבניכם.

ואי

ברביעה ראשונה. יורה שלש רביעות הן: בכירה, שניה ושלישית. ראשונה – בי"ז במרחשון, שניה – בכ"ג, שלישית – בר"ח כסליו: ברד מלקה אותו. שעתיד ברד ליפול סמוך לרביעה *ראשונה ומה שנזרע כבר הוקשה, והברד שוברו; והנזרע בשניה עדיין רך הוא ואינו נשבר בשביל הברד, כענין שנאמר "והפשתה והשעורה נכתה והחטה והכוסמת לא נכו" (שמות ט): שדפון. מלקה הרך ואינו משדף הקשה: אלמא ידעי. דברים האמורים בין החיים: לחצר מות. לבית הקברות: בצנורא דדשא. בחור מפתן הבית שהדלת סובב אותו: מסרקאי. מסרק שלי: גובתא. קנה, ובשביל שמתה ילדה אמרה כן לעגמת נפש: בהדי פלניתא דאתיא למחר. לקבורה: אלמא ידעי. מה שעושין, שידעה זו שזו גוססת ונטויה למות: דלמא דומה. מלאך שהוא ממונה על המתים קדים ומכריז להו: עכשיו יבא פלוני. אבל שאר דברי החיים אינם יודעים: בעינא אבא. מבקש אני את אבא, כך היה שמו: א"ל. המתים נגלו לו כאילו הם חוץ מקבריהם ויושבים בעגולה: חזייה. שמואל ללוי *חברו שהיה יושב חוץ לישיבה של שאר מתים: כל כי הנך שני. מספר השנים שלא נכנסת בישיבתו של רבי אפס במסכת כתובות בפרק "הנושא את האשה" (דף קג:): חזייה. שמואל לאבוה דקא בכי וחייך: דלעגל אתית. במהרה תקבר: באמתא דריחיא. כל בנין מושב הרחיים קרוי אמת הרחיים: אלמא ידעי. מי חשוב בין החיים: זאת הארץ. במיתת משה כתיב: ואי

דילמא דומה הוא דקדים מכריז להו. במסכת סנהדרין בפרק כל ישראל יש להן חלק (דף לד) אמרי' אמר ר' יוחנן אותו מלאך שהוא ממונה על הרוחות דומה שמו: **ת"ש** דאבוה דשמואל הוו מפקדי גביה זוזי דיתמי אמר ליה דאמרו לי כל הנך שני דלא עיילת למתיבתא דר' אפס הכא נמי לא תיעול. איתיה לפירושה במסכת כתובות בפרק הנושא את האשה (דף קג) דתנו רבנן בשעת פטירתו של רבי כו' אמר להם לחכמי ישראל אני צריך נכנסו חכמי ישראל אצלו אמר להם אל תספדוני בעיירות והושיבו ישיבה לאחר ל' יום שמעון בני חכם גמליאל בני נשיא חנינא בר חמא ישב בראש ודאמרי' עלה לא קביל עליה ר' חנינא שהיה ר' אפס גדול ממנו ב' שנים ומחצה יתיב ר' אפס ברישא ויתיב ר' חנינא אבראי ואתא לוי יתיב גביה ומשום הכא לא עיילוה ללוי למתיבתא דרקיעא עד דבעא שמואל רחמי עליה ועיילוה:

הגהות הב"ח

(א) רש"י ד"ה שתי וכו' מתות הס"ד ואח"כ מ"ה בואי ונשוט ונלע:

גליון הש"ס

גמ' ואף ר' יונתן הדר ביה. עי' סוטה דף לד ע"ב תוס' ד"ה אבותי: **רש"י** ד"ה ונחת כו' כדי לעסוק בתורה. עי' ב"ק דף פ"ב ע"ב תוס' ד"ה אתא:

[כלומר שתא קדמיתא ערוך ועי' תוי"ט ב"ב פ"ו מ"ג]

ובתרגום רב יוסף בד"ה א' יא איתא שטבל מחמת שנגע בשרץ אחד

[נ"ל שניה]

[עיין תוס' ב"ק פב: ד"ה אתא]

[כמס' עו"ג מו. כתב רש"י ד"ה בני רבי חייא יהודה וחזקי' שמן]

[סוטה דף י. סנהדרין מח:]

ס"א הכירו

נ"א צנורא

[כתובות עז:]

יחזקאל כא · דברים יז · איוב יד · שם · דברים לד · [אבות דר"נ פ"ג]

ואי ס"ד דלא ידעי – כי אמר להו: מאי הוי? – אלא מאי, דידעי? – למה ליה למימר להו? – לאחזוקי ליה טיבותא למשה. אמר רבי יצחק: כל המספר אחרי המת כאלו מספר אחרי האבן. איכא דאמרי: דלא ידעי; ואיכא דאמרי: דידעי ולא איכפת להו. איני?! והא אמר רב פפא: חד אישתעי מילתא בתריה דמר שמואל ונפל קניא מטללא ובזעא לארנקא דמוחיה! שאני צורבא מרבנן, דקודשא בריך הוא תבע ביקריה. אמר רבי יהושע בן לוי: כל המספר אחר *מטתן של תלמידי חכמים נופל בגיהנם, שנא': "והמטים עקלקלותם יוליכם ה' את פועלי האון שלום על ישראל", אפילו בשעה ששלום על ישראל "יוליכם ה' את פועלי האון". תנא דבי ר' ישמעאל: אם ראית תלמיד חכם שעבר עבירה בלילה – אל תהרהר אחריו ביום, שמא עשה תשובה. 'שמא' סלקא דעתך? אלא: ודאי עשה תשובה. והני מילי – בדברים שבגופו, אבל בממונא – עד דמהדר למריה.§ ואמר ר' יהושע בן לוי: [א]בכ"ד מקומות בית דין מנדי' על כבוד הרב, וכולן שנינו במשנתנו. אמר ליה ר' אלעזר: היכא? אמר ליה: לכי תשכח. נפק דק ואשכח תלת: המזלזל בנטילת ידים, והמספר אחר מטתן של תלמידי חכמי', והמגיס דעתו כלפי מעלה. [ב]המספר אחר מטתן של תלמידי חכמים מאי היא? *דתנן, הוא היה אומר: אין משקין לא את הגיורת ולא את המשוחררת; וחכמים אומרים: [ג]משקין. ואמרו לו: מעשה בכרכמית, שפחה משוחררת בירושלים והשקוה שמעיה ואבטליון! – ואמר להם: דוגמא השקוה; ונדוהו, ומת בנדויו, וסקלו בית דין את ארונו. [ד]והמזלזל בנטילת ידים מאי היא? *דתנן, א"ר יהודה: חס ושלום שעקביא בן מהללאל נתנדה, שאין עזרה ננעלת על כל אדם בישראל בחכמה ובטהרה וביראת חטא כעקביא בן מהללאל. אלא את מי נדו – את אלעזר בן חנוך שפקפק בנטילת ידים; וכשמת – שלחו בית דין והניחו אבן גדולה על ארונו, *ללמדך: [ה]שכל המתנדה ומת בנדויו – ב"ד סוקלין את ארונו. המגיס דעתו כלפי מעלה מאי היא? *דתנן, שלח לו שמעון בן שטח לחוני המעגל: צריך אתה להתנדות, ואלמלא חוני אתה גוזרני עליך נדוי, אבל מה אעשה שאתה *מתחטא לפני המקום ועושה לך רצונך כבן שמתחטא לפני אביו ועושה לו רצונו, ועליך הכתוב אומר "ישמח אביך ואמך ותגל יולדתך". ותו ליכא? והא איכא דתני רב יוסף: *תודוס איש רומי [ו]הנהיג את בני רומי להאכילן גדיים מקולסין בלילי פסחים; שלח ליה שמעון בן שטח: אלמלא תודוס אתה גוזרני עליך נדוי, שאתה מאכיל את ישראל קדשים בחוץ! – *במשנתנו קאמרינן, והא ברייתא היא. – ובמתני' ליכא?! והא איכא הא *דתנן: חתכו חוליות ונתן חול בין חוליא לחוליא, ר' אליעזר מטהר, [ז]וחכמים מטמאים, וזהו תנורו של עכנאי; מאי עכנאי? אמר רב יהודה אמר שמואל: מלמד, שהקיפוהו הלכות כעכנאי זה וטמאוהו; ותניא: *אותו היום הביאו כל טהרות שטיהר ר"א ושרפום לפניו, ולבסוף ברכוהו! – אפילו הכי, נדוי במתני' לא תנן. אלא בכ"ד מקומות היכא משכחת לה? – ר' יהושע בן לוי מדמה מילתא למילתא, ור' אלעזר לא מדמה מילתא למילתא.§ "נושאי המטה וחלופיהן".§ *ת"ר: [ח]אין מוציאין את המת סמוך לק"ש, ואם התחילו אין מפסיקין. איני?! והא רב יוסף אפקוהו סמוך לק"ש! – *אדם חשוב שאני.§ שלפני המטה ושלאחר המטה.§ ת"ר: [ט]העוסקים בהספד, בזמן שהמת מוטל לפניהם – נשמטין אחד אחד וקורין, אין המת מוטל לפניהם – הן יושבין וקורין והוא יושב ודומם, הם עומדים ומתפללין והוא עומד ומצדיק עליו את הדין, ואומר: רבון העולמים, הרבה חטאתי לפניך ולא נפרעת ממני אחד מני אלף, יהי רצון מלפניך ה' אלהינו שתגדור פרצותינו ופרצות כל עמך בית ישראל ברחמים. אמר אביי: ['] לא מבעי ליה לאיניש למימר הכי, *דארשב"ל, וכן תנא משמיה דרבי יוסי: לעולם אל יפתח אדם פיו לשטן; ואמר רב יוסף: מאי קראה – שנאמר: "כמעט כסדום היינו", מאי אהדר להו נביא – "שמעו דבר ה' קציני סדום".§ "קברו את המת וחזרו וכו'". אם יכולים להתחיל ולגמור את כולה – אין, אבל פרק אחד או פסוק אחד – לא. ורמינהו: קברו את המת וחזרו, אם יכולין להתחיל ולגמור אפילו פרק אחד או פסוק אחד! הכי נמי קאמר: [י]אם יכולין להתחיל ולגמור אפי' פרק אחד או אפילו פסוק אחד עד שלא יגיעו לשורה – יתחילו ואם לאו – לא יתחילו.§

העומדים

רש"י

ואי ס"ד דלא ידעי. אין מבינין כלום אלא צערא דגופא: המספר אחר המת. בגנותו של מת אחר מיתתו: קניא מטללא. קנה גדול וכבד נפל מן הגג: טללא. גג: ארנקא דמוחיה. כיס שהמוח מונח בו: והמטים עקלקלותם. לעיל מיניה כתיב "היטיבה ה' לטובים" וסמיך ליה "והמטים עקלקלותם", והמכריעים את חובותם יותר על זכיותם להטותם לכף חובה: יוליכם ה' את פועלי האון. לגיהנם: בכ"ד מקומות. השתא משמע מלינו שנדו חכמים בני אדם בכ"ד מקומות לכבוד הרב לפי שלא נשאו כבוד לרבם: הוא היה אומר. עקביא בן מהללאל במסכת עדיות: אין משקין. אם קינא לה בעלה ונסתרה: לא את הגיורת. ד'בני ישראל' אמור בפרשה (במדבר ה) – פרט לאשת גר ועבד משוחרר: בכרכמית. כך שמה, או על שם מקומה: דוגמא השקוה. על שהיו (א)דומים להם הם השקוה, שהיו שמעיה ואבטליון מבני בניו של סנחריב כדאמרינן בגיטין בפרק "הנזקין" (דף נז:): ר' יהודה. פליג אדלעיל דקתני שנדו את עקביא: שאין עזרה ננעלת. בפרק ה' דפסחים (דף סד.), שהיו שערי העזרה ננעלים כששוחטין פסחים של כל כת וכת, שהפסח נשחט בג' כתות: על כל אדם בישראל. כלומר: כשהיתה ננעלת עליהם, והיינו כשנתמלאה פה לפה לא היה בכולם אדם חשוב בחכמה ויראת חטא כעקביא: אלעזר בן חנוך שפקפק. זילזל, והיינו נמי לכבוד הרב שעבר ע"פ הגוזרים על הידים: אלמלא חוני אתה. שיצא שמך בגדולה ובחשיבות: צריך אתה להתנדות. לפי שהטריח לפני המקום על עסק גשמים "לא כך שאלתי" כמה פעמים וכבוד המקום כבוד הרב הוא: מתחטא. לשון חוטא, נקל בלבו לחטוא לאביו ולהטריחו על תאותו: מקולסים. צלויים כשהן שלמין, ותולין כרעיהן וקרסוליהן וקרביהם סביבותן בשפוד, ועל שם כך קורהו מקולס שהוא לשון מזויין, כדמתרגם "וכובע נחשת על ראשו" (שמואל א יז) – וקולסא דנחשא: בלילי פסחים. זכר לפסח שצולהו שלם, שנאמר בו "על כרעיו ועל קרבו" (שמות יב), כלומר עם כרעיו ועם קרבו: גוזרני עליך נדוי. והיינו נמי לכבוד הרב, שאסרו חכמים את הדבר לפי שהוא קרוב להאכיל את ישראל קדשים בחוץ שהרואה סבור שהקדישו לשם פסח: חתכו חוליות. תנור של חרס שהוא עשוי ככלי ומטלטל, ותחלתברייתו מן הטיט ומצרפו בכבשן כשאר קדרות, ואם נטמא הצריכו הכתוב נתיצה, ואם נתנו בענין זה שחתכו סביב סביב כחוליות עגולות, וחזר וחיברו בטיט של חול בין חוליא לחוליא, רבי אליעזר מטהר עולמית שאינו עוד כלי חרס, שלא נצרף בכבשן, וחכמים מטמאין: בעכנאי. כנחש זה שכורך עצמו בעגולה: כל טהרות. שנעשו בתנור זה או שנגעו באוירו. והיה רבי אליעזר מטהרן, והם שרפום: וברכוהו. לפי שהרבה מאד לחלוק בדבר זה כדאמרינן בבבא מציעא בפרק "הזהב" (דף נט:): נדוי במתני' לא תנן. הא דברכוהו – בברייתא הוא דקתני לה: מדמה מילתא למילתא. כל מקום שראה במתניתין שנחלק היחיד על הרבים מחלוקת גדולה, או אחד מן החכמים שמדבר קשה כנגד גדול הימנו: אומר ראוי היה כאן נדוי: אין מוציאין את המת. לקברו: סמוך לקריאת שמע. לפי שמתבטלין מן הקריאה: אין המת מוטל לפניהם. שהמת בבית אחר והם מספידין אותו כאן. ויש מפרשין: שנתון לצד אחר: והוא יושב ודומם. הקהל: למימר הכי. לא נפרעת ממני, דמשמע הפרע:

הרואה

תוספות

אפי' בשעה ששלום על ישראל. והיינו לאחר מיתתו, דלא אתו לאנצויי בהדי המספרים בגנותם. מהכא משמע דאיירי לאחר מיתה: דוגמא השקוה. פרש"י: לפי שהיתה גיורת כמותם, שהיו גרים. וכן משמע בירושלמי דמועד קטן (פ"ג): מהו דוגמא – דכוות'. בערוך פירש: *דוגמא השקוה – מי לבע, אבל לא היו מרים ממש, ולא מחקו התורה עליה אלא ליראה אותה:

מדלגין

עין משפט נר מצוה

ט א מיי' פ"ז מהלכות תלמוד תורה הלכה יד טוש"ע יו"ד סימן שלד סעיף מג:
י ב מיי' שם והלכה יב טוש"ע יו"ד סימן רמג סעיף ז ובסימן שלד סעיף מז:
יא ג מיי' פ"ב מהלכות סוטה הלכה ו:
יב ד מיי' פ"ו מהלכות ברכות הלכה י"ט סמג עשין כז טור שו"ע או"ח סי' קנח סעיף ט:
יג ה מיי' פ"ז מהלכות ת"ת הלכה ד טוש"ע יו"ד סימן שלד סעיף ג:

[בשם רב האי גאון והערוך גרס דוכתא ופי' כפירש"י ע"ש ערך דגם]

יד ו מיי' פ"ח מהלכות חמץ ומצה הלכה יא טוש"ע או"ח סימן תעו סעיף א:
טו ז מיי' פי"ב מהלכות כלים הלכה ה:
טז ח מיי' פ"ד מהלכות ק"ש הלכה ד סמג עשין יח טוש"ע או"ח סימן עב סעיף ב טור שו"ע יו"ד סימן שנח סעיף ב:
יז ט מיי' שם הלכה ה סמג שם טוש"ע או"ח סי' עב סעיף ג [וביו"ד סימן שמ"ד סעיף יב]: [י] [רמ"א בהגה' שו"ע יו"ד סי' שעו סעיף ב]:
יח י מיי' שם הלכה ו סמג שם טוש"ע שם סעיף ד:

[עי' פירש"י דהכא אמנם במשנה דתענית לא פי' כלום אלא הנקרא פורפייש בלע"ז אכן במנחות סז. כתב רש"י ד"ה ונתחטא נטייל כמו בן מתחטא לפני אביו ע"כ אבל בבכורות נז: כתב רש"י סד"ה והכתיב נתחטא לשון ירידה וחבירו במס' תענית בן המתחטא לפני אביו ע"כ ודע דהרע"ב מ"ח פ"ג דתענית כתב מתחטא מתגעגע וכתב התוי"ט דלשון ארמית היא כמ"ש בערוך כי הילדים רכים ת"י ארוס טלייא מחטיין]

מסורת הש"ס

תורה אור: תהלים קכה; משלי כג; ישעיה א

עדיות פ"ה מ"ו
שם פסחים סד:
שם מ"ק טו.
תענית דף יט.
פסחים נג. ע"ש ביצה כג. ע"ש תוספתא שם פ"ב
[עירובין דף סג. מנחות לח: כתובות קט.] עדיות פ"ה מ"ז כלים פ"ה מ"י ב"מ נט
ב"מ דף נט:
שמחות פ"י
[שבת דף לג. קמב. פסחים קי. מו"ק יח: יב. מגילה כב. כתובות נב: סו. ב"מ עג. מס' ע"ג ח: כח. מח: חולין קלז:]
לקמן ס. כתובות ח:

הגהות הב"ח

(א) רש"י ד"ה דוגמא השקוה על שהיו הם דומין לה השקוה:

גליון הש"ס

גמ' ואיכא מאי קלאה עבד כמעשה בסדום. עיין מו"ק דף יח ע"א תוס' ד"ה ולמשהייתא:

רב נסים גאון

מעשה בתודוס איש רומי שהנהיג את בני רומי לאכול גדיי' מקולסים בלילי פסחים. גרסינן במסכת פסחים בפ' מקום שנהגו (ד' נג) איבעיא להו תודוס איש רומי גברא רבה הוה או בעלי אגרופים הוה תא שמע את זו דרש תודוס איש רומי כו' שמע מינה גברא רבה הוה שמע מינה ר' יוסי בר אבין אמר מטיל מלאי לכים של תלמידי חכמים הוה דאמר ר' יוחנן כל המטיל מלאי לכים של תלמידי חכמים זוכה ויושב בישיבה של מעלה שנא' (קהלת ז) כי בצל החכמה בצל הכסף ובגמרא דבני מערבא (מו"ק פ"ג ה"א) אמרי מהו תודוס אמר ר' חנינא דהוה משלח פרנסתן דרבנן: חתכו חוליות ונתן חול בין חוליא לחוליא ר' אליעזר מטהר וחכמים מטמאין וזהו תנורו של עכנאי ואמר רב יהודה אמר שמואל למה נקרא שמו עכנאי שהקיפוהו דברים כעכנא וטמאוהו. איתא מיפרשא בבבא מציעא בפרק הזהב (דף נט) ומי שלא עיין בה לשם אינה מתפרשת לו מיכן לפי שלא הוזכר ממנה כאן אלא כפי הצורך בענין נמנו וברכוהו בלבד וכלל המעשה כולו לשם פירשוהו ולפי שהוא קשה ומשתבשין בפירושה ישר בעיני לפרש תורף דבריה בקיצור כפי שלמדתי מדברי אדוננו האיי גאון ז"ל החלוקה היתה בין ר' אליעזר והחכמים חבריו בתנור שנעשה חוליות של טיט מתחלתו ואחר כן הניחו אותן החוליות אחת על גבי חברתה עד שנגמר התנור ועמד על מתכונתו וכשהיו מרכיבין החוליות אחת על גבי חברתה היו נותנין חול בנתים סבר ר' אליעזר כי זה התנור הואיל והחול נתון בין כל חוליא וחוליא וכשמבקש אדם לפורקו ולהחזירו חוליות כמו שהיה מתחלה יכול הוא לפי כי חוליות שלו לא נדבקו זו בזו ולא נצמדו זו לזו ולפיכך יהא דינו עכשיו בשעה שהוא מוקם כדין שהיה לחוליות שלו קודם הקמתו ואם נפל באוירו של זה התנור שרץ אינו מטמא ולא יהא דינו כדין התנור שחוליותיו מצומדין ומדובקין זו בזו שאמר בו הכתוב (ויקרא יא) תנור וכירים יותץ והחכמים החולקים עליו לא היה אצלם הפרש בין נתן חול בין החוליות שלו בין לא נתן אלא בין כך ובין כך טמא הוא אצלם כדין שאר כלי חרש שמיטמאין מאוירן והיו דנין כנגד ר' אליעזר על זה הדבר ונשאו ונתנו בה הרבה ורצה ר' אליעזר להביא ראיה לדבריו ולסייעם מדרך שהיא נוהגת כמנהג סימנים וראיות והיא מדמית למעשה מופת ולא קיבלום החכמים ולא נתקיימו אצלם לפי שכן דרכו של עולם להתנהג בביוצא בהן ולפיכך אמרו לו אין מביאין ראיה מן החרוב ואין מביאין ראיה מאמת המים כלומר כי אין בזה דבר שהוא סותר למנהגו של עולם ומשנה סדרי בראשית כדי שיהא לך לראיה אלא לעולם אין ההלכה מתקיימת אלא לפי מה שנתברר מן הקבלה של מרובין והיינו דברי חכמים ובגמרא דאלו מגלחים דבני מערבא (הלכה א) הזכירו זה המעשה ואמר ר' אליעזר אמר ר' חנינא משנתנה לא נתנה אלא אחרי רבים להטות ולית לר' אליעזר ידע

שאחרי

"העומדים בשורה וכו'". § *ת"ר: אשורה הרואה פנימה – פטורה, ושאינה רואה פנימה – חייבת, רבי יהודה אומר: הבאים מחמת האבל – פטורין, מחמת עצמן – חייבין. § אמר רב יהודה אמר רב: בהמוצא כלאים בבגדו פושטן אפי' בשוק, מ"ט – °"אין חכמה ואין תבונה ואין עצה לנגד ה'" – *כ"מ שיש חילול השם אין חולקין כבוד לרב. מתיבי: גקברו את המת וחזרו, ולפניהם ב' דרכים, אחת טהורה ואחת טמאה, בא בטהורה – באין עמו בטהורה, בא בטמאה – באין עמו בטמאה, משום כבודו. אמאי? לימא: "אין חכמה ואין תבונה לנגד ה'". תרגמה רבי אבא בבית הפרס דרבנן. דאמר *רב יהודה אמר שמואל: דמנפח אדם בית הפרס והולך; ואמר רב יהודה בר אשי משמיה דרב: הבית הפרס שנדש טהור. § ת"ש, דאמר ר' אלעזר בר צדוק: ומדלגין היינו על גבי ארונות של מתים לקראת מלכי ישראל, ולא לקראת מלכי ישראל בלבד אמרו אלא אפי' לקראת מלכי אומות העולם, שאם יזכה – יבחין בין מלכי ישראל למלכי אומות העולם. אמאי? לימא: "אין חכמה ואין תבונה ואין עצה לנגד ה'"! כדרבא, דאמר רבא: דבר תורה, אהל, כל שיש בו חלל טפח – חוצץ בפני הטומאה, ושאין בו חלל טפח – אינו חוצץ בפני הטומאה, ורוב ארונות יש בהן חלל טפח, וגזרו על שיש בהן משום שאין בהן, ומשום כבוד מלכים לא גזרו בהו רבנן. § ת"ש: *גדול כבוד הבריות שדוחה [את] לא תעשה שבתורה. ואמאי? לימא: "אין חכמה ואין תבונה ואין עצה לנגד ה'"! – תרגמה רב בר שבא קמיה דרב כהנא בלאו °"דלא תסור". אחיכו עליה: לאו ד"לא תסור" דאורייתא היא! אמר רב כהנא: *גברא רבה אמר מילתא לא תחיכו עליה, כל מילי דרבנן אסמכינהו על לאו ד"לא תסור", ומשום כבודו שרו רבנן. § *ת"ש: °"והתעלמת מהם" – פעמים שאתה מתעלם מהם ופעמים שאין אתה מתעלם מהם; הא כיצד – אם זהיה כהן והיא בבית הקברות, או היה זקן ואינה לפי כבודו, או שהיתה מלאכתו מרובה משל חברו, לכך נאמר: "והתעלמת". אמאי? לימא: "אין חכמה ואין תבונה ואין עצה לנגד ה'"! שאני התם, דכתיב: "והתעלמת מהם". וליגמר מינה! – *איסורא מממונא לא ילפינן. § ת"ש: °"ולאחותו" *מה תלמוד לומר? הרי שהיה הולך לשחוט את פסחו ולמול את בנו ושמע שמת לו מת, יכול יחזור ויטמא – אמרת לא יטמא. יכול כשם שאינו מטמא להם כך אינו מטמא למת מצוה, ת"ל: "ולאחותו" – לאחותו הוא דאינו מטמא, אבל

תורה אור: משלי כא | דברים יז | דברים כב | במדבר ו

רש"י

הרואה פנימה. את חלל ההקף אחורי שורה הפנימית, והאבל יושב שם: מחמת עצמן. ולא מחמת כבוד, שלא באו לנחם אלא לראות את המאורע: אין חכמה. חשובה נגד ה': אחת טמאה. שיש בה קבר: בא בטהורה. האבל: בבית הפרס. דלא מטמא אלא מדרבנן. והוא שדה שנחרש בו קבר, וחשו חכמים שמא דלדלו כלי המחרישה את העצמות, והדורס עליהן מסיטן, ועצם כשעורה מטמא במגע ובמשא ולא באהל, וכיון דמדרבנן הוא דאסור. רבנן הוא דאחלוה ליקרייהו גבי אבל: מנפח אדם. לפניו, שאם הי' שם עצם – ירחפנו. דאי דאורייתא הוא לא הוינן מזלזלינן ביה כולי האי למיסמך אנפיחה. והך בדיקה – לעושה פסח אישתרי, ולא לאוכלי תרומה, כדאמרינן ב"חומר בקדש" (חגיגה דף כה:): שנדש. ברגלים: לקראת מלכי ישראל. הרי לכבוד הבריות עוברים על "נפש לא יטמא" (ויקרא כא) דהא ר' אלעזר בר צדוק כהן הוה כדאמרינן בבכורות (דף לו.): מדלגין. מארון לארון: דבר תורה. הלכה למשה מסיני: אינו חוצץ בפני הטומאה. דנקראת טומאה רצוצה, ובוקעת ועולה: את לא תעשה. קס"ד כל ל"ת קאמר: בלאו דלא תסור וגו'. אחיכו עליה. אינהו סבור דאפי' אמרו לו דבר תורה והוא עומד בפני הכבוד – יעבור עליו, והא האי נמי דאורייתא הוא: כל מילי דרבנן וכו'. והכי קאמר להו: דבר שהוא מדברי סופרים נדחה מפני כבוד הבריות, וקרי ליה ל"ת – משום דכתיב לא תסור. ודקא קשיא לכו דאורייתא הוא. רבנן אחלוה ליקרייהו לעבור על דבריהם היכא דאיכא כבוד הבריות, כגון לטלטל בשבת אבנים של בית הכסא לקנוח (שבת דף פא:), או מי שנפסקה ציצית טליתו בכרמלית לא הצריכו להניח טליתו שם וליכנס לביתו ערום (מנחות דף לח.): והיא בבית הקברות. האבדה: ואינה לפי כבודו. אין האבדה חשובה לפי כבודו להשיבה: או שהיתה מלאכתו מרובה. שדמי בטול מלאכתו לרדוף אחריה יתרים על דמי האבדה, ולא ירצו הבעלים להשיב לו יותר ממה שמשיב להם, ונמצא הוא מפסיד: ונגמר מינה. לגבי כלאים, דאמרן: פושטן אפילו בשוק: ממונא. קל מאיסורא: ולאחותו מה תלמוד לומר. בנזיר כתיב "כל ימי הזירו לה' על נפש מת לא יבא", וסמיך לי' "לאביו ולאמו לאחיו ולאחותו לא יטמא להם" דהא כולהו בכלל "על נפש מת לא יבא" היו, ולמה יצאו? 'לאביו' – פרט למת מצוה, 'לאמו' מה תלמוד לומר? משום מת מצוה לא איצטריך, דמ'לאביו' נפקא, ודרשי ליה בספרי ללמוד שאם היה נזיר זה כהן, דהוו עליה שתי קדושות אף הוא, לאמו הוא דלא יטמא, אבל מטמא הוא למת מצוה. 'לאחיו' מה תלמוד לומר? הרי שהיה כ"ג והוא נזיר, אף הוא 'לאחיו' לא יטמא, אבל מטמא למת מצוה. ו'לאחותו' מה תלמוד לומר? אם אינו ענין לזה, תנהו ענין למי שהולך לשחוט את פסחו ולמול את בנו שמטמא למת מצוה: ושמע שמת לו מת. מקרוביו, יכול יטמא להם: אמרת לא יטמא. הואיל ועונת שחיטת הפסח היא, וחלה עליו חובת הפסח שהוא בכרת אם יטמא בטל מלעשות פסח. ולמול את בנו נמי (א)מצות כרת היא. ואית דאמרי בערבי פסחים נמי קאמר, דמילת זכריו מעכב הפסח:

תוספות

מדלגין היינו על גבי ארונות. תימה לפ"ה דפי' גולל = כיסוי של ארון, דתני': *"כל אשר יגע על פני השדה" לרבות גולל ודופק, וא"כ גם הגולל מטמא באהל, והיאך היו מדלגין עליו? וי"ל: דלא קשה, דהא תני' בשמחות (פ"ד הלכה כא): *כל טומאה שאין הנזיר מגלח עליה – אין כהן מוזהר עליה, וגולל ודופק אין נזיר מגלח עליהן, כדתנן במס' נזיר פרק "כהן גדול" (דף נד.). והיה אומר ר"ת דליתי' להני כללי, דהא אמר התם: רביעית דם אין הנזיר מגלח עליו עד שיהא חצי לוג, ואפילו הכי כהן מוזהר עליו, כדאמרינן בפרק "בהמה המקשה" (חולין דף עב.) דרביעית דם הבא מב' מתים טמא. ומפקינן ליה מ"על כל נפשות מת לא יבא". וי"ל: דהתם מכל מקום הוי שם טומאה שהנזיר מגלח עליה, אבל גולל ודופק אינו כלל בנזיר, ולכך אין כהן מוזהר עליו. אי נמי, הא ברייתא סברה כזקנים הראשונים [נזיר נג.] שהיו אומרים רביעית דם גם בתגלחת נזיר, ומיהו, תימה אמאי אין המת מטמא באהל, כיון שהכסוי עצמו מקבל טומאה, דכל דבר המקבל טומאה – אינו חוצץ בפני הטומאה, אם כן מטמא באהל! וי"ל: דאין מטמא אלא צד חיצון שבו, אבל צד פנימי – טהור, כדתנן במסכת אהלות בפט"ו (משנה ט): חבית שהיא מלאה משקין טהורים ומוקפת צמיד פתיל ועשאה גולל לקבר, הנוגע בה מטמא טומאת שבעה והחבית והמשקין טהורין – לפי שצד פנימי כולו טהור. ומיהו, תימה לפ"ה דפירש בפ"ק דעירובין (דף טו)(ב) גבי אין עושין מבעלי חיים גולל ודופק לקבר, ואי גולל היינו כסוי הארון וכי עושין מבעלי חיים כסוי לארון?(ג) ע"כ פר"ת: דגולל היינו מצבה, וכן דרך בני אדם ליתן בהמה על הקבר לסימן עד שיתנו עליו מצבה*):

רוב ארונות יש להם חלל טפח. וצ"ל שראש הארון פתוח, שאם היה סתום, אדרבה, כי יש בו פותח טפח – מטמא, ואפילו בצד הריקן שבו, כדאמרינן במסכת אהלות בפ"ז (מ"א): נפש אטומה, הנוגע בה מן הצדדין – טהור, פי' בצד הריקן, מפני שטומאה בוקעת ועולה בוקעת ויורדת, ואם היה מקום הטומאה טפח ע"ט(ד) על רום טפח – הנוגע בה מכל מקום טמא, מפני שהוא כקבר סתום. אלמא, בקבר סתום אינו מטמא כל סביביו אלא כשיש עליו טפח, אבל בטומאה רצוצה אינו מטמא אלא כנגד הטומאה ולא מצד הריקן. ובפרק "המוכר פירות" (ב"ב דף ק:) יש להאריך **):

ולאחותו מה ת"ל. גבי נזיר כתיב "על (כל נפשות) [נפש] מת לא יבא" וכתיב בתריה "לאביו ולאמו לאחיו ולאחותו לא יטמא", וכולהו יתירי נינהו דמנפש מת נפקא, ודרשינן: 'לאביו' מה תלמוד לומר? לגופיה לא איצטריך – דהא מ"נפש מת" נפקא כולהו, ולא בא אלא להוציא מת מצוה שמותר לטמא בו. 'לאמו' מה תלמוד לומר? לגופיה לא איצטריך, ולהתיר מת מצוה דמלאביו נפקא, אלא להביא שאם היה נזיר וכהן שיש עליו שתי קדושות – אין הכתוב מזהירו מלטמא אלא לאמו, אבל מטמא הוא למת מצוה. 'לאחיו' מה תלמוד לומר? שאם היה כהן גדול ונזיר דקדושתו חמור, דגם בלא נזירות אסור לטמא לקרוביו, אעפ"כ: לאחיו הוא דאינו מטמא, אבל מטמא הוא למת מצוה, ואם אינו ענין לנזיר גרידא ולא לכהן הדיוט נזיר, תנהו ענין לכ"ג נזיר. 'ולאחותו' מה תלמוד לומר? הרי שאם היה כ"ג ונזיר והלך לשחוט פסחו ולמול את בנו, דאיכא מצות טובא, אפ"ה 'לאחותו' הוא דאינו מטמא, אבל מטמא למת מצוה: **אמרת לא יטמא.** מפני שקאי על אדם שהוא נזיר וכהן גדול ועושה פסח, משמע דעושה פסח גרידא – רשאי לטמא לקרובים. ותימה, דבזבחים (פי"ב דף ק.) גבי מעשה דיוסף הכהן שמתה אשתו בערב פסח וטמאוהו אחיו בע"כ, ופריך מהך ברייתא דהכא דקאמר לא יטמא, ומאי פריך? דילמא שאני הכא דמיירי דכל קדושות האלו בו, כדפרישי', אבל עושה פסחו גרידא, אימא רשאי לטמא! על כן נראה לפרש: אמרת לא

*) [בשבת קנב: ד"ה עד שיסתם כתבו תוס' ביתר ביאור ע"ש וע"ע תוס' כתובות דף ד: ד"ה עד ותוס' סוכה כג. ד"ה ולא ותוס' סנהדרין מז: ד"ה משיסתום.]
**) [וע"ע תוס' נזיר נג: ותוס' ב"ב ק: ד"ה ורוזו]

עין משפט נר מצוה

יט א מיי' פ"ה מהלכות ק"ש הלכה ו סמג עשין יח טוש"ע או"ח סימן עג סעיף ה: [ובתוספתא פ"ג דמכות]

כ ב מיי' פ"י מהלכות כלאים הלכה כט סמג לאוין רפג טוש"ע יו"ד סימן שג:

כא ג מיי' פ"ג מהלכות אבל הלכה יד טוש"ע יו"ד סימן שעב סעיף ח:

כב ד ה מיי' פ"ו מהל' קרבן פסח הלכה ח:

כג ו מיי' פ"ג מהלכות אבל הלכה יד טור יו"ד סימן שעד:

כד ז מיי' פי"א מהלכות אבדה הלכה יג [והלכה יג וכו' פ"ב] סמג עשין עד טוש"ע חו"מ סימן רסג סעיף ב ג.

רב נסים גאון

שאחרי רבים להטות לא הקפיד אלא על ידי ששרפו טהרותיו בפניו פירוש עכנה נקבה של נחשים זה שנתכוונו לדמותו לדברים בעכנה מפני שהקיפו דבריהן עליו בראיות ברורות שאין עליהן פירכא והתקיפו עליו באתקפות מחוורות ששוברין דבריו ולא מצא מהן מנוס בעכנה זו שאם מקפת על שום דבר וסוגרת עליו לא יהיה לו ממנה מפלט ודבוותה התם בבבא קמא בפרק הגוזל בתרא (דף קיז) עכנה עכנה (פתחו) [פתח] פיך ויכנס הרב אצל התלמיד. וזה שאמרו יצאת בת קול ואמרה מה לכם אצל ר' אליעזר שהלכה כמותו בכ"מ ראיתי בב' תשובות האחת כי בת קול לא אמרה שהלכה כמותו בדבר זה אלא בכל מקום סתם הוא שאמרה ואפשר לומר כי בכל מקום וזולתו זה המקום היתה כוונתה או מה שדומה לו שמעון שאין הלכה כר' אליעזר בזה הדבר ויהיו דברי בת קול נכוחים וקיימים והשנית שלא היתה הכוונה אלא לנסות את החכמים אם יניחו הקבלה שבידם והגמרא שבפיהם בשביל בת קול ואם לאו ודומה למה שכתב (דברים יג) כי מנסה ה' אלהיכם אתכם והנה נודע עם כל זאת שאמר ר' יהושע (דברים ל) לא בשמים היא כלומר כי כבר נתנה לנו תורת ה' תמימה בסיני והודיעו כי אינו מחליף ואין בתורתנו חסרון ולא ספק כדי שנצטרך אל ראיה מן השמים וכל מקום בתלמוד שיש בו ור' יהושע היא דאמר אין משגיחין בבת קול מיכן היא עיקרו והברכה שבירכוהו לר' אליעזר שהוא כינוי לנידוי פירשו במסכת סנהדרין בסוף פרק ד' מיתות (דף סח) כי בשעת פטירתו התירוהו כמו שאמרו עמד ר' יהושע על רגליו ואמר הותר הנדר הותר הנדר: **העומדים בשורה הפנימיים פטורים.** במס' סנהדרין בפרק כהן גדול (דף יט) אמרינן אמר ר' יהודה משאית את ... אשיה רבה מבית עילמין דהוציא ואמר לה אין שורה פחותה מי' בני אדם ואין אבלים מן המנין: **תרגמה ר' אבא בבית הפרס דרבנן.** איתיה לפירושא דבית הפרס במס' אהלות (פרק יח מ"ב) במתניתין ובתוספתא (פרק יז) ובפרק משקין בית השלחין (מו"ק ה:) תניא ג' בית הפרס הן שדה שאבד בה קבר ושדה שנחרש בה קבר ושדה בוכין מאי שדה בוכין א"ר יהושע בר אבא משמיה דעולא שדה שמפטירין בה מתים ... [illegible]

מסורת הש"ס

תוספתא פ"ב שמחות פ"ב

[עירובין מא: סנהדרין פב. שבועות ל:]

עירובין דף ל: פסחים דף לב: מו"ק דף כב: חגיגה דף כה: כתובות דף כח: בכורות דף כט: נדה דף נז. [ועיין בכל המקומות ותמצא שינוי נוסחאות באמוראים]

מנחות דף לז: [שבת פא: לד: מגילה ג: עירובין מא:]

[גיטין דף נה: נדה דף ג:]

סנהדרין דף יח: ב"מ דף ל.

[כתובות מ: מו: קדושין ג: ב"מ כ:] מגילה ג: נזיר מח: סנהדרין לה: זבחים ק.

הגהות הב"ח

(א) רש"י ד"ה אמרת וכו' נמי מלוה שוב בה כרת היא: (ב) תוס' ד"ה מדלגין וכו' תימה לפ"ה דלאמרינן פ"ק דעירובין אין כל"ל ותיבת גבי נמחק: (ג) בא"ד כסוי לארון. נ"ב עי' כתובות דף ד: ד"ה עד שיסתום ובס"פ שואל קנב מפור' יותר וע"ש: (ד) ד"ה רוב וכו' טפח על טפח ברום טפח וכו':

גמרא

תורה אור

א אֲבָל מְטַמֵּא הוּא לְמֵת מִצְוָה, אַמַּאי? לֵימָא: "אֵין חָכְמָה וְאֵין תְּבוּנָה וְאֵין עֵצָה לְנֶגֶד ה'". – שָׁאנֵי הָתָם, דִּכְתִיב "וּלְאַחוֹתוֹ" – וְלִיגְמַר מִינָּהּ! – *שֵׁב וְאַל תַּעֲשֶׂה שָׁאנֵי.§ אֲמַר לֵיהּ רַב פַּפָּא לְאַבָּיֵי: מַאי שְׁנָא רִאשׁוֹנִים דְּאִתְרְחִישׁ לְהוּ נִיסָּא, וּמַאי שְׁנָא אֲנַן דְּלָא מִתְרְחִישׁ לָן נִיסָּא? *אִי מִשּׁוּם תְּנוּיֵי – בִּשְׁנֵי דְּרַב יְהוּדָה כּוּלֵּי תְּנוּיֵי בִּנְזִיקִין הֲוָה, וַאֲנַן קָא מַתְנִינַן שִׁיתָּא סִדְרֵי! וְכִי הֲוָה מָטֵי רַב יְהוּדָה בְּעוּקְצִין *"הָאִשָּׁה שֶׁכּוֹבֶשֶׁת יָרָק בַּקְּדֵרָה" וְאָמְרִי לַהּ *"זֵיתִים שֶׁכְּבָשָׁן בְּטַרְפֵיהֶן טְהוֹרִים" אָמַר: "הֲוָיוֹת דְּרַב וּשְׁמוּאֵל קָא חָזֵינָא הָכָא", וַאֲנַן קָא מַתְנִינַן בְּעוּקְצִין תְּלֵיסַר מְתִיבָתָא! וְאִילּוּ רַב יְהוּדָה, כִּי הֲוָה שָׁלֵיף חַד מְסָאנֵיהּ – אָתֵי מִטְרָא, וַאֲנַן קָא מְצַעֲרִינַן נַפְשִׁין וּמְצַוְּחִינַן קָא צָוְחִינַן – וְלֵית דְּמַשְׁגַּח בָּן! – אֲמַר לֵיהּ: קַמָּאֵי הֲווּ קָא מָסְרִי נַפְשַׁיְיהוּ אַקְּדוּשַּׁת הַשֵּׁם, אֲנַן לָא מָסְרִינַן נַפְשִׁין אַקְּדוּשַּׁת הַשֵּׁם. כִּי הָא דְּרַב אַדָּא בַּר אַהֲבָה חַזְיַיהּ לְהַהִיא כּוּתִית דַּהֲוַת לְבִישָׁא *כַּרְבַּלְתָּא בְּשׁוּקָא, סְבַר דְּבַת יִשְׂרָאֵל הִיא, קָם קַרְעֵיהּ מִינָּהּ; אִגַּלַּאי מִילְּתָא דְּכוּתִית הִיא, שַׁיְּימוּהָ בְּאַרְבַּע מְאָה זוּזֵי. א"ל: מַה שְּׁמֵךְ? אֲמַרָה לֵיהּ: מָתוּן. אֲמַר לָהּ: מָתוּן מָתוּן אַרְבַּע מְאָה זוּזֵי שָׁוְיָא.§ רַב גִּידֵּל הֲוָה רָגִיל דַּהֲוָה קָא אָזֵיל וְיָתֵיב אַשַּׁעֲרֵי דִּטְבִילָה, אֲמַר לְהוּ: הָכִי טְבִילוּ וְהָכִי טְבִילוּ. אָמְרִי לֵיהּ רַבָּנַן: לָא קָא מִסְתְּפֵי מָר מִיֵּצֶר הָרָע?!(א) אֲמַר לְהוּ: דָּמְיָין בְּאַפַּאי כִּי קָאקֵי חִיוָּרֵי. *ר' יוֹחָנָן הֲוָה רָגִיל דַּהֲוָה קָא אָזֵיל וְיָתֵיב *אַשַּׁעֲרֵי דִּטְבִילָה, אֲמַר: כִּי סָלְקָן בְּנוֹת יִשְׂרָאֵל וְאָתְיָין מִטְּבִילָה מִסְתַּכְּלָן בִּי, וְנֶהֱוֵי לְהוּ זַרְעָא דְּשַׁפִּירֵי כְּוָותִי. אָמְרִי לֵיהּ רַבָּנַן: לָא קָא מִסְתְּפֵי מָר מֵעֵינָא בִּישָׁא?! אֲמַר לְהוּ: אֲנָא *מִזַּרְעָא דְּיוֹסֵף קָא אָתֵינָא, דְּלָא שָׁלְטָא בֵּיהּ עֵינָא בִּישָׁא, דִּכְתִיב: [בראשית מט] "בֵּן פֹּרָת יוֹסֵף בֵּן פֹּרָת עֲלֵי עָיִן", וְאָמַר רַבִּי אַבָּהוּ: אַל תִּקְרֵי "עֲלֵי עָיִן" אֶלָּא "עוֹלֵי עָיִן". רַבִּי יוֹסֵי בְּרַבִּי חֲנִינָא אָמַר מֵהָכָא: [שם מח] "וְיִדְגּוּ לָרֹב בְּקֶרֶב הָאָרֶץ" מַה דָּגִים שֶׁבַּיָּם מַיִם מְכַסִּין עֲלֵיהֶם וְאֵין עַיִן הָרָע שׁוֹלֶטֶת בָּהֶם – אַף זַרְעוֹ שֶׁל יוֹסֵף אֵין עַיִן הָרָע שׁוֹלֶטֶת בָּהֶם. ואב"א: עַיִן שֶׁלֹּא רָצְתָה לָזוּן מִמַּה שֶּׁאֵינוֹ שֶׁלּוֹ – אֵין עַיִן הָרָע שׁוֹלֶטֶת בּוֹ.§

מתני' ב נָשִׁים וַעֲבָדִים וּקְטַנִּים פְּטוּרִין מִקְּ"שׁ וּמִן

רש"י

אֲבָל מְטַמֵּא הוּא לְמֵת מִצְוָה. וְהוּא כְּבוֹד הַבְּרִיּוֹת, וְדוֹחֶה דְּבַר תּוֹרָה: שֵׁב וְאַל תַּעֲשֶׂה שָׁאנֵי. דְּבָרִים רַבִּים הִתִּירוּ לַעֲקוֹר דְּבַר תּוֹרָה מִפְּנֵי סְיָיג וּמִפְּנֵי כְּבוֹד הַבְּרִיּוֹת, הֵיכָא דְּאֵינוֹ עוֹקֵר דָּבָר בְּמַעֲשֶׂה יָדַיִם, אֶלָּא יוֹשֵׁב בִּמְקוֹמוֹ, וּדְבַר תּוֹרָה נֶעֱקָר מֵאֵלָיו. כְּגוֹן תְּקִיעַת שׁוֹפָר וְלוּלָב בְּשַׁבָּת, וְסָדִין בְּצִיצִית, וְדִכְוָותַיְיהוּ טוּבָא בִּיבָמוֹת (דף צ:). אֲבָל מְעַקֵּר בְּיָדַיִם – לָא. וְהַלּוֹבֵשׁ כִּלְאַיִם עוֹקְרוֹ בְּמַעֲשֶׂה מַמָּשׁ, שֶׁהוּא לוֹבְשׁוֹ. וְטוּמְאַת גּוּפֵי' שֶׁהוּתְּרָה לְכֹהֵן וּלְנָזִיר לִיטַּמֵּא לְמֵת מִצְוָה, דְּקָא מְעַקֵּר בְּיָדַיִם מִפְּנֵי כְּבוֹד הַבְּרִיּוֹת דְּלָאו שֵׁב וְאַל תַּעֲשֶׂה הוּא, הַיְינוּ טַעֲמָא דְּלָא גָּמְרִינַן מִינֵּיהּ – דְּהָתָם (ג) לָאו כְּבוֹד הַבְּרִיּוֹת הוּא דְּדָחֵי לָא תַּעֲשֶׂה דִּידֵיהּ. דְּמֵעִיקָּרָא כְּשֶׁנִּכְתַּב ל"ת דְּטוּמְאָה – לֹא עַל מֵת מִצְוָה נִכְתַּב, כְּשֵׁם שֶׁלֹּא נִכְתַּב עַל הַקְּרוֹבִים. אֲבָל הֲשָׁבַת אֲבֵדָה וּפֶסַח – לְכָל יִשְׂרָאֵל נֶאֱמַר, וְאֵצֶל כְּבוֹד הַבְּרִיּוֹת נִתְּנוּ לִדְחוֹת, ע"כ הַיְינוּ דִּדְחִיָּיתָן אֵינָהּ בְּיָדַיִם אֶלָּא בִּישִׁיבָתוֹ תִּדָּחֶה הַמִּצְוָה. אֲבָל כִּלְאַיִם דְּבְמַעֲשֵׂה יָדָיו יִדָּחֶה – הִזְהִיר בְּאַזְהָרָתוֹ: בִּנְזִיקִין הֲוָה. לֹא הָיוּ גְּדוֹלִים בְּכָל גְּמָרָא שֶׁל ד' סְדָרִים אֶלָּא *בְּתַלְמוּד בָּבָא שֶׁלָּנוּ. וְהַאי מִילְּתָא נָקַט הָכָא מִשּׁוּם דְּמַיְירֵי שֶׁמּוֹסְרִין נַפְשָׁם עַל קְדוּשַּׁת הַשֵּׁם, וְעַד הַשְׁתָּא אַיְירֵי נָמֵי בְּמִי שֶׁמְּבַזֶּה עַצְמוֹ עַל קְדוּשַּׁת הַשֵּׁם לִפְשׁוֹט כִּלְאַיִם בַּשּׁוּק: הָאִשָּׁה שֶׁכּוֹבֶשֶׁת יָרָק אוֹ זֵיתִים שֶׁכְּבָשָׁן בְּטַרְפֵיהֶן. מִשְׁנָה הִיא בְּמַס' עוּקְצִין*: טְהוֹרִים. שֶׁמּוֹסְקִין זֵיתִים עִם הֶעָלִין כְּדֵי לְאָחְזָן בָּהֶן, דַּהֲווּ לְהוּ עָלִין יָד לַזֵּיתִים לְהָבִיא לָהֶם טוּמְאָה, כִּדְאָמְרִינַן בְּ"הָעוֹר וְהָרוֹטֶב" (דף קיח.) שֶׁהַיָּד מְבִיאָה טוּמְאָה עַל הָאוֹכֶל. וְאִם כְּבָשָׁן בְּטַרְפֵיהֶן בְּחוֹמֶץ – בָּטְלָה תּוֹרַת יָד מִן הֶעָלִין, לְפִי שֶׁהַכְּבִישָׁה מְרַכַּכְתָּן וּמְרַכַּכְתָּן וְאֵינָן רְאוּיִן שׁוּב לֶאֱחוֹז בָּהֶן: הֲוָיוֹת דְּרַב וּשְׁמוּאֵל קָא חָזֵינָא הָכָא. כְּלוֹמַר: טַעַם הַמִּשְׁנָיוֹת הַלָּלוּ קָשֶׁה עָלַי כְּכָל הַקּוּשְׁיוֹת שֶׁהָיוּ שְׁנֵי רַבּוֹתַי מִתְקַשִּׁין בָּהֶן בְּכָל הַגְּמָ': בִּתְלֵיסַר מְתִיבָתָא. בְּי"ג פָּנִים, יֵשׁ בֵּינֵינוּ מִשְׁנָה וּבָרַיְיתָא שֶׁל שִׁשָּׁה סְדָרִים, וּמַסֶּכֶת עוּקְצִין גַּם הִיא בְּי"ג פָּנִים כְּגוֹן מִשְׁנַת רַבִּי וְר' חִיָּיא וּמִשְׁנַת בַּר קַפָּרָא וְלֵוִי וְתַנָּא דְּבֵי שְׁמוּאֵל. וְהָכִי אָמְרִינַן בְּמַסֶּכֶת נְדָרִים: (דף מא.) רַבִּי מַתְנֵי הִלְכְתָא בְּי"ג פָּנִים: כַּרְבַּלְתָּא. שֵׁם לְבוּשׁ חָשׁוּב כְּמוֹ "פַּטְּשֵׁיהוֹן וְכַרְבְּלָתְהוֹן" (דניאל ג): מָתוּן מָתוּן. לְשׁוֹן מָאתַן: ד' מֵאוֹת. ב' פְּעָמִים ב' מֵאוֹת. כְּלוֹמַר: הַשֵּׁם גָּרַם לִי. לָשׁוֹן אַחֵר: מָתוּן מָתוּן לְשׁוֹן הַמְתָּנָה; אִם הִמְתַּנְתִּי הָיִיתִי מִשְׂתַּכֵּר ד' מֵאוֹת זוּז: כִּי קָאקֵי חִיוָּרֵי. אַוָּוזִים לְבָנִים: ר' יוֹחָנָן. אָדָם יָפֶה תּוֹאַר הָיָה, דְּאָמְרִי' בְּ"הַשּׂוֹכֵר אֶת הַפּוֹעֲלִים" (דף פד.) שׁוּפְרֵיהּ דְּר' אַבָּהוּ מֵעֵין שׁוּפְרֵיהּ וְכוּ': עוּלֵי עַיִן. מְסוּלָּקִין מִן הָעַיִן שֶׁאֵינָהּ שׁוֹלֶטֶת בָּהֶן: שֶׁלֹּא רָצְתָה לָזוּן. לֵיהָנוֹת מֵאֵשֶׁת אֲדוֹנָיו: **מתני'** נָשִׁים וַעֲבָדִים וּקְטַנִּים פְּטוּרִים מִקְּ"שׁ. שֶׁהִיא מ"ע שֶׁהַזְּמַן גְּרָמָא, וְקַיְ"ל בְּקִדּוּשִׁין (דף כט.) דְּנָשִׁים פְּטוּרוֹת מִדְּאוֹרַיְיתָא. וּתְפִילִּין נָמֵי מ"ע שֶׁהַזְּמַן גְּרָמָא. דְּקָסָבַר לַיְלָה וְשַׁבָּת לָאו זְמַן תְּפִילִּין נִינְהוּ: קְטַנִּים. אֲפִי' קָטָן שֶׁהִגִּיעַ לְחִינּוּךְ לֹא הִטִּילוּ עַל אָבִיו לְחַנְּכוֹ בְּק"ש, לְפִי שֶׁאֵינוֹ מָצוּי תָּמִיד כְּשֶׁמַּגִּיעַ זְמַן ק"ש:

תוספות

לא יטמא – אפי' עושה פסחו גרידא. וא"ת: מהיכא פשיטא ליה אמרת לא יטמא? וי"ל כדפירש"י: דלא אתי עשה שאין בו כרת כטומאת קרובים, וידחה עשה שיש בו כרת כגון עושה פסח, וגם מילה שייך בה כרת. וא"ת: התם דפריך על מעשה דיוסף הכהן, מנ"ל [לתלמודא] דהכא מיירי בעושה פסחו לחוד? וי"ל: מדלא כייל גבי עושה פסחו כמו גבי אחרים מי שהיה נזיר וכהן הדיוט. דמעיקרא נקט נזיר לחוד, ואח"כ נזיר וכהן הדיוט וכו'. וא"ת: מנא ליה (לתלמודא) דהאי קרא בעושה פסחו ולמול את בנו? הא קרא כתיב בנזיר! וי"ל: אם אינו ענין בנזיר, דהא כתיבי פסוקים אחרים דמטמא במת מצוה, תנהו ענין להולך לשחוט פסחו וכו'. והשר מקוצי מיישב פירש"י: דמיירי הכא דיש בו כל הקדושות הללו כו'. ומ"מ פריך התם גבי יוסף הכהן, דע"כ אף בעושה פסח גרידא אינו רשאי לטמא. דאי ס"ד עושה פסח מטמא לקרובים, 'ולאחותו' למה לי למימר דמטמא למת מצוה? כיון דמטמא לקרובים אלמא עושה פסחו אינו מעלה עליו שום חומרא טפי – א"כ פשיטא דמטמא למת מצוה. וכי תימא: מכל מקום צריך קרא דמטמא למת מצוה, מפני שיש בו ג' קדושות נזיר וכהן ועושה פסח. ולעולם אימא לך דעושה פסח גרידא מטמא לקרובים – לא היא, דהא כבר שמעינן מלאביו ולאמו ולאחיו דנזיר וכ"ג לא מהני מידי למת מצוה. א"כ, ע"כ קראי לא אצטריכו אלא למעלה דפסח. ולמה לי, פשיטא דאי מטמא לקרובים – כ"ש למת מצוה. ואע"ג דאצטריך קרא ד'לאמו' לכהן הדיוט ונזיר דמטמא למת מצוה, אע"ג דכתב קרא דמטמא לקרובים ואצטריך קרא שהן ב' קדושות אע"ג דשמעינן כבר דמעלה דנזיר לא מהני מידי למת מצוה מ'לאביו', ה"מ – כהן דקדושתו קדושת עולם, ומשום הכי יש לנו לומר כי יש לו שתי קדושות דטפי קדושה ולכך אצטריך קרא. אבל עושה פסח שקדושתו לפי שעה, אם אתה מתיר לו לקרובים – ה"ה למת מצוה מכ"ש, דמאי חזית ליתן לו קדושה טפי גבי מת מצוה יותר מן הקרובים. א"נ יש לפרש בקוצר הברייתא; מדתניא גרידא על ישראל נזיר, ואח"כ נזיר וכהן הדיוט, ואח"כ נזיר וכ"ג, וא"כ מסברא יש לנו לומר (כי יש) דאינו מטמא לקרובים כמו נזיר וכלהו אינך, ודוק מעלמך: **שב** ואל תעשה שאני. וא"ת: נזיר וכ"ג קום עשה הוא דיטמא למת! ותירץ רש"י: דקרא גלי לן דלאו ד"לא יטמא" לא נאמר גבי מת מצוה. ולא נהירא, דא"כ כל מקום דאמרי' שעשה דוחה ל"ת, לקרי שב ואל תעשה וכו' והיאך קרי ליה דחייה? אימא שאינו דחייה, דהתם לא נאמר הלאו! ועוד: דהא מילה ותמיד ופסח דדחו שבת כדאמרינן פרק "אלו דברים" (פסחים דף סט:) אלמא: מקרי שפיר דחייה! אלא נראה: דמנזיר לא גמרינן, דמה לנזיר – שכן ישנו בשאלה; וכן מכהן, מה לכהן – שכן לאו שאינו שוה בכל: **זיתים** שכבשן בטרפיהן טהורים. פירש הקונטרס: כיון דכבשן בקדרה בטלים מתורת יד להביא טומאה. ולא נהירא, דא"כ מאי האי דקאמר עלה שלא נכבשו אלא למראה, מה נתינת טעם יש דבטלינהו מתורת יד? לכך נראה לפרש: דטהורים משום כבישה בקדרה, שלא נכבשו אלא למראה. כלומר: מה שכבש העלין עמהן – לא כבשן אלא להראות שהזיתים נאים וחדשים, ומשום הכי טהורים. אבל כבשן להיות ראויין לאכילה – משעה שיהו מתוקנין לראיית אכילה טמאים: **תליסר** מתיבתא. יש מפרשין: תליסר ישיבות יש בנו שבקיאים. ותליסר לאו דוקא, אלא לשון הרגיל בגמ' כמו תליסר (חולין מד:) זוזי פשיטי. ורש"י פי' בע"א*): **וקטנים** פטורין מק"ש. פירש הקונטרס: קטן שהגיע לחנוך. ולא נהירא, דהא פרק "לולב הגזול" (סוכה דף מב.) אמרי': קטן היודע לשמור תפילין אביו חייב לקנות לו תפילין, אלמא כשהגיע לחנוך דשייכי ביה תפילין – חייב בתפילין. ובק"ש נמי יש לחייבו יותר מסתמא, מדאשכחן התם קטן היודע לדבר אביו מלמדו תורה ופסוק ראשון של ק"ש. ונראה לר"ת: דמיירי בקטן שלא הגיע לחנוך. ומיהו, סיפא דקתני וחייבין בתפלה היה ר"י ר"ל: דמיירי בקטן שהגיע לחנוך. דאי לא הגיע – לא הוו להו לחייבו בתפלה. ולא נהירא, דאם כן לא הוו להו קטנים דומיא דנשים ועבדים, שפטורים בכל ענין וקטנים אינם פטורים אלא בשלא הגיע, ואין יודע לשמור תפיליו. ופי' ר"ת: דודאי איירי הכל בקטן שלא הגיע לחנוך, וחייבין דסיפא – קאי אנשים ועבדים לחוד, אבל קטנים פטורים מכל וכל כיון דלא הגיע לחנוך. וא"ת: א"כ אמאי תנא קטנים בהדי נשים ועבדים, כיון דאין שוין כדפרישית? וי"ל: דכן דרך התנא לשנות יחד נשים ועבדים וקטנים שלא הגיעו לחנוך, כמו: נשים ועבדים וקטנים פטורים מסוכה (סוכה דף כח.):

בתפלה

*) וע"ע רש"י שבת קיט. ד"ה תריסר וצ"ל תליסר ותוס' ב"ב קלג: ד"ה עליתא ורש"י ותוס' חולין נה: ד"ה תריסר וצ"ל תליסר:

רב נסים גאון

לאביו ולאמו לאחיו ולאחותו לא יטמא זה שדבר הכתוב בכל אלו הקרובין צריך היה הדבר להזכיר את כולם שאי אפשר שיזכיר דבר שאין בו תלמוד כדכתיב (דברים לב) כי לא דבר רק הוא מכם ואין לנו דרך לידע לאיזה תלמוד נכתבו כולם אלא מקבלת החכמים ז"ל לפי שאם באנו לעיין בהם מדרך דעתנו היה עולה על לבנו כי בהזכירו את האב שמעלתו למעלה מכולם והאם עם הבנים חייבים בכבודו לא היה צריך להזכיר את השאר והיינו אומרים אם הזהיר הכתוב מליטמא לאב שהוא עדיף מכולם כל שכן לשאר קרובין שהם פחותין ממנו ולא היינו יודעין מה צורך היה לו להזכיר האם והאח והאחות עד ששמענו קבלה של חכמים שבירורם ופירושם ואמרו כי לאביו ולאמו צריך הדבר להזכיר את שניהם שאם היה מזכיר את אחד מהן לא היינו למדין ממנו חברו לפי שכל אחד מהם יש לו מעלה מיוחדת לו ואינה כחברו שהאב עדיף מן האם שבנו מיוחס אחריו ולא אחר האם והאם יש לה יתרון על האב מפני שהיא ודאי אמו ואביו אינו ודאי אלא חזקה שאפשר שתזנה אמו ותהר לזנונים ויהיה זה הבן מאיש אחר זולתי בעלה ולפיכך הוצרך לומר לאביו ולאמו ואיתא במסכת נזיר בפרק כהן גדול ונזיר אינן מטמאין לקרוביהן (דף מט) לאביו ולאמו למה לי צריכא דאי כתב רחמנא אביו הוה אמינא היינו טעמא דלא מיטמא ליה משום דחזקה בעלמא הוא אבל אמו (היא) דוודאי ילדתיה ליטמא לה ואי כתב רחמנא אמו הוה אמינא אמו היא דלא מיטמי לה דלא אזיל זרעה בתרה אבל אביו כיון דאמר רחמנא (במדבר א) למשפחותם לבית אבותם אימא ליטמי ליה קמ"ל ועוד אמרו (שם דף מח) אם הוצרך לומר אביו ואמו למה הזכיר עוד את אחיו והלא אין צריך להזכירו מפני שהוא גלמד מאביו ואמו זה שהזכיר את אחיו לא לצורך עצמו נאמר אלא ללמד על מת מצוה שאין לו קוברין נאמר שמותר לנזיר להטמא לו ולהתעסק בקבורתו כדתניא לאחיו אינו מיטמא אבל מטמא למת מצוה ונשתיירה עדיין אחותו ושאלנו עליה למה הוצרך הכתוב עוד להזכירה ולאחותו מה תלמוד והשבנו כי הוצרך להזכירה ללמוד ממנה תוספת תלמוד שהנזיר אפי' אם היה הולך לעשות מצוה ונזדמן לו מת מצוה שיניח את המצוה שהיה סובר לעשותה ויטמא למת מצוה ויתעסק בו עד שיקברו ולפיכך הזכיר הכתוב את אחותו כי כשהזכיר אחיו למדנו כי הנזיר מטמא למת מצוה בזמן שאינו מתעסק למצוה אחרת והוצרכנו עוד לידע אם בזמן כשהוא עוסק במצוה יניחנה ויתעסק במת מצוה אם לאו אתא ולאחותו ללמד כי מת מצוה קודם כמו שאמרו הרי שהיה הולך לשחוט את פסחו ולמול את בנו כו' ת"ל ולאחותו לאחותו הוא דאינו מיטמא אבל מיטמא למת מצוה ודרשינן ליה תו בדרך אחרת לאביו לאביו הוא דאינו מיטמא אבל מיטמא למת מצוה ולאמו שאם היה כהן והוא נזיר לאמו אינו מיטמא אבל מיטמא למת מצוה לאחיו שאם היה כהן גדול והוא נזיר לאחיו אינו מטמא אבל מטמא למת מצוה ולאחותו מה תלמוד לומר הרי שהיה הולך לשחוט פסחו ולמול את בנו כו' מכל מקום ולאחותו בא ללמדנו מה שכבר הזכרנו: **ואילו** רב יהודה כי מטי גבי האשה שכובשת ירק בקדרה. זו המשנה בתחלת פרק שני דמסכת טהרות. ואמרי

עין משפט נר מצוה

כה א מיי' פ"ג מהלכות אבל הלכה ח טור שו"ע יו"ד סימן שע"ד סעיף ח:

כו ב מיי' פ"ד מהלכות ק"ש סמג עשין יח טור ושו"ע או"ח סימן ע סעיף א ג:

מסורת הש"ס

[עי' תוס' ב"מ ל: ד"ה אלא ותוס' שבועות ל: ד"ה אבל ועי' יבמות ז: תוד"ה כולהו]

טהרות פ"ב משנה א

עוקצין פ"ב משנה א [ועי' רש"י סנה' קו: ורש"י בתענית כד:]

[ובסנהדרין ובתענית פירש"י בסדר נזיקין ע"ש]

[פי' בגד אדום כגון כרבלתא דתרנגולא שאין דרך בנות ישראל להתכסות בו שקוה פריצות ומביא לדבר עבירה. ערוך]

ב"מ פד. [כל הענין וע"ש]

[עי' תוס' ב"מ פד. ד"ה יתיב]

לקמן נה: סוטה לו: ב"ב קיח:

[רש"א וח"מ]

[פי' רב"י דתענית כד: ובסנהדרין קו:]

הגהות הב"ח

(א) גמ' לא קא מסתפי מר מיצר הרע. נ"ב הא דלא אמרו ליה מעינא בישא כדאמרי' גבי ר' יוחנן היינו משום דר"י הוה שפיר ושייך ביה עינא בישא משא"כ רב גידל ... אמאי לא ... לא קא מסתפי מר מיצר הרע משום דר"י ... עיניו ... בתענית ... ינוקא דל ... לי עיני: (ב) רש"י ד"ה אלא שב ואל תעשה וכו' דהתם לאו ... הבריות וכו' ... לדחייתן:

גליון הש"ס

גמ' רב גידל הוה רגיל כו' ויתיב כו'. עי' תו' פסחים קי ע"ב ד"ה האי מאן:

תורה אור

ומן התפילין, וחייבין בתפלה ובמזוזה ובברכת המזון. § גמ' "ק"ש", פשיטא! מצות עשה שהזמן גרמא הוא, *וכל מצות עשה שהזמן גרמא נשים פטורות! —מהו דתימא: הואיל ואית בה מלכות שמים – קמ"ל. "ומן התפלין". § פשיטא! – מהו דתימא: הואיל ואתקש למזוזה – קמ"ל. § "וחייבין בתפלה". § דרחמי נינהו. (א) —מהו דתימא: הואיל וכתיב בה "ערב ובקר וצהרים", כמצות עשה שהזמן גרמא דמי – קמ"ל. § "ובמזוזה" פשיטא! —מהו דתימא: הואיל ואתקש לתלמוד תורה – קמשמע לן. "ובברכת המזון" פשיטא! —מהו דתימא: הואיל וכתיב "בתת ה' לכם בערב בשר לאכל ולחם בבקר לשבע" כמצות עשה שהזמן גרמא דמי – קמ"ל. § *אמר רב אדא בר אהבה: נשים חייבות בקדוש היום דבר תורה. —אמאי? מצות עשה שהזמן גרמא הוא, וכל מצות עשה שהזמן גרמא נשים פטורות! —אמר אביי מדרבנן. —א"ל רבא: והא "דבר תורה" קאמר! ועוד, כל מצות עשה נחייבינהו מדרבנן! – אלא אמר רבא: אמר קרא "זכור" "ושמור" – כל שישנו בשמירה ישנו בזכירה, והני נשי, הואיל ואיתנהו בשמירה – איתנהו בזכירה. § א"ל רבינא לרבא: נשים בברכת המזון, דאורייתא או דרבנן? למאי נפקא מינה – לאפוקי רבים ידי חובתן. אי אמרת (בשלמא) דאורייתא – אתי דאורייתא ומפיק דאורייתא, (אלא *אי) אמרת דרבנן – הוי "שאינו מחוייב בדבר", *וכל שאינו מחוייב בדבר – אינו מוציא את הרבים ידי חובתן. מאי? ת"ש, *באמת אמרו: *בן מברך לאביו, ועבד מברך לרבו, ואשה מברכת לבעלה; אבל אמרו חכמים: תבא מארה לאדם שאשתו ובניו מברכין לו. אי אמרת בשלמא דאורייתא – אתי דאורייתא ומפיק דאורייתא, אלא אי אמרת דרבנן – אתי דרבנן ומפיק דאורייתא?! – ולטעמיך, קטן בר חיובא הוא?! – אלא, הכי במאי עסקינן – כגון שאכל שיעורא דרבנן, דאתי דרבנן ומפיק דרבנן. דרש רב עוירא, זמנין אמר לה משמיה דר' אמי וזמנין אמר לה משמיה דר' אסי: אמרו מלאכי השרת לפני הקב"ה: רבש"ע, כתוב בתורתך "אשר לא ישא פנים ולא יקח שחד", והלא אתה נושא פנים לישראל, דכתיב: "ישא ה' פניו אליך". אמר להם: וכי לא אשא פנים לישראל?! שכתבתי להם בתורה: "ואכלת ושבעת וברכת את ה' אלהיך", והם מדקדקים [על] עצמם *עד כזית ועד כביצה. § מתני' בעל קרי מהרהר בלבו ואינו מברך לא לפניה ולא לאחריה; ועל המזון מברך לאחריו ואינו מברך לפניו. רבי יהודה אומר: מברך לפניהם ולאחריהם. גמ' אמר רבינא, זאת אומרת: הרהור כדבור דמי. דאי סלקא דעתך לאו כדבור דמי, למה מהרהר? —אלא מאי הרהור כדבור דמי, יוציא בשפתיו! —*כדאשכחן בסיני. ורב חסדא אמר: *הרהור לאו כדבור דמי. דאי סלקא דעתך הרהור כדבור דמי – יוציא בשפתיו! —אלא מאי – הרהור לאו כדבור דמי, למה מהרהר? —אמר רבי אלעזר: כדי שלא יהו כל העולם עוסקין בו והוא יושב ובטל. —ונגרוס בפרקא אחרינא! (ב) —אמר רב אדא בר אהבה: בדבר שהצבור עוסקין בו. והרי

ומן התפילין. משום דקסבר קטן אינו יודע לשמור גופו שלא יפיח בהן: וחייבין בתפלה. דתפלה רחמי היא, ומדרבנן היא, ותקנוה אף לנשים ולחנוך קטנים: ובמזוזה ובברכת המזון. מזוזה מצות עשה שלא הזמן גרמא ובגמרא פריך: פשיטא: ברכת המזון. בגמרא בעי לה דאורייתא או דרבנן: גמ' מהו דתימא נקיש תפלין למזוזה. דכתיב "וקשרתם" "וכתבתם", מה מזוזה נשים חייבות – אף תפילין נשים חייבות, קמשמע לן: הכי גרסינן: תפלה דרחמי נינהו. ולא גרס פשיטא, דהא לאו דאורייתא היא: נקיש מזוזה לתלמוד תורה. דכתיב (דברים יא) "ולמדתם אותם את בניכם" וסמיך ליה "וכתבתם". מה תלמוד תורה נשים פטורות – ואע"ג דאין הזמן גרמא – רחמנא פטרינהו, דכתיב "את בניכם" ולא בנותיכם – אף מזוזה נשים פטורות, קמ"ל דנשים חייבות, דכתיב "למען ירבו ימיכם" גברי בעו חיי נשי לא בעו חיי? בתמיה: קדוש היום מ"ע שהזמן גרמא הוא. "זכור את יום השבת לקדשו" (שמות כ) – זכרהו על היין: בשמירה. ד"לא תעשה מלאכה" (שם): והני נשי איתנהו בשמירה. דתנן (קדושין דף כט.): כל מצות לא תעשה, בין שהזמן גרמא בין שאין הזמן גרמא – נשים חייבות, דהשוה הכתוב אשה לאיש לכל עונשים שבתורה: נשים בברכת המזון דאורייתא. דכתיב "ואכלת ושבעת", (דברים ח), והוה ליה מצות עשה שאין הזמן גרמא: או דרבנן. דכתיב "על הארץ הטובה אשר נתן לך" (שם), והארץ לא נתנה לנקבות להתחלק. ואי משום בנות צלפחד – חלק אביהם הם דנטלו, שהיה מיוצאי מצרים: בן. קטן: מברך. ברכת המזון לאביו, אם אין אביו יודע לברך: שיעורא דרבנן. כגון כזית לר"מ וכביצה לרבי יהודה, דמדאורייתא "ואכלת ושבעת וברכת" כתיב, אבל בשיעור כי האי – לא מחייב אלא מדרבנן, והלכך אתי קטן דרבנן ומפיק גדול: עד כזית עד כביצה. עד כזית לר"מ, עד כביצה לר' יהודה. דתנן (לקמן דף מה.): עד כמה מזמנין, ר"מ אומר עד כזית. ר' יהודה אומר: עד כביצה: מתני' בעל קרי. מתקנת עזרא ואילך שתקן טבילה לבעלי קריין לעסוק בתורה, כדאמרינן בב"ק בפרק "מרובה" (דף פב:): מהרהר. ק"ש בלבו, כשמגיע זמן המקרא: ואינו מברך. אפילו בהרהור: לא לפניה ולא לאחריה. כיון דברכות לאו מדאורייתא מחייב, לא אצרכוהו רבנן: ועל המזון מברך לאחריו. דחיובא דאורייתא הוא: ואינו מברך לפניו. דלאו דאורייתא הוא: רבי יהודה אומר וכו'. בגמ' מפרש לה: גמ' כדבור דמי. וכל אדם נמי יוצא ידי חובתו בהרהור: למה מהרהר. מה מועיל: כדאשכחן בסיני. שהפרישן מאשה דכתיב "אל תגשו אל אשה" (שמות יט). ועל פרשה זו סמך עזרא לתקן טבילה לבעלי קריין קודם שיעסקו בתורה, דכתיב (דברים ד) "והודעתם לבניך" וסמיך ליה "יום אשר עמדת לפני ה' אלהיך בחורב", כדאמרינן לקמן בפרקין (דף כב.): אלא

בתפלה פשיטא כיון דכתיב "ערב ובקר וצהרים אשיחה ואהמה" – כמצות עשה שהזמן גרמא הוי, קמ"ל דרחמי נינהו. ורש"י לא גריס ליה, שהרי תפלה דרבנן היא, ומאי מ"ע שייכי ביה? ומ"מ יש ליישב, דהא הלל דרבנן ונשים פטורות מהאי טעמא, דמצות עשה שהזמן גרמא הוא. כדאמרינן בסוכה (דף לח.): מי שהיה עבד ואשה או קטן מקרין אותו – עונה אחריהן מה שהם אומרים, דאין השומע פטור מקריאתן, כיון שהם פטורים: אית דגרסי בברכת המזון פשיטא. ומשני: כיון דכתיב "בתת ה' לכם בערב בשר לאכול ולחם בבקר לשבוע" כמ"ע שהזמן גרמא הוא, קמ"ל: נשים בברכת המזון דאורייתא או דרבנן. פי' הקונטרס: דסלקא דעתך דלא מחייבי מדאורייתא משום דכתיב "על הארץ הטובה" ונשים לא נטלו חלק בארץ. ומה שנטלו בנות צלפחד – חלק אביהם נטלו. ותימה: כהנים ולוים נמי תבעי, שהרי לא נטלו חלק בארץ, וא"כ לא יוציאו אחרים ידי חובתן בברכת המזון! אלא י"ל: דטעמא משום דכתיב "על בריתך שחתמת בבשרנו ועל תורתך שלמדתנו", ונשים ליתנהו לא בברית ולא בתורה. ואמרינן לקמן (דף מט.): מי שלא אמר ברית ותורה בברכת המזון – לא יצא ידי חובתו. והשתא קא מבעיא ליה כיון דלא מצו למימר ברית ותורה, לא הוו אלא מדרבנן, או דלמא כיון דלא שייך בהו – הוי שפיר דאורייתא. והא דלקמן – מיירי באנשים, דשייכי בברית ותורה: בעל קרי מהרהר בלבו ואינו מברך לא לפניה ולא לאחריה. פי': אפילו בהרהור, כדמשמע בגמ'. והיינו טעמא דשרינא טפי בק"ש מברכות – משום דק"ש דאורייתא וברכות דרבנן. ואפי' למ"ד ק"ש דרבנן – היינו היכא דהזכיר יציאת מצרים, אבל מתניתין שלא הזכיר יציאת מצרים, שלא התירו לו לומר "אמת ויציב". והוי ק"ש דאורייתא, ו"אמת ויציב" דרבנן – שהרי הזכיר יציאת מצרים בק"ש. ואין להקשות: נתקן דלימא "אמת ויציב" ולא לימא ק"ש! דהא עדיף דלימא ק"ש, דאית ביה נמי מלכות שמים: יוציא בשפתיו. כיון דשרית ליה הרהור אע"פ שהוא כדבור לענין לצאת ידי ק"ש, כמו כן מקרי דבור לענין דמקרי עוסק בתורה, ומדשרית ליה להרהר, אע"פ שהוא בעל קרי – תתיר לו גם דבור: כדאשכחן בסיני. פירוש: אף ע"ג דכדבור דמי לענין יציאה, מ"מ לאו כדבור דמי לענין שיהא בעל קרי אסור להרהר, כדאשכחן בסיני דהיה שם דבור והיו צריכין לטבול. ואע"פ שהיו שותקין – שומע כעונה [סוכה לח:]: ורב חסדא אמר לאו כדבור דמי. ר"ח פירש דהלכה כרב חסדא, מדתרלי רב אדא ורבי אלעזר למלתיה – שמע מיניה כותיה קיימי, ולא יצא בקריאת שמע בהרהור: והרי

כז א מיי' פ"ד מהלכות תפילין הלכה יג סמג עשין כב טוש"ע או"ח סימן לח סעיף ג:
כח ב מיי' פ"א מהל' תפלה הלכה ב סמג עשין יט טוש"ע או"ח סימן קו סעיף ב:
כט ג מיי' פ"ה מהל' מזוזה הלכה י סמג עשין כג טוש"ע יו"ד סימן רצא סעיף ג:
ל ד מיי' פ"ה מהלכות ברכות הלכה א סמג עשין כז טוש"ע או"ח סימן קפו סעיף א ב:
לא ה מיי' פ"כ מהל' שבת הלכה ג סמג עשין כט טוש"ע או"ח סימן רעא סעיף ב:
[ה מיי' פ"ה מה' ברכות הלכה א' טוש"ע שם:]
לב ו מיי' פ"ה מהלכות ברכות הלכה טו:
לג ז ח מיי' פ"ה שם הלכה טו וטז סמג עשין כז טוש"ע או"ח סימן קפו סעיף ב:
לד ט מיי' פ"ד מהל' ק"ש הלכה ח סמג עשין יט טוש"ע או"ח סימן פח:
לה י ב טוש"ע או"ח סי' סה סעיף ג (ד):

רב נסים גאון

לה זיתים שבשבן בסורפיתן וזו המשנה בתחלת פרק ב' דמסכת עוקצין: ורב יהודה בי הוה שליף חד מסאניה אתי מיטרא. איתה לפירושה במסכת תענית בפרק סדר תעניות האלו (דף כד) והיינו דאמר' רב יהודה הוה חזי הנך בי תרי דהוו קא פרצי בריפתא אמר שמע מינה איכא שבעא בעלמא יהב עיניה הוה כפנא אמרו ליה רבנן לרב כהנא בריה דרב נחוניא שמעיה מר דשכיח קמיה נעשייה דליפוק לשוקא כיון דנפק לשוקא חזא כינופיא אמר להו מאי האי [א"ל] אכוספא דתמרי דקא מזדבן אמר שמע מינה איכא כפנא אמר ליה לשמעיה שלוף לי מסאני שלף ליה חד מסאנא בעא למישלף אידך אתא אלהיו כו' ובתוך כל הדר הדבר הרבה אבדנק דמסכת נדה (דף יג) אמרי' (קרי) [דקרן] שאני רב יהודה דמאריה עליה אין זה ילוד אשה: ר' יוחנן הוה אזיל ויתיב אשערי טבילה אמר כי סלקן בנות ישראל מטבילה נפגען בי דניהוי להו בני שפירי כוותי. אתה מוצא שהכירו שבח יופיו בבבא מציעא בפרק השוכר את הפועלים (דף פד) אמר ר' יוחנן אנא אשתיירי משפירי ירושלים האי מאן דבעי מיחזי שופריה דר' יוחנן נייתי כסא דכספא מבי סלקי כו': קריאת שמע מצות עשה שהזמן גרמא וכל מצות עשה שהזמן גרמא נשים פטורות וכל מצות עשה שלא הזמן גרמא אחד אנשים ואחד נשים חייבין. פירושו בברייתא (קידושין דף לג) איזו היא מצות עשה שהזמן גרמא סוכה ולולב שופר וציצית ותפלין והיא מצות עשה שלא הזמן גרמא מזוזה ומעקה ומציאת אבדה ושלוח הקן: אקיש מזוזה לתלמוד תורה מה תלמוד תורה פטירי אף מזוזה נמי פטירי קמ"ל. הא נמי איתה בפירקא קמא דקידושין (דף לד) דאקשינן הרי תלמוד תורה פריה ורביה ופדיון הבן דמצות עשה שלא הזמן גרמא ונשים פטורות ואמרינן (שם דף ל) ותלמוד תורה גופיה מנלן דכתיב ולמדתם אותם את בניכם ולא בנותיכם: כדאשכחן בסיני מה סיני דבור אסור הרהור מותר. במסכת שבת בפרק ר' עקיבא (דף פו) אמרי' אמר אביי בר אבין ור' חנינא בר אבין דאמרי תרווייהו ניתנה תורה לטבולי יום ואמר עלה אמימר ראויה קאמינא ואעפ"כ מי שאירע לו קרי בלילי ו' בסיון דההיא שתא כבר שמע את הדברות ולא סגיא דלא הרהר בלבו:
רבי

קדושין דף כט. [וש"נ]
[שבועות דף כ: ע"ש]

הגהות הב"ח

(א) גמ' דרחמי נינהו (מהו דתימא וכו' קמ"ל) תא"מ ונ"ב ברוב הספרים לא גרסי ליה: (ב) שם ונגרוס בפרק' אחרינ'. נ"ב בהל' דרך ארץ כדלקמן בדף כ"ב:

[נ"ל ואי]
ר"ה דף כט.
[עי' תוס' לעיל טו. ד"ה ור' יהודה]

גליון הש"ס

גמ' ומן התפלין פשיטא. עיין תוס' עירובין דף צו ע"א ד"ה לא ס"ל: שם ובמזוזה פשיטא. עיין יומא דף י"א ע"ב ואם כן לא הוה פשיטא דלא נימא למעט מן ביתך ולא ביתה. ועט"ק: שם נשים בבהמ"ז דאורייתא. עיין לקמן בכסמוך פשיטא. א"ל רבינא לרבא נשים בבהמ"ז דאורייתא או דרבנן. ועי' בבהמ"ז דאורייתא. עי' תשובת חו"מ סימן קס"ט: שם ולטעמיך קטן. ע' בר"ן מגילה (ובדף הספר רס"ב א) בשם הרמב"ן וש"ע. ואח"ז ראיתי בהרמב"ן במלחמות שי"ל גירסא אחרת כאן: שם לאתי דרבנן ומפיק דרבנן. עי' תוס' ד"ה בר"ה ועירובין ע"ב ד"ה דילמא ומגילה יט ע"ב ד"ה ור"י: שם אמר רבינא זאת אומרת. עי' בטורי אבן מגילה יט ע"ב בד"ה ר"י מכשיר:

וַהֲרֵי תְּפִלָּה דְּדָבָר שֶׁהַצִּבּוּר עֲסוּקִין בּוֹ, וּתְנַן: *הָיָה עוֹמֵד בַּתְּפִלָּה וְנִזְכַּר שֶׁהוּא בַּעַל קֶרִי – לֹא יַפְסִיק אֶלָּא יְקַצֵּר, טַעְמָא דְּאַתְחֵיל, הָא לָא אַתְחֵיל – לֹא יַתְחִיל! שָׁאנֵי תְּפִלָּה, דְּלֵית בָּהּ מַלְכוּת שָׁמַיִם. וַהֲרֵי בִּרְכַּת הַמָּזוֹן לְאַחֲרָיו, דְּלֵית בָּהּ מַלְכוּת שָׁמַיִם, וּתְנַן: עַל הַמָּזוֹן מְבָרֵךְ לְאַחֲרָיו וְאֵינוֹ מְבָרֵךְ לְפָנָיו! אֶלָּא: ק"ש וּבִרְכַּת הַמָּזוֹן – דְּאוֹרָיְיתָא, וּתְפִלָּה – דְּרַבָּנַן.§ אָמַר רַב יְהוּדָה:(א) *מִנַּיִן לְבִרְכַּת הַמָּזוֹן לְאַחֲרֶיהָ מִן הַתּוֹרָה – שֶׁנֶּאֱמַר: °"וְאָכַלְתָּ וְשָׂבָעְתָּ וּבֵרַכְתָּ". מִנַּיִן לְבִרְכַּת הַתּוֹרָה לְפָנֶיהָ מִן הַתּוֹרָה – שֶׁנֶּאֱמַר: °"כִּי שֵׁם ה' אֶקְרָא הָבוּ גֹדֶל לֵאלֹהֵינוּ". אָמַר ר' יוֹחָנָן: לָמַדְנוּ בִּרְכַּת הַתּוֹרָה לְאַחֲרֶיהָ מִן בִּרְכַּת הַמָּזוֹן מִקַּל וָחוֹמֶר, וּבִרְכַּת הַמָּזוֹן לְפָנֶיהָ מִן בִּרְכַּת הַתּוֹרָה מִקַּל וָחוֹמֶר; בִּרְכַּת הַתּוֹרָה לְאַחֲרֶיהָ מִן בִּרְכַּת הַמָּזוֹן מִקַּל וָחוֹמֶר: וּמַה מָּזוֹן שֶׁאֵין טָעוּן לְפָנָיו – טָעוּן לְאַחֲרָיו, תּוֹרָה שֶׁטְּעוּנָה לְפָנֶיהָ – אֵינוֹ דִּין שֶׁטְּעוּנָה לְאַחֲרֶיהָ; וּבִרְכַּת הַמָּזוֹן לְפָנֶיהָ מִן בִּרְכַּת הַתּוֹרָה מק"ו: וּמַה תּוֹרָה שֶׁאֵין טְעוּנָה לְאַחֲרֶיהָ – טְעוּנָה לְפָנֶיהָ, מָזוֹן שֶׁהוּא טָעוּן לְאַחֲרָיו – אֵינוֹ דִּין שֶׁיְּהֵא טָעוּן לְפָנָיו. אִיכָּא לְמִפְרַךְ:(ב) מַה לַּמָּזוֹן – שֶׁכֵּן נֶהֱנֶה, וּמַה לַּתּוֹרָה – שֶׁכֵּן חַיֵּי עוֹלָם! וְעוֹד, תְּנַן: עַל הַמָּזוֹן מְבָרֵךְ לְאַחֲרָיו וְאֵינוֹ מְבָרֵךְ לְפָנָיו! תְּיוּבְתָּא.§ אָמַר רַב *יְהוּדָה: סָפֵק קָרָא קְרִיאַת שְׁמַע סָפֵק לֹא קָרָא – °אֵינוֹ חוֹזֵר וְקוֹרֵא, סָפֵק אָמַר "אֱמֶת וְיַצִּיב" סָפֵק לֹא אָמַר – חוֹזֵר וְאוֹמֵר "אֱמֶת וְיַצִּיב". °מַאי טַעְמָא – קְרִיאַת שְׁמַע דְּרַבָּנַן, 'אֱמֶת וְיַצִּיב' דְּאוֹרָיְיתָא. –מְתִיב רַב יוֹסֵף: °"וּבְשָׁכְבְּךָ וּבְקוּמֶךָ"! –אָמַר לֵיהּ אַבַּיֵי: הַהוּא בְּדִבְרֵי תוֹרָה כְּתִיב. תְּנַן: בַּעַל קֶרִי מְהַרְהֵר בְּלִבּוֹ וְאֵינוֹ מְבָרֵךְ לֹא לְפָנֶיהָ וְלֹא לְאַחֲרֶיהָ, וְעַל הַמָּזוֹן – מְבָרֵךְ לְאַחֲרָיו וְאֵינוֹ מְבָרֵךְ לְפָנָיו. וְאִי ס"ד "אֱמֶת וְיַצִּיב" דְּאוֹרָיְיתָא – לְבָרוּךְ לְאַחֲרֶיהָ! מַאי טַעְמָא מְבָרֵךְ – אִי מִשּׁוּם יְצִיאַת מִצְרַיִם – הָא אַדְכַּר לֵיהּ בִּקְרִיאַת שְׁמַע. וְנֵימָא הָא וְלָא לִבָּעֵי הָא! –קְרִיאַת שְׁמַע עֲדִיפָא, דְּאִית בָּהּ תַּרְתֵּי. ור' אֶלְעָזָר אָמַר: אסָפֵק קָרָא קְרִיאַת שְׁמַע סָפֵק לֹא קָרָא – חוֹזֵר וְקוֹרֵא ק"ש, סָפֵק הִתְפַּלֵּל סָפֵק לֹא הִתְפַּלֵּל – אֵינוֹ חוֹזֵר וּמִתְפַּלֵּל. וְרַבִּי יוֹחָנָן אָמַר: *בוּלְוַאי שֶׁיִּתְפַּלֵּל אָדָם כָּל הַיּוֹם כּוּלּוֹ.§ וְאָמַר רַב יְהוּדָה אָמַר שְׁמוּאֵל: גהָיָה עוֹמֵד בַּתְּפִלָּה וְנִזְכַּר שֶׁהִתְפַּלֵּל – פּוֹסֵק, וַאֲפִילּוּ בְּאֶמְצַע בְּרָכָה. –אִינִי?! וְהָאָמַר רַב נַחְמָן: כִּי הֲוֵינַן בֵּי רַבָּה בַּר אֲבוּהּ, בְּעַן מִינֵּיהּ, הָנֵי בְּנֵי בֵּי רַב דְּטָעוּ וּמַדְכְּרֵי דְּחוֹל בְּשַׁבָּת, מַהוּ שֶׁיִּגְמְרוּ? וַאֲמַר לָן: דגּוֹמְרִין כָּל אוֹתָהּ בְּרָכָה! –הָכִי הָשְׁתָּא! הָתָם – גַּבְרָא בַּר חִיּוּבָא הוּא, וְרַבָּנַן הוּא דְּלָא אַטְרְחוּהוּ מִשּׁוּם כְּבוֹד שַׁבָּת, אֲבָל הָכָא – הָא צַלֵּי לֵיהּ. וְאָמַר רַב יְהוּדָה אָמַר שְׁמוּאֵל: ההִתְפַּלֵּל וְנִכְנַס לְבֵיהַכ"נ וּמָצָא צִבּוּר שֶׁמִּתְפַּלְּלִין, אִם יָכוֹל לְחַדֵּשׁ בָּהּ דָּבָר – יַחֲזוֹר וְיִתְפַּלֵּל, וְאִם לָאו – אַל יַחֲזוֹר וְיִתְפַּלֵּל. וּצְרִיכָא: דְּאִי אַשְׁמְעִינַן קַמַּיְיתָא, ה"מ – יָחִיד וְיָחִיד, או

רש"י

אֶלָּא יְקַצֵּר. כָּל בְּרָכָה וּבְרָכָה: דְּלֵית בָּהּ מַלְכוּת שָׁמַיִם. אֵין "מֶלֶךְ הָעוֹלָם" בַּבְּרָכוֹת שֶׁל י"ח: ה"ג: וַהֲרֵי בִּרְכַּת הַמָּזוֹן לְפָנֶיהָ דְּאִית בָּהּ מַלְכוּת שָׁמַיִם כו'. לִישָּׁנָא אַחֲרִינָא: שָׁאנֵי תְּפִלָּה דְּלֵית בָּהּ מַלְכוּת שָׁמַיִם. קַבָּלַת מַלְכוּת שָׁמַיִם, כִּדְאִיתָא בק"ש שֶׁמְּקַבֵּל עָלָיו אֶת הַשֵּׁם לְאָדוֹן וּלְמֶלֶךְ מְיוּחָד. וּלְהַאי לִישָּׁנָא גָּרְסִינַן: וַהֲרֵי בִּרְכַּת הַמָּזוֹן לְאַחֲרָיו דְּלֵית בָּהּ מַלְכוּת שָׁמַיִם. וְלָשׁוֹן זֶה נִרְאֶה שֶׁהוּא עִיקָּר, מִדְּמְשַׁנֵּי לֵיהּ: אֶלָּא ק"ש וּבִרְכַּת הַמָּזוֹן דְּאוֹרָיְיתָא וְהַאי בִּלְאַחֲרָיו עָסְקִינַן. וְאִי לְלִישָּׁנָא קַמָּא – הָא לָא אָיְירֵי בְּבִרְכַּת הַמָּזוֹן לְאַחֲרָיו בְּדְאַתְקַפְתֵּיהּ, דְּלְהַדְרִי תַּלְמוּדָא עִילָּוֵיהּ. אֶלָּא ק"ש וּבִרְכַּת הַמָּזוֹן דְּאוֹרָיְיתָא כו'. וְאִית דְּגָרְסִי הָכָא בִּלְשׁוֹן קוּשְׁיָא: ק"ש דְּרַבָּנָן הִיא, אֶלָּא ק"ש דְּאִית בָּהּ מַלְכוּת שָׁמַיִם, וּבִרְכַּת הַמָּזוֹן דְּאוֹרָיְיתָא – לְאַפּוּקֵי תְּפִלָּה דְּרַבָּנָן, וְאֵין בָּהּ מַלְכוּת שָׁמַיִם. לְמַאן דְּגָרַס הָכִי מְפָרְשִׁינַן לְקַמָּן "בְּשָׁכְבְּךָ וּבְקוּמֶךָ" – בְּדִבְרֵי תוֹרָה כְּתִיב: כִּי שֵׁם ה' **אֶקְרָא**. כְּשֶׁבָּא מֹשֶׁה לִפְתּוֹחַ בְּדִבְרֵי שִׁירָה אָמַר לָהֶם לְיִשְׂרָאֵל: אֲנִי אֲבָרֵךְ תְּחִלָּה, וְאַתֶּם עֲנוּ אַחֲרַי אָמֵן. "כִּי שֵׁם ה' אֶקְרָא" בִּבְרָכָה, אַתֶּם – "הָבוּ גוֹדֶל לֵאלֹהֵינוּ" בְּאָמֵן. הָכִי מְפָרְשִׁי לָהּ בְּמַסֶּכֶת יוֹמָא (דף לז.): **שֶׁאֵינוֹ** טָעוּן לְפָנָיו. כְּלוֹמַר: שֶׁלֹּא מָצִינוּ לוֹ מִקְרָא מְפוֹרָשׁ לְבָרֵךְ לְפָנָיו: טָעוּן לְאַחֲרָיו. כִּדְכְתִיב "וְאָכַלְתָּ וְשָׂבָעְתָּ וּבֵרַכְתָּ": תּוֹרָה שֶׁטְּעוּנָה לְפָנֶיהָ. כִּדְאָמְרַן: **אִיכָּא** לְמִפְרַךְ. בִּתְרַוַּיְיהוּ. כְּשֶׁאַתָּה בָּא לִלְמוֹד תּוֹרָה מִן הַמָּזוֹן אִיכָּא לְמִפְרַךְ: מַה לְּמָזוֹן – שֶׁכֵּן נֶהֱנֶה. וּכְשֶׁאַתָּה בָּא לִלְמוֹד מָזוֹן מִן הַתּוֹרָה, אִיכָּא לְמִפְרַךְ: מַה לַּתּוֹרָה – שֶׁכֵּן חַיֵּי הָעוֹלָם הַבָּא: ק"ש דְּרַבָּנָן. לְקַמָּן פָּרֵיךְ לָהּ: **אֱמֶת וְיַצִּיב דְּאוֹרָיְיתָא הִיא**. שֶׁמַּזְכִּיר בָּהּ יְצִיאַת מִצְרַיִם, דְּחִיּוּבָא דְּאוֹרָיְיתָא הִיא, דִּכְתִיב "לְמַעַן תִּזְכֹּר אֶת יוֹם צֵאתְךָ מֵאֶרֶץ מִצְרַיִם" (דברים טז): דְּאִית בָּהּ תַּרְתֵּי. יְצִיאַת מִצְרַיִם וּמַלְכוּת שָׁמַיִם: חוֹזֵר וְקוֹרֵא ק"ש. קָסָבַר: ק"ש דְּאוֹרָיְיתָא הִיא: וּלְוַאי שֶׁיִּתְפַּלֵּל אָדָם כָּל הַיּוֹם. בַּהֲלָכוֹת גְּדוֹלוֹת פָּסַק: הֲלָכָה כְּרַבִּי יוֹחָנָן בְּסָפֵק, וַהֲלָכָה כִּשְׁמוּאֵל בְּוַדַּאי הִתְפַּלֵּל: מַהוּ שֶׁיִּגְמְרוּ. אֶת הַבְּרָכָה אִם נִזְכַּר בְּאֶמְצַע הַבְּרָכָה בְּאַחַת מִן הַבְּרָכוֹת שֶׁטָּעָה: יָחִיד וְיָחִיד. כְּשֶׁהִתְפַּלֵּל תְּחִלָּה הָיָה יָחִיד, וּכְשֶׁשָּׁכַח שֶׁהִתְפַּלֵּל וְהִתְחִיל לְהִתְפַּלֵּל הָיָה כְּיָחִיד: או

תוספות

והרי תפלה דדבר שהצבור כו'. וא"ת: אמאי שבק בבא דק"ש דקאי בגווה, דדבר שהצבור עסוקין בו וקתני אינו מברך לפניה כו'? וי"ל: משום רבותא דתפלה, פריך מיניה, אע"ג דתפלה מעומד ונראה לכל שאין זה עומד כמותם אפילו הכי אמרינן: אם לא התחיל לא יתחיל. וא"ת: כיון דלא ידע טעמא דבסמוך, יקשה גם לרבינא מה לי ק"ש וברכת המזון יותר מתפלה? וי"ל: דלרבינא ניחא, כיון דהרהור כדבור דמי – יש להצריכו בק"ש ובברכת המזון שהם מדאורייתא, יותר מתפלה דרבנן. אבל לרב חסדא, כיון דהרהור אינו כלום, רק שלא יהא יושב ובטל – מה לי ק"ש מה לי תפלה: **הא אי לא אתחיל** לא יתחיל. וא"ת: אימא דבדבור קאמר, הא בהרהור שפיר דמי? וי"ל: דמשמע דלא יתחיל – אפי' בהרהור, מדלא קאמר: יקצר בדבור או יהרהר באריכות: **הכי** גרסי': **אלא ק"ש וברכת המזון דאורייתא ותפלה דרבנן**, ולא גרסינן מידי בתר הכי עד אמר רב יהודה אמר רב. פי' הקונטרס: ק"ש דאורייתא כיון שאינו אומר 'אמת ויציב' כדפי' במתניתין. ויש ספרים גורסים *ק"ש דרבנן הוא. ומשני: אלא ק"ש אית בה מלכות שמים, וברכת המזון דאורייתא ותפלה דרבנן, וכן הגירסא בפ"ה. וקשה, דבמתניתין פי' דק"ש דאורייתא לכולי עלמא, כיון שלא אמר 'אמת ויציב', דבהכי איירי מתניתין. וגם יש ספרים גורסים שאני תפלה דלית בה מלכות שמים. והרי ברכת המזון דלית בה מלכות שמים – ותנן: על המזון מברך לאחריו וכו'; אלא היינו טעמא דק"ש אית בה מלכות שמים, וברכת המזון דאורייתא, ותפלה דרבנן. וגם על גירסא זו קשה כדפירש': **ספק** לא אמר אמת ויציב – חוזר. ותימה: הא ע"כ צריך לומר שהוא מסופק גם מק"ש. שאם היה ברור לו מק"ש וספק מ'אמת ויציב' – לא יהיה מן התורה, כיון שהזכיר יציאת מצרים בק"ש. ואם כן, הואיל ומסופק משניהם יחזור לק"ש דאית בה תרתי, מלכות שמים ויציאת מצרים, דהכי עדיף מלומר 'אמת ויציב', דליכא אלא חדא כדאמר בסמוך גבי מתני'. ואומר ר"י: דודאי מתני' גבי בעל קרי שידענו בו שלא אמר ק"ש ולא 'אמת ויציב' כלל, ואנו רוצים להתיר לו, הלכך טוב הוא יותר שיאמר ק"ש דאיכא תרתי. אבל הכא, שהוא ספק אם אמר 'אמת ויציב', ומספקא ליה אם אמר שניהם כדפרישית – טוב הוא יותר שיאמר 'אמת ויציב' מלומר ק"ש. דכשיאמר 'אמת ויציב' שמא יש לתלות שתקן הכל. דאם קרא כבר 'אמת ויציב' – גם קרא ק"ש כבר, דמסתמא התפלל כדרך תפלה ק"ש ואח"כ 'אמת ויציב' – ויצא ידי שתיהן. וכי נמי תימא דלא אמר כבר שתיהן – מ"מ שמא אמר ק"ש ולא אמר 'אמת ויציב' שזה יכול להיות, ועתה כשיאמר 'אמת ויציב' – נמצא שהשלים הכל. וכי תימא: שמא לא קרא לא זה ולא זה? כיון דספיקא הוא – כולי האי לא אטרחוהו רבנן לחזור שניהם. אבל אם יאמר ק"ש – אין זו תקנה גמורה כל כך, דשמא קרא ק"ש אחרת ולא יצא כלל במה שעושה עתה. ואם ברור שלא אמר כבר ק"ש, אם כן לא אמר נמי 'אמת ויציב' – שאין רגילות לומר 'אמת ויציב' בלא ק"ש, ואם כן כשיאמר מעתה ק"ש לא תקן כלל ולא יצא מדי ספקו. עוד אמר הר"ר שמעון דמיירי שפיר שאינו מסופק אלא מ'אמת ויציב' אבל ברור הוא שקרא ק"ש. ואפילו הכי הוי 'אמת ויציב' דאורייתא, שר"ל ספק לא אמר 'אמת ויציב' עם פרשת ציצית שמסופק אי לא אמר לא פרשת ציצית ולא 'אמת ויציב' ואם כן לא הזכיר כלל יציאת מצרים וכולה מילתא דיציאת מצרים קרי ליה 'אמת ויציב', לפי דטעם 'אמת ויציב' הוי משום יציאת מצרים והלכך הוי פרשת ציצית בכלל 'אמת ויציב': **ההוא** בדברי תורה כתיב. והא דאמרינן לעיל בפרק קמא (דף ב.): בערב משום דכתיב "ובשכבך" אסמכתא בעלמא הוא*:

ורבי יוחנן אמר: ולואי שיתפלל אדם כל היום. אומר ר"י דהלכה כרבי יוחנן, ודוקא בספק התפלל; °אבל ודאי התפלל – לא. *תדע, דהא מסתמא לא פליג אהא דאמר רב יהודה אמר שמואל בסמוך ונזכר שהתפלל פוסק וכו'. וכן אם יכול לחדש דבר בתפלתו:

עין משפט נר מצוה

לו א מיי' פ"ב מהלכות ק"ש הלכה יג סמג עשין יט טוש"ע או"ח סימן סז:
לז ב ג מיי' פ"י מהל' תפלה הלכה ו סמג עשין יט טוש"ע או"ח סימן קז סעיף א:
לח ד מיי' שם הלכה ז סמג שם טוש"ע או"ח סי' רסח סעיף ב:
לט ה מיי' פ"א מהלכות תפלה הלכה ט סמג שם טוש"ע או"ח סימן קז סעיף א:

[עיין תוס' סוטה לב: ד"ה ורבי]

[ועי' תוס' סוטה לב ע"ב ד"ה ורבי ותוס' מנחות מג ע"ב ד"ה ואיזו]

גליון הש"ס

גמ' אינו חוזר וקורא. עי' ברבינו יונה לעיל פ"ב י"א ד"ה באמצע: **שם** מ"ט ק"ש דרבנן. עי' בב"ק פז ע"א תוס' ד"ה וכן היה ר"י פוטרו מכל המצות האמורות בתורה ובסוטה לב ע"ב תוס' ד"ה ורבי ובמנחות מג ע"ב תוס' ד"ה ואיזו: **רש"י** ד"ה שאינו כו' כלומר שלא מצינו. וכיוצא בזה בב"מ פח ע"ב ועיין קדושין טו ע"ב תוס' ד"ה א"ק: **תוס'** ד"ה ור"י כו' אבל ודאי התפלל. עי' לקמן כט ע"א תוס' ד"ה מפני:

מסורת הש"ס

לקמן דף כב:
מגילה דר"י פ' בא ולקמן דף מח: ע"ש
דברים ח
שם לב
[ל רב יהודה אמר שמואל וכן איתא בריי"ף וברא"ש]
שם ו
פסחים דף נד:
[כ"ב תוס' לקמן כט. ד"ה מפני]

הגהות הב"ח

(א) גמ' אמר ר' יהודה אמר רב מנין לברכת המזון: (ב) שם מה למזון. נ"ב עיין לקמן בפ' שלשה שאכלו סוף דף מח:

עין משפט נר מצוה

מסורת הש"ס

תורה אור

או צבור וצבור, אבל יחיד לגבי צבור כמאן דלא צלי דמי – קמ"ל; ואי אשמעינן הכא – משום דלא אתחיל בה, אבל התם דאתחיל בה, אימא לא – צריכא.§ אמר רב הונא: הנכנס לבית הכנסת ומצא צבור שמתפללין, אאם יכול להתחיל ולגמור עד שלא יגיע ש"ץ ל"מודים" – יתפלל, ואם לאו – אל יתפלל; ריב"ל אמר: באם יכול להתחיל ולגמור עד שלא יגיע ש"צ לקדושה – יתפלל, ואם לאו – אל יתפלל. במאי קא מפלגי? מר סבר: יחיד אומר קדושה; ומר סבר: אין יחיד אומר קדושה. *וכן אמר רב אדא בר אהבה: *מנין שאין היחיד אומר קדושה – שנאמר: °"ונקדשתי בתוך בני ישראל" – גכל דבר שבקדושה לא יהא פחות מעשרה. מאי משמע? דתני *רבנאי אחוה דרבי חייא בר אבא: אתיא "תוך" "תוך". כתיב הכא: "ונקדשתי בתוך בני ישראל" וכתיב התם: °"הבדלו מתוך העדה הזאת", *מה להלן עשרה, אף כאן עשרה. ודכולי עלמא מיהת מפסק לא פסיק. איבעיא להו: מהו להפסיק ל"יהא שמו הגדול מבורך"? כי אתא רב דימי אמר, ר' יהודה *ור"ש תלמידי דרבי יוחנן אמרי: לכל אין מפסיקין, חוץ מן "יהא שמו הגדול מבורך", שאפילו עוסק במעשה מרכבה – פוסק. ולית דהלכתא כותיה.§ "ר' יהודה אומר, מברך לפניהם ולאחריהם". למימרא דקסבר רבי יהודה בעל קרי מותר בדברי תורה? והאמר ריב"ל: מנין לבעל קרי שאסור בדברי תורה – *שנאמר: °"והודעתם לבניך ולבני בניך" וסמיך ליה "יום אשר עמדת וגו'" – מה להלן בעלי קריין אסורין, אף כאן – בעלי קריין אסורין! וכי תימא: *רבי יהודה *לא דריש סמוכים, והאמר *רב יוסף: אפילו מאן דלא דריש סמוכים בכל התורה – במשנה תורה דריש. דהא רבי יהודה לא דריש סמוכין בכל התורה כולה, ובמשנה תורה דריש. ובכל התורה כולה מנא לן דלא דריש – דתניא, *בן עזאי אומר: נאמר °"מכשפה לא תחיה" ונאמר "כל שוכב עם בהמה מות יומת", סמכו ענין לו, לומר: מה שוכב עם בהמה בסקילה – האף מכשפה נמי בסקילה; אמר ליה ר' יהודה: וכי מפני שסמכו ענין לו נוציא לזה לסקילה?! אלא: אוב וידעוני בכלל כל המכשפים היו, ולמה יצאו – להקיש להן, ולומר לך: מה אוב וידעוני בסקילה – אף מכשפה בסקילה. ובמשנה תורה מנא לן דדריש – דתניא, רבי אליעזר אומר: *ונושא אדם אנוסת אביו ומפותת אביו, אנוסת בנו ומפותת בנו. ר' יהודה אוסר באנוסת אביו ובמפותת אביו. ואמר רב גידל אמר רב: מאי טעמא דר' יהודה, דכתיב: °"לא יקח איש את אשת אביו ולא יגלה (את) כנף אביו" – כנף שראה אביו לא יגלה. וממאי דבאנוסת אביו כתיב – דסמיך ליה: "ונתן האיש השוכב עמה וגו'"! אמרי: אין, במשנה תורה דריש. והני סמוכין מבעי ליה לאידך דריב"ל, דאמר ריב"ל: *כל המלמד לבנו תורה – מעלה עליו הכתוב כאלו קבלה מהר חורב, שנאמר: °"והודעתם לבניך ולבני בניך", וכתיב בתריה: "יום אשר עמדת לפני ה' אלהיך בחורב".§ *תנן: זב שראה קרי, ונדה שפלטה שכבת זרע, המשמשת וראתה *דם צריכין טבילה; ורבי יהודה פוטר. עד כאן לא פטר רבי יהודה אלא בזב שראה קרי – דמעיקרא לאו בר טבילה הוא, אבל בעל קרי גרידא מחייב! וכי תימא, ה"ה דאפילו בעל קרי גרידא נמי פטר רבי יהודה; והאי דקא מפלגי בזב שראה קרי – להודיעך כחן דרבנן, אימא סיפא: המשמשת וראתה *דם צריכה טבילה, למאן קתני לה? אילימא לרבנן – פשיטא! השתא ומה זב שראה קרי דמעיקרא לאו בר טבילה הוא – מחייבי רבנן, המשמשת וראתה *דם – דמעיקרא בת טבילה היא – לא כל שכן! אלא לאו ר' יהודה היא, ודוקא קתני לה משמשת

(ויקרא כב; במדבר טז; דברים ד; שמות כב; דברים כג)

או צבור וצבור. בין בראשונה בין בשניה היה עם הצבור, כגון עשרה אחר עשרה, וזה עמהם בשתיהן, ששכח שהתפלל עם הראשונים: רב הונא סבר. יחיד המתפלל עם הצבור אומר "קדוש". הלכך: אם לא גמר עד שלא יגיע ש"ץ ל"קדוש" – לית לן בה. אבל "מודים", אף על פי שיחיד אומר "מודים", אם אינו אומרו עם הצבור – הרואה את כולם כורעים והוא אינו כורע, נראה ככופר במי שחבריו משתחוין לו: מפסק לא פסיק. תפלתו לקדושה לענות עם הצבור, וכן ל"מודים": במשנה תורה דריש. והאי קרא במשנה תורה הוא נאמר: מכשפה לא תחיה. ולא פירש באיזו מיתה תמות, ונאמר אצלו "כל שוכב עם בהמה מות יומת": סמכו ענין לו. סמכתו פרשת "מכשפה לא תחיה" לשוכב עם בהמה: מה שוכב עם בהמה בסקילה. כדאמרינן לה בסנהדרין פרק "ד' מיתות" (דף נד:) בגזרה שוה ד"תהרוגו" דהכא מ"כי הרוג תהרגנו" דמסית, אף מכשף בסקילה: אמר ליה רבי יהודה: וכי מפני שסמכו הענין. לשוכב עם בהמה, נוציא זה המכשף לסקילה שהיא חמורה מכל מיתות שבתורה? אלא מקרא מפורש יש לו במקום אחר שהוא בסקילה: אוב וידעוני בכלל. "לא תחיה" דכל המכשפים היו, ולמה יצאו בפני עצמן כשהפרישן לסקילה, כדכתיב "באבן ירגמו אותם דמיהם בם" – להקיש אליהם את כל הכלל. שזו מדה בתורה, שכל דבר שהיה בכלל ויצא מן הכלל ללמד – לא ללמד על עצמו, יצא אלא ללמד על הכלל כולו יצא: זב שראה קרי וכו'. לענין טבילה שתקן עזרא לבעלי קריין לעסוק בתורה קאי, ולשאר טמאים לא הוצרך. וקאמר הכא: דאם יש לו טומאה אחרת עם הקרי, שאינו יכול לצאת ממנה בטבילה זו כגון זב ונדה שהם טמאים טומאת שבעה – אפילו הכי צריך לטבול לקריו קודם שיעסוק בתורה: פולטת שכבת זרע. הרי היא כבעל קרי: ורבי יהודה פוטר.(א) קס"ד דאין טבילה זו מטהרתו מכל וכל: המשמשת למאן קתני לה. להשמיענו כח מי הוצרכו לחלוק בה: אילימא לרבנן. להודיעך כחן דמחייבי בה: השתא זב שראה קרי. שקדמתו טומאת הזיבה מעיקרא: דמעיקרא. בשעה שראה קרי לאו בר טבילה הוא, ומחייבי ליה רבנן טבילה לקרי לדברי תורה: משמשת

עד שלא יגיע שליח צבור למודים. וטעמא – לפי שצריך לשוח עם הצבור, שלא יראה ככופר במי שהצבור משתחוין לו. והוא הדין נמי אם יגיע ל'מודים' כששליח צבור יגיע ל'מודים', דשפיר דמי – כיון שהוא משתחוה עם חביריו, אבל אין גמרא פסיקא ליה כי האי גוונא. אבל אין נראה דמשום 'מודים' דרבנן נקט הכי שמצוה לענות – שזה לא מצינו לו עיקר בגמ'. ור"ת היה רגיל כשהיה מתפלל ביחיד, כשהחזן מגיע ל'מודים' – היה כורע עם הקהל בלא אמירה כלל. ודוקא באמצע ברכה, אבל בסוף ברכה – לא, דאמר לקמן (דף לד.) דאסור לשחות בסוף כל ברכה וברכה. מיהו, לכתחלה אין לעשות כן, כדמשמע הכא. וכתב רש"י בסוכה פרק "לולב הגזול" (דף לח:): דאדם המתפלל, ושמע מפי החזן קדיש או קדושה – אינו יכול להפסיק ולענות עם הצבור, אלא ישתוק ויתכוין מעט דשומע כעונה. וי"ל: דלכתחלה אין לעשות כן, דענייה חשיבא טפי הדור מצוה. ור"ת ור"י היו אומרים: דאדרבה, אי שומע כעונה – הוי הפסקה אם שותק. ומ"מ, נהגו העם לשתוק ולשמוע, וגדול המנהג. בירושלמי פרק "תפלת השחר" קאמר: לא התפלל(ב) ובא ומצאן מתפללים מוסף, אם היה יודע שיהיה מתפלל וגומר עד שלא יתחיל ש"ץ כדי לענות אמן – מתפלל, אם לאו – לא יתפלל. באיזה אמן אמרו? פליגי ביה תרי אמוראי, חד אמר: באמן של 'האל הקדוש' וחד אמר: באמן של 'שומע תפלה'. ולא פליגי, כאן – בחול, כאן – בשבת. והא דאמרינן באמן של 'שומע תפלה' – היינו בחול. לכך יש ליזהר לענות אמן ב'האל הקדוש', וגם לענות אמן ב'שומע תפלה'. ומתוך הירושלמי משמע שהיו רגילין לומר י"ח ברכות שלמות במוסף של חול, כגון בר"ח ובחול המועד, ומיהו, אנן סמכינן אהא דאמר פרק "תפלת השחר", (לקמן דף כט.) דקאמר תמני סרי תקון תשסרי לא תקון. ומה שאנו אומרים 'ענגו' בין גואל לרופא לא קשה, שאינו אלא לש"ץ, אבל יחיד כוללה ב'ש"ת'. ועוד אומר הר"ר חיים: דאיתא בתוספתא (דפ' ח"ה) בהדיא כמנהגנו, דקאמר התם: ימים שיש בהן קרבן מוסף – כגון ר"ח וח"ה ערבית ושחרית – מתפלל י"ח שלמות ואומר מעין המאורע בעבודה, ואם לא אמר – מחזירים אותו. ובמוספים מתפלל שבע, ואומר קדושת היום באמצע, ובירושלמי נמי, י"ל דטעות סופר הוא, ול"ג של מוסף. אלא: בא ומצאן מתפללין. וכן משמע בירושלמי "פרק מי שמתו" דגם זו המימרא כתובה שם ולא הזכיר של מוסף כלל: אין יחיד מתפלל קדושה. וכן הלכה. אבל המתפלל י"ח עם החזן, לכשיגיע ש"ץ לקדושה יאמר עם השליח צבור "נקדש", וכל הקדושה משלם יכול לענות עם הצבור, דאין זה קרוי יחיד: ונחזי

מ א [טוש"ע או"ח סי' קט סעיף א]:
ב מיי' פ"י מהלכות תפלה הלכה טז סמג עשין יט טור שו"ע או"ח סימן קט סעיף א:
מא ג מיי' פ"ח שם הלכה ו טור שו"ע או"ח סימן נה סעיף א:
מב ד מיי' פ"ו שם הלכה טז טור שו"ע או"ח סימן קד סעיף ז:
מג ה מיי' פי"א מהל' ע"ג הלכה טו סמג לאוין נה טור יו"ד סימן קעט:
מד ו מיי' פ"ב מהלכות איסורי ביאה הי"ג טוש"ע אה"ע סי' טו:

רב נסים גאון

ר' יהודה דלא דריש סמוכין בכל התורה ובמשנה תורה דריש. פירשו לטעמא דמילתא בפרק ט"ו נשים (דף ד) ואמרי ובמשנה תורה מאי טעמא דריש איבעית אימא משום דמוכח ואיבעית אימא משום דמופנה:

[אולי צ"ל ור"ש בן לקיש וע' כתובות קיא:]

[עי' תוס' יבמות דף ד. ד"ה וכי מפני ותוס' קדושין נג. ד"ה וסמיך ליה]

הגהות הב"ח

(א) רש"י ד"ה ור' יהודה פוטר קסבר לאין: (ב) תוס' ד"ה עד וכו' בירושלמי וכו' לא התפלל שחרית ובא:

[תיבת וכן ליתא בריי"ף]
מגילה דף כג:
[שם ע"ש סנה' עד: ע"ש]
[צ"ל ואתיא עדה עדה דכתיב עד מתי לעדה הרעה הזאת מה להלן וכו' כך איתא במגילה]
[ע' תוספות ב"ק פב: ד"ה אתא]
[פסחים כח:]
יבמות דף ד.
שם סנהדרין דף סז:
יבמות ד. לז. וע"ש במשנה
[קדו' ל. ע"ש]
שם ד
לקמן כו.
[נ"ל נדה]
[נ"ל נדה]
[נ"ל נדה]

משמשת וראתה נדה אינה צריכה טבילה, אבל בעל קרי גרידא – מחייב! לא תימא "מברך" אלא "מהרהר". ומי אית ליה לרבי יהודה הרהור?! והתניא: בעל קרי שאין לו מים לטבול – קורא קריאת שמע, ואינו מברך לא לפניה ולא לאחריה, ואוכל פתו ומברך לאחריה ואינו מברך לפניה, אבל מהרהר בלבו ואינו מוציא בשפתיו, דברי רבי מאיר. רבי יהודה אומר: בין כך ובין כך מוציא בשפתיו. אמר רב נחמן בר יצחק: עשאן ר' יהודה כהלכות דרך ארץ.§ דתניא:* °"והודעתם לבניך ולבני בניך", וכתיב בתריה "יום אשר עמדת לפני ה' אלהיך בחורב", מה להלן באימה וביראה וברתת ובזיע אף כאן באימה וביראה וברתת ובזיע; מכאן אמרו: *[א]הזבים והמצרעים ובאין על נדות – מותרים לקרות בתורה ובנביאים ובכתובים, לשנות במשנה וגמרא ובהלכות ובאגדות, אבל בעלי קריין אסורים; רבי יוסי אומר: שונה הוא ברגיליות ובלבד שלא *יציע את המשנה; רבי יונתן בן יוסף אומר: מציע הוא את המשנה ואינו מציע את(א) הגמרא; רבי נתן בן *אבישלום אומר: אף מציע את הגמרא ובלבד שלא יאמר אזכרות שבו; רבי יוחנן הסנדלר תלמידו של רבי עקיבא משום ר"ע אומר: לא יכנס למדרש כל עיקר ואמרי לה: לא יכנס לבית המדרש כל עיקר; ר' יהודה אומר: שונה הוא בהלכות דרך ארץ. מעשה ברבי יהודה שראה קרי והיה מהלך על גב הנהר. אמרו לו תלמידיו: רבינו, שנה לנו פרק אחד בהלכות דרך ארץ! ירד וטבל ושנה להם. אמרו לו: לא כך למדתנו רבינו: שונה הוא בהלכות דרך ארץ?! אמר להם: אע"פ שמיקל אני על אחרים, מחמיר אני על עצמי.§ תניא, ר' יהודה בן בתירא היה אומר: *אין דברי תורה מקבלין טומאה. מעשה בתלמיד אחד שהיה מגמגם למעלה מרבי יהודה בן בתירא. אמר ליה: בני, פתח פיך ויאירו דבריך; שאין דברי תורה מקבלין טומאה שנאמר °"הלא כה דברי כאש נאם ה'" מה אש אינו מקבל טומאה אף דברי תורה אינן מקבלין טומאה.§ אמר מר: מציע את המשנה ואינו מציע את הגמרא. מסייע ליה לרבי אלעאי; דאמר רבי אלעאי אמר ר' אחא בר יעקב משום רבינו: הלכה, מציע את המשנה ואינו מציע את הגמרא. כתנאי: מציע את המשנה ואינו מציע את הגמרא, דברי רבי מאיר; רבי יהודה בן גמליאל אומר משום רבי חנינא בן גמליאל: זה וזה אסור; ואמרי לה: זה וזה מותר. מ"ד זה וזה אסור – כרבי יוחנן הסנדלר, מ"ד זה וזה מותר – כרבי יהודה בן בתירא.§ *אמר רב נחמן בר יצחק נהוג עלמא כהני תלת סבי: כרבי אלעאי בראשית הגז, כרבי יאשיה בכלאים, כרבי יהודה בן בתירא בד"ת. כרבי אלעאי בראשית הגז – דתניא, *רבי אלעאי אומר: [ב]ראשית הגז אינו נוהג אלא בארץ. כרבי יאשיה בכלאים – כדכתיב: °"(כרמך) לא תזרע [כרמך] כלאים", *רבי יאשיה אומר: [ג]לעולם *אינו חייב עד שיזרע חטה ושעורה וחרצן במפולת יד. כרבי יהודה בן בתירא בדברי תורה, דתניא, רבי יהודה בן בתירא אומר: [ד]אין דברי תורה מקבלין טומאה.§ כי אתא זעירי, אמר: בטלוה לטבילותא, ואמרי לה: בטלוה לנטילותא. מאן דאמר "בטלוה לטבילותא" – כרבי יהודה בן בתירא. מאן דאמר "בטלוה לנטילותא" – כי הא *דרב חסדא לייט אמאן דמהדר אמיא בעידן צלותא.§ תנו רבנן: בעל קרי שנתנו עליו תשעה קבין מים – טהור; נחום איש גם זו לחשה לרבי עקיבא, ורבי עקיבא לחשה לבן עזאי, ובן עזאי יצא ושנאה לתלמידיו בשוק. פליגי בה תרי אמוראי במערבא, רבי יוסי בר אבין ורבי יוסי בר זבידא: חד תני 'שנאה' וחד תני 'לחשה'. מאן דתני 'שנאה' משום בטול תורה, ומשום בטול פריה ורביה. ומאן דתני 'לחשה' – [ה]שלא יהו תלמידי חכמים מצויים אצל נשותיהם כתרנגולים. אמר רבי ינאי: שמעתי שמקילין בה ושמעתי שמחמירין בה, [ו]וכל המחמיר בה על עצמו מאריכין לו ימיו ושנותיו. אמר ריב"ל: מה טיבן של טובלי שחרין? – מה טיבן?! הא איהו דאמר: בעל קרי אסור בדברי תורה! –הכי קאמר: מה טיבן בארבעים סאה? אפשר בתשעה קבין, מה טיבן בטבילה? אפשר בנתינה! אמר רבי חנינא: גדר גדול גדרו בה, דתניא: מעשה באחד שתבע אשה לדבר עבירה. אמרה לו: ריקא! יש לך ארבעים סאה שאתה טובל בהן?! מיד פירש.§ אמר להו: רב הונא לרבנן: רבותי, מפני מה אתם מזלזלין בטבילה זו? אי משום צינה, אפשר במרחצאות! אמר ליה רב חסדא: *[ז]וכי יש טבילה בחמין?! אמר ליה: רב אדא בר אהבה קאי כוותך. רבי זירא הוה יתיב באגנא דמיא בי מסותא. אמר ליה לשמעיה: זיל ואייתי לי תשעה קבין ושדי עלואי. אמר ליה רבי חייא בר אבא: למה ליה למר כולי האי? והא יתיב בגווייהו! אמר ליה: כארבעים סאה; מה ארבעים סאה בטבילה ולא בנתינה אף [ח]תשעה קבין בנתינה ולא בטבילה.§ רב נחמן תקן חצבא בת תשעה קבין. כי אתא רב דימי אמר, רבי עקיבא ורבי יהודה גלוסטרא אמרו: לא שנו אלא לחולה לאונסו, אבל לחולה המרגיל ארבעים סאה. אמר רב יוסף: אתבר חצביה דרב נחמן. כי אתא רבין אמר: *באושא הוה עובדא בקילעא

תורה אור: דברים ד · ירמיה כג · דברים כב

משמשת וראתה נדה. דטומאת קרי קדמה, וכשראתה הקרי ראויה היתה לטבול מיד: לא כל שכן. דלא אתיא טומאת נדה שהיא אחרונה, ומפקעה לטבילה שנתחייבה בה כבר: אלא לאו רבי יהודה. קתני להודיעך דאפי' היכא דקדם הקרי – אתיא טומאת נדה ומפקעה טבילה, דאין טבילה אלא המטהרת; ואי לרבי יהודה לית ליה תקנת עזרא, למה ליה לאשמעינן בהא? כל בעלי קריין נמי לא בעי טבילה לדברי תורה! הלכך, על כרחך דוקא קתני לה: לא תימא. במתני' 'מברך' אלא 'מהרהר': עשאן ר' יהודה. לברכת המזון: בהלכות ד"א. שמותר לשנותה בעל קרי, כדבריו: מה להלן באימה. דכתיב "וירא העם וינועו וגו'" (שמות כ): מכאן אמרו. כל הטמאים מותרים בתורה, שאף הם יכולים להיות באימה וברתת. אבל בעל קרי אינו אלא מתוך קלות ראש וחשות הדעת: ובועלי נדות. אם טבלו לקריין לדברי תורה הטבילה אינה עולה להם לטהרם מטומאת בועל נדה שהיא שבעת ימים, אבל לתקנת עזרא עולה להם כדתנן במתניתין "זב שראה קרי ונדה כו' צריכין טבילה": ברגיליות. במשניות השגורות בפיו, שהוא מוציאן מפיו במרוצה ואין צריך להאריך בהן: שלא יציע. בטעמי פירושיהן: ואינו מציע את המדרש גרסי'. מפני שצריך הוא תמיד להזכיר בו את הפסוקים שהוא דורש: אזכרות. שבמקראות הנדרשים: לא יכנס למדרש כל עיקר. לא להציע ולא לשנות, אבל לבית המדרש הוא נכנס ושותק: הלכות דרך ארץ. כגון דרכן של ת"ח שהיא ברייתא, ופרק "בן עזאי" הנותן ארבעה דברים אל לבו: מגמגם וקורא. בעל קרי היה: נראה בעיני דה"ג: א"ר אלעאי הלכה כו'. ולא גרסינן מסייע ליה: משום רבינו. רב: כי הנך תלת סבי. וכולהו לקולא: אינו נוהג אלא בארץ. בשחיטת חולין יליף טעמא, בפרק "הזרוע": חטה ושעורה וחרצן. שלשתן במפולת יד, דהוו להו כלאי זרעים וכלאי הכרם כאחת: לטבילותא. דבעלי קריין: חד תני. בן עזאי, לחשה לתלמידים: משום בטול פריה ורביה. שהיו נמנעים מתשמיש מפני טורח הטבילה: שמקילין בה. במרחצאות, או בנתינת תשעה קבין: שמחמירין בה. בארבעים סאה: של טובלי שחרין. בעלי קריין הטובלין שחרית: והא איהו אמר כו'. לעיל בריש שמעתין: אפשר בנתינה. תשעה קבין. ואע"ג דלא תנא לקמן אלא בחולה, (ב)סתם תלמידי חכמים חולים הם, כדאמר במסכת נדרים (דף מט:), כמאן מצלינן אקלירי ואמריעי כרבי יוסי. קלירי – חולין, מריעי – רבנן: גדר גדול גדרו. במה שהצריכו בארבעים סאה: שתבע אשה. אותה אשה פנויה היתה, וחכמים גזרו על היחוד אף על הפנויה: אתם מזלזלים. לנהוג כרבי יהודה בן בתירא: אפשר במרחצאות. חמין: קאי כוותך. דבעי טבילה זו במקוה כשאר טבילות: באגנא דמיא. גיגית: תקן חצבא. ליתן מים לתלמידים עליהם שחרית קודם קריאת התורה: לא שנו. דסגי בנתינה אלא בחולה שראה קרי לאונסו: המרגיל. וממשיך את הקרי עליו, שמשמש מטתו: אתבר חצביה. אינו צריך לנו, דחולה לאונסו לא שכיח: בקילעא

מסורת הש"ס:
[כל זה וגם ד"ה לכ"ש וגם ד"ה אלא לאו שייכים לסוף ע"ב לעיל בסמוך]
[מ"ק טו.]
תוספתא פ"ב
[בערוך ערך לע פי' שלא ילמד לאחרים ודבר זה אנו לומדין מק"ו מסיני אם ללמוד אסור ללמד כל"ש]
במס' ד"א פ"ג
[עי' תוס' ב"ק פ"ב: ד"ה אתא]
חולין קלו:
שם: וקלח:
קדושין לט. חולין פב: קלו: בכורות נד.
לעיל טו.
[תענית יג.]
[גי' הערוך באושא הוה בקילעא דר' הושעיא וכו'. באושא פי' חולה:]

עין משפט נר מצוה:
מה א מיי' פ"ד מהלכות ק"ש הלכה ח סמג עשין יח טוש"ע או"ח סימן פח:
מו ב מיי' פ"י מהלכות בכורים הלכה א סמג עשין קמג טוש"ע י"ד סי' שלג סעיף א:
מז ג מיי' פ"ח מהלכות כלאים הלכה יג סמג לאוין רפ טוש"ע י"ד סי' רצו סעיף א:
מח ד מיי' פ"ד מהל' ק"ש הלכה ח ופ"ד מהל' תפלה הל' ד (ופ"א מהל' ברכות הל' ט) ופ"י מהל' ספר תורה הל' ח סמג עשין יח טוש"ע א"ח סי' פח טוש"ע י"ד סי' רפב סעיף ט:
מט ה מיי' פ"ה מהלכות דעות הל' ד ופ"ד מהלכות תפלה הלכה ד סמג לאוין פא טוש"ע או"ח סי' פח וסי' רמ סעיף א וטוש"ע אה"ע סי' כה סעיף ב:
נ ו טור א"ח סי' רמא:
נא ז טוש"ע י"ד סימן רא סעיף עה:
נב ח טור א"ח בב"י סי' פח:

[עיין תוספות יומא לח: ד"ה ולא ותוס' כתובות קז: ד"ה שני]

רב נסים גאון
מה ארבעים סאה בטבילה ולא בנתינה. פירשו בברייתא דשיעור מקוה שכשר לטבילה מ' סאה ואיתה להא ברייתא בפרק ערבי פסחים (דף קט) ובעירובין בפרק מבוי (דף יד): **עזרא** תיקן להן טבילה לבעלי קריין. זו אחת מי' תקנות שתיקן עזרא ומפרשא בבבא קמא בפ' מרובה (דף פב) ובגמ' דהקורא את המגילה עומד דבני מערבא (הלכה א):

[עי' ברש"י קדושין לט. ד"ה לא קי"ל וכו' וטעמיה דרבי יאשיה לא ידענא וכו' ועי' תוס' בקדושין שם ובכורות נ"ד. סד"ה לגן ובתוס' חולין פב: ד"ה ולאפוקי מה שכתבו בזה]

הגהות הב"ח
(א) גמ' מציע את (הגמ') תז"מ. ונ"ב גי' רש"י המדרש וכן בכל העמוד: (ב) רש"י ד"ה אפשר וכו' דלא תנא לה אלא בחולה. נ"ב בסמוך בסוף עמוד זה:

גליון הש"ס
רש"י ד"ה ובועלי נדות אם טבלו לקריין. עי' מ"ל פ"ג מהל' ביאת המקדש:

בְּקִילְעָא דְּרַב אוֹשַׁעְיָא, אָתוּ וְשַׁאֲלוּ לְרַב אַסִי, אֲמַר לְהוּ: לֹא שָׁנוּ אֶלָּא לַחוֹלֶה הַמַּרְגִּיל, אֲבָל לַחוֹלֶה לְאוֹנְסוֹ פָּטוּר מִכְּלוּם. א"ר יוֹסֵף: אִצְטְמִיד חַצְבֵיהּ דְּרַב נַחְמָן.§ מִכְּדִי כּוּלְּהוּ אֲמוֹרָאֵי וְתַנָּאֵי בְּדְעֶזְרָא קָמִיפַּלְגִי, וְנֶחֱזֵי עֶזְרָא הֵיכִי תַּקֵּן! אֲמַר אַבַּיֵי: עֶזְרָא תַּקֵּן לְבָרִיא הַמַּרְגִּיל מ' סְאָה, וּבָרִיא לְאוֹנְסוֹ – ט' קַבִּין. וְאָתוּ אֲמוֹרָאֵי וּפְלִיגִי בְּחוֹלֶה; מָר סְבַר: חוֹלֶה הַמַּרְגִּיל כְּבָרִיא הַמַּרְגִּיל, וְחוֹלֶה לְאוֹנְסוֹ כְּבָרִיא לְאוֹנְסוֹ; וּמָר סְבַר: חוֹלֶה הַמַּרְגִּיל כְּבָרִיא לְאוֹנְסוֹ, וְחוֹלֶה לְאוֹנְסוֹ פָּטוּר מִכְּלוּם. אֲמַר רָבָא: נְהִי דְּתַקֵּן עֶזְרָא טְבִילָה, נְתִינָה מִי תַּקֵּן? וְהָאָמַר מָר: *עֶזְרָא תַּקֵּן טְבִילָה לְבַעֲלֵי קְרָיִין! אֶלָּא אָמַר רָבָא: עֶזְרָא תַּקֵּן טְבִילָה לְבָרִיא הַמַּרְגִּיל מ' סְאָה. וְאָתוּ רַבָּנַן וְהִתְקִינוּ לְבָרִיא לְאוֹנְסוֹ ט' קַבִּין. וְאָתוּ אֲמוֹרָאֵי וְקָא מִיפַּלְגִי בְּחוֹלֶה; מָר סְבַר: חוֹלֶה הַמַּרְגִּיל כְּבָרִיא הַמַּרְגִּיל, וְחוֹלֶה לְאוֹנְסוֹ כְּבָרִיא לְאוֹנְסוֹ; וּמָר סְבַר: לְבָרִיא הַמַּרְגִּיל מ' סְאָה וְחוֹלֶה הַמַּרְגִּיל כְּבָרִיא לְאוֹנְסוֹ, ט' קַבִּין, אֲבָל לְחוֹלֶה לְאוֹנְסוֹ – פָּטוּר מִכְּלוּם. אָמַר רָבָא: אהִלְכְתָא, בָּרִיא הַמַּרְגִּיל וְחוֹלֶה הַמַּרְגִּיל – אַרְבָּעִים סְאָה, וּבָרִיא לְאוֹנְסוֹ – תִּשְׁעָה קַבִּין, אֲבָל לַחוֹלֶה לְאוֹנְסוֹ – פָּטוּר מִכְּלוּם.§ *ת"ר: בַּעַל קֶרִי שֶׁנָּתְנוּ עָלָיו ט' קַבִּין מַיִם–טָהוֹר; בד"א–לְעַצְמוֹ, אֲבָל לַאֲחֵרִים–אַרְבָּעִים סְאָה; ר' יְהוּדָה אוֹמֵר: מ' סְאָה מִכָּל מָקוֹם. ר' יוֹחָנָן וריב"ל ור"א ור' יוֹסִי בר' חֲנִינָא, חַד מֵהַאי זוּגָא וְחַד מֵהַאי זוּגָא אֲרֵישָׁא. חַד אֲמַר: הָא דְּאָמַרְתְּ "בַּמֶּה דְּבָרִים אֲמוּרִים לְעַצְמוֹ אֲבָל לַאֲחֵרִים מ' סְאָה" – לֹא שָׁנוּ אֶלָּא לַחוֹלֶה הַמַּרְגִּיל, אֲבָל לַחוֹלֶה לְאוֹנְסוֹ – ט' קַבִּין; וְחַד אֲמַר: כֹּל לַאֲחֵרִים – אֲפִילּוּ חוֹלֶה לְאוֹנְסוֹ – עַד דְּאִיכָּא מ' סְאָה. וְחַד מֵהַאי זוּגָא וְחַד מֵהַאי זוּגָא אַסֵּיפָא. חַד אֲמַר: הָא דְּאָמַר רַבִּי יְהוּדָה "מ' סְאָה מִכָּל מָקוֹם" – לֹא שָׁנוּ אֶלָּא בְּקַרְקַע, אֲבָל בְּכֵלִים – לֹא; וְחַד אֲמַר: אֲפִי' בְּכֵלִים נַמִּי. בִּשְׁלָמָא לְמ"ד אֲפִי' בְּכֵלִים – הַיְינוּ דְּקָתָנֵי: "ר' יְהוּדָה אוֹמֵר מ' סְאָה מִכָּל מָקוֹם" אֶלָּא לְמ"ד "בְּקַרְקַע – אִין, בְּכֵלִים – לָא" "מִכָּל מָקוֹם" לְאֵתוּיֵי מַאי? – לְאֵתוּיֵי מַיִם שְׁאוּבִין. רַב פַּפָּא וְרַב הוּנָא בְּרֵיהּ דְּרַב יְהוֹשֻׁעַ וְרָבָא (בְּרַבִּי) בַּר שְׁמוּאֵל כְּרִיכוּ רִיפְתָא בַּהֲדֵי הֲדָדֵי. א"ל רַב פַּפָּא: הֲבוּ לִי לְדִידִי לְבָרוּךְ, דִּנְפוּל עִילָּוַאי ט' קַבִּין. אֲמַר לְהוּ רָבָא (בְּרַבִּי) [בַּר] שְׁמוּאֵל, תְּנֵינָא: בַּמֶּה דְּבָרִים אֲמוּרִים – לְעַצְמוֹ, אֲבָל לַאֲחֵרִים – מ' סְאָה; אֶלָּא, הֲבוּ לִי לְדִידִי לְבָרוּךְ, דִּנְפוּל עִילָּוַאי אַרְבָּעִים סְאָה. אֲמַר לְהוּ רַב הוּנָא: הֲבוּ לִי לְדִידִי לְבָרוּךְ, דְּלֵיכָּא עִילָּוַאי לָא הַאי וְלָא הַאי. רַב חָמָא טָבֵיל בְּמַעֲלֵי יוֹמָא דְּפִסְחָא לְהוֹצִיא רַבִּים יְדֵי חוֹבָתָן. וְלֵית הִלְכְתָא כְּוָותֵיהּ.§

מתני' *הָיָה עוֹמֵד בַּתְּפִלָּה וְנִזְכַּר שֶׁהוּא בַּעַל קֶרִי – לֹא יַפְסִיק, אֶלָּא יְקַצֵּר. יָרַד בלִטְבּוֹל, אִם יָכוֹל לַעֲלוֹת וּלְהִתְכַּסּוֹת וְלִקְרוֹת עַד שֶׁלֹּא תֵּהֵא הָנֵץ הַחַמָּה – יַעֲלֶה וְיִתְכַּסֶּה וְיִקְרָא, וְאִם לָאו – יִתְכַּסֶּה בַּמַּיִם וְיִקְרָא; וְלֹא יִתְכַּסֶּה לֹא בַּמַּיִם הָרָעִים וְלֹא *בְּמֵי הַמִּשְׁרָה, עַד שֶׁיַּטִּיל לְתוֹכָן מַיִם. *וְכַמָּה יַרְחִיק מֵהֶן וּמִן הַצּוֹאָה – ד' אַמּוֹת.§

גמ' ת"ר: הָיָה עוֹמֵד בַּתְּפִלָּה וְנִזְכַּר שֶׁהוּא בַּעַל קֶרִי – לֹא יַפְסִיק אֶלָּא יְקַצֵּר. הָיָה קוֹרֵא בַּתּוֹרָה וְנִזְכַּר שֶׁהוּא בַּעַל קֶרִי – אֵינוֹ מַפְסִיק וְעוֹלֶה, אֶלָּא מְגַמְגֵּם וְקוֹרֵא; ר"מ אוֹמֵר: אֵין בַּעַל קֶרִי רַשַּׁאי לִקְרוֹת בַּתּוֹרָה יוֹתֵר מג' פְּסוּקִים. תַּנְיָא אִידָךְ: גהָיָה עוֹמֵד בַּתְּפִלָּה וְרָאָה צוֹאָה כְּנֶגְדּוֹ – מְהַלֵּךְ לְפָנָיו עַד שֶׁיִּזְרְקֶנָּה לַאֲחוֹרָיו ד' אַמּוֹת. וְהַתַנְיָא: לִצְדָדִין! –ל"ק: דהָא – דְּאֶפְשָׁר, הָא – דְּלָא אֶפְשָׁר. ההָיָה מִתְפַּלֵּל וּמָצָא צוֹאָה בִּמְקוֹמוֹ, אָמַר רַבָּה: אע"פ שֶׁחָטָא – תְּפִלָּתוֹ תְּפִלָּה. מַתְקִיף לֵיהּ רָבָא: וְהָא °"זֶבַח רְשָׁעִים תּוֹעֵבָה"! אֶלָּא אָמַר רָבָא: הוֹאִיל וְחָטָא, *אע"פ שֶׁהִתְפַּלֵּל – תְּפִלָּתוֹ תּוֹעֵבָה*.§ ת"ר: והָיָה עוֹמֵד בַּתְּפִלָּה וּמַיִם שׁוֹתְתִין עַל בִּרְכָּיו – פּוֹסֵק עַד שֶׁיִּכְלוּ הַמַּיִם, וְחוֹזֵר וּמִתְפַּלֵּל. לְהֵיכָן חוֹזֵר? רַב חִסְדָּא וְרַב הַמְנוּנָא, חַד אָמַר: חוֹזֵר לָרֹאשׁ; וְחַד אָמַר: זלַמָּקוֹם שֶׁפָּסַק. לֵימָא בְּהָא קָמִיפַּלְגִי,

מָר

רש"י

בְּקִילְעָא. כְּנִיסַת הַבַּיִת, חֶדֶר שֶׁלִּפְנֵי הַטְּרַקְלִין שֶׁקּוֹרִין פורטיג"ו בְּלַעַ"ז: אִצְטְמִיד. נִתְחַזְּקוּ שְׂפָתָיו וְנִגְמְדוּ, כְּלוֹמַר: נוֹרֶךְ לָנוּ עוֹד בּוֹ: וְקָא מִיפַּלְגִי אֲמוֹרָאֵי. רַב דִּימִי וְרָבִין: דְּאָמַר מָר. גַּבֵּי עֶשֶׂר תַּקָּנוֹת, בְּב"ק בְּפֶרֶק 'מְרוּבֶּה': אָמַר רָבָא הִלְכְתָא וְכוּ'. אַפְּלוּגְתָּא דַּאֲמוֹרָאֵי הוּא דְּפָסַק רָבָא דִּפְלִיגִי אַלִּיבָּא דְּרַבָּנָן. מִיהוּ, הַשְׁתָּא אֲנַן כְּרַבִּי יְהוּדָה בֶּן בְּתֵירָא נָהֲגִינַן כְּדַאֲמַר רַב נַחְמָן לְעֵיל, וְרַב נַחְמָן בַּר יִצְחָק בָּתְרָא הֲוָה: לְעַצְמוֹ. לַעֲסוֹק בַּתּוֹרָה לְעַצְמוֹ, אֲבָל לְלַמֵּד לַאֲחֵרִים – מ' סְאָה: ור"י אוֹמֵר מ' סְאָה מ"מ. מ' סְאָה שֶׁאָמְרוּ בְּכָל עִנְיָן שֶׁהֵן, וּלְקַמָּן מְפָרֵשׁ לָהּ: חַד מֵהַאי זוּגָא וְחַד מֵהַאי זוּגָא. פְּלִיגִי אֲרֵישָׁא בְּפֵירוּשָׁא דְּמִילְּתָא דְּת"ק: אַסֵּיפָא. דְּר' יְהוּדָה: ל"ש אֶלָּא בְּקַרְקַע. לָא תֵּימָא מ"מ דְּר' יְהוּדָה לְאַכְשׁוּרֵי בִּכְלִי אָתָא, דְּאֵין כָּשֵׁר אֶלָּא מ' סְאָה בְּקַרְקַע, וּלְקַמָּן בָּעֵי: א"כ מַאי מ"מ: אֲבָל לַאֲחֵרִים מ' סְאָה. וְהָכָא נָמֵי דִּלְאַפּוּקֵי אֲחֵרִים יְדֵי חוֹבָתָן – כַּלַּאֲחֵרִים דָּמֵי: דִּנְפוּל עִילָּוַאי. לָאו דַּוְקָא, אֶלָּא טָבַלְתִּי בְּמ' סְאָה: לָא הַאי וְלָא הַאי. לֹא הוּצְרַכְתִּי לֹא לָזוּ וְלֹא לָזוּ, שֶׁלֹּא רָאִיתִי קֶרִי: טָבַל. וּבֵירֵךְ רָגִיל הָיָה לַעֲשׂוֹת כֵּן, דְּהוּ"ל לְלַמֵּד אֲחֵרִים. וּבִשְׁאָר יְמוֹת הַשָּׁנָה לֹא הָיָה טוֹבֵל, אֶלָּא נוֹתֵן עָלָיו ט' קַבִּין: וְלֵית הִלְכְתָא כְּוָותֵיהּ. דְּכִי הֵיכִי דִּלְעַצְמוֹ בִּנְתִינָה – לַאֲחֵרִים נָמֵי בִּנְתִינָה. אִי נָמֵי, דְּקיי"ל כְּרַבִּי יְהוּדָה בֶּן בְּתֵירָא:

מתני' לֹא יַפְסִיק. תְּפִלָּתוֹ לְגַמְרֵי אֶלָּא יְקַצֵּר כָּל בְּרָכָה וּבְרָכָה וְאוֹמֵר כָּל הַבְּרָכוֹת בְּקוֹצֶר: בַּמַּיִם הָרָעִים. מַיִם סְרוּחִים: עַד שֶׁיִּתֵּן לְתוֹכָן מַיִם. וּבַגְּמָרָא (ד' כה:) (א)מְפָרֵשׁ: כַּמָּה מַיָּא רָמֵי וְאָזֵיל? וּמְפָרֵשׁ לָהּ בְּחַסּוּרֵי מְחַסְּרָא וְהָכִי קָתָנֵי: לֹא יִקְרָא אֵצֶל מֵי רַגְלַיִם עַד שֶׁיִּתֵּן לְתוֹכָן מַיִם: וְכַמָּה יַרְחִיק מֵהֶם. מִמֵּי רַגְלַיִם:

גמ' מְגַמְגֵּם. בִּמְרוּצָה: יוֹתֵר מג' פְּסוּקִים. כְּגוֹן בְּבֵית הַכְּנֶסֶת דְּאִי אֶפְשָׁר לִפְחוֹת. כְּדִתְנַן (מגילה פ"ג ד' כג:): הַקּוֹרֵא בַּתּוֹרָה לֹא יִפְחוֹת מִשְּׁלֹשָׁה פְּסוּקִים: וְהַתַנְיָא לִצְדָדִין. א"נ לְהַלֵּךְ עַד שֶׁיִּזְרְקֶנָּה לַאֲחוֹרָיו. אֶפְשָׁר. שֶׁיֵּלֵךְ לְפָנָיו, עַד שֶׁתְּהֵא לַאֲחוֹרָיו: לֹא אֶפְשָׁר. כְּגוֹן יֵשׁ נָהָר לְפָנָיו – מִסְתַּלֵּק לַצְּדָדִים:

תוספות

ונחזי עזרא היכן תקן. בהרבה מקומות(ב) גבי שאר תקנות לא פריך גמרא הכי, אלא שאני הכא דלדבר הרגיל בכל יום הוא, על כן אנו זכורים: **ולית** הלכתא כוותיה. דטבילה בכל יום ארבעים סאה, אלא אפילו לאחרים נמי סגי בתשעה קבין, אי נמי, הכי פירושו: ולית הלכתא כוותיה אלא כר' יהודה בן בתירא, דאמר דברי תורה אין מקבלין טומאה. וי"מ: דוקא לתורה, אבל לתפלה צריך *טבילה. ופי' ר"י: דלא שנא. והטובל בערב יוה"כ אין לו לברך, והמברך הוה ברכה לבטלה:

***אלא** דכולי עלמא חוזר לראש. וה"ה דהו"מ לאוקמי דכולי עלמא אין חוזר לראש. ומדלא מוקי הכי ש"מ דהלכה דחוזר לראש. וכן לקמן, (ג)בהדיא אמר ר' אבהו חוזר לראש. ותימה, דבמסכת ר"ה (דף לד:) א"ר יוחנן שמע תשע תקיעות בט' שעות ביום יצא, אלמא: תקיעות מצטרפות אע"ג דשהה כדי לעשות כולם. וכן במגילה (פ"ב ד' יח:) נמי, דאמרינן אמר רב אין הלכה כרבי מונא, דאמר אם שהה חוזר לראש, דקאמר נקוט דרב בידך! ואומר השר מקוצי: דיש לחלק, דשאני הכא דאין ראוי לקרות. וכן לקמן (ד' כד:) דרבי אבהו אזל במבואות המטונפות, דהתם כ"ע מודו דחוזר לראש, אבל היכא דגברא חזי, כמו מגילה ושופר, כולי עלמא מודו דאינו חוזר לראש אלא למקום שפסק. ורבינו יהודה פירש:(ד) דהכא לא מצי למימר דכולי עלמא דאין חוזר לראש, ובדשהה קמיפלגי, דהא לכ"ע הוי גברא חזי כיון דאינו חוזר לראש, אבל ודאי אי הו"מ למימר הכי – הוה אמר ליה:

והא זבח רשעים תועבה. פר"י: דדוקא במקום שהיה יכול להסתפק ולתלות שיש שם צואה:

אע"פ שהתפלל תפלתו תועבה. והוי מעוות לא יוכל לתקן. ור"י פי': דיחזור ויתפלל:

ממתין עד שיכלו המים. במשתין על גבי קרקע, או ע"ג בגדים ואין שם טופח על מנת להטפיח; כדגרסינן לקמן (ד' כה.) כגון דעביד טיף טיף, שנבלעין מהרה, כן פי' הרב רבי יוסף. ומיהו נראה, אפילו אם יש בהן טופח על מנת להטפיח – מותרין, כיון דמדאורייתא אינן אסורין אלא כנגד העמוד בלבד, ורבנן הוא דגזור, וכיון שעומד כבר בתפלתו – לא אטרחוהו רבנן לחזור בתפלה:

חיישינן

תורה אור

עין משפט נר מצוה

נג א מיי' פ"ד מהל' תפלה הלכה ו:

נד ב מיי' פ"ב מהלכות ק"ש הלכה ז:

נה ג ד מיי' פ"ד מהל' תפלה הל' ט סמג עשין י"ט טוש"ע או"ח סימן פא סעיף ב:

[ע' תוספו' חולין קכב: ד"ה לגבל]

[שייך לדף כג.]

נו ה מיי' וסמג שם טוש"ע או"ח סימן עו סעיף ח:

נז ו ז מיי' שם הל' יג סמג שם טוש"ע א"ח סימן עח:

רב נסים גאון

היה עומד בתפלה ונזכר שהוא בעל קרי לא יפסיק. אמרי' עלה בתלמוד ארץ ישראל [פ"ג הלכה ה'] מתניתא ברבים אבל בינו לבין עצמו מפסיק וכר' מאיר ברם כר' יהודה אפי' בינו לבין עצמו אינו מפסיק כשאין לו מים לטבול אבל יש לו מים לטבול אפי' ר' יהודה מודה שהוא מפסיק:

הגהות הב"ח

(א) במשנה רש"י ד"ה עד שיתן וכו' ובגמ' פריך כמה: (ב) תוס' ד"ה ונחזי וכו' בהרבה מקומות. נ"ב בפרק אין עומדין דף ל"ג גבי הבדלה פריך תלמודא נמי הכי וצריך לומר ג"כ כמ"ש התוספות הכא: (ג) ד"ה אלא וכו' וכן לקמן. נ"ב סוף דף כ"ה: (ד) בא"ד ורבינו יהודה פירש. נ"ב עיין בספר נחלת צבי סימן ו' ס"ה תמצא באור לדברים אלו:

[ע' פירש"י לקמן כה: ד"ה מי המשרה]

משלי כא

נ"א מאי תקנתא להדר ולצלי

ב"ק פב.

תוספתא פ"ב ע"ש

[לעיל כח.]

מגילה כז:

[עי' תוס' ערכין טז. ד"ה סכור]

דְּמַר סָבַר. כָּל הַמַּפְסִיק בִּתְפִלָּתוֹ אִם שָׁהָה כְּדֵי לִגְמוֹר כּוּלָּהּ – חוֹזֵר לָרֹאשׁ. כִּדְאָמְרִינַן גַּבֵּי ק"ש לְקַמָּן בְּפִירְקִין (דף כד:), וּבְשָׁהָה קָא מִיפַּלְגִי הָכָא: הַאי אִם לֹא שָׁהָה מִיבָּעֵי לֵיהּ. בְּמִילְּתָא דְּרַב חִסְדָּא וְרַב הַמְנוּנָא מִיבָּעֵי לֵיהּ לְאִיפְלוּגֵי בֵּין שָׁהָה לְלֹא שָׁהָה, וּמִדְּלָא אִפְלִיג שְׁמַע מִינַּהּ: אֲפִילּוּ בִּדְלָא שָׁהָה קָאָמַר: גַּבְרָא דְּחוּיָא הוּא. כְּשֶׁהִתְחִיל לְהִתְפַּלֵּל וְהָיָה צָרִיךְ לִנְקָבָיו דָּחוּי הוּא מִלְּהִתְפַּלֵּל, הִלְכָּךְ מַה שֶּׁהִתְפַּלֵּל אֵינָהּ תְּפִלָּה – וְחוֹזֵר לָרֹאשׁ: וּמַר סָבַר גַּבְרָא חֲזְיָא. אַע"פ שֶׁאֵינוֹ יָכוֹל לְהַמְתִּין עַד שֶׁיְּסַיֵּים תְּפִלָּתוֹ – תְּפִלָּה רְאוּיָה הִיא מַה שֶּׁהִתְפַּלֵּל קוֹדֶם שְׁתִיָּתָהּ: וְעַד כַּמָּה. יָכוֹל לְהַעֲמִיד עַצְמוֹ מִנְּקָבָיו שֶׁיְּהֵא מוּתָּר לְהַתְחִיל בִּתְפִלָּה: אִיכָּא דְּמַתְנֵי. לְהָאִי, 'בַּמֶּה דְּבָרִים אֲמוּרִים' בְּמַתְנִיתָא גּוּפָא, וְלָא מִשְּׁמַעְתָּא דְּרַב זְבִיד וְרַב יְהוּדָה. וְכִי קָיְירֵי אִינְהוּ – בְּשִׁיעוּרָא הוּא דְּקָיְירֵי: שְׁמוֹר עַצְמְךָ שֶׁלֹּא תֶּחֱטָא. וְתִצְטָרֵךְ רַגְלְךָ לָלֶכֶת אֶל בֵּית הָאֱלֹהִים לְהָבִיא חַטָּאת: הֱוֵי קָרוֹב לִשְׁמוֹעַ. תְּשׁוּבָה בַּהֲבָאַת קָרְבָּנְךָ, מִתֵּת אוֹתוֹ כַּכְּסִילִים בְּלֹא תְּשׁוּבָה: שְׁמוֹר נְקָבֶיךָ. מִבֵּין רַגְלֶיךָ, כְּמוֹ "לְהָסֵךְ אֶת רַגְלָיו", (שמואל א כד) שְׁמוֹר נְקָבֶיךָ שֶׁלֹּא יָפִיחוּ: בֵּית הַכִּסֵּא קָבוּעַ. שֶׁיֵּשׁ בּוֹ צוֹאָה, וְכָל בָּתֵּי כִסְאוֹת שֶׁבַּגְּמָרָא עַל פְּנֵי הַשָּׂדֶה הֵם, בְּלֹא חֲפִירָה: עֲרַאי. שֶׁזֶּה מַתְחִיל עַכְשָׁיו לַעֲשׂוֹתוֹ בֵּית הַכִּסֵּא: חוֹלֵץ וְנִפְנֶה לְאַלְתַּר. וְיֹאחֵז תְּפִילִּין בְּיָדוֹ, כִּדְאָמְרִינַן לְקַמָּן. וּבְקָבוּעַ נַמִּי אוֹחֲזָן בְּיָדוֹ, אֶלָּא שֶׁצָּרִיךְ לְחָלְצָן בְּרִחוּק ד' אַמּוֹת, שֶׁבִּזְמַן שֶׁהֵם בְּרֹאשׁוֹ הֵם בְּגָלוּי וּגְנַאי הַדָּבָר: מַהוּ שֶׁיִּכָּנֵס בִּתְפִילָּיו. כְּשֶׁהֵן בְּרֹאשׁוֹ קָאָמַר: שֶׁמָּא יִפְנֶה בָּהֶן. גְּדוֹלִים: בַּחוֹרִים הַסְּמוּכִים לְבֵית הַכִּסֵּא. לִפְנִים מִן הַגָּדֵר בְּשָׂדֶה שֶׁהוּא נִפְנֶה בָּהּ, נוֹתְנָן בַּחוֹרִים שֶׁבַּכּוֹתֶל: בַּחוֹרִים הַסְּמוּכִים לִרְשׁוּת הָרַבִּים. חוֹרֵי כּוֹתְלֵי מְחִיצוֹת הַשָּׂדֶה, שֶׁאֵין עַכְבָּרִים מְצוּיִין בִּמְקוֹם הִילּוּךְ בְּנֵי אָדָם, וְהוּא יִכָּנֵס לַאֲחוֹרֵי הַגָּדֵר לִפְנוֹת: גּוֹלְלָן. בִּרְצוּעוֹת שֶׁלָּהֶן: שֶׁלֹּא תֵּצֵא רְצוּעָה. שֶׁיֵּשׁ בָּהּ קְדוּשָּׁה שֶׁהֲרֵי בָּהֶן הוּא קוֹשְׁרָן, וּבַקֶּשֶׁר נִרְאֶה בַּעֲשִׂיָּיתוֹ כְּמִין דָּלֶ"ת עַל שֵׁם אַחַת מֵאוֹתִיּוֹת שֶׁל שַׁדַּי, וְהַשִּׁי"ן עֲשׂוּיָה בְּכוֹתְלֵי הַקְּצִיצָה הַחִיצוֹנָה, וְהַיּוּ"ד עֲשׂוּיָה בְּרֹאשׁ רְצוּעַת תְּפִילִּין שֶׁל יָד, וּרְצוּעָה קְטַנָּה מְאֹד כָּפוּף רֹאשָׁהּ וְנִרְאֵית כְּמִין יוּ"ד: וְאוֹחֲזָן בִּימִינוֹ. שֶׁלֹּא בְּבִגְדוֹ, כְּדֵי שֶׁלֹּא יִפְּלוּ: בַּיּוֹם. כְּשֶׁהוּא חוֹלְצָן בִּשְׁבִיל בֵּית הַכִּסֵּא גּוֹלְלָן כְּמִין סֵפֶר כִּדְאָמְרַן: וּבַלַּיְלָה. כְּשֶׁהוּא חוֹלְצָן בְּבֵיתוֹ עַל מְנָת לְהַצְנִיעַ עַד הַבֹּקֶר: עוֹשֶׂה לָהֶם כִּיס טֶפַח. דְּהַלָּלוּ טֶפַח, דְּחָשִׁיב הַכְּלִי אֹהֶל לְהַפְסִיק בֵּינָם לַקַּרְקַע: לֹא שָׁנוּ. דְּבָעֵי טֶפַח אֶלָּא בִּכְלִי שֶׁהוּא כְּלְיָין. כִּיס הֶעָשׂוּי לְצָרְכָּן; דִּכְלְיָין קָרוֹב לִהְיוֹת בָּטֵל אֶצְלָם, הִילְכָּךְ בָּעִינַן דָּבָר הַנִּיכָּר שֶׁיְּהֵא חוֹצֵץ בִּפְנֵיהֶם: שֶׁהֲרֵי פַּכִּין קְטַנִּים מַצִּילִין. בְּהֶיקֵּף צָמִיד פָּתִיל בְּאֹהֶל הַמֵּת, וְאַף עַל גַּב דְּלָא הָווּ טֶפַח – חָיְילִי: אָמַר הוֹאִיל וְשָׁרוּנְהוּ רַבָּנָן. לְאוֹחֲזָן בְּיָדוֹ מִשּׁוּם שְׁמִירָתָן: נִנְטְרָן

תורה אור

מָר סָבַר: *אִם שָׁהָה כְּדֵי לִגְמוֹר אֶת כּוּלָּהּ – חוֹזֵר לָרֹאשׁ; וּמָר סָבַר: לְמָקוֹם שֶׁפָּסַק. אֲמַר רַב אַשִׁי: הַאי "אִם שָׁהָה"? 'אִם לֹא שָׁהָה' מִיבָּעֵי לֵיהּ! – *אֶלָּא, [א]דְּכוּלֵּי עָלְמָא אִם שָׁהָה כְּדֵי לִגְמוֹר אֶת כּוּלָּהּ – חוֹזֵר לָרֹאשׁ, *וְהָתָם בִּדְלָא שָׁהָה קָמִיפַּלְגִי; דְּמָר סָבַר: גַּבְרָא דְּחוּיָא הוּא, וְאֵין רָאוּי, וְאֵין תְּפִלָּתוֹ תְּפִלָּה; וּמָר סָבַר: גַּבְרָא חֲזְיָא הוּא, וּתְפִלָּתוֹ תְּפִלָּה. § תָּנוּ רַבָּנַן: [ב]הַנִּצְרָךְ לִנְקָבָיו – אַל יִתְפַּלֵּל, וְאִם הִתְפַּלֵּל – תְּפִלָּתוֹ תּוֹעֵבָה. אָמַר רַב זְבִיד וְאִיתֵּימָא רַב יְהוּדָה: לֹא שָׁנוּ אֶלָּא שֶׁאֵינוֹ יָכוֹל לִשְׁהוֹת בְּעַצְמוֹ, אֲבָל אִם יָכוֹל לִשְׁהוֹת בְּעַצְמוֹ – תְּפִלָּתוֹ תְּפִלָּה. וְעַד כַּמָּה? –אָמַר רַב שֵׁשֶׁת: [ג]עַד פַּרְסָה. אִיכָּא דְּמַתְנֵי לָהּ אַמַּתְנִיתָא: בַּמֶּה דְּבָרִים אֲמוּרִים – כְּשֶׁאֵין יָכוֹל לַעֲמוֹד עַל עַצְמוֹ, אֲבָל אִם יָכוֹל לַעֲמוֹד עַל עַצְמוֹ – תְּפִלָּתוֹ תְּפִלָּה. וְעַד כַּמָּה? אָמַר רַב זְבִיד: (א) *עַד פַּרְסָה. אָמַר רַבִּי שְׁמוּאֵל בַּר נַחְמָנִי אָמַר רַבִּי יוֹנָתָן: *[ד]הַנִּצְרָךְ לִנְקָבָיו הֲרֵי זֶה לֹא יִתְפַּלֵּל, מִשּׁוּם שֶׁנֶּאֱמַר: °"הִכּוֹן לִקְרַאת אֱלֹהֶיךָ יִשְׂרָאֵל". וְאָמַר רַבִּי שְׁמוּאֵל בַּר נַחְמָנִי אָמַר רַבִּי יוֹנָתָן: מ"ד °"שְׁמוֹר רַגְלְךָ כַּאֲשֶׁר תֵּלֵךְ אֶל בֵּית הָאֱלֹהִים" שְׁמוֹר עַצְמְךָ שֶׁלֹּא תֶּחֱטָא, וְאִם תֶּחֱטָא – הָבֵא קָרְבָּן לְפָנַי. "וְקָרוֹב לִשְׁמֹעַ *(דִּבְרֵי חֲכָמִים)", אָמַר רָבָא: הֱוֵי קָרוֹב לִשְׁמוֹעַ דִּבְרֵי חֲכָמִים שֶׁאִם חוֹטְאִים מְבִיאִים קָרְבָּן וְעוֹשִׂים תְּשׁוּבָה; "מִתֵּת הַכְּסִילִים [זָבַח]" – אַל תְּהִי כַּכְּסִילִים שֶׁחוֹטְאִים וּמְבִיאִים קָרְבָּן וְאֵין עוֹשִׂים תְּשׁוּבָה; "כִּי אֵינָם יוֹדְעִים לַעֲשׂוֹת רָע", אִי הָכִי, צַדִּיקִים נִינְהוּ! אֶלָּא, אַל תְּהִי כַּכְּסִילִים שֶׁחוֹטְאִים וּמְבִיאִים קָרְבָּן, וְאֵינָם יוֹדְעִים אִם עַל הַטּוֹבָה הֵם מְבִיאִים אִם עַל הָרָעָה הֵם מְבִיאִים; אָמַר הקב"ה: בֵּין טוֹב לְרַע אֵינָן מַבְחִינִים, וְהֵם מְבִיאִים קָרְבָּן לְפָנַי?! רַב אַשִׁי וְאִיתֵּימָא רַב חֲנִינָא בַּר פַּפָּא אָמַר: שְׁמוֹר נְקָבֶיךָ בְּשָׁעָה שֶׁאַתָּה עוֹמֵד בִּתְפִלָּה לְפָנַי. § תָּנוּ רַבָּנַן: *[ה]הַנִּכְנָס לְבֵית הַכִּסֵּא – חוֹלֵץ תְּפִילָּיו בְּרִחוּק ד' אַמּוֹת, וְנִכְנָס. אָמַר רַב אַחָא בַּר רַב הוּנָא אָמַר רַב שֵׁשֶׁת: לֹא שָׁנוּ אֶלָּא בֵּית הַכִּסֵּא קָבוּעַ, אֲבָל בֵּית הַכִּסֵּא עֲרַאי – חוֹלֵץ וְנִפְנֶה לְאַלְתַּר. [ו]וּכְשֶׁהוּא יוֹצֵא – מַרְחִיק ד' אַמּוֹת וּמַנִּיחָן, מִפְּנֵי שֶׁעֲשָׂאוֹ בֵּית הַכִּסֵּא קָבוּעַ. אִיבַּעְיָא לְהוּ: מַהוּ שֶׁיִּכָּנֵס אָדָם בִּתְפִילִּין לְבֵית הַכִּסֵּא קָבוּעַ לְהַשְׁתִּין מַיִם? רָבִינָא שָׁרֵי, רַב אַדָּא בַּר מַתְנָא [ז]אָסַר. אָתוּ שַׁיְילוּהּ לְרָבָא, אֲמַר לְהוּ: אָסוּר, חָיְישִׁינַן שֶׁמָּא יִפָּנֶה בָּהֶן; וְאָמְרִי לָהּ: שֶׁמָּא יָפִיחַ בָּהֶן. תַּנְיָא אִידָךְ: הַנִּכְנָס לְבֵית הַכִּסֵּא קָבוּעַ – חוֹלֵץ תְּפִילָּיו בְּרִחוּק ד' אַמּוֹת, וּמַנִּיחָן בַּחַלּוֹן הַסָּמוּךְ לִרְשׁוּת הָרַבִּים וְנִכְנָס, וּכְשֶׁהוּא יוֹצֵא – מַרְחִיק ד' אַמּוֹת וּמַנִּיחָן, דִּבְרֵי בֵּית שַׁמַּאי. וּבֵית הִלֵּל אוֹמְרִים: אוֹחֲזָן בְּיָדוֹ וְנִכְנָס; ר"ע אוֹמֵר: אוֹחֲזָן בְּבִגְדוֹ וְנִכְנָס. בְּבִגְדוֹ ס"ד?! זִימְנִין מִישְׁתְּלֵי לְהוּ וְנָפְלֵי! אֶלָּא אֵימָא: אוֹחֲזָן בְּבִגְדוֹ וּבְיָדוֹ וְנִכְנָס, וּמַנִּיחָם בַּחוֹרִין הַסְּמוּכִים לְבֵית הַכִּסֵּא; [ח] וְלֹא יַנִּיחֵם בַּחוֹרִין הַסְּמוּכִים לִרְשׁוּת הָרַבִּים, שֶׁמָּא יִטְּלוּ אוֹתָם עוֹבְרֵי דְּרָכִים וְיָבֹא לִידֵי חֲשָׁד. וּמַעֲשֶׂה בְּתַלְמִיד אֶחָד שֶׁהִנִּיחַ תְּפִילָּיו בַּחוֹרִין הַסְּמוּכִים לִרְשׁוּת הָרַבִּים, וּבָאת זוֹנָה אַחַת וּנְטָלָתַן, וּבָאת לְבֵית הַמִּדְרָשׁ וְאָמְרָה: רְאוּ מַה נָּתַן לִי פְּלוֹנִי בִּשְׂכָרִי! כֵּיוָן שֶׁשָּׁמַע אוֹתוֹ תַּלְמִיד כָּךְ, עָלָה לְרֹאשׁ הַגַּג וְנָפַל וּמֵת. בְּאוֹתָהּ שָׁעָה הִתְקִינוּ [ח]שֶׁיְּהֵא אוֹחֲזָן בְּבִגְדוֹ וּבְיָדוֹ וְנִכְנָס. § תָּנוּ רַבָּנַן: בָּרִאשׁוֹנָה הָיוּ מַנִּיחִין תְּפִילִּין בַּחוֹרִין הַסְּמוּכִין לְבֵית הַכִּסֵּא, וּבָאִין עַכְבָּרִים וְנוֹטְלִין אוֹתָן. הִתְקִינוּ שֶׁיְּהוּ מַנִּיחִין אוֹתָן בַּחַלּוֹנוֹת הַסְּמוּכוֹת לִרְשׁוּת הָרַבִּים, וּבָאִין עוֹבְרֵי דְּרָכִים וְנוֹטְלִין אוֹתָן; הִתְקִינוּ שֶׁיְּהֵא אוֹחֲזָן בְּיָדוֹ וְנִכְנָס. אָמַר רַבִּי מְיָאשָׁא *בְּרֵיהּ דריב"ל: הֲלָכָה, [ט]גּוֹלְלָן כְּמִין סֵפֶר וְאוֹחֲזָן בִּימִינוֹ כְּנֶגֶד לִבּוֹ. אָמַר רַב יוֹסֵף בַּר מַנְיוּמֵי אָמַר רַב נַחְמָן: וּבִלְבַד [י]שֶׁלֹּא תְּהֵא רְצוּעָה יוֹצֵאת מִתַּחַת יָדוֹ טֶפַח. אָמַר רַבִּי יַעֲקֹב בַּר אַחָא אָמַר רַבִּי זֵירָא: [כ]לֹא שָׁנוּ אֶלָּא שֶׁיֵּשׁ שָׁהוּת בַּיּוֹם לְלָבְשָׁן, אֲבָל אֵין שָׁהוּת בַּיּוֹם לְלָבְשָׁן – עוֹשֶׂה לָהֶן כְּמִין כִּיס טֶפַח, וּמַנִּיחָן. *אָמַר רַבָּה בַּר בַּר חָנָה אָמַר רַבִּי יוֹחָנָן: בַּיּוֹם – גּוֹלְלָן כְּמִין סֵפֶר וּמַנִּיחָן בְּיָדוֹ כְּנֶגֶד לִבּוֹ, וּבַלַּיְלָה – עוֹשֶׂה לָהֶן כְּמִין כִּיס טֶפַח, וּמַנִּיחָן. אָמַר אַבָּיֵי: [ל]לֹא שָׁנוּ אֶלָּא בִּכְלִי שֶׁהוּא כְּלְיָין, אֲבָל בִּכְלִי שֶׁאֵינוֹ כְּלְיָין – אֲפִילּוּ פָּחוֹת מִטֶּפַח. אָמַר מָר זוּטְרָא וְאִיתֵּימָא רַב אַשִׁי: תֵּדַע, שֶׁהֲרֵי פַּכִּין קְטַנִּים מַצִּילִין בְּאֹהֶל הַמֵּת. וְאָמַר רַבָּה בַּר בַּר חָנָה: כִּי הֲוָה אָזְלִינַן בָּתְרֵיהּ דְּרַבִּי יוֹחָנָן, כִּי הֲוָה בָּעֵי לְמֵיעַל לְבֵית הַכִּסֵּא, כִּי הֲוָה נָקֵיט סִפְרָא דְּאַגַּדְתָּא – הֲוָה יָהֵיב לָן, כִּי הֲוָה נָקֵיט תְּפִילִּין – לָא הֲוָה יָהֵיב לָן, אָמַר: הוֹאִיל וְשָׁרוּנְהוּ רַבָּנַן – נִינְטְרָן

חיישינן שמא יפנה בהן ואסור. ודוקא בבית הכסא קבוע חיישינן שמא יפנה בהן, אבל בבית הכסא עראי שאין רגילים לפנות שם – מותר להשתין בהן, ולא חיישינן שמא יפנה בהן. והא דתניא לקמן "לא ישתין בהן אפילו בבית הכסא עראי" – היינו דוקא כשאוחזן בידו, דחיישינן שמא ישפשף בהן הניצוצות אם יפלו מים על רגליו, או יגע באמה:

שהרי פכין קטנים מצילין באהל המת. ועל כרחך מטעם אויר הוא, דאי לית בהו אויר כלל לא היו מצילין, דהוי כמו אוכלין שגבלן בטיט, °שמקבלין טומאה באהל המת:

דבריס

נח א מיי' פ"ד מהל' תפלה הלכה יג סמג עשין יט טוש"ע או"ח סימן קד סעיף ה:
נט ב ג מיי' שם הל' י' סמג שם טוש"ע או"ח סימן צב סעיף א:
ס ד מיי' וסמג שם טוש"ע שם סעיף א ג:
סא ה ו מיי' פ"ד מהל' תפילין הלכה יז סמג עשין כב טוש"ע או"ח סימן מג סעיף ה [רב אלפס כאן ובהל' תפילין דף עה]:
סב ז מיי' וסמג שם טוש"ע שם סעיף א:
[ח מיי' שם]:
סג ח ט י מיי' וסמג שם טור שו"ע שם סעיף ה':
סד כ ל מיי' שם הלכה יט סמג שם טוש"ע שם סעיף ו:

ואיתימא רב יהודה עד פרסה כצ"ל רש"ל

רב נסים גאון

פכין קטנים מצילין באהל המת. עיקרה בסיפרי (פרשת חקת) וכל כלי פתוח בכלי חרש הכתוב מדבר מה ת"ל פתוח ואפילו כל שהוא (והואיל והוא) [הוא] טמא באהל המת לפיכך אם יהיה מוקף בצמיד פתיל מציל על מה שבתוכו כדמפרש התם נמי וכל כלי פתוח מיכן אמרו כלים מצילין בצמיד פתיל באהל המת ואמרו עוד טמא הוא אין ת"ל הוא אלא הוא שיציל על עצמו ובשבת בפ' אמר רבי עקיבא (דף פד) ובבבא קמא בפ' כיצד הרגל מועדת (דף כה) גרסי' תניא מפץ במת מנין ודין הוא ומה פכין קטנים שטהורין בזב טמאין במת:

[בר בריה כצ"ל וכ"ה בשאלתות פ' בא וכן איתא לקמן כד:]

הגהות הב"ח

(א) גמ' איכא דמתני לה במתניתא וכו' אמר רב זביד אמר רב יהודה עד פרסה:

גליון הש"ס

תום' ד"ה שהרי וכו' שמקבלין טומאה באהל המת. כדאיתא זבחים דף ג ע"א:

[לקמן כד: ר"ה לד:]

[ג"ל כב: תוס' ד"ה אלא]

תוספתא פ"ב

[טעות הדפוס וע' הגוהת בעין יעקב]

שבת סב.

[עי' דרכה בכ"ח נ"ל קודם אחא ר' יעקב בר אחא רש"ל]

עמוס ד | קהלת ד

סה א מיי' פ"ה מהל' תפלה הלכה ה סמג עשין יט טור שו"ע או"ח סימן צז סעיף א:
סו ב מיי' פ"ד מהלכות תפילין הלכה יח סמג עשין כב טור ושו"ע או"ח סימן מג סעיף א:
סז ג מיי' שם הל' טו סמג שם טוש"ע א"ח סימן מד:
סח ד מיי' פ"ה מהלכו' תפלה הלכה ה סמג עשין יט טוש"ע או"ח סימן צז סעיף א:
סט ה מיי' פ"ה מהל' דעות ה"ו טור שו"ע או"ח סימן ג סעיף ד:
ע ו מיי' פ"ד מהלכות דעות הלכה ב:
עא ז ח מיי' פ"ד מהל' תפילין הלכה טז סמג עשין כב טוש"ע או"ח סימן מ סעיף א:
עב ט מיי' שם הל' ט סמג שם טוש"ע או"ח סי' מב סעיף ג:
עג י כ מיי' שם הל' כד סמג שם טוש"ע או"ח סי' מ סעיף ג:

דברים שהתרתי לך כאן כו'. ולא בעי לשנויי דברים שהתרתי לך בבית הכסא עראי אסרתי לך בקבוע – דאסור לפנות בגדולים והתפילין בראשו, אבל להשתין מותר, משום דלא אשכחן בברייתא, אבל הך דטפח וטפחיים – אשכחן ליה בברייתא בהדיא. הר"ר יוסף: והא

נִנְטְרָן. אָמַר רָבָא: כִּי הֲוָה אָזְלִינַן בָּתְרֵיהּ דר"נ כִּי הֲוָה נָקֵיט סִפְרָא דְּאַגַּדְתָּא – יָהֵיב לָן, כִּי הֲוָה נָקֵיט תְּפִילִּין – לָא יָהֵיב לָן, אָמַר: הוֹאִיל וְשָׁרוּנְהוּ רַבָּנַן – נִינְטְרַן.§ ת"ר: *אלֹא יֹאחַז אָדָם תְּפִילִּין בְּיָדוֹ וס"ת בִּזְרוֹעוֹ וְיִתְפַּלֵּל, בוְלֹא יַשְׁתִּין בָּהֶן מַיִם, *גוְלֹא יִישַׁן בָּהֶן לֹא שֵׁינַת קֶבַע וְלֹא שֵׁינַת עֲרַאי. אָמַר שְׁמוּאֵל: דסַכִּין, וּמָעוֹת, וּקְעָרָה, וְכִכָּר, הֲרֵי אֵלּוּ כַּיּוֹצֵא בָּהֶן. אָמַר רָבָא אָמַר רַב שֵׁשֶׁת: לֵית הִלְכְתָא כִּי הָא מַתְנִיתָא – דב"ש הִיא. דְּאִי ב"ה – הַשְׁתָּא בֵּית הַכִּסֵּא קָבוּעַ שָׁרֵי, בֵּית הַכִּסֵּא עֲרַאי מִיבַּעְיָא?! מֵיתִיבִי: "דְּבָרִים שֶׁהִתַּרְתִּי לְךָ כָּאן, אָסַרְתִּי לְךָ כָּאן", מַאי לָאו תְּפִילִּין? אִי אָמְרַתְּ בִּשְׁלָמָא בֵּית הִלֵּל – "הִתַּרְתִּי לְךָ כָּאן" – קָבוּעַ, "אָסַרְתִּי לְךָ כָּאן" – בֵּית הַכִּסֵּא עֲרַאי; אֶלָּא אִי אָמְרַתְּ ב"ש – הָא לָא שָׁרוּ וְלָא מִידֵי! –כִּי תַּנְיָא הַהִיא לְעִנְיַן טֶפַח וְטִפְחַיִים. דְּתָנֵי חֲדָא: כְּשֶׁהוּא נִפְנֶה – מְגַלֶּה לַאֲחוֹרָיו טֶפַח וּלְפָנָיו טְפָחַיִים. וְתַנְיָא אִידָךְ: לַאֲחוֹרָיו טֶפַח, וּלְפָנָיו וְלֹא כְלוּם! מַאי לָאו אִידֵי וְאִידֵי בְּאִישׁ, וְלָא קַשְׁיָא: כָּאן לִגְדוֹלִים, כָּאן לִקְטַנִּים. – וְתִסְבְּרָא?! אִי בִּקְטַנִּים לַאֲחוֹרָיו טֶפַח לָמָּה לִי! אֶלָּא, אִידֵי וְאִידֵי בִּגְדוֹלִים, וְלָא קַשְׁיָא: ההָא בְּאִישׁ, הָא בְּאִשָּׁה. –אִי הָכִי, הָא דְּקָתָנֵי עֲלַהּ: *"זֶהוּ ק"ו שֶׁאֵין עָלָיו תְּשׁוּבָה", מַאי "אֵין עָלָיו תְּשׁוּבָה"? דַּרְכָּא דְּמִלְּתָא הָכִי אִיתָא! אֶלָּא לָאו – תְּפִילִּין, וּתְיוּבְתָּא דְּרָבָא אָמַר רַב שֵׁשֶׁת, תְּיוּבְתָּא. מִכׇּל מָקוֹם קַשְׁיָא: הַשְׁתָּא בֵּית הַכִּסֵּא קָבוּעַ שָׁרֵי, בֵּית הַכִּסֵּא עֲרַאי לֹא כׇּל שֶׁכֵּן?! –הָכִי קָאָמַר: בֵּית הַכִּסֵּא קָבוּעַ דְּלֵיכָּא נִיצוֹצוֹת – שָׁרֵי, בֵּית הַכִּסֵּא עֲרַאי דְּאִיכָּא נִיצוֹצוֹת – אָסְרִי. אִי הָכִי, אַמַּאי 'אֵין עָלָיו תְּשׁוּבָה'? תְּשׁוּבָה מְעַלַּיְתָא הִיא! –הָכִי קָאָמַר: הָא מִלְּתָא תֵּיתֵי לַהּ בְּתוֹרַת טַעְמָא וְלָא תֵּיתֵי לַהּ בְּק"ו, דְּאִי אָתְיָא לַהּ בְּתוֹרַת ק"ו – זֶהוּ ק"ו שֶׁאֵין עָלָיו תְּשׁוּבָה.§ *ת"ר: והָרוֹצֶה לִיכָּנֵס לִסְעוּדַּת קֶבַע – מְהַלֵּךְ עֲשָׂרָה פְּעָמִים ד' אַמּוֹת, אוֹ ד' פְּעָמִים י' אַמּוֹת, וְיִפָּנֶה, ואח"כ נִכְנָס. אָמַר ר' יִצְחָק: הַנִּכְנָס לִסְעוּדַּת קֶבַע – חוֹלֵץ תְּפִילָּיו ואח"כ נִכְנָס. וּפְלִיגָא דר' חִיָּיא, דא"ר חִיָּיא: זמַנִּיחָן עַל שֻׁלְחָנוֹ, וְכֵן הָדוּר לוֹ. וְעַד אֵימַת? אָמַר רַב נַחְמָן בַּר יִצְחָק: חעַד זְמַן בְּרָכָה.§ תָּנֵי חֲדָא: צוֹרֵר אָדָם תְּפִילָּיו עִם מְעוֹתָיו בְּאַפַּרְקָסוּתוֹ, וְתַנְיָא אִידָךְ: לֹא יָצוּר! לָא קַשְׁיָא: הָא – דְּאַזְמְנֵיהּ, הָא – דְּלָא אַזְמְנֵיהּ; *דְּאָמַר רַב חִסְדָּא: טהַאי סוּדָרָא דִּתְפִילִּין דְּאַזְמְנֵיהּ לְמֵיצַר בֵּיהּ תְּפִילִּין, צַר בֵּיהּ תְּפִילִּין – אָסוּר לְמֵיצַר בֵּיהּ פְּשִׁיטֵי, אַזְמְנֵיהּ וְלָא צַר בֵּיהּ, צַר בֵּיהּ וְלָא אַזְמְנֵיהּ – שָׁרֵי לְמֵיצַר בֵּיהּ זוּזֵי. וּלְאַבַּיֵי, דְּאָמַר *הַזְמָנָה מִילְּתָא הִיא, אַזְמְנֵיהּ אע"ג דְּלָא צַר בֵּיהּ; צַר בֵּיהּ, אִי אַזְמְנֵיהּ – אָסִיר, אִי לָא אַזְמְנֵיהּ – לָא.§ בְּעָא מִינֵּיהּ רַב יוֹסֵף בְּרֵיהּ דְּרַב נְחוּנְיָא מֵרַב יְהוּדָה: מַהוּ שֶׁיַּנִּיחַ אָדָם תְּפִילָּיו תַּחַת מְרַאֲשׁוֹתָיו? יתַּחַת מַרְגְּלוֹתָיו לָא קָא מִיבַּעְיָא לִי – שֶׁנּוֹהֵג בָּהֶן מִנְהַג בִּזָּיוֹן, כִּי קָא מִיבַּעְיָא לִי – תַּחַת מְרַאֲשׁוֹתָיו, מַאי? –א"ל, הָכִי אָמַר שְׁמוּאֵל: כמוּתָּר, אֲפִילּוּ אִשְׁתּוֹ עִמּוֹ. מֵיתִיבִי: לֹא יַנִּיחַ אָדָם תְּפִילָּיו תַּחַת מַרְגְּלוֹתָיו מִפְּנֵי שֶׁנּוֹהֵג בָּהֶם דֶּרֶךְ בִּזָּיוֹן, אֲבָל מַנִּיחָן תַּחַת מְרַאֲשׁוֹתָיו; וְאִם הָיְתָה אִשְׁתּוֹ עִמּוֹ – אָסוּר; הָיָה מָקוֹם שֶׁגָּבוֹהַּ ג' טְפָחִים אוֹ נָמוּךְ ג' טְפָחִים – מוּתָּר. תְּיוּבְתָּא דִּשְׁמוּאֵל! תְּיוּבְתָּא. אָמַר רָבָא: אע"ג דְּתַנְיָא תְּיוּבְתָּא דִּשְׁמוּאֵל – הִלְכְתָא כְּוָותֵיהּ. מ"ט?

כָּל

נִנְטְרָן. יִשְׁמְרוּנִי. אַכְנִיס עִמִּי וְיִשְׁמְרוּנִי מִן הַמַּזִּיקִין: לֹא יֶאֱחוֹז בְּיָדוֹ וְכוּ' וְיִתְפַּלֵּל. שֶׁאֵין דַּעְתּוֹ מְיוּשֶּׁבֶת עָלָיו בַּתְּפִלָּה, שֶׁהֲרֵי לִבּוֹ תָּמִיד עֲלֵיהֶן שֶׁלֹּא יִפְּלוּ מִיָּדוֹ: וְלֹא יִישַׁן בָּהֶן. שֶׁמָּא [א] יָפִיחַ: הֲרֵי אֵלּוּ כַּיּוֹצֵא בָּהֶן. לְעִנְיַן תְּפִלָּה, שֶׁדּוֹאֵג עֲלֵיהֶן שֶׁלֹּא תִּפּוֹל הַסַּכִּין וְתַזִּיקֶנּוּ, וְהַקְּעָרָה תִּשָּׁפֵךְ, וְהַמָּעוֹת יֹאבְדוּ, וְהַכִּכָּר יִטָּנֵף: לֵית הִלְכְתָא כִּי הָא מַתְנִיתָא. דְּקָתָנֵי "לֹא יַשְׁתִּין בִּתְפִילִּין": דְּבֵית שַׁמַּאי הִיא. דְּאָמְרִי לְעֵיל "מַנִּיחָן בַּחַלּוֹן הַסָּמוּךְ לָר"ה וְלֹא יַכְנִיס בְּיָדוֹ וְיִכָּנֵס": דְּאִי ב"ה. הָא אָמְרִי לְעֵיל "אוֹחֲזָן בְּיָדוֹ וְנִכְנָס": בֵּית הַכִּסֵּא עֲרַאי. כְּגוֹן לְהַשְׁתִּין" שֶׁאֵין אָדָם הוֹלֵךְ בִּשְׁבִילָם לְבֵית הַכִּסֵּא. וְהַפַּעַם הַזֹּאת נַעֲשֶׂה הַמָּקוֹם הַזֶּה בֵּית הַכִּסֵּא תְּחִלָּה: שֶׁהִתַּרְתִּי לְךָ כָּאן. בְּבֵית הַכִּסֵּא קָבוּעַ: אָסַרְתִּי לְךָ כָּאן. בְּבֵית הַכִּסֵּא עֲרַאי: מַאי לָאו תְּפִילִּין. שֶׁאָמְרוּ בֵּית הִלֵּל "אוֹחֲזָן בְּיָדוֹ וְנִכְנָס לְבֵית הַכִּסֵּא קָבוּעַ", וּלְהַשְׁתִּין בָּהֶם אָסְרוּ, כִּדְמְפָרֵשׁ טַעְמָא לְקַמָּן: הָא לָא שָׁרוּ. בְּבֵית הַכִּסֵּא קָבוּעַ: כִּי תַּנְיָא הַהִיא. לָאו לְעִנְיַן תְּפִילִּין תַּנְיָא, אֶלָּא לְעִנְיַן גִּלּוּי טֶפַח וְטִפְחַיִים. דִּלִגְדוֹלִים אֵינוֹ מְגַלֶּה אֶלָּא טֶפַח, וְלִקְטַנִּים מְגַלֶּה טְפָחַיִים. וַעֲלַהּ קָאֵי, גִּלּוּי טְפָחַיִים שֶׁהִתַּרְתִּי לְךָ כָּאן – אָסַרְתִּי לְךָ כָּאן: לַאֲחוֹרָיו טֶפַח. וְלֹא יוֹתֵר, מִשּׁוּם צְנִיעוּת: וּלְפָנָיו טְפָחַיִים. מִשּׁוּם קִילּוּחַ מֵי רַגְלַיִם הַנִּתָּזִין לְמֵרָחוֹק: מַאי לָאו כו'. וְהַיְינוּ דְּקָאָמַר לְעֵיל: דְּבָרִים שֶׁהִתַּרְתִּי לְךָ בְּבֵית הַכִּסֵּא עֲרַאי, אָסַרְתִּי לְךָ בְּקָבוּעַ: אֶלָּא אִידֵי וְאִידֵי בִּגְדוֹלִים. וּמִתּוֹךְ שֶׁהוּא דּוֹחֵק עַצְמוֹ לִגְדוֹלִים הוּא בָּא לִידֵי קְטַנִּים. הִלְכָּךְ: בְּאִישׁ מִלַּאֲחוֹרָיו טֶפַח, וּמִלְּפָנָיו טְפָחַיִים; וּבְאִשָּׁה מִלְּפָנֶיהָ וְלֹא כְלוּם. וְהָכִי קָאָמַר: הָא דִּלְעֵיל דְּבָרִים שֶׁאָסַרְתִּי לְךָ בְּאִשָּׁה, הִתַּרְתִּי לְךָ בְּאִישׁ: אִי הָכִי. דִּלְעִנְיַן טֶפַח וְטִפְחַיִים קָתָנֵי, דְּבָרִים שֶׁהִתַּרְתִּי לְךָ כָּאן אָסַרְתִּי לְךָ כָּאן: הָא דְּקָתָנֵי עֲלַהּ. בְּסֵיפָא דִּידַהּ, וְזֶה הוּא ק"ו שֶׁאֵין עָלָיו תְּשׁוּבָה. כְּדָבָר הַזֶּה יֵשׁ לְךָ לַהֲשִׁיבֵנִי ק"ו, וְאֵין לִי עָלָיו תְּשׁוּבָה לְהַחֲזִיר לְךָ. אִי אָמְרַתְּ בִּשְׁלָמָא בִּתְפִילִּין קָאָמַר, וּכְדְאָמְרַן, וּב"ה הִיא – הַיְינוּ דְּקָתָנֵי דְּיֵשׁ כָּאן לְהַקְשׁוֹת קַל וָחוֹמֶר: הַשְׁתָּא בֵּית הַכִּסֵּא קָבוּעַ שָׁרֵי – בֵּית הַכִּסֵּא עֲרַאי מִיבַּעְיָא! וְאֵין לִי תְּשׁוּבָה לַהֲשִׁיבְךָ עָלָיו. אֶלָּא אִי אָמְרַתְּ לְעִנְיַן טֶפַח וְטִפְחַיִים, מַאי ק"ו יֵשׁ לְהַקְשׁוֹת כָּאן: אוֹרְחָא דְּמִילְּתָא הָכִי הֲוָה. שֶׁהָאִישׁ צָרִיךְ לְגַלּוֹת לְפָנָיו וְלֹא הָאִשָּׁה: תְּיוּבְתָּא דְּרָבָא אָמַר רַב שֵׁשֶׁת. דְּאָמַר בֵּית שַׁמַּאי הִיא וְלֹא בֵּית הִלֵּל, דְּאִם כֵּן לֹא מַשְׁכַּחַת מִידֵי לְאוֹקְמַהּ הַךְ בָּרַיְיתָא דְּקָתָנֵי "מַאי שֶׁהִתַּרְתִּי לְךָ כָּאן אָסַרְתִּי לְךָ כָּאן": דְּלֵיכָּא נִיצוֹצוֹת. שֶׁיְּהֵא צָרִיךְ לְשַׁפְשֵׁף בִּימִינוֹ מֵעַל רַגְלָיו: בֵּית הַכִּסֵּא עֲרַאי. לִקְטַנִּים: דְּאִיכָּא נִיצוֹצוֹת. הַנִּיתָּזִין עַל גַּבֵּי רַגְלָיו. וְאָמְרִינַן בְּמַסֶּכֶת יוֹמָא (דף ל.): מִצְוָה לְשַׁפְשְׁפָן, שֶׁאָסוּר לְאָדָם שֶׁיֵּלֵךְ בְּנִיצוֹצוֹת שֶׁעַל גַּבֵּי רַגְלָיו, שֶׁמָּא יֵרָאֶה כִּכְרוּת שָׁפְכָה וְנִמְצָא מוֹצִיא לַעַז עַל בָּנָיו שֶׁהֵם מַמְזֵרִים. הִילְכָּךְ, אִי אֶפְשָׁר לֶאֱחוֹז תְּפִילִּין בְּיָדוֹ: הָא מִילְּתָא. דִּתְפִילִּין דְּבֵית הַכִּסֵּא עֲרַאי וְקָבוּעַ: תֵּיתֵי לַהּ בְּתוֹרַת טַעְמָא. לְהַתִּיר בְּבֵית הַכִּסֵּא קָבוּעַ אֶת הָאָסוּר בְּבֵית הַכִּסֵּא עֲרַאי מִשּׁוּם טַעְמָא דְּנִיצוֹצוֹת: דְּאִי אַתְיָא לַהּ בְּתוֹרַת ק"ו. לוֹמַר: דִּין הוּא לְהָקֵל בְּבֵית הַכִּסֵּא עֲרַאי קַל וּלְהַחֲמִיר בְּבֵית הַכִּסֵּא[א] חָמוּר וְלֹא תֵּזִיל בָּתַר טַעְמָא אֶלָּא בָּתַר חוּמְרָא וְקוּלָּא, וַאֲנַן עָבְדִינַן אִיפְּכָא – אֵין לִי עָלָיו מַה לַּהֲשִׁיבְךָ, שֶׁאֵין לִי לוֹמַר שֶׁיְּהֵא בְּשׁוּם מָקוֹם בֵּית הַכִּסֵּא עֲרַאי חָמוּר מִן הַקָּבוּעַ, שֶׁאוּכַל לַהֲשִׁיבְךָ: אִם הִתַּרְתִּי בְּקָבוּעַ שֶׁהוּא קַל בְּדָבָר פְּלוֹנִי – נַתִּיר בְּשֶׁל עֲרַאי שֶׁהוּא חָמוּר בּוֹ. אֲבָל טַעְמָא אִיכָּא לְמַאי דְּעָבְדִינַן, דְּהָכָא אִיכָּא נִיצוֹצוֹת וְהָכָא לֵיכָּא. וְדָבָר זֶה לָאו קַל וָחוֹמֶר, לֹא קַל וְלֹא חָמוּר: הַנִּכְנָס לִסְעוּדַּת קֶבַע. וּגְנַאי הוּא שֶׁיִּצְטָרֵךְ לִנְקָבָיו בְּתוֹךְ הַסְּעוּדָּה: מְהַלֵּךְ עֲשָׂרָה פְּעָמִים כו'. וּבְכׇל פַּעַם וּפַעַם בּוֹדֵק עַצְמוֹ וְיוֹשֵׁב אוּלַי יוּכַל לְהִפָּנוֹת שֶׁהַהִילּוּךְ מוֹרִיד הַגְּדוֹלִים לַנֶּקֶב: חוֹלֵץ תְּפִילָּיו. שֶׁמָּא יִשְׁתַּכֵּר בַּסְּעוּדָּה וְיִתְגַּנֶּה בִּתְפִילָּיו: וְכֵן הָדוּר לוֹ. שֶׁיְּהוּ מְזוּמָּנִים לוֹ, וְיַחֲזוֹר וְיַנִּיחֵם בִּשְׁעַת בְּרָכָה: בְּאַפַּרְקְסוּתֵיהּ. סוּדָר שֶׁל רֹאשׁוֹ: עִם מְעוֹתָיו. לֹא עִם הַמָּעוֹת מַמָּשׁ, אֶלָּא שְׁנֵי קְשָׁרִים זֶה אֵצֶל זֶה: ה"ג: הָא דְּאַזְמְנֵיהּ הָא דְּלָא אַזְמְנֵיהּ. לְהַאי סוּדָר לִתְפִילִּין, דְּכֵיוָן דְּאַזְמְנֵיהּ – שׁוּב אָסוּר לָצוּר בּוֹ מָעוֹת, מֵאַחַר שֶׁהִקְצוּ לְכָךְ: צַר בֵּיהּ. אִי אַזְמְנֵיהּ – אִין, אִי לָא אַזְמְנֵיהּ – לָא קָדֵישׁ וּשְׁרֵי לְמֵיצַר בֵּיהּ. דְּהָכִי תַּנְיָא בְּהֶדְיָא בְּסַנְהֶדְרִין (מח.): הִנִּיחַ בּוֹ תְּפִילָּיו יָנִיחַ בּוֹ מָעוֹת: וּלְאַבַּיֵי דְּאָמַר הַזְמָנָה מִילְּתָא הִיא. גַּבֵּי אוֹרֵג בֶּגֶד לַמֵּת, בְּסַנְהֶדְרִין בְּפֶרֶק "נִגְמַר הַדִּין" (ד' מז:): מַהוּ שֶׁיַּנִּיחַ תְּפִילָּיו תַּחַת מְרַאֲשׁוֹתָיו. בַּלַּיְלָה כְּשֶׁהוּא יָשֵׁן: אִם הָיָה מָקוֹם גָּבוֹהַּ ג' טְפָחִים. לְמַעְלָה מֵרַאֲשׁוֹתָיו, וְעָלָיו נוֹתֵן הַתְּפִילִּין אוֹ לְמַטָּה מֵרַאֲשׁוֹתָיו יוֹצֵא מָקוֹם מִן הַמִּטָּה:

כָּל

סוכה מא:

[שם כו.]

[ב"מ לה.]

שבת פב.

סנהדרין מח.

[שם מז: מח. מגילה כ מנחות לד:]

רב נסים גאון

ולאביי דאמר הזמנה מילתא היא. עיקר דבריו של אביי במס' סנהדרין בפ' נגמר הדין (דף מז) איתמר האורג בגד למת אביי אמר אסור ורבא אמר מותר אביי אמר אסור הזמנה מילתא היא:

הגהות הב"ח

(א) רש"י ד"ה דאי אתיא וכו' בבית הכסא קבוע חמור:

גליון הש"ס

רש"י ד"ה ולא יישן בהן שמא יפיח. עיין סוכה ד' כו ע"א ול"ע:

הגהות הגר"א

[א] רש"י ד"ה ולא ייש בהן שמא יפיח. כצ"ל:

כָּל לִנְטוּרִינְהוּ טְפֵי עָדִיף.(א) וְהֵיכָא מַנַּח לְהוּ? – אָמַר ר' יִרְמְיָה: אבֵּין כַּר לְכֶסֶת שֶׁלֹּא כְּנֶגֶד רֹאשׁוֹ. וְהָא תָּנֵי רַבִּי חִיָּיא: מַנִּיחָן בְּכוֹבַע תַּחַת מְרַאֲשׁוֹתָיו! דְּמַפֵּיק לֵיהּ לְמוֹרְשָׁא דְּכוֹבַע לְבַר. *בַּר קַפָּרָא צַיֵּיר לְהוּ בְּכִילְתָא וּמַפֵּיק לְמוֹרְשְׁהוֹן לְבַר. רַב שֵׁישָׁא בְּרֵיהּ דְּרַב אִידִי במַנַּח לְהוּ אַשַּׁרְשִׁיפָא וּפָרֵים סוּדָרָא עִילָּוַיְיהוּ. אָמַר רַב הַמְנוּנָא בְּרֵיהּ דְּרַב יוֹסֵף: זִימְנָא חֲדָא הֲוָה קָאֵימְנָא קַמֵּיהּ דְּרָבָא וַאֲמַר לִי: זִיל אַיְיתִי לִי תְּפִילִּין. וְאַשְׁכַּחְתִּינְהוּ בֵּין כַּר לְכֶסֶת שֶׁלֹּא כְּנֶגֶד רֹאשׁוֹ, וַהֲוָה יָדַעְנָא [ב]דְּיוֹם טְבִילָה הֲוָה, וּלְאַגְמוֹרַן *הֲלָכָה לְמַעֲשֶׂה הוּא דַּעֲבַד.§ בָּעֵי מִינֵּיהּ רַב יוֹסֵף בְּרֵיהּ דְּרַב נְחוּנְיָא מֵרַב יְהוּדָה: שְׁנַיִם שֶׁיְּשֵׁנִים בְּמִטָּה אַחַת, מַהוּ שֶׁזֶּה יַחֲזִיר פָּנָיו וְיִקְרָא ק"ש, וְזֶה יַחֲזִיר פָּנָיו וְיִקְרָא ק"ש? א"ל הָכִי אָמַר שְׁמוּאֵל: וַאֲפִילּוּ אִשְׁתּוֹ עִמּוֹ. מַתְקִיף לָהּ רַב יוֹסֵף: אִשְׁתּוֹ וְלֹא מִבָּעְיָא אַחֵר?! גאַדְּרַבָּה! *אִשְׁתּוֹ כְּגוּפוֹ, דאַחֵר לָאו כְּגוּפוֹ! מֵיתִיבִי: שְׁנַיִם שֶׁיְּשֵׁנִים בְּמִטָּה אַחַת – זֶה מַחֲזִיר פָּנָיו וְקוֹרֵא, וְזֶה מַחֲזִיר פָּנָיו וְקוֹרֵא; וְתַנְיָא אַחֲרִיתִי: הַיָּשֵׁן בְּמִטָּה וּבָנָיו וּבְנֵי בֵיתוֹ בְּצִדּוֹ – הֲרֵי זֶה לֹא יִקְרָא ק"ש אא"כ הָיְתָה טַלִּית מַפְסֶקֶת בֵּינֵיהֶן. וְאִם הָיוּ בָּנָיו וּבְנֵי בֵיתוֹ קְטַנִּים – מוּתָּר. בִּשְׁלָמָא לְרַב יוֹסֵף לָא קַשְׁיָא: הָא – בְּאִשְׁתּוֹ, הָא – בְּאַחֵר. אֶלָּא לִשְׁמוּאֵל קַשְׁיָא! –אָמַר לָךְ שְׁמוּאֵל: לְרַב יוֹסֵף מִי נִיחָא?! וְהַתַּנְיָא: הָיָה יָשֵׁן בְּמִטָּה,(ג) וּבָנָיו וּבְנֵי בֵיתוֹ בְּמִטָּה – לֹא יִקְרָא ק"ש אא"כ הָיְתָה טַלִּיתוֹ מַפְסֶקֶת בֵּינֵיהֶן! אֶלָּא מַאי אִית לָךְ לְמֵימַר – אִשְׁתּוֹ לְרַב יוֹסֵף תַּנָּאֵי הִיא, לְדִידִי נַמִי תַּנָּאֵי הִיא.§ אָמַר מָר: "זֶה מַחֲזִיר פָּנָיו וְקוֹרֵא ק"ש". וְהָא אִיכָּא עַגָּבוֹת! מְסַיַּיע לֵיהּ לְרַב הוּנָא, דא"ר הוּנָא: עַגָּבוֹת אֵין בָּהֶם מִשּׁוּם עֶרְוָה. לֵימָא מְסַיַּיע לֵיהּ לְרַב הוּנָא: *ההָאִשָּׁה יוֹשֶׁבֶת וְקוֹצָה לָהּ חַלָּתָהּ עֲרוּמָּה מִפְּנֵי שֶׁיְּכוֹלָה לְכַסּוֹת פָּנֶיהָ בְּקַרְקַע, אֲבָל לֹא הָאִישׁ. תַּרְגְּמָהּ רַב נַחְמָן בַּר יִצְחָק: וכְּגוֹן שֶׁהָיוּ פָּנֶיהָ טוּחוֹת בְּקַרְקַע.§ אָמַר מָר: ז"אִם הָיוּ בָּנָיו וּבְנֵי בֵיתוֹ קְטַנִּים – מוּתָּר." וְעַד כַּמָּה? –אָמַר רַב חִסְדָּא: תִּינוֹקֶת בַּת שָׁלֹשׁ שָׁנִים וְיוֹם אֶחָד, וְתִינוֹק בֶּן ט' שָׁנִים וְיוֹם אֶחָד. אִיכָּא דְּאָמְרִי: חתִּינוֹקֶת בַּת י"א שָׁנָה וְיוֹם אֶחָד, וְתִינוֹק בֶּן שְׁתֵּים עֶשְׂרֵה שָׁנָה וְיוֹם אֶחָד, *אִידִי וְאִידִי עַד כְּדֵי °"שָׁדַיִם נָכֹנוּ וּשְׂעָרֵךְ צִמֵּחַ". אָמַר לֵיהּ רַב כָּהֲנָא לְרַב אַשִׁי: הָתָם אָמַר רָבָא "אע"ג דִּתְיוּבְתָּא דִּשְׁמוּאֵל הִלְכְתָא כְּוָותֵיהּ דִּשְׁמוּאֵל", הָכָא מַאי? –אָמַר לֵיהּ: *אַטּוּ כּוּלְּהוּ בְּחָדָא מַחְתָּא מַחְתִּינְהוּ?! אֶלָּא: הֵיכָא דְּאִיתְּמַר אִיתְּמַר, וְהֵיכָא דְּלָא אִיתְּמַר לָא אִיתְּמַר. א"ל רַב מָרִי לְרַב פָּפָּא: שֵׂעָר יוֹצֵא בְּבִגְדוֹ מַהוּ? קְרָא עֲלֵיהּ: שֵׂעָר, שֵׂעָר.§ א"ר יִצְחָק: טֶפַח בְּאִשָּׁה עֶרְוָה. לְמַאי? אִילֵימָא לְאִסְתַּכּוֹלֵי בָּהּ – וְהָא *א"ר שֵׁשֶׁת: לָמָּה מָנָה הַכָּתוּב תַּכְשִׁיטִין שֶׁבַּחוּץ עִם תַּכְשִׁיטִין שֶׁבִּפְנִים – לוֹמַר לָךְ: טכָּל הַמִּסְתַּכֵּל בְּאֶצְבַּע קְטַנָּה שֶׁל אִשָּׁה כְּאִילּוּ מִסְתַּכֵּל בִּמְקוֹם הַתּוֹרֶף! יאֶלָּא: בְּאִשְׁתּוֹ, וּלְק"ש. אָמַר רַב חִסְדָּא: שׁוֹק בְּאִשָּׁה עֶרְוָה, שֶׁנֶּאֱמַר: °"גַּלִּי שׁוֹק עִבְרִי נְהָרוֹת", וּכְתִיב °"תִּגָּל עֶרְוָתֵךְ וְגַם תֵּרָאֶה חֶרְפָּתֵךְ". *אָמַר שְׁמוּאֵל: כקוֹל בְּאִשָּׁה עֶרְוָה, שֶׁנֶּא' °"כִּי קוֹלֵךְ עָרֵב וּמַרְאֵךְ נָאוֶה". אָמַר רַב שֵׁשֶׁת: לשֵׂעָר בְּאִשָּׁה עֶרְוָה, שֶׁנֶּא' °"שַׂעְרֵךְ כְּעֵדֶר הָעִזִּים".§ אָמַר ר' חֲנִינָא: אֲנִי רָאִיתִי אֶת רַבִּי שֶׁתָּלָה תְּפִלָּיו. מֵיתִיבִי: מהַתּוֹלֶה תְּפִלָּיו יִתָּלוּ לוֹ חַיָּיו. *דּוֹרְשֵׁי חֲמוּרוֹת אָמְרוּ °"וְהָיוּ חַיֶּיךָ תְּלֻאִים לְךָ מִנֶּגֶד" זֶה הַתּוֹלֶה תְּפִלָּיו! –לָא קַשְׁיָא, הָא – בִּרְצוּעָה, הָא – בִּקְצִיצָה. וְאִיבָּעֵית אֵימָא: לֹא שְׁנָא רְצוּעָה וְלֹא שְׁנָא קְצִיצָה – אָסוּר, וְכִי תָּלֵה רַבִּי – נבְּכִיסְתָּא תָּלֵה. אִי הָכִי, מַאי לְמֵימְרָא? – מַהוּ דְּתֵימָא: תִּיבָּעֵי הֲנָחָה כְּסֵפֶר תּוֹרָה, קמ"ל.§ וְאָמַר ר' חֲנִינָא: אֲנִי רָאִיתִי אֶת רַבִּי סשֶׁגִּיהֵק וּפִיהֵק, וְנִתְעַטֵּשׁ, וְרָק וּמְמַשְׁמֵשׁ

תורה אור

יחזקאל טז | ישעיה מז | שם | שיר ב | שם ד | דברים כח

רש"י

כָּל לְנָטוּרִינְהוּ טְפֵי עָדִיף. לְהוּ מִבִּזְיוֹנֵי, (ג)כַּמָּה שֶׁהוּא מוּזְהָר עַל שְׁמִירָתָן מִן הָעַכְבָּרִים וּמִן הַגַּנָּבִים טְפֵי עָדִיף לְהוּ מִבִּזְיוֹנֵי: בְּכוֹבַע. הוּא הַכִּיס שֶׁלָּהֶם: לְמוֹרְשָׁא דְכוֹבַע. שֶׁהַתְּפִילִּין נִכָּרִין בִּבְלִיטָתָן בִּקְצֵה הַכִּיס, וְהוּא כְּמוֹרָשָׁא: צַיֵּיר לְהוּ בְּכִילְתָא. בִּירִיעָה הַפְּרוּסָה סְבִיבוֹת מִטָּתוֹ קוֹשְׁרָן: וּמַפֵּיק לְמוֹרְשְׁהוֹן לְבַר. בְּלִיטַת הַקֶּשֶׁר שֶׁהַתְּפִילִּין בּוֹלְטִין מִן הַיְרִיעָה הָיָה הוֹפֵךְ לְצַד הַחוּץ, וְלֹא לְצַד הַמִּטָּה: אַשַּׁרְשִׁיפָא. סַפְסָל: יוֹם טְבִילָה הֲוָה. יוֹם שֶׁטָּבְלָה אִשְׁתּוֹ, דַּהֲוָה לֵיהּ לֵיל תַּשְׁמִישׁ. וְהַיְינוּ כִּשְׁמוּאֵל דְּאָמַר אֲפִילּוּ אִשְׁתּוֹ עִמּוֹ: וּלְאַגְמוֹרַן הֲלָכָה לְמַעֲשֶׂה. מַה שֶּׁשִּׁנָּה לַהֲבִיאָם לוֹ לֹא עָשָׂה אֶלָּא לְלַמְּדֵנִי הֲלָכָה לַעֲשׂוֹת מַעֲשֶׂה כִּשְׁמוּאֵל: וַאֲפִילּוּ אִשְׁתּוֹ עִמּוֹ. (ד)שֶׁיַּחֲזִיר פָּנָיו. דְּכָל זְמַן שֶׁהֵן פּוֹנִים פָּנִים כְּנֶגֶד פָּנִים, פְּשִׁיטָא לֵיהּ דְּאָסוּר, דְּאִיכָּא הִרְהוּר נְגִיעַת עֶרְוָה עַל יְדֵי אֵבְרֵי תַּשְׁמִישׁ: אִשְׁתּוֹ כְּגוּפוֹ. וְרָגִיל בָּהּ, וְלֵיכָּא הִרְהוּר כּוּלֵּי הַאי: בִּשְׁלָמָא לְרַב יוֹסֵף. דְּאָמַר אִשְׁתּוֹ הִיא דִּשְׁרְיָא, אֲבָל אַחֵר – לֹא, מְתָרֵץ לְהוּ לְמַתְנִיתָא הָא בְּאִשְׁתּוֹ, הָא בְּאַחֵר. וְהָא דְּקָתָנֵי בְּנֵי בֵיתוֹ – אֵינוֹ אִשְׁתּוֹ: הָיָה יָשֵׁן בְּמִטָּה וּבְנֵי בֵיתוֹ. וְאִשְׁתּוֹ בִּכְלָל בֵּיתוֹ: לְדִידִי נַמִי. בֵּין אִשְׁתּוֹ בֵּין אַחֵר, פְּלוּגְתָּא דְּהָנֵי תַּנָּאֵי הִיא: הָא אִיכָּא עַגָּבוֹת. דְּנָגְעֵי אַהֲדָדֵי: וְקוֹצָה חַלָּתָהּ עֲרוּמָּה. וְאַף עַל פִּי שֶׁעָרוֹם אָסוּר לְבָרֵךְ, אִשָּׁה יוֹשֶׁבֶת מוּתֶּרֶת, שֶׁבִּישִׁיבָתָהּ פָּנֶיהָ שֶׁלְּמַטָּה מְכוּסִּים בְּקַרְקַע: אֲבָל לֹא הָאִישׁ. מִפְּנֵי שֶׁהַבֵּיצִים וְהַגִּיד בּוֹלְטִין וְנִרְאִין. וְאַף עַל פִּי שֶׁמְּגוּלּוֹת עַגְבוֹתֶי' – וְהַיְינוּ סִיַּיעְתָּא: כְּגוֹן שֶׁהָיוּ פָּנֶיהָ טוּחוֹת. דְּבוּקוֹת וּמְכוּסּוֹת בְּקַרְקַע. טוּחוֹת מַשְׁמַע לְשׁוֹן שְׁעִיעוּת, טִיחַ חָלָק שֶׁאֵינוֹ בּוֹלֵט, אפלטיירש"א בלע"ז: בַּת שָׁלֹשׁ וּבֶן תֵּשַׁע. שֶׁהוּא זְמַן שֶׁהֵן בָּאִין לִכְלַל בִּיאָה: בַּת י"א וּבֶן י"ב. זְמַן שֶׁהֵן בָּאוֹת לִכְלַל שְׂעָרוֹת וּשְׁדֵיהֶן נְכוֹנִים, שֶׁמִּשָּׁם וָאֵילָךְ בָּאוֹת לִכְלַל [בִּיאָה] שֶׁאָדָם מִתְאַוֶּה לָהֶן: הָתָם אָמַר רָבָא. גַּבֵּי תְּפִילִּין תַּחַת מְרַאֲשׁוֹתָיו דְּקָאָמַר שְׁמוּאֵל אֲפִי' אִשְׁתּוֹ עִמּוֹ, הֲלָכָה כִּשְׁמוּאֵל: הָכָא. גַּבֵּי שְׁנַיִם שֶׁהֵם יְשֵׁנִים, דְּקָא שָׁרֵי שְׁמוּאֵל בְּאִשְׁתּוֹ עִמּוֹ, מַאי: מַחְתָּא מַחְתִּינְהוּ. בַּאֲרִיגָה אַחַת *אֲרַגְתָּם: יָצָא שְׂעָרוֹ בְּבִגְדוֹ. שֶׁנִּקַּב בִּגְדוֹ כְּנֶגֶד זְקַן הַתַּחְתּוֹן, וְיָצָא מִן הַשֵּׂעָר בַּנֶּקֶב, מַהוּ? מִי הָוֵי עֶרְוָה לִקְרוֹת ק"ש כְּנֶגְדּוֹ אוֹ לֹא: שֵׂעָר שֵׂעָר. כְּלוֹמַר: מַה בְּכָךְ: לְאִסְתַּכּוֹלֵי בָּהּ. אִם אֵשֶׁת אִישׁ הִיא: תַּכְשִׁיטִין שֶׁבִּפְנִים. כּוּמָז דְּפוּס שֶׁל בֵּית הָרֶחֶם שֶׁהָיוּ עוֹשִׂין לִבְנוֹתֵיהֶן, וְנוֹקְבִין כָּתְלֵי בֵּית הָרֶחֶם כְּדֶרֶךְ שֶׁנּוֹקְבִין אֶת הָאָזְנַיִם וְתוֹחֲבִין אוֹתוֹ, כְּדֵי שֶׁלֹּא יִזְדַּקְּקוּ לָהֶן זְכָרִים: עִם תַּכְשִׁיטִין שֶׁבַּחוּץ. אֶצְעָדָה וְצָמִיד; הֵן הֱבִיאוּ אוֹתָן עַל כַּפָּרַת הִרְהוּר עֲבֵירָה שֶׁנִּסְתַּכְּלוּ בִּבְנוֹת מִדְיָן: לְאִשְׁתּוֹ וּלְק"ש. אִם טֶפַח מְגוּלֶּה בָּהּ – לֹא יִקְרָא ק"ש כְּנֶגְדָּהּ: שׁוֹק. *בְּאֵשֶׁת אִישׁ: עֶרְוָה. לְהִסְתַּכֵּל, וְכֵן בְּאִשְׁתּוֹ לְק"ש: גַּלִּי שׁוֹק. וּכְתִיב בָּתְרֵיהּ תִּגָּל עֶרְוָתֵךְ: קוֹלֵךְ עָרֵב. מִדְּמִשְׁתַּבַּח לָהּ קְרָא בְּגַוֵּיהּ – שְׁמַע מִינָּהּ תַּאֲוָה הִיא: הַתּוֹלֶה תְּפִילָּיו. בְּיָתֵד, יִתָּלוּ חַיָּיו: דּוֹרְשֵׁי רְשׁוּמוֹת. קְשָׁרִים וּסְתוּמִים הַכְּלוּלִים בַּתּוֹרָה. דּוֹרְשֵׁי חֲמוּרוֹת גָּרְסִינַן, וְהִיא הִיא: זֶה הַתּוֹלֶה תְּפִילָּיו. שֶׁהַתּוֹרָה חַיָּיו שֶׁל אָדָם (ה)וְרָמַז לְךָ הַכָּתוּב שֶׁיִּתָּלוּ חַיָּיו: בִּרְצוּעָה. וְהַקְּצִיצָה לְמַטָּה, גְּנַאי הוּא לָהֶם. אֲבָל תּוֹלֶה הוּא אוֹתָם בַּקְּצִיצָה, וּתְהֵא הַקְּצִיצָה מוּנַּחַת עַל הַיָּתֵד וְהָרְצוּעָה לְמַטָּה: בְּכִיסְתָּא תָּלֵה. בְּתוֹךְ תִּיקָן הָיוּ, וְתָלָה הַתִּיק: שֶׁגִּיהֵק. ריט"ייר בלע"ז, פְּעָמִים שֶׁאָדָם מוֹצִיא מִגּוּפוֹ לְפִיו נְפִיחָה מִתּוֹךְ שָׂבְעוֹ וְרֵיחָהּ כְּרֵיחַ הַמַּאֲכָל שֶׁאָכַל: פִּיהֵק. באליי"ר בלע"ז, חִיךְ מַלְקוֹחָיו פּוֹתֵחַ לְהוֹצִיא רוּחַ הַפֶּה מָלֵא, כְּאָדָם שֶׁרוֹצֶה לִישׁוֹן אוֹ שֶׁעָמַד מִשֵּׁינָה: וְנִתְעַטֵּשׁ. סטרנוד"ר בלע"ז. וְיֵשׁ שֶׁדּוֹרְשִׁים גִּיהֵק נוֹטָרִיקוֹן גֵּו הֵקִיס סטריליי"ר פִּיהֵק – פִּיו הֵקִיס: וְרָק. ע"ג קַרְקַע: וּמְמַשְׁמֵשׁ

תוספות

והא תני רבי חייא מניחן בכובע תחת מראשותיו. ואם תאמר: אימא בכובע שלא כנגד ראשו, שהרי בברייתא דלעיל נמי תני "תחת מראשותיו" ולא פריך מיניה, משום דמצינן לפרושי שלא כנגד ראשו! ואומר(ו) הרב: דא"כ מאי איריא בכובע? אפילו שלא בכובע נמי. אלא ש"מ דמיירי אפילו כנגד ראשו! ומ"מ קשיא לישני דמיירי באשתו עמו, דבעיא כלי בתוך כלי! וצ"ע:

שנים שהיו ישנים במטה. וא"ת: והלא רואה ערות עצמו! וי"ל: שיוציא ראשו לחוץ. וא"ת: והרי לבו רואה את הערוה! וי"ל: דקסבר לבו רואה את הערוה מותר, אי נמי: חולץ בגדו כנגד לבו:

והתניא היה ישן במטה ובני ביתו וכו'. פי' רש"י: אשתו בכלל ביתו. ולא נהירא, חדא: דלא אשכחן אשתו °דמקריא בני ביתו. ועוד, לפירושו הו"ל והא קתני כאן, כיון דהברייתא דלעיל קאי, אבל מדקאמר "והתניא" משמע דברייתא אחרת היא! ואומר ה"ר יוסף דגרסינן "היה ישן במטה ואשתו ישנה בלדו – לא יחזיר פניו ויקרא אא"כ היתה טלית מפסקת בינו לבינה": וממשמש

עין משפט נר מצוה

עד א מיי' וסמג טוש"ע שם:

עה ב טוש"ע או"ח סימן רמ סעיף (ו) [א]:

עו ג מיי' פ"ג מהלכות ק"ש הלכה יח סמג עשין יח טוש"ע או"ח סימן עג סעיף ב:

עז ד מיי' שם טוש"ע שם סעיף א:

עח ה ו מיי' פ"א מהל' ברכות הלכה ט סמג עשין כז טור שו"ע או"ח סי' עד סעיף ד וכסי' רו סעיף ג' [ובי"ד סי' שכח סעיף א]:

עט ז מיי' פ"ג מהלכות ק"ש הלכה יח סמג עשין יח טור שו"ע או"ח סימן עג סעיף ג:

פ ח מיי' שם הל' יט טוש"ע שם סעיף ד:

פא ט מיי' פכ"א מהל' איס"ב הל' ב סמג לאוין קכו טוש"ע אה"ע סי' כא סעיף א:

פב י מיי' פ"ג מהל' ק"ש הל' טז סמג עשין יח טוש"ע או"ח סי' עה סעיף א:

פג כ [מיי' פכ"א מהל' איס"ב הלכה ב טוש"ע] שם סעי' ג טוש"ע אה"ע סי' כא סעי' א:

פד ל [מיי' שם] טוש"ע או"ח סי' עה סעיף ב וטוש"ע אה"ע שם:

פה מ נ מיי' פ"ד מהל' תפילין הל' ט סמג עשין כב טוש"ע או"ח סי' מ סעיף א:

פו ס מיי' פ"ד מהלכות תפלה הל' יא סמג עשין יט טוש"ע א"ח סי' לז סעיף א:

מסורת הש"ס

בשאלתות פ' בא איתא רב פפא

[שבת נג. ביצה כט: ב"ב קל: ע"ג עד. סנהדרין יח.]

[כתובות סו. מנחות לג: בכורות לה:]

חלה פ"ב משנה ג

[קדושין פא:]

[חולין נח: פירש"י ביתר ביאור ע"ש]

שבת סד:

[קדושין ע.]

[פסחים נז. חולין קלד:]

[ע' ב"ח בא"ח סי' ע"ה פי' על דברי רש"י הנ"ל]

[שבת קמח. פסחים מב. חולין נח:]

רב נסים גאון

מסייעא ליה לרב הונא דאמר רב הונא עגבות אין בהן משום ערוה. הא מילתא מיפרשא בפ' ב' דמס' חלה בגמ' דבני מערבא (הלכה א') הדא אמרה עגבות אין בהם משום ערוה הדא דאיתמר לברכה אבל להביט אפי' כל שהוא אסור להביט כהדה דתני המסתכל בעקיבה של אשה כמסתכל בבית הרחם והמסתכל בבית הרחם כאילו בא עליה: **והאמר** רב ששת למה מנה הכתוב תכשיטין שבחוץ עם תכשיטין שבפנים. מפרשי' לה במס' שבת בפ' במה אשה (ד' סד) ונקרב את קרבן ה' אמר ר' אלעזר עגיל זה דפוס של דדין כומז זה דפוס של בית הרחם אמר ליה רבא אטו מקרא לא שמעת מיניה כומז כאן מקום זמה והנה כבר הזכיר

הגהות הב"ח (א) גמרא טפי עדיף מבזיוני והיכא: (ב) שם היה ישן במטה ובני ביתו כצ"ל ותיבת ובניו נמחק: (ג) רש"י ד"ה כל לנטורינהו וכו' מבזיוני כיון שהוא: (ד) ד"ה ואפילו אשתו עמו והוא שיחזיר: (ה) ד"ה זה התולה תפילין שהתפילין חיים של אדם. נ"ב בפרק התכלת דף מ"ד ואמר ריש לקיש כל המניח תפילין מאריך ימים שנאמר אדני עליהם יחיו: (ו) תוס' ד"ה והא תני וכו' ואומר הרב רבינו יוסף לא"כ:

גליון הש"ס תוס' ד"ה והתניא כו' דלא אשכחן אשתו דמקריא בני ביתו. עי' פסחים דף נט ע"ב תוס' ד"ה ולא יפחתו. ועי' פר"ח או"ח בלקוטיו (סימן רל"ח):

ממשמש בבגדו, אבל לא היה מתעטף, *וכשהוא מפהק – היה מניח ידו על סנטרו. מיתיבי: המשמיע קולו בתפלתו – הרי זה מקטני אמנה, המגביה קולו בתפלתו – הרי זה מנביאי השקר, מגהק ומפהק – הרי זה מגסי הרוח. המתעטש בתפלתו – סימן רע לו, ויש אומרים:(א) ניכר שהוא מכוער. הרק בתפלתו – כאילו רק בפני המלך! –בשלמא מגהק ומפהק לא קשיא: כאן – לאונסו, כאן – לרצונו, אלא מתעטש אמתעטש קשיא! –מתעטש אמתעטש נמי לא קשיא: כאן – מלמעלה, כאן – מלמטה; דאמר רב זירא: הא מילתא *אבלעא לי בי רב המנונא, *ותקילא לי ככולי תלמודאי: המתעטש בתפלתו – סימן יפה לו, כשם שעושים לו נחת רוח מלמטה כך עושין לו נחת רוח מלמעלה. אלא רק ארק קשיא! –רק ארק נמי לא קשיא: אפשר כדרב יהודה; דאמר רב יהודה: היה עומד בתפילה ונזדמן לו רוק – מבליעו בטליתו, ואם טלית נאה הוא – מבליעו באפרקסותו. רבינא הוה קאי אחורי דרב אשי, נזדמן לו רוק, פתקיה לאחוריה. א"ל: לא סבר לה מר להא דרב יהודה "מבליעו באפרקסותו"?! –א"ל: אנא אנינא דעתאי. § המשמיע קולו בתפלתו הרי זה מקטני אמנה. § אמר רב הונא: לא שנו אלא שיכול לכוון את לבו בלחש, אבל אין יכול לכוון את לבו בלחש – מותר; וה"מ – ביחיד, אבל בציבור – אתי למיטרד ציבורא. § רבי אבא הוה קא משתמיט מיניה דרב יהודה, דהוה קא בעי למיסק לארעא דישראל, *דאמר רב יהודה: כל העולה מבבל לא"י עובר בעשה, שנאמר: °"בבלה יובאו ושמה יהיו עד יום פקדי אותם נאם ה'". אמר: איזיל ואשמע מיניה מילתא *מבית וועדא, והדר אפיק. אזל אשכחיה לתנא דקתני קמיה דרב יהודה: היה עומד בתפלה ונתעטש – ממתין עד שיכלה *הרוח וחוזר ומתפלל, איכא דאמרי: היה עומד בתפלה וביקש להתעטש – מרחיק לאחריו ד' אמות ומתעטש, וממתין עד שיכלה הרוח, וחוזר ומתפלל; ואומר: רבש"ע, יצרתנו נקבים נקבים חלולים חלולים, גלוי וידוע לפניך חרפתנו וכלימתנו בחיינו, ובאחריתנו רמה ותולעה; ומתחיל ממקום שפסק. [א] אמר ליה:(ב) *אילו לא באתי אלא לשמוע דבר זה – דיי. § ת"ר: היה ישן בטליתו ואינו יכול להוציא את ראשו מפני הצנה – חוצץ בטליתו על צוארו וקורא ק"ש. וי"א: על לבו. ותנא קמא – הרי לבו רואה את הערוה! קסבר: לבו רואה את הערוה מותר. § אמר רב הונא א"ר יוחנן: היה מהלך במבואות המטונפות – מניח ידו על פיו וקורא ק"ש. א"ל רב חסדא: האלהים! אם אמרה לי ר' יוחנן בפומיה – לא צייתנא ליה. איכא דאמרי, אמר רבה בר בר חנה אמר ריב"ל: היה מהלך במבואות המטונפות – מניח ידו על פיו וקורא ק"ש. א"ל ר' חסדא: האלהים! אם אמרה לי ריב"ל בפומיה – לא צייתנא ליה. ומי אמר ר' הונא הכי? והאמר רב הונא: ת"ח אסור לו לעמוד במקום הטנופת – לפי שאי אפשר לו לעמוד בלי הרהור תורה! – לא קשיא, כאן – בעומד, כאן – במהלך. ומי אמר רבי יוחנן הכי? והאמר *רבה בר בר חנה א"ר יוחנן: בכל מקום מותר להרהר בדברי תורה – חוץ מבית המרחץ ומבית הכסא! וכי תימא, הכא נמי, כאן בעומד כאן במהלך; איני?! והא *רבי אבהו הוה קא אזיל בתריה דרבי יוחנן, והוה קא קרי ק"ש, כי מטא במבואות המטונפות אשתיק. א"ל לר' יוחנן: להיכן אהדר? *א"ל: אם שהית כדי לגמור את כולה – חזור לראש! הכי קאמר ליה: לדידי – לא סבירא לי, לדידך דסבירא לך – אם שהית כדי לגמור את כולה חזור לראש. תניא כותיה דרב הונא, תניא כותיה דרב חסדא. תניא כותיה דרב הונא: המהלך במבואות המטונפות – מניח ידו על פיו ויקרא ק"ש. תניא כותיה דרב חסדא: *היה מהלך במבואות המטונפות – לא יקרא ק"ש; ולא עוד אלא שאם היה קורא ובא – פוסק. לא פסק מאי? – אמר ר' מיאשה בר בריה דריב"ל: עליו הכתוב אומר °"וגם אני נתתי להם חקים לא טובים ומשפטים לא יחיו [בהם]". ר' אסי אמר:(ג) °"הוי מושכי העון בחבלי השוא". רב אדא בר אהבה אמר מהכא: °"כי דבר ה' בזה". ואם פסק מה שכרו? אמר ר' אבהו עליו הכתוב אומר: °"ובדבר הזה תאריכו ימים". § אמר רב הונא: היתה טליתו חגורה לו על מתניו – מותר לקרות ק"ש. תניא נמי הכי: היתה טליתו, של בגד ושל עור ושל שק, חגורה על מתניו – מותר לקרות ק"ש; אבל

רש"י

וממשמש בבגדו. להעביר הכינה העוקצתו: אבל לא היה מתעטף. אם נפלה טליתו כשהוא מתפלל – לא היה נוטלה ומתעטף, שלא להפסיק: על סנטרו. מנטו"ן בלע"ז. שלא תראה פתיחת פיו: הרי זה מקטני אמנה. כאילו אין הקב"ה שומע תפלת לחש(ד) ומגביה הרבה: הרי זה מנביאי השקר. דכתיב ויקראו בקול גדול (מלכים א' י"ח): המגהק והמפהק הרי זה מגסי הרוח. וי"א: ניכר שהוא מכוער גרסינן: אלא עטוש אעטוש קשיא. דאין עטוש אלא לאונסו: למטה. מפיח בקול: ותקילא לי ככולי תלמודאי. שקולה עלי וחביבה, לפי שהיה רגיל להתעטש: כשם שעושים לו נחת רוח. שהעטוש נחת רוח לאדם: כך עושים לו נחת רוח מלמעלה. מן השמים, למלאות שאלתו: אפשר כדר' יהודה. להבליע באפרקסותו = סודר שבראשו, ושני ראשין תלויין בפניו: פתקיה. זרקו: מישתמיט מיניה. לא היה נראה אליו, לפי שהיה רבי אבא חפץ לעלות לא"י ורב יהודה אוסר לו, לפיכך לא היה נכנס לבית המדרש: ואשמע מיניה מילתא. מבחוץ: מבית וועדא. מבית המדרש: ונתעטש. מלמטה: עד שיכלה הרוח. מגופו, שנודף מאותו רוח: וחוזר לתפלה. למקום שפסק: ואומר. בתוך התפלה, דהא מופסקת ועומדת כבר על ידי הרוח, לפיכך יכול להפסיק נמי ולומר דבר זה באמצע: חוצץ בטליתו על צוארו. מה שיש מן הטלית ולמעלה מן כתפיו מדביק בצוארו, ובישן ערום קאמר: לדידי לא סבירא לי. לא הייתי מזקיקו להפסיק: בחבלי השוא. בחבלים שאינם חזקים, אלא נוחין להנתק הן מושכין העון על עצמם: אף זה. על ידי דבור בעלמא הוא נענש: ובדבר הזה. בשביל דבור זה שנזהרתם עליו, תאריכון ימים: היתה טליתו חגורה על מתניו. לכסותו ממתניו ולמטה, אע"פ שממתניו ולמעלה הוא ערום – קורא ק"ש: אבל

תוספות

וממשמש בבגדו. פרש"י: להעביר הכינה העוקצתו, אבל לא מתעטף אם נפלה טליתו, ותרי מילי נינהו. ור"ח פי' דחדא מילתא היא; פי' ממשמש בבגדו – תקן(ה) שלא יפול מעל ראשו, אבל אם נפל מעל ראשו – לא היה מתעטף, שהרי היא הפסקה אם מתעטף כיון שנפל לגמרי, אבל לתקן קצת שלא יפול – לא הוי הפסקה:

ואומר רבון העולמים. מיד באמצע תפלתו, ואח"כ מתחיל ממקום שפסק:

אמר ליה לדידי לא סבירא לי. פירוש: משום תרתי מילי, חדא: דסבירא דאינו חוזר לראש, דאמר רבי יוחנן (ר"ה דף ל"ד:): שמע תשע תקיעות בתשע שעות יצא. ועוד, דסבירא לי מניח ידו על פיו, ואם כן הוי ליה ראוי, אלא לדידך דסבירא לך דחייב להפסיק וכו':

בחבלי השוא. כלומר: בחנם מושכים עליהם עון, כי טוב היה שלא היו מקיימין אותו כלל:

*פסק רבינו חננאל כרב חסדא דאסור לקרות ק"ש אפילו צואה תחת בגדו על בשרו, וס"ל "כל עצמותי תאמרנה" (תהלים לה), דאע"ג דר' חסדא תלמיד דר' הונא הוה, לחומרא אזלינן. ורב אלפס פסק כרב הונא, מדאקשי גמרא מיניה ביומא פרק "הממונה" (ד' ל.): לית

עין משפט נר מצוה

פז א טוש"ע או"ח סי' צז סעיף ג:
פח ב טוש"ע שם סעי' ד:
פט ג [טור שו"ע שם ס"א]
ד [מיי' פ"ד מהל' תפלה הל' יא טוש"ע] שם סעיף א:
צ ה טוש"ע או"ח סי' קג סעיף ג:
צא ו ז מיי' פ"ד מהל' תפלה הלכה יא סמג עשין יט טור שו"ע או"ח סימן צז סעיף ב:
צב ח ט מיי' פ"ה שם הלכה ט סמג שם טוש"ע או"ח סימן קא סעיף ב:
צג י מיי' פ"ד שם הל' יא סמג שם טוש"ע או"ח סי' קג סעי' א:
צד כ מיי' שם הל' יב טוש"ע שם סעי' ב:
צה ל מיי' פ"ג מהלכות ק"ש הלכה יז סמג עשין יח טוש"ע או"ח סימן עד סעיף א:
צו מ ש"ע י"ד סי' רמו סעיף כו בהגה:
צז נ מיי' שם הלכה ד סמג שם טוש"ע א"ח סימן פה סעיף ב:
צח ס ע מיי' שם הלכה יד ופ"ב שם הל' יב טוש"ע או"ח סימן פה סעי' א וסי' סה סעי' א וסי' עח:
צט פ מיי' פ"ג שם הל' יז סמג שם טוש"ע א"ח סי' עד סעיף ו:

רב נסים גאון

הזכיר טבעת שהוא תכשיט שבחוץ עם כומז שהוא תכשיט שבפנים ובתר הכי הוזכרה שמעתא דרב ששת והתם היא עיקרה ולא הוזכרה בכאן אלא כדי להקשות ממנה:

הגהות הב"ח

(א) גמ' המגהק והמפהק וכו' ויש אומרים (ניכר שהוא מכוער) תא"מ ונ"ב ס"א שהוא עכרן: (ב) שם אמר אילו כצ"ל ותיבת ליה נמחק: (ג) שם ר' אסי אמר מהכא הוי מושכי: (ד) רש"י ד"ה הרי זה וכו' לחש הס"ד ואח"כ מ"ה המגביה הרבה הרי זה מנביאי: (ה) תום' ד"ה וממשמש וכו' תקן בגדו שלא יפול:

גליון הש"ס

תום' ד"ה פסק ר"ח וכו' דאע"ג דר"ח וכו'. עי' בב"מ (דף ל"ג ע"א):

מסורת הש"ס

תיבת וכשהוא מפהק ליתא מן הגמ' אלא מפירש"י נכתב בגמ' רש"א

ס"א איבעי לי

[מנחות יז.]

ירמיה כז

שבת מא. כתובות קי:

מבית וועדא ואתי ואזיל כצ"ל רש"א

[כ"ה ברא"ש אבל בטוש"ע איתא הריח]

[לעיל טז. שבת מא.]

שבת מ. קנ. קדושין לג. ע"ג מד: זבחים קב:

ר"ה לד:

[לעיל כג.]

תוספתא פ"ב

יחזקאל כ

ישעיה ה

במדבר טו

דברים לב

הגהות הגר"א

[א] גמרא (ומתחיל ממקום שפסק) תא"מ (וכ"מ בתוס' ורא"ש ותר"י דל"ג לה):

אֲבָל ^אלִתְפִלָּה – עַד שֶׁיְּכַסֶּה אֶת לִבּוֹ.§ וא"ר הוּנָא: ^בשָׁכַח וְנִכְנַס בִּתְפִילִּין לְבֵית הַכִּסֵּא – מַנִּיחַ יָדוֹ עֲלֵיהֶן עַד שֶׁיִּגְמוֹר. עַד שֶׁיִּגְמוֹר ס"ד?! –אֶלָּא כִּדְאָמַר ר"נ בַּר יִצְחָק: עַד שֶׁיִּגְמוֹר עַמּוּד רִאשׁוֹן. וְלִפְסוֹק לְאַלְתַּר וְלֵיקוּם! –מִשּׁוּם דרשב"ג; *דְּתַנְיָא, רשב"ג אוֹמֵר: עַמּוּד הַחוֹזֵר מֵבִיא אֶת הָאָדָם לִידֵי הִדְרוֹקָן. סִילוֹן הַחוֹזֵר – מֵבִיא אֶת הָאָדָם לִידֵי יֵרָקוֹן.§ *אִתְּמַר: צוֹאָה עַל בְּשָׂרוֹ, אוֹ יָדוֹ מוּנַּחַת בְּבֵית הַכִּסֵּא; רַב הוּנָא אָמַר: ^גמוּתָּר לִקְרוֹת ק"ש; רַב חִסְדָּא אָמַר: אָסוּר לִקְרוֹת ק"ש. אָמַר רָבָא: מ"ט דְּרַב הוּנָא – דִּכְתִיב °"כֹּל הַנְּשָׁמָה תְּהַלֵּל יָהּ". וְרַב חִסְדָּא אָמַר: אָסוּר לִקְרוֹת ק"ש. מ"ט דְּרַב חִסְדָּא – דִּכְתִיב °"כָּל עַצְמוֹתַי תֹּאמַרְנָה ה' מִי כָמוֹךָ".§ אִתְּמַר: רֵיחַ רַע שֶׁיֵּשׁ לוֹ עִיקָּר, רַב הוּנָא אָמַר: ^דמַרְחִיק ד' אַמּוֹת וְקוֹרֵא ק"ש; וְרַב חִסְדָּא אָמַר: מַרְחִיק ד' אַמּוֹת מִמָּקוֹם שֶׁפָּסַק הָרֵיחַ, וְקוֹרֵא ק"ש. תַּנְיָא כְּוָתֵיהּ דְּרַב חִסְדָּא: לֹא יִקְרָא אָדָם ק"ש, לֹא כְּנֶגֶד צוֹאַת אָדָם וְלֹא כְּנֶגֶד צוֹאַת כְּלָבִים, וְלֹא כְּנֶגֶד צוֹאַת חֲזִירִים, וְלֹא כְּנֶגֶד צוֹאַת תַּרְנְגוֹלִים, *וְלֹא ^הכְּנֶגֶד [א] צוֹאַת אַשְׁפָּה שֶׁרֵיחָהּ רַע; וְאִם ^והָיָה מָקוֹם גָּבוֹהַּ עֲשָׂרָה טְפָחִים אוֹ נָמוּךְ עֲשָׂרָה טְפָחִים – יוֹשֵׁב בְּצִדּוֹ וְקוֹרֵא ק"ש, וְאִם לָאו – מַרְחִיק מְלֹא עֵינָיו; ^זוְכֵן לִתְפִלָּה. רֵיחַ רַע שֶׁיֵּשׁ לוֹ עִיקָּר – מַרְחִיק ד' אַמּוֹת מִמְּקוֹם הָרֵיחַ, וְקוֹרֵא ק"ש. אָמַר רָבָא, לֵית הִלְכְתָא כִּי הָא מַתְנִיתָא *(בְּכָל הָנֵי שְׁמַעְתָּתָא) אֶלָּא כִּי הָא *דְּתַנְיָא: ^חלֹא יִקְרָא אָדָם ק"ש לֹא כְּנֶגֶד צוֹאַת אָדָם [ב] וְלֹא כְּנֶגֶד צוֹאַת חֲזִירִים וְלֹא כְּנֶגֶד צוֹאַת כְּלָבִים בִּזְמַן שֶׁנָּתַן עוֹרוֹת לְתוֹכָן. בָּעוּ מִינֵּיהּ מֵרַב שֵׁשֶׁת: רֵיחַ רַע שֶׁאֵין לוֹ עִיקָּר מַהוּ? אֲמַר לְהוּ: ^טאַתּוּ חֲזוּ הָנֵי צִיפֵּי דְּבֵי רַב, דְּהָנֵי גָּנוּ וְהָנֵי גָּרְסִי. וה"מ – ^יבְּדִבְרֵי תוֹרָה, אֲבָל בק"ש – לֹא; וְדִבְרֵי תוֹרָה נַמִּי לֹא אֲמָרַן ^כאֶלָּא דְּחַבְרֵיהּ, אֲבָל דִּידֵיהּ – לָא.§ אִתְּמַר, צוֹאָה עוֹבֶרֶת; אַבַּיֵּי אָמַר: מוּתָּר לִקְרוֹת ק"ש; רָבָא אָמַר: ^לאָסוּר לִקְרוֹת ק"ש. אָמַר אַבַּיֵּי מְנָא אָמֵינָא לַהּ – *דִּתְנַן: ^מהַטָּמֵא עוֹמֵד תַּחַת הָאִילָן וְהַטָּהוֹר עוֹבֵר – טָמֵא, טָהוֹר עוֹמֵד תַּחַת הָאִילָן וְטָמֵא עוֹבֵר – טָהוֹר, וְאִם עָמַד – טָמֵא; וְכֵן בְּאֶבֶן הַמְנוּגַּעַת. וְרָבָא אָמַר לָךְ: הָתָם – בִּקְבִיעוּתָא תַּלְיָא מִילְּתָא, דִּכְתִיב: °"בָּדָד יֵשֵׁב מִחוּץ לַמַּחֲנֶה מוֹשָׁבוֹ", הָכָא: °"וְהָיָה מַחֲנֶיךָ קָדוֹשׁ" אָמַר רַחֲמָנָא, וְהָא לֵיכָּא.§ א"ר פָּפָּא: ^נפִּי חֲזִיר כְּצוֹאָה עוֹבֶרֶת דָּמֵי. פְּשִׁיטָא! –לָא צְרִיכָא,[ס] אע"ג דְּסָלֵיק מִנַּהֲרָא. א"ר יְהוּדָה: סָפֵק צוֹאָה – אֲסוּרָה; סָפֵק מֵי רַגְלַיִם – מוּתָּרִים. א"ד, אָמַר רַב יְהוּדָה: ^סספק צוֹאָה, בַּבַּיִת – מוּתֶּרֶת, בָּאַשְׁפָּה – אֲסוּרָה; סָפֵק מֵי רַגְלַיִם – אֲפִילּוּ בָּאַשְׁפָּה נַמִּי מוּתָּרִין. סָבַר לַהּ כִּי הָא דְּרַב הַמְנוּנָא, דְּאָמַר רַב הַמְנוּנָא: ^עלֹא אָסְרָה תּוֹרָה אֶלָּא כְּנֶגֶד עַמּוּד בִּלְבַד, וּכְדְרַבִּי יוֹנָתָן. דר' יוֹנָתָן רָמֵי: כְּתִיב °"וְיָד תִּהְיֶה לְךָ מִחוּץ לַמַּחֲנֶה וְיָצָאתָ שָׁמָּה חוּץ", וּכְתִיב: °"וְיָתֵד תִּהְיֶה לְךָ וגו' וְכִסִּיתָ אֶת צֵאָתֶךָ"! הָא כֵּיצַד – כָּאן בִּגְדוֹלִים, כָּאן בִּקְטַנִּים; אַלְמָא: קְטַנִּים לֹא אָסְרָה תּוֹרָה אֶלָּא כְּנֶגֶד עַמּוּד בִּלְבַד. הָא נָפוּל לְאַרְעָא – שָׁרֵי, וְרַבָּנַן הוּא דִּגְזָרוּ בְּהוּ, וְכִי גְּזָרוּ בְּהוּ רַבָּנַן – בְּוַדָּאָן, אֲבָל בִּסְפֵקָן לֹא גְּזוּר. וּבְוַדָּאָן עַד כַּמָּה? אָמַר רַב יְהוּדָה אָמַר שְׁמוּאֵל: כָּל זְמַן שֶׁמְּטַפְּחִין; וְכֵן אָמַר רַבָּה בב"ח א"ר יוֹחָנָן: כָּל זְמַן שֶׁמְּטַפְּחִין; וְכֵן אָמַר עוּלָּא: כָּל זְמַן שֶׁמְּטַפְּחִין. גְּנִיבָא מִשְּׁמֵיהּ דְּרַב אָמַר: כָּל זְמַן שֶׁרִשּׁוּמָן נִיכָּר. א"ר יוֹסֵף: שָׁרָא לֵיהּ מָרֵיהּ לִגְנִיבָא! הַשְׁתָּא צוֹאָה, אָמַר רַב יְהוּדָה אָמַר רַב: כֵּיוָן שֶׁקָּרְמוּ פָּנֶיהָ מוּתָּר, מֵי רַגְלַיִם מִיבַּעְיָא?! – א"ל אַבַּיֵּי: מַאי חָזֵית דְּסָמְכַתְּ אַהָא – סְמוֹךְ אַהָא! דְּאָמַר רַבָּה בַּר רַב הוּנָא אָמַר רַב: צוֹאָה, אֲפִילּוּ כְּחֶרֶס – אֲסוּרָה. וְהֵיכִי דָּמֵי צוֹאָה כְּחֶרֶס? אָמַר רַבָּה בב"ח א"ר יוֹחָנָן: כָּל זְמַן שֶׁזּוֹרְקָהּ וְאֵינָהּ נִפְרֶכֶת; וא"ד: כָּל זְמַן שֶׁגּוֹלְלָהּ וְאֵינָהּ נִפְרֶכֶת. אָמַר רָבִינָא: הֲוָה קָאֵימְנָא קַמֵּיהּ דְּרַב יְהוּדָה מִדִּיפְתִּי, חֲזָא צוֹאָה, אָמַר לִי: עַיֵּין אִי קָרְמוּ פָּנֶיהָ אִי לֹא. א"ד, הָכִי א"ל: עַיֵּין אִי מִפְלַאי אַפְלוּיֵי. מַאי הָוֵי עֲלַהּ? אִתְּמַר: צוֹאָה כְּחֶרֶס; אֲמֵימָר אָמַר: אֲסוּרָה; וּמָר זוּטְרָא אָמַר: מוּתֶּרֶת. אָמַר רָבָא, ^פהִלְכְתָא: צוֹאָה כְּחֶרֶס אֲסוּרָה, וּמֵי רַגְלַיִם כָּל זְמַן שֶׁמְּטַפְּחִין. מֵיתִיבֵי: מֵי רַגְלַיִם כָּל זְמַן שֶׁמְּטַפְּחִין – אֲסוּרִין, נִבְלְעוּ אוֹ יָבְשׁוּ – מוּתָּרִים; מַאי לָאו 'נִבְלְעוּ' דּוּמְיָא 'דְּיָבְשׁוּ', מָה יָבְשׁוּ – דְּאֵין רִשּׁוּמָן נִיכָּר, אַף נִבְלְעוּ – דְּאֵין רִשּׁוּמָן נִיכָּר, הָא רִשּׁוּמָן נִיכָּר – אָסוּר, אע"ג דְּאֵין מְטַפְּחִין! – וּלְטַעֲמֵיךְ, אֵימָא רֵישָׁא: כָּל זְמַן שֶׁמְּטַפְּחִין הוּא דְּאָסוּר, הָא רִשּׁוּמָן נִיכָּר – שָׁרֵי! – *אֶלָּא: מֵהָא לֵיכָּא לְמִשְׁמַע מִינַּהּ. לֵימָא כְּתַנָּאֵי: כְּלִי שֶׁנִּשְׁפְּכוּ מִמֶּנּוּ מֵי רַגְלַיִם – אָסוּר לִקְרוֹת ק"ש כְּנֶגְדּוֹ, וּמֵי רַגְלַיִם עַצְמָן שֶׁנִּשְׁפְּכוּ – נִבְלְעוּ – מוּתָּר, לֹא נִבְלְעוּ – אָסוּר; ר' יוֹסֵי אוֹמֵר: כָּל זְמַן שֶׁמְּטַפְּחִין. מַאי 'נִבְלְעוּ' וּמַאי 'לֹא נִבְלְעוּ' דְּקָאָמַר ת"ק? אִילֵימָא נִבְלְעוּ – דְּאֵין מְטַפְּחִין, לֹא נִבְלְעוּ – דִּמְטַפְּחִין, וַאֲתָא ר' יוֹסֵי לְמֵימַר: כ"ז שֶׁמְּטַפְּחִין הוּא דְּאָסוּר, הָא רִשּׁוּמָן נִיכָּר שָׁרֵי! – הַיְינוּ ת"ק! אֶלָּא: 'נִבְלְעוּ' – דְּאֵין רִשּׁוּמָן נִיכָּר, 'לֹא נִבְלְעוּ' – דְּרִשּׁוּמָן נִיכָּר, וַאֲתָא ר' יוֹסֵי לְמֵימַר: כ"ז שֶׁמְּטַפְּחִין הוּא דְּאָסוּר, הָא רִשּׁוּמָן נִיכָּר – שָׁרֵי! –לָא, דכ"ע כ"ז שֶׁמְּטַפְּחִין הוּא דְּאָסוּר, הָא רִשּׁוּמָן נִיכָּר – שָׁרֵי

וְהָכָא

תורה אור (marginal references): תהלים קנ; שם לה; ויקרא יג; דברים כג; שם; שם

רש"י

אֲבָל לִתְפִלָּה. צָרִיךְ הוּא לְהַרְאוֹת אֶת עַצְמוֹ כְּעוֹמֵד לִפְנֵי הַמֶּלֶךְ וְלַעֲמוֹד בְּאֵימָה, אֲבָל ק"ש אֵינוֹ מְדַבֵּר לִפְנֵי הַמֶּלֶךְ: הִדְרוֹקָן. חוֹלִי הַמַּגְבִּיהַּ אֶת הַכֶּרֶס: סִילוֹן. שֶׁל מֵי רַגְלַיִם: יֵרָקוֹן. חוֹלִי שֶׁשְּׁמוֹ גלניי"ה: יָדָיו בְּבֵית הַכִּסֵּא. מְחִילָה יֵשׁ בֵּינוֹ לְבֵין בֵּית הַכִּסֵּא, וּפָשַׁט יָדָיו לְפָנִים מִן הַמְּחִילָה: כֹּל הַנְּשָׁמָה. הַפֶּה וְהַחוֹטֶם בִּכְלַל הַהִילּוּל, וְלֹא שְׁאָר אֵבָרִים: שֶׁיֵּשׁ לוֹ עִיקָּר. שֶׁהַצּוֹאָה מוּנַּחַת שָׁם וּמַסְרַחַת; וְשֶׁאֵין לוֹ עִיקָּר – הַפָּחַת רוּחַ: מַרְחִיק ד' אַמּוֹת. מִן הָעִיקָּר, וְאַע"פ שֶׁהָרֵיחַ בָּא אֵלָיו, וּכְגוֹן שֶׁהִיא לַאֲחוֹרָיו, שֶׁאֵינוֹ רוֹאֶה אוֹתָהּ: מִמָּקוֹם שֶׁפָּסַק הָרֵיחַ. שֶׁהָרֵיחַ כָּלֶה שָׁם: לֹא כְּנֶגֶד צוֹאַת אָדָם כו'. וְאַע"פ שֶׁאֵין רֵיחַ: לֵית הִלְכְתָא כִּי הָא מַתְנִיתָא. דִּלְעֵיל, דְּאָסַר צוֹאַת כְּלָבִים וַחֲזִירִים כְּשֶׁאֵין בָּהֶם עוֹרוֹת: בִּזְמַן שֶׁיֵּשׁ בָּהֶן עוֹרוֹת. אַצּוֹאַת כְּלָבִים וַחֲזִירִים קָאֵי, שֶׁדַּרְכָּן לִתֵּן בְּעִבּוּד הָעוֹרוֹת. אֲבָל צוֹאַת אָדָם – אֲפִי' בְּלֹא עוֹרוֹת, שֶׁהֲרֵי אֵין דַּרְכָּן לִתֵּן שָׁם הִלְכָּךְ ע"כ בְּלֹא עוֹרוֹת קָאָמַר: שֶׁאֵין לוֹ עִיקָּר. הַפָּחַת רוּחַ: צִיפֵּי. מַחְצָלוֹת, שֶׁל בֵּית הַמִּדְרָשׁ: דְּהָנֵי גָּנוּ וְהָנֵי גָּרְסֵי. וְאַע"פ שֶׁדֶּרֶךְ הַיְשֵׁנִים לְהָפִיחַ: וה"מ לִגְרָסָא. מִשּׁוּם דְּלֹא אֶפְשָׁר: אֲבָל לק"ש. יֵצֵא לַחוּץ וְיִקְרָא: אֲבָל לְדִידֵיהּ. הַפִּיחַ הוּא עַצְמוֹ, מַמְתִּין עַד שֶׁיִּכְלֶה הָרֵיחַ: צוֹאָה עוֹבֶרֶת. אָדָם שֶׁנּוֹשְׂאִים לְפָנָיו גְּרָף שֶׁל רְעִי לְהַעֲבִירוֹ: מוּתָּר לִקְרוֹת. וא"צ לְהַפְסִיק: הַטָּמֵא עוֹמֵד תַּחַת הָאִילָן. וְלֹא בְּנוֹשֵׂא אֶת הַמֵּת קָאֵי, דְּמֵת לֹא שְׁנָא עוֹמֵד וְל"ש יוֹשֵׁב וְל"ש הוֹלֵךְ – אֹהֶל הוּא. וְגַבֵּי מְצוֹרָע קָתָנֵי לָהּ בת"כ, דְּגַלֵּי בֵּיהּ רַחֲמָנָא יְשִׁיבָה דִּכְתִיב בָּדָד יֵשֵׁב מִחוּץ לַמַּחֲנֶה מוֹשָׁבוֹ. [מוֹשָׁבוֹ] טָמֵא. מִכָּאן אָמְרוּ: עוֹמֵד נַמִּי כְּיוֹשֵׁב דָּמֵי, דְּקָבִיעַ, אֲבָל מְהַלֵּךְ לֹא קָבִיעַ: אֶבֶן הַמְנוּגַּעַת. הֲרֵי הִיא כִּמְצוֹרָע, שֶׁהֶקִּישָׁהּ הַכָּתוּב זֹאת הַתּוֹרָה לְכָל נֶגַע הַצָּרַעַת וְלַנֶּתֶק וּלְצָרַעַת הַבֶּגֶד וְלַבָּיִת (ויקרא יד): פְּשִׁיטָא. דְּפִי חֲזִיר אֵינוֹ בְּלֹא צוֹאָה: בַּבַּיִת מוּתָּר. דְּאֵין דֶּרֶךְ לְהַנִּיחַ צוֹאָה בַּבַּיִת: לֹא אָסְרָה תּוֹרָה. בְּמֵי רַגְלַיִם, לִקְרוֹת, אֶלָּא כְּנֶגֶד עַמּוּד הַקִּלּוּחַ בִּלְבַד: וְיָצָאתָ שָׁמָּה חוּץ. וְלֹא הִצְרִיכוּ כִּסּוּי וּכְתִיב וְכִסִּיתָ: עַד כַּמָּה. יְהוּ עַל גַּבֵּי קַרְקַע וִיהֵא אָסוּר: שָׁרָא לֵיהּ מָרֵיהּ. יִמְחוֹל לוֹ רִבּוֹנוֹ, דְּוַדַּאי שֶׁקֶר הֵעִיד מִשְּׁמֵיהּ דְּרַב. הַיְּבֵשָׁה נִפְרֶכֶת הִיא יוֹתֵר מִן הַלַּחָה: אִיכָּא דְּאָמְרֵי. חוּמְרָא הִיא, אַף ע"פ שֶׁאָדָם זוֹרְקָהּ נִפְרֶכֶת, הוֹאִיל וְאֵינָהּ נִפְרֶכֶת מִגִּלְגּוּל – לַחָה הִיא: קָרְמוּ. לְשׁוֹן קְרוּם, טיל"א, כְּלוֹמַר: גֶּלֶד מְעַט: אִי מִפְּלַאי אַפְּלוּיֵי. אִם יֵשׁ בָּהּ סְדָקִים סְדָקִים – יְבֵשָׁה הִיא, וְשָׁרֵי: מַאי הָוֵי עֲלַהּ. דְּמֵי רַגְלַיִם: נִבְלְעוּ. בָּאָרֶץ: יָבְשׁוּ. עַל גַּבֵּי אֲבָנִים בַּחַמָּה: בְּטוֹפֵחַ

תוספות

לית הלכתא כי הא מתניתא אלא כי הא דתניא כו'. פרש"י: לית הלכתא כי הא מתניתא דלעיל דאסרה צואת כלבים וחזירים אפי' בשאין בהם עורות, אבל בצואת אדם לא שייך ואסור בכל ענין. משמע אבל בצואת תרנגולים לא איירי רבא, ובאידך ברייתא לא גרס צואת תרנגולים כלל ולא פליג בהא אמתניתא דלעיל, ולפי זה יש לאסור צואת תרנגולין. ואומר רבינו יהודה: דדוקא כשהן בלול שלהם, שיש שם סרחון גדול, אבל בתרנגולים ההולכים בבית – אין חוששין. ובירושלמי* יש דגאדומים בלבד יש לחוש, *ולא ידעינן לפרש. ועוד קאמר מרחיקין מגללי בהמה ד' אמות, ר' שמואל ברבי יצחק אומר: ובלבד של חמור:

ריח רע שאין לו עיקר. י"מ דבתי כסאות שלנו בעומק, אם יש בהן מחילה מפסקת, הויא כמו ריח רע שאין לו עיקר, כמו בתי כסאות דפרסאי לקמן (ד' כו.): והרי

(marginal reference: פ"ג הל' ה')

ק א [מיי' פ"ד מהלכות תפלה הלכה ז] וטוש"ע שם ובסי' נח סעיף א:

קא ב מיי' פ"ד מהל' תפלין הל' כ סמג עשין כב טוש"ע א"ח סי' מג סעיף א:

קב ג מיי' פ"ג מהל' ק"ש הלכה יא טוש"ע או"ח סימן עו סעיף ד:

קג ד מיי' שם הל' יב סמג עשין יח טור שו"ע א"ח סי' עט סעיף א:

קד ה שם סעיף א: [בגדולת מרדכי פירש לפי שבארץ אדום היו השעורים מצויים כלאי' כתובות סד: והיו מאכילין התרנגולין שעורי' וצואתן מסרחת וע' ב"י סי' עט]

קה ו [מיי' שם הלכה ט טוש"ע]. שם סעי' ב:

קו ז מיי' פ"ד מהלכות תפלה הלכה ח סמג שם טור שו"ע או"ח סי' ל סעיף כו:

קז ח מיי' פ"ג מהלכות ק"ש הל' ו סמג שם טור שו"ע אורח חיים סימן עט סעיף [א] ד:

קח ט י כ [מיי' שם הל' יד טור שו"ע] שם סעיף ט:

קט ל מיי' שם הלכה יג סמג שם טוש"ע א"ח סימן עו סעיף ג:

קי מ מיי' פ"י מהלכות טומאת צרעת הל' יב: תוספתא פ"ב

קיא נ מיי' פ"ג מהל' ק"ש הלכה יג סמג עשין יח טוש"ע או"ח סימן עו סעיף ג:

קיב ס ע מיי' שם הל' טו [וע"ש בכ"מ] טור שו"ע שם סעי' ז:

קיג פ מיי' שם הל' ז סמג שם טוש"ע או"ח סי' פב סעי' א [וסעיף ב]:

רב נסים גאון

ריח רע שיש לו עיקר. גרסי בני מערבא [בפירקין הלכה ה] אמר רב חסדא* מסוף ריח רע ד' אמות הדא דאיתמר לאחריו אבל לפניו עד מקום שעיניו רואות כהדא ר' בא וחבריה הוו יתבין קמי פונדקייה ברמשא אמרין מהו למימר מילי דאורייה אמרין מכיון דאילו הוה בימא הוינן חמין ליה ואסור ברם כדון אסור:

גליון הש"ס

גמ' כאן בקטנים. ע' בכורות מ"ד ע"ב תוס' ד"ה אימתי: רש"י ד"ה בזמן שיש כו' שדרכן לתתן כו'. עי' ברש"י כתובות ע"ז ע"א ד"ה מקמץ וצ"ע: שם בעבוד העורות. וכן איתא בילקוט פ' בא בפסוק ולא יחרץ כלב לשונו. ולא עוד אלא שזכו לעבד עורות מצואתן ולכתוב בהם סת"ס:

בכורות מז: לקמן סב: תמיד כז:

יומא ל.

ולא כנגד אשפה כצ"ל (ח"מ)

[בריי"ף וברא"ש ליתא]

קדושין לג: נגעים פי"ג משנה ז תוספתא דנגעים פ"ו ת"כ פרשה מצורע

הגהות הגר"א

[א] גמ' ולא כנגד אשפה כצ"ל. [ב] שם (ולא כנגד צואת חזירים) תא"מ ונ"ב בתוספתא ל"ג לה:

[שבת קכא. וע"ש ברש"י מגלה כב. כז. יבמות עו: נדרים ס: עב. וע"ש ב"מ כו: ל. לד. פא: ב"ב קד. קלג: קסב: ע"ג כב. עב. שבועות לח. זבחים פט: מנחות קה. נדה לג: וע' היטב קדושין ה:]

וְהָכָא, בְּטוֹפֵחַ עַל מְנָת לְהַטְפִּיחַ אִיכָּא בֵּינַיְיהוּ.§ "יָרַד לִטְבּוֹל, אִם יָכוֹל לַעֲלוֹת כו'". לֵימָא תְּנָא סְתָמָא כר' אֱלִיעֶזֶר, דְּאָמַר: *עַד הָנֵץ הַחַמָּה! –אפי' תֵּימָא ר' יְהוֹשֻׁעַ, וְדִלְמָא כְּוָתִיקִין; *דא"ר יוֹחָנָן: וָתִיקִין הָיוּ גּוֹמְרִין אוֹתָהּ עִם הָנֵץ הַחַמָּה.§ "וְאִם לָאו – יִתְכַּסֶּה בַּמַּיִם וְיִקְרָא". וַהֲרֵי לִבּוֹ רוֹאֶה אֶת הָעֶרְוָה! –א"ר אֶלְעָזָר, וְאִי תֵּימָא ר' אַחָא בַּר אַבָּא בַּר אַחָא מִשּׁוּם רַבֵּינוּ: [א]בְּמַיִם עֲכוּרִין שָׁנוּ, דְּדָמוּ כְּאַרְעָא סְמִיכְתָּא, שֶׁלֹּא יִרְאֶה לִבּוֹ עֶרְוָתוֹ. ת"ר: מַיִם צְלוּלִין – יֵשֵׁב בָּהֶן עַד צַוָּארוֹ וְקוֹרֵא; וי"א: עוֹכְרָן בְּרַגְלוֹ, ות"ק – וַהֲרֵי לִבּוֹ רוֹאֶה אֶת הָעֶרְוָה! –קָסָבַר: לִבּוֹ רוֹאֶה אֶת הָעֶרְוָה – מוּתָּר. וַהֲרֵי עֲקֵבוֹ רוֹאֶה אֶת הָעֶרְוָה! –קָסָבַר: עֲקֵבוֹ רוֹאֶה אֶת הָעֶרְוָה – מוּתָּר. אִתְּמַר: עֲקֵבוֹ רוֹאֶה אֶת הָעֶרְוָה – מוּתָּר. נוֹגֵעַ, אַבָּיֵי אָמַר: אָסוּר, וְרָבָא אָמַר: מוּתָּר. רַב זְבִיד מַתְנֵי לָהּ לְהָא שְׁמַעְתָּא הָכִי. רַב חִינָּנָא בְּרֵיהּ דְּרַב אִיקָא מַתְנֵי לָהּ הָכִי: נוֹגֵעַ – דִּבְרֵי הַכֹּל אָסוּר; רוֹאֶה, אַבָּיֵי אָמַר: אָסוּר, רָבָא אָמַר: מוּתָּר, *לֹא נִתְּנָה תּוֹרָה לְמַלְאֲכֵי הַשָּׁרֵת. [ב]וְהִלְכְתָא: נוֹגֵעַ – אָסוּר, רוֹאֶה – מוּתָּר.§ אָמַר רָבָא: [ג]צוֹאָה בַּעֲשָׁשִׁית – מוּתָּר לִקְרוֹת ק"ש כְּנֶגְדָּהּ, [ד]עֶרְוָה בַּעֲשָׁשִׁית – אָסוּר לִקְרוֹת ק"ש כְּנֶגְדָּהּ. צוֹאָה בַּעֲשָׁשִׁית מוּתָּר לִקְרוֹת ק"ש כְּנֶגְדָּהּ – דְּצוֹאָה בְּכִיסּוּי תַּלְיָא מִילְּתָא, וְהָא מִיכַּסְיָא; עֶרְוָה בַּעֲשָׁשִׁית אָסוּר לִקְרוֹת ק"ש כְּנֶגְדָּהּ °"וְלֹא יִרְאֶה בְךָ עֶרְוַת דָּבָר" (דברים כג) אָמַר רַחֲמָנָא, וְהָא קָמִיתַחְזְיָא.§ אָמַר אַבָּיֵי: [ה]צוֹאָה כָּל שֶׁהוּא – מְבַטְּלָהּ בְּרוֹק; אָמַר רָבָא: [ו]וּבְרוֹק עָבֶה. אָמַר רָבָא: [ז]צוֹאָה בְּגוּמָא – מַנִּיחַ סַנְדָּלוֹ עָלֶיהָ וְקוֹרֵא ק"ש. בָּעָא מָר בְּרֵיהּ דְּרָבִינָא: [ח]צוֹאָה דְּבוּקָה בְּסַנְדָּלוֹ מַאי? תֵּיקוּ.§ *אָמַר רַב יְהוּדָה: [ט]גּוֹי עָרוֹם – אָסוּר לִקְרוֹת ק"ש כְּנֶגְדּוֹ. מַאי אִירְיָא גּוֹי, אֲפִילּוּ יִשְׂרָאֵל נַמִי! – יִשְׂרָאֵל – פְּשִׁיטָא לֵיהּ דְּאָסוּר, אֶלָּא גּוֹי אִיצְטְרִיכָא לֵיהּ; מַהוּ דְּתֵימָא: הוֹאִיל וּכְתִיב בְּהוּ °"אֲשֶׁר בְּשַׂר חֲמוֹרִים בְּשָׂרָם" (יחזקאל כג), אֵימָא כַּחֲמוֹר בְּעָלְמָא הוּא – קמ"ל: דְּאִינְהוּ נַמִי אִיקְּרוּ עֶרְוָה, דִּכְתִיב °"וְעֶרְוַת אֲבִיהֶם לֹא רָאוּ" (בראשית ט).§ "וְלֹא יִתְכַּסֶּה לֹא בַּמַּיִם הָרָעִים וְלֹא בְּמֵי הַמִּשְׁרָה, עַד שֶׁיַּטִּיל לְתוֹכָן מַיִם". וְכַמָּה מַיָּא רָמֵי וְאָזֵיל? אֶלָּא ה"ק: [י]לֹא יִתְכַּסֶּה לֹא בַּמַּיִם הָרָעִים וְלֹא בְּמֵי הַמִּשְׁרָה כְּלָל; וּמֵי רַגְלַיִם – עַד שֶׁיַּטִּיל לְתוֹכָן מַיִם, וְיִקְרָא. ת"ר: *כַּמָּה יַטִּיל לְתוֹכָן מַיִם – כָּל שֶׁהוּא; ר' זַכַּאי אוֹמֵר: [כ]רְבִיעִית. אָמַר רַב נַחְמָן: מַחֲלוֹקֶת – לְבַסּוֹף, אֲבָל בַּתְּחִילָּה – כָּל שֶׁהֵן; וְרַב יוֹסֵף אָמַר: [ל]מַחֲלוֹקֶת – לְכַתְּחִילָּה, אֲבָל לְבַסּוֹף – דִּבְרֵי הַכֹּל רְבִיעִית. אָמַר לֵיהּ רַב יוֹסֵף לְשַׁמָּעֵיהּ: אַיְיתִי לִי רְבִיעִיתָא דְּמַיָּא, כר' זַכַּאי. *ת"ר: [מ]גְּרַף שֶׁל רְעִי וַעֲבִיט שֶׁל מֵי רַגְלַיִם – אָסוּר לִקְרוֹת ק"ש כְּנֶגְדָּן, וְאַף ע"פ שֶׁאֵין בָּהֶן כְּלוּם, וּמֵי רַגְלַיִם עַצְמָן – עַד שֶׁיַּטִּיל לְתוֹכָן מַיִם. וְכַמָּה יַטִּיל לְתוֹכָן מַיִם? כָּל שֶׁהוּא; ר' זַכַּאי אוֹמֵר: רְבִיעִית. בֵּין לִפְנֵי הַמִּטָּה בֵּין לְאַחַר הַמִּטָּה; רַבָּן שִׁמְעוֹן בֶּן גַּמְלִיאֵל אוֹמֵר: לְאַחַר הַמִּטָּה – קוֹרֵא, לִפְנֵי הַמִּטָּה – אֵינוֹ קוֹרֵא, אֲבָל מַרְחִיק הוּא אַרְבַּע אַמּוֹת וְקוֹרֵא; ר"ש בֶּן אֶלְעָזָר אוֹמֵר: אפי' בַּיִת מֵאָה אַמָּה – לֹא יִקְרָא עַד שֶׁיּוֹצִיאֵם, אוֹ שֶׁיַּנִּיחֵם תַּחַת הַמִּטָּה. אִיבַּעְיָא לְהוּ: הֵיכִי קָאָמַר(א) [אַחַר הַמִּטָּה – קוֹרֵא מִיָּד, לִפְנֵי הַמִּטָּה – מַרְחִיק אַרְבַּע אַמּוֹת וְקוֹרֵא], אוֹ דִּילְמָא הָכִי קָאָמַר: לְאַחַר הַמִּטָּה – מַרְחִיק ד' אַמּוֹת וְקוֹרֵא, לִפְנֵי הַמִּטָּה – אֵינוֹ קוֹרֵא כְּלָל? ת"ש, דְּתַנְיָא ר"ש בֶּן אֶלְעָזָר אוֹמֵר: [נ]אַחַר הַמִּטָּה – קוֹרֵא מִיָּד, לִפְנֵי הַמִּטָּה – מַרְחִיק אַרְבַּע אַמּוֹת; רַבָּן שִׁמְעוֹן בֶּן גַּמְלִיאֵל אוֹמֵר: אפי' בַּיִת מֵאָה אַמָּה – לֹא יִקְרָא עַד שֶׁיּוֹצִיאֵם אוֹ שֶׁיַּנִּיחֵם תַּחַת הַמִּטָּה. בְּעַיִין אִיפְּשִׁיטָא לָן, מַתְנְיָיתָא קַשְׁיָין אַהֲדָדֵי! –אֵיפוֹךְ בָּתְרַיְיתָא. –מָה חָזֵית דְּאַפְכַתְּ בָּתְרַיְיתָא? אֵיפוֹךְ קַמַּיְיתָא! –מַאן שָׁמְעַתְּ לֵיהּ דְּאָמַר: *כּוּלֵּיהּ בַּיִת כְּאַרְבַּע אַמּוֹת דָּמֵי – ר"ש בֶּן אֶלְעָזָר הִיא.§ אָמַר רַב יוֹסֵף, בְּעַאי מִינֵּיהּ מֵרַב הוּנָא: מִטָּה פָּחוֹת מִשְּׁלֹשָׁה – פְּשִׁיטָא לִי דִּכְלָבוּד דָּמֵי; שְׁלֹשָׁה, אַרְבָּעָה, חֲמִשָּׁה, שִׁשָּׁה, שִׁבְעָה, שְׁמוֹנָה, תִּשְׁעָה, מַהוּ? א"ל: לָא יָדַעְנָא. עֲשָׂרָה, וַדַּאי לָא מִיבַּעְיָא לִי. אָמַר אַבָּיֵי: שַׁפִּיר עֲבַדְתְּ דְּלָא אִיבַּעְיָא לָךְ, כָּל עֲשָׂרָה רְשׁוּתָא אַחֲרִיתִי הִיא. אָמַר רָבָא, הִלְכְתָא: פָּחוֹת מִשְּׁלֹשָׁה – כִּלְבוּד דָּמֵי, עֲשָׂרָה – רְשׁוּתָא אַחֲרִיתִי הִיא, מִשְּׁלֹשָׁה עַד עֲשָׂרָה – הַיְינוּ דִּבְעָא מִינֵּיהּ רַב יוֹסֵף מֵרַב הוּנָא וְלָא פְּשַׁט לֵיהּ. אָמַר רַב: הֲלָכָה כר"ש בֶּן אֶלְעָזָר; וְכֵן אָמַר בַּאלִי א"ר יַעֲקֹב *בְּרָהּ דְּבַת שְׁמוּאֵל: הֲלָכָה כְּרַבִּי שִׁמְעוֹן בֶּן אֶלְעָזָר; וְרָבָא אָמַר: אֵין הֲלָכָה כר"ש בֶּן אֶלְעָזָר.§ רַב אַחַאי אִיעַסַּק לֵיהּ לִבְרֵיהּ בֵּי רַב יִצְחָק בַּר שְׁמוּאֵל בַּר מָרְתָא, עַיְילֵיהּ לַחוּפָּה וְלָא הֲוָה מִסְתַּיְיעָא מִילְּתָא. אֲזַל בָּתְרֵיהּ לְעַיּוּנֵי, חֲזָא סֵפֶר תּוֹרָה דְּמַנְּחָא. אֲמַר לְהוּ: אִילּוּ הַשְׁתָּא לָא אֲתַאי סַכַּנְתּוּן לִבְרִי! דְּתַנְיָא: [ס]בַּיִת שֶׁיֵּשׁ בּוֹ סֵפֶר תּוֹרָה אוֹ תְּפִילִּין – אָסוּר לְשַׁמֵּשׁ בּוֹ אֶת הַמִּטָּה עַד שֶׁיּוֹצִיאֵם אוֹ שֶׁיַּנִּיחֵם כְּלִי בְּתוֹךְ כְּלִי. אָמַר אַבָּיֵי: לֹא שָׁנוּ [ע]אֶלָּא בִּכְלִי שֶׁאֵינוֹ כְּלִיָין, אֲבָל בִּכְלִי שֶׁהוּא כְּלִיָין – אֲפִילּוּ עֲשָׂרָה מָאנֵי כְּחַד מָאנָא דָּמֵי. אָמַר רָבָא: גְּלִימָא אַקַּמְטְרָא

רש"י

בטופח ע"מ להטפיח איכא בינייהו. ת"ק בעי על מנת להטפיח, ור' יוסי מחמיר: לימא תנא סתמא כר' אליעזר. והלכה כמותו: דילמא לותיקין. קאמרה מתני' עם הנץ החמה, אבל לכ"ע עד שלש שעות: והרי לבו רואה את הערוה. קס"ד כל אבר שאין דרכו לראות את הערוה, [ורואה] אותו בשעה שקורא בתורה, קרינן ביה ולא יראה בך ערות דבר: לא נתנה תורה למלאכי השרת. שאין להם ערוה, על כרחנו יש לנו ערוה, ואין אנו יכולים להשמר מכל זה: (ג)כל שהוא. מעט: ברוק. רוקק עליה ומכסה אותה ברוק: בעששית. לנטירנ"א בלע"ז. כלומר: מחילת זכוכית או קלף דק מפסיק בינתיים והיא נראית: בכסוי תליא מילתא. וכסית את צאתך: מים הרעים. סרוחים: *מי המשרה. ששורים שם הפשתן והקנבוס והם מסריחים: וכמה מיא רמי ואזיל. כמה ישליך לתוכם ויבטלם, הלא מרובין הם: ומי רגלים. מועטין, והם בכלי, והוא בא לקרות ק"ש אצלם: לבסוף. שמי רגלים בכלי וזה נותן לתוכן מים, בההיא קאמר ר' זכאי רביעית: אבל לבתחלה. שקדמו המים למי רגלים, דברי הכל כל שהוא. שכשמטיל מי רגלים בכלי לבסוף ראשון ראשון שנופל לתוך המים מתבטל, ואע"פ שהם רבים והולכין – כבר בטלו: אייתי לי רביעתא. אפי' בתחלה: גרף ועביט. שניהם כלי חרס הם, אלא של רעי קרוי גרף, ושל מי רגלים קרוי עביט: אסור לקרות ק"ש כנגדם. הואיל ומיוחדין לכך, ואע"פ שאין בתוכן כלום: ומי רגלים עצמן. בכלי שאינו מיוחד להם: בין לפני המטה. שאין המטה מפסקת בינו לבינם: בין לאחר המטה. שהמטה מפסקת ביניהם – אסור: או שיניחם תחת המטה. גרסינן – ולא גרסינן כלי בתוך כלי: תחת המטה. כאילו היו טמונים בארץ: היכי קאמר. רשב"ג: בעיין איפשיטא לן. שאלתנו נתפרשה לה בחלוק שבין לפני המטה ולאחר המטה: מתנייתא מיהו קשיין. שהוחלפה שיטתן: מאן שמעת ליה וכו'. לא ידעתי היכן היא: פשיטא לי. כמניחן תחת המטה ורגליה קצרים, שאין הימנה ולקרקע שלשה טפחים, כלבוד דמי, והרי הן כטמונים: עשרה ודאי. לא שאלתי ממנו – דנראה כאילו אינה תחתיה, מאחר שיש הפסק כל כך אין זה כסוי: עייליה לחופה ולא הוה מסתייעא מילתא. דנשואין, שלא היה יכול לבעול: סכנתון לברי. כמעט סכנתם את בני למות בעונש העון: אפילו עשרה מאני. וכולן כליין כחד מאנא דמי:

אַקַּמְטְרָא

תוספות

והרי לבו רואה את הערוה. פירש ר"י: מדפריך גמרא הכי בפשיטות משמע דלבו רואה את הערוה אסור. אלא דרבינו שמעיה תלמידו של רש"י פסק כת"ק, דלבו רואה את הערוה מותר. ומיהו בסמוך משמע דאסור, דלא פליגי הני אמוראי אלא בעקבו רואה את הערוה אבל בלבו רואה את הערוה – כ"ע מודו דאסור: והלכתא נוגע עקבו אסור. וטעמא דגזרינן נוגע עקבו – שמא יגע בידיו: גרף של רעי. פי' רש"י: של חרס בלוע. משמע לפירושו: אבל כלי דלא בלע כגון זכוכית – אפשר דשרי[א]: ובלבד שיטיל בהן רביעית מים. אבל בגרף אפשר דלא מהני מים:

ספר

עין משפט נר מצוה

קיד א מיי' פ"ב (ופ"ג) מהל' ק"ש הלכה ז סמג עשין יח טוש"ע או"ח סי' עד סעיף ב:

קטו ב מיי' שם פ"ג הלכה יז טוש"ע שם סעיף ה:

קטז ג מיי' שם הלכה י סמג שם טוש"ע א"ח סי' עו סעיף א:

קיז ד מיי' שם הלכה טז סמג שם טוש"ע א"ח סי' עה סעיף ה:

קיח ה ו מיי' שם הלכה יא סמג שם טוש"ע או"ח סי' עו סעיף ו:

קיט ז ח מיי' שם טוש"ע שם סעי' ב:

קכ ט מיי' שם הלכה טז סמג שם טוש"ע או"ח סי' עה סעיף ד:

קכא י מיי' שם פ"ג הלכה ז טוש"ע או"ח סי' עד סעיף ב (וסימן פו):

קכב כ ל מיי' שם פ"ג הלכה י טוש"ע או"ח סי' עז סעיף א:

קכג מ (נ) מיי' שם הל' יב סמג שם טוש"ע או"ח סימן פז סעיף א: [נ טור שם]:

קכד ס ע מיי' פ"ד מהל' תפילין הל' כד ופ"י מהל' ס"ת הל' ז סמג עשין כב טוש"ע או"ח סימן מ סעיף ב ובסי' רמ סעיף ו [ובי"ד סי' רפב ס"ח]:

רב נסים גאון

לימא תנן סתמא כר' אליעזר דאמר עד הנץ החמה. (דאמר) [עיקר] מחלוקת ר' אליעזר ור' יהושע בפירקא קמא (דף ט) דהא מסכתא: מאן שמעת ליה דאמר כל הבית כולו כד' אמות דמי ר' שמעון בן אלעזר. עיקר דבריו של ר' שמעון בן אלעזר בתוספתא דעירובין (פ"ז) ובגמרא בפרק עושין פסין (דף כג.) אמר רבי שמעון בן אלעזר כל אויר שתשמישו לדירה כגון דיר וסהר ומוקצה וחצר אפילו בית ה' כורין אפילו בית י' כורין מותר שמעינן מיהא דר' שמעון היה מתיר לטלטל כל כי האי שיעור' מפני שתשמישו לדירה וכולו כד' אמות דמי ליה: אמר רב יוסף בעו מיניה מרב הונא פחות מג' כלבוד דמי. עיקרא דהא מילתא דכל פחות מג' כלבוד דמי שנוי במשנה ובהרבה מקומות וגם בתוספתא ואנו מזכירים מה שנמצא בידינו במסכת כלאים בפרק קרחת הכרם (משנה ד) שנינו מחיצת הקנים אם אין בין קנה לקנה ג' טפחים כדי שיכנס הגדי הרי זה כמחיצה ובתוספתא נמי דכוותה ובפרק קמא דעירובין (דף טז:) מקיפין ג' חבלים כו' מקיפין בקנים ובלבד שלא יהא בין קנה לחברו ג' טפחים ובגמרא דהאי פירקא (שם דף טז.) תא שמע ג' מדות במחיצה כו' והיא שנויה בתוספת' כלאים (פרק ד) ובמתני' (סוכה פרק א דף טז.) המשלשל דפנות מלמעלה למטה אם גבוהות מן הארץ ג' טפחים פסולה משום דנפקא לה מתורת לבוד והא דאמרינן הכא עשרה רשותא אחריתי היא איתיה לעיקרא בפירקא קמא דשבת (דף ו.) בברייתא דתנו רבנן ד' רשויות לשבת כו' [וכן בסוכה דף ה ע"ש]:

מסורת הש"ס

[לעיל ט:]

לעיל דף ט: לקמן כו.

[דיבור זה ודבור הקודם שייך לעיל במשנה כב:]

יומא ל. קדושין נד. [מעילה יז:]

[שבת קנ. ע"ש]

[נזיר לח.]

תוספתא פ"ב

[עירובין מב:]

[ע' פירש"י לעיל טז. ד"ה ברה]

הגהות הגר"א

[א] בתוס' סד"ה גרף נמחק ב' נקודו' ההפסק (דד"ה גרף וד"ה בלבד הוא דבור אחד וכ"ה בדפו"י וכ"מ במרדכי ולא כרש"א):

הגהות הב"ח (א) גמ' היכי קאמר רשב"ג אחר המטה: (ב) רש"י ד"ה כל שהוא וד"ה ברוק נ"ל אחר ד"ה בכסוי:

גליון הש"ס **רש"י** ד"ה אבל כו' כבר בטלו. עי' ע"ג דף עג ע"א תוס' ד"ה כי אתא: **רש"י** ד"ה מאן שמעת ליה כו' לא ידעתי כו'. וכן ברש"י שבת טז: ד"ה למ"ד. יז. ד"ה הניחא. מט: ד"ה לא זזו. קז: ד"ה הטפיין. קלח: ד"ה באדם וד"ה זה הקן. ערובין מ: ד"ה דרב אחא. פסחים לד: ד"ה תנא [פ"א. ד"ה אבל]. קטז: ברשב"ם ד"ה נאות. יומא יט. ד"ה שער הדלקה. עב: ד"ה הא כמ"ד: פה. ד"ה ולוי הסדר. סוכה כז: ד"ה שלא העמיד. כח. ד"ה שיחות. כט. ד"ה בשביל. מז. ד"ה שיר. נב: ד"ה שבעה. ביצה טו: ד"ה ופירותיה. כה: ד"ה נלף. תענית סוף פ"ב ד"ה שמעיה. מגילה יז. ד"ה נבואה. סוטה לז: ד"ה אלא זה. מט. ד"ה זיו החכמה. קדושין ל. ד"ה לא א"א. סנהדרין יז. ד"ה טורמוסין. מח: ד"ה והלא. ע: ד"ה כפת. שבועות לז. ד"ה לא א"א. זבחים כב. ד"ה והא תנא. נו: ד"ה לב' ימים. מנחות קה: ד"ה שמעינן. חולין [מו: ד"ה נגרר] נ: ד"ה אסטומכא. נב. ד"ה בר זכאי. נה: ד"ה והרי. קכו: ד"ה גולל. קלא. ד"ה תשעה. ערכין י. ד"ה ולא מוסיפין. יא: ד"ה אלא. יג. ד"ה מתשעה. תמורה טו: ד"ה כיולא. כח: ד"ה נעבד נמי:

תורה אור

אַקַּמְטְרָא – אכְּכְלִי בְּתוֹךְ כְּלִי דָּמֵי. אָמַר רַבִּי יְהוֹשֻׁעַ בֶּן לֵוִי: ס"ת – צָרִיךְ לַעֲשׂוֹת לוֹ מְחִיצָה עֲשָׂרָה. מָר זוּטְרָא אִיקְּלַע לְבֵי רַב אַשִׁי, חַזְיֵיהּ לְדוּכְתֵּיהּ דְּמָר בַּר רַב אַשִׁי דְּמַנַּח בֵּיהּ סֵפֶר תּוֹרָה וְעָבֵיד לֵיהּ מְחִיצָה עֲשָׂרָה. אָמַר לֵיהּ: כְּמַאן – כְּרַבִּי יְהוֹשֻׁעַ בֶּן לֵוִי? באֵימַר דְּאָמַר רַבִּי יְהוֹשֻׁעַ בֶּן לֵוִי – דְּלֵית לֵיהּ בֵּיתָא אַחֲרִינָא, מָר הָא אִית לֵיהּ בֵּיתָא אַחֲרִינָא! אָמַר לֵיהּ: *לָאו אַדַּעְתַּאי.§ "כַּמָּה יַרְחִיק מֵהֶן וּמִן הַצּוֹאָה – אַרְבַּע אַמּוֹת". אָמַר רָבָא אָמַר רַב סְחוֹרָה אָמַר רַב הוּנָא: גלֹא שָׁנוּ אֶלָּא לַאֲחוֹרָיו, אֲבָל לְפָנָיו – מַרְחִיק מְלֹא עֵינָיו, וְכֵן לִתְפִלָּה. אִינִי?! וְהָא אָמַר רַפְרָם בַּר פַּפָּא אָמַר רַב חִסְדָּא: עוֹמֵד אָדָם כְּנֶגֶד בֵּית הַכִּסֵּא וּמִתְפַּלֵּל! –הָכָא בְּמַאי עָסְקִינַן – בְּבֵית הַכִּסֵּא שֶׁאֵין בּוֹ צוֹאָה. אִינִי?! וְהָאָמַר *רַב יוֹסֵף בַּר חֲנִינָא: דבֵּית הַכִּסֵּא שֶׁאָמְרוּ – אע"פ שֶׁאֵין בּוֹ צוֹאָה, וּבֵית הַמֶּרְחָץ שֶׁאָמְרוּ – אע"פ שֶׁאֵין בּוֹ אָדָם! –אֶלָּא, הָכָא בְּמַאי עָסְקִינַן: בַּחֲדָתִי. *–וְהָא מִיבַּעְיָא לֵיהּ לְרָבִינָא: ההִזְמִינוֹ לְבֵית הַכִּסֵּא מַהוּ, יֵשׁ זִימּוּן אוֹ אֵין זִימּוּן? –כִּי קָא מִיבַּעְיָא לֵיהּ לְרָבִינָא – לְמֵיקַם עֲלֵיהּ לְצַלּוֹיֵי בְּגַוֵּיהּ. אֲבָל כְּנֶגְדּוֹ – לֹא. אָמַר רָבָא: והָנֵי בָּתֵּי כִסְאֵי דְּפָרְסָאֵי, אע"ג דְּאִית בְּהוּ צוֹאָה – כִּסְתוּמִין דָּמוּ.§ **מתני'** *זָב שֶׁרָאָה קֶרִי, וְנִדָּה שֶׁפָּלְטָה שִׁכְבַת זֶרַע, וְהַמְשַׁמֶּשֶׁת שֶׁרָאֲתָה נִדָּה – [ז] צְרִיכִין טְבִילָה, וְרַבִּי יְהוּדָה (ז) פּוֹטֵר. **גמ'** אִיבַּעְיָא לְהוּ: בַּעַל קֶרִי שֶׁרָאָה זִיבָה, לר' יְהוּדָה מַהוּ? כִּי פָּטַר רַבִּי יְהוּדָה הָתָם בְּזָב שֶׁרָאָה קֶרִי – דְּמֵעִיקָּרָא לָאו בַּר טְבִילָה הוּא, אֲבָל בַּעַל קֶרִי שֶׁרָאָה זִיבָה, דְּמֵעִיקָּרָא בַּר טְבִילָה הוּא – מְחַיֵּיב, אוֹ דִּילְמָא לָא שְׁנָא? –תָּא שְׁמַע: הַמְשַׁמֶּשֶׁת וְרָאֲתָה נִדָּה צְרִיכָה טְבִילָה, וְרַבִּי יְהוּדָה פּוֹטֵר. וְהָא מְשַׁמֶּשֶׁת וְרָאֲתָה נִדָּה כְּבַעַל קֶרִי שֶׁרָאָה זִיבָה דָּמְיָא, וְקָא פָּטַר רַבִּי יְהוּדָה – ש"מ. תָּנֵי רַבִּי חִיָּיא בְּהֶדְיָא: בַּעַל קֶרִי שֶׁרָאָה זִיבָה – צָרִיךְ טְבִילָה, וְרַבִּי יְהוּדָה פּוֹטֵר.§

הדרן עלך מי שמתו

תְּפִלַּת הַשַּׁחַר עַד חֲצוֹת, ר' יְהוּדָה אוֹמֵר: חעַד ד' שָׁעוֹת. תְּפִלַּת *הַמִּנְחָה עַד הָעֶרֶב; רַבִּי יְהוּדָה אוֹמֵר עַד פְּלַג הַמִּנְחָה. תְּפִלַּת הָעֶרֶב אֵין לָהּ קֶבַע; *וְשֶׁל מוּסָפִים כָּל הַיּוֹם, °(ר' יְהוּדָה אוֹמֵר: עַד ז' שָׁעוֹת)? **גמ'** וּרְמִינְהוּ: מִצְוָתָהּ טעִם הָנֵץ הַחַמָּה, כְּדֵי שֶׁיִּסְמוֹךְ גְּאוּלָּה לִתְפִלָּה וְנִמְצָא מִתְפַּלֵּל בַּיּוֹם! –כִּי תַּנְיָא הַהִיא – לְוָתִיקִין, *דא"ר יוֹחָנָן: וְתִיקִין הָיוּ גּוֹמְרִים אוֹתָהּ עִם הָנֵץ הַחַמָּה. וכ"ע עַד חֲצוֹת וְתוּ לָא?! וְהָאָמַר רַב מָרִי בְּרֵיהּ דְּרַב הוּנָא בְּרֵיהּ דר' יִרְמְיָה בַּר אַבָּא אָמַר רַבִּי יוֹחָנָן: יטָעָה וְלֹא הִתְפַּלֵּל עַרְבִית – מִתְפַּלֵּל בְּשַׁחֲרִית שְׁתַּיִם, כשַׁחֲרִית – מִתְפַּלֵּל בְּמִנְחָה שְׁתַּיִם! –כּוּלֵּי יוֹמָא מְצַלֵּי וְאָזֵיל, עַד חֲצוֹת – יָהֲבִי לֵיהּ שְׂכַר תְּפִלָּה בִּזְמַנָּהּ, מִכָּאן וְאֵילָךְ – לשְׂכַר תְּפִלָּה יָהֲבִי לֵיהּ, שְׂכַר תְּפִלָּה בִּזְמַנָּהּ – לָא יָהֲבִי לֵיהּ.§ אִיבַּעְיָא לְהוּ: טָעָה וְלֹא הִתְפַּלֵּל מִנְחָה, מַהוּ שֶׁיִּתְפַּלֵּל עַרְבִית ב'? את"ל טָעָה וְלֹא הִתְפַּלֵּל עַרְבִית מִתְפַּלֵּל שַׁחֲרִית ב' – מִשּׁוּם דְּחַד יוֹמָא הוּא, דִּכְתִיב °"וַיְהִי עֶרֶב וַיְהִי בֹקֶר יוֹם אֶחָד", אֲבָל הָכָא – תְּפִלָּה בִּמְקוֹם קָרְבָּן הִיא, וְכֵיוָן דְּעָבַר יוֹמוֹ בָּטֵל קָרְבָּנוֹ; אוֹ דִּילְמָא, כֵּיוָן דִּצְלוֹתָא רַחֲמֵי הִיא – כָּל אֵימַת דְּבָעֵי מְצַלֵּי וְאָזֵיל? –ת"ש: דְּאָמַר רַב הוּנָא בַּר יְהוּדָה א"ר יִצְחָק א"ר יוֹחָנָן: מטָעָה וְלֹא הִתְפַּלֵּל מִנְחָה – מִתְפַּלֵּל עַרְבִית ב', וְאֵין בָּזֶה מִשּׁוּם "דְּעָבַר יוֹמוֹ בָּטֵל קָרְבָּנוֹ". מֵיתִיבִי: °"מְעֻוָּת נלֹא יוּכַל לִתְקֹן וְחֶסְרוֹן לֹא יוּכַל לְהִמָּנוֹת"; *"מְעֻוָּת לֹא יוּכַל לִתְקֹן" – זֶה שֶׁבִּטֵּל ק"ש שֶׁל עַרְבִית וק"ש שֶׁל שַׁחֲרִית, אוֹ תְּפִלָּה שֶׁל עַרְבִית, אוֹ תְּפִלָּה שֶׁל שַׁחֲרִית; "וְחֶסְרוֹן לֹא יוּכַל לְהִמָּנוֹת" – זֶה שֶׁנִּמְנוּ חֲבֵירָיו לִדְבַר מִצְוָה וְלֹא נִמְנָה עִמָּהֶם! –א"ר יִצְחָק א"ר יוֹחָנָן: הָכָא בְּמַאי עָסְקִינַן – סשֶׁבִּטֵּל בְּמֵזִיד. אָמַר רַב אַשִׁי: דַּיְקָא נָמֵי דְּקָתָנֵי "בִּטֵּל" וְלֹא קָתָנֵי "טָעָה" – ש"מ.§

תָּנוּ

רש"י

אַקַּמְטְרָא. אַרְגָּז שֶׁל סְפָרִים. וּבִמְגִילָּה (דף כו:) קַמְטְרֵי דְּסִפְרֵי, וְכֵן תַּרְגּוּם יוֹנָתָן וּבְגִנְזֵי בְּרוֹמִים (יחזקאל כז) – חֲלָמִין דְּזְהִירִין מַחֲתִין בְּקַמְטְרִין, וכן לַאֲשֶׁר עַל הַמֶּלְתָּחָה (מלכים ב י) – לִדְעַל קַמְטְרָא: כִּכְלִי בְּתוֹךְ כְּלִי דָּמֵי. דְּהָא גְּלִימָא לָאו כֶּלְיָין הוּא: מְחִיצָה עֲשָׂרָה. וְאִם לָאו – לֹא יְשַׁמֵּשׁ: לְדוּכְתֵּיהּ. בִּמְקוֹם מִטָּתוֹ: לָאו אַדַּעְתַּאי. לֹא נָתַתִּי לִבִּי: כְּנֶגֶד בֵּית הַכִּסֵּא. בְּרָחוֹק אַרְבַּע אַמּוֹת: דְּלֵית בֵּהּ צוֹאָה. שֶׁפִּינּוּ אוֹתָהּ: בֵּית הַמֶּרְחָץ. אָסוּר לְהַרְהֵר בּוֹ: דְּפָרְסָאֵי. בַּחֲפִירָה הָיוּ, וּפִיהֶם בְּרָחוֹק מִן הַגּוּמָא וְהוּא בְּשִׁיפּוּעַ, וְהָרְעִי מִתְגַּלְגֵּל וְנוֹפֵל לְגוּמָא: **מתני'** זָב שֶׁרָאָה קֶרִי. אע"פ שֶׁטָּמֵא טוּמְאַת שִׁבְעָה מִשּׁוּם זִיבָה, וְאֵין טְבִילָה זוֹ מְטַהַרְתּוֹ – אפ"ה צָרִיךְ טְבִילָה לְדִבְרֵי תוֹרָה, כְּתַקָּנַת עֶזְרָא מִשּׁוּם קֶרִי. וְכֵן נִדָּה, אִם בָּאָה לְהִתְפַּלֵּל: שֶׁפָּלְטָה שִׁכְבַת זֶרַע. הֲרֵי הִיא כְּבַעַל קֶרִי, כִּדְאַשְׁכְּחַן בְּסִינַי שְׁלֹשֶׁת יָמִים אַל תִּגְּשׁוּ אֶל אִשָּׁה (שמות יט), לְפִי שֶׁשִּׁכְבַת זֶרַע מְטַמֵּא בִּפְלִיטָתוֹ כָּל שְׁלֹשָׁה, וּלְאַחַר מִכָּאן כְּבָר הִסְרִיחַ בְּגוּפָהּ וְאֵין רָאוּי עוֹד לְהַזְרִיעַ לִהְיוֹת עוֹד וָלָד נוֹצָר הֵימֶנָּה. וה"פ: נִדָּה שֶׁפָּלְטָה עַתָּה הַתַּשְׁמִישׁ שֶׁשִּׁמְּשָׁה אֶתְמוֹל קוֹדֶם שֶׁרָאֲתָה: וְרַבִּי יְהוּדָה פּוֹטֵר. קָא סָלְקָא דַּעְתָּךְ הָשְׁתָּא הוֹאִיל וְטוּמְאַת זִיבָה קוֹדֶמֶת, וַהֲרֵי הוּא טָמֵא טוּמְאָה חֲמוּרָה, וְאֵינוֹ אוֹסַרְתּוֹ בְּדִבְרֵי תוֹרָה, כְּדְאָמְרִינַן בְּפִרְקִין הַזָּבִים וְהַמְּצוֹרָעִים מוּתָּרִים, תּוּ לֹא אָתְיָא טוּמְאַת קֶרִי דְּקִילָּא וְאָסְרָה לֵיהּ: **גמ'** לָאו בַּר טְבִילָה הוּא. לְדִבְרֵי תוֹרָה, ואע"פ שֶׁטּוּמְאָתוֹ חֲמוּרָה, וְתוּ לֹא אָתֵי קֶרִי וּמַצְרִיךְ לֵיהּ:

הַדְרָן עֲלָךְ מִי שֶׁמֵּתוֹ

תְּפִלַּת הַשַּׁחַר: עַד הָעֶרֶב. עַד חֲשֵׁכָה: עַד פְּלַג הַמִּנְחָה. בַּגְּמָרָא מְפָרֵשׁ לָהּ: אֵין לָהּ קֶבַע. כָּל הַלַּיְלָה זְמַנָּהּ, וּבַגְּמָרָא מְפָרֵשׁ מַאי לְשׁוֹן אֵין לָהּ קֶבַע: **גמ'** מִצְוָתָהּ. שֶׁל קְרִיאַת שְׁמַע: לְוָתִיקִין. הַמַּקְדִּימִין לְמִצְוֹת וּמְחַזְּרִים לַעֲשׂוֹת דָּבָר בִּזְמַנּוֹ וּמִצְוָתוֹ, מַקְדִּימִים (א) לְאַחַר הָנֵץ הַחַמָּה לְהִתְפַּלֵּל. וְכִי תְּנַן בְּמתני' – לַמְאַחֲרִים, שֶׁלֹּא יְאַחֵר יוֹתֵר מֵחֲצוֹת, שֶׁמִּשָּׁם וָאֵילָךְ עָבַר הַזְּמַן: וְכוּלֵּי עָלְמָא. שְׁאָר הַמִּתְפַּלְּלִין הַמְאַחֲרִין עַד חֲצוֹת יְכוֹלִין לְאַחֵר וְתוּ לֹא: בְּמִנְחָה. הַיְינוּ אַחַר חֲצוֹת: אִם תִּימְצֵי לוֹמַר. כְּלוֹמַר: אִם תְּשִׁיבֵנִי בִּשְׁאֵלָתִי מִמַּה שֶּׁאָמַרְנוּ טָעָה וְלֹא הִתְפַּלֵּל עַרְבִית וכו': וְכֵיוָן דְּעָבַר יוֹמוֹ בָּטֵל קָרְבָּנוֹ. וְאֵינוֹ מַקְרִיבוֹ בְּיוֹם אַחֵר אִם זְמַנּוֹ קָבוּעַ, כְּגוֹן: *מוּסָפִים שֶׁל כָּל יוֹם וְיוֹם: מַדְּדִיל

תוספות

ספר תורה עושה לו מחיצה. ודוקא ספר תורה, וגם בחומשים יש להחמיר כמו בספר תורה, אבל בשאר ספרים דיין בכסוי בעלמא: הדרן עלך מי שמתו

תפלת השחר עד חצות וכו' תפלת המנחה עד הערב. וא"ת: אמאי לא קתני גבי תפלת המנחה כל היום, כמו גבי תפלת המוספין? וי"ל: דזמן מוספין הוא כל היום, אפילו משחרית, שהרי קרבנות יכול להקריב מיד אחר התמיד – א"כ גם תפלת מוספין יכול להתפלל מיד מן הבקר, מה שאין כן במנחה, (ב) אלא משש שעות ומחצה, והכי נמי בפ"ק דע"ג (ד' ד:): לא ליצלי איניש צלותא דמוספין בתלת שעי קמייתא בריש שתא ביחיד כו', אלמא: בשאר ימות השנה יכול להתפלל. ולהכי מקדים תפלת המנחה לתפלת המוספין, משום שהיא תדירה בכל יום, אע"פ שתפלת מוספין קודמת:

טעה ולא התפלל ערבית מתפלל בשחרית שתים. וא"ת: והאמר רב לקמן (ד' כז:): תפלת ערבית רשות, וקי"ל כותיה באיסורי! ועוד קשה, דאמר לקמן (ד' ל:): טעה ולא התפלל "יעלה ויבוא" בלילה – אין מחזירים אותו, משום דאין מקדשין את החדש בלילה, ולמה ליה האי טעמא, תיפוק ליה דתפלת ערבית רשות! וי"ל: הא דאמרינן דתפלת ערבית רשות – היינו לגבי מצוה אחרת והיא עוברת, דאז אמרינן תדחה תפלת ערבית מפניה, אבל לחנם אין לו לבטלה. *ומיהו, אם איחר עד המנחה נראה דעבר זמנו בטל קרבנו, כיון ששהה כל כך, ולאחר ב' תפלות לא מצינו שתיקנו חכמים לחזור ולהתפלל אם שכח. ואפילו תפלה אחת אם בטל במזיד – לא יוכל לתקן, ובסמוך קרי ליה מעוות לא יוכל לתקון:

איבעיא להו טעה ולא התפלל תפלת מנחה כו'. לא בעי אם טעה ולא התפלל תפלת מוסף – דהא ודאי אינו מתפלל בערבית, דהיאך יקרא את הקרבנות וכבר עבר זמן מוסף! וגם לא תיקנו שבע ברכות של מוסף אלא משום "ונשלמה פרים שפתינו", וזה ודאי "עבר זמנו בטל קרבנו". אבל שאר תפלות דרחמי נינהו, ולואי שיתפלל אדם כל היום כולו, ואין כאן "עבר זמנו" בתפלה אחרת:

טעה

עין משפט נר מצוה

קכה א [טוש"ע שם ושם] ב מיי' פ"י מהל' ס"ת הלכה ז טוש"ע או"ח סימן רמ סעיף ו [ובי"ד שם]:

קכו ג מיי' פ"ג מהל' ק"ש הל' ח' טוש"ע או"ח סי' עט סעיף א:

קכז ד מיי' שם הלכ' ב' סמג עשין יח טוש"ע או"ח סימן פג סעיף א:

קכח ה מיי' שם הלכה ג טוש"ע שם סעיף ב:

קכט ו טוש"ע שם סעיף ד:

קל ז מיי' פ"ד מהל' ק"ש הלכה ח ופ"ד מהל' תפלה הל' ה (סמג עשין יח טור או"ח סי' פח):

א ח ט מיי' פ"ג מהל' תפלה הלכה א סמג עשין יט טוש"ע או"ח סי' פט סעיף א:

ב י מיי' שם הלכה ט סמג שם טוש"ע או"ח סי' קח סעיף ב:

ג כ מיי' שם טוש"ע שם סעיף א:

ד ל מיי' שם הל' א טוש"ע או"ח סי' פט סעיף א:

ה מ מיי' שם הל' ט טוש"ע או"ח סי' קח סעיף ב וסימן רלד סעיף ב:

ו נ ס מיי' שם הל' ח טוש"ע שם סי' קח סעיף ז:

מסורת הש"ס

[שבת לה. ע"ש בפירש"י עירובין נה: ביצה כב. קידושין לג. פא: כתובות ס: סנהדרין ה: מנחות לה: חולין ו.]

שבת י. [ושם איתא ר' יוסי]

[נדרים ז. שבת י.]

לעיל דף כה:

[ע' תוס' לקמן כז. ד"ה ושלו]

תמידין

בראשית א

קהלת א

חגיגה דף ט:

[וע"ע תוס' יומא פז: ד"ה והאמר ותוס' חגיגה ט: ד"ה אין]

[ע' תוס' פסחים קז. ד"ה סמוך וכו' שני טעמים שנקרא תפלת המנחה]

נ"א ל"ג

לעיל דף ט: ודף כה:

הגהות הב"ח

(א) רש"י ד"ה לותיקין וכו' מקדימין (א ב) להתפלל לאחר הנץ החמה וכי תנן: (ב) תוס' ד"ה תפלת וכו' מש"כ במנחה דאינה אלא משש:

ז א מיי' פ"ו [פ"י] מהל' תפלה הלכה טו סמג עשין יט טוש"ע או"ח סימן קח סעי' ט:
ח ב מיי' שם טוש"ע שם סעיף י:
ט ג מיי' שם הלכה ח סמג שם טור וש"ע או"ח סי' קיד סעיף ה:
י ד מיי' שם הלכה ט סמג שם טוש"ע או"ח סי' קיז סעיף ד:
יא ה מיי' שם הלכה יד טוש"ע או"ח סימן רלד סעיף א:
יב ו מיי' פ"א מהלכות תפלה הלכה ה ו טוש"ע או"ח סימן נח סעיף ד [רב אלפס ברכות פ"ג דף יד ב]:
יג ז ח מיי' פ"ג שם הל' ד סמג שם טוש"ע או"ח סי' רל"ג סעיף א:

טעה ולא התפלל מנחה בע"ש וכו' טעה ולא התפלל מנחה בשבת מתפלל ערבית שתים. דהיינו של מוצאי שבת ומבדיל בראשונה וכו'. כתב רבינו יהודה: אם טעה ולא הזכיר ר"ח במנחה – לא יתפלל עוד בלילה. דלמה יתפלל עוד, הרי כבר התפלל כל תפלת המנחה מבעוד יום, לבד ר"ח שלא הזכיר, א"כ אין מרויח כלום אם יחזור ויתפלל במוצאי ר"ח. הרי לא יזכיר עוד תפלת ר"ח, וי"ח כבר התפלל. ולא דמי להא דאמר הכא: טעה ולא התפלל מנחה בשבת דמתפלל ערבית בחול שתים, פירוש: של חול, משום שלא התפלל כלל, א"כ ירויח תפלת י"ח כשמתפלל במ"ש, אע"פ שלא יזכיר של שבת. וא"ת: והלא הוא מתפלל יותר ממה שהוא חייב להתפלל, שלא היה לו להתפלל כי אם ז' ברכות והוא מתפלל י"ח! בכך אין לחוש, שגם בשבת היה דין שיתפלל כל י"ח, רק שלא הצריכוהו מפני הטורח. נמצא שמרויח כל תפלתו. אבל כשטעה ולא הזכיר של ר"ח, כבר התפלל – א"כ לא ירויח כלום אם יתפלל במוצאי ר"ח. (דהא) [וה"ה] נמי אם התפלל במנחה בשבת י"ח שלמות ולא הזכיר של שבת – נראה דלמ"ש לא יתפלל שתים, דכבר התפלל י"ח ברכות. ומיהו ברב אלפס לא משמע כן, דאפי' היכא דאינו מרויח כלום מצריך להתפלל פעם אחרת. וזה לשונו, שכתב אהא דקאמר שמבדיל בראשונה ואינו מבדיל בשניה, ואם לא הבדיל בראשונה והבדיל בשניה – שניה עלתה לו, ראשונה לא עלתה לו, דאיבעי ליה לאקדומי תפלת שניה ברישא (דהכי) [דהיא] חובה; וכיון דלא אבדיל ברישא ואבדיל בבתרייתא גלי דעתיה דהך בתרייתא היא חובה, הלכך בעי למהדר ולצלויי זימנא אחריתי כדי להקדים חובת שעתיה ברישא. ואי אבדיל בתרוייהו, אע"ג דלא מיבעי ליה למעבד הכי – לא מחוייב לאהדורי, ואי לא אבדיל אפילו בחדא מנהון – לא מהדרינן ליה, דתניא: טעה ולא הזכיר הבדלה ב'חונן הדעת' – אין מחזירין אותו, מפני שיכול לאומרה על הכוס. עכ"ל. אלמא: דמצריך להתפלל זימנא אחריתי, אף על גב שלא יחזור ויתפלל פעם שניה יותר מבראשונה. כך היה נראה לה"ר משה מאלאוו"ר מתוך לשון האלפסי:

קשיא. תימה: אמאי לא משני דמיירי קודם שהעשירו? דאמרינן לקמן בפרק "אין עומדין" (דף לג.): העשירו קבעוה על הכוס! וי"ל: דלא אשכחן ברייתא דנשנית בין שתי תקנות:

יצחק תקן תפלת המנחה. ואע"ג דאמרינן (יומא כח:): צלותא דאברהם מכי שחרי כתלי! וי"ל: היינו אחר שתקנה יצחק:

ואין שיחה אלא תפלה שנאמר "תפלה לעני כי יעטוף". תימה: דבפ"ק דע"ז (ד' ז: וע"ש) מוכיח דשיחה [זו] תפלה מדכתיב ביצחק "לשוח בשדה"! י"ל: דכיוצא בו מצינו במגילה (פ"ק ד' יג.) "ויהי אומן את הדסה" ואין הדסים אלא צדיקים דכתיב "והוא עומד בין ההדסים", ובפרק "חלק" (סנהדרין ד' נג.) הוא אומר להיפך:

יעקב תקן תפלת ערבית. תימה. דאמר בפרק גיד הנשה (חולין ד' צא:): "וילך חרנה", כי מטי לחרן בעי למיהדר, אמר: אפשר שעברתי במקום וכו', אלמא דהתם מוכח דהתפלל ערבית ביום, מאחר שהתפלל כבר והוה דעתיה למהדר; וקשה למתניתין דפרק קמא, דקאמר שאינו[3] זמן תפלה עד צאת הכוכבים! ולפי מה שפירשנו דקי"ל כר' יהודה דאמר עד פלג המנחה – ניחא, ויפה מנהג שלנו, *דאדרבה טוב להתפלל מבעוד יום קצת:

עד פלג המנחה. תימה: מנא ליה הא? בשלמא עד תשע שעות ומחצה דעד אותו זמן הוי תפלת המנחה – ניחא, דהיינו מנחה קטנה, אבל הא מנא ליה? וי"ל: דר' יהודה ס"ל דתפלה כנגד קטרת תקנוה, דכתיב "תכון תפלתי קטרת לפניך" (תהלים קמא):

איבעיא להו עד ועד בכלל וכו'. תימה: דאמר בנדה פרק "הרואה כתם" (ד' נח:): כל שיעורי חכמים להחמיר חוץ מכגרים של כתמים, אלמא – עד ולא עד בכלל! וי"ל: אי אמרי' עד ועד בכלל יש בו גם חומרא שיתפלל ולא אמרי' עבר זמנו בטל קרבנו, ואפי' במזיד:

תנו רבנן: [א]טעה ולא התפלל מנחה בערב שבת – מתפלל בליל [א] שבת שתים, [ב]טעה ולא התפלל מנחה בשבת – מתפלל במוצאי שבת שתים של חול, מבדיל בראשונה ואינו מבדיל בשניה, ואם הבדיל בשניה ולא הבדיל בראשונה – שניה עלתה לו, ראשונה לא עלתה לו. למימרא, דכיון דלא אבדיל בקמייתא כמאן דלא צלי דמי ומהדרינן ליה? ורמינהו: *טעה [ג]ולא הזכיר גבורות גשמים בתחיית המתים ושאלה [ד]בברכת השנים – מחזירין אותו, הבדלה [ה]בחונן הדעת – אין מחזירין אותו, מפני שיכול לאומרה על הכוס! –קשיא.§ איתמר, רבי יוסי ברבי חנינא אמר: תפלות אבות תקנום; רבי יהושע בן לוי אמר: [ו]תפלות כנגד תמידין תקנום. תניא כוותיה דר' יוסי ברבי חנינא, ותניא כוותיה דרבי יהושע בן לוי. תניא כוותיה דרבי יוסי בר' חנינא: אברהם תקן תפלת שחרית – שנא' "וישכם אברהם בבקר אל המקום אשר עמד שם" *ואין עמידה אלא תפלה, שנאמר: "ויעמד פינחס ויפלל"; יצחק תקן תפלת מנחה – שנאמר: "ויצא יצחק לשוח בשדה לפנות ערב", ואין שיחה אלא תפלה, שנאמר: "תפלה לעני כי יעטף ולפני ה' ישפך שיחו"; יעקב תקן תפלת ערבית – שנאמר: "ויפגע במקום וילן שם", *ואין פגיעה אלא תפלה, שנאמר: "ואתה אל תתפלל בעד העם הזה ואל תשא בעדם רנה ותפלה ואל תפגע בי".§ ותניא כוותיה דר' יהושע בן לוי: *מפני מה אמרו תפלת השחר עד חצות – שהרי תמיד של שחר קרב והולך עד חצות; ורבי יהודה אומר: עד ארבע שעות, שהרי תמיד של שחר קרב והולך עד ארבע שעות. ומפני מה אמרו תפלת המנחה עד הערב – שהרי תמיד של בין הערבים קרב והולך עד הערב; רבי יהודה אומר: עד פלג המנחה, שהרי תמיד של בין הערבים קרב והולך עד פלג המנחה. ומפני מה אמרו תפלת הערב אין לה קבע – שהרי אברים ופדרים שלא נתעכלו מבערב קרבים והולכים כל הלילה; ומפני מה אמרו של מוספין כל היום – שהרי קרבן של מוספין קרב כל היום; רבי יהודה אומר: עד שבע שעות, שהרי קרבן מוסף קרב והולך עד שבע שעות. ואיזו היא [ז]מנחה גדולה – משש שעות ומחצה ולמעלה; ואיזו היא מנחה קטנה – מתשע שעות ומחצה ולמעלה. איבעיא להו: רבי יהודה פלג מנחה קמא קאמר, או פלג מנחה אחרונה קאמר? תא שמע: דתניא, ר' יהודה אומר: [ח]פלג המנחה אחרונה אמרו, והיא י"א שעות חסר רביע. נימא תיהוי תיובתיה דר' יוסי בר' חנינא! אמר לך ר' יוסי בר' חנינא: לעולם אימא לך תפלות אבות תקנום, ואסמכינהו רבנן אקרבנות. דאי לא תימא הכי – תפלת מוסף לר' יוסי בר' חנינא מאן תקנה? אלא: תפלות אבות תקנום, ואסמכינהו רבנן אקרבנות.§ רבי יהודה אומר: עד ארבע שעות. איבעיא להו: *עד ועד בכלל, או דילמא, עד ולא עד בכלל? תא שמע: ר' יהודה אומר עד פלג המנחה. אי אמרת בשלמא עד ולא עד בכלל – היינו דאיכא בין ר' יהודה לרבנן, אלא אי אמרת עד ועד בכלל – ר' יהודה היינו

מבדיל בראשונה. פעם ראשונה מתפלל בשביל תפלה של עכשיו – לפיכך אומר בה הבדלה בחונן הדעת, והשניה היא בשביל תשלומי תפלת שבת – אינו מבדיל בה: שניה עלתה לו. בשביל תפלת מ"ש, וראשונה לא עלתה לו שאינה כלום, שאין לו להקדים [א]תפלה שעבר זמנה לתפלה שזמנה עכשיו. והשניה נמי לא עלתה לו לשל שבת, הואיל והבדיל בה גילה דעתו שאינה של שבת, והיא תחשב לשל ערבית: אבות תקנום. כדקתני בברייתא לקמיה: כנגד תמידים תקנום. אנשי כנסת הגדולה: רבי יהודה. ס"ל שאין תמיד של שחר קרב אלא עד ארבע שעות: אברים. של עולות: ופדרים. של שאר קרבנות, שנזרק דמן קודם שקיעת החמה, קרבין כל הלילה וכנגדן תקנו תפלת ערבית: מנחה גדולה. אם בא להקדים תמיד של בין הערבים אינו יכול להקדימו קודם שש שעות ומחצה, דבין הערבים כתיב ביה מכי ינטו צללי ערב, משהחמה נוטה למערב, דהיינו משש שעות ומחצה ולמעלה. דאמר מר: חצי שש וחצי שבע – חמה עומדת בראש כל אדם, באמצע הרקיע (פסחים ד' צד.): מנחה קטנה. זמן תמיד של בין הערבים בכל יום מתשע שעות ומחצה ולמעלה, כדתנן בתמיד נשחט (ד' נח.): נשחט בשמונה ומחצה וקרב בתשע ומחצה, והתם מפרש טעמא: פלג מנחה אחרונה. חלק את ב' שעות ומחצה הנותרים ביום, ותמצא פלג אחרון של מנחה מי"א שעות חסר רביע ולמעלה: דאי לא תימא הכי. דמודה רבי יוסי ברבי חנינא דרבנן אסמכינהו אקרבנות: תפלת המוספין מאן תקנה. אלא: ע"כ רבנן אסמכינהו אקרבנות, וכי עיינו במוספין ולא מצאו תפלה כנגדה – עמדו הם ותקנוה: עד ועד בכלל. לרבי יהודה הוא דקא בעי, דאילו לרבנן – עד ולא עד בכלל:

תא

תוספתא פ"ג לקמן כט. לג. (תענית ג:)
[לעיל ו:]
[תענית ז: ח. סוטה יד. סנהדרין לה:]
תוספתא פ"ג ע"ש
[עירובין פב: פסחי' קיז: ר"ה ל: סוכה מח: נזיר ו: מנחות סח: חולין מו. נג: ערכין יח: נדה נח:]
[ועיין פסקי תוס' פרק הקומץ רבה סימן קיח]

בראשית יט; תהלים קו; בראשית כד; תהלים קב; בראשית כח; ירמיה ז

תורה אור

הגהות הגר"א
[א] גמ' בליל שבת שתים. נ"ב שתים של שבת. גירסת רי"ף ושאר פוסקים.

הגהות הב"ח
(א) רש"י ד"ה שניה עלתה וכו' שאין לו להקדים. נ"ב פירוש דודאי הוא לא הקדים ראשונה לתשלומין א"כ מסתמא [דעתו היה] על חובה ולשם [חובה לא] עלתה משום דלא הבדיל בה ע"כ [כתב רש"י] אח"כ אם כן דאמרינן דמסתמא דעתו [היה בראשונה לחובה] רק דלא עלתה לו משום דלא הבדיל בה א"כ תעלה שניה לשם שבת דהרי לא הקדים תפלת תשלומין לחובה ע"ז משני רש"י דהואיל דהבדיל בשניה גילה דעתו שאינה של שבת והיא תחשב לשל ערבית ר"ל בשעה שהתפלל ראשונה אמרינן דעתו היה לשם חובה אבל כשהתפלל והבדיל בשניה אז גילה דעתו שהיא תהי' של ערבי' וק"ל ועי' באשר"י: (ב) תוס' ד"ה יעקב וכו' דפרק קמא דקאמר שאינו. נ"ב [אע"ג דלא] אמרו זמן דצאת הכוכבים אלא לענין [ק"ש מ"מ] כיון דקי"ל דצריך גם כן לסמוך גאולה לתפלה [בערבית] א"כ בע"כ דתפלת ערבית אחר צאת הכוכבים:

גליון הש"ס
גמ' תפלות אבות תקנום. עי' תענית (דף כ"ח ע"א) ברש"י ד"ה הללו: **שם** ואין שיחה אלא תפלה. בשאלתות דרא"ג פ' לך לך איתא שנאמר אשפוך לפניו שיחי. וכן הוא בתוס' ע"ג (דף ז' ע"ב) ד"ה ואין: **תוס'** ד"ה ואין כו' ובפרק חלק הוא אומר להיפך. וכן בסנה' (ד' צ"ו ע"ב) ואין כסף אלא צדיקים שנאמר ואכרה לי. ובחולין (דף צ"ב ע"א) אומר בהיפך:

הַיְינוּ רַבָּנַן! אֶלָּא מַאי? *עַד וְלֹא עַד בִּכְלָל – אֵימָא סֵיפָא וְשֶׁל מוּסָפִין כָּל הַיּוֹם, ר׳ יְהוּדָה אוֹמֵר: עַד שֶׁבַע שָׁעוֹת; וְתַנְיָא: *הָיוּ לְפָנָיו שְׁתֵּי תְּפִלּוֹת, אַחַת שֶׁל מוּסָף וְאַחַת שֶׁל מִנְחָה – מִתְפַּלֵּל שֶׁל מִנְחָה וְאַחַר כָּךְ שֶׁל מוּסָף, שֶׁזּוֹ תְּדִירָה וְזוֹ אֵינָהּ תְּדִירָה; רַבִּי יְהוּדָה אוֹמֵר: מִתְפַּלֵּל שֶׁל מוּסָף וְאַחַר כָּךְ שֶׁל מִנְחָה, שֶׁזּוֹ עוֹבֶרֶת וְזוֹ אֵינָהּ עוֹבֶרֶת. אִי אָמְרַתְּ בִּשְׁלָמָא עַד וְעַד בִּכְלָל – הַיְינוּ דְּמַשְׁכַּחַתְּ לְהוּ שְׁתֵּי תְּפִלּוֹת בַּהֲדֵי הֲדָדֵי; אֶלָּא אִי אָמְרַתְּ עַד וְלֹא עַד בִּכְלָל – הֵיכִי מַשְׁכַּחַתְּ לְהוּ שְׁתֵּי תְּפִלּוֹת בַּהֲדֵי הֲדָדֵי? כֵּיוָן דְּאָתְיָא לָהּ שֶׁל מִנְחָה אָזְלָא לָהּ שֶׁל מוּסָפִין! –אֶלָּא מַאי, עַד וְעַד בִּכְלָל? קַשְׁיָא רֵישָׁא: מַאי אִיכָּא בֵּין רַבִּי יְהוּדָה לְרַבָּנַן? –מִי סָבְרַתְּ דְּהַאי ׳פְּלַג מִנְחָה׳ פְּלַג אַחֲרוֹנָה קָאָמַר?! פְּלַג רִאשׁוֹנָה קָאָמַר, וְהָכִי קָאָמַר: אֵימַת נָפֵיק פְּלַג רִאשׁוֹנָה וְעָיֵיל פְּלַג אַחֲרוֹנָה? מִכִּי נָפְקִי י״א שָׁעוֹת חָסֵר רְבִיעַ.§ אָמַר רַב נַחְמָן: אַף אֲנַן נַמִי תְּנֵינָא, *רַבִּי יְהוּדָה בֶּן בָּבָא הֵעִיד חֲמִשָּׁה דְּבָרִים: [א]שֶׁמְּמָאֲנִין אֶת הַקְּטַנָּה, וְשֶׁמַּשִּׂיאִין [ב]אֶת הָאִשָּׁה עַל פִּי עֵד אֶחָד, וְעַל [ג]תַּרְנְגוֹל שֶׁנִּסְקַל בִּירוּשָׁלַיִם עַל שֶׁהָרַג אֶת הַנֶּפֶשׁ, וְעַל [ד]יַיִן בֶּן אַרְבָּעִים יוֹם שֶׁנִּתְנַסֵּךְ עַל גַּבֵּי הַמִּזְבֵּחַ, *וְעַל [ה]תָּמִיד שֶׁל שַׁחַר שֶׁקָּרַב בְּאַרְבַּע שָׁעוֹת; שְׁמַע מִינַּהּ: [ו]׳עַד׳ וְעַד בִּכְלָל, שְׁמַע מִינַּהּ. אָמַר רַב כָּהֲנָא: [ז]הֲלָכָה כְּרַבִּי יְהוּדָה, הוֹאִיל *וּתְנַן בִּבְחִירְתָּא כְּוָותֵיהּ.§ "וְעַל תָּמִיד שֶׁל שַׁחַר שֶׁקָּרַב בְּאַרְבַּע שָׁעוֹת". מַאן תָּנָא לְהָא, *דִּתְנַן: °"וְחַם הַשֶּׁמֶשׁ וְנָמָס" – בְּאַרְבַּע שָׁעוֹת. אַתָּה אוֹמֵר בְּאַרְבַּע שָׁעוֹת, אוֹ אֵינוֹ אֶלָּא בְּשֵׁשׁ שָׁעוֹת? כְּשֶׁהוּא אוֹמֵר: °"כְּחֹם הַיּוֹם" – הֲרֵי שֵׁשׁ שָׁעוֹת אָמוּר, הָא מָה אֲנִי מְקַיֵּים "וְחַם הַשֶּׁמֶשׁ וְנָמָס" – בְּאַרְבַּע שָׁעוֹת. מַנִּי? לֹא רַבִּי יְהוּדָה וְלֹא רַבָּנַן! אִי רַבִּי יְהוּדָה עַד אַרְבַּע שָׁעוֹת נַמִי צַפְרָא הוּא, אִי רַבָּנַן – עַד חֲצוֹת נַמִי צַפְרָא הוּא! –אִי בָּעֵית אֵימָא: רַבִּי יְהוּדָה, אִי בָּעֵית אֵימָא: רַבָּנַן. אִי בָּעֵית אֵימָא רַבָּנַן – אָמַר קְרָא: "בַּבֹּקֶר בַּבֹּקֶר" – חַלְּקֵהוּ לִשְׁנֵי בְקָרִים; וְאִי בָּעֵית אֵימָא רַבִּי יְהוּדָה, הַאי בֹּקֶר יְתֵירָא – לְהַקְדִּים לוֹ שָׁעָה אַחַת. דְּכוּלֵּי עָלְמָא מִיהָא "וְחַם הַשֶּׁמֶשׁ וְנָמָס" בְּאַרְבַּע שָׁעוֹת, מַאי מַשְׁמַע? אָמַר רַבִּי אַחָא בַּר יַעֲקֹב, אָמַר קְרָא: "וְחַם הַשֶּׁמֶשׁ וְנָמָס", אֵיזוֹ הִיא שָׁעָה שֶׁהַשֶּׁמֶשׁ חַם וְהַצֵּל צוֹנֵן? הֱוֵי אוֹמֵר בְּאַרְבַּע שָׁעוֹת.§ "תְּפִלַּת הַמִּנְחָה עַד הָעֶרֶב וכו׳". אָמַר לֵיהּ רַב חִסְדָּא לְרַב יִצְחָק: הָתָם אָמַר רַב כָּהֲנָא "הֲלָכָה כְּרַבִּי יְהוּדָה הוֹאִיל וּתְנַן בִּבְחִירְתָּא כְּוָותֵיהּ", הָכָא מַאי? אִישְׁתִּיק וְלֹא אֲמַר לֵיהּ וְלֹא מִידֵּי. אָמַר רַב חִסְדָּא: נֶחֱזֵי אֲנַן, מִדְּרַב מְצַלֵּי שֶׁל שַׁבָּת בְּעֶרֶב שַׁבָּת מִבְּעוֹד יוֹם – ש״מ הֲלָכָה כְּרַבִּי יְהוּדָה. אַדְּרַבָּה, מִדְּרַב הוּנָא וְרַבָּנַן לֹא הֲווּ מְצַלּוּ עַד אוּרְתָּא, שְׁמַע מִינַּהּ אֵין הֲלָכָה כְּרַבִּי יְהוּדָה! הַשְׁתָּא דְּלֹא אִתְּמַר הִלְכְתָא לֹא כְּמָר וְלֹא כְּמָר, [ח]דַּעֲבַד כְּמָר – עֲבַד, וְדַעֲבַד כְּמָר – עֲבַד.§ רַב אִיקְּלַע לְבֵי גְנִיבָא וְצַלֵּי שֶׁל שַׁבָּת בְּעֶרֶב שַׁבָּת, וַהֲוָה מְצַלֵּי רַבִּי יִרְמְיָה בַּר אַבָּא לַאֲחוֹרֵיהּ דְּרַב, וְסַיֵּים רַב וְלֹא פַּסְקֵיהּ לִצְלוֹתֵיהּ דְּרַבִּי יִרְמְיָה. שְׁמַע מִינַּהּ תְּלָת: שְׁמַע מִינַּהּ [ט]מִתְפַּלֵּל אָדָם שֶׁל שַׁבָּת בְּעֶרֶב שַׁבָּת, וּשְׁמַע מִינַּהּ מִתְפַּלֵּל תַּלְמִיד אֲחוֹרֵי רַבּוֹ, וּשְׁמַע מִינַּהּ [י]אָסוּר לַעֲבוֹר כְּנֶגֶד הַמִּתְפַּלְּלִין. מְסַיַּיע לֵיהּ לְרַבִּי יְהוֹשֻׁעַ בֶּן לֵוִי, דְּאָמַר רַבִּי יְהוֹשֻׁעַ בֶּן לֵוִי: אָסוּר לַעֲבוֹר כְּנֶגֶד הַמִּתְפַּלְּלִין. –אִינִי?! וְהָא רַבִּי אַמִּי וְרַבִּי אַסִּי חָלְפִי! – רַבִּי אַמִּי וְרַבִּי אַסִּי חוּץ לְאַרְבַּע אַמּוֹת הוּא דְּחָלְפִי. – וְרַבִּי יִרְמְיָה הֵיכִי עָבֵיד הָכִי? וְהָא אָמַר רַב יְהוּדָה אָמַר רַב: לְעוֹלָם אַל יִתְפַּלֵּל אָדָם

לא

שמות טז · בראשית יח

רש״י

הַיְינוּ רַבָּנָן. דקס״ד, רַבִּי יְהוּדָה פְּלַג אַחֲרוֹן שֶׁל מִנְחָה אַחֲרוֹנָה קָאָמַר: מִתְפַּלֵּל שֶׁל מִנְחָה וכו׳. רַבָּנָן לְטַעֲמַיְיהוּ, דְּאָמְרִי: תְּפִלַּת הַמּוּסָפִים כָּל הַיּוֹם, כְּמוֹ שֶׁל מִנְחָה, הִלְכָּךְ תָּדִיר קוֹדֵם. ור׳ יְהוּדָה לְטַעְמֵיהּ דְּאָמַר מוּסָפִין עַד שֶׁבַע שָׁעוֹת וְתוּ לָא, וְהָוְיָא לָהּ מִצְוָה עוֹבֶרֶת, וְשֶׁל מִנְחָה יֵשׁ לָהּ עוֹד שָׁהוּת עַד פְּלַג הַמִּנְחָה: שְׁתֵּי תְּפִלּוֹת בַּהֲדֵי הֲדָדֵי. אֲבָל הָאַחֲרוֹן שֶׁל שָׁעָה שְׁבִיעִית הוּא זְמַן לִשְׁתֵּיהֶן, דְּהָא אָמַר מִנְחָה גְּדוֹלָה מִשֵּׁשׁ שָׁעוֹת וּמֶחֱצָה וּלְמַעְלָה: הֵיכִי מַשְׁכַּחַת לָהּ. הֲרֵי עָבַר זְמַן הַמּוּסָפִים מִשֶּׁעָבְרָה שָׁעָה שִׁשִּׁית: פְּלַג רִאשׁוֹנָה. שֶׁל מִנְחָה אַחֲרוֹנָה וְעַד בִּכְלָל; וְאַף עַל גַּב דְּתַנָּא יָהֵיב סִימָנָא לִפְלַג אַחֲרוֹנָה דְּקָתָנֵי: אֵיזוֹ פְּלַג מִנְחָה מי״א שָׁעוֹת חָסֵר רְבִיעַ, ה״ק כו׳: אַף אֲנַן נָמֵי תַּנִּינָא. לְרַבִּי יְהוּדָה עַד וְעַד בִּכְלָל: שֶׁמְּמָאֲנִין אֶת הַקְּטַנָּה׳. קְטַנָּה שֶׁהִשִּׂיאַתָּה אִמָּהּ לְאַחַר מִיתַת אָבִיהָ, דְּמִדְּאוֹרָיְיתָא אֵין קִדּוּשֶׁיהָ כְּלוּם; שֶׁהֲרֵי קְטַנָּה אֵינָהּ בַּת דַּעַת, וְאֶת אִמָּהּ לֹא זִכְּתָה תּוֹרָה לִהְיוֹת לָהּ כֹּחַ לְקַדְּשָׁהּ אֶלָּא לָאָב, שֶׁנֶּאֱמַר אֶת בִּתִּי נָתַתִּי לָאִישׁ הַזֶּה (דברי׳ כב). וּמִיהוּ, רַבָּנָן תַּקִּינוּ לָהּ קִדּוּשִׁין לְהַצְרִיכָהּ מֵיאוּן, כְּדֵי שֶׁיִּשָּׂאוּהָ וְלֹא תֵּצֵא לִזְנוּת. לְפִיכָךְ, אִם מֵיאֲנָה לְאַחַר זְמַן וְאָמְרָה אִי אֶפְשִׁי בּוֹ – יוֹצֵאת וּמוּתֶּרֶת לְכָל אָדָם, וְאֵינָהּ צְרִיכָה הֵימֶנּוּ גֵּט. וְהֵעִיד ר׳ יְהוּדָה בֶּן בָּבָא שֶׁפְּעָמִים שֶׁמִּצְוָה עַל בֵּית דִּין לְלַמְּדָהּ שֶׁתְּמָאֵן בּוֹ, כְּגוֹן: שְׁנֵי אַחִים נְשׂוּאִין שְׁתֵּי אֲחָיוֹת יְתוֹמוֹת, אַחַת גְּדוֹלָה וְקִדּוּשֶׁיהָ קִדּוּשֵׁי תּוֹרָה וְאַחַת קְטַנָּה שֶׁאֵין קִדּוּשֶׁיהָ אֶלָּא מִדְּרַבָּנָן, וּמֵת בַּעֲלָהּ שֶׁל גְּדוֹלָה בְּלֹא בָּנִים וְנָפְלָה לִפְנֵי אָחִיו לְיִבּוּם, וְנִמְצֵאת זְקוּקָה לוֹ מִן הַתּוֹרָה, וְזִיקָה זוֹ אוֹסֶרֶת אֶת אִשְׁתּוֹ עָלָיו מִשּׁוּם אֲחוֹת זְקוּקָה שֶׁהִיא כַּאֲחוֹת אִשְׁתּוֹ. וא״ר אֱלִיעֶזֶר בְּמַסֶּכֶת יְבָמוֹת (דף קט.): מְלַמְּדִין קְטַנָּה זוֹ שֶׁתְּמָאֵן בְּבַעְלָהּ, וְתַעֲקוֹר קִדּוּשֶׁיהָ לְמַפְרֵעַ, וְתַעֲשֶׂה כָּל בְּעִילוֹתֶיהָ כְּאִלּוּ הֵן שֶׁל זְנוּת כְּדֵי לְהַתִּיר אֶת בַּעְלָהּ לְיַבֵּם אֶת אֲחוֹתָהּ, דִּתְנַן: נוֹשְׂאִין עַל הָאֲנוּסָה וְעַל הַמְפוּתָּה (יבמות דף נז.) – וְהֵעִיד רַבִּי יְהוּדָה בֶּן בָּבָא כַּיּוֹם שֶׁנִּשְׁנֵית עֵדִיּוֹת שֶׁהֲלָכָה כר״א: ע״פ עֵד אֶחָד. שֶׁאָמַר לָהּ: מֵת בַּעְלֵךְ בִּמְדִינַת הַיָּם (יבמות דף קכב.): שֶׁנִּסְקַל תַּרְנְגוֹל. שֶׁנִּיקֵּר קָדְקֳדוֹ שֶׁל תִּינוֹק בְּמָקוֹם שֶׁהַמּוֹחַ רוֹפֵף, וְנִיקֵּב אֶת מוֹחוֹ, וּסְקָלוּהוּ כְּמִשְׁפַּט שׁוֹר שֶׁנָּגַח אֶת הָאָדָם, דִּכְתִיב (שמות כא) הַשּׁוֹר יִסָּקֵל וְגָמְרִינַן בג״ש שׁוֹר שׁוֹר מִשַּׁבָּת, לַעֲשׂוֹת כָּל בְּהֵמָה חַיָּה וָעוֹף כְּשׁוֹר (ב״ק ד׳ נד:): וְעַל יַיִן בֶּן אַרְבָּעִים יוֹם. שֶׁיָּצָא מִכְּלַל יַיִן מִגִּתּוֹ, וּבָא לִכְלַל יַיִן גָּמוּר וְקָרֵינַן בֵּיהּ נֶסֶךְ שֵׁכָר (במדבר כח): בְּאַרְבַּע שָׁעוֹת. וְתוּ לֹא, אַלְמָא כְּרַבִּי יְהוּדָה ס״ל, וְקָאָמַר בְּאַרְבַּע שָׁעוֹת; אַלְמָא לְרַבִּי יְהוּדָה עַד וְעַד בִּכְלָל: הֲלָכָה כְּרַבִּי יְהוּדָה. דמתני׳, דְּאֵין תָּמִיד שֶׁל שַׁחַר קָרֵב לְאַחַר אַרְבַּע שָׁעוֹת, וה״ה לִתְפִלָּה: בִּבְחִירְתָּא. עֵדִיּוֹת קָרֵי בְּחִירְתָּא, שֶׁהֲלָכָה כְּאוֹתָן עֵדִיּוֹת: כְּשֶׁהוּא אוֹמֵר כְּחוֹם הַיּוֹם הֲרֵי שֵׁשׁ שָׁעוֹת אָמוּר. כְּלוֹמַר: מָצִינוּ בְּמָקוֹם אַחֵר שֶׁשִּׁינָּה הַכָּתוּב בִּלְשׁוֹנוֹ וְאָמַר וְהוּא יוֹשֵׁב פֶּתַח הָאֹהֶל כְּחוֹם הַיּוֹם, וְלֹא אָמַר כְּחוֹם הַשֶּׁמֶשׁ אֶלָּא הַיּוֹם; מַשְׁמַע כָּל הַמְּקוֹמוֹת חַמִּין בֵּין חַמָּה בֵּין צֵל – הוּא מְדַבֵּר בְּשָׁעָה שִׁשִּׁית: הָא מָה אֲנִי מְקַיֵּים וְחַם הַשֶּׁמֶשׁ. דְּמַשְׁמַע: הַשֶּׁמֶשׁ חַם וְהַצֵּל צוֹנֵן: בְּאַרְבַּע שָׁעוֹת. דְּאִילּוּ קוֹדֶם אַרְבַּע שָׁעוֹת, אַף הַשֶּׁמֶשׁ צוֹנֵן: מַנִּי. הָא דְּמַשְׁמַע דְּאַרְבַּע לָאו בֹּקֶר הוּא, דְּהָא כְּתִיב וַיִּלְקְטוּ אוֹתוֹ בַּבֹּקֶר בַּבֹּקֶר וְחַם הַשֶּׁמֶשׁ וְנָמָס הַנּוֹתָר, וּמִדְּמוֹקֵי וְנָמָס בְּאַרְבַּע שָׁעוֹת מִכְּלָל דְּלָאו זְמַן לְקִיטָה הוּא, וְלָאו בֹּקֶר מִיקְרֵי: אַרְבַּע שָׁעוֹת נָמֵי צַפְרָא הוּא. דְּהָא אָמְרַתְּ עַד וְעַד בִּכְלָל, וְגַבֵּי תָּמִיד כְּתִיב תַּעֲשֶׂה בַבֹּקֶר: לִשְׁנֵי בְקָרִים. שֶׁלֹּא הָיוּ לוֹקְטִים אֶלָּא בְּשָׁלֹשׁ שָׁעוֹת רִאשׁוֹנוֹת, שֶׁהוּא בֹּקֶר רִאשׁוֹן: הָתָם אָמַר רַב כָּהֲנָא. גַּבֵּי תְּפִלַּת הַשַּׁחַר: שֶׁל שַׁבָּת בְּעֶרֶב שַׁבָּת. שֶׁקִּיבֵּל עָלָיו שַׁבָּת מִבְּעוֹד יוֹם: שְׁמַע מִינַּהּ. כְּרַבִּי יְהוּדָה ס״ל, דְּאָמַר מִפְּלַג הַמִּנְחָה אָזֵיל לֵיהּ זְמַן תְּפִלַּת הַמִּנְחָה וְעָיֵיל לֵיהּ זְמַן תְּפִלַּת עַרְבִית: וְלֹא פַּסְקֵיהּ לִצְלוֹתֵיהּ. כְּלוֹמַר: לֹא הִפְסִיק בֵּין רַבִּי יִרְמְיָה וְלַכּוֹתֶל, לַעֲבוֹר לְפָנָיו וְלֵישֵׁב בִּמְקוֹמוֹ, אֶלָּא עָמַד עַל עָמְדוֹ:

כנגד

תוספות

תא שמע ושל מוספין כל היום ורבי יהודה אומר עד שבע שעות ותניא היו לפניו וכו׳. ולא גרסינן אימא סיפא ושל וכו׳, שאינו במשנה, שדברי רבי יהודה שאמר "עד שבע שעות" אינו במשנה, ויש ספרים שהגיהו אותו במשנה, ומיהו בכל הספרים הישנים אינו. וא״ת: ורבי למה לא הזכיר אותו במשנה? וי״ל: משום דלא ס״ל כוותיה בהא דאמר עד שבע שעות, אבל בהא דקאמר עד ארבע שעות ס״ל כוותיה, משום דתנן בבחירתא כוותיה. ובההיא דפלג המנחה נמי, משום דאמרינן לקמן דעבד כמר עבד ודעבד כמר עבד, דהכי פירושא דעבד כר׳ יהודה (עבד) דאמר מפלג המנחה ליליא הוא עבד, ומשום הכי מנחה לא. אבל אין לפרש הכל בתפלת המנחה, ועבד כרבי יהודה שהתפלל מנחה קודם פלג, דפשיטא דרבנן מודו בשיעורו דרבי יהודה:

דרב צלי של שבת בע״ש. תימה: דהא אמרינן בפרק "במה מדליקין" (ד׳ כג:) ובלבד שלא יקדים ושלא יאחר! ויש לומר: דהתם בשאינו מקבל עליו שבת מיד, אבל הכא איירי שמקבל עליו שבת מיד הלכך לא הויא הקדמה. וטעמא משום דס״ל כרבי יהודה, וכן הנך דלקמן שהתפללו של מ״ש בשבת היינו משום דסבירא להו כרבי יהודה לענין תפלת הערב, שהיא שעה ורביע קודם הלילה, אעפ״כ [אין] אסור לעשות מלאכה[א] *במ״ש מיד לאחר פלג המנחה. וכן לענין תוספת שבת (*וט׳ בלא) וי״ה, דקי״ל שהוא מן התורה, *אם כן לא צריך שיעור גדול כל כך:

ולא

[בע״] · [ויו״] · [אפ״ה]

עין משפט נר מצוה

יד א מיי׳ פ״ז מהלכות יבום וחליצה הלכה טו טוש״ע אה״ע סימן קעה סעיף יא:

טו ב מיי׳ פי״ב מהל׳ גרושין הלכה טו סמג עשין נ טוש״ע אה״ע סי׳ יז סעיף ג:

טז ג מיי׳ פ״י מהלכות נזקי ממון הלכה ב סמג עשין סו:

יז ד מיי׳ פ״ו מהל׳ איסורי מזבח הל׳ ט:

יח ה מיי׳ פ״א מהל׳ תמידין הל׳ ב סמג עשין קל:

יט ו ז מיי׳ פ״ג מהל׳ תפלה [הל׳ א] סמג עשין יט טוש״ע או״ח סי׳ פ״ט סעיף א:

כ ח מיי׳ שם הלכה ד סמג שם טוש״ע או״ח סי׳ רלג סעיף א:

כא ט מיי׳ שם הלכה ז סמג עשין כט טור שו״ע או״ח סימן רסז סעיף ב:

כב י מיי׳ פ״ה מהל׳ תפלה הלכה ו סמג עשין יט טוש״ע או״ח סי׳ קב סעיף ד:

רב נסים גאון

העיד ר׳ יהודה בן בבא על חמשה דברים. הא דתני על התרנגול שנסקל בירושלים [על] שהרג את הנפש כבר מפורש בתלמוד ארץ ישראל במסכת עירובין בפרק המוצא תפילין (הלכה א) והכי גרסינן ראו (נ״א ראה) מוחו של תינוק רופף והלך וניקרו וזה הדבר ידוע הוא כי התינוקות מוחיהן פתוחין ונראה להן רפרוף מתחת העור שעל המוח ניקר אותו מקום עד שנקבו והרגו לתינוק וזה התרנגול ראוי להורגו מן הכתוב כי אין הפרש לשורו לתרנגלו וכל בעלי חיים שברשותו אכולהי אמר רחמנא סקל יסקל השור: **הואיל** ותנן (בבתריתא) [בבחירתא] כוותיה ומאי היא מס׳ עדיות פ״ו מ״א שזו המשנה שנויה בה העיד ר׳ יודה בן בבא:

גליון הש״ס

גמ׳ שממאנין את הקטנה. הקטנות כל״ל [וכמבואר בנדה ח]: **שם** ועל תמיד של שחר. עי׳ ברש״י משלי לא ועי׳ מנחות ד׳ סד ע״ב תוס׳ ד״ה ועל: **שם** לאחוריה דרב. תפלה של חול. כן הוא בבה״ג:

מסורת הש״ס

[ע׳ תוס׳ חולין נה. ד״ה כל שיעורי]

לקמן דף כח.

עדיות פ״ו משנה א נדה דף ח.

[ע׳ תוס׳ מנחות סד: ד״ה ועל]

[קדושין נב: בכורות כו.]

מכילתא דר״י פרשת בשלח

הגהות הב״ח

(א) תוס׳ ד״ה דרב וכו׳ מלאכה במ״ש נ״ב דלאכתי יום הוא וכן לענין תוספת שבת אין צריך להוסיף קודם פלג המנחה:

עין משפט
נר מצוה

כג א מיי׳ פ״ה מהל׳ ת״ת הלכה ו סמג עשין יב טוש״ע או״ח סי׳ ל סעיף כד [וכי״ד סימן רמב סעיף טז]:
כד ב מיי׳ שם הל׳ ה סמג עשין יג טוש״ע יו״ד סי׳ רמב סעיף יז:
לעיל לחומרא כנ״ל רש״א
כה ג מיי׳ שם הל׳ ב טוש״ע שם סעי׳ ג:
כו ד מיי׳ שם הלכה ט טוש״ע שם סעי׳ כד:
כז ה מיי׳ שם טוש״ע או״ח סימן ל סעיף כה:
כח ו ז שו״ע א״ח סימן רסג סעיף יד:
כט ח מיי׳ פ״ג מהלכות תפלה הל׳ ז (ופכ״ט מהלכות שבת הל׳ י״א) סמג עשין כט טור שו״ע א״ח סי׳ רסז סעיף ב:
ל ט מיי׳ וסמג שם טור שו״ע או״ח סי׳ רלג סעיף ג:
לא י מיי׳ פ״ג מהלכות תפלה הלכה ו:
לב כ מיי׳ פ״א מהל׳ תפלה הלכה ו ופ״ג הל׳ ו ז ופ״ט הלכה ט סמג עשין יט טור או״ח סי׳ רלה רלו רלז:

לא כנגד רבו ולא אחורי רבו; ותניא, רבי אליעזר אומר: המתפלל אחורי רבו, והנותן שלום לרבו, והמחזיר שלום לרבו, *והחולק על ישיבתו של רבו, והאומר *דבר שלא שמע מפי רבו – גורם לשכינה שתסתלק מישראל! – שאני רבי ירמיה בר אבא, דתלמיד חבר הוה. והיינו *דקאמר ליה רבי ירמיה בר אבא לרב: 'מי בדלת'? אמר ליה: אין, בדילנא, ולא אמר, 'מי בדיל מר'.§ ומי בדיל?! והאמר רבי אבין: פעם אחת התפלל רבי של שבת בערב שבת, ונכנס למרחץ ויצא ושנה לן פרקין ועדיין לא חשכה! *אמר רבא: ההוא דנכנס להזיע, וקודם גזירה הוה. איני?! והא אביי שרא ליה לרב דימי בר ליואי לכברויי סלי! – ההוא טעותא הואי. – וטעותא מי הדרא?! והא אמר אבידן: פעם אחת נתקשרו שמים בעבים, כסבורים העם לומר חשכה הוא, ונכנסו לבית הכנסת והתפללו של מוצאי שבת בשבת, ונתפזרו העבים וזרחה החמה, ובאו ושאלו את רבי, ואמר: הואיל והתפללו – התפללו! – שאני צבור, דלא מטרחינן להו.§ א״ר חייא בר אבין: רב צלי של שבת בערב שבת, רבי יאשיה מצלי של מוצאי שבת בשבת. רב צלי של שבת בערב שבת. אומר קדושה על הכוס, או אינו אומר קדושה על הכוס? ת״ש: דאמר רב נחמן אמר שמואל: מתפלל אדם של שבת בערב שבת ואומר קדושה על הכוס. והלכתא כוותיה. רבי יאשיה מצלי של מוצאי שבת בשבת. אומר הבדלה על הכוס או אינו אומר הבדלה על הכוס? ת״ש דאמר רב יהודה אמר שמואל: מתפלל אדם של מוצאי שבת בשבת, ואומר הבדלה על הכוס. אמר ר׳ זירא אמר רבי אסי אמר ר׳ אלעזר א״ר חנינא אמר רב: בצד עמוד זה התפלל ר׳ ישמעאל בר׳ יוסי של שבת בערב שבת. כי אתא עולא, אמר: בצד תמרה הוה ולא בצד עמוד הוה, ולא ר׳ ישמעאל ברבי יוסי הוה אלא ר׳ אלעזר בר׳ יוסי הוה, ולא של שבת בערב שבת הוה אלא של מוצאי שבת בשבת הוה.§ "תפלת הערב אין לה קבע". מאי "אין לה קבע"? אילימא דאי בעי מצלי כוליה ליליא – ליתני תפלת הערב כל הלילה! אלא מאי "אין לה קבע"? כמאן דאמר: *תפלת ערבית רשות. דאמר רב יהודה אמר שמואל: תפלת ערבית, רבן גמליאל אומר: חובה, ר׳ יהושע אומר: *רשות. אמר אביי: הלכה כדברי האומר חובה. ורבא אמר: הלכה כדברי האומר רשות.§ ת״ר מעשה בתלמיד אחד שבא לפני ר׳ יהושע, א״ל: תפלת ערבית רשות או חובה? אמר ליה רשות. בא לפני רבן גמליאל, א״ל: תפלת ערבית רשות או חובה? א״ל: חובה. א״ל: והלא ר׳ יהושע אמר לי רשות! א״ל: *המתן עד שיכנסו בעלי תריסין לבית המדרש. כשנכנסו בעלי תריסין, עמד השואל ושאל: תפלת ערבית רשות או חובה? א״ל רבן גמליאל: חובה. אמר להם רבן גמליאל לחכמים: כלום יש אדם שחולק בדבר זה? אמר ליה ר׳ יהושע: לאו. א״ל: והלא משמך אמרו לי רשות! אמר ליה: יהושע, עמוד על רגליך ויעידו בך! עמד רבי יהושע על רגליו ואמר: אלמלא אני חי והוא מת – יכול החי להכחיש את המת, ועכשיו שאני חי והוא חי – היאך יכול החי להכחיש את החי? היה רבן גמליאל יושב ודורש, ור׳ יהושע עומד על רגליו, עד שרננו כל העם ואמרו לחוצפית התורגמן: עמוד! ועמד.§ אמרי: עד כמה נצעריה וניזיל? בר״ה אשתקד צעריה, בבכורות במעשה דר׳ צדוק צעריה, הכא נמי צעריה, תא ונעבריה! מאן נוקים ליה? נוקמיה לרבי יהושע? בעל מעשה הוא; נוקמיה לר׳ עקיבא? דילמא עניש ליה, דלית ליה זכות אבות; אלא נוקמיה לר׳ אלעזר בן עזריה, דהוא חכם והוא עשיר והוא עשירי לעזרא. הוא חכם – דאי מקשי ליה מפרק ליה, והוא עשיר – דאי אית ליה לפלוחי לבי קיסר אף הוא איזיל ופלח, והוא עשירי לעזרא – דאית ליה זכות אבות ולא מצי עניש ליה. אתו ואמרו ליה: ניחא ליה למר דליהוי ריש מתיבתא? אמר להו: איזיל ואימליך באינשי ביתי. אזל ואמליך בדביתהו. אמרה ליה: דלמא

(לעיל ד: שבת ט:)

רש״י

כנגד רבו. אלא רבו, ומראה כאילו הם שוים: אחורי רבו. נמי יוהרא הוא: שלום לרבו. כשאר כל אדם שלום עליך ולא אמר לו שלום עליך רבי: והיינו דקאמר ליה. אותו היום שהתפלל רב של שבת בערב שבת אמר ליה רבי ירמיה: מי בדלת מן המלאכה הואיל וקבלת עליך שבת בתפלתך: ולא אמר ליה מי בדיל מר. שמע מינה: תלמיד חבר הוי ליה: לבית המרחץ. סלקא דעתך – לאחר שגזרו על הזיעה ועל הרחיצה בשבת, כדאמרי׳ במסכת שבת בפרק כירה שהסיקוה (ד׳ מ.). אלמא: אע״ג דצלי, לא בדיל מאיסורי שבת: אמר רבא להזיע. נכנס להזיע מחמת חום בית המרחץ, ולא נתן עליו מים: וקודם גזרה. עד שלא גזרו על הזיעה. ובכל דוכתא דאמרינן כדאמר רבא להזיע כו׳ – מהכא אמרינן: לכברויי סלי. לעשן אותן בגפרית לאחר שהתפלל של שבת בערב שבת: טעותא הואי. לא קבל עליו תוספת שבת משעת תפלה מדעת, אלא יום המעונן היה וכסבור חשכה ואחר כך זרחה חמה: הואיל והתפללו התפללו. ולא הצריכם להתפלל משתחשך, אלמא: תפלה היא; ואע״פ שלא הותרו במלאכה, התם הוא דלא לעבור על ד״ת, אבל לענין תוספת אע״ג דבטעות הוה, תוספת הוא ע״י תפלה, הואיל ואמר תפלה קבלה היא: בעלי תריסין. חכמים המנצחים זה את זה בהלכה: היאך יכול החי להכחיש את החי. על כרחי אני צריך להודות שאמרתי לו רשות: התורגמן. שהיה עומד לפני רבן גמליאל ומשמיע לרבים את הדרשה מפי רבן גמליאל: עמוד. שתוק: אשתקד. שנה שעברה: בראש השנה. במסכת ראש השנה (דף כה.), שאמר לו: גוזר אני עליך שתבא אצלי במקלך ובמעותיך ביום הכפורים שחל להיות בחשבונך: בבכורות. במסכת בכורות (דף לו.): במעשה דרבי צדוק. בבכורות הוא. ר׳ צדוק הוה ליה בוכרא, ואמר ליה רבן גמליאל לר׳ יהושע: עמוד על רגליך כו׳ כי הכא: תא ונעבריה. בוא ונעביר אותו מן הנשיאות: בעל מעשה הוא. והוה ליה לרבן גמליאל צערא טפי: לית ליה זכות אבות. ודילמא עניש ליה רבן גמליאל: מעברין לך. יורידוך מן הנשיאות בשביל אחר:
ה״ג

תוספות

ולא אחורי רבו. פירש רש״י: משום יוהרא. ויש מפרש: שנראה כמשתחוה לרבו: והנותן שלום לרבו והמחזיר שלום. פירוש: כשאר בני אדם, שאינו אומר 'שלום עליך רבי' והיינו דאמרינן: (ב״ק דף עג:) כדי שאילת תלמיד לרב. אי נמי, ההוא לכתחלה קאמר, ובתלמיד חבר דשרי, ככל הני דלקמן: הואיל והתפללו וכו׳. הכא נמי נימא *לענין(א) חומרא ואמאי שרי ליה. ובקונטרס פי׳ בפנים אחר: שאני צבור. אע״ג דלא מטא זמן *אין(ב) איסורא איסור בעשיית מלאכה, אף על גב דטעותא הוא: צלי של מוצאי שבת וכו׳. יש לומר דהכא מיירי שיש לו צורך מצוה לעשות במוצאי שבת, כגון ללכת למול תינוק ולא יהיה לו יין להבדלה אם לא יקדים, דודאי צריך להוסיף מחול על הקדש דאורייתא, אבל בחנם לא. ופשיטא שלא היו ממהרים להבדיל ולהתפלל של מוצאי שבת בשבת, דגם במלאכה אסור עם חשיכה: הלכה כדברי האומר רשות. לאו דוקא רשות, אלא כדפרישית לעיל (ד׳ כו.); ולכך נקרא רשות – לבטלה עבור מצוה אחרת העוברת: והלכתא כוותיה דרב. ונראה דלכך תקנו פסוקים וקדיש בין גאולה לתפלה, דרשות היא: [ע׳ תוס׳ לעיל ד: ד״ה אמר ר״י]: ושל

רב נסים גאון

אמר רבא [כו׳] להזיע וקודם גזירה. איתה מיפרשה במס׳ שבת בפ׳ כירה (דף מ.) אמר ר׳ שמעון בן פזי אמר ר׳ יהושע בן לוי משום בר קפרא בתחלה היו רוחצין בחמין שהוחמו מערב שבת כו׳ ראו שאין הדבר עומד התירו להן חמי טבריא ועדיין זיעה במקומה עומדת הודיענו בכאן כי רבי שהתפלל של שבת בערב שבת כבר קיבלה לשבת עילויה ואיחייב לשבות ונאסרו עליו החמין לרחוץ בהן ולא נכנס במרחץ אלא להזיע בלבד וזה המעשה היה קודם שגזרו חכמים על הזיעה לפי מה שיש בהלכה שהזכרנוה אסרו להן להזיע. אמרי [עד] כמה נצעריה וניזיל בר״ה צעריה בבכורות צעריה. האי דצעריה בראש השנה שנוי הוא בפרק אם אינן מכירין אותו (דף כה.) דתנן ועוד באו שנים ואמרו ראינוהו בזמנו שלח לו רבן גמליאל גוזר אני עליך שתבא אצלי במקלך ובמעותיך ביום הכפורים שחל להיות בחשבונך ובבכורות (עוד) בפרק כל פסולי המוקדשים (דף לו.) פירשו מעשה (אחר) [אחד] שאירע לר׳ יהושע עם רבן גמליאל דכסיף ליה קמי רבנן והעמידו על רגליו ברבים עד שנכנסה קנאה בלבו כל העם שהיו לשם ושיתקו את המתורגמן וזו היא הגירסא של זו המעשה ר׳ צדוק הוה ליה בוכרא רמא ליה שערי בסלי נצרין של ערבה קלופה בהדי דאכיל איבוע שיפותיה אתא לקמיה דר׳ יהושע אמר ליה כלום חלקנו בין בור לחבר אמר ליה הין בא לפני רבן גמליאל אמר ליה לאו אמר ליה והלא ר׳ יהושע אמר לי הין אמר לו המתן עד שיכנסו בעלי תריסין לבית המדרש כיון שנכנסו עמד השואל ושאל כלום חלקנו בין בור לחבר אמר לו ר׳ יהושע לאו אמר לו רבן גמליאל והלא משמך אמרו לי הין אמר לו עמוד על רגליך ויעידו בך עמד ר׳ יהושע על רגליו ואמר אלמלי אני (מת) [חי] והוא (חי) [מת] יכול החי להכחיש את (החי) [המת] עכשיו שאני חי והוא חי היאך חי יכול להכחיש את החי] היה רבן גמליאל יושב ודורש ור׳ יהושע עומד עד שריננו כל העם ואמרו לחוצפית התורגמן העמד: נוקי לר׳ עקיבא לית ליה זכות אבות. איתה בסנהדרין בפרק כל ישראל יש להן חלק (דף לו) מבני בניו של סיסרא למדו תורה בירושלים ומאן אינון ר׳ עקיבא ואיתה נמי בפ׳ הניזקין דמסכת גיטין (דף נז:) נוקי לר׳ אלעזר בן עזריה שהוא חכם ועשיר והוא עשירי לעזרא הסופר. החכמה שלו גלויה היא וידועה הלא תראה היאך אמר ר׳ יהושע אין דור יתום שר׳ אלעזר בן עזריה שרוי בתוכו באותה המעשה האמור במסכת חגיגה בפרק א׳ (דף ג) והעושר שלו נמי כבר גרסי׳ בפרק (במה אשה) [נ״ל במה בהמה] (שבת דף נד) י״ב אלפי עגלי הוה מעשר ר׳ אלעזר בן עזריה מעדריה כל שתא ובמס׳ קדושין בפרק האיש מקדש (דף מט) על מנת שאני עשיר אין אומרים כר׳ אלעזר בן חרסום וכר׳ אלעזר בן עזריה וייחוסו לעזרא הסופר נמי איתה במנחות באות מצה (דף נג) אמרו ליה רבנן לר׳ פרידא (רב עוירא) [ר׳ עזרא] בריה דרב אבטולס דהוא עשירי לר׳ אלעזר בן עזריה דהוא עשירי לעזרא קאי אבבא ובגמרא דפירקין דבני מערבא [הלכה ח] וגם (בפסחים בפרק תמיד) [נ״ל בתענית פ״ד ה״א] גרסינן הלכו ומינו את ר׳ אלעזר בן עזריה בן י״ז שנה ונתמלא כל ראשו שיבה והיה ר׳ עקיבא יושב ומצטער ואומר לא שהוא בן תורה יותר ממני אלא שהוא בן גדולים יותר ממני אשרי אדם שזכו לו אבותיו אשרי אדם שיש לו יתד להתלות בה ומה היתה יתידתו של ר׳ אלעזר בן עזריה שהיה עשירי לעזרא:

מסורת הש״ס

חלק קו. וע״ש
סוכה דף כז: וסוף מסכת כלה
[עירובין מ:]
[ביצה לב.]
ס״א רשות והלכתא כדברי האומר חובה ורב אמר הלכה כדברי האומר רשות ע׳ יומא דף פז:
[בכורות לו. וע״ש בתוס׳]

הגהות הב״ח

(א) תוס׳ ד״ה הואיל וכו׳ נמי נימא לענין מלאכה ואמאי שרי: (ב) ד״ה שאני וכו׳ אין איסור בעשיית כנ״ל ותיבת איסורא נמחק:

גליון הש״ס

גמ׳ והמחזיר שלום לרבו. ברי״ף וברא״ש ליתא להא והמחזיר שלום לרבו: שם דתלמיד חבר הוה. עיין קדושין ד׳ מ״ו ע״א תוס׳ ד״ה נראין: שם וקודם גזרה הוה. ע׳ שבת ד׳ מ׳ ע״ב ברש״י ד״ה דהא מעשה. וברשב״א בחדושיו שם:

וזה

דִּלְמָא מְעַבְּרִין לָךְ? אָמַר לָהּ: [לִשְׁתַּמֵּשׁ אֱינָשׁ] יוֹמָא חֲדָא בְּכָסָא דְּמוֹקְרָא וּלְמָחָר לִיתְּבַר. אֲמַרָה לֵיהּ: לֵית לָךְ חִיוָּרְתָּא. הַהוּא יוֹמָא בַּר תְּמָנֵי סְרֵי שְׁנֵי הֲוָה, אִתְרְחִישׁ לֵיהּ נִיסָּא וְאַהֲדַרוּ לֵיהּ תְּמָנֵי סְרֵי דָּרֵי חִיוָּרְתָּא. הַיְינוּ דְּקָאָמַר ר' אֶלְעָזָר בֶּן עֲזַרְיָה: *הֲרֵי אֲנִי "כְּבֶן" שִׁבְעִים שָׁנָה, וְלֹא "בֶּן" שִׁבְעִים שָׁנָה.§ תָּנָא; אוֹתוֹ הַיּוֹם סִלְּקוּהוּ לְשׁוֹמֵר הַפֶּתַח [א]וְנִתְּנָה לָהֶם רְשׁוּת לַתַּלְמִידִים לִיכָּנֵס. שֶׁהָיָה ר"ג מַכְרִיז וְאוֹמֵר: *כָּל תַּלְמִיד שֶׁאֵין תּוֹכוֹ כְּבָרוֹ – לֹא יִכָּנֵס לְבֵית הַמִּדְרָשׁ. הַהוּא יוֹמָא אִתּוֹסְפוּ כַּמָּה סַפְסְלֵי. א"ר יוֹחָנָן: פְּלִיגִי בָּהּ אַבָּא יוֹסֵף בֶּן דּוֹסְתַּאי וְרַבָּנַן, חַד אָמַר: אִתּוֹסְפוּ אַרְבַּע מְאָה סַפְסְלֵי; וְחַד אָמַר: שְׁבַע מְאָה סַפְסְלֵי. הֲוָה קָא חָלְשָׁא דַּעְתֵּיהּ דר"ג, אָמַר: דִּלְמָא ח"ו מָנַעְתִּי תּוֹרָה מִיִּשְׂרָאֵל. אַחֲזוּ לֵיהּ בְּחֶלְמֵיהּ חַצְבֵי חִיוָּרֵי דְּמַלְיָין קִטְמָא. וְלָא הִיא, הַהִיא לְיַתּוּבֵי דַּעְתֵּיהּ הוּא דְּאַחֲזוּ לֵיהּ.§ תָּנָא: עֵדֻיּוֹת בּוֹ בַּיּוֹם נִשְׁנֵית, וְכָל הֵיכָא דְּאָמְרִינַן "בּוֹ בַּיּוֹם" – הַהוּא יוֹמָא הֲוָה. וְלֹא הָיְתָה הֲלָכָה שֶׁהָיְתָה תְּלוּיָה בְּבֵית הַמִּדְרָשׁ שֶׁלֹּא פֵּירְשׁוּהָ. וְאַף ר"ג לֹא מָנַע עַצְמוֹ מִבֵּית הַמִּדְרָשׁ אֲפִילּוּ שָׁעָה אַחַת, דִּתְנַן: *בּוֹ בַּיּוֹם בָּא יְהוּדָה גֵּר עַמּוֹנִי לִפְנֵיהֶם בְּבֵית הַמִּדְרָשׁ, אָמַר לָהֶם:[א] מָה אֲנִי לָבֹא בַּקָּהָל? א"ל ר"ג: אָסוּר אַתָּה לָבֹא בַּקָּהָל; א"ל ר' יְהוֹשֻׁעַ: [ב]מוּתָּר אַתָּה לָבֹא בַּקָּהָל. א"ל ר"ג: וַהֲלֹא כְּבָר נֶאֱמַר: °"לֹא יָבֹא עַמּוֹנִי וּמוֹאָבִי בִּקְהַל ה'"! א"ל ר' יְהוֹשֻׁעַ: וְכִי עַמּוֹן וּמוֹאָב בִּמְקוֹמָן הֵן יוֹשְׁבִין?![ב] *כְּבָר עָלָה סַנְחֵרִיב מֶלֶךְ אַשּׁוּר וּבִלְבֵּל אֶת כָּל הָאוּמּוֹת, שֶׁנֶּאֱמַר: °"וְאָסִיר גְּבֻלֹת עַמִּים וַעֲתוּדוֹתֵיהֶם שׁוֹסֵתִי וְאוֹרִיד כַּאַבִּיר יוֹשְׁבִים", *וְכָל דְּפָרֵישׁ – מֵרוּבָּא פָּרֵישׁ. אָמַר לוֹ ר"ג: וַהֲלֹא כְּבָר נֶאֱמַר: °"וְאַחֲרֵי כֵן אָשִׁיב אֶת שְׁבוּת בְּנֵי עַמּוֹן נְאֻם ה'" – וּכְבָר שָׁבוּ. אָמַר לוֹ ר' יְהוֹשֻׁעַ: וַהֲלֹא כְּבָר נֶאֱמַר: °"וְשַׁבְתִּי אֶת שְׁבוּת עַמִּי יִשְׂרָאֵל" – וַעֲדַיִין לֹא שָׁבוּ. מִיָּד הִתִּירוּהוּ לָבֹא בַּקָּהָל.§ אר"ג: הוֹאִיל וְהָכִי הֲוָה, אֵיזִיל וַאֲפַיְּיסֵיהּ לר' יְהוֹשֻׁעַ. כִּי מְטָא לְבֵיתֵיהּ, חֲזִינְהוּ לְאַשִּׁיתָא דְּבֵיתֵיהּ דְּמַשְׁחֲרָן. א"ל: °מִכּוֹתְלֵי בֵּיתְךָ אַתָּה נִיכָּר שֶׁפֶּחָמִי אַתָּה. א"ל: אוֹי לוֹ לַדּוֹר שֶׁאַתָּה פַּרְנָסוֹ, *שֶׁאִי אַתָּה יוֹדֵעַ בְּצַעֲרָן שֶׁל ת"ח [ג]בַּמֶּה הֵם מִתְפַּרְנְסִים וּבַמֶּה הֵם נִזּוֹנִים. אָמַר לוֹ: נַעֲנֵיתִי לָךְ, מְחוֹל לִי! לֹא אַשְׁגַּח בֵּיהּ. עֲשֵׂה בִּשְׁבִיל כְּבוֹד אַבָּא! פַּיֵּים. אָמְרוּ: מַאן נֵיזִיל וְלֵימָא לְהוּ לְרַבָּנַן? אֲמַר לְהוּ הַהוּא כּוֹבֵס: אֲנָא אָזֵילְנָא. שְׁלַח לְהוּ ר' יְהוֹשֻׁעַ לְבֵי מִדְרָשָׁא: מַאן דְּלָבֵישׁ מַדָּא יִלְבַּשׁ מַדָּא, וּמַאן דְּלָא לָבֵישׁ מַדָּא יֵימַר לֵיהּ לְמַאן דְּלָבֵישׁ מַדָּא 'שְׁלַח מַדָּךְ וַאֲנָא אֶלְבְּשֵׁיהּ'?! אֲמַר לְהוּ ר"ע לְרַבָּנַן: טְרוֹקוּ גַּלֵּי, דְּלָא לֵיתוּ עַבְדֵי דר"ג וּלְצַעֲרוּ לְרַבָּנַן. א"ר יְהוֹשֻׁעַ: מוּטָב דְּאֵיקוּם וְאֵיזִיל אֲנָא לְגַבַּיְיהוּ. אֲתָא, טְרַף אַבָּבָא. א"ל: [ד]מַזֶּה בֶּן מַזֶּה יַזֶּה, וְשֶׁאֵינוֹ לֹא מַזֶּה וְלֹא בֶּן מַזֶּה יֹאמַר לְמַזֶּה בֶּן מַזֶּה: מֵימֶיךָ מֵי מְעָרָה וְאֶפְרְךָ אֵפֶר מִקְלֶה? א"ל ר"ע: רַבִּי יְהוֹשֻׁעַ, נִתְפַּיַּיסְתָּ? כְּלוּם עָשִׂינוּ אֶלָּא בִּשְׁבִיל כְּבוֹדְךָ! לְמָחָר אֲנִי וְאַתָּה נַשְׁכִּים לְפִתְחוֹ. אָמְרֵי: הֵיכִי נַעֲבֵיד? נַעַבְרֵיהּ – *גְּמִירִי: מַעֲלִין בַּקֹּדֶשׁ וְאֵין מוֹרִידִין! נִדְרוֹשׁ מָר חֲדָא שַׁבְּתָא וּמָר חֲדָא שַׁבְּתָא – אָתֵי לְקַנְּאוּיֵי! אֶלָּא: לִדְרוֹשׁ ר"ג *תְּלָתָא שַׁבְּתֵי, וראב"ע חֲדָא שַׁבְּתָא. וְהַיְינוּ דְּאָמַר מָר: *שַׁבָּת שֶׁל מִי הָיְתָה – שֶׁל ראב"ע הָיְתָה. וְאוֹתוֹ תַּלְמִיד – ר' שִׁמְעוֹן בֶּן יוֹחַאי הֲוָה.§ [ה]"וְשֶׁל מוּסָפִין כָּל הַיּוֹם". א"ר יוֹחָנָן: [ו]°וְנִקְרָא פּוֹשֵׁעַ. ת"ר: *הָיוּ לְפָנָיו שְׁתֵּי תְּפִלּוֹת, אַחַת שֶׁל מִנְחָה וְאַחַת שֶׁל מוּסָף – מִתְפַּלֵּל שֶׁל מִנְחָה וְאח"כ מִתְפַּלֵּל שֶׁל מוּסָף, שֶׁזּוֹ תְּדִירָה וְזוֹ אֵינָהּ תְּדִירָה. ר' יְהוּדָה אוֹמֵר: מִתְפַּלֵּל שֶׁל מוּסָף וְאח"כ מִתְפַּלֵּל שֶׁל מִנְחָה, שֶׁזּוֹ מִצְוָה עוֹבֶרֶת וְזוֹ מִצְוָה שֶׁאֵינָהּ עוֹבֶרֶת. *א"ר יוֹחָנָן, [ז]הֲלָכָה: מִתְפַּלֵּל שֶׁל מִנְחָה וְאח"כ מִתְפַּלֵּל שֶׁל מוּסָף. ר' זֵירָא °כִּי הֲוָה חָלֵישׁ מִגִּירְסֵיהּ, הֲוָה אָזֵיל וְיָתֵיב אַפִּתְחָא דְּבֵי ר' נָתָן בַּר טוֹבִי, אָמַר: כִּי חָלְפֵי רַבָּנַן אָז אֵיקוּם מִקַּמַּיְיהוּ וַאֲקַבֵּל אַגְרָא. נְפַק אֲתָא ר' נָתָן בַּר טוֹבִי, א"ל: מַאן אֲמַר הֲלָכָה בֵּי מִדְרָשָׁא? א"ל, הָכִי א"ר יוֹחָנָן: אֵין הֲלָכָה כר' יְהוּדָה דְּאָמַר: מִתְפַּלֵּל אָדָם שֶׁל מוּסָף ואח"כ מִתְפַּלֵּל שֶׁל מִנְחָה. א"ל: רַבִּי יוֹחָנָן אֲמָרָהּ?! אָמַר לֵיהּ: אִין. *תְּנָא מִינֵּיהּ אַרְבְּעִין זִמְנִין. א"ל: חֲדָא הִיא לָךְ, אוֹ חֲדַת הִיא לָךְ? א"ל: חֲדַת הִיא לִי, מִשּׁוּם דִּמְסַפְּקָא לִי בר' יְהוֹשֻׁעַ בֶּן לֵוִי.§ אריב"ל: [ח]כָּל הַמִּתְפַּלֵּל תְּפִלָּה שֶׁל מוּסָפִין לְאַחַר שֶׁבַע שָׁעוֹת לר' יְהוּדָה, עָלָיו הַכָּתוּב אוֹמֵר: °"נוּגֵי מִמּוֹעֵד אָסַפְתִּי מִמֵּךְ הָיוּ". מַאי מַשְׁמַע דְּהַאי "נוּגֵי" לִישָּׁנָא דְּתַבְרָא הוּא? כִּדְמְתַרְגֵּם רַב יוֹסֵף: "תַּבְרָא אָתֵי עַל שַׂנְאֵיהוֹן דְּבֵית יִשְׂרָאֵל עַל דְּאַחֲרוּ זִמְנֵי מוֹעֲדַיָּא דְּבִירוּשְׁלֵים". א"ר אֶלְעָזָר: כָּל הַמִּתְפַּלֵּל תְּפִלָּה שֶׁל שַׁחֲרִית לְאַחַר אַרְבַּע שָׁעוֹת לר' יְהוּדָה, עָלָיו הַכָּתוּב אוֹמֵר: "נוּגֵי מִמּוֹעֵד אָסַפְתִּי מִמֵּךְ הָיוּ". מַאי מַשְׁמַע דְּהַאי "נוּגֵי" לִישָּׁנָא דְּצַעֲרָא הוּא? דִּכְתִיב: °"דָּלְפָה נַפְשִׁי מִתּוּגָה". רַב נַחְמָן בַּר יִצְחָק אָמַר, מֵהָכָא: °"בְּתוּלֹתֶיהָ נוּגוֹת וְהִיא מַר לָהּ".
רַב

רש"י

ה"ג. דִּלְמָא מְעַבְּרִין לָךְ? אָמַר לָהּ: יוֹמָא חֲדָא בְּכָסָא דְּמוֹקְרָא וּלְמָחָר לִיתְּבַר. ול"ג מַעֲלִין בַּקֹּדֶשׁ: **כָּסָא** דְּמוֹקְרָא. *כּוֹס זְכוּכִית יְקָרָה שֶׁקּוֹרִין לָהּ בִּלְשׁוֹן יִשְׁמָעֵאל ערקי"א. וְאוֹמְרִים בְּנֵי אָדָם בְּמָשָׁל הֶדְיוֹט: יוֹם אֶחָד יִשְׁתַּמֵּשׁ בּוֹ בְּעָלָיו וְיִתְכַּבֵּד בּוֹ, וְאִם יִשָּׁבֵר – יִשָּׁבֵר: **לֵית לָךְ חִיוַּרְתָּא.** אֵין לְךָ שְׂעָרוֹת לְבָנוֹת שֶׁל זִקְנָה, וְנָאֶה לְדַרְשָׁן לִהְיוֹת זָקֵן: **י"ח דָּרֵי חִיוַּרְתָּא.** י"ח שׁוּרוֹת שֶׁל זִקְנָה: **קָא חָלְשָׁא דַּעְתֵּיהּ דר"ג.** כְּשֶׁרָאָה שֶׁנִּתּוֹסְפוּ הַיּוֹם תַּלְמִידִים רַבִּים, וְהָיָה דּוֹאֵג שֶׁלֹּא יֵעָנֵשׁ בַּמֶּה שֶּׁמְּנָעָם בְּיָמָיו מִלָּבֹא: **דְּמַלְיָין קִטְמָא.** כְּלוֹמַר: אַף אֵלּוּ אֵינָם רְאוּיִם: **תְּלוּיָה.** בְּסָפֵק, שֶׁלֹּא פֵּירְשׁוּהָ. מִתּוֹךְ שֶׁרַבּוּ הַתַּלְמִידִים רַב הַחִדּוּד וְהַפִּלְפּוּל: **לְאַשִּׁיתָא** דְּבֵיתֵיהּ דְּמַשְׁחֲרָן. כּוֹתְלֵי בֵּיתוֹ שֶׁל ר' יְהוֹשֻׁעַ שֶׁהָיוּ שְׁחוֹרוֹת: **שֶׁפֶּחָמִי אַתָּה.** עוֹשֶׂה פֶּחָמִים. וְי"א: נַפָּח: **נַעֲנֵיתִי לָךְ.** דִּבַּרְתִּי לְמוּלְךָ יוֹתֵר מִן הָרָאוּי: **דְּלָבִישׁ מַדָּא.** הָרָגִיל לִלְבּוֹשׁ הַמְּעִיל יִלְבַּשׁ. כְּלוֹמַר: הָרָגִיל בִּנְשִׂיאוּת יִהְיֶה נָשִׂיא: **מַזֶּה בֶּן מַזֶּה.** כֹּהֵן בֶּן כֹּהֵן, יַזֶּה אֶת מֵי חַטָּאת: **אֵפֶר מִקְלֶה.** אֵפֶר הַקָּלוּי בְּתַנּוּרִים וְכִירוֹת, כְּלוֹמַר: אֵפֶר סְתָם: **שַׁבָּת שֶׁל מִי הָיְתָה.** בְּמַסֶּכֶת חֲגִיגָה: **וְאוֹתוֹ תַּלְמִיד.** שֶׁשָּׁאַל תְּפִלַּת עַרְבִית רְשׁוּת אוֹ חוֹבָה רשב"י הוּא: **וְנִקְרָא פּוֹשֵׁעַ.** הַמְּאַחֵר כָּ"כ: **מִתְפַּלֵּל שֶׁל מִנְחָה.** מֵאַחַר שֶׁהִגִּיעַ זְמַנָּהּ, כְּדֵי לְהַקְדִּימָהּ בִּתְחִלַּת זְמַנָּהּ, שֶׁלֹּא יִקָּרֵא פּוֹשֵׁעַ גַּם עָלֶיהָ: **ואח"כ שֶׁל מוּסָפִין.** הוֹאִיל וְאִיחֵר, *זְמַנָּהּ אֵינוֹ עוֹבֵר. דְּהָא אָמְרֵי רַבָּנַן וְשֶׁל מוּסָפִים כָּל הַיּוֹם: **שֶׁזּוֹ מִצְוָה עוֹבֶרֶת.** ר' יְהוּדָה לְטַעְמֵיהּ, דְּאָמַר עַד שֶׁבַע שָׁעוֹת וְתוּ לֹא: **כִּי חָלְפִי רַבָּנַן.** תַּלְמִידִים הַיּוֹצְאִים מִבֵּית ר' נָתָן: **מַאן אֲמַר הֲלָכָה בֵּי מִדְרָשָׁא.** מִי מִבְּנֵי הַיְשִׁיבָה אָמַר בְּבֵית הַמִּדְרָשׁ שֶׁהֲלָכָה כר' יְהוּדָה: **חֲדָא הִיא לָךְ אוֹ חֲדַת הִיא לָךְ.** אַחַת הִיא לָךְ – שֶׁלֹּא לָמַדְתָּ דָּבָר מִשְּׁמוֹ שֶׁל ר' יוֹחָנָן אֶלָּא זוֹ בִּלְבַד, לָכֵן חֲבִיבָה הִיא לְךָ; אוֹ חֲדָשָׁה הִיא לָךְ, שֶׁהָיִיתָ סָבוּר שֶׁאֶחָד מִן הָאֲחֵרִים אֲמָרָהּ: ה"ג. **א"ל חֲדַת הִיא לִי דִּמְסַפְּקָא לִי** בר' יְהוֹשֻׁעַ בֶּן לֵוִי. סָבוּר הָיִיתִי שֶׁרַבִּי יְהוֹשֻׁעַ בֶּן לֵוִי אֲמָרָהּ: **אָמַר** ריב"ל. גָּרְסִי' וְל"ג דְּאָמַר: **מִמּוֹעֵד.** מֵחֲמַת שֶׁהֶעֱבִירוּ מוֹעֲדֵי הַתְּפִלּוֹת וְהַחַגִּים, יִהְיוּ נוּגִים וַאֲסוּפִים וְכָלִים:
לא

תוספות

וְשֶׁל מוּסָפִין כָּל הַיּוֹם. הִקְשָׁה הָרַב רַבֵּינוּ שִׁמְשׁוֹן ז"ל, דְּאָמְרִי' בְּפֶרֶק "תָּמִיד נִשְׁחָט" (דף נח.): מוּסָפִין בְּשֵׁשׁ, בְּזִיכִין בְּשֶׁבַע! וְכ"ת: ה"מ לְמִצְוָה, אֲבָל דִּיעֲבַד כָּל יוֹמָא נַמִי זִמְנֵיהּ הוּא, הֲרֵי *בִּתְמוּרָה (פ"ג ד' יד) מַשְׁמַע שֶׁהַמּוּסָפִין הָיוּ נִשְׁחָטִין עִם הַתָּמִיד וְנִקְטָרִין עִמּוֹ! וְתֵירֵץ: דְּהָתָם מַיְירֵי בְּשַׁבָּת*:

הֲלָכָה מִתְפַּלֵּל שֶׁל מִנְחָה וְאח"כ מִתְפַּלֵּל שֶׁל מוּסָף. מִכָּאן יֵשׁ לִיזָּהֵר בְּיוה"כ לְהִתְפַּלֵּל תְּפִלַּת שַׁחֲרִית קוֹדֶם שֵׁשׁ שָׁעוֹת וּמֶחֱצָה, דְּהַיְינוּ קוֹדֶם שֶׁיַּגִּיעַ שְׁעַת הַמִּנְחָה, דְּאִלְּ"כ הָיוּ צְרִיכִין לְהִתְפַּלֵּל תְּפִלַּת הַמִּנְחָה קוֹדֶם. וְהָרִ"י אוֹמֵר דְּאֵינוֹ צָרִיךְ, דְּהָא דְּקָאָמַר שֶׁיִּתְפַּלֵּל תְּפִלַּת הַמִּנְחָה קוֹדֶם – הַיְינוּ כְּשֶׁיֵּשׁ לוֹ לַעֲשׂוֹת צְרָכָיו, שֶׁלֹּא יוּכַל לְהִתְפַּלֵּל תְּפִלַּת הַמִּנְחָה בִּזְמַנָּהּ וְצָרִיךְ לְהִתְפַּלֵּל שְׁנֵיהֶם מִיָּד, כְּגוֹן שֶׁהָיָה לוֹ לֵילֵךְ לִסְעוּדָה גְּדוֹלָה, כְּמוֹ לְנִשּׂוּאִין, וּמִתְיָירֵא שֶׁמָּא יִמְשׁוֹךְ בִּסְעוּדָתוֹ אוֹ שֶׁיִּשְׁתַּכֵּר. אֲבָל אִם הָיָה לוֹ שָׁהוּת לְהִתְפַּלֵּל אַחַר תְּפִלַּת מוּסָף תְּפִלַּת הַמִּנְחָה בִּזְמַנָּהּ, אֵין לוֹ לְהַקְדִּים תְּפִלַּת הַמִּנְחָה אֶלָּא יִתְפַּלֵּל כַּסֵּדֶר, מוּסָף וְאח"כ מִנְחָה:

כִּדְמְתַרְגֵּם רַב יוֹסֵף עַל דְּאַחֲרוּ זִמְנֵי מוֹעֲדַיָּא. וְאִי מַשְׁמַע בִּרְגָלִים אֵין שַׁיָּיךְ לוֹמַר לְשׁוֹן אִיחוּר, שֶׁהֲרֵי אֵין לָהֶם תַּשְׁלוּמִין, אֶלָּא ע"כ בִּתְפִלָּה מַשְׁמַע קְרָא:
כיון

מסורת הש"ס

[ועי' פירש"י לקמן לח. ד"ה כסא]

לעיל פ"א דף יב:

[דוגמתו יומא עב:]

[יומא נב. ועי' תוס' מגילה יב: ותוס' יבמות עו: ובסוטה ט. ד"ה מנימין]

[ידים פ"ד מ"ד]

[יומא פד: יבמות טז: כתובות טו. קדושין עג. זבחים עג.]

דברים כג; ישעיה י; ירמיה מט; עמוס ט

[יומא יב: עג. מגילה ט: כא: הוריות יב: שבת כא: (תמיד לא:) מנחות לט. צט. ושם מפיק לה מקרא וע"ע לשון גמירי]

[יותר נכון לגרוס תרתי וכ"ה בהקדמת הרמב"ם לפי' המשניות ביבמות]

חגיגה ג. [לעיל כז.]

[זבחים יב. לא.]

[פסחים עב. מגילה ז: כתובות כב: נ.]

צפניה ג

תהלים קיט; איכה א

נ"ל וזמנה רש"ל

ס"א ואוי לה לספינה שאתה קברניטה

הגהות הב"ח

(א) גמ' אמר להם (מה אני) תא"מ. ונ"ב ס"א מותר: (ב) שם במקומן הן יושבין והלא כבר:

גליון הש"ס

גמ' מכותלי ביתך. עיין תשב"ץ ח"א ענין קמב: **שם** ונקרא פושע. עיין לקמן (דף מ"ג ע"ב): **שם** כי הוה חליש מגירסא. עיין עירובין (דף כ"ח ע"ב):

עין משפט נר מצוה

לג א מיי' פ"ד מהלכות ת"ת הלכה א טוש"ע יו"ד סי' רמו סעיף ז:

[נ"ל ביומא ד' ע. כ"כ המג"א סימן רפ"א] עיין רש"ל ורש"א

לד ב מיי' פי"ב מהל' איסורי ביאה הלכה כה סמג לאוין קטז טוש"ע אה"ע סימן ד סעיף י:

לה ג מיי' פ"א מהל' ת"ת הלכה ט ופ"י מהל' מתנות עניים הלכה יח:

לו ד מיי' פ"א מהל' מלכים הל' ז טוש"ע י"ד סימן רמה סעיף כב בהגהה:

לז ה ו מיי' פ"ג מהל' תפלה הלכה ה סמג עשין יט טוש"ע או"ח סימן רפו סעיף א:

לח ז מיי' שם הל' יא טוש"ע שם סעיף ד:

לט ח שם סעיף א:

מס' ידים פ"ד משנה ד'

רב נסים גאון

וזה שאמרו כל בו ביום דאמרינן ההוא יומא איתמר. יש במשנה הרב' מזה הענין כגון האי דתנן במס' ידים (פ"ג מ"ה) אמ' ר' שמעון בן עזאי מקובל אני מפי ע"ב זקנים ביום שהושיבו את ר' אלעזר בן עזריה בראש ששיר השירים וקהלת מטמאין את הידי' אמר ר' עקיבא חס ושלום וכו' (פ"ד מ"א) בו ביום נמנו וגמרו על עריבת [הרגלים] בו ביום אמרו [משנה ב] כל הזבחים וכו' ובתוספתא [ידים פ"ב] בו ביום עמד יהודה גר עמוני: **אמר** רבן גמליאל השתא איזיל ואפייסיה לר' יהושע אזל חזינהו לאשיתא דביתיה דהוו קא משחרן כו'. ופירשו בגמרא דבני מערבא אזל ואשכח לר' יהושע יתיב עביד מחטין אמר ליה מן אילין את חיי אמר ליה עד כדון את בעי מידע אוי לדור שאתה פרנסו. והאי דאמר ליה עשה בשביל כבוד בית אבא כלומר בשביל הלל הזקן שהיה מזרע דוד כדגרסינן בפ' יציאות השבת (דף טו) הלל ושמעון גמליאל ושמעון נהגו נשיאותן בפני הבית ק' שנה וזה רבן גמליאל הנזכר בכאן הוא בנו של רבן שמעון בן גמליאל שהוא רביעי להלל הזקן דהוי ליה רבן גמליאל חמישי להלל ובנו רבן שמעון ששי להלל ובנו ר' יהודה הנשיא שהוא רבי והוא רבינו הקדוש הוי שביעי להלל הזקן ואיתא במסכת שבת בפרק במה בהמה (דף נו) רבי דאתי מדוד מהפך בזכותיה דדוד ובגמרא דפרק אחרון דתענית דבני מערבא (הלכה ב) אמרי אמר לוי מגילת יוחסין מצאו בירושלים וכתוב בה הלל מן דדוד ואיתא בפ' אע"פ שאמרו בכתובות (ד' סב) בדקו במשפחות רבי אתי משפטיה בן אביטל. והאי דאמרינן אעפ"כ לא עברוה לר' אלעזר בן עזריה פירשו בתלמוד ארץ ישראל אלא מינו אותו אב בית דין והיינו דאמר מר שבת של מי היתה של ר' אלעזר בן עזריה היתה ואיתא בפירקא קמא דחגיגה (דף ג) תנו רבנן מעשה בר' יוחנן בן ברוקא ור' אלעזר חסמא שהלכו להקביל את פני ר' יהושע בפקיעין אמר להם מה חידוש היה היום בבית המדרש אמרו לו תלמידיך אנחנו ומימיך אנו שותין אמר להן אעפ"כ אי אפשר לבית המדרש בלא חידוש שבת של מי היתה אמרו לו שבת של ר' אלעזר בן עזריה:

עין משפט
נר מצוה

לט א ב מיי' פ"י מהל' תפלה הלכה יו סמג עשין יט טוש"ע או"ח סימן ל סעיף י:
מ ג מיי' פ"ו שם הלכה ד סמג שם טוש"ע או"ח סימן רפו סעיף ג:
מא ד מיי' וסמג שם טור שו"ע א"ח סי' רלב סעיף ג:
מב ה מיי' פ"י מהל' ברכות הלכה כג כד סמג עשין כז טוש"ע או"ח סי' קי סעיף ח:
מג ו טור ושו"ע או"ח סימן א סעיף א:
מד ז מיי' פ"ב מהל' תפלה הלכה ב סמג עשין יט טור שו"ע א"ח סי' קי סעיף א:
מה ח ט מיי' פ"ה שם הלכה יב סמג שם טוש"ע א"ח סימן קיג סעיף ז:
מו י כ מיי' שם טוש"ע שם סעיף ה:

רב נסים גאון

רבן גמליאל אומר בכל יום אדם מתפלל י"ח. בתלמוד ארץ ישראל הזכירו עוד טעמים אחרים (כעין) [אולי צ"ל על שתקנו] י"ח תוספת על מה שיש בתלמודינו דאמרינן ר' חנניה בשם ר' פינחס כנגד י"ח פעמים שאבות כתובין בתורה אברהם יצחק ויעקב אם יאמר לך אדם י"ט הן אמור לו והנה ה' נצב עליו לית הוא מינהון אם יאמר לך אדם י"ז הן אמור לו ויקרא בהן שמי ושם אבותי מינהון הוא ר' שמואל בר נחמני בשם ר' יונתן כנגד י"ח ציוויים שכתב בפרשת משכן שני אמר ר' חייא בר אדא ובלבד מן ואתו אהליאב בן אחיסמך עד סופיה דסיפרא: היה יושב בספינה או באסדא. בגמ' דבני מערבא גרסי היא ואסדא היא רפסודות דכתיב (דברי הימים ב ב) ונביאם לך רפסודות על ים יפו:

הגהות הב"ח

(א) גמ' אזכרות שבק"ש ר' תנחום א"ר יהושע בן לוי אמר כנגד: (ב) רש"י ד"ה שיתפקקו וכו' מן הפקק ולמעלה:

גליון הש"ס

גמ' כשחלה ר"א. במס' דרך ארץ רבה פ"ג איתא ר"א בן עזריה. וע"ש עוד איזה שינויים: שם הני י"ח כנגד מי. עי' מדרש תנחומא ר"פ וירא עוד איזה טעמים. ושם איתא דריב"ל אמר נגד י"ח אזכרות שאמר דוד בהבו לה' בני אלים:

תוספות

כיון שהגיע זמן תפלת המנחה אסור לטעום כלום וכו'. ואית ליה לרבי יהושע מפסיקין, ואפילו מן האכילה, ולא היא:

לייט

גמרא

רב אויא חליש ולא אתא לפרקא דרב יוסף. למחר כי אתא, בעא אביי לאנוחי דעתיה דרב יוסף. א"ל: מ"ט לא אתא מר לפרקא? א"ל: דהוה חליש לבאי ולא מצינא. א"ל: אמאי לא טעמת מידי ואתית? א"ל: לא סבר לה מר להא דרב הונא? דאמר רב הונא: אסור לו לאדם שיטעום כלום קודם שיתפלל תפלת המוספין! -א"ל: איבעי ליה למר לצלויי צלותא דמוספין ביחיד, ולטעום מידי ולמיתי! -א"ל: ולא סבר לה מר להא דא"ר יוחנן: [א]אסור לו לאדם שיקדים תפלתו לתפלת הצבור?! -א"ל: לאו אתמר עלה: א"ר אבא: [ב]בצבור שנו?! ולית הלכתא; [ג]לא כרב הונא ולא [ד]כריב"ל; כרב הונא - הא דאמרן, כריב"ל - דאריב"ל: *כיון שהגיע זמן תפלת המנחה, אסור לו לאדם שיטעום כלום קודם שיתפלל תפלת המנחה.§ **מתני'** ר' נחוניא בן הקנה היה מתפלל בכניסתו לבית המדרש וביציאתו תפלה קצרה. אמרו לו: מה מקום לתפלה זו? אמר להם: בכניסתי אני מתפלל שלא יארע דבר תקלה על ידי, וביציאתי אני נותן הודאה על חלקי. **גמ'** ת"ר: [ה]בכניסתו מהו אומר? יהי רצון מלפניך ה' אלהי שלא יארע דבר תקלה על ידי, ולא אכשל בדבר הלכה וישמחו בי חברי, ולא אומר [א] על טמא טהור ולא על טהור טמא, ולא יכשלו חברי בדבר הלכה ואשמח בהם. ביציאתו מהו אומר? מודה אני לפניך ה' אלהי ששמת חלקי מיושבי בית המדרש ולא שמת חלקי מיושבי קרנות, שאני משכים והם משכימים - אני משכים לדברי תורה והם משכימים לדברים בטלים, אני עמל והם עמלים - אני עמל ומקבל שכר והם עמלים ואינם מקבלים שכר, אני רץ והם רצים - אני רץ לחיי העולם הבא והם רצים לבאר שחת.§ ת"ר: °כשחלה ר' אליעזר, נכנסו תלמידיו לבקרו. אמרו לו: רבינו, למדנו אורחות חיים ונזכה בהן לחיי העולם הבא. אמר להם: הזהרו בכבוד חבריכם, ומנעו בניכם מן ההגיון, והושיבום בין ברכי תלמידי חכמים, וכשאתם מתפללים - דעו לפני מי אתם עומדים, ובשביל כך תזכו לחיי העולם הבא. וכשחלה רבי יוחנן בן זכאי, נכנסו תלמידיו לבקרו. כיון שראה אותם התחיל לבכות. אמרו לו תלמידיו: נר ישראל, עמוד הימיני, פטיש החזק, מפני מה אתה בוכה? אמר להם: אילו לפני מלך בשר ודם היו מוליכין אותי, שהיום כאן ומחר בקבר, שאם כועס עלי - אין כעסו כעס עולם, ואם אוסרני - אין איסורו איסור עולם, ואם ממיתני - אין מיתתו מיתת עולם, ואני יכול לפייסו בדברים ולשחדו בממון - אעפ"כ הייתי בוכה; ועכשיו שמוליכים אותי לפני ממ"ה הקב"ה, שהוא חי וקיים לעולם ולעולמי עולמים, שאם כועס עלי - כעסו כעס עולם, ואם אוסרני - איסורו איסור עולם, ואם ממיתני - מיתתו מיתת עולם, ואיני יכול לפייסו בדברים ולא לשחדו בממון; ולא עוד, אלא שיש לפני שני דרכים, אחת של גן עדן ואחת של גיהנם, ואיני יודע באיזו מוליכים אותי - ולא אבכה?! אמרו לו: רבינו, ברכנו! אמר להם: יהי רצון [ו]שתהא מורא שמים עליכם כמורא בשר ודם. אמרו לו תלמידיו: עד כאן?! -אמר להם: ולואי! תדעו, כשאדם עובר עבירה אומר: "שלא יראני אדם". בשעת פטירתו, אמר להם: פנו כלים מפני הטומאה, והכינו כסא לחזקיהו מלך יהודה שבא.§ **מתני'** רבן גמליאל אומר: בכל יום ויום מתפלל אדם שמנה עשרה. רבי יהושע אומר: מעין י"ח. ר"ע אומר: [ז]אם שגורה תפלתו בפיו - מתפלל י"ח, ואם לאו - מעין י"ח. ר"א אומר: העושה תפלתו קבע אין תפלתו תחנונים. ר' יהושע אומר: ההולך במקום סכנה מתפלל תפלה קצרה, ואומר: הושע ה' את עמך את שארית ישראל, בכל פרשת העבור *יהיו צרכיהם לפניך, ברוך אתה ה' שומע תפלה. היה רוכב על החמור - ירד ויתפלל, ואם אינו יכול לירד - יחזיר את פניו, ואם אינו יכול להחזיר את פניו - יכוין את לבו כנגד בית קדשי הקדשים. היה מהלך בספינה או באסדא - יכוין את לבו כנגד בית קדשי הקדשים.§ **גמ'** °הני י"ח כנגד מי? א"ר הלל בריה דר' שמואל בר נחמני: *כנגד י"ח אזכרות שאמר דוד °ב"הבו לה' בני אלים". רב יוסף אמר: כנגד י"ח אזכרות שבקריאת שמע.(א) א"ר תנחום אמר רבי יהושע בן לוי: כנגד שמונה עשרה חוליות שבשדרה. ואמר ר' תנחום אמר רבי יהושע בן לוי: [ח]המתפלל צריך שיכרע עד שיתפקקו כל חוליות שבשדרה; עולא אמר: [ט]עד כדי שיראה איסר כנגד לבו; רבי חנינא אמר: [י]כיון שנענע ראשו שוב אינו צריך. אמר רבא: [כ]והוא - דמצער נפשיה ומחזי כמאן דכרע.§ הני תמני סרי, תשסרי הוין! אמר רבי לוי: ברכת הצדוקים ביבנה תקנוה. כנגד מי תקנוה? א"ר לוי: לרבי הלל בריה דרבי שמואל בר נחמני - כנגד °"אל הכבוד הרעים", לרב יוסף - כנגד "אחד" שבקריאת שמע; לר' תנחום א"ר יהושע בן לוי - כנגד חוליא קטנה שבשדרה. ת"ר: *שמעון הפקולי הסדיר י"ח ברכות לפני רבן גמליאל על הסדר ביבנה. אמר להם ר"ג לחכמים: כלום יש אדם שיודע לתקן ברכת הצדוקים? עמד שמואל הקטן ותקנה, לשנה אחרת שכחה.

והשקיף

רש"י

לא על לפרקא דרב יוסף. שהיה ראש הישיבה בפומבדיתא, והיה דורש בשבת קודם תפלת המוספין, ולאחר הדרשה היו הולכים לבית הכנסת ומתפללים תפלת המוספין: בצבור שנו. אם הוא בבהכ"נ עם הצבור, לא יקדים להתפלל: **מתני'** מה מקום. כלומר: מה טיבה: **גמ'** ולא אכשל. וישמחו חברי על כשלוני. הרי רעות שתים, שיבאו על ידי שאגרום להם *שיענשו: מיושבי קרנות. חנונים, או עמי הארץ, שעוסקים בדבר שיחה: מההגיון. לא תרגילום במקרא יותר מדאי, משום דמשכא. לשון אחר: משיחת ילדים: דעו לפני מי וכו'. כדי שתתפללו ביראה ובכוונה: עמוד הימיני. שני עמודים העמיד שלמה באולם, שם הימני יכין ושם השמאלי בועז (מלכים א ז). הימיני לעולם חשוב: פטיש. המפוצץ, פי"ק בלע"ז: אוסרני. חובש אותי: מיתת עולם. לעוה"ב: הייתי בוכה. מאימת משפטו, אם לדין מוליכין אותי לפניו: עד כאן. בתמיה, כלומר: ולא יותר ממורא בשר ודם? ולואי. שיהא כמורא בשר ודם, שאם כן תחדלו מעבירות הרבה: עבירה. בסתר, ממורא הבריות, ויודע שהכל הוא גלוי להקב"ה, ואינו מניח בכך: מפני הטומאה. טומאת אהל המת בכל הבית: לחזקיהו שבא. אלי ללוותי: **מתני'** מעין שמנה עשרה. בגמרא מפרש: הושע ה' וכו'. זו תפלה קצרה: בכל פרשת העבור כו'. מפרש בגמרא: אם אינו יכול לירד. שאין לו מי שיאחז את חמורו: יחזיר את פניו. לצד ירושלים: באסדא. כמו ותשם בסד רגלי (איוב יג) = בית הסהר שקורין ליפ"ש בלע"ז. לשון אחר: עצים הקשורים זה עם זה הרבה יחד, ובלשון מקרא קורא אותם רפסודות (ד"ה ב) ובלע"ז - רדיי"ל, ובלשון אשכנז - ולו"ס ומשיטן בנהר להוליכן ממקום למקום ויכולין להלך עליהן כמו בספינה: **גמ'** הבו לה' בני אלים. שהוא רמז לאבות וגבורות וקדושת השם, כדאמרינן בראש השנה (דף לב.): מנין שאומרים אבות? ת"ל הבו לה' בני אלים כו': שיתפקקו. שיראו הפקקים, הם הקשרים. כמו ששנינו* (ב"ב פ:) בקנים ובגפנים מן הפקק (ב)שלמעלה, והיא הקשר שחלל הקנה פקוק וסתום שם: איסר. שני קמטים, אחד מלמטה ואחד מלמעלה וכאיסר רוחב בשר באמצע: דמצער נפשיה. שהוא ניכר שחפץ לכרוע, אלא שהוא מצטער: ביבנה תקנוה. לאחר זמן מרובה: הפקולי. מוכר פקולי צמר גפן שקורין קיטו"ן:

מסורת הש"ס

[ע' כתי"ע]
שבת דף ע:
[תענית כה: ב"ק פא.]
נ"י ויהיו
תוספתא פ"ג
תהלים כט
שם
מגילה יז:

הגהות הגר"א

[א] גמ' ולא אומר על טמא טהור ולא על טהור טמא. כל זה נ"ל למעלה קודם ולא אכשל:

תורה אור

וְהִשְׁקִיף בָּהּ שְׁתַּיִם וְשָׁלֹשׁ שָׁעוֹת וְלֹא הֶעֱלוּהוּ. אַמַּאי לֹא הֶעֱלוּהוּ? וְהָאָמַר רַב יְהוּדָה אָמַר רַב: [א]טָעָה בְּכָל הַבְּרָכוֹת כֻּלָּן – אֵין מַעֲלִין אוֹתוֹ, בְּבִרְכַּת הַצְּדוּקִים – מַעֲלִין אוֹתוֹ, חָיְישִׁינַן שֶׁמָּא מִין הוּא! שָׁאנֵי שְׁמוּאֵל הַקָּטָן, דְּאִיהוּ תַּקְנָהּ. וְנֵיחוּשׁ דִּלְמָא הֲדַר בֵּיהּ! אָמַר אַבַּיֵי, גְּמִירִי: טָבָא לָא הָוֵי בִּישָׁא. וְלָא?! וְהָכְתִיב °"וּבְשׁוּב צַדִּיק מִצִּדְקָתוֹ וְעָשָׂה עָוֶל"! הַהוּא רָשָׁע מֵעִיקָּרוֹ, אֲבָל צַדִּיק מֵעִיקָּרוֹ – לֹא. וְלָא?! וְהָא *תְּנַן: אַל תַּאֲמִין בְּעַצְמְךָ עַד יוֹם מוֹתְךָ, שֶׁהֲרֵי *יוֹחָנָן כ"ג שִׁמֵּשׁ בִּכְהוּנָּה גְּדוֹלָה שְׁמוֹנִים שָׁנָה וּלְבַסּוֹף נַעֲשָׂה צְדוֹקִי! *אָמַר אַבַּיֵי: הוּא יַנַּאי הוּא יוֹחָנָן. רָבָא אָמַר: יַנַּאי לְחוּד וְיוֹחָנָן לְחוּד, יַנַּאי – רָשָׁע מֵעִיקָּרוֹ, וְיוֹחָנָן – צַדִּיק מֵעִיקָּרוֹ. הָנִיחָא לְאַבַּיֵי, אֶלָּא לְרָבָא קַשְׁיָא! אָמַר לָךְ רָבָא: צַדִּיק מֵעִיקָּרוֹ נַמִי, דִּלְמָא הֲדַר בֵּיהּ. אִי הָכִי, אַמַּאי לֹא אַסְקוּהוּ? שָׁאנֵי שְׁמוּאֵל הַקָּטָן דְּאַתְחֵיל בָּהּ. דְּאָמַר רַב יְהוּדָה אָמַר רַב, וְאִיתֵּימָא רַבִּי יְהוֹשֻׁעַ בֶּן לֵוִי: [ב]לֹא שָׁנוּ אֶלָּא שֶׁלֹּא הִתְחִיל בָּהּ, אֲבָל הִתְחִיל בָּהּ – גּוֹמְרָהּ.§ הָנֵי שֶׁבַע דְּשַׁבְּתָא כְּנֶגֶד מִי? א"ר חֲלַפְתָּא בֶּן שָׁאוּל: כְּנֶגֶד שִׁבְעָה קוֹלוֹת שֶׁאָמַר דָּוִד עַל הַמַּיִם. הָנֵי תֵּשַׁע דר"ה כְּנֶגֶד מִי? א"ר יִצְחָק דְּמִן קַרְטִיגְנִין: כְּנֶגֶד תִּשְׁעָה אַזְכָּרוֹת שֶׁאָמְרָה חַנָּה בִּתְפִלָּתָהּ, דְּאָמַר מַר: *בְּרֹאשׁ הַשָּׁנָה נִפְקְדָה שָׂרָה רָחֵל וְחַנָּה. הָנֵי עֶשְׂרִים וְאַרְבַּע דְּתַעֲנִיתָא כְּנֶגֶד מִי? א"ר חֶלְבּוֹ: כְּנֶגֶד כ"ד רְנָנוֹת *שֶׁאָמַר שְׁלֹמֹה בְּשָׁעָה שֶׁהִכְנִיס אָרוֹן לְבֵית קָדְשֵׁי הַקֳּדָשִׁים. אִי הָכִי, כָּל יוֹמָא נַמִי נֵמְרִינְהוּ! אֵימַת אֲמָרִינְהוּ שְׁלֹמֹה – בְּיוֹמָא דְּרַחֲמֵי, אֲנַן נַמִי בְּיוֹמָא דְּרַחֲמֵי אָמְרִי לְהוּ.§ "רַבִּי יְהוֹשֻׁעַ אוֹמֵר מֵעֵין שְׁמוֹנֶה עֶשְׂרֵה". מַאי מֵעֵין שְׁמוֹנֶה עֶשְׂרֵה? רַב אָמַר: מֵעֵין כָּל בְּרָכָה וּבְרָכָה, וּשְׁמוּאֵל אָמַר: [ג]"הֲבִינֵנוּ ה' אֱלֹהֵינוּ לָדַעַת דְּרָכֶיךָ, וּמוֹל אֶת לְבָבֵנוּ לְיִרְאָתֶךָ, וְתִסְלַח לָנוּ לִהְיוֹת גְּאוּלִים, וְרַחֲקֵנוּ מִמַּכְאוֹבֵינוּ, וְדַשְּׁנֵנוּ בִּנְאוֹת אַרְצֶךָ, וּנְפוּצוֹתֵינוּ מֵאַרְבַּע תְּקַבֵּץ, וְהַתּוֹעִים עַל דַּעְתְּךָ יִשָּׁפֵטוּ, וְעַל הָרְשָׁעִים תָּנִיף יָדֶיךָ, וְיִשְׂמְחוּ צַדִּיקִים בְּבִנְיַן עִירֶךָ וּבְתִקּוּן הֵיכָלֶךָ וּבִצְמִיחַת קֶרֶן לְדָוִד עַבְדֶּךָ וּבַעֲרִיכַת נֵר לְבֶן יִשַׁי מְשִׁיחֶךָ, טֶרֶם נִקְרָא [א] אַתָּה תַעֲנֶה, בָּרוּךְ אַתָּה ה' שׁוֹמֵעַ תְּפִלָּה". *לַיְיט עֲלָהּ אַבַּיֵי אַמַּאן דִּמְצַלֵּי "הֲבִינֵנוּ".§ אָמַר רַב נַחְמָן אָמַר שְׁמוּאֵל: [ד]כָּל הַשָּׁנָה כּוּלָּהּ מִתְפַּלֵּל אָדָם "הֲבִינֵנוּ", חוּץ מִמּוֹצָאֵי שַׁבָּת וּמִמּוֹצָאֵי יָמִים טוֹבִים, מִפְּנֵי שֶׁצָּרִיךְ לוֹמַר הַבְדָּלָה בְּ"חוֹנֵן הַדַּעַת". מַתְקִיף לָהּ רַבָּה בַּר שְׁמוּאֵל: וְנֵימְרָהּ בְּרָכָה רְבִיעִית בִּפְנֵי עַצְמָהּ! מִי לֹא תְּנַן, *ר"ע אוֹמֵר: אוֹמְרָהּ בְּרָכָה רְבִיעִית בִּפְנֵי עַצְמָהּ; ר' אֱלִיעֶזֶר אוֹמֵר: בְּהוֹדָאָה! *אַטּוּ כָּל הַשָּׁנָה כּוּלָּהּ מִי עָבְדִינַן כְּר' עֲקִיבָא, דְּהַשְׁתָּא נַמִי נַעֲבֵיד?! כָּל הַשָּׁנָה כּוּלָּהּ מַאי טַעְמָא לָא עָבְדִינַן כר"ע – תְּמָנֵי סְרֵי תַּקּוּן, תְּשַׁסְרֵי לָא תַּקּוּן; הָכָא נַמִי – שְׁבַע תַּקּוּן, תְּמָנֵי לָא תַּקּוּן. מַתְקִיף לָהּ מָר זוּטְרָא: וְנִכְלְלָהּ מִכְּלַל "הֲבִינֵנוּ ה' אֱלֹהֵינוּ הַמַּבְדִּיל בֵּין קֹדֶשׁ לְחוֹל"! קַשְׁיָא.§ אָמַר רַב בֵּיבַי בַּר אַבַּיֵי: [ה]כָּל הַשָּׁנָה כּוּלָּהּ מִתְפַּלֵּל אָדָם "הֲבִינֵנוּ" חוּץ מִימוֹת הַגְּשָׁמִים, מִפְּנֵי שֶׁצָּרִיךְ לוֹמַר שְׁאֵלָה בְּבִרְכַּת הַשָּׁנִים. מַתְקִיף לָהּ מָר זוּטְרָא: וְנִכְלְלָהּ מִכְּלַל "וְדַשְּׁנֵנוּ בִּנְאוֹת אַרְצֶךָ וְתֵן טַל וּמָטָר"! אָתֵי לְאִטְרוּדֵי. אִי הָכִי, הַבְדָּלָה בְּ"חוֹנֵן הַדַּעַת" נַמִי אָתֵי לְאִטְרוּדֵי! אָמְרִי: הָתָם כֵּיוָן דְּאָתְיָא בִּתְחִלַּת צְלוֹתָא – לָא מִטְרִיד, הָכָא כֵּיוָן דְּאָתְיָא בְּאֶמְצַע צְלוֹתָא – מִטְרִיד. מַתְקִיף לָהּ רַב אָשֵׁי: וְנֵימְרָהּ בְּ"שׁוֹמֵעַ תְּפִלָּה"! דא"ר תַּנְחוּם אָמַר רַב אַסִּי: טָעָה וְלֹא הִזְכִּיר גְּבוּרוֹת גְּשָׁמִים בִּתְחִיַּית הַמֵּתִים – מַחֲזִירִין אוֹתוֹ, שְׁאֵלָה בְּבִרְכַּת הַשָּׁנִים – אֵין מַחֲזִירִין אוֹתוֹ, מִפְּנֵי שֶׁיָּכוֹל לְאוֹמְרָהּ בְּ"שׁוֹמֵעַ תְּפִלָּה", וְהַבְדָּלָה בְּ"חוֹנֵן הַדַּעַת" – אֵין מַחֲזִירִין אוֹתוֹ, מִפְּנֵי שֶׁיָּכוֹל לְאוֹמְרָהּ עַל הַכּוֹס! – טָעָה שָׁאנֵי.§ גּוּפָא, א"ר תַּנְחוּם אָמַר רַב אַסִּי: טָעָה וְלֹא הִזְכִּיר גְּבוּרוֹת גְּשָׁמִים בִּתְחִיַּית הַמֵּתִים – מַחֲזִירִין אוֹתוֹ, שְׁאֵלָה בְּבִרְכַּת הַשָּׁנִים – אֵין מַחֲזִירִין אוֹתוֹ, מִפְּנֵי שֶׁיָּכוֹל לְאוֹמְרָהּ בְּ"שׁוֹמֵעַ תְּפִלָּה", וְהַבְדָּלָה בְּ"חוֹנֵן הַדַּעַת" – אֵין מַחֲזִירִין אוֹתוֹ, מִפְּנֵי שֶׁיָּכוֹל לְאוֹמְרָהּ עַל הַכּוֹס. מֵיתִיבֵי: *טָעָה [ו]וְלֹא הִזְכִּיר גְּבוּרוֹת גְּשָׁמִים בִּתְחִיַּית הַמֵּתִים – מַחֲזִירִין אוֹתוֹ, שְׁאֵלָה [ז]בְּבִרְכַּת הַשָּׁנִים – מַחֲזִירִין אוֹתוֹ, וְהַבְדָּלָה [ח]בְּ"חוֹנֵן הַדַּעַת" – אֵין מַחֲזִירִין אוֹתוֹ, מִפְּנֵי שֶׁיָּכוֹל לְאוֹמְרָהּ עַל הַכּוֹס! ל"ק: הָא בְּיָחִיד, הָא בְּצִבּוּר. בְּצִבּוּר מ"ט לֹא – מִשּׁוּם דְּשָׁמְעָהּ מִשְּׁלִיחַ צִבּוּר, אִי הָכִי, הַאי 'מִפְּנֵי שֶׁיָּכוֹל לְאוֹמְרָהּ בְּ"שׁוֹמֵעַ תְּפִלָּה"' – "מִפְּנֵי שֶׁשּׁוֹמֵעַ מִשְּׁלִיחַ צִיבּוּר" מִיבְּעֵי לֵיהּ! אֶלָּא, אִידִי וְאִידִי בְּיָחִיד, ול"ק: [ט]הָא – דְּאִדְּכַר קוֹדֶם "שׁוֹמֵעַ תְּפִלָּה", הָא

רש"י

וְהִשְׁקִיף. חָשַׁב לִזְכּוֹר אוֹתָהּ. לְשׁוֹן סוֹכֶה, כְּדִמְתַרְגְּמִינָן "וַיַּשְׁקֵף" וְאִסְתְּכֵי (בראשית יט): רָשָׁע מֵעִיקָּרוֹ. וְשָׁב מֵרִשְׁעָתוֹ, פְּעָמִים שֶׁחוֹזֵר וְנַעֲשָׂה רָשָׁע: הוּא יַנַּאי. שֶׁשָּׁנִינוּ בְּקִידּוּשִׁין (פ"ג דף סו.) שֶׁהָרַג חַכְמֵי יִשְׂרָאֵל: יַנַּאי רָשָׁע מֵעִיקָּרוֹ. וְנַעֲשָׂה צַדִּיק, וְחָזַר לְרִשְׁעָתוֹ: דְּאַתְחִיל בָּהּ. הִתְחִיל לְאוֹמְרָהּ וְטָעָה בְּאֶמְצָעִיתָהּ: לֹא שָׁנוּ. הָא דְּאָמַר רַב יְהוּדָה מַעֲלִין אוֹתוֹ: שִׁבְעָה קוֹלוֹת. בְּמִזְמוֹר קוֹל ה' עַל הַמַּיִם (תהלים כט): שֶׁאָמְרָה חַנָּה. בְּפָרָשַׁת עָלַץ לִבִּי (ש"א ב): כ"ד רְנָנוֹת. בְּפָרָשַׁת וַיַּעֲמוֹד שְׁלֹמֹה (מלכים א ח). רִנָּה, תְּפִלָּה, תְּחִנָּה כֻּלְּהוֹן כ"ד אִיכָּא: בְּיוֹמָא דְּרַחֲמֵי. שֶׁהוּצְרַךְ לְבַקֵּשׁ רַחֲמִים, שֶׁדָּבְקוּ שְׁעָרִים זֶה בָּזֶה וְלֹא הָיוּ מַנִּיחִין לְהַכְנִיס אָרוֹן לְבֵית קָדְשֵׁי הַקֳּדָשִׁים, כִּדְאָמְרִי' בְּמוֹעֵד קָטָן (דף ט.): מֵעֵין כָּל בְּרָכָה. אוֹמֵר בְּקוֹצֶר, וּמְבָרֵךְ עַל כָּל אַחַת וְאַחַת: הֲבִינֵנוּ. וְאֵינוֹ מְבָרֵךְ אֶלָּא שׁוֹמֵעַ תְּפִלָּה בְּכָל הַבְּרָכוֹת שֶׁבֵּין שָׁלֹשׁ רִאשׁוֹנוֹת לְשָׁלֹשׁ אַחֲרוֹנוֹת. הֲבִינֵנוּ כְּנֶגֶד אַתָּה חוֹנֵן, וּמוֹל אֶת לְבָבֵנוּ כְּנֶגֶד הֲשִׁיבֵנוּ, לִסְלוֹחַ לָנוּ – כְּנֶגֶד סְלַח לָנוּ, לִהְיוֹת גְּאוּלִים – כְּנֶגֶד גְּאוּלָּה, וְכֵן כּוּלָּם: בִּנְאוֹת אַרְצֶךָ. לְשׁוֹן נָוֶה, כְּמוֹ בִּנְאוֹת דֶּשֶׁא יַרְבִּיצֵנִי (תהלים כג), וְהוּא כְּנֶגֶד בִּרְכַּת הַשָּׁנִים: וְהַתּוֹעִים עַל דַּעְתְּךָ. הָעוֹבְרִים עַל דְּבָרֶיךָ: יִשָּׁפֵטוּ. כְּנֶגֶד צְדָקָה וּמִשְׁפָּט. לָשׁוֹן אַחֵר: וְהַתּוֹעִים בְּמִשְׁפָּט עַל דַּעְתְּךָ יִשָּׁפְטוּ, הֲשִׁיבֵם לְלַמְּדָם לִשְׁפּוֹט כִּדְבָרֶיךָ, וְכֵן עִיקָּר נִרְאֶה לִי וְכֵן בה"ג: לַיְיט עֲלָהּ אַבַּיֵי. לְפִי שֶׁמְּדַלֵּג הַבְּרָכוֹת וְכוֹלְלָן בִּבְרָכָה אַחַת: כָּל הַשָּׁנָה מִי עָבְדִינַן כְּרַבִּי עֲקִיבָא. כְּלוֹמַר: כְּשֶׁאָנוּ מִתְפַּלְּלִין י"ח שְׁלֵמוֹת מִי עָבְדִינַן כְּר' עֲקִיבָא לוֹמַר בְּרָכָה רְבִיעִית בִּפְנֵי עַצְמָהּ, דְּהַשְׁתָּא כְּשֶׁמִּתְפַּלְּלִין הֲבִינֵנוּ נַעֲבֵיד כְּוָתֵיהּ: שֶׁבַע תַּקּוּן. שָׁלֹשׁ רִאשׁוֹנוֹת וְשָׁלֹשׁ אַחֲרוֹנוֹת וַהֲבִינֵנוּ: וְנִכְלְלָהּ. לְהַבְדָּלָה: מִכְּלָל. בְּתוֹךְ הֲבִינֵנוּ, כְּדֶרֶךְ שֶׁהוּא כּוֹלְלָהּ בְּחוֹנֵן הַדַּעַת. וְיֹאמַר: הֲבִינֵנוּ ה' אֱלֹהֵינוּ הַמַּבְדִּיל בֵּין קֹדֶשׁ לְחוֹל לָדַעַת דְּרָכֶיךָ: לְאִטְרוּדֵי. לִטְעוֹת: בִּתְחִלַּת. הַתְּפִלָּה יָכוֹל אָדָם לְכַוֵּין דַּעְתּוֹ יוֹתֵר מִן הָאֶמְצַע: גְּבוּרוֹת גְּשָׁמִים. הַזְכָּרָה בְּעָלְמָא הִיא, לְפִיכָךְ מַחֲזִירִין אוֹתוֹ, שֶׁאֵינָהּ תְּפִלָּה שֶׁיָּכוֹל לְאוֹמְרָהּ בְּשׁוֹמֵעַ תְּפִלָּה: בְּיָחִיד. מַחֲזִירִין אוֹתוֹ: בְּצִבּוּר. יָחִיד הַמִּתְפַּלֵּל עִם הַצִּבּוּר: דְּאִדְּכַר קוֹדֶם ש"ת. אֵין מַחֲזִירִין אוֹתוֹ, שֶׁיָּכוֹל לְאוֹמְרָהּ בְּשׁוֹמֵעַ תְּפִלָּה: תַּחֲנוּנִים

תוספות

לייט עלה אביי אמאן דמצלי הבינננו. והכי קי"ל. ויש ספרים דמסיק: ה"מ במתא, אבל בדרך שרי, כדמשמע במכילתין(א) גבי רבי יוסי וכו':

ונכללה בהבינננו. והא דאמרינן בפ"ק דנדה (דף ח:): כל השנה כולה מתפלל אדם י"ח, חוץ ממוצאי יה"כ מפני טורח צבור מפני התענית, וי"א שמתפללים י"ח שלימות מפני שצ"ל הבדלה ב'חונן הדעת'. ותימה: אמאי לא פריך ונכללה ב'הבינננו'? – וי"ל: דלא דמי, דהתם כל השנה כולה מתפלל י"ח ואין לנו להקשות ונכללה מכלל, כדי לשנות המנהג של כל השנה. אבל הכא, שכל השנה מתפלל 'הבינננו', פריך שפיר: למה לי לשנות המנהג בשביל 'אתה חוננתנו' ונכללה ב'הבינננו':

מפני שיכול לאומרה בשו"ת. כדאמר (לקמן לא.): (עו"ג דף ח) שואל אדם צרכיו ב'שו"ת'. ודוקא צרכיו, כגון שיש לו חולה בתוך ביתו או שצריך שדהו מים דהוא מעין תפלה, וכן שאלה. אבל הזכרה והבדלה ושאר שבחים – אסור שאינה מעין 'שו"ת'. ונראה שכל האומר "ברוך אתה ה' שו"ת" אחר שסיים דברי תחנונים מיושב – מגונה, כדאמרי' (מגילה דף יח.): מכאן ואילך אסור לספר בשבחו של מקום, כלומר: להוסיף ברכות על אלו. ואפילו אם בא להתפלל שמנה עשרה עוד פעם אחרת – אסור שנראה כמוסיף על הברכות. והא דאמר לעיל (דף כא.): ולואי שיתפלל אדם כל היום(ב) – היינו דוקא ספק התפלל, אבל ודאי – אוקמינן לעיל שפוסק אפי' באמצע ברכה, כשמואל בפרק "מי שמתו" (שם). ומה שש"ץ חוזר ומתפלל – היינו להוציא רבים ידי חובתן, ומה שמתפלל בלחש – היינו כדי להסדיר תפלתו, כדמוקמינן בפרק בתרא דר"ה (דף לד:):

עין משפט נר מצוה

מז א ב מיי' פ"י מהל' תפלה הל' ג סמג עשין יט טוש"ע או"ח סי' קכ"ו סעיף א:

מח ג ד ה מיי' פ"ב שם הל' ג ד סמג שם טוש"ע או"ח סימן קי סעיף א:

מט ו מיי' פ"י שם הל' ח סמג שם טוש"ע א"ח סי' קיד סעיף ה:

נ ז מיי' שם הלכה ט סמג שם טוש"ע א"ח סי' קיז סעיף ד:

נא ח מיי' שם הל' יד סמג שם טוש"ע א"ח סימן רצד סעיף א:

נב ט מיי' שם הל' ט סמג שם טוש"ע א"ח סימן קי"ז סעיף ה:

רב נסים גאון

הני כ"ד דתעניתא כנגד מי אמר ר' חלבו כנגד כ"ד רננות שאמר שלמה. הא מילתא פרושה בתלמוד ארץ ישראל בפירקין ובפרק ב' דתענית (הלכה ב) ר' חלבו ור' שמואל כנגד כ"ד פעמים רנה תפלה תחנה שכתובין בפרשת שלמה ואית בגמרא בפ' משקין בית השלחין (מועד קטן דף ט) ובפרק כל ישראל יש להם חלק (דף קז) בשעה שבנה שלמה את בית המקדש ובקש להכנים ארון לבית קדש הקדשים דבקו שערים זה בזה אמר כ"ד רננות כו':

הגהות הב"ח

(א) תום' ד"ה לייט וכו' במכילתין. נ"ב לעיל בפ"ק דף ג' וע"ש בתוס' בד"ה היה לך: (ב) ד"ה מפני וכו' היינו דווקא בספק התפלל אבל בוודאי התפלל אוקמינן:

הגהות הגר"א

[א] טרם נקרא אתה תענה. נ"ב כי אתה עונה בכל כו'. גי' רי"ף ורא"ש ועיין רמב"ם:

מסורת הש"ס: יחזקאל יח | [אבות פ"ב מ"ד] | [יומא ט.] | נ"ל ואמר | [ר"ה יא. יבמות סד:] | [שבת ל. מ"ק ט. סנהדרין קז:] | [קדושין לג: וש"נ] | לקמן לג. נדה ח. | [לקמן לג:] | תוספתא פ"ג לעיל כו: לקמן לג. תענית ג:

הא – דאדכר בתר "שומע תפלה".§ אמר רבי תנחום אמר רב אסי אמר ר' יהושע בן לוי: אטעה ולא הזכיר של ר"ח בעבודה – חוזר לעבודה, נזכר בהודאה – חוזר לעבודה, ב"שים שלום" – חוזר לעבודה, ואם סיים – חוזר לראש. אמר רב פפא בריה דרב אחא בר אדא: הא דאמרן "סיים חוזר לראש" – לא אמרן אלא שעקר רגליו, אבל לא עקר רגליו – חוזר לעבודה. א"ל: מנא לך הא? א"ל: מאבא מרי שמיע לי, ואבא מרי מרב. אמר רב נחמן בר יצחק: הא דאמרן "עקר רגליו חוזר לראש" – לא אמרן אלא שאינו רגיל לומר תחנונים אחר תפלתו, אבל רגיל לומר תחנונים אחר תפלתו – חוזר לעבודה. איכא דאמרי, אמר רב נחמן בר יצחק: בהא דאמרן כי לא עקר רגליו חוזר לעבודה – לא אמרן אלא שרגיל לומר תחנונים אחר תפלתו, אבל אם אינו רגיל לומר תחנונים אחר תפלתו – חוזר לראש.§ "ר' אליעזר אומר: העושה תפלתו קבע וכו'". מאי 'קבע'? א"ר יעקב בר אידי אמר רבי אושעיא: גכל שתפלתו דומה עליו כמשוי; ורבנן אמרי: דכל מי שאינו אומרה בלשון תחנונים; רבה ורב יוסף דאמרי תרוייהו: כל שאינו יכול לחדש בה דבר. א"ר זירא: אנא יכילנא לחדושי בה מילתא, ומסתפינא דלמא מטרידנא. אביי בר אבין ור' חנינא בר אבין דאמרי תרוייהו: כל שאין מתפלל עם דמדומי חמה, דא"ר חייא בר אבא א"ר יוחנן: *מצוה הלהתפלל עם דמדומי חמה; וא"ר זירא: מאי קראה – °"ייראוך עם שמש ולפני ירח דור דורים". (תהלים עב) *לייטי עלה במערבא אמאן דמצלי עם דמדומי חמה, מאי טעמא? דלמא מיטרפא ליה שעתא.§ "רבי יהושע אומר, המהלך במקום סכנה מתפלל תפלה קצרה וכו' בכל פרשת העבור". מאי 'פרשת העבור'? אמר רב חסדא אמר מר עוקבא: אפי' בשעה שאתה מתמלא עליהם עברה כאשה עוברה – יהיו כל צרכיהם לפניך. איכא דאמרי, אמר רב חסדא אמר מר עוקבא: אפילו בשעה שהם עוברים על דברי תורה – יהיו כל צרכיהם לפניך. ת"ר: *המהלך במקום גדודי חיה ולסטים מתפלל תפלה קצרה. ואיזה היא תפלה קצרה? ר' אליעזר אומר: "עשה רצונך בשמים ממעל, ותן נחת רוח ליראיך מתחת, והטוב בעיניך עשה, בא"י שומע תפלה". ר' יהושע אומר: [א] "שמע שועת עמך ישראל ועשה מהרה בקשתם, בא"י שומע תפלה". רבי אלעזר ברבי צדוק אומר: "שמע צעקת עמך ישראל ועשה מהרה בקשתם, בא"י שומע תפלה". אחרים אומרים: "צרכי עמך ישראל מרובין ודעתם קצרה, יהי רצון מלפניך ה' אלהינו שתתן לכל אחד ואחד כדי פרנסתו ולכל גויה וגויה די מחסורה, [ב] ברוך אתה ה' שומע תפלה". אמר רב הונא: והלכה כאחרים.§ אמר ליה אליהו לרב יהודה אחוה דרב סלא חסידא: זלא תרתח ולא תחטי, לא תרוי ולא תחטי, וכשאתה יוצא לדרך – המלך בקונך וצא. מאי 'המלך בקונך וצא'? אמר רבי יעקב אמר רב חסדא: זו תפלת הדרך. ואמר רבי יעקב אמר רב חסדא: כל היוצא לדרך צריך להתפלל תפלת הדרך. מאי תפלת הדרך? חיהי רצון מלפניך ה' אלהי שתוליכני לשלום ותצעידני לשלום ותסמכני לשלום, [ג] ותצילני מכף כל אויב ואורב בדרך, ותשלח ברכה במעשי ידי, [ד] ותתנני לחן לחסד ולרחמים בעיניך ובעיני כל רואי, [ה] בא"י שומע תפלה. אמר אביי: טלעולם לישתף

רש"י

תחנונים. כגון אלהי נצור לשוני מרע שאנו אומרים בעמידה אחר תפלה: אבל אם אינו רגיל. הויא סיום תפלתו כעקירה, אפילו לא עקר: כמשוי. והיינו לשון קבע, חוק קבוע הוא עלי להתפלל וצריך אני לצאת ידי חובתי(א): מי שאינו יכול. לכוין לבו לשאול צרכיו: לחדש בה דבר. בבקשתו, והיינו לשון קבע – כיום (ב)כן אתמול כן מחר: דילמא מטרידנא. שמא אטעה, ולא אדע לחזור למקום שהפסקתי: שאינו מתפלל עם דמדומי חמה. והיינו לשון קבע – תפלתו עליו חוק קבוע לצאת ידי חובה, ואינו מקפיד לחזר אחר שעת מצוה ועת רצון: עם דמדומי חמה. תפלת יוצר עם הנץ החמה, ותפלת המנחה עם שקיעת החמה: ייראוך עם שמש. זו תפלת יוצר(ג): ולפני ירח. זו מנחה: לייטי במערבא. על מי שמשהה תפלת המנחה עד דמדומי חמה, שמא תטרף לו השעה ע"י אונס ועבר הזמן: בכל פרשת העבור וכו'. כמו פרישת העבור: אפי' בשעה שאתה מתמלא עליהם עברה כאשה עוברה. והכי משמע בכל עניני פרישת העבור כגון עברה *בעברה: יהיו כל צרכיהם. גלויים לפניך לרחם עליהם: אפילו בשעה שהם עוברים. ולשון פרשת העבור – שהן פורשין לעבירה: עשה רצונך בשמים. שאין שם חטא, ואין רצונך עליהם אלא לטוב, ועבור לתחתונים על רצונך: ותן. להם ליראיך: נחת רוח. שלא יתערבב רוחם על ידי הבריות, כגון ע"י חיות ולסטים: והטוב בעיניך עשה. חטה להם. ודוגמא זו מצינו בספר שופטים: (י) ויאמרו בני ישראל חטאנו עשה אתה לנו (כטוב) [ככל הטוב] בעיניך אך הצילנו וגו': שועת. לשון גניחה יותר מתפלה: ודעתם קצרה. ואינם יודעים לפרש צרכיהם: לא תרתח ולא תחטי. לא תכעוס, שמתוך הכעס אתה בא לידי חטא: לא תרוי. לא תשתכר ביין: המלך. טול רשות:

תוספות

הא דאדכר (אחר) [בתר] שומע תפלה. אז ודאי מחזירין אותו. מיהו, אם לא עקר רגליו – אינו צריך לחזור לראש, ולא לברכת השנים, אלא חוזר ל'שומע תפלה'. וכן משמע בירושלמי פ' "אין עומדין", דקאמר: אם לא שאל בברכת השנים מחזירין אותו, ולהיכן חוזר? ר' שמעון בשם ר' יוחנן אמר: בר"ח אם עקר רגליו חוזר לראש, ואם לאו – חוזר לעבודה, ה"נ, אם עקר רגליו – חוזר לראש, ואם לאו – חוזר ל'שומע תפלה'. אלמא משמע בהדיא דאינו חוזר אלא ל'שומע תפלה' כי לא עקר רגליו. מיהו הירושלמי פליג אגמרא דידן בגבורות גשמים; דהכא קתני: "לא הזכיר גבורות גשמים מחזירין אותו", ולא קאמר לאומרו ב'שומע תפלה', ובירושל' קאמר: אם לא שאל בברכת השנים – אומרה ב'שומע תפלה'. ודכוותה אם לא הזכיר גבורות גשמים בתחיית המתים – מזכיר ב'שומע תפלה'. ומה אם שאלה שהיא מדוחק אומרה ב'שומע תפלה', הזכרה שהיא מריוח לא כ"ש. אלמא דבהדיא איתא התם דחוזר בגבורות גשמים ל'שומע תפלה'! ואפשר להיות שהגמרא שלנו לא חשש לפרשו – משום הקל וחומר, כדאיתא בירושלמי. והא דקתני: לא הזכיר גבורות גשמים מחזירין אותו – איירי שלא הזכיר כלל ב'שומע תפלה', והא ליתא, דהא במסקנא מוקי האי מימרא בנזכר קודם שומע תפלה משום פירכא דשאלה. ובירושלמי קאמר: היה עומד בטל והזכיר של גשם מחזירין אותו, פי' בימות הקיץ, ופריך: והא תניא: בטל וברוחות לא חייבו חכמים להזכיר, והכי פריך: כי היכי דאם לא הזכיר כלל מטל אינו עיכוב, ואם היה רוצה להזכיר – מזכיר, ה"נ, אם עמד בטל והזכיר של גשם – אין לחוש, דלא גרע מלא הזכיר טל כלל. ומשני: דלא דמי ההוא דמקל ומללי, להההוא דמללי ולא מקל. פי': מקלל, כלומר: אינו דומה כשעומד בטל והזכיר של גשם – שהוא סימן קללה, למי שאינו מזכיר כלל לא טל ולא גשם, שאינו מקלל. וכן הלכה למעשה: שאם עומד בשל טל והזכיר של גשם – דמחזירין אותו, ואם לא הזכיר משניהם כלל – אין מחזירין אותו. והדר קאמר בירושלמי: קאי בגשם ואדכר בטל על – אין מחזירין אותו. ופריך מהכא, והתניא: או שלא הזכיר גבורות גשמים מחזירין אותו, ומשני: הא דאדכר, הא דלא(ד) אדכר, הא דלא אדכר לא טל ולא מטר לכך מחזירין אותו, הא דהזכיר של טל ומטר. ולא נהירא, דפשיטא אם הזכיר שניהם – דאין מחזירין אותו, ואם לא הזכיר כלל – פשיטא דמחזירין אותו! אלא ודאי יש לפרש: הא דאדכר טל, הא דלא אדכר כלל לא טל ולא מטר, לפיכך מחזירין אותו. אבל אם הזכיר טל אף בימות הגשמים – אין מחזירין אותו. לכך יש בני אדם שאומרים כל שעה טל מתוך שהם רגילים, אם כן בימות הגשמים אם שכח 'מוריד הגשם' – אין מחזירין אותו: טעה ולא הזכיר של ראש חדש בעבודה חוזר לעבודה. ובהלכות גדולות פי': דוקא ביחיד, אבל בצבור אינו חוזר מפני ששומעה מש"צ. מיהו, צריך לדקדק מפי החזן כל אות ואות של תפלה אע"פ שהוא בקי, דהא אמרינן בראש השנה (פ"ד דף לד:): כשם שמוציא את שאינו בקי – כך מוציא הבקי. ואע"ג דאמרינן התם: לא פטר רבן גמליאל אלא העם שבשדות, משום דאניסי וטרידי אבל *טעה – לא, יש לומר: היינו שלא התפלל כלל, אבל היכא שהתפלל כבר – לא חשבינן ליה כאילו לא התפלל כלל. וה"ה לכל דבר שמחזירין אותו אי הדר [illegible] משלוחא דצבורא מראש ועד סוף – נפיק. והרב ר"מ פסק: דוקא שכח להזכיר של ר"ח, אבל שכח ברכה שלמה – מחזירין אותו, ואינו יוצא בשמיעתו משליח צבור (וע"ע תוס' ר"ה לד: ד"ה כן): איכא דאמרי אמר רב נחמן וכו'. רב אלפס פסק כאיכא דאמרי, דברגיל לומר תחנונים ולא עקר רגליו – אינו חוזר לראש, ואם אינו רגיל – גם כי לא עקר רגליו – חוזר לראש, ואם עקר גם כי רגיל לומר תחנונים כמו 'אלהי נצור לשוני' חוזר לראש:

כל שאינו יכול לומר תחנונים. פי' ר"ח: דאם יכול לומר לשון תחנונים, אפי' עליו כמשא – הוי תפלה מעליא, דלא בעינן אלא לשון תחנונים בלבד:

והיכי

עין משפט נר מצוה

נד א ב מיי' פ"י מהל' תפלה הלכה י סמג עשין יט טוש"ע או"ח סי' תכב סעיף א:

נה ג ד מיי' פ"ד שם הלכה טז סמג שם טוש"ע או"ח סימן צח סעיף ג:

נו ה מיי' פ"ג שם הל' ד סמג שם טוש"ע או"ח סי' פט סעיף א ובסי' רלג סעיף א:

נז ו מיי' פ"ד שם הל' יט סמג שם טוש"ע או"ח סי' קי סעיף ג:

נח ז מיי' פ"א מהלכות דעות הלכה ד ופ"ב הלכה ג:

נט ח ט מיי' פ"י מהל' ברכות [ע"ש ולא תמצא והב"י סי' קי תמה על הרמב"ם שהשמיטו] סמג עשין (כז) [יט] טוש"ע או"ח סימן קי סעיף ד:

מסורת הש"ס

(וע' רש"ל בחדושי אגדה)

שבת קיח:

[קדושין לג: ושם נסמן]

תוספתא פ"ג

[בעיר לא כל"ל וכ"ה שם ברא"ש]

הגהות הב"ח

(א) רש"י ד"ה כמשוי וכו' ידי חובתי הס"ד ואחר כך מתחיל הדבור מי שאינו אומר בלשון תחנונים. מי שאינו: (ב) ד"ה לחדש וכו' קבע כהיום כן: (ג) ד"ה ייראוך וכו' תפלת יוצר. נ"ב ע' לעיל ד' ט ע"ב פירש"י דקאי אק"ש: (ד) תום' ד"ה הא דאדכר וכו' דלא אדכר פירוש הא דלא אדכר לא טל ולא מטר לכך מחזירין אותו הא דאדכר דהזכיר:

הגהות הגר"א

[א] גמ' (רי"א שמע שועת עמך ישראל ועשה מהרה בקשתם בא"י ש"ת) תא"מ ונ"ב בתוספתא ל"ג לה: [ב] שם די מחסורה. נ"ב והטוב בעיניך עשה. גירסת רי"ף ורמב"ם ורא"ש: [ג] שם ותסמכני לשלום. נ"ב ותחזירני לביתי לשלום: [ד] שם (ותשלח ברכה במעשה ידי) תא"מ: [ה] שם ובעיני כל רואי. נ"ב כי אתה שומע כו'. טור:

תורה אור

לִישַׁתֵּף אֱינָשׁ נַפְשֵׁיהּ בַּהֲדֵי צִבּוּרָא. הֵיכִי נֵימָא? – יְהִי רָצוֹן מִלְּפָנֶיךָ ה' אֱלֹהֵינוּ שֶׁתּוֹלִיכֵנוּ לְשָׁלוֹם וכו'. אֵימַת מְצַלֵּי? – אָמַר רַבִּי יַעֲקֹב אָמַר רַב חִסְדָּא: [א]מִשָּׁעָה שֶׁמְּהַלֵּךְ בַּדֶּרֶךְ. עַד כַּמָּה? –אָמַר רַבִּי יַעֲקֹב אָמַר רַב חִסְדָּא: [ב]עַד פַּרְסָה. וְהֵיכִי מְצַלֵּי לָהּ? –רַב חִסְדָּא אָמַר: מְעוּמָּד; רַב שֵׁשֶׁת אָמַר: [ג]אֲפִילּוּ מְהַלֵּךְ. רַב חִסְדָּא וְרַב שֵׁשֶׁת הָווּ קָאָזְלִי בְּאוֹרְחָא, קָם רַב חִסְדָּא וְקָא מְצַלֵּי. א"ל רַב שֵׁשֶׁת לְשַׁמָּעֵיהּ: מַאי קָא עָבֵיד רַב חִסְדָּא? אָמַר לֵיהּ: קָאֵי וּמְצַלֵּי. א"ל: אוֹקְמַן נַמִי לְדִידִי וְאַצַּלֵּי, *מִהְיוֹת טוֹב אַל תִּקָּרֵא רָע.§ מַאי אִיכָּא בֵּין "הֲבִינֵנוּ" לִתְפִלָּה קְצָרָה? – [ד]הֲבִינֵנוּ – בָּעֵי לְצַלּוֹיֵי ג' קַמַּיָּיתָא וג' בַּתְרַיְיתָא, וְכִי מָטֵי לְבֵיתֵיהּ לָא בָּעֵי לְמֶהְדַּר לְצַלּוֹיֵי; בִּתְפִלָּה קְצָרָה – לָא בָּעֵי לְצַלּוֹיֵי לֹא ג' קַמַּיָּיתָא וְלֹא ג' בַּתְרַיְיתָא, וְכִי מָטֵי לְבֵיתֵיהּ בָּעֵי לְמֶהְדַּר לְצַלּוֹיֵי. וְהִלְכְתָא: [ה]הֲבִינֵנוּ – מְעוּמָּד, תְּפִלָּה קְצָרָה – בֵּין מְעוּמָּד בֵּין מְהַלֵּךְ.§ "הָיָה רוֹכֵב עַל הַחֲמוֹר וכו'". ת"ר: *הָיָה רוֹכֵב עַל הַחֲמוֹר וְהִגִּיעַ זְמַן תְּפִלָּה, אִם יֵשׁ לוֹ מִי שֶׁיֹּאחַז אֶת חֲמוֹרוֹ – יֵרֵד לְמַטָּה וְיִתְפַּלֵּל, וְאִם לָאו – יֵשֵׁב בִּמְקוֹמוֹ וְיִתְפַּלֵּל; רַבִּי אוֹמֵר: [ו]בֵּין כָּךְ וּבֵין כָּךְ – יֵשֵׁב בִּמְקוֹמוֹ וְיִתְפַּלֵּל, לְפִי שֶׁאֵין דַּעְתּוֹ מְיוּשֶּׁבֶת עָלָיו. אָמַר רָבָא וְאִיתֵּימָא רַבִּי יְהוֹשֻׁעַ בֶּן לֵוִי: הֲלָכָה כְּרַבִּי.§ ת"ר: *[ז]סוּמָא וּמִי שֶׁאֵינוֹ יָכוֹל לְכַוֵּין אֶת הָרוּחוֹת – יְכַוֵּין לִבּוֹ כְּנֶגֶד אָבִיו שֶׁבַּשָּׁמַיִם, שנא' °"וְהִתְפַּלְלוּ אֶל ה'" [מלכים א ח]; הָיָה [ח]עוֹמֵד בחו"ל – יְכַוֵּין אֶת לִבּוֹ כְּנֶגֶד אֶרֶץ יִשְׂרָאֵל שנא': °"וְהִתְפַּלְלוּ אֵלֶיךָ דֶּרֶךְ אַרְצָם" [שם]; הָיָה עוֹמֵד בְּאֶרֶץ יִשְׂרָאֵל – יְכַוֵּין אֶת לִבּוֹ כְּנֶגֶד יְרוּשָׁלַיִם, שֶׁנֶּאֱמַר: °"וְהִתְפַּלְלוּ אֶל ה' דֶּרֶךְ הָעִיר אֲשֶׁר בָּחַרְתָּ" [שם]; הָיָה עוֹמֵד בִּירוּשָׁלַיִם – יְכַוֵּין אֶת לִבּוֹ כְּנֶגֶד בֵּית הַמִּקְדָּשׁ, שֶׁנֶּאֱמַר: °"וְהִתְפַּלְלוּ אֶל הַבַּיִת הַזֶּה" [דה"ב ו]; הָיָה עוֹמֵד בְּבֵית הַמִּקְדָּשׁ – יְכַוֵּין אֶת לִבּוֹ כְּנֶגֶד בֵּית קׇדְשֵׁי הַקֳּדָשִׁים, שֶׁנֶּאֱמַר: °"וְהִתְפַּלְלוּ אֶל הַמָּקוֹם הַזֶּה" [מלכים א ח]; הָיָה עוֹמֵד בְּבֵית קׇדְשֵׁי הַקֳּדָשִׁים – יְכַוֵּין אֶת לִבּוֹ כְּנֶגֶד בֵּית הַכַּפּוֹרֶת; הָיָה עוֹמֵד אֲחוֹרֵי בֵּית הַכַּפּוֹרֶת – יֵרָאֶה עַצְמוֹ כְּאִילּוּ לִפְנֵי הַכַּפּוֹרֶת; נִמְצָא: עוֹמֵד בַּמִּזְרָח – מַחֲזִיר פָּנָיו לַמַּעֲרָב, בַּמַּעֲרָב – מַחֲזִיר פָּנָיו לַמִּזְרָח, בַּדָּרוֹם – מַחֲזִיר פָּנָיו לַצָּפוֹן, בַּצָּפוֹן – מַחֲזִיר פָּנָיו לַדָּרוֹם; נִמְצְאוּ כׇּל יִשְׂרָאֵל מְכַוְּונִין אֶת לִבָּם לְמָקוֹם אֶחָד. א"ר אָבִין וְאִיתֵּימָא ר' אָבִינָא: מַאי קְרָאָה – °"כְּמִגְדַּל דָּוִיד צַוָּארֵךְ בָּנוּי לְתַלְפִּיּוֹת" [שיר ד], תֵּל שֶׁכׇּל פִּיּוֹת פּוֹנִים בּוֹ.§ אֲבוּהּ דִּשְׁמוּאֵל וְלֵוִי [ט]כִּי הָווּ בָּעוּ לְמִיפַּק לְאוֹרְחָא הָווּ מַקְדְּמִי וּמְצַלּוּ, וְכִי הֲוָה מָטֵי זְמַן ק"ש קָרוּ. כְּמַאן; כִּי הַאי תַּנָּא – דְּתַנְיָא: *הַשְׁכִּים לָצֵאת לַדֶּרֶךְ – מְבִיאִין לוֹ שׁוֹפָר וְתוֹקֵעַ, לוּלָב וּמְנַעְנֵעַ, מְגִילָּה וְקוֹרֵא בָּהּ, וּכְשֶׁיַּגִּיעַ זְמַן ק"ש קוֹרֵא. הִשְׁכִּים לֵישֵׁב בְּקָרוֹן אוֹ בִּסְפִינָה – מִתְפַּלֵּל, וּכְשֶׁיַּגִּיעַ זְמַן ק"ש קוֹרֵא; רשב"א אוֹמֵר: בֵּין כָּךְ וּבֵין כָּךְ קוֹרֵא ק"ש וּמִתְפַּלֵּל, כְּדֵי שֶׁיִּסְמוֹךְ גְּאוּלָּה לִתְפִלָּה. בְּמַאי קָמִיפַּלְגִי? – [י]מָר סָבַר: תְּפִלָּה מְעוּמָּד עָדִיף; וּמָר סָבַר: מִסְמַךְ גְּאוּלָּה לִתְפִלָּה עָדִיף. מָרֵימָר וּמָר זוּטְרָא הָווּ מְכַנְּפִי בֵּי עַשְׂרָה בְּשַׁבְּתָא דְּרִגְלָא וּמְצַלּוּ, וַהֲדַר נָפְקִי לְפִרְקָא. רַב אַשִׁי מְצַלֵּי בַּהֲדֵי צִבּוּרָא בְּיָחִיד מְיוּשָּׁב, כִּי הֲוָה אָתֵי לְבֵיתֵיהּ הָדַר וּמְצַלֵּי מְעוּמָּד. אָמְרִי לֵיהּ רַבָּנַן: וְלַעֲבִיד מָר כְּמָרֵימָר וּמָר זוּטְרָא! –אֲמַר לְהוּ: טְרִיחָא לִי מִלְּתָא. –וְלַעֲבִיד מָר כַּאֲבוּהּ דִּשְׁמוּאֵל וְלֵוִי! –אֲמַר לְהוּ: לָא חָזֵינָא לְהוּ לְרַבָּנַן קַשִּׁישֵׁי מִינַּן דְּעָבְדִי הָכִי.§

מתני' ר' אֶלְעָזָר בֶּן עֲזַרְיָה אוֹמֵר: אֵין תְּפִלַּת הַמּוּסָפִין אֶלָּא בְּחֶבֶר עִיר, וחכ"א: [כ]בְּחֶבֶר עִיר וְשֶׁלֹּא בְּחֶבֶר עִיר; ר' יְהוּדָה אוֹמֵר מִשְּׁמוֹ: כׇּל מָקוֹם שֶׁיֵּשׁ שָׁם חֶבֶר עִיר – יָחִיד פָּטוּר מִתְּפִלַּת הַמּוּסָפִין. **גמ'** ר' יְהוּדָה הַיְינוּ ת"ק! אִיכָּא בֵּינַיְיהוּ: יָחִיד שֶׁלֹּא בְּחֶבֶר עִיר; ת"ק סָבַר: פָּטוּר, ור' יְהוּדָה סָבַר: חַיָּיב. א"ר הוּנָא בַּר חִינָּנָא אָמַר ר' חִיָּיא בַּר רַב: הֲלָכָה כר' יְהוּדָה שֶׁאָמַר מִשּׁוּם ראב"ע. א"ל רַב חִיָּיא בַּר אָבִין: שַׁפִּיר קָאָמְרַתְּ, דַּאֲמַר שְׁמוּאֵל: מִיָּמַי לֹא מְצַלֵּינָא צְלוֹתָא דְּמוּסָפִין בְּיָחִיד בִּנְהַרְדְּעָא

רש"י

לִישַׁתֵּף נַפְשֵׁיהּ. אַל יִתְפַּלֵּל תְּפִלָּה קְצָרָה בִּלְשׁוֹן יָחִיד אֶלָּא בִּלְשׁוֹן רַבִּים, שֶׁמִּתּוֹךְ כָּךְ תְּפִלָּתוֹ נִשְׁמַעַת: עַד כַּמָּה. זְמַנָּהּ לְהִתְפַּלֵּל: עַד פַּרְסָה אֲבָל לֹא לְאַחַר שֶׁהָלַךְ פַּרְסָה. וה"ג מְפָרֵשׁ: עַד כַּמָּה יְבַקֵּשׁ לֵילֵךְ שֶׁיְּהֵא צָרִיךְ לְהִתְפַּלֵּל – עַד פַּרְסָה, אֲפִי' אֵין לוֹ לֵילֵךְ אֶלָּא עַד פַּרְסָה, אֲבָל דֶּרֶךְ פָּחוֹת מִפַּרְסָה – אֵין צָרִיךְ לְהִתְפַּלֵּל תְּפִלָּה זוֹ: רַב שֵׁשֶׁת. סוּמָא עֵינַיִם הֲוָה: מִהְיוֹת טוֹב אַל תִּקָּרֵא רָע. הוֹאִיל וַאֲנִי יָכוֹל לְהִתְפַּלֵּל מְעוּמָּד, שֶׁהֲרֵי חֲבוּרָתִי עוֹמֶדֶת, לֹא אֶקָּרֵא רָע לְהִתְפַּלֵּל מְהַלֵּךְ, וְאַע"פ שֶׁמּוּתָּר: וְכִי מָטֵי לְבֵיתֵיהּ בָּעֵי מֶהְדַּר לְצַלּוֹיֵי. שֶׁהֲרֵי לֹא הִתְפַּלֵּל כְּלוּם מִתְּפִלַּת י"ח: שֶׁאֵין דַּעְתּוֹ מְיוּשֶּׁבֶת עָלָיו. שֶׁקָּשֶׁה עָלָיו עִכּוּב הַדֶּרֶךְ: לְכַוֵּין אֶת הָרוּחוֹת. לְצַד אֶרֶץ יִשְׂרָאֵל, כְּדְבָעֵינַן לְמֵימַר תֵּל שֶׁהַכֹּל פּוֹנִים בּוֹ: אֲחוֹרֵי בֵּית הַכַּפּוֹרֶת. בְּמַעֲרַב הָעֲזָרָה הָיוּ י"א אַמָּה חָלָל מִכּוֹתֶל בֵּית קׇדְשֵׁי הַקֳּדָשִׁים לְכוֹתֶל מַעֲרָבִי שֶׁל עֲזָרָה, וְהָעוֹמֵד שָׁם מַחֲזִיר פָּנָיו לְבֵית הַכַּפּוֹרֶת לְמִזְרָח: הָווּ מַקְדְּמֵי. קוֹדֶם הַיּוֹם: בְּקָרוֹן וּבִסְפִינָה. אִיכָּא בְּעִתּוּתָא דְּמַיָּא: קוֹרֵא ק"ש. יַמְתִּין עַד שֶׁיַּגִּיעַ זְמַן ק"ש וְיִקְרָאֶנָּה, וְאַח"כ יִתְפַּלֵּל: תְּפִלָּה מְעוּמָּד עָדִיף. שֶׁיָּכוֹל לְכַוֵּין אֶת לִבּוֹ. לְפִיכָךְ הָיוּ מַקְדִּימִין לְהִתְפַּלֵּל מְעוּמָּד בְּבֵיתָם, שֶׁלֹּא יִצְטָרְכוּ לְהִתְפַּלֵּל בַּדֶּרֶךְ בִּמְהַלֵּךְ: בְּשַׁבְּתָא דְּרִגְלָא. שֶׁלִּפְנֵי פֶּסַח וַעֲצֶרֶת וְסוּכּוֹת. וּמָרֵימָר בְּעִירוֹ וּמָר זוּטְרָא בְּעִירוֹ, הָיוּ הַדַּרְשָׁנִים. וְשַׁחֲרִית הָיוּ הָעָם הוֹלְכִים לְבֵית הַמִּדְרָשׁ, וּכְשֶׁמַּגִּיעַ זְמַן ק"ש – קוֹרִין, וְהַדַּרְשָׁן דּוֹרֵשׁ וְהָעָם נִשְׁמָטִים וּמִתְפַּלְלִים אִישׁ אִישׁ לְבַדּוֹ. וְלָכָךְ, הֵם הָיוּ מְאַסְּפִין לָהֶם י' שַׁחֲרִית קוֹדֶם שֶׁיֵּלְכוּ לְבֵית הַמִּדְרָשׁ וְקוֹרִין ק"ש וּמִתְפַּלְלִים בִּסְמִיכַת גְּאוּלָּה לִתְפִלָּה, וְהָדַר נָפְקִי לְפִרְקָא וְדָרְשֵׁי: וּמְצַלֵּי בַּהֲדֵי צִבּוּרָא. ל"ג: רַב אַשִׁי. הָיָה רֹאשׁ יְשִׁיבָה בְּמָתָא מַחְסְיָא וְדוֹרֵשׁ. וְהוּא לֹא הָיָה מִתְפַּלֵּל קוֹדֶם בֵּית הַמִּדְרָשׁ, אֶלָּא כְּשֶׁמַּגִּיעַ זְמַן ק"ש לוֹחֵשׁ הַרְבֵּה יַחַד לַמְתוּרְגְּמָן הָעוֹמֵד לְפָנָיו, וּבְעוֹד שֶׁהַמְתוּרְגְּמָן מַשְׁמִיעַ לָרַבִּים הוּא קוֹרֵא אֶת שְׁמַע, וְסוֹמֵךְ גְּאוּלָּה לִתְפִלָּה וּמִתְפַּלֵּל מְיוּשָּׁב. שֶׁלֹּא הָיָה רוֹצֶה לָצֵאת, שֶׁלֹּא לְהַטְרִיחַ אֶת הַצִּבּוּר לָקוּם מִפָּנָיו: בַּהֲדֵי צִבּוּרָא. בְּשָׁעָה שֶׁהַצִּבּוּר נִשְׁמָטִין וּמִתְפַּלְּלִין. אִי נָמֵי: בַּהֲדֵי צִבּוּרָא – כְּמוֹ שֶׁהוּא יוֹשֵׁב בְּתוֹךְ הַצִּבּוּר, כְּלוֹמַר שֶׁאֵינוֹ יוֹצֵא. וְכִי הֲוָה אָתֵי לְבֵיתֵי' חוֹזֵר וּמִתְפַּלֵּל מְעוּמָּד לְכַוֵּין אֶת לִבּוֹ: טְרִיחָא לִי מִילְּתָא. לְאַחֵר בֵּית הַמִּדְרָשׁ עַד שֶׁאֶתְפַּלֵּל: וְלַעֲבִיד מַר כַּאֲבוּהּ דִּשְׁמוּאֵל וְלֵוִי. שֶׁמִּתְפַּלְּלִין קוֹדֶם הַיּוֹם בְּבֵיתָם מְעוּמָּד וְלֹא תִּצְטָרֵךְ לב' תְּפִלּוֹת. וּמִשּׁוּם מִסְמַךְ גְּאוּלָּה לִתְפִלָּה, כֵּיוָן דְּמַצְלוּ קוֹדֶם ק"ש – לָא קַפְּדֵי: לָא חֲזֵינַן לְהוּ לְרַבָּנַן קַשִּׁישֵׁי מִינַּן דְּעָבְדֵי הָכֵי. שֶׁיַּקְדִּימוּ תְּפִלָּה לִקְרִיאַת שְׁמַע. הִלְכָּךְ: כֵּיוָן דְּמַמְתִּין מִתְּפִלָּה עַד זְמַן ק"ש, מִצְוָה לִסְמוֹךְ תְּפִלָּה אַחַר גְּאוּלָּה, לְפִיכָךְ מִתְפַּלֵּל מְיוּשָּׁב בִּמְקוֹמוֹ. וּלְפִי שֶׁאֵין דַּעְתּוֹ מְיוּשֶּׁבֶת עָלָיו כ"כ – צָרִיךְ לַחֲזוֹר וּלְהִתְפַּלֵּל בְּבֵיתוֹ: מתני' אֵין תְּפִלַּת הַמּוּסָפִין אֶלָּא בְּחֶבֶר עִיר. לֹא תִּקְנוּהָ אֶלָּא בְּצִבּוּר. חֶבֶר עִיר – חֲבוּרַת הָעִיר, אֲבָל לֹא לְיָחִיד: מִשְּׁמוֹ. שֶׁל ראב"ע: כׇּל מָקוֹם כו'. וּבגמ' פָּרֵיךְ: הַיְינוּ ת"ק אַלִּיבָּא דראב"ע: גמ' יָחִיד שֶׁלֹּא בְּחֶבֶר עִיר. יָחִיד הַדָּר בְּעִיר שֶׁאֵין שָׁם עֲשָׂרָה, לת"ק אַלִּיבָּא דְּרַבִּי אֶלְעָזָר דְּאָמַר לֹא תִּקְנוּהָ אֶלָּא בַּעֲשָׂרָה – יָחִיד זֶה פָּטוּר, וּלְרַבִּי יְהוּדָה אֵין יָחִיד פָּטוּר אֶלָּא בְּמָקוֹם עֲשָׂרָה, שֶׁשְּׁלִיחַ צִבּוּר פּוֹטְרוֹ: בִּנְהַרְדְּעָא

תוספות

והיכי מצלי לה. אתפלת הדרך קאי. ורב ששת אמר אפי' מהלך. וקי"ל כרב ששת. ומיהו, בתוספ' פסק ה"ר יוסף כרב חסדא, וכן רב אלפס פי', דרב חסדא עדיפא ליה טפי:

מאי איכא בין הבינונו לתפלה קצרה. תימה: לימא דאיכא בינייהו, דתפלה קצרה אינו מתפלל אלא במקום סכנה. ו"הבינונו" מתפלל אפילו שלא במקום סכנה! וי"ל דהכי קא בעי: מאי בינייהו, כל א' במקומו, תפלה קצרה במקום סכנה, ו"הבינונו" שלא במקום סכנה:

הלכה כרבי. שלא ירד למטה. ואפי' שלא במקום סכנה, ואפילו במהלך מתפלל, ואינו צריך להחזיר פניו כנגד ירושלים:

היה עומד בח"ל יכוין כנגד ארץ ישראל. ול"ג לבו, דאפניו קאי; כדקתני סיפא: היה עומד במזרח מחזיר פניו למערב:

לתלפיות תל שכל פיות פונים בו. וכהן שמעתתא קי"ל. וכן מסקינן ב"לא יחפור" (ב"ב כה:) דקאמר: אתון דקיימיתון לצפונא דא"י – אדרימו. ולא כהני אמוראי דלעיל (שם) דפליגי אי השכינה במזרח או במערב. עכשיו אנו במערבה של א"י. על כן אנו פונין למזרח:

אבוה דשמואל ולוי הוו מקדמי ומצלו. פירש רש"י: קודם עמוד השחר. ולא נראה, דאם כן לא היו יוצאין בו כלל,(א) דעדיין אינו יום! לכך נראה כפי' ר"ח: דמשעלה עמוד השחר קאמר, והוו מקדמי קודם הנץ החמה קאמר, ועדיין אינו עיקר זמן תפלה:

מסמך גאולה לתפלה עדיף. מלהתפלל מעומד, והכי פסקי בה"ג הלכה כר"ש בן אלעזר. ומשמע די"ח ברכות מותר להתפלל בדרך במהלך, ואין צריך לעמוד. וא"ת: ומ"ש מהבינונו, דמסקינן לעיל דמעומד דוקא? וי"ל: דשאני הבינונו שהיא קצרה, ואין כאן בטול דרך כ"כ כמו בי"ח ברכות. ועוד פירש הר"ס: דהכא כי הדר לביתיה מצלי מעומד, כדאמרינן בסמוך: רב אשי מצלי בהדי צבורא ביחיד מיושב כדי לקרות ק"ש בשעתא; וכי הדר לביתי' מצלי מעומד. ור"ח פסק כאבוה דשמואל ולוי; ומיהו, מדקאמר רב אשי "לא חזינן לרבנן קשישי דקא עבדי הכי" משמע דאין הלכה כמותם:

אין

עין משפט נר מצוה

ס א ב טוש"ע א"ח סי' קי סעיף ז:
סא ג שם סעיף ד:
סב ד ה מיי' פ"ב מהל' תפלה ה"ב [וספ"ד] טוש"ע שם סעיף א ג:
סג ו מיי' פ"ה שם הלכה ב סמג עשין יט טור שו"ע או"ח סי' צד סעיף ד:
סד ז מיי' שם הלכה ג טוש"ע שם סעיף ג:
סה ח מיי' שם הלכה ג טוש"ע שם סעיף א:
סו ט י טוש"ע או"ח סי' פט סעיף ח:
סז כ טוש"ע או"ח סי' רפו סעיף ב:

רב נסים גאון

אמר ליה אוקמן לדידי נמי ואצלי מהיות טוב אל תקרא רע. התם בבבא קמא בפרק מרובה (ד' פא) אמרינן מהלכין בשבילי הרשות שלמה אמרה כדתניא הרי שכלו פירותיו מן השדה ואינו מניח בני אדם ליכנס בתוך שדהו מה הבריות אומרות עליו מה הנאה יש לו לפלוני ומה הבריות מזיקות אותו עליו הכתוב אומר מהיות טוב אל תקרא רע ומתמהינן מהיות טוב אל תקרא רע קרא הוא ומתרצי' אין כתיב כי האי גוונא (משלי ג) אל תמנע טוב מבעליו:

הגהות הב"ח

(א) תוס' ד"ה אבוה וכו' לא היו יוצאין כלל בתפלה דיום כיון דעדיין אינו יום:

גליון הש"ס

גמ' היה עומד אחורי בית הכפורת. עי' ברבינו יונה פ"ק דף ו' ע"א ובדף הספר דף ה' ע"ב: **רש"י** ד"ה בשבתא דרגלא וכו' ועצרת. עי' לעיל י"ז ע"ב ברש"י ד"ה שבתא ותוס' שם ד"ה תרי זימני:

מסורת הש"ס

[ב"ק פא:]
תוספתא פ"ג
תוספתא פ"ג
תוספתא פ"ג

עין משפט נר מצוה

סח א מיי' פ"ד מהל' תפלה הלכה טו ופ"י הלכה א [טוש"ע או"ח סימן קא סעיף א]:
סט ב מיי' פ"ח מהלכות תפלה הלכה ג סמג עשין יט טוש"ע א"ח סי' נ סעיף יח:
ע ג מיי' פ"ד שם הל' טו סמג שם (טוש"ע או"ח סי' קא סעיף א):
עא ד ה מיי' פ"י שם הלכה יב סמג שם טוש"ע או"ח סימן קכו סעיף ג:
עב ו מיי' שם הל' טו סמג שם טור שו"ע או"ח סי' קה:
עג ז ח מיי' שם הלכה יא סמג שם טוש"ע או"ח סי' תכב סעיף א:
א ט מיי' פ"ד שם הל' טז סמג שם טוש"ע או"ח סי' צג סעי' ב:
ב י מיי' פ"ה שם הל' ה סמג שם טוש"ע א"ח סימן צח סעיף ו:

[הרי"ף ורא"ש לא גרסי זה וע' בטור סימן קכ"ו ותכ"ב]

גמרא

בנהרדעא, לבר מההוא יומא דאתא פולמוסא דמלכא למתא ואטרידו רבנן ולא צלו, וצלי לי ביחיד, והואי יחיד שלא בחבר עיר. יתיב רבי חנינא קרא קמיה דר' ינאי, ויתיב וקאמר: הלכה כר' יהודה שאמר משום ר' אלעזר בן עזריה. א"ל: *פוק קרא קראיך לברא! דאין הלכה כרבי יהודה שאמר משום ראב"ע. א"ר יוחנן: אני ראיתי את רבי ינאי דצלי והדר צלי. א"ל רבי ירמיה לר' זירא: [א]ודילמא מעיקרא לא כוון דעתיה, ולבסוף כוון דעתיה? א"ל: *חזי מאן גברא רבא דקמסהיד עליה! *ר' אמי ור' אסי [ב]אע"ג דהוו להו תליסר בי כנישתא בטבריא, לא הוו מצלו אלא ביני עמודי היכא דהוו גרסי. איתמר, רב יצחק בר אבדימי משום רבינו אמר: הלכה כר' יהודה שאמר משום ראב"ע. רבי חייא בר אבא צלי והדר צלי. א"ל רבי זירא: מאי טעמא עביד מר הכי? אילימא משום דלא כוון מר דעתיה – והאמר ר"א: [ג]לעולם ימוד אדם את עצמו, אם *יכול לכוין את לבו – יתפלל, ואם לאו – אל יתפלל! –אלא דלא אדכר מר דריש ירחא, והתניא: טעה ולא הזכיר של ר"ח (א) [א] בערבית – אין מחזירין אותו מפני שיכול לאומרה בשחרית, [ד]בשחרית – אין מחזירין אותו מפני שיכול לאומרה במוספין, *במוספין – אין מחזירין אותו מפני שיכול לאומרה במנחה! –א"ל: לאו איתמר עלה, א"ר יוחנן, – [ה]בצבור שנו.§ כמה ישהה בין תפלה לתפלה? רב הונא ור"ח, חד אמר: [ו]כדי שתתחונן דעתו עליו; וחד אמר: כדי שתתחולל דעתו עליו. מאן דאמר כדי שתתחונן דעתו עליו – דכתיב: °"ואתחנן אל ה'"; ומ"ד כדי שתתחולל דעתו עליו – דכתיב °"ויחל משה". אמר רב ענן אמר רב: [ז]טעה ולא הזכיר של ר"ח ערבית – אין מחזירין אותו, לפי שאין בית דין מקדשין את החדש אלא ביום. אמר אמימר: מסתברא מילתא דרב בחדש מלא, אבל בחדש חסר – מחזירין אותו. א"ל רב אשי לאמימר: מכדי רב טעמא קאמר, [ח]מה לי חסר ומה לי מלא! אלא, לא שנא.§

(דברים ג; שמות לב)

הדרן עלך תפלת השחר

אין [ט]עומדין להתפלל אלא מתוך כובד ראש. חסידים הראשונים היו שוהין שעה אחת ומתפללין, כדי שיכוונו לבם לאביהם שבשמים. °אפי' המלך שואל בשלומו לא ישיבנו, ואפי' נחש כרוך על עקבו לא יפסיק.§ **גמ'** מנא ה"מ? א"ר אלעזר; דאמר קרא: °"והיא מרת נפש". –ממאי? דילמא חנה שאני, דהות מרירא לבא טובא! אלא א"ר יוסי בר' חנינא מהכא: °"ואני ברב חסדך אבוא ביתך אשתחוה אל היכל קדשך ביראתך". –ממאי, דילמא דוד שאני, דהוה מצער נפשיה ברחמי טובא! –אלא אמר ר' יהושע בן לוי, מהכא: °"השתחוו לה' בהדרת קדש", אל תקרי בהדרת אלא בחרדת. – ממאי? דילמא לעולם אימא לך, הדרת ממש, כי הא דרב יהודה הוה מציין נפשיה והדר מצלי! – אלא א"ר נחמן בר יצחק מהכא: °"עבדו את ה' ביראה וגילו ברעדה".§ *מאי "וגילו ברעדה"? א"ר אדא בר מתנא אמר *רבה: במקום גילה שם תהא רעדה. אביי הוה יתיב קמיה דרבה, חזייה דהוה קא בדח טובא, אמר: "וגילו ברעדה" כתיב! א"ל: אנא תפילין מנחנא. ר' ירמיה הוה יתיב קמיה דר' זירא, חזייה דהוה קא בדח טובא אמר ליה, °"בכל עצב יהיה מותר" כתיב! – א"ל: אנא תפילין מנחנא מר בריה דרבינא עבד הילולא לבריה, חזנהו לרבנן דהוו קבדחי טובא, אייתי

(שמואל א א; תהלים ה; שם כט; שם ב; יומא ד:; [רב כל']; משלי יד)

רש"י

בנהרדעא. לפי שיש שם צבור, והשליח פוטרני: פולמוסא. חיל: דצלי והדר צלי. ולמה ליה ב' תפלות? אלא: אחת של שחרית ואחת של מוספין, ש"מ לית ליה דראב"ע: ודילמא מעיקרא לא כוון דעתיה. ותרווייהו דשחרית: מאן גברא רבא דקמסהיד עליה. רבי יוחנן שהעיד על הדבר, יפה דקדק שבשביל תפלת המוספין היתה: משום רבינו. רב: בצבור שנו. דאין מחזירין, משום דשמע ליה מש"צ, ואיכא מקצת הזכרה, אבל ביחיד צריך לחזור. ובה"ג מפרש לה בש"צ משום טירחא דצבורא, אבל יחיד הדר: טעה ולא הזכיר במוספין. שהתפלל אתה חוזר: כמה ישהה בין תפלה לתפלה. מי שיש עליו לחזור ולהתפלל, או משום דטעה או משום מוספין, כמה ישהה בין זו לזו: שתתחונן. שתהא דעתו מיושבת לערוך דבריו בלשון תחנה: שתתחולל. לשון חילוי; והיא היא, אלא בלישנא בעלמא פליגי: בחדש מלא. כשהחדש שעבר מלא עושין ר"ח ב' ימים, הלכך יכול לאומרה למחר דערבית של מחר ר"ח גמור יותר מן הראשון: מכדי טעמא קאמר. שאין מקדשין את החדש בלילה:

הדרן עלך תפלת השחר

כובד ראש. הכנעה: שוהין שעה אחת. במקום שבאו להתפלל גמ' אשתחוה אל היכל קדשך ביראתך. מתוך יראה: מציין נפשיה. מקשט עצמו בבגדיו: עבדו את ה' ביראה. תפלה, שהיא לנו במקום עבודה, עשו אותה ביראה: *בכל עצב יהיה מותר. כשאדם מראה את עצמו עצב – יהיה לו שכר: דהוה קא בדח טובא. יותר מדאי, ונראה כפורק עול: תפילין מנחנא. והם עדות שממשלת קוני ומוראו עלי: כסא

([יבמות מ. כתובות נו.]; [חולין ז.]; לעיל דף ח.; [ע' תוס' לקמן לד: ד"ה יכוין]; [דבורי רש"י נתהפכו בזה])

תוספות

*ה"ג: **אין** הלכה כרבי יהודה שאמר משום ראב"ע. אלא הלכה כרבנן, וכן פסק ר"ח. דלהכי מייתי(ב) רבי אמי ור' אסי שהיו מתפללים ביחיד כרבנן ביני עמודי דגרסי, לאשמעינן דהלכה כרבנן: **והתניא** טעה ולא הזכיר של ר"ח בערבית אין מחזירין אותו. ל"ג ליה. דהא אמרינן בסמוך טעה ולא הזכיר של ר"ח – אין מחזירין אותו, לפי שאין מקדשין כו'. אי נמי: אי איתא – אגב אחרינא נקט ליה:

כמה ישהה בין תפלה לתפלה. כגון: אדם שטעה ורוצה להתפלל שנית, וכן בין תפלת שחרית לתפלת המוספין: **כדי** שתתחולל דעתו עליו. ומפרש בירושלמי דהיינו כשילך ארבע אמות: **לפי** שאין מקדשין את החדש כו'. פי' לעיל בריש פרקין (דף כו.): מה שמקשין ותיפוק ליה משום רשות! משום דהיינו דוקא לעשות מצוה אחרת עוברת. וי"מ: דוקא בלילה ראשונה אין מחזירין אותו – לפי שאין מקדשין החדש בלילה, אבל בלילה שניה מחזירין אותו – שכבר מקודש מיום שלפניו, ולא נראה לחלק:

מסתברא מילתא דרב בחדש מלא. כלומר: שהיה אותו שלפניו מלא, דאז יכול לאומרה בערבית של מחר שהוא עיקר. והיה אומר ה"ר יצחק: לכל דבר שאמרו חכמים "אין מחזירין אותו" – כגון יעלה ויבא בערבית ועל הנסים – לא מיבעיא אם עקר רגליו(ג) ופתח בברכה שלאחריה – דאין מחזירין אותו, אלא אפילו לא עקר אלא שסיים אותה ברכה שתקנו בה לאומרה – אין מחזירין אותו. ולא נהירא לרבינו אלחנן, דהא חזינן בברכת המזון דאותן שאמרו חכמים מחזירין, וגם אותן שאין מחזירין – שוין, היכא דלא עקר רגליו, כדאמר לקמן (דף מט.) אם שכח של שבת וסיים הברכה כולה ועדיין לא התחיל בברכת 'הטוב והמטיב' – אומר ברוך אשר נתן שבתות למנוחה כו'. וקאמר נמי התם: אם טעה ולא הזכיר של ר"ח קודם שעקר רגליו, דהיינו קודם שיתחיל ברכת 'הטוב והמטיב' דאותה קורא עקר רגליו, אומר: ברוך אשר נתן ראשי חדשים וכו'. אלמא: היכא דלא עקר – אלו ואלו שוין, ואם עקר רגליו שהתחיל בברכת 'הטוב והמטיב' של שבת – חוזר לראש, ושל ר"ח – מעוות לא יוכל לתקון, והכי נמי: יחזור(ד) באותה ברכה, אם לא התחיל בברכה שלאחריה. ומיהו, אין ראיה מהתם, דשאני התם בברכת המזון שכבר בירך ג' ברכות, וברכת 'הטוב והמטיב' לאו דאורייתא היא, על כן אין מחזירין אותו לגמרי כי אין דומה שם הפסק כל כך. ואין להביא ממנו ראיה לי"ח ברכות, דאם יחזירוהו בדבר שאין לו לחזור – הוי כמו הפסקה. ועוד, דאין להביא ראיה לכאן; דאם היית אומר היכא שלא עקר רגליו בי"ח ברכות שהיה לו לחזור – א"כ היה צריך לחזור לרצה, ואין זה הגון. ומיהו, אומר ר"י דראה את ר"ת דהיכא דלא עקר רגליו חוזר ל'רצה', אפי' בדברים שאין מחזירין, כגון 'על הנסים', וכן עמא דבר:

הדרן עלך תפלת השחר

אל תקרי בהדרת אלא בחרדת. תימה: אמאי לא מוכח בהדיא מדכתיב בתריה "חילו מלפניו כל הארץ"? וי"ל: היינו קרא דכתיב במזמור "הבו לה' בני אלים", ומההוא קרא בעי להוכיח במסכת מגילה (דף יז:) שאומרים אבות וגבורות וקדושת השם, וי"ח ברכות תקנו כנגד האזכרות, ומשום הכי דייק מאותו קרא שכתוב באותה פרשה אבל אותו ד"חילו" וגו' אינו כתוב באותה פרשה:
אייתי

הגהות הב"ח

(א) גמ' ולא הזכיר של ר"ח (בערבית וכו'. בשחרית) תא"מ. ונ"ב ס"א אין זה: (ב) תום' ד"ה אין הלכה כו' דלכי מייתי הכא רבי אמי וכו' ביחיד ביני עמודי היכא דהוו גרסי כצ"ל ותיבת כרבנן נמחק: (ג) [illegible] עקר רגליו ופתח נ"ב פי' או פתח: (ד) בא"ד וה"נ יחזור לאותה ברכה:

הגהות הגר"א

[א] גמ' של ר"ח בערבית. נ"ב רי"ף וש"פ ל"ג אלא בשחרית אין כו' לבד:

גליון הש"ס

מתני' אפי' המלך. עי' יומא י"ט ע"ב תוס' ד"ה כס:

אייתי כסא דמוקרא, בת ארבע מאה זוזי, ותבר קמייהו, ואעציבו. רב אשי עבד הילולא לבריה, חזנהו לרבנן דהוו קא בדחי טובא, אייתי כסא *דזוגיתא חיורתא ותבר קמייהו, ואעציבו. אמרו ליה רבנן לרב המנונא זוטי בהלולא דמר בריה דרבינא: לישרי לן מר! –אמר להו: ווי לן דמיתנן, ווי לן דמיתנן! אמרי ליה: אנן מה נעני בתרך? –א"ל: *הי תורה והי מצוה דמגנו עלן? א"ר יוחנן משום רשב"י: אאסור לאדם שימלא שחוק פיו בעולם הזה, שנאמר: °"אז ימלא שחוק פינו ולשוננו רנה", אימתי – בזמן ש"יאמרו בגוים הגדיל ה' לעשות עם אלה". אמרו עליו על ר"ל, שמימיו לא מלא שחוק פיו בעוה"ז מכי שמעה מר' יוחנן רביה.§ ת"ר: באין עומדין להתפלל לא מתוך דין, ולא מתוך דבר הלכה, אלא מתוך הלכה פסוקה. והיכי דמי הלכה פסוקה? אמר אביי: כי הא דר' זירא, *דאמר ר' זירא: גבנות ישראל החמירו על עצמן, *שאפילו רואות טיפת דם כחרדל – יושבת עליה שבעה נקיים. רבא אמר: כי הא דרב הושעיא, דאמר רב הושעיא: *מערים דאדם על תבואתו ומכניסה במוץ שלה, כדי שתהא בהמתו אוכלת ופטורה מן המעשר. ואב"א: כי הא דרב הונא, *דא"ר הונא א"ר זעירא: ההמקיז דם בבהמת קדשים – אסור בהנאה, ומועלין בו. רבנן עבדי כמתניתין, רב אשי עביד כברייתא.§ ת"ר: *ואין עומדין להתפלל לא מתוך עצבות, ולא מתוך עצלות, ולא מתוך שחוק, ולא מתוך שיחה, ולא מתוך קלות ראש, ולא מתוך דברים בטלים – אלא *מתוך שמחה של מצוה. וכן לא יפטר אדם מחברו לא מתוך שיחה, ולא מתוך שחוק, ולא מתוך קלות ראש, ולא מתוך דברים בטלים – אלא מתוך [א] דבר הלכה, שכן מצינו בנביאים הראשונים שסיימו דבריהם בדברי שבח ותנחומים. [ב] וכן תנא *מרי בר בריה דרב הונא בריה דר' ירמיה בר אבא: אל יפטר אדם מחבירו אלא מתוך דבר הלכה, שמתוך כך זוכרהו. כי הא *דרב כהנא אלוייה לרב שימי בר אשי מפום נהרא עד בי צניתא דבבל; כי מטא להתם, א"ל: מר, ודאי דאמרי אינשי: הני צניתא דבבל איתנהו מאדם הראשון ועד השתא? א"ל: אדכרתן מילתא דרבי יוסי ברבי חנינא, דאמר ר' יוסי ברבי חנינא: מאי דכתיב °"בארץ אשר לא עבר בה איש ולא ישב אדם שם", וכי מאחר דלא עבר היאך ישב? אלא לומר לך: כל ארץ שגזר עליה אדם הראשון לישוב – נתישבה, וכל ארץ שלא גזר עליה אדם הראשון לישוב – לא נתישבה. רב מרדכי אלוייה *לרבי שימי בר אשי מהגרוניא ועד בי כיפי, ואמרי לה: עד בי דורא.§ ת"ר: *המתפלל יצריך שיכוין את לבו לשמים. אבא שאול אומר, סימן לדבר: °"תכין לבם תקשיב אזנך". תניא, *א"ר יהודה: כך היה מנהגו של ר"ע, חכשהיה מתפלל עם הציבור – היה מקצר ועולה, מפני טורח צבור, טוכשהיה מתפלל בינו לבין עצמו – אדם מניחו בזוית זו ומוצאו בזוית אחרת, וכל כך למה – מפני כריעות והשתחויות.§ א"ר חייא בר אבא: *ילעולם יתפלל אדם בבית שיש בו חלונות, שנאמר: °"וכוין פתיחן ליה וגו'". *יכול יתפלל אדם כל היום כלו – כבר מפורש על ידי דניאל: °"וזמנין תלתא וגו'". יכול משבא לגולה הוחלה? – כבר נאמר: °"די הוא עבד מן קדמת דנא". יכול יתפלל אדם לכל רוח שירצה? – ת"ל °"(לקבל) [נגד] ירושלם". יכול יהא כוללן בבת אחת – כבר מפורש ע"י דוד, דכתיב: °"ערב ובקר וצהרים וגו'". יכול ישמיע קולו בתפלתו? – כבר מפורש על ידי חנה, שנאמר: °"וקולה לא ישמע". יכול *ישאל אדם צרכיו ואח"כ יתפלל? – כבר מפורש על ידי שלמה, שנאמר: °"לשמע אל הרנה ואל התפלה", "רנה" – זו תפלה, "תפלה" –זו בקשה. אין אומר דבר *(בקשה) אחר אמת ויציב, אבל כאחר התפלה – אפי' כסדר וידוי של יה"כ אומר. איתמר נמי, אמר רב חייא בר אשי אמר רב: *אע"פ שאמרו שואל אדם צרכיו ב"שומע תפלה" אם בא לומר אחר תפלתו, אפילו כסדר של יה"כ – אומר.§ אמר רב המנונא: כמה הלכתא גברוותא איכא למשמע מהני קראי דחנה: °"וחנה היא מדברת על לבה" – למכאן למתפלל צריך שיכוין לבו. "רק שפתיה נעות" – ממכאן למתפלל שיחתוך בשפתיו. "וקולה לא ישמע" – נמכאן, שאסור להגביה קולו בתפלתו. "ויחשבה עלי לשכרה" – סמכאן, *ששכור אסור להתפלל, "ויאמר אליה עלי עד מתי תשתכרין וגו'" – א"ר אלעזר: מכאן, לרואה בחברו

דבר

רש"י

כסא דמוקרא. *כוס של זכוכית לבנה: לישרי לן מר. שירה: הי תורה והי מצוה דמגנו עלן. היכן התורה שעסקנו והיכן המצות שאנו מקיימין, שיגינו עלינו מדינה של גיהנם: הלכה פסוקה. שאינה צריכה עיון, שלא יהא מהרהר בה בתפלתו: יושבת עליה ז' נקיים. לבד מאותו יום שפוסקת. והתורה לא הצריכה ז' נקיים אלא לזבה, שנאמר ואם טהרה מזובה, ואין זבה אלא הרואה שלשה ימים רצופין בתוך י"א יום שבין נדה לנדה: ומכניסה. בבית: במוץ שלה. קודם שיזרה אותה, שאין מתחייב במעשר מן התורה אלא בראיית פני הבית ומשנמרח בכרי. אבל לפני מירוח אין ראיית פני הבית קובעתו. דגבי תרומה ומעשר כתיב דגן – ראשית דגנך (דברים יח) והוא המירוח. לפיכך כשמכניסה לבית קודם מירוח לא הוקבעה למעשר מן התורה, ורבנן הוא דאסרו אכילת קבע בדבר שלא נגמר מלאכתו, אבל אכילת עראי לא אסרו. ומאכל בהמה עראי הוא, דתנן במסכת פאה (פ"א מ"ו): מאכיל לבהמה חיה ועוף עד שימרח. הלכך: בהמתו אוכלת ופטורה, אבל איהו אסור באכילת קבע: אסור בהנאה ומועלין בו. ואע"ג דקי"ל אין מועלין בדמים, ויליפינן לה מקראי במסכת יומא (דף נט:) ובשחיטת חולין (דף קיז.), ה"מ – כשנשחטו בעזרה דאיכא למימר נתתיו לכם על המזבח לכפר (ויקרא יז), לכפר נתתיו לך ולא למעילה. אבל בדם הקזה – מועלין. כלומר: אם נהנה – מביא קרבן מעילה. והנך הויין הלכות פסוקות שאין עליהן קושיות ותירוצים שיהא צריך להרהר בהן: כמתניתין. מתוך כובד ראש: כברייתא. מתוך הלכה פסוקה: שיחה. ליצנות: מתוך קלות ראש. חילוף של כובד ראש. מתוך זחות לב ועתק: אלא מתוך שמחה(א). כגון דברי תנחומים של תורה; כגון סמוך לגאולת מצרים, או סמוך לתהלה לדוד שהוא של שבח ותנחומין, כגון רצון יראיו יעשה, שומר ה' את כל אוהביו, וכגון מקראות הסדורות בתפלת ערבית: כי לא יטוש ה' את עמו, וכיוצא בהן: אלוייה. ליוהו בדרך: צניתא. דקלים: אדכרתן מילתא כו'. וזה שאומרים מימות אדם הראשון הם, שהוא גזר על אותו מקום לישוב דקלים: אם תכין לבם. אז תקשיב אזנך: זמנין תלתא. שחרית, מנחה וערבית: יכול משבא לגולה הוחלה. התפלה הזאת. הוחלה כמו נתחלה, אבל קודם לכן לא היה רגיל בכך: יכול יהא כוללן. לשלש תפלות הללו בשעה אחת: יכול ישאל צרכיו. כגון ברכות דאתה חונן עד ש"ת, ואח"כ יתפלל שלש ברכות ראשונות, שהן של שבח: רנה זו תפלה. של שבח: בקשה. שאלת צרכיו: אחר אמת ויציב. קודם ג' ראשונות: שצריך

תוספות

אייתי כסא דזוגיתא חיורתא. מכאן נהגו לשבר זכוכית בנשואין: *במקום גילה שם תהא רעדה. פשוטו של מקרא: עבדו את ה' ביראה, וכשיבא יום רעדה תגילו. והכי מפורש בירושלמי: עבדו את ה' ביראה היינו תפלה דאיקרי עבודה, *כדתניא בספרי (פ' עקב) "ולעבדו בכל לבבכם"–זו תפלה:

המקיז דם בבהמת קדשים וכו'. וקשה, דאמר בפ"ג דע"ז (דף מד.) גבי דמים חילונים ודמים פנימיים של קרבנות: אלו ואלו נמכרים לגננים לזבל, אלמא דאין מועלין בהן! *וי"ל: דהתם היינו לאחר זריקת דמים וכבר נתכפרו בעלים, מה שאין כן הכא: רבנן עבדי כמתניתין. וכותייהו קי"ל. ולכן אין מתפללין מתוך קלות ראש ושחוק, אלא מתוך כובד ראש ושמחה של מצוה, כגון שעסק בדברי תורה. ולכן נהגו לומר פסוקי דזמרה ואשרי קודם תפלה: רב אשי עביד כברייתא. ירושלמי: לא יעמוד ויתפלל אלא מתוך דבר הלכה, א"ר ירמיה: העוסק בצרכי צבור כעוסק בדברי תורה דמי: שכן מצינו בנביאים הראשונים שסיימו דבריהם בדברי שבח ותנחומין. ומקשה בירושלמי חוץ מירמיה וכו', והא כתיב "כי אם מאס מאסתנו" (איכה ה). מיהו *מההוא קראי דסוף תרי עשר וקהלת לא פריך מידי, שחושבו בטוב בדברי תנחומין, ולא איירי בפורענות דישראל: ומוצאו בזוית אחרת. תימה: דאמר לקמן (דף לד.): הבא לשחות בסוף כל ברכה וברכה מלמדין אותו שלא ישחה! ותירץ הר"ר יוסף: דהכא איירי בתחנונים שהיה אומר אחר י"ח ברכות. ולא נהירא, דהא מי"ח קאמר! ונראה להר"י דודאי בסוף כל ברכה אסור לשחות, אבל באמצע הברכה מיהא מותר לשחות, ובהכי איירי הכא, וכשהיה מגיע לסוף הברכה היה זוקף. ולכך נהגו העולם בראש השנה וביום הכפורים שמתפללין זכרנו, ובכן תן, ותמלוך – ששוחים כשמגיעים לפסוקים. ובסוף ברכה זוקפין, שאין לשחות בסוף ברכות אלא היכא דתקון:

דבר

מסורת הש"ס: [ע' לעיל כח. פירש"י ד"ה כסא] | [ע' תוס' שבת כ: ד"ה אמר ותו' ב"מ כט: וחולין פד: ד"ה בזוגיתא] | עיין בעין יעקב הגירסא | תהלים קכו | [עפירש"י ותו' במגילה שם] | פסחים קד ע. מנחות מז: נדה טז: [ע"ז מח:] | מעילה יב: [ע"ש] | תוספתא פ"ג | שבת ל: פסחים קיז. | עירובין סד. | סוטה מו: | ירמיה ב | תהלים י | תוספתא פ"ג | תוספתא שם | לקמן לד: | דניאל ו | תוספתא שם | שם | שם | תהלים נה | שמואל א א | ע"ז ז: | מלכים א ח | רי"ף ורא"ש ל"ג | ע"ז ח. | שמואל א א | עירובין סד.

עין משפט נר מצוה

ג א טוש"ע א"ח סימן תקס סעיף ה:

[וכ"א להדיא תענית ב.]

ד ב מיי' פ"ד מהלכות תפלה הלכה יח סמג עשין יח טוש"ע או"ח סי' צג סעיף ג:

[וע' תוס' יומא נט: ד"ה הוא ותוס' מעילה יב: ד"ה המקיז]

ה ג מיי' פי"א מהלכות איסורי ביאה הל' ד סמג לאוין קיא טוש"ע י"ד סי' קפג:

[רב אלפס כאן ובשבועות פ"ב דף רפ"ט]

ו ד מיי' פ"ג מהל' מעשר הלכה ו טוש"ע י"ד סימן שלא סעיף פד:

ז ה מיי' פ"ב מהלכות מעילה הלכה יא סמג עשין רי:

ח ו מיי' פ"ד מהלכות תפלה הל' יח סמג עשין יט טוש"ע א"ח סי' צג סעיף ב:

ט ז מיי' שם הלכה טז סמג שם טוש"ע א"ח סימן נח סעי' א':

י ח מיי' פ"ו שם הלכה ב טוש"ע א"ח סי' צג סעיף יא:

יא ט טור א"ח סי' קד:

יב י מיי' פ"ה מהלכות תפלה הלכה ו סמג שם טוש"ע א"ח סימן צ סעיף ד:

יג כ מיי' פ"ו שם הל' ב טוש"ע א"ח סימן קיט סעיף א:

יד ל מיי' פ"ד שם הל' טו סמג שם טוש"ע א"ח סי' נח סעי' א:

טו מ נ מיי' פ"ה שם הלכה ט סמג שם טור שו"ע א"ח סי' קא סעיף ב:

טז ס מיי' פ"ד שם הל' יז סמג שם טור וש"ע א"ח סי' צט סעיף א:

הגהות הב"ח

(א) רש"י ד"ה אלא מתוך שמחה של מצוה כגון:

הגהות הגר"א

[א] גמ' אלא מתוך דבר הלכה. רשום קו על תיבת דבר הלכה וכ"ב שמחה של מצוה: [ב] שם (וכן) תז"מ:

[לרב אשי כ"ה בסוטה וכ"כ רש"י בגיטין נט. ד"ה זילו ע"ש שכך מוכח וע"ע ברש"י ביצה ו. ד"ה א"ל]

גליון הש"ס

גמ' כבר מפורש על ידי חנה. עי' יומא עג ע"א: שם יכול ישאל אדם צרכיו. עי' לקמן לב ע"א:

עין משפט נר מצוה

יז א מיי' פ"ו מהלכות דעות הלכה ז סמג עשין יא:

[שייך לעיל עמוד א]

יח ב מיי' פ"ג מהלכות סוטה הלכה כב:

יט ג מיי' פ"ה מהל' תפלה הלכה ו סמג עשין יט טוש"ע או"ח סימן קב סעיף א:

כ ד ה מיי' פ"ט מהל' ביאת המקדש הלכה ו ופ"ה מהל' מעשה הקרבנו' הל' א ופ"א מהל' פסולי המוקדשין הלכה א סמג לאוין שט:

כא ו מיי' פ"ו מהלכות ת"ת הלכה ג סמג עשין יג טוש"ע יו"ד סימן רמב סעיף ד:

כב ז ח מיי' (פ"ל מהל' שבת הל' ט) ופ"א מהל' תענית הל' יב סמג עשין ג טוש"ע או"ח סי' רפח סעיף ד:

גמרא

*דבר שאינו הגון צריך להוכיחו. "ותען חנה ותאמר לא אדוני" – אמר עולא ואיתימא רבי יוסי ברבי חנינא, אמרה ליה: לא אדון אתה בדבר זה, ולא רוח הקודש שורה עליך, שאתה חושדני בדבר זה. איכא דאמרי, הכי אמרה ליה: לא אדון אתה, לאו איכא שכינה ורוח הקודש גבך, שדנתני לכף חובה ולא דנתני לכף זכות, מי לא ידעת דאשה קשת רוח אנוכי?! "ויין ושכר לא שתיתי" – אמר רבי אלעזר: מכאן, לנחשד בדבר שאין בו שצריך להודיעו. "אל תתן את אמתך לפני בת בליעל" – אמר רבי אלעזר: מכאן, לשכור שמתפלל כאילו עובד ע"ז, כתיב הכא "לפני בת בליעל", וכתיב התם "יצאו אנשים בני בליעל מקרבך", מה להלן ע"ז, אף כאן – ע"ז. "ויען עלי ויאמר לכי לשלום" – אמר רבי אלעזר: מכאן, לחושד את חברו בדבר שאין בו שצריך לפייסו; ולא עוד, אלא שצריך לברכו, שנאמר: "ואלהי ישראל יתן את שלתך". § "ותדר נדר ותאמר ה' צבאות", אמר רבי אלעזר: מיום שברא הקב"ה את עולמו, לא היה אדם שקראו להקב"ה "צבאות" עד שבאתה חנה וקראתו צבאות; אמרה חנה לפני הקב"ה: רבש"ע, מכל צבאי צבאות שבראת בעולמך קשה בעיניך שתתן לי בן אחד?! משל למה הדבר דומה – למלך בשר ודם שעשה סעודה לעבדיו, בא עני אחד ועמד על הפתח, אמר להם: תנו לי פרוסה אחת! ולא השגיחו עליו; דחק ונכנס אצל המלך. א"ל: אדוני המלך, מכל סעודה שעשית קשה בעיניך ליתן לי פרוסה אחת?! "אם ראה תראה", א"ר אלעזר: אמרה חנה לפני הקב"ה: רבש"ע, אם 'ראה' – מוטב, ואם לאו – 'תראה', אלך ואסתתר בפני אלקנה בעלי, וכיון דמסתתרנא משקו לי מי סוטה, ואי אתה עושה תורתך פלסתר, שנאמר: "ונקתה ונזרעה זרע". הניחא למאן דאמר אם היתה עקרה נפקדת – שפיר, אלא למאן דאמר אם היתה יולדת בצער יולדת בריוח, נקבות – יולדת זכרים, שחורים – יולדת לבנים, קצרים – יולדת ארוכים, מאי איכא למימר? *דתניא: "ונקתה ונזרעה זרע" – מלמד, שאם היתה עקרה נפקדת, דברי ר' ישמעאל; א"ל רבי עקיבא: אם כן, ילכו כל העקרות כולן ויסתתרו, וזו שלא קלקלה *נפקדת! אלא: מלמד שאם היתה יולדת בצער – יולדת בריוח, קצרים – יולדת ארוכים, שחורים – יולדת לבנים, אחד – יולדת שנים. מאי "אם ראה תראה" – *דברה תורה כלשון בני אדם. § "בעני אמתך", "אל תשכח את אמתך", "ונתתה לאמתך". א"ר יוסי בר' חנינא: ג' אמתות הללו למה אמרה חנה לפני הקב"ה: רבש"ע, *שלשה בדקי מיתה בראת באשה, ואמרי לה: שלשה דבקי מיתה, ואלו הן: נדה וחלה והדלקת הנר, כלום עברתי על אחת מהן. § "ונתתה לאמתך זרע אנשים" מאי 'זרע אנשים'? אמר רב: גברא בגוברין; ושמואל אמר: זרע שמושח שני אנשים, ומאן אינון – שאול ודוד; ורבי יוחנן אמר: זרע ששקול כשני אנשים, ומאן אינון – משה ואהרן, שנאמר: "משה ואהרן בכהניו ושמואל בקוראי שמו"; ורבנן אמרי: "זרע אנשים" – זרע שמובלע בין אנשים. כי אתא רב דימי, אמר: לא ארוך ולא גוץ, (א) ולא קטן ולא אלם, ולא צחור ולא גיחור, ולא חכם ולא טפש. § "אני האשה הנצבת עמכה בזה", – אמר ריב"ל: מכאן, שאסור לישב בתוך ארבע אמות של תפלה. "אל הנער הזה התפללתי", – א"ר אלעזר: שמואל מורה הלכה לפני רבו היה, שנאמר: "וישחטו את הפר ויביאו את הנער אל עלי", משום ד"וישחטו את הפר" הביאו הנער אל עלי?! אלא, אמר להן עלי: קראו כהן, ליתי ולשחוט. חזנהו שמואל דהוו מהדרי בתר כהן למישחט, אמר להו: למה לכו לאהדורי בתר כהן למישחט? שחיטה בזר כשרה! אייתוהו לקמיה דעלי, אמר ליה: מנא לך הא? אמר ליה: *מי כתיב "ושחט הכהן"?! "והקריבו הכהנים" כתיב! מקבלה ואילך מצות כהונה; מכאן לשחיטה שכשרה בזר. אמר ליה: מימר שפיר קא אמרת, מיהו, מורה הלכה בפני רבך את – וכל *המורה הלכה בפני רבו חייב מיתה. אתיא חנה וקא צווחה קמיה: "אני האשה הנצבת עמכה בזה וגו'". אמר לה: שבקי לי דאענשיה, ובעינא רחמי ויהיב לך רבא מיניה. אמרה ליה: "אל הנער הזה התפללתי". § "וחנה היא מדברת על לבה" – אמר רבי אלעזר משום רבי יוסי בן זמרא: על עסקי לבה. אמרה לפניו: רבונו של עולם, כל מה שבראת באשה לא בראת דבר אחד לבטלה, עינים לראות, ואזנים לשמוע, חוטם להריח, פה לדבר, ידים לעשות בהם מלאכה, רגלים להלך בהן, דדים להניק בהן; דדים הללו שנתת על לבי למה, לא להניק בהן?! תן לי בן ואניק בהן. ואמר רבי אלעזר משום רבי יוסי בן זמרא: כל היושב בתענית בשבת – קורעין לו גזר דינו של שבעים שנה, ואף על פי כן חוזרין ונפרעין ממנו דין עונג שבת. *מאי תקנתיה? אמר רב נחמן בר יצחק: ליתיב תעניתא לתעניתא. § ואמר רבי אלעזר: חנה הטיחה דברים כלפי מעלה, שנאמר: "ותתפלל על ה'" – מלמד, שהטיחה דברים כלפי מעלה. ואמר רבי אלעזר: אליהו הטיח דברים כלפי מעלה, שנאמר: "ואתה הסבת את לבם אחרנית". א"ר שמואל בר רבי יצחק: מנין שחזר הקב"ה והודה לו לאליהו – דכתיב

תורה אור

דברים יג; במדבר ה; תהלים צט; מלכים א יח

רש"י

שצריך להודיעו. הנחשד צריך לנקות את עצמו, ולהודיע את חושדו שאין בו אותו דבר מגונה: לפני בת בליעל. אל תתנני כבת בליעל לחשדני בשכרות: ואסתתר. אתייחד עם אחרים, ויחשדוני בעלי: פלסתר. שקר: שלש אמתות. דריש להו לשון מיתה: בדקי מיתה. שהאשה נבדקת בהן בשעת הסכנה, שאם ימלא בה אחד מהם תמות: נדה וחלה והדלקת נר. של שבת, על ג' עבירות הללו נשים מתות. וטעמא יליף במסכת שבת (ד' לא:): שמובלע בין אנשים. רב דימי מפרש לה: לא ארוך ולא גוץ וכו': אלם. פי': עב: *צחור. רו"ש בלע"ז: גיחור. שהוא לבן יותר מדאי: ולא חכם. יותר מדאי, שלא יהיה תימה בעיני הבריות, ומתוך שנדברין בו שולטת בו עין הרע: הנצבת עמכה. משמע אף הוא עמה בעמידה: אל הנער הזה. על זה ולא לאחר. מכאן שחטא לעלי ורצה לענשו ולהתפלל שיתן לה בן אחר: והקריבו הכהנים. אמרו בפרק קמא דחגיגה (דף יא.): והקריבו — זה קבלת הדם: של שבעים שנה. כלומר: אפילו נגזר עליו מנעוריו. לפי שתענית קשה בשבת, לפי שהכל מתענגים בו והוא מתענה: תעניתא לתעניתא. יתענה למחר: ותתפלל על ה'. כך כתוב הוא במקרא, ולא גרסינן הכא אל תקרי: שחזר והודה לאליהו. לדבריו הודה לאחר זמן, בנבואת נביאים אחרים:

דכתיב

תוספות

דבר שאינו הגון. פירוש: אע"ג דליכא איסורא דאורייתא. דאי איכא איסורא דאורייתא, פשיטא, "הוכח תוכיח" כתיב (ויקרא יט):

גברא בגוברין. פי': אדם שיהא חשוב לימנות בין אנשים:

*מכאן ששכור אסור להתפלל. ירושלמי במסכת תרומות, פרק קמא: רבי זירא בעי קמיה דרבי אמי: שכור מהו שיברך? א"ל: "ואכלת ושבעת וברכת", ואפילו מדומדם. פירוש: ואפי' הוא שתוי ושכור כל כך שאינו יכול לדבר כראוי, דהכי משמע "ושבעת וברכת":

מכאן שאסור לישב בד' אמות של תפלה. בין מלפניו (בין מלאחריו) ובין מן הצדדין. ופירשו תשובת הגאונים דוקא ביושב ובטל, אבל אם היה עוסק בק"ש ובברכותיה וכיוצא בהם – אפילו יושב שפיר דמי:

[עמכה] עמך משמע בתוך ארבע אמות – משום דכתיב עמכה מלא בה"א, כלומר: שלא היה יושב בתוך ארבע אמות שלה, כי אם בחמישית:

מורה הלכה בפני רבך את. ואף ע"פ שלא למד עדיין בפניו, מ"מ גדול הדור היה, ובא ללמוד לפניו:

כל היושב בתענית בשבת. פירש ר"ח: בתענית חלום, וכן איתא במדרש תהלים. וכשיושב בתענית חלום בשבת פי' בה"ג שאומר 'עננו' באלהי נצור, ואפילו קובע ברכה לעצמו, כיון שאינו בתוך י"ח:

גדולה

מסורת הש"ס

ערכין טז:

[צחור שהוא לבן. גי' רו"ש בלע"ז כצ"ל ו... [ברש"י] לקמן נח: וגב... בכורות דף מה: פירש"י לקמן נט: במעדני יו"ט לקמן נח...

סוטה כו. [וכס מוסף... הסיטה וע"ש בת... ובתוס' מנחות יז: ולע"...

שבת לב.

עירובין סג.

[תענית יב:]

ג"א נפסדת

[יבמות עא. כתובות סז: קדושין יז: גיטין מא: נדרים ג. ב"מ לא: נד: ע"ז כז. סנהדרין נו. סד: פה: ל: מכות יב. זבחים קח: כריתות יא. ערכין ג. נדה לב: מד.]

זבחים לב. [יומא כז. מנחות יט.]

הגהות הב"ח

(א) גמ' ולא קטן. נ"ב פי' שהוא דק ביותר ולא אלם פירוש שהוא עב הרבה לשון ואלים:

גליון הש"ס

תוס' ד"ה מורה וכו' ובא ללמוד לפניו. עי' תה"ד סימן קל"ח:

דכתיב ואשר הרעותי. רישא דקרא אוספה הצולעה והנדחה אקבצה ואשר הרעותי – אני גרמתי להם שבראתי יצר הרע: אלמלא שלש מקראות הללו. שמעידין שיש ביד הקדוש ברוך הוא לתקן יצרנו, ולהסיר יצר הרע ממנו: נתמוטטו רגלינו במשפט. אבל עכשיו יש לנו פתחון פה. שהוא גרם לנו שברא יצר הרע: הטיח. לשון זריקה, כמו כמטחוי קשת (בראשית כא): אין ארי נוהם. שמח ומשתגע ומזיק: מלי כריסיה זני בישי. מילוי הכרס הוא ממיני חטאים הרעים. זני מתרגמינן למיניהו – לזנוהי (בראשית א): הרף ממני. הרפהו שיש כח בידו למחול ע"י תפלה: הניחה לי. משמע שהיה אוחז בו: שלש רגלים. אברהם יצחק ויעקב: שהחלהו. הפליל בו, אנוי"ר בלע"ז: נדרו. דבורו שאמר ואכלם: שמסר עצמו למיתה. ויחל לשון חלל: שהחלה עליהם מדת רחמים. כמו יחולו על ראש יואב (ש"ב ג), לשון הניח: שאחזתו אחילו. גרס: אשתא דגרמי. מוליי"ר בלע"ז: אשר נשבעת להם בך. שנאמר בעקדת יצחק בי נשבעתי (בראשית כב): עד כאן. עד ככוכבי השמים: מכאן ואילך דברי הרב. אמר לו אעשה כדבריך: דברים שאמרת לי. בסנה אמרת לי אעלה אתכם מעני מצרים אל ארץ טובה ורחבה (שמות ג): החייתני. בפני האומות: עלה

תורה אור

[סוכה נב: ע"ש] [מגילה כז:] [יומא פו: סנהדרין קב.]

(מיכה ד) דכתיב: °"ואשר הרעתי".§ *אמר רבי חמא ברבי חנינא: אלמלא שלש
מקראות הללו – נתמוטטו רגליהם של שונאי ישראל: חד, דכתיב: "ואשר
(ירמיה יח) הרעתי", וחד, דכתיב: °"הנה כחמר ביד היוצר כן אתם בידי בית ישראל"; וחד,
(יחזקאל לו) דכתיב: °"והסרתי את לב האבן מבשרכם ונתתי לכם לב בשר". רב פפא
(שם) אמר, מהכא: °"ואת רוחי אתן בקרבכם ועשיתי את אשר בחקי תלכו". ואמר
(במדבר יא) רבי אלעזר: משה הטיח דברים כלפי מעלה, שנאמר: °"ויתפלל משה אל ה'",
אל תקרי "אל" ה' אלא "על" ה', שכן דבי רבי אליעזר בן יעקב *קורין לאלפי"ן(א)
(דברים א) עייני"ן ולעייני"ן אלפי"ן. דבי רבי ינאי אמרי, מהכא: °"ודי זהב", מאי "ודי זהב"? אמרי
*דבי ר' ינאי, כך אמר משה לפני הקב"ה: רבונו של עולם, בשביל כסף וזהב
שהשפעת להם לישראל עד שאמרו די – הוא גרם שעשו את העגל. אמרי דבי
ר' ינאי: אין ארי נוהם מתוך קופה של תבן אלא מתוך קופה של בשר. אמר
רבי אושעיא: משל, לאדם שהיתה לו פרה כחושה ובעלת אברים, האכילה
כרשינין והיתה מבעטת בו. אמר לה: מי גרם ליך שתהא מבעטת בי – אלא
כרשינין שהאכלתיך. אמר רבי חייא בר אבא אמר ר' יוחנן: משל, לאדם אחד
שהיה לו בן, הרחיצו וסכו, והאכילו והשקהו, ותלה לו כיס על צוארו, והושיבו
על פתח של זונות, מה יעשה אותו הבן שלא יחטא? אמר רב אחא בריה
(הושע יג) דרב הונא אמר רב ששת: היינו דאמרי אינשי "מלי כריסיה זני בישי" שנאמר: °"כמרעיתם וישבעו שבעו
(דברים ח) וירם לבם על כן שכחוני"; רב נחמן אמר, מהכא: °"ורם לבבך ושכחת את ה'"; ורבנן אמרי, מהכא: °"ואכל (דברים לב)
(שם לב) ושבע ודשן ופנה"; ואי בעית אימא, מהכא: °"וישמן ישורון ויבעט". אמר רבי שמואל בר נחמני אמר רבי
(הושע ב) יונתן: מנין שחזר הקדוש ברוך הוא והודה לו למשה – שנאמר: °"וכסף הרביתי *להם וזהב עשו לבעל".§ (נ"ל לה)
(שמות לב) °"וידבר ה' אל משה לך רד" מאי "לך רד"? אמר רבי אלעזר, אמר לו הקדוש ב"ה למשה: משה, רד מגדולתך!
כלום נתתי לך גדולה אלא בשביל ישראל, ועכשיו ישראל חטאו(ב) – אתה למה לי? מיד תשש כוחו של משה
(דברים ט) ולא היה לו כח לדבר. וכיון שאמר: °"הרף ממני ואשמידם", אמר משה: דבר זה תלוי בי – מיד עמד ונתחזק
בתפלה ובקש רחמים. משל, למלך(ג) שכעס על בנו והיה מכהו מכה גדולה, והיה אוהבו יושב לפניו ומתירא
לומר לו דבר. אמר המלך: אלמלא אוהבי זה שיושב לפני הרגתיך! אמר: דבר זה תלוי בי – מיד עמד
(שמות לב) והצילו. °"ועתה הניחה לי ויחר אפי בהם ואכלם ואעשה אותך לגוי גדול וגו'" – אמר רבי אבהו: אלמלא מקרא
כתוב אי אפשר לאומרו; מלמד, שתפסו משה להקדוש ברוך הוא כאדם שהוא תופס את חבירו בבגדו,
(שם) ואמר לפניו: רבונו של עולם, אין אני מניחך עד שתמחול ותסלח להם. °"ואעשה אותך לגוי גדול וגו'" –
אמר רבי אלעזר, אמר משה לפני הקדוש ב"ה: רבונו של עולם, ומה כסא של שלש רגלים אינו יכול
לעמוד לפניך בשעת כעסך, כסא של רגל אחד על אחת כמה וכמה! ולא עוד אלא שיש בי בושת פנים
(שם) מאבותי. עכשיו יאמרו: ראו פרנס שהעמיד עליהם, בקש גדולה לעצמו ולא בקש עליהם רחמים. °"ויחל
משה את פני ה'" – אמר רבי אלעזר:(ד) מלמד שעמד משה בתפלה לפני הקדוש ברוך הוא עד שהחלהו; *ורבא [אולי צ"ל ורב]
[נ"ל שהתיר וכ"ה בילקוט ובע"י והוא נכון כדאיתא נדרים עז: וב"ב קכ: וע' תוספות בכורות לז. ד"ה מפירין] אמר: עד *שהפר לו נדרו, כתיב הכא "ויחל" וכתיב התם °"לא יחל דברו", *ואמר מר: הוא אינו מיחל אבל (במדבר ל חגיגה י)
אחרים מחלין לו. ושמואל אמר מלמד שמסר עצמו למיתה עליהם שנאמר: °"ואם אין מחני נא מספרך". (שמות לב)
*אמר רבא אמר רב יצחק: מלמד שהחלה עליהם מדת רחמים. ורבנן אמרי: מלמד שאמר משה לפני [רב יצחק אמ' מלמד כו' כצ"ל וכ"ה בילקוט ובע"י]
הקב"ה: רבש"ע, *חולין הוא לך מעשות כדבר הזה. "ויחל משה את פני ה'". תניא, רבי אליעזר הגדול אומר: [ע"ז ז.]
מלמד שעמד משה בתפלה לפני הקדוש ברוך הוא עד שאחזתו אחילו. *מאי אחילו? אמר רבי אלעזר: (גיטין ע.)
(שם) אש של עצמות. מאי אש של עצמות? אמר אביי: אשתא דגרמי. °"זכר לאברהם ליצחק ולישראל עבדיך אשר
נשבעת להם בך". מאי 'בך' – אמר רבי אלעזר: אמר משה לפני הקדוש ב"ה: רבונו של עולם, אלמלא נשבעת
להם בשמים ובארץ הייתי אומר כשם ששמים וארץ בטלים – כך שבועתך בטלה. ועכשיו שנשבעת להם
בשמך הגדול, מה שמך הגדול חי וקיים לעולם ולעולמי עולמים – כך שבועתך קיימת לעולם ולעולמי עולמים.
(שם) °"ותדבר אליהם ארבה את זרעכם ככוכבי השמים וכל הארץ הזאת אשר אמרתי". האי "אשר אמרתי"? "אשר אמרת"
מיבעי ליה! – אמר רבי אלעזר: עד כאן דברי תלמיד מכאן ואילך – דברי הרב. ורבי שמואל בר נחמני אמר: אלו
ואלו דברי תלמיד,(ה) אלא כך אמר משה לפני הקדוש ברוך הוא: רבונו של עולם, דברים שאמרת לי "לך אמור
(במדבר יד) להם לישראל" בשמי הלכתי ואמרתי להם בשמך, עכשיו מה אני אומר להם? °"מבלתי יכלת ה'", "יכול ה'" מיבעי
ליה! – אמר רבי אלעזר, אמר משה לפני הקב"ה: רבש"ע, עכשיו יאמרו אומות העולם: תשש כחו כנקבה
ואינו יכול להציל. אמר הקב"ה למשה: והלא כבר ראו נסים וגבורות שעשיתי להם על הים! – אמר לפניו:
רבונו של עולם, עדיין יש להם לומר: למלך אחד – יכול לעמוד, לשלשים ואחד מלכים – אינו יכול לעמוד.
(שם) אמר ר' יוחנן: מנין שחזר הקדוש ברוך הוא והודה לו למשה – שנאמר: °"ויאמר ה' סלחתי כדבריך". תני דבי רבי
(שם) ישמעאל: כדבריך עתידים אוה"ע לומר כן. אשרי תלמיד שרבו מודה לו. °"ואולם חי אני". אמר רבא אמר רב יצחק:
(ע"ז ז:) מלמד, שאמר לו הקדוש ב"ה למשה: משה, החייתני בדבריך.§ *דרש רבי שמלאי: א לעולם יסדר אדם שבחו
(דברים ג) של הקב"ה ואחר כך יתפלל. מנלן – ממשה דכתיב °"ואתחנן אל ה' בעת ההיא"; וכתיב "ה' אלהים אתה החלות
להראות את עבדך את גדלך ואת ידך החזקה אשר מי אל בשמים ובארץ אשר יעשה כמעשיך וכגבורותיך", וכתיב
בתריה "אעברה נא ואראה את הארץ הטובה וגו'". (סימן: מעשי"ם, צדק"ה, קרב"ן, כה"ן, תעני"ת, מנע"ל, ברז"ל).§
אמר

עין משפט נר מצוה

כג א מיי' פ"א מהלכות תפלה הלכה ב:

הגהות הב"ח

(א) גמ' קורין לאלפי"ן. נ"ב פרש"י פי' הקורא שומד דהיינו בדרש' אבל בתפלה איסורא איכא ע"ש ד' כ"ד ע"ב: (ב) שם ועכשיו ישראל חטאו (אתה למה לי) תא"מ ונ"ב ס"א למה לך גדולה: (ג) שם משל למלך כ"ו שכעס: (ד) שם א"ר אלעזר (מלמד שעמד וכו' שהחלהו) תא"מ ונ"ב ס"א מלמד שהתפלל משה עד שהחלה אביי אמר עד שהחלה להקב"ה: (ה) שם דברי תלמיד הן אלא:

רב נסים גאון

ואולם חי אני אמר לו הקב"ה למשה משה החייתני בדבריך. זה הדבר קשה היה בפני התלמידים והיו מלעיזים בו עלינו החולקין על דברי רבותינו ז"ל ואמנם כי פשוטו של זה הדבר נראה שאינו מתקבל על הדעת שמשתבשין בה ואני ברחמי שמיא פירשתיה פירוש צח וביארתי טעמיה ביאור יפה שהוא שוה לענין הכתוב ולסברא והרי אנו מזכירין המימרא כללא כדגרסי' בגמ' ואחר כן נאמר פירושה (במדבר יד) מבלתי יכולת ה' יכול ה' מיבעי ליה אמר ר' אלעזר אמר משה לפני הקב"ה רבש"ע עכשיו יאמרו אומות העולם תשש [כחו] כנקבה ואין בו כח להצילם אמר לו הקב"ה והודה למשה שנא'

בן עמרם והלא כבר ראו נסים וגבורות שעשיתי על הים אמר לפניו רבונו של עולם יאמרו לפני מלך אחד יכול לעמוד בפני ל"א (מלך) [מלכים] אינו יכול לעמוד אמר ר' יוחנן מנין שחזר הקב"ה והודה למשה שנא' (שם) ויאמר ה' סלחתי כדבריך תנא דבי ר' ישמעאל כדבריך עתידין אומות העולם לומר אשרי תלמיד שרבו מודה לו ואולם חי אני אמר רבא א"ר יצחק אמר לו הקב"ה למשה משה החייתני בדבריך עד כאן היא הדרשה שנאמרה בזה הפסוק ופירושה אנו מזכירין דע לך כי החיים והיכולת שתי מדות הן ממדותיו של הקב"ה שהן מדות עצמו וגדולתו שאינן נחלפין ממנו כלל כי הכח והיכולת אינם נמצאים אלא במי שהוא חי ומי שהוא חי העולמים שלא יתמו שנותיו אי אפשר שלא יהיה יכול וזה הדבר אע"פ שהוא שריר ומקויים בסברא יש לו חיזוק מן הכתוב והיינו דכתב רחמנא (דברים לב) כי אשא אל שמים ידי ואמרתי חי אנכי לעולם פתח בזכרון היד שהוא היכולת וסיים בזכר החיים ואמר חי אנכי לעולם קיימת לו היכולת מפני שהוא חי העולמים ובעת שאירע מעשה המרגלים ואמר הקב"ה להשמידם לאומתו נגש הנביא עליו השלום בתפלה בעדם ואמר בכלל דבריו מבלתי יכולת ה' ולפי שידע הקב"ה כי אמת דבר וכי אם הוא משמיד את העם במדבר ואינו מכבש לפניהן את ארץ כנען האומות אומרים עליו כי קצרה ידו ותשש כחו ואינו יכול לעמוד כנגד ל"א (מלך) [מלכים] ולגרשם מפני בניו ולפיכך קבל תפלתו בעדם ונעתר לו ואמר לו סלחתי כדבריך ואמר לו אחר כן ואולם חי אני הודיע לנביאו שבודאי אילו השמידם לעם היו האומות אומרים שאין לו יכולת ולא היו מכירין גבורתו והואיל ואין מתברר להם שהוא יכול גם כן אין מתברר להם שהוא חי והנה בשביל עתירת הנביא בעד העם הודו האומות כי יש להקב"ה החיים לעלמין ונתברר להם שהוא חי וקיים וזכה הנביא לשבח בשביל זה הדבר כי בשביל עתירתו נודעה גדולתו של מלכנו ועצמו וגבורתו ונתפרסמו בקצות הארץ ונתברר ונתקיים כי הקב"ה יתעלה שמו חי בעצמו ולפיכך א"ל רחמנא ואולם חי אני אחר שאמר כדברך תיכף לה ודרשי ליה רבנן החייתני בדבריך כלומר שבשביל עתירתך גרם הדבר ונתברר לאומות שאני חי וזה הוא צד התירוץ של זה הדבר והיה נעלם מאד וסייעני הקב"ה לגלותו ולפרשו ולא ראיתי אדם שקדמני לזה התירוץ וזה הפירוש יהיה שמור בידך:

תורה אור

אָמַר ר' אֶלְעָזָר: גְּדוֹלָה תְּפִלָּה יוֹתֵר מִמַּעֲשִׂים טוֹבִים. שֶׁאֵין לְךָ גָּדוֹל בְּמַעֲשִׂים טוֹבִים יוֹתֵר מִמֹּשֶׁה רַבֵּינוּ, אעפ"כ לֹא נַעֲנָה אֶלָּא בִּתְפִלָּה, שֶׁנֶּאֱמַר: °"אַל תּוֹסֶף דַּבֵּר אֵלַי" וְסָמִיךְ לֵיהּ "עֲלֵה רֹאשׁ הַפִּסְגָּה". וא"ר אֶלְעָזָר: גְּדוֹלָה תַּעֲנִית יוֹתֵר מִן הַצְּדָקָה. מַאי טַעְמָא – זֶה בְּגוּפוֹ וְזֶה בְּמָמוֹנוֹ. וא"ר אֶלְעָזָר: גְּדוֹלָה תְּפִלָּה יוֹתֵר מִן הַקָּרְבָּנוֹת שנא' °"לָמָּה לִּי רֹב זִבְחֵיכֶם" וּכְתִיב "וּבְפָרִשְׂכֶם כַּפֵּיכֶם"(א). א"ר יוֹחָנָן: *°כָּל כֹּהֵן שֶׁהָרַג אֶת הַנֶּפֶשׁ לֹא יִשָּׂא אֶת כַּפָּיו, שנא' °"יְדֵיכֶם דָּמִים מָלֵאוּ".§ *וא"ר אֶלְעָזָר: מִיּוֹם שֶׁחָרַב בֵּית הַמִּקְדָּשׁ נִנְעֲלוּ שַׁעֲרֵי תְפִלָּה, שֶׁנֶּאֱמַר: °"גַּם כִּי אֶזְעַק וַאֲשַׁוֵּעַ שָׂתַם תְּפִלָּתִי", ואע"פ שֶׁשַּׁעֲרֵי תְפִילָּה נִנְעֲלוּ שַׁעֲרֵי דִמְעָה לֹא נִנְעֲלוּ, שֶׁנֶּאֱמַר: °"שִׁמְעָה תְפִלָּתִי ה' וְשַׁוְעָתִי הַאֲזִינָה אֶל דִּמְעָתִי אַל תֶּחֱרַשׁ". רָבָא לֹא גָּזַר תַּעֲנִיתָא בְּיוֹמָא דְעֵיבָא מִשּׁוּם שנא' °"סַכֹּתָה בֶעָנָן לָךְ מֵעֲבוֹר תְּפִלָּה". וא"ר אֶלְעָזָר: מִיּוֹם שֶׁחָרַב בֵּית הַמִּקְדָּשׁ נִפְסְקָה חוֹמַת בַּרְזֶל בֵּין יִשְׂרָאֵל לַאֲבִיהֶם שֶׁבַּשָּׁמַיִם, שנא' °"וְאַתָּה *קַח לְךָ מַחֲבַת בַּרְזֶל וְנָתַתָּה אוֹתָהּ קִיר בַּרְזֶל בֵּינְךָ וּבֵין הָעִיר".§ א"ר חָנִין א"ר חֲנִינָא: כָּל הַמַּאֲרִיךְ בִּתְפִלָּתוֹ אֵין תְּפִלָּתוֹ חוֹזֶרֶת רֵיקָם. מְנָא לָן – מִמֹּשֶׁה רַבֵּינוּ שנא': °"וָאֶתְפַּלֵּל אֶל ה'", וּכְתִיב בָּתְרֵיהּ "וַיִּשְׁמַע ה' אֵלַי גַּם בַּפַּעַם הַהִיא". אִינִי?! וְהָא *א"ר חִיָּיא בַּר אַבָּא א"ר יוֹחָנָן: כָּל הַמַּאֲרִיךְ בִּתְפִילָּתוֹ וּמְעַיֵּין בָּהּ – סוֹף בָּא לִידֵי כְּאֵב לֵב, שנא': °"תּוֹחֶלֶת מְמֻשָּׁכָה מַחֲלָה לֵב" מַאי תַּקַּנְתֵּיהּ – יַעֲסוֹק בַּתּוֹרָה, שנא' °"וְעֵץ חַיִּים תַּאֲוָה בָאָה" וְאֵין עֵץ חַיִּים אֶלָּא תּוֹרָה, שֶׁנֶּאֱמַר: °"עֵץ חַיִּים הִיא לַמַּחֲזִיקִים בָּהּ"! – לָא קַשְׁיָא, ב[ה]א – דְּמַאֲרִיךְ וּמְעַיֵּין בָּהּ, הָא – דְּמַאֲרִיךְ וְלֹא מְעַיֵּין בָּהּ. א"ר חָמָא בר' חֲנִינָא: אִם רָאָה אָדָם שֶׁהִתְפַּלֵּל וְלֹא נַעֲנָה יַחֲזוֹר וְיִתְפַּלֵּל שֶׁנֶּאֱמַר: °"קַוֵּה אֶל ה' חֲזַק וְיַאֲמֵץ לִבֶּךָ וְקַוֵּה אֶל ה'". ת"ר, אַרְבָּעָה צְרִיכִין חִזּוּק וְאֵלּוּ הֵן: תּוֹרָה, וּמַעֲשִׂים טוֹבִים, תְּפִלָּה וְדֶרֶךְ אֶרֶץ. תּוֹרָה וּמַעֲשִׂים טוֹבִים מִנַּיִן – שנא' °"רַק חֲזַק וֶאֱמַץ מְאֹד לִשְׁמֹר *וְלַעֲשׂוֹת כְּכָל הַתּוֹרָה". 'חֲזַק' – בַּתּוֹרָה, 'וֶאֱמַץ' – בְּמַעֲשִׂים טוֹבִים. תְּפִלָּה מִנַּיִן – שנא' "קַוֵּה אֶל ה' חֲזַק וְיַאֲמֵץ לִבֶּךָ וְקַוֵּה אֶל ה'"; דֶּרֶךְ אֶרֶץ מִנַּיִן – שנא' °"חֲזַק וְנִתְחַזַּק בְּעַד עַמֵּנוּ וגו'".§ °"וַתֹּאמֶר צִיּוֹן עֲזָבַנִי ה' וה' שְׁכֵחָנִי". הַיְינוּ עֲזוּבָה הַיְינוּ שְׁכוּחָה! אָמַר ר"ל, אָמְרָה כְּנֶסֶת יִשְׂרָאֵל לִפְנֵי הקב"ה: רבש"ע, אָדָם נוֹשֵׂא אִשָּׁה עַל אִשְׁתּוֹ רִאשׁוֹנָה – זוֹכֵר מַעֲשֵׂה הָרִאשׁוֹנָה, אַתָּה עֲזַבְתַּנִי וּשְׁכַחְתַּנִי. –אָמַר לָהּ הקב"ה: בִּתִּי, י"ב מַזָּלוֹת בָּרָאתִי בָּרָקִיעַ וְעַל כָּל מַזָּל וּמַזָּל בָּרָאתִי לוֹ שְׁלֹשִׁים חַיִל וְעַל כָּל חַיִל וְחַיִל בָּרָאתִי לוֹ שְׁלֹשִׁים לִגְיוֹן וְעַל כָּל לִגְיוֹן וְלִגְיוֹן בָּרָאתִי לוֹ שְׁלֹשִׁים רַהֲטוֹן וְעַל כָּל רַהֲטוֹן וְרַהֲטוֹן בָּרָאתִי לוֹ שְׁלֹשִׁים קַרְטוֹן וְעַל כָּל קַרְטוֹן וְקַרְטוֹן בָּרָאתִי לוֹ שְׁלֹשִׁים גַּסְטְרָא וְעַל כָּל גַּסְטְרָא וגַסְטְרָא תָּלִיתִי בּוֹ שְׁלֹשׁ מֵאוֹת וְשִׁשִּׁים וַחֲמִשָּׁה אַלְפֵי רִבּוֹא כּוֹכָבִים כְּנֶגֶד יְמוֹת הַחַמָּה – וְכוּלָּן לֹא בָּרָאתִי אֶלָּא בִּשְׁבִילֵךְ וְאַתְּ אָמַרְתְּ עֲזַבְתַּנִי וּשְׁכַחְתַּנִי?! °"הֲתִשְׁכַּח אִשָּׁה עוּלָהּ" אָמַר הקב"ה: כְּלוּם אֶשְׁכַּח עוֹלוֹת אֵילִים [א] וּפִטְרֵי רְחָמִים שֶׁהִקְרַבְתְּ לְפָנַי בַּמִּדְבָּר?! אָמְרָה לְפָנָיו: רבש"ע, הוֹאִיל וְאֵין שִׁכְחָה לִפְנֵי כִּסֵּא כְבוֹדֶךָ שֶׁמָּא לֹא תִשְׁכַּח לִי מַעֲשֵׂה הָעֵגֶל? –אָמַר לָהּ: °"גַּם אֵלֶּה תִשְׁכַּחְנָה". אָמְרָה לְפָנָיו: רבש"ע, הוֹאִיל וְיֵשׁ שִׁכְחָה לִפְנֵי כִּסֵּא כְבוֹדֶךָ שֶׁמָּא תִּשְׁכַּח לִי מַעֲשֵׂה סִינַי? – אָמַר לָהּ: °"וְאָנֹכִי לֹא אֶשְׁכָּחֵךְ". וְהַיְינוּ דא"ר אֶלְעָזָר א"ר אוֹשַׁעְיָא: מַאי דִּכְתִיב "גַּם אֵלֶּה תִשְׁכַּחְנָה" – זֶה מַעֲשֵׂה הָעֵגֶל, "וְאָנֹכִי לֹא אֶשְׁכָּחֵךְ" – זֶה מַעֲשֵׂה סִינַי.§ "חֲסִידִים הָרִאשׁוֹנִים הָיוּ שׁוֹהִין שָׁעָה אַחַת". מְנָא הָנֵי מִילֵּי? א"ר יְהוֹשֻׁעַ ב"ל: אָמַר קְרָא °"אַשְׁרֵי יוֹשְׁבֵי בֵיתֶךָ". וְאָמַר ר' יְהוֹשֻׁעַ ב"ל: הַמִּתְפַּלֵּל צָרִיךְ לִשְׁהוֹת שָׁעָה אַחַת אַחַר תְּפִלָּתוֹ שנא' °"אַךְ צַדִּיקִים יוֹדוּ לִשְׁמֶךָ יֵשְׁבוּ יְשָׁרִים אֶת פָּנֶיךָ". תַּנְיָא נַמִי הָכִי: גהַמִּתְפַּלֵּל צָרִיךְ שֶׁיִּשְׁהֶא שָׁעָה אַחַת קוֹדֶם תְּפִלָּתוֹ, וְשָׁעָה אַחַת אַחַר תְּפִלָּתוֹ. קוֹדֶם תְּפִלָּתוֹ מִנַּיִן – שנא' "אַשְׁרֵי יוֹשְׁבֵי בֵיתֶךָ". לְאַחַר תְּפִלָּתוֹ מִנַּיִן – דִּכְתִיב "אַךְ צַדִּיקִים יוֹדוּ לִשְׁמֶךָ יֵשְׁבוּ יְשָׁרִים אֶת פָּנֶיךָ". תָּנוּ רַבָּנַן: חֲסִידִים הָרִאשׁוֹנִים הָיוּ שׁוֹהִין שָׁעָה אַחַת וּמִתְפַּלְּלִין שָׁעָה אַחַת וְחוֹזְרִין וְשׁוֹהִין שָׁעָה אַחַת. וְכִי מֵאַחַר שֶׁשּׁוֹהִין תֵּשַׁע שָׁעוֹת בַּיּוֹם בִּתְפִלָּה, תּוֹרָתָן הֵיאַךְ מִשְׁתַּמֶּרֶת, וּמְלַאכְתָּן הֵיאַךְ נַעֲשֵׂית? אֶלָּא מִתּוֹךְ שֶׁחֲסִידִים הֵם – תּוֹרָתָם מִשְׁתַּמֶּרֶת וּמְלַאכְתָּן מִתְבָּרֶכֶת.§ "אֲפִילּוּ דהַמֶּלֶךְ שׁוֹאֵל בִּשְׁלוֹמוֹ לֹא יְשִׁיבֶנּוּ". אָמַר רַב יוֹסֵף: הלֹא שָׁנוּ אֶלָּא לְמַלְכֵי יִשְׂרָאֵל אֲבָל לְמַלְכֵי אוּמּוֹת הָעוֹלָם פּוֹסֵק. מֵיתִיבִי: והַמִּתְפַּלֵּל וְרָאָה אַנָּס בָּא כְּנֶגְדּוֹ, רָאָה קָרוֹן בָּא כְּנֶגְדּוֹ – לֹא יְהֵא מַפְסִיק אֶלָּא מְקַצֵּר וְעוֹלֶה! – לָא קַשְׁיָא: הָא – זדְּאֶפְשָׁר לְקַצֵּר (*יְקַצֵּר, וְאִם לָאו – פּוֹסֵק.) ת"ר: מַעֲשֶׂה בְּחָסִיד אֶחָד שֶׁהָיָה מִתְפַּלֵּל בַּדֶּרֶךְ, בָּא הֶגְמוֹן אֶחָד וְנָתַן לוֹ שָׁלוֹם וְלֹא הֶחֱזִיר לוֹ שָׁלוֹם, הִמְתִּין לוֹ עַד שֶׁסִּיֵּים תְּפִלָּתוֹ. לְאַחַר שֶׁסִּיֵּים תְּפִלָּתוֹ א"ל: רֵיקָא, וַהֲלֹא כָּתוּב בְּתוֹרַתְכֶם °"רַק הִשָּׁמֶר לְךָ וּשְׁמֹר נַפְשְׁךָ" וּכְתִיב °"וְנִשְׁמַרְתֶּם מְאֹד לְנַפְשֹׁתֵיכֶם", כְּשֶׁנָּתַתִּי לְךָ שָׁלוֹם לָמָּה לֹא הֶחֱזַרְתָּ לִי שָׁלוֹם? אִם הָיִיתִי חוֹתֵךְ רֹאשְׁךָ בְּסַיִף מִי הָיָה תּוֹבֵעַ אֶת דָּמְךָ מִיָּדִי?! א"ל: הַמְתֵּן לִי עַד שֶׁאֲפַיֶּיסְךָ בִּדְבָרִים. א"ל: אִילּוּ הָיִיתָ עוֹמֵד לִפְנֵי מֶלֶךְ בָּשָׂר וָדָם וּבָא חֲבֵרְךָ וְנָתַן לְךָ שָׁלוֹם – הָיִיתָ מַחֲזִיר

עֲלֵה רֹאשׁ הַפִּסְגָּה. בִּדְבַר תְּפִלָּה זוֹ נִתְרַצֵּיתִי לְהַרְאוֹתְךָ אוֹתָהּ: וּבְפָרִשְׂכֶם כַּפֵּיכֶם. אִי לָאו דִּגְדוֹלָה תְּפִלָּה, כֵּיוָן דְּאָמַר לָמָּה לִּי רוֹב זִבְחֵיכֶם לָמָּה לִי תּוּ וּבְפָרִשְׂכֶם? הָא אֲפִילּוּ זִבְחֵיהֶם לָא נִיחָא לֵיהּ: אַל תֶּחֱרַשׁ. מִדְּלָא (ג) כְּתִיב אֶת דִּמְעָתִי תִּרְאֶה, ש"מ: נִרְאֵית הִיא לְפָנָיו, וְאֵין צָרִיךְ לְהִתְפַּלֵּל אֶלָּא שֶׁתִּתְקַבֵּל לְפָנָיו: וְנָתַתָּה אוֹתָהּ קִיר בַּרְזֶל. סִימָן לִמְחִיצַּת בַּרְזֶל הַמַּפְסֶקֶת בֵּינוֹ לְבֵינָם: וּמְעַיֵּין בָּהּ. מְצַפֶּה שֶׁתֵּעָשֶׂה בַּקָּשָׁתוֹ עַל יְדֵי הַאֲרָכָתוֹ, סוֹף שֶׁאֵינָהּ נַעֲשֵׂית וְנִמְצֵאת תּוֹחֶלֶת מְמוּשֶּׁכֶת חִנָּם. וְהִיא כְּאֵב לֵב כְּשֶׁאָדָם מְצַפֶּה וְאֵין תַּאֲוָתוֹ בָּאָה: תּוֹחֶלֶת. לְשׁוֹן חִלּוּי וְתִקְוָה: וְעֵץ חַיִּים תַּאֲוָה בָאָה. סוֹפוֹ שֶׁל מִקְרָא הוּא: קַוֵּה. וְהִתְחַזֵּק, וְלֹא תִּמְשׁוֹךְ יָדְךָ, אֶלָּא חֲזוֹר וְקַוֵּה: צְרִיכִין חִזּוּק. שֶׁיִּתְחַזֵּק אָדָם בָּהֶם תָּמִיד בְּכָל כֹּחוֹ: דֶּרֶךְ אֶרֶץ. אִם אוּמָּן הוּא – לְאוּמָּנוּתוֹ, אִם סוֹחֵר הוּא – לִסְחוֹרָתוֹ, אִם אִישׁ מִלְחָמָה הוּא – לְמִלְחַמְתּוֹ: שְׁלֹשִׁים חַיִל. רָאשֵׁי גְּיָיסוֹת וַחֲבוּרוֹת חֲלוּקוֹת: לִגְיוֹן וְקַרְטוֹן וְגַסְטְרָא. שֵׁמוֹת שֶׁל שְׂרָרָה, כְּגוֹן שִׁלְטוֹן, וְהֶגְמוֹן, וְדוּכָּס, וּפֶחָה: עוּלָהּ. כְּמוֹ עוֹלוֹת וְקָרְבָּנוֹת: גַּם אֵלֶּה. מַעֲשֵׂה הָעֵגֶל שֶׁאָמְרוּ אֵלֶּה אֱלֹהֶיךָ יִשְׂרָאֵל (שמות לב): וְאָנֹכִי זֶה מַעֲשֵׂה סִינַי. שֶׁנֶּאֱמַר בּוֹ אָנֹכִי ה' אֱלֹהֶיךָ (שמות כ): יוֹשְׁבֵי בֵיתֶךָ. וְהָדָר יְהַלְלוּךָ: יוֹדוּ לִשְׁמֶךָ. וְהָדָר יֵשְׁבוּ יְשָׁרִים אֶת פָּנֶיךָ: תֵּשַׁע שָׁעוֹת. לְשָׁלֹשׁ תְּפִלּוֹת: תּוֹרָתָם מִשְׁתַּמֶּרֶת. בְּתוֹךְ לִבָּם, שֶׁאֵין תַּלְמוּדָם מִשְׁתַּכֵּחַ: אֲבָל לְמַלְכֵי אוּמּוֹת הָעוֹלָם פּוֹסֵק. שֶׁלֹּא יַהַרְגֵהוּ: הָא דְּאֶפְשָׁר בְּקִצּוּר. כְּגוֹן שֶׁסָּמוּךְ לִגְמוֹר תְּפִלָּתוֹ: אֲבָל

גדולה תפלה יותר ממעשים טובים. בלא תפלה, שהרי משה רבינו ע"ה אף על פי שהיו בידו מעשים טובים הוצרך לתפלה:

כל המאריך בתפלתו ומעיין בה. פירוש: שמצפה שתבא בקשתו לפי שכוון בתפלתו. תימה: דהכא משמע דעיון תפלה לאו מעליותא הוא. וכן משמע פ' "הרואה" (לקמן נה.): ג' דברים מזכירין עונותיו של אדם, וקאמר עיון תפלה. ולא כן משמע בפ' "מפנין" (שבת קכז.) דקאמר: אדם אוכל פירותיהן בעוה"ז, וקא חשיב עיון תפלה, אלמא מעליותא הוא! וכן משמע "בגט פשוט" (ב"ב קסד:), דקאמר: משלשה דברים אין אדם ניצול בכל יום וקאמר: עיון תפלה, פירוש: שאין אדם מעיין בה, אם כן משמע שהוא טוב! וי"ל: דתרי עיון תפלה יש: עיון תפלה דהכא – המצפה שתבא בקשתו, ועיון תפלה דהתם – שמכוין את לבו לתפלה*:

אל דמעתי אל תחרש. פרש"י: דדייק מדיוקא, מדלא קאמר "ודמעתי תראה" ש"מ שהיא נראית בכל פעם, ואין להתפלל רק שתתקבל:

קודם תפלתו מנין שנא' "אשרי יושבי ביתך". ולפיכך תקנו לומר זה הפסוק קודם תהלה לדוד, לאפוקי מהנהו דאמרי 'אשרי' הרבה: אבל

עין משפט נר מצוה

כד א מיי' פט"ו מהל' תפלה הלכה ג סמג עשין כ טוש"ע או"ח סי' קכח סעיף לה:

כה ב טוש"ע או"ח סי' נח סעיף ה:

כו ג מיי' פ"ד מהל' תפלה הלכה טז סמג עשין יט טור וש"ע או"ח סי' נג סעיף א:

כז ד ה מיי' פ"ו שם הל' ט סמג שם טור וש"ע או"ח סימן קד סעיף א:

כח ו מיי' שם טוש"ע שם סעיף ב:

כט ז מיי' שם טוש"ע שם סעיף א:

ב"מ נט.

[וע"ע תוס' שבת קיח: וכר"ה טז: וב"ב קסד:]

רב נסים גאון

אפילו המלך שואל בשלומו לא ישיבנו. ושנינו עוד בתוספתא הכותב את השם אפי' המלך שואל בשלומו לא ישיבנו היה כותב ה' או ו' שמות כיון שגמר אחד מהן משיב שאילת שלום ואיתא להא ברייתא בגמרא דבני מערבא דפירקין: **תנו** רבנן מעשה בחסיד אחד שהיה מתפלל בדרך. אית בבבא קמא בפ' הגוזל (דף קג.) כל מעשה בחסיד אחד אינו אלא ר' יהודה בן בבא או ר' יהודה בר' אילעאי ואיתא דכוותה בתמורה (דף טו) בפרק יש בקרבנות הצבור:

נ"ל לעשות

הגהות הב"ח

(א) גמ' שנאמר ובפרשכם וגו' ודורש דחוח: (ב) רש"י ד"ה אל תחרש מדלא. נ"ב ובב"מ דף נ"ט פי' בע"א ע"ש:

הגהות הגר"א

[א] גמ' עולות (אילים תז"מ ונ"ב אשים:

גליון הש"ס

גמ' כל כהן שהרג. בהגהה מוהרי"ב זצ"ל וכן בתוס' יבמות (דף ז.) ד"ה שנאמר. וע' בתוי"ט סוף פרק ז' דבכורות: **תוס'** ד"ה גדולה וכו' בלא תפלה. וע' תשובת מהרשד"ם חא"ח סי' ל':

[ברב אלפס אי' והא דלא אפשר לקצר אפשר לקצר מקצר ואי לא מפסיק]

מסורת הש"ס

[ע' תוס' סנהדרין לה: בתוס' דיבמות ז. שנאמר]

בן אדם קח לך כו"ל

לקמן נה.

שם ג

תהלים כז

יהושע א

שמואל ב י ישעיה מט

שם

שם

שם

תהלים פד

שם קמ

דברים ישעיה א שם מיכה ג תהלים לט איכה ג יחזקאל ד דברים ט משלי יג שם דברים ד

גמרא

מחזיר לו?! – א"ל: לאו. ואם היית מחזיר לו, מה היו עושים לך? א"ל: היו חותכים את ראשי בסייף. – א"ל: והלא דברים ק"ו, ומה אתה שהיית עומד לפני מלך בשר ודם *שהיום כאן ומחר בקבר – כך, אני שהייתי עומד לפני מלך מלכי המלכים הקב"ה שהוא חי וקיים לעד ולעולמי עולמים – על אחת כמה וכמה! מיד נתפייס אותו הגמון, ונפטר אותו חסיד לביתו לשלום.§ "אפי' נחש כרוך על עקבו לא יפסיק". אמר רב ששת: לא שנו אלא נחש, אבל עקרב – פוסק. מיתיבי: *נפל לגוב אריות אין מעידין עליו שמת, נפל לחפירה מלאה נחשים ועקרבים – מעידין עליו שמת! – שאני התם, דאגב איצצא מזקי. א"ר יצחק: ראה שוורים פוסק, דתני רב אושעיא: *מרחיקין משור תם חמשים אמה, ומשור מועד – כמלוא עיניו. תנא משמיה דר' מאיר: ריש תורא בדיקולא – סליק לאגרא, ושדי דרגא מתותך. אמר שמואל: הני מילי – בשור שחור וביומי ניסן, מפני שהשטן מרקד לו בין קרניו. ת"ר: *מעשה במקום אחד שהיה ערוד והיה מזיק את הבריות, באו והודיעו לו לר' חנינא בן דוסא. אמר להם: הראו לי את חורו! הראוהו את חורו, נתן עקבו על פי החור, יצא ונשכו ומת אותו ערוד. נטלו על כתפו והביאו לבית המדרש. אמר להם: ראו בני, אין ערוד ממית אלא החטא ממית. באותה שעה אמרו: אוי לו לאדם שפגע בו ערוד ואוי לו לערוד שפגע בו ר' חנינא בן דוסא.§

מתני' *מזכירין גבורות גשמים בתחיית המתים ושאלה בברכת השנים, והבדלה בחונן הדעת; *ר"ע אומר: אומרה ברכה רביעית בפני עצמה; רבי אליעזר אומר: בהודאה.§

גמ' "מזכירין גבורות גשמים". מאי טעמא? *אמר רב יוסף: מתוך ששקולה כתחיית המתים, לפיכך קבעוה בתחיית המתים. "ושאלה בברכת השנים". מאי טעמא? אמר רב יוסף: מתוך שהיא פרנסה לפיכך קבעוה בברכת פרנסה. "הבדלה בחונן הדעת". מ"ט? א"ר יוסף: מתוך שהיא חכמה קבעוה בברכת חכמה; ורבנן אמרי: מתוך שהיא חול לפיכך קבעוה בברכת חול.§ א"ר אמי: גדולה דעה שנתנה בתחלת ברכה של חול. וא"ר אמי: גדולה דעה שנתנה בין שתי אותיות, שנאמר: "כי אל דעות ה'". וכל מי שאין בו דעה אסור לרחם עליו, שנאמר: "כי לא עם בינות הוא על כן לא ירחמנו עושהו". אמר רבי אלעזר: גדול מקדש שנתן בין ב' אותיות, שנאמר: "פעלת ה' מקדש ה'". וא"ר אלעזר: כל אדם שיש בו דעה – כאילו נבנה בית המקדש בימיו; דעה נתנה בין שתי אותיות, מקדש נתן בין שתי אותיות. מתקיף לה *רב אחא קרחינאה: אלא מעתה, גדולה נקמה שנתנה בין שתי אותיות שנאמר: "אל נקמות ה'"! – אמר ליה: אין, במילתה מיהא גדולה היא. והיינו דאמר עולא: שתי נקמות הללו למה? אחת לטובה ואחת לרעה, לטובה – דכתיב: "הופיע מהר פארן", לרעה – דכתיב: "אל נקמות ה' אל נקמות הופיע".§ "רבי עקיבא אומר אומרה ברכה רביעית כו'". א"ל רב שמן בר אבא לר' יוחנן: מכדי אנשי כנסת הגדולה תקנו להם לישראל ברכות ותפלות קדושות והבדלות, נחזי(א) היכן תקון. – א"ל: בתחלה קבעוה בתפלה, העשירו – קבעוה על הכוס, הענו – חזרו וקבעוה בתפלה, והם אמרו: *המבדיל בתפלה צריך שיבדיל על הכוס. איתמר נמי, אמר ר' חייא בר אבא אמר רבי יוחנן: אנשי כנסת הגדולה תקנו להם לישראל ברכות ותפלות קדושות והבדלות. בתחלה קבעוה בתפלה, העשירו – קבעוה על הכוס, חזרו והענו – קבעוה בתפלה, והם אמרו: המבדיל בתפלה צריך שיבדיל על הכוס. איתמר נמי, רבה ורב יוסף דאמרי תרוייהו: המבדיל בתפלה צריך שיבדיל על הכוס. אמר *רבא, *ומותבינן אשמעתין: *טעה ולא הזכיר גבורות גשמים בתחיית המתים ושאלה בברכת השנים – מחזירין אותו, והבדלה בחונן הדעת – אין מחזירין אותו, מפני שיכול לאומרה על הכוס! – לא תימא "מפני שיכול לאומרה על הכוס" אלא אימא "מפני שאומרה על הכוס". איתמר נמי, אמר רבי בנימין בר יפת: שאל ר' יוסי את ר' יוחנן בצידן ואמרי לה, ר' שמעון בן יעקב דמן צור את ר' יוחנן, ואנא שמעית: המבדיל בתפלה, צריך שיבדיל על הכוס או לא? ואמר ליה: צריך שיבדיל על הכוס.§ איבעיא להו: המבדיל על הכוס, מהו שיבדיל בתפלה? – אמר רב נחמן בר יצחק, קל וחומר מתפלה: ומה תפלה דעיקר תקנתא היא – אמרי: המבדיל בתפלה צריך שיבדיל על הכוס; המבדיל על הכוס, דלאו עיקר תקנתא היא – לא כ"ש?! תני ר' *אחא אריכא קמיה דרב חיננא: המבדיל בתפלה משובח יותר ממי שיבדיל על הכוס, ואם הבדיל בזו ובזו – *ינוחו לו ברכות על ראשו. – הא גופא קשיא! אמרת, המבדיל בתפלה משובח יותר ממי שיבדיל על הכוס, אלמא: תפלה לחודה סגי, והדר תני: אם הבדיל בזו ובזו – ינוחו לו ברכות על ראשו, וכיון דנפיק ליה בחדא – איפטר, והויא *ברכה שאינה צריכה; ואמר רב ואיתימא ר"ל, ואמרי לה ר' יוחנן ור"ל דאמרי תרוייהו: כל המברך ברכה שאינה צריכה – עובר משום: "לא תשא"! אלא, אימא הכי: אם הבדיל בזו ולא הבדיל בזו – ינוחו לו ברכות על ראשו. בעא מיניה רב חסדא מרב ששת: טעה בזו ובזו* מהו? – אמר ליה: טעה בזו ובזו – חוזר לראש.

אמר

רש"י

אבל עקרב פוסק. ונוטלו. לפי שהעקרב *מסוכן לעקוץ יותר משהנחש מוכן לישוך: **אין מעידין עליו.** לומר לאשתו: מת בעליך, להתירה לינשא, פעמים שאין האריות רעבים ואין אוכלין אותו: **נחשים ועקרבים.** או זה או זה, מעידים עליו שמת, אלמא: מועד הנחש לישוך: **אגב איצצא.** כשנופל עליהם ודוחקם הזיקוהו: **שור תם.** שלא נגח אדם: **מועד.** שנגח ג' פעמים: **בדיקולא.** סל, שתולין בו תבן בראשו ואוכל: **ושדי דרגא.** לאו דוקא, אלא כלומר, הזהר ממנו הרבה: **ביומי ניסן.** מתוך שעברו ימי הסתיו שהארץ יבשה, ועכשיו רואה אותה מליאה דשאים זחה דעתו עליו, ונכנס בו יצר הרע: **ערוד.** מן הנחש והצב בא, שנזקקין זה עם זה ויוצא מביניהם ערוד*: **את חורו.** שהוא יוצא משם: **ומת הערוד.** מצאתי בה"ג, אמרי במערבא: כשהערוד נושך את האדם אם הערוד קודם למים – מת האדם; ואם האדם קודם למים – מת הערוד. ונעשה נס לר' חנינא ונקבע מעין מתחת עקבו: **מתני' מזכירין גבורות גשמים.** משיב הרוח, שאינו לשון בקשה אלא לשון הזכרה ושבח: **ושואלין.** ותן טל ומטר, לשון בקשה: **והבדלה בחונן הדעת.** במוצאי שבת אתה חוננתנו: **גמ' מתוך שהיא חכמה.** החכם יודע להבדיל בין קדש לחול ובין טמא לטהור: **בין שתי אותיות.** בין שתי הזכרות: **במילתה מיהא גדולה היא.** במקום שצריכה נקמה – דבר גדול הוא: **שתי נקמות הללו למה.** אחת לרעה – להנקם מן הגוים שלא קבלו את התורה: **ואחת לטובה.** כדאמרינן בב"ק (דף לח.): מפארן הופיע והפקיר ממונן לישראל; שור של ישראל שנגח שור של גוי – פטור: **הופיע.** גלה והפקיר, כשלא קבלו את התורה: *__העשירו.__ לקנות יין: **קבעוה על הכוס.** ואז נשתכח תקנת עזרא, וכשחזרו והענו – קבעוה בתפלה, ונחלקו היאך יאמרוה: **בתחלה.** כשעלו מן הגולה והיו דחוקים: **קדושות.** קידוש היום: **מפני שיכול.** משמע: אם ירצה שלא לחזור ולהתפלל, הא אם אמרה בתפלה – א"נ לאומרה על הכוס: **ואנא שמעית.** אני שמעתי: **חוזר לראש.** לתפלה ולכוס:

הלכתא

תוספות

אבל עקרב פוסק. בירושלמי קאמר דאם היה נחש מרתיע לבא כנגדו – פוסק, לפי שבא כנגדו בכעס מתכוין להזיקו. ומיהו לא מלינו אם פסק שיחזור לראש, מדלא קאמר: ואם פסק חוזר לראש, אבל לתחלת ברכה מיהא יחזור. ואם טעה בג' ראשונות או בג' אחרונות – חוזר לתחלת הג': באבות – בראשונות, ובעבודה – באחרונות, כדאמרינן לקמן בפרקין (דף לד.):

אמר

עין משפט נר מצוה

ל א ב מיי' פ"ו מהל' תפלה הלכה ט (סמג עשין יט) טוש"ע או"ח סי' קד סעיף ג:

לא ג מיי' פי"ג מהל' גירושין הלכה יז (סמג לאוין ל) טוש"ע אה"ע סי' יז סעי' כט:

לב ד ה (מיי' פ"ו מהל' תפלה סמג עשין יט) טוש"ע או"ח סימן קד סעיף ד:

לג ו מיי' פ"ב מה' תפלה הלכה טו סמג שם טוש"ע או"ח סי' קיד סעי' א:

לד ז מיי' שם הל' טו סמג שם טוש"ע או"ח סי' קיז סעי' א:

לה ח ט מיי' שם הלכה ד יב סמג שם טוש"ע או"ח סימן רצד סעי' א:

לו י מיי' פ"י שם הלכה ח סמג שם טוש"ע או"ח סי' קיד סעי' ה:

לז כ מיי' שם הל' ט סמג שם טוש"ע או"ח סי' קיז סעי' ד:

לח ל מיי' שם הל' יד סמג שם טוש"ע או"ח סי' רצד סעיף א:

לט מ טור או"ח שם:

מ נ מיי' פ"א מהל' ברכות הלכה טו סמג עשין כז טוש"ע או"ח סי' רו סעי' ו ובסי' רטו סעי' ד [רב אלפס לקמן פ"ח]:

מא ס טוש"ע או"ח סי' רצד סעיף א:

לעיל כט. נדה ח.

רב נסים גאון

אפי' נחש כרוך על עקבו לא יפסיק אמר רב ששת לא שנו אלא נחש אבל עקרב פוסק. בתלמוד ארץ ישראל פירשו טעמא דמלתא ואמרי חוא עקרב מפסיק למה משום דמחיא וחזרה ומחיא: **באותה** שעה אמרו אוי לו לאדם שפגע בו ערוד ואוי לו לערוד שפגע בו ר' חנינא בן דוסא. פירשו עוד בתלמוד ארץ ישראל ואמרו מאי עיסקא דהדין חברברה אלא כד הוא נכית לבר נשא אין בר נשא קדים למיא חברברה מיית ואין חברברה קדים למיא בר נשא מיית אמרון ליה תלמידוי רבי ולא הרגשתה יבא עלי ממה שהיה לבי מכוון בתפלתי לא הרגשתי אמר ר' יצחק בן אלעזר ברא לו הקב"ה מעיין מתחת כפות רגליו לקיים מה שנאמר (תהלים קמה) רצון יראיו יעשה: **מזכירין** גבורות גשמים בתחיית המתים. פירשו בתלמוד ארץ ישראל כשם שתחיי' המתים חיים לעולם כך ירידת גשמים חיים לעולם ר' חייא בר אבא שמע ליה מן הדא קרייה (הושע ו) יחיינו מיומים ונדעה נרדפה לדעת את ה' ויבא כגשם לנו ובבראשית רבה דר' הושעיא (פרשה יג) ר' חייא בר אבא אמר שקולה כנגד תחיית המתים ר' אבא בריה דר' חייא בר אבא אף חכמים קבעו אותה בתחיית המתים בזו יד ובזו יד בזו פתיחה ובזו פתיחה בזו יד (יחזקאל לז) היתה עלי יד ה' ובזו יד (תהלים קמה) פותח את ידך בזו פתיחה (יחזקאל לז) הנני פותח את קברותיכם ר' יודן בשם ר' אלעזר בר אבינה בזו שירה ובזו שירה (ישעיה מב) ירונו יושבי סלע ובזו שירה (תהלים סה) יתרועעו אף ישירו:

הגהות הב"ח (א) גמ' ניחזי היכן תיקון. נ"ב בפרק מי שמתו. דף כב ע"ב גבי טבילת בעלי קרי פריך תלמודא נמי הכי וע"ש בתוס':

גליון הש"ס **גמ'** נתן עקבו על פי החור. עיין יפה מראה בתענית (פרק ג סימן יז) ד"ה מפלתו:

אמר ליה רבינא לרבא: הלכתא מאי? – אמר ליה: כי קידוש, מה קידוש אף על גב דמקדש בצלותא מקדש אכסא, אף הבדלה נמי – אע״ג דמבדיל בצלותא מבדיל אכסא.§ "ר׳ אליעזר אומר: בהודאה". ר׳ זירא הוה רכיב חמרא, הוה קא שקיל ואזיל ר׳ חייא בר אבין בתריה. אמר ליה, ודאי דאמריתו משמיה דר׳ יוחנן: הלכה כר׳ אליעזר ביום טוב שחל להיות אחר השבת? – אמר ליה: [א] אין. *הלכה – מכלל דפליגי! –ולא פליגי?! והא פליגי רבנן! –איכא דפליגי רבנן – בשאר ימות השנה, ביום טוב שחל להיות אחר השבת מי פליגי? –והא פליג ר׳ עקיבא! *–אטו כל השנה כולה מי עבדינן כר׳ עקיבא, דהשתא ניקו ונעביד כוותיה?! כל השנה כולה מאי טעמא לא עבדינן כרבי עקיבא? – דתמני סרי תקון, תשסרי לא תקון, הכא נמי – שב תקון, תמני לא תקון! –אמר ליה: לאו "הלכה" אתמר, אלא "מטין" אתמר. [ב] *דאתמר, ר׳ יצחק בר אבדימי אמר משום רבנו: הלכה, ואמרי לה: מטין. ר׳ יוחנן אמר: מודים; ור׳ חייא בר אבא אמר: נראין. אמר ר׳ זירא: נקוט דרבי חייא בר אבא בידך. *דדייק וגמר שמעתא מפומא דמרה שפיר כרחבא דפומבדיתא. דאמר רחבא *אמר ר׳ יהודה: אהר הבית סטיו כפול היה, והיה סטיו לפנים מסטיו. אמר רב יוסף: אנא לא האי ידענא ולא האי ידענא, אלא מדרב ושמואל ידענא דתקינו לן מרגניתא בבבל: בותודיענו ה׳ אלהינו את משפטי צדקך ותלמדנו לעשות חקי רצונך, ותנחילנו זמני ששון וחגי נדבה [ד] ותורישנו קדושת שבת וכבוד מועד וחגיגת הרגל. בין קדושת שבת לקדושת יום טוב הבדלת ואת יום השביעי מששת ימי המעשה קדשת, הבדלת וקדשת את עמך ישראל בקדושתך, ותתן לנו וכו׳.§ **מתני׳** *האומר *ג"על קן ציפור יגיעו רחמיך" ו"על טוב יזכר שמך", ד"מודים" "מודים" –משתקין אותו.§ **גמ׳** בשלמא "מודים" "מודים" משתקין אותו – משום דמיחזי כשתי רשויות, ו"על טוב יזכר שמך" – נמי משמע על הטובה ולא על הרעה, *ותנן: החייב אדם לברך על הרעה כשם שמברך על הטובה. אלא, "על קן צפור יגיעו רחמיך" מ״ט? – פליגי בה תרי אמוראי במערבא, רבי יוסי בר אבין ורבי יוסי בר זבידא; חד אמר: מפני שמטיל קנאה במעשה בראשית, וחד אמר: מפני שעושה מדותיו של הקדוש ברוך הוא רחמים, ואינן אלא גזרות. ההוא דנחית קמיה דרבה ואמר: אתה חסת על קן צפור אתה חוס ורחם עלינו. אמר רבה: כמה ידע האי צורבא מרבנן לרצויי למריה! –א״ל אביי: והא "משתקין אותו" תנן! *ורבה נמי – לחדודי לאביי הוא דבעי.§ ההוא דנחית קמיה דר׳ חנינא, ואמר: האל הגדול הגבור והנורא והאדיר והעזוז והיראוי החזק והאמיץ והודאי והנכבד. המתין לו עד דסיים, כי סיים א״ל: סיימתינהו לכולהו שבחי דמרך?! למה לי כולי האי? אנן הני תלת דאמרינן – אי לאו דאמרינהו משה רבנו באורייתא, ואתו אנשי כנסת הגדולה ותקנינהו בתפלה – לא הוינן יכולין למימר להו, ואת אמרת כולי האי ואזלת! משל, למלך בשר ודם שהיו לו אלף אלפים דינרי זהב, והיו מקלסין אותו בשל כסף, והלא גנאי הוא לו.§ ואמר *רבי חנינא: *והכל בידי שמים – חוץ מיראת שמים, שנאמר: °"ועתה ישראל מה ה׳ אלהיך שואל מעמך כי אם ליראה". אטו יראת שמים מילתא זוטרתא היא?! והא״ר חנינא משום ר׳ שמעון בן יוחי: אין לו להקב״ה בבית גנזיו אלא אוצר של יראת שמים, שנאמר: °"יראת ה׳ היא אוצרו"! – אין, לגבי משה מילתא זוטרתא היא. דאמר ר׳ חנינא: משל, לאדם שמבקשים ממנו כלי גדול ויש לו – דומה עליו ככלי קטן, קטן ואין לו – דומה עליו ככלי גדול.§ "מודים מודים – משתקין אותו". אמר ר׳ *זירא, חכל האומר "שמע" "שמע" – כאומר "מודים" "מודים" דמי. מיתיבי: הקורא את שמע וכופלה – הרי זה מגונה. מגונה הוא דהוי, שתוקי לא משתקינן ליה! – לא קשיא: הא – דאמר מילתא מילתא ותני לה, והא – דאמר פסוקא פסוקא ותני ליה. אמר ליה רב פפא לאביי: ודילמא מעיקרא לא כוון דעתיה, ולבסוף כוון דעתיה? –אמר ליה: חברותא

הלכתא מאי. המבדיל בתפילה צריך שיבדיל על הכוס, או לא: ביום טוב שחל להיות אחר השבת. שאין מתפללין אתה חוננ: ה״ג הלכה מכלל דפליגי, ולא פליגי, והא פליגי רבנן אימר דפליגי רבנן בשאר ימות השנה בי״ט שחל להיות אחר השבת, מי פליגי והא פליג ר״ע אטו כל השנה מי עבדינן כר״ע דהשתא נעביד וכו׳ – והכי *פריך: א״ל רבי זירא: [ג] הלכה מכלל דפליגי?! בתמיה, ופריך הגמרא: ולא פליגי? והא פליגי רבנן וכו׳: והא פליג ר׳ עקיבא. לומרה ברכה רביעית לעצמה, ואצטרי׳ למימר הלכה כר״א לאפוקי מדר״ע: אטו כל השנה כולה מי עבדינן כר״ע דהשתא נעביד כוותיה. דאצטריך למימר הלכה כר״א: הלכה. מ״ד הלכה – דרשינן לה בפרקין, ומ״ד מטין – מדרש לא דרשינן ברבים, אבל אורויי מורינן ליחיד לעשות כר״א בי״ט שחל להיות בא׳ בשבת, ומ״ד נראין – אורויי נמי לא מורינן, ואי עביד לא מהדרינן עובדא: מודים. חכמים לר״א בי״ט שחל להיות אחר השבת: נקוט דר׳ חייא בר אבא בידך. שהוא מדקדק בלשון רבו, וקובע בו סימנים שלא יתחלף לו נראין במטין או במודים: כרחבא. שהיה מדקדק בלשון רבו ואומר סטיו כפול היה ואע״פ שבלשון משנה קורהו אצטבא, בפסחים ובסוכה על גב האצטבא, הוא דקדק בלשון רבו ולא אמר אצטבא כפולה היתה. יש פותרין הא דרחבא מדאמר ר׳ יהודה דדייק ספיקי דרבוותיה אי מדרבי יהודה אי מדרב יהודה. וקשיא לי בגוה טובא, חדא – דרחבא לא ראה רבי יהודה מימיו, לא רבי יהודה ברבי אלעאי ולא ר׳ יהודה *נשיאה. ועוד: כולהו אמוראי נמי הגה״ה דייקו לומר דבר בשם אומרו. ועוד: ליכא למימר מהא דדייק לישנא דשמעתא, אלא ספיקי דרבוותא: סטיו כפול. אצטבאות זו לפנים מזו, בהיקף עגול, לישב שם: לא האי ידענא כו׳. לא נראין ולא מודים ולא מטים: ותודיענו. לומר במקום ותתן לנו ולהשיגע בין קדושת שבת לקדושת י״ט וכו׳ הבדלת וקדשת את עמך ישראל בקדושתך יאמר ותתן לנו ה׳ אלהינו מועדים לשמחה וכו׳, ומסיים מקדש ישראל והזמנים: **מתני׳** האומר. בתפלתו: על קן צפור יגיעו רחמיך. אנשים שהיו מראים עצמם כמתכוונים להעמיק בלשון תחנונים, ואומרים: רחום וחנון אתה, ועל קן צפור יגיעו רחמיך, שאמרת לשלח את האם. או שאומר: על טוב שאתה עושה לנו יזכר שמך, או שאומר: מודים מודים – משתקין אותו: **גמ׳** שמטיל קנאה. לומר: על אלה חס, ולא על שאר בריותיו: מדותיו. מצותיו, והוא לא לרחמים עשה, אלא להטיל על ישראל חקי גזרותיו; להודיע שהם עבדיו ושומרי מצותיו וגזרות חוקותיו, אף בדברי׳ שיש לשטן ולגוים להשיב עליהם, ולומר מה צורך במצוה זו: ורבה נמי לחדודי לאביי הוא דבעי. שישיב לו מה שהשיב: אי לאו דאמרינהו משה. האל הגדול הגבור והנורא אשר לא ישא פנים ולא יקח שוחד (דברים י): ותקנינהו בתפלה. כשהתפלל עזרא על מעל הגולה, בספר עזרא (נחמיה ט): הכל בידי שמים. כל הבא על האדם ביד הקב״ה; כגון ארוך, קצר, עני, עשיר, חכם, שוטה, לבן, שחור, הכל בידי שמים. הוא אבל צדיק ורשע אינו בא על ידי שמים, את זו מסר בידו של אדם, ונתן לפניו שני דרכים, והוא יבחר לו יראת שמים: מילתא מילתא ותני לה. כל תיבה ותיבה חוזר ושונה – מגונה הוי, שתוקי לא משתקינן ליה, שאין זה דומה למקבל עליו שתי מלכיות, אלא למתלוצץ. אמר פסוק שלם ותני ליה – משתקינן ליה, דמחזי כשתי רשויות: חברותא

מב א מיי׳ פ״ה מהל׳ בית הבחירה הל׳ א:

מג ב מיי׳ פ״ב מהל׳ תפלה הלכה יב סמג עשין יט טוש״ע או״ח סי׳ תלא סעיף ב:

[נ״ל פירושא]

מד ג מיי׳ פ״ט מהל׳ תפלה הל׳ ז סמג שם:

מה ד מיי׳ שם הלכה ד סמג שם טוש״ע או״ח סימן קכא סעיף ב:

מו ה מיי׳ פ״י מהלכות ברכות הלכה ג סמג עשין כז טוש״ע או״ח סימן רכב סעיף ג:

מז ו מיי׳ פ״ט מהל׳ תפלה הל׳ ז טוש״ע או״ח סימן קיג סעיף ט:

מח ז מיי׳ פ״ה מהל׳ תשובה הל׳ א:

מט ח מיי׳ פ״ב מהל׳ ק״ש הלכה יא סמג עשין יח טוש״ע או״ח סי׳ סא סעיף ט:

רב נסים גאון

אמר ר׳ זירא נקוט דר׳ חייא בר אבא בידך דגמר שמעתתא מפומיה דרביה. איתא בפרק כיצד מברכין על הפירות (דף לח) מה ענין בנימין בר יפת אצל ר׳ חייא בר אבא ר׳ חייא בר אבא דייק שמעתא מפומיה דרביה ר׳ חייא בר אבא כל ל׳ יומין הוה מהדר לתלמודיה קמיה דר׳ יוחנן רביה ואית דכוותה בפ׳ כיסוי הדם (דף פו) דשחיטת חולין ובפ׳ המביא אשם תלוי דכריתות (דף כז): **מודים** מודים משתקין אותו. בתלמוד ארץ ישראל נתנו הפרש בזה הדבר ואמרו הדה דאיתמר בצבור אבל ביחיד תחנונים הם ובגמ׳ דמגילה (ירושלמי פרק ד הלכה י) אמרו ודכוותה אמן אמן שמע שמע:

[ברב אלפס וברא״ש סדר המשנה דהכא בזה״ל האומר יברכוך טובים הרי זה דרך המינות האומר על קן צפור וכו׳ וע״ש פירש״י ורבינו יונה וכן במה שפי׳ הרא״ש ודע שכסדר הזה נשנית ג״כ במשנה דמגילה כה. מכוון ממש]

הגהות הגר״א

[א] גמ׳ (א״ל אין) תא״מ: [ב] צ״ל איתמר: [ג] רש״י ד״ה ה״ג כו׳ (א״ל ר׳ זירא) תא״מ: [ד] גמ׳ (ותנחילנו זמני ששון וחגי נדבה) תא״מ ונ״ב ברמב״ם ל״ג לה:

נדה טז: מגילה כה.

דברים י

גליון הש״ס

גמ׳ אלא מטין אתמר. עיין תשובת דבר שמואל (סימן קיד): **במתני׳** האומר על קן צפור. ע׳ זוה״ק פ׳ אמור על פסוק אדם ובהמה תושיע ה׳. ובמדרש רבה פרשת כי תצא (פ״ו):

תורה אור

[שבת קו: וש״ס נסמן]

[לעיל כט.]

עירובין מו:

[לקמן לח: פסחים נב:]

פסחים יג: נב: סוכה מח.

מגילה כה.

לקמן דף נד. [וש״נ]

[עירובין יג. מגילה שם נזיר נט: זבחים יג. חולין מג: נדה לד: מה.]

[ע׳ תוס׳ מגילה ותוס׳ נדה]

ישעיה לג

מגילה שם [סוכה נג:]

חברותא כלפי שמיא. מנהג שנוהג אדם בחברו ינהג אצל המקום, ולא יזהר בתפלתו: מחינן ליה. כלומר: מלמדין אותו שיכוין ומכין אותו אם ירגיל בכך: מרזפתא. קורנס, "ויפשם את המקבת בידם" מתרגמינן "מרזפתא" (שופטים ד): מתני' ולא יהא סרבן באותה שעה. לפי שאחר יורדין לפני התיבה כשאומרים לו "לך רד" צריך לסרב פעם אחת, כלומר איני כדאי לכך, כדאמרי' לקמן בשמעתין. אבל זה – לא יסרב, מפני שגנאי הוא שתהא התפלה מופסקת כל כך: מתחלת הברכה שטעה זה. אם דלג א' מן הברכות ואמר אחרת, ואינו יודע לשוב ולאחוז סדרו – יתחיל העובר תחתיו אותה ברכה שדלג זה, ואומר משם ולהלן: לא יענה אמן אחר הכהנים. הש"ץ בסוף כל ברכה וברכה: מפני הטירוף. שלא תטרף דעתו ויטעה. לפי שהש"ץ הוא צריך להתחיל ברכה שניה, ולומר לפני הכהנים כל תיבה ותיבה, כדאמרינן במס' סוטה (דף לט:). ובעניתו אמן לא יוכל לכוין מהר ולהתחיל בברכה שלאחריו: אם אין שם כהן אלא הוא. החזן: לא ישא את כפיו. שמא לא יוכל לחזור לתפלתו לדעת לכוין להתחיל ב"שים שלום", שדעתו מטורפת מאימת הצבור: ואם הבטחתו. כלומר: אם בטוח הוא שאין דעתו מטורפת מאימת הצבור: גמ' יסרב. כשאומרים לו לך, יעשה עצמו כלא רוצה, כלומר: איני כדאי: שהקדיחתו. לשון שריפה, כמו כי אש קדחה באפי (דברים לב): מהבהב. כלומר: מזמין עצמו כמו נגער לעמוד: אין להן סדר. ואם דלג ברכה אחת ואח"כ נזכר בה – אומרה, אף שלא במקומה: מתחלת הברכה שטעה זה. ומתוך מילא משמע דנומר ממנה והלאה, אלמא על סדרה צריך לחזור ולאומרה: חדא ברכתא נינהו. ודקתני מתני' מתחלת הברכה שטעה זה – היינו אתה חונן: ונפטר. נוטל רשות: א"צ להזכיר שמו. של חולה: תחלה וסוף. במודים, ולך נאה להודות:

כהן

*אמר 'מודים מודים' – משתקין אותו. ירושלמי: הדא דתימא – בצבור, אבל ביחיד – תחנונים הם: *אמר פסוקא וכפליה. פי' בקונטרס: משתקין אותו דמחזי כעושה ב' רשויות. ובה"ג ובפר"ח מפרש איפכא: פסוקא – אין משתקין אותו, מיהו מגונה הוי. אך לשון הגמרא לא משמע כפי'. ואותן בני אדם שאומרים ב' או ג' פעמים שמע ישראל ביוה"כ – משתקין אותם לפירש"י, ולפר"ח – מגונה מיהא הוי. או שמא אין לחוש רק כשקורא ק"ש בעונתה, ומקבל עליו עול מלכות שמים, ומ"מ טוב שלא לומר, אך מה שאומרים "ה' הוא האלהים" ז' פעמים ביוה"כ ויום ערבה, כנגד ז' רקיעים משבחים לבורא שהוא דר למעלה מז' – מנהג כשר הוא. וגם מצינו בקרא שתי פעמים "ה' הוא האלהים" גבי אליהו (מלכים א יח): מהיכן הוא מתחיל? מתחלת הברכה שטעה בה. ירושלמי: בטיטי אשתתק באופנים, אתון שיילון לר' בון, אמר להו בשם ריב"ל: זה שעבר תחתיו יתחיל ממקום שפסק. ופריך: והתנן מתחיל מתחלת הברכה שטעה בה! אמר להו: מכיון דעניתון קדושת השם, כמי שהוא תחלת הברכה דמי: לא יענה אמן אחר הכהנים מפני הטרוף. תימה: תיפוק ליה דמפסיק תפלה אם עונה אמן! וי"ל: מאחר שלא אמר האי טעמא, ש"מ דעניית אמן לא חשיב ליה הפסקה – מאחר שצורך תפלה הוא. אבל לקרות כהנים לדוכן אומר ר"ת שאין ש"צ יכול לקוראם, דחשיב הפסקה לתפלה אם קוראם, אלא אחד מבני הקהל קוראם. והא דאמרינן בסוטה פ' "אלו נאמרים" (ד' לח.): לשנים קורא כהנים וכו' – לאו אשליח צבור קאי, אלא אחזן. כדתניא בספרי (פרשת נשא) "אמור להם" – מלמד שהחזן אומר להם: אמרו. וחזן לאו היינו שליח צבור; דחזן היינו המתעסק בצרכי צבור. וכן משמע נמי בסוטה (ד' לט:), דלאו אשליח צבור קאי; דמעיקרא קאמר "אין הכהנים רשאין להתחיל בברכה עד שיכלה הדבור מפי הקורא", פי': הקורא 'כהנים' ואח"כ אומר: אין שליח צבור רשאי וכו', משמע דשנים הם. ויש שהיו רוצים לומר דכמו כן אין ש"צ רשאי להקרות 'יברכך' לכהנים, דכמו כן הוי הפסקה. אמנם רבינו יהודה פי' דבהדיא יש במדרש "טעמי יתרות וחסרות": "אמור להם" – מלמד ששליח צבור אומר להם על כל דבור ודבור. וכן יש שרוצים להתיר לשליח צבור עצמו לקרות 'כהנים', אפילו לפי' ר"ת.

תורה אור

*חברותא כלפי שמיא מי איכא?! אי לא כוון דעתיה מעיקרא – מחינן ליה במרזפתא דנפחא עד דמכוין דעתיה.§ מתני' (*האומר יברכוך טובים – הרי זה דרכי מינות.) [א]העובר לפני התיבה וטעה – יעבור אחר תחתיו, ולא [ב]יהא סרבן באותה שעה. מהיכן [ג]הוא מתחיל? מתחלת הברכה שטעה *זה. [ד]העובר לפני התיבה לא יענה אמן אחר הכהנים מפני הטרוף, [ה]ואם אין שם כהן אלא הוא – לא ישא את כפיו. *ואם הבטחתו שהוא נושא את כפיו וחוזר לתפלתו – רשאי. גמ' ת"ר: [ו]העובר לפני התיבה – צריך לסרב, ואם אינו מסרב – דומה לתבשיל שאין בו מלח, ואם מסרב יותר מדאי – דומה לתבשיל שהקדיחתו מלח. כיצד הוא עושה – פעם ראשונה יסרב, שניה *מהבהב, שלישית – פושט את רגליו ויורד. *ת"ר: שלשה רובן קשה ומיעוטן יפה, ואלו הן: שאור, ומלח, וסרבנות.§ אמר רב הונא: [ז]טעה בשלש ראשונות – חוזר לראש, באמצעיות – חוזר ל"אתה חונן", באחרונות – חוזר ל"עבודה"; ורב אסי אמר: אמצעיות אין להן סדר. מתיב רב ששת: "מהיכן הוא חוזר – מתחלת הברכה שטעה זה", *תיובתא דרב הונא! –אמר לך רב הונא: אמצעיות – כולהו חדא ברכתא נינהו. אמר רב יהודה: [ח]לעולם אל ישאל אדם צרכיו לא בשלש ראשונות, ולא בשלש אחרונות, אלא באמצעיות. דא"ר חנינא: ראשונות – דומה לעבד שמסדר שבח לפני רבו, אמצעיות – דומה לעבד שמבקש פרס מרבו, אחרונות – דומה לעבד שקבל פרס מרבו [ט]ונפטר והולך לו.§ *ת"ר: מעשה בתלמיד אחד *שירד לפני התיבה בפני רבי אליעזר והיה מאריך יותר מדאי. א"ל תלמידיו: רבינו, כמה ארכן הוא זה! – אמר להם: כלום מאריך יותר ממשה רבינו?! דכתיב ביה: (דברים ט) "את ארבעים היום ואת ארבעים הלילה וגו'". שוב מעשה בתלמיד א' שירד לפני התיבה בפני ר"א והיה מקצר יותר מדאי. א"ל תלמידיו: כמה קצרן הוא זה! א"ל: כלום מקצר יותר ממשה רבינו?! דכתיב: (במדבר יב) "אל נא רפא נא לה". א"ר יעקב אמר רב חסדא: כל המבקש רחמים על חבירו אין צריך להזכיר שמו, שנאמר: "אל נא רפא נא לה", ולא קמדכר שמה דמרים.§ ת"ר: *[י]אלו ברכות שאדם שוחה בהן: באבות תחלה וסוף, בהודאה תחלה וסוף, ואם בא לשוח בסוף כל ברכה וברכה ובתחלת כל ברכה וברכה – מלמדין אותו שלא ישחה. אר"ש בן פזי אריב"ל משום בר קפרא: הדיוט – כמו שאמרנו. כהן

דמה דפי' דהויא הפסקה – היינו דוקא בימיהם, מיד כשסיימו ברכת הודאה לא היו אומרים: "או"א אבותינו ברכנו בברכה", כדמשמע בסוטה (שם) דקאמר: אין הקורא רשאי לקרות כהנים עד שיכלה אמן מפי הצבור, פי': אמן שעונין בסיום ברכת הודאה, אלמא משמע שלא היו אומרים אלא כהנים מיד. אבל עכשיו, שהורגלו לומר 'אלהינו' בלשון ברכה ותפלה – אין זה הפסק, דלא גרע מעניית אמן דהכא דלא חשיבא הפסק, כדפרישית*: אמצעיות אין להן סדר. פי' בקונטרס: ואם דלג ברכה אחת ואחר כך נזכר בה שלא במקומה – אומרה במקום שנזכר. ולא נהירא; דהא תנן במגילה (פ"ב ד' יז.): "הקורא את המגילה למפרע לא יצא", ותניא (שם): וכן בהלל, וכן בק"ש, וכן בתפלה! לכך נראה כפירוש רשב"ם ורב אלפס, ד'אין להן סדר' דקאמר – היינו שיתחיל במקום שדלג הברכה, ומשם ואילך יאמר הכל על הסדר, אבל ודאי לא יתחיל ב'אתה חונן' כמו בג' ראשונות וג' אחרונות שחוזר לראש. וראיה, מדתניא בתוספתא דמכילתין: *הקורא את שמע והשמיט בה פסוק אחד – לא יקרא אותו פסוק בפני עצמו, אלא מתחיל מאותו פסוק ואילך וגומר עד סופה. ותניא נמי בפ"ב דמגילה (ד' יח:) שאם השמיט פסוק א' במגילה – שקורא על הסדר מאותו פסוק ואילך, והתם משוי תפלה למגילה לענין הך מילתא כדפרישית. ובה"ג פסק כרב אסי, דאמר אמצעיות אין להם סדר; חדא – דרב הונא כתלמיד לגבי רב אסי כדאמרינן בכמה מקומות אמר רב הונא אמר רב אסי: ועוד – דלרב הונא צריך לדחוק ולשנויי מתניתין דכולהו חדא ברכתא נינהו, ואשנויי דחיקי לא ניקום ונסמוך. ועוד – דרב אסי ורב ששת קיימי בחד שיטתא, ועוד – דבשל סופרים הלך אחר המיקל. וא"כ אדם שטעה ודלג ברכה אחת באמצעיות, או שלא אמר 'המלך המשפט' בין ר"ה ליוה"כ, דקי"ל בפ"ק (דף יב:) דמחזירין אותו – לא יחזור ל'אתה חונן', אלא לאותה ברכה שדלג, ומשם ואילך יאמר על הסדר, כדפי' רשב"ם. והיכא שטעה בג' ראשונות: כגון שטעה בחתימתן, או לא הזכיר בין ר"ה ליוה"כ בברכת אבות, 'זכרנו' או בחתיית המתים 'מי כמוך', או שלא אמר 'המלך הקדוש' חוזר לראשונה. והיכא שטעה בשלש אחרונות: כגון שטעה כמו כן בחתימתן, או שלא הזכיר בין ראש השנה ליוה"כ בשים שלום 'בספר חיים טובים', או 'וכתוב לחיים טובים' בהודאה – חוזר ל'עבודה'. וטעמא: דכיון שכולה שבח – הוי כברכה א'. ותענית צבור שש"צ קובע ברכה לעצמו, שאומר 'עננו' בין 'גואל' ל'רופא', אם שכחה ונזכר בה קודם סיום תפלה – אין מחזירין אותו, כיון שהיה צריך לחזור ולומר על הסדר כפי' רשב"ם א"כ הויא ברכה לבטלה אם מחזירין אותו. אבל לפי' הקונטרס היה אומרה במקום שנזכר, ואין כאן ברכה לבטלה: אל ישאל אדם צרכיו לא בג' ראשונות ולא בג' אחרונות. פי' ר"ת ורבינו האי: דוקא ליחיד, אבל צרכי צבור – שואלין. ולכך אנו אומרים 'זכרנו' וקרובץ ו'יעלה ויבא' בהם. ותדע דדוקא יחיד קאמר, שהרי עיקר ברכות אחרונות צרכי צבור הם*: מלמדין אותו שלא ישחה. וא"ת: ישחה, ומה בכך! וי"ל: שלא יבא לעקור דברי חכמים, שלא יאמרו כל אחד מחמיר כמו שהוא רוצה, ואין כאן תקנת חכמים. וחיישינן(א) ליוהרא:

קידה

[שייך לדף לג:]
[ג"ז שייך לשם]

נ א מיי' פ"י מהלכות תפלה הלכה ג סמג עשין יט טוש"ע או"ח סי' קכו סעיף ב:
נא ב מיי' שם טוש"ע שם ובסי' נג סי"ז:
נב ג מיי' שם הלכה ד סמג שם טוש"ע שם סימן קיט סעיף ג ובסי' קכו סעיף ב:
נג ד מיי' פי"ד מהל' נשיאת כפים הל' ה סמג עשין כ טוש"ע או"ח סימן קכח סעיף יט:
נד ה מיי' שם פט"ו הלכה י טוש"ע שם סעיף כ:
נה ו טוש"ע או"ח סי' נג סעיף טז:
נו ז מיי' פ"י מהל' תפלה הלכה א ד סמג עשין יט טוש"ע או"ח סי' קכו סעיף ב:
נז ח מיי' פ"א שם הלכה ד ופ"ו שם הל' ג סמג שם טוש"ע או"ח סי' קיב סעיף א:
נח ט מיי' פ"ה שם הל' יא סמג עשין יט טוש"ע או"ח סי' קכג סעיף א:
נט י מיי' פ"ה שם הל' יוד סמג שם טוש"ע או"ח סי' קיג סעיף א:

רב נסים גאון

תנו רבנן אלו ברכות שאדם שוחה בהן כו'. פי' בתלמוד ארץ ישראל בפ' מאימתי קורין הכל שוחין בהודאה עם שליח צבור ר' זעירא אמר ובלבד במודים כו' תני ובלבד שלא ישוח יותר מדאי ובגמ' דד' אבות נזיקין (בבא קמא דף טז) איתא שדרו של אדם לסוף (ע') [שבע] שנה נעשה נחש והני מילי הוא דלא כרע במודים ובגמ' דסוטה בפ' אלו נאמרים בכל לשון (דף מ) אמרי בזמן ששליח צבור אומר מודים העם מה הם אומרים:

הגהות הב"ח

(א) תום' ד"ה מלמדין וכו' וחיישינן ליוהרא. נ"ב כלומר ועוד חיישינן ליוהרא:

[וע"ע תוס' מנחות מד. ד"ה כל כהן כו']

גליון הש"ס

רש"י ד"ה מתחלת הברכה וכו' וממילא כו'. עיין בקרבן נתנאל שמלא גירסא בקלף. תיובתא דרב אסי לימא תהוי תיובתא דר"ה אמר לך ר"ה: גמ' אר"ש בן פזי אריב"ל. במדרש רבה בראשית פרשה לט איתא ריב"ע בשם ריב"ל אמר כ"ג תחלת כל ברכה שוחה והמלך בתחלת כל ברכה ובסוף כל ברכה שוחה. רבי סימון בשם ריב"ל אמר המלך משהיה כורע לא היה נזקף:

מגילה דף כה.
שם [ועמש"ש לעיל לג: גירסת הרי"ף ורא"ש]
נ"א בה
[סוטה לח:]
[פירוש יונתן בראשון]
גיטין ע. ע"ש
[נ"ל תיובתא דרב אסי לימא תהוי תיובתא דרב הונא וכו' כך הוה הגירסא לפני רש"י וע' בסוף ס' קרבן נתנאל]
מכילתא דר"י פרשת בשלח
[לפי שמצוה להתפלל במקום נמוך כדאיתא לעיל י: הלכך קתני ירד ע' רש"י ר"ה לב. ד"ה ירדו]
במדבר יב
[תוספתא פ"א]
[פ"ב]
[וע"ע תוס' ע"ג ת. ד"ה אם כאן]

תורה אור

כהן גדול – בסוף כל ברכה וברכה, והמלך – תחלת כל ברכה וברכה וסוף כל ברכה וברכה. אמר רבי יצחק בר נחמני, לדידי מפרשא לי מיניה דריב"ל: אהדיוט – כמו שאמרנו, כהן גדול – תחלת [א] כל ברכה וברכה, המלך – כיון שכרע, שוב אינו זוקף, שנאמר: °"ויהי ככלות שלמה להתפלל וגו' קם מלפני (מלכים א ח) מזבח ה' מכרע על ברכיו". ת"ר: *בקידה – על אפים, שנאמר: °"ותקד בת שבע אפים ארץ", (שם א) כריעה – על ברכים, שנאמר: "מכרע על ברכיו", השתחואה – זו פשוט ידים ורגלים, שנאמר: °"הבוא נבוא אני ואמך ואחיך להשתחות לך (בראשית לז) ארצה". *אמר רב חייא בריה דרב הונא: חזינא להו לאביי ורבא גדמצלו אצלויי.§ תני חדא: הכורע בהודאה הרי זה משובח; ותניא אידך: הרי זה מגונה! לא קשיא: הא – בתחלה, הא – לבסוף. רבא כרע בהודאה תחלה וסוף. אמרי ליה רבנן: אמאי קא עביד מר הכי? – אמר להו: חזינא לרב נחמן דכרע, וחזינא ליה לרב ששת דקא עבד הכי. – והתניא: הכורע בהודאה הרי זה מגונה! – ההיא – בהודאה שבהלל. – והתניא: הכורע בהודאה ובהודאה של הלל הרי זה מגונה! – כי תניא ההיא – בהודאה דברכת המזון.§ **מתני'** המתפלל וטעה – סימן רע לו, ואם שליח צבור הוא – סימן רע לשולחיו, מפני *ששלוחו של אדם כמותו. אמרו עליו על ר' חנינא בן דוסא, שהיה מתפלל על החולים ואומר, "זה חי וזה מת". אמרו לו: מנין אתה יודע? אמר להם: אם שגורה תפלתי בפי – יודע אני שהוא מקובל, ואם לאו – יודע אני שהוא מטורף.§ **גמ'** אהייא? א"ר חייא אמר רב ספרא משום חד דבי רבי: באבות. איכא דמתני לה אברייתא: המתפלל דצריך שיכוין את לבו בכולן, ואם אינו יכול לכוין בכולן – יכוין את לבו באחת; א"ר חייא אמר רב ספרא משום חד דבי רבי: באבות. "אמרו עליו על רבי חנינא וכו'". מנא הני מילי? א"ר יהושע בן לוי, דאמר קרא: °"בורא ניב שפתים שלום שלום לרחוק ולקרוב אמר (ישעיה נז) ה' ורפאתיו". א"ר חייא בר אבא *א"ר יוחנן: הכל הנביאים כולן לא נתנבאו אלא למשיא בתו לתלמיד חכם (סנהדרין צט.) ולעושה פרקמטיא לת"ח ולמהנה ת"ח מנכסיו, אבל תלמידי חכמים עצמן – °"עין לא ראתה אלהים זולתך (שם סד) יעשה למחכה לו". ואמר רבי חייא בר אבא אמר רבי יוחנן: וכל הנביאים כולן לא נתנבאו אלא לימות המשיח, אבל לעולם הבא – "עין לא ראתה אלהים זולתך". ופליגא דשמואל, *דאמר שמואל: זאין בין העוה"ז (שבת סג. קנא: פסחים סח. סנהדרין שם [ודף לא:]) לימות המשיח אלא שעבוד מלכויות בלבד, שנאמר: °"כי לא יחדל אביון מקרב הארץ". (דברים טו) וא"ר חייא בר אבא א"ר יוחנן: כל הנביאים כולן לא נתנבאו אלא לבעלי תשובה, אבל צדיקים גמורים – "עין לא ראתה אלהים זולתך". ופליגא דר' אבהו, דא"ר רבי אבהו: מקום חשבעלי תשובה עומדין – צדיקים גמורים אינם עומדין, שנאמר: °"שלום שלום לרחוק ולקרוב". (ישעיה נז) לרחוק ברישא והדר לקרוב. ורבי יוחנן אמר לך: מאי "רחוק" – שהיה רחוק מדבר עבירה מעיקרא, ומאי "קרוב" – שהיה קרוב לדבר עבירה(א) ונתרחק ממנו השתא. *מאי "עין לא ראתה?" (סנהדרין שם) אמר רבי יהושע בן לוי: זה יין המשומר בענביו מששת ימי בראשית; רבי *שמואל בר נחמני אמר: זה ([שם איתא ר"ל]) עדן שלא שלטה בו עין כל בריה. שמא תאמר, אדם הראשון היכן היה? – בגן. ושמא תאמר: הוא גן, הוא עדן – תלמוד לומר: °"ונהר יוצא מעדן להשקות את הגן", גן לחוד ועדן לחוד.§ (בראשית ב) ת"ר: מעשה שחלה בנו של ר"ג, שגר שני ת"ח אצל רבי חנינא בן דוסא לבקש עליו רחמים. כיון שראה אותם עלה לעלייה ובקש עליו רחמים. בירידתו, אמר להם: לכו – שחלצתו חמה. אמרו לו: וכי נביא אתה?! אמר להן: לא נביא אנכי ולא בן נביא אנכי, אלא כך מקובלני: אם שגורה תפלתי בפי – יודע אני שהוא מקובל, ואם לאו – יודע אני שהוא מטורף. ישבו וכתבו וכוונו אותה שעה. וכשבאו אצל ר"ג, אמר להן: העבודה! לא חסרתם ולא הותרתם, אלא כך היה מעשה, באותה שעה חלצתו חמה ושאל לנו מים לשתות. ושוב מעשה ברבי חנינא בן דוסא שהלך ללמוד תורה אצל ר' יוחנן בן זכאי, וחלה בנו של ריב"ז. אמר לו: חנינא בני, בקש עליו רחמים ויחיה. הניח ראשו בין ברכיו ובקש עליו רחמים – וחיה. אמר רבי יוחנן בן זכאי: אלמלי הטיח בן זכאי את ראשו בין ברכיו כל היום כולו – לא היו משגיחים עליו. אמרה לו אשתו: וכי חנינא גדול ממך?! אמר לה: לאו, אלא הוא דומה כעבד לפני המלך, ואני דומה כשר לפני המלך.§ *ואמר רבי חייא בר אבא אמר ([לעיל לא. ע"ש]) רבי יוחנן: טאל יתפלל אדם אלא בבית שיש שם חלונות, שנאמר: °"וכוין פתיחן ליה בעליתה (לקבל) (דניאל ו) [נגד] ירושלם". אמר רב כהנא: יחציף עלי מאן דמצלי בבקתא. ואמר רב כהנא: *כחציף עלי מאן דמפרש (סוטה ז: ע"ש) חטאיה, שנאמר: °"אשרי נשוי פשע כסוי חטאה".§ (תהלים לב)

הדרן עלך אין עומדין

כהן גדול בסוף כל ברכה. כל מה שהוא גדול ביותר צריך להכניע ולהשפיל עצמו: **אינו זוקף.** עד שיגמור: **קם מלפני מזבח ה' מכרוע.** רישיה דקרא "ויהי ככלות שלמה" להתפלל והדר "קם מכרוע": **ארצה.** לשון משתטח משמע: **דמצלו אצלויי.** כשנופלין על פניהם אין פושטין ידיהם ורגליהם, אלא מטין על צדיהן: **בתחלה.** **כורע:** **חזינא** לרב נחמן דכרע. **תחלה וסוף:** בהודאה דהלל. "הודו לה' כי טוב": **מתני' אם שגורה.** אם סדורה תפלתי בפי במרוצה ואיני נכשל, ותחנתי נובעת מלבי אל פי, כל מה שאני חפץ להאריך בתחנונים: **שהוא מטורף.** החולה לשון אחר: [*לשון] טורפין לו תפלתו בפניו*, (כצ"ל תוי"ט) כלומר: התפלה שהתפללו עליו מטורפת וטרודה ממנו ואינה מקובלת: ((לעיל ה:) מגילה כב: שבועות טז:) **גמ' אהייא.** בהיכא, ובאיזו מן הברכות הוי טעות בסימן רע: **באבות.** שהוא תחלת התפלה, רמז הוא שאין חפץ בה: **בורא ניב שפתים.** כשהניב בריא באדם – אז מובטח על השלום: ([מגילה כב: ע"ש]) **לא נתנבאו.** הטובות והנחמות: **עין לא ראתה.** לא נראית ולא נגלית לשום נביא: **רחוק.** שהיה רחוק כל ימיו מן העבירה, דהיינו צדיק מעיקרו: **חלצתו חמה.** שלפתו, ניטלה מגופו החמה, הוא החולי הקודחו. חלצתו – לשון *חלץ מהם: ([הושע ה]) **לא חסרתם.** **שעה:** **כעבד.** בן בית, נכנס ויוצא שלא ברשות: **כשר לפני המלך.** שאינו רגיל לבא לפניו: ([חגיגה י: קדושין מח: מג. נדרים עב: נזיר יב: ב"מ נו. מנחות נג:]) **חלונות.** שגורמין לו שיכוין לבו, שהוא מסתכל כלפי שמים ולבו נכנע: **דמצלי בבקתא.** בבקעה, שכשהוא במקום צניעות חלה עליו אימת מלך, ולבו נשבר:

הדרן עלך אין עומדין

קידה על אפים. ומייתי קרא. אע"ג דאשכחן נמי בענין אחר, יש לומר דקים ליה מקבלה דקידה על אפים, ומייתי קרא דמסייעו: **חזינא** לאביי ורבא דמצלו אצלויי. פירוש: שהיו מטין על צדיהן: **יכוין** לבו באחת מהן. והא דאמרי' בסוף פרק "ת"ה" (דף ל:) לעולם ימוד אדם דעתו אם יכול לכוין – יתפלל, ואם לאו – אל יתפלל, יש לפרש התם נמי באחת מהן: **חציף** עלי מאן דמצלי בבקתא. וא"ת: הכתיב "ויצא יצחק *לשוח בשדה" (בראשית כד), י"ל: דהתם מיירי בהר המוריה, כדאמרי' בפסחים פרק "האשה" (ד' פח.): לא כיצחק שקראו שדה וכו'. א"נ: בקתא דהכא מיירי בבקעה, במקום שרגילין שם בני אדם לעבור והולכי דרכים: **כסוי** חטאה. וטעמא: לפי שאז מתבייש על חטאו. אבל אם מפרש חטאיו דומה שאינו מתבייש עליו, ואמרינן לעיל פרק קמא (ד' יב:): כל העושה דבר ומתבייש – מוחלים לו מיד:

הדרן עלך אין עומדין

ס א מיי' פ"ה מהלכות תפלה הלכה י:
סא ב מיי' שם הל' יג סמג עשין יט:
סב ג מיי' שם הל' יד ופ"ט שם הלכה ה טוש"ע או"ח סי' קלא סעיף א:
סג ד מיי' פ"י מהלכות תפלה סמג שם טור שו"ע או"ח סימן קא סעיף א:
[כוונת התו' מהא דאמרי' לעיל כו: ואין שיחה אלא תפלה]
סד ה מיי' פ"ו מהלכות דעות הלכה ב:
סה ו מיי' פ"ח מהל' תשובה הל' ז:
סו ז מיי' פ"ט מהלכות תשובה הל' ב ופי"ב מהל' מלכים הל' ב:
סז ח מיי' פ"ז מהל' תשובה הלכה ד:
סח ט מיי' פ"ה מהל' תפלה הלכה ו סמג עשין יט טוש"ע או"ח סי' צ סעיף ד:
סט י טוש"ע שם סעי' ה:
ע כ מיי' פ"ב מהל' תשובה הל' ה טוש"ע או"ח סי' תרז סעיף ב:

רב נסים גאון

אמר ר' חייא בריה דרב הונא חזינא לאביי ורבא דכי נפלי על אנפיהו מצלו אצלויי. איתא במס' מגילה בפ' הקורא את המגילה עומד יושב (דף כב) רב איקלע (לבית) [לבבל] בתענית צבור נפל כולי עלמא על אפייהו רב לא נפל מאי טעמא רצפה של אבנים היתה ומשום אבן משכית אית דאמר דמשום האי טעמא הוו אביי ורבא מצלו אצלויי. במס' ע"ז בגמ' דבני מערבא בפ' ר' ישמעאל (הלכה א) אמרו עליה אי אתה משתחוה אבל אתה משתחוה על אבני בית המקדש רב מפקד לדבי רב אחא ר' אמי מפקד לאנשי ביתיה כד תהוון נפקין לתעניתא לא תהוון רבעין כאורחכון ר' יונה רבע על סיטריה ר' אחא רבע על סיטריה: **אמר** רב (ששת) [כהנא] חציף עלאי מאן דמפרש חטאיה שנא' (תהלים לב) אשרי נשוי פשע כסוי חטאה. אית בפרק יום הכפורים (דף פו) רב רמי כתיב אשרי נשוי פשע כסוי חטאה וכתיב (משלי כח) מכסה פשעיו לא יצליח לא קשיא כאן בחטא מפורסם כאן בחטא שאינו מפורסם רב זוטרא בר טוביה אמר לא קשיא כאן בעבירות שבין אדם לחבירו כאן בעבירות שבין אדם למקום:

הגהות הב"ח

(א) גמ' לדבר עבירה מעיקרא ונתרחק:

הגהות הגר"א

[א] גמ' כהן גדול תחלת. נ"ב וסוף: